Modern
REAL ESTATE
Practice in Georgia
FIRST EDITION UPDATE

Fillmore W. Galaty

Wellington J. Allaway

Robert C. Kyle

Roy T. Black and Joseph S. Rabianski,
Consulting Editors

Dearborn™
Real Estate Education

This publication is designed to provide accurate and authoritative information in regard to the subject matter covered. It is sold with the understanding that the publisher is not engaged in rendering legal, accounting, or other professional advice. If legal advice or other expert assistance is required, the services of a competent professional should be sought.

President: Dr. Andrew Temte
Chief Learning Officer: Dr. Tim Smaby
Vice President, Real Estate Education: Asha Alsobrooks
Development Editor: **Chris Kugler**

MODERN REAL ESTATE PRACTICE IN GEORGIA FIRST EDITION UPDATE
© 2010 by Kaplan, Inc.
Published by DF Institute, Inc., d/b/a Dearborn™ Real Estate Education
332 Front St. S., Suite 501
La Crosse, WI 54601
www.dearbornRE.com

Printed in the United States of America
11   12   10   9   8   7   6   5   4   3   2
ISBN: 978-1-4277-2641-4 / 1-4277-2641-8
PPN: 1511-551A

Contents

Preface

Modern Real Estate Practice is the nationwide industry standard for real estate education. Whether you are preparing for a licensing examination, fulfilling a college or university requirement, looking for specific guidance to buy or sell a home, or expanding your understanding of this fascinating field, you can rely on *Modern Real Estate Practice* for accurate and comprehensive information in an easy-to-use format.

Modern Real Estate Practice in Georgia is based on the 17th edition of the national text described above. This book goes one step further by providing up-to-date information specific to Georgia real estate principles and practices. *Modern Real Estate Practice in Georgia* stands out as one-of-a-kind in its field by gathering in one place all of the relevant materials regarding real estate in general and Georgia specifically.

■ KEY FEATURES

- **Georgia-specific laws and practice issues** are clearly highlighted in each chapter for classroom and study emphasis.
- **Key terms** at the beginning of each chapter include Georgia-specific terms.
- **Questions** at the end of each chapter, where appropriate, include Georgia-specific questions.
- **Chapter 14, Georgia Real Estate License Law,** covers all necessary information and references relating to the practice of real estate in Georgia. End-of-chapter questions focus solely on Georgia real estate law and practice.
- **Sample exams** in the back of the book include a 50-question Georgia sample exam with an Answer Key, including explanations.
- **Key Point Reviews,** bulleted key point summaries, provide students with a quick review tool of the most essential content covered in each chapter.
- **Math FAQs** explains in depth how to solve common real estate problems involving fractions, decimals, percentages, and measurements. Twenty-five sample questions are included.

■ A FINAL NOTE

We like to hear from our readers. Like the hundreds of instructors who have helped us develop each edition and like the real estate professionals who have been willing to share their expertise, you are a partner in the *Modern Real Estate Practice* series. The only way we can be sure we've succeeded and know what we need to improve is if you tell us.

Did the book help you? Has your understanding of the real estate industry increased? How did you do in your course or on your license exam? What additional or different information would improve the book? Please indicate that you used the 1st Edition Update of *Modern Real Estate Practice in Georgia* and send your remarks to Dearborn™ Real Estate Education, Attention: Editorial Group, 332 Front Street South, Suite 501, La Crosse, WI 54601 or e-mail your comments to *contentinquiries@dearborn.com.*

Thank you for your help and for joining the ranks of successful *Modern Real Estate Practice in Georgia* users!

The Publisher

Acknowledgments

■ *MODERN REAL ESTATE PRACTICE IN GEORGIA*

Like a real estate transaction, this book is the product of teamwork and cooperation among professionals. The authors express their gratitude and appreciation to the instructors and other real estate professionals whose invaluable suggestions and advice helped shape *Modern Real Estate Practice in Georgia*.

■ Consulting Editors: Roy T. Black, PhD, JD, Professor, Goizueta Business School, Emory University
Joseph S. Rabianski, PhD, CRE, Professor of Real Estate, Georgia State University
■ Content Consultant: Judith A. Nolde, JD, Madison, WI
■ Reviewers: William J. Aaron, CEO, Director, Barney Fletcher Realty U, Atlanta, GA
Patricia Johnson, DREI, ABR, AIS, CRB, GRI, SRES, Buford, GA

■ *REVIEWERS—MODERN REAL ESTATE PRACTICE*

Modern Real Estate Practice would not have been possible without the guidance of the following real estate instructors and professionals:

William (Bill) J. Aaron, Barney Fletcher Enterprises, Atlanta, GA

W. Thomas Anderson III, Weichert School of Real Estate, Brick, NJ

John Ashby, Ashby's Real Estate Institute, Washington D.C.

Christopher Ashe, Coach Unlimited, Litchfield, CT

Doris Barrell, GRI, DREI, Grand Island, FL

Marty Baum, 1st USA School of Real Estate, Mesa, AZ

Chuck Byers, Pioneer Real Estate School, Meridian, ID

Wayne Camp, Camp Real Estate School, Mountain Home, AR

Linda L. Crawford, Real Estate Education Consultant, Gainesville, FL

William Hatch, PhD, GRI, North Idaho College

John (Wayne) Hite, Blue Ridge Community College, Staunton, VA

Deborah Long, DREI, Long Talks, Chapel Hill, NC

Gail Lyons, Boulder Real Estate Services, Ltd., Boulder, CO

Mark Munizzo, Equity Network, Frankfort, IL

Katherine Pancak, University of Connecticut

Teresa Sirico, ABR, GRI, CRS, New Haven Real Estate School, CT

Ben C. Scheible, Truckee Meadows Community College, Reno, NV

Marie S. Spodek, DREI, Professional Real Estate Services, David City, NE

Dennis Tosh, FNC, Inc., Oxford, MS

Steve Willoughby, Steve Willoughby Seminars, Casper, WY

The authors thank the following individuals for sharing their comments, suggestions, and classroom experiences regarding *Modern Real Estate Practice* and its ancillary products. Their responses to the online survey and questionnaire were an integral part of the development of the 17th edition.

Jennifer Aamodt

Karen Ameen

Mitchell Appelrouth

Donna Austin

Hope Bailey

Jim Barry

Susan Barry

Kenneth Bellville

Stuart Bernstein

Darryl Bradshaw

Julie Caputo

Dick Clemmer

George Collins

Kim Cook

Allan Creighton

Ted Cucuro

Vernon R. Damron

James A. Deibert

R. Patrick Diamond

Doug Embree

Loretta Everhart

Alfred E. Fabian

Daniel Flowers

Michelle Francis

Helen Fridenstine

Bill Frost

Harold Fuhrman

A. David Geldhof

Lynette Glatzer

Dr. Lawrence Hasbrouck

Mary Hibbler-Kee

Martha Hilton

Jay Hooper

Richard Howard

Cynthia Hull

Joanne Jamrose

Sandra Johnson

Michael James Johnston

Karen Keating-Volke

Janice Knott

Mike Krein

Susan Lanham

Craig Larabee

Janet Lofty

Leanne Long

Tim McColly

Gail Minga

Jack Oliver

Ray Padgett

Larry Pearlo

Jane Reiser

Sondra Rich

John D. Rinehart

Susan Rinker

Barbara Sander

Clarence Schnick

Geraldine W. Scott

April Sepulveda

Jean Smith

Gerald Steltzler

Michael Tax

Rodger Thixton

Robert Valentine

Ruth Vella

John Vincze

Dwight Wells

Rawlin Westover

Jennifer Winfield

Harry Winning, Jr.

John Wright

W. Curtis York, Jr.

Introduction to the Real Estate Business

■ **LEARNING OBJECTIVES** *When you have finished reading this chapter, you should be able to:*

■ **identify** the various careers available in real estate and the professional organizations that support them.

■ **describe** the five categories of real property.

■ **explain** the operation of supply and demand in the real estate market.

■ **distinguish** the economic, political, and social factors that influence supply and demand.

■ **define** the following *key terms:*

broker	market	supply and demand
community association manager	salesperson	

■ A VERY BIG BUSINESS

Real estate transactions are taking place all around you, all the time. When a commercial leasing company rents space in a mall or the owner of a building rents an apartment to a retired couple, it's a real estate transaction. If an appraiser gives an expert opinion of the value of farmland or a bank lends money to a professional corporation to purchase an office building, it's a real estate transaction. Most common of all, when an American family sells its old home and buys a new one, the family takes part in the real estate industry. Consumers of real estate services include buyers and sellers of homes, tenants and landlords, investors and developers. Nearly everyone, at some time, is involved in a real estate transaction.

All this adds up to big business—complex transactions that involve billions of dollars every year in the United States alone. The services of millions of highly trained individuals are required: attorneys, bankers, trust company representatives, abstract and title insurance company agents, architects, surveyors, accountants, tax experts, and many others, in addition to buyers and sellers. All these people depend on the skills and knowledge of licensed real estate professionals.

■ REAL ESTATE: A BUSINESS OF MANY SPECIALIZATIONS

Despite the size and complexity of the real estate business, many people think of it as being made up of brokers and salespersons only. Actually, the real estate industry is much broader than that. Appraisal, property management, financing, subdivision and development, counseling, and education are all separate businesses within the real estate field. To succeed in a complex industry, every real estate professional must have a basic knowledge of these specialties.

Brokerage—*Brokerage* is the business of bringing people together in a real estate transaction. A **broker** acts as a point of contact between two or more people in negotiating the sale, purchase, or rental of property. A *broker* is defined as a person or company licensed to buy, sell, exchange, or lease real property for others and to charge a fee for these services. A broker may be the agent of the buyer or the seller or of both, or the broker may not be anyone's agent. The property may be residential, commercial, or industrial. A salesperson is a licensee employed by or associated with the broker. The **salesperson** conducts brokerage activities on behalf of the broker. The broker, however, is ultimately responsible for the salesperson's acts. Brokerage is discussed in Chapter 5.

Appraisal—*Appraisal* is the process of estimating a property's market value, based on established methods and the appraiser's professional judgment. Although their training will give brokers some understanding of the valuation process, lenders generally require a professional appraisal, and property sold by court order requires an appraiser's expertise. Appraisers must have detailed knowledge of the methods of valuation. In many states, appraisers must be licensed or certified to carry out local transactions. Appraisers must be licensed or certified for many federally related transactions. Appraisal is covered in Chapter 19.

Property management—A *property manager* is a person or company hired to maintain and manage property on behalf of its owner. By hiring a property manager, the owner is relieved of such day-to-day management tasks as finding new tenants, collecting rents, altering or constructing new space for tenants, ordering repairs, and generally maintaining the property. The scope of the manager's work depends on the terms of the individual employment contract, known as a *management agreement*. Whatever tasks are specified, the basic responsibility of the property manager is to protect the owner's investment and maximize the owner's return on his or her investment. Property management is discussed in Chapter 18.

| In Georgia |

Community association management—Georgia has a separate license and education requirement for the **community association manager.** *Community association* means an organization of owners in a residential or mixed use common interest real property or realty association in which membership is mandatory as an incident of ownership within the development. Such organizations include condominiums, cooperatives, and homeowners' associations. *Community association management services* means the provision of management or administrative services in the operation of the affairs of a community association, including, but not limited to, collecting, controlling, or disbursing the funds; obtaining insurance; arranging for association property maintenance; and overseeing the daily operations of the association. A *community association manager* is one who acts on behalf of a real estate broker in providing only community association management services. In Georgia, a licensed broker, associate broker, or salesperson may also perform community association management services.

Financing—*Financing* is the business of providing the funds that make real estate transactions possible. Most transactions are financed by means of mortgage loans or trust deed loans secured by the property. Individuals involved in financing real estate may work in commercial banks, savings associations, and mortgage banking and mortgage brokerage companies. A growing number of real estate brokerage firms affiliate with mortgage brokers to provide consumers with *one-stop-shopping* real estate services. Financing issues are examined in Chapter 15 and Chapter 16.

Subdivision and development—*Subdivision* is the splitting of a single property into smaller parcels. *Development* involves the construction of *improvements* on the land. These improvements may be either on site or off site. Off-site improvements, such as water lines and storm sewers, are made on public lands to serve the new development. On-site improvements, such as new homes or swimming pools, are made on individual parcels. While subdivision and development normally are related, they are independent processes that can occur separately. Subdivision and development are discussed further in Chapter 20.

Home inspection—*Home inspection* is a profession that allows practitioners to combine their interest in real estate with their professional skills and training in the construction trades or in engineering. Professional *home inspectors* conduct a thorough visual survey of a property's structure, systems, and site conditions and prepare an analytical report that is valuable to both purchasers and homeowners. Increasingly wary consumers are relying on the inspector's report to help them make purchase decisions. Frequently, a real estate sales contract will be contingent upon the inspector's report. While professional home inspectors are usually prohibited from practicing real estate, many of them are also licensed as real estate agents. Some of the things inspectors typically look for in a property are discussed in Chapter 22.

Counseling—*Counseling* involves providing clients with competent independent advice based on sound professional judgment. A real estate counselor helps clients choose among the various alternatives involved in purchasing, using, or investing in property. A counselor's role is to furnish clients with the information needed to make informed decisions. Professional real estate counselors must have a high degree of industry expertise.

Education—*Real estate education* is available to both practitioners and consumers. Colleges and universities, private schools, and trade organizations all conduct real estate courses and seminars, from the principles of a prelicensing program to the technical aspects of tax and exchange law. State licensing laws establish the minimum educational requirements for obtaining—and keeping—a real estate license. Continuing education helps ensure that licensees keep their skills and knowledge current.

Other areas—Many other real estate career options are available. Practitioners will find that real estate specialists are needed in a variety of business settings. Lawyers who specialize in real estate are always in demand. Large corporations with extensive land holdings often have their own real estate and property tax departments. Local governments must staff both zoning boards and assessment offices.

■ PROFESSIONAL ORGANIZATIONS

Many trade organizations serve the real estate business. The largest is the National Association of REALTORS® (NAR), whose Web site is *www.realtor.org*. The NAR is composed of state (Georgia Association of REALTORS® (GAR)), regional, and local Boards of REALTORS®. The NAR also sponsors various affiliated organizations that offer professional designations to brokers, salespersons, appraisers, and others who complete required courses in areas of special interest. Members subscribe to a Code of Ethics and, if eligible, are entitled to be known as REALTORS® or REALTOR-ASSOCIATES®.

The NAR has the following nine affiliated Institutes, Societies, and Councils:

1. Counselors of Real Estate (CRE)
2. Commercial Investment Real Estate Institute (CIREI)
3. Institute of Real Estate Management (IREM)
4. Real Estate Brokerage Managers Council
5. REALTORS® Land Institute (RLI)

6. REALTORS® National Marketing Institute (RNMI)
   A. Certified Real Estate Brokerage Manager (CRB)
   B. Certified Residential Specialist (CRS)
7. Council of Residential Specialists (CRS)
8. Society of Industrial and Office REALTORS® (SIOR)
9. Women's Council of REALTORS® (WCR)

The National Association of Real Estate Brokers (NAREB), whose members are known as *Realtists*, also adheres to a Code of Ethics. The NAREB arose out of the early days of the civil rights movement as an association of racial minority real estate brokers in response to the conditions and abuses that eventually gave rise to fair housing laws. Today, The NAREB remains dedicated to equal housing opportunity. The Empire Board of Realtists (EREB) is the Georgia affiliate of NAREB.

Other professional associations include the Appraisal Institute, the American Society of Appraisers (ASA), the National Association of Independent Fee Appraisers (NAIFA), and the Real Estate Educators Association (REEA). The Georgia Real Estate Educators Association (GREEA) promotes high standards in real estate education, camaraderie among members, and opportunities for professional development.

The growth in buyer brokerage, discussed in Chapter 5, led to the formation of organizations such as the Real Estate Buyer's Agent Council (REBAC), now associated with the NAR, and the National Association of Exclusive Buyer's Agents (NAEBA). Other organizations include the Building Owners and Managers Association (BOMA), and Certified Commercial Investment Managers (CCIM). Home inspectors may be members of the American Society of Home Inspectors® (ASHI), a national professional organization. Members of the ASHI are expected to comply with its Standards of Practice and Code of Ethics.

■ TYPES OF REAL PROPERTY

Five Categories of Real Property
1. Residential
2. Commercial
3. Industrial
4. Agricultural
5. Special-Purpose

Just as there are areas of specialization within the real estate industry, there are different types of property in which to specialize. Real estate can be classified as

■ *residential*—all property used for single-family or multifamily housing, whether in urban, suburban, or rural areas;
■ *commercial*—business property, including office space, shopping centers, stores, theaters, hotels, and parking facilities;
■ *industrial*—warehouses, factories, land in industrial districts, and power plants;
■ *agricultural*—farms, timberland, ranches, and orchards; or
■ *special-purpose*—churches, schools, cemeteries, and government-held lands.

The market for each of these types of property can be subdivided into the *sales market*, which involves the transfer of title and ownership rights, and the *rental market*, in which space is used temporarily by lease.

IN PRACTICE   Although it is possible for a single real estate firm or an individual real estate professional to perform all the services and handle all classes of property discussed in this chapter (unless restricted by a state's license law), this is rarely done. While such general services may be available in small towns, most firms and professionals specialize to some degree, especially in urban areas. Some licensees perform only one service for one type of property, such as residential sales or commercial leasing.

■ THE REAL ESTATE MARKET

A **market** is a place where goods can be bought and sold. A market may be a specific place, such as the village square. It also may be a vast, complex, worldwide economic system for moving goods and services around the globe. In either case, the function of a market is to provide a setting in which supply and demand can establish market value, making it advantageous for buyers and sellers to trade.

Supply and Demand

Prices for goods and services in the market are established by the operation of **supply and demand.** Essentially, *when supply increases and demand remains stable, prices go down; when demand increases and supply remains stable, prices go up.* Greater supply means producers need to attract more buyers, so they lower prices. Greater demand means producers can raise their prices because buyers compete for the product.

> When supply increases and demand remains stable, prices go down.
>
> When demand increases and supply remains stable, prices go up.

■ FOR EXAMPLE   Here's how one broker describes market forces: "In my 17 years in real estate, I've seen supply and demand in action many times. When a car maker relocated its factory to my region a few years back, hundreds of people wanted to buy the few higher-bracket houses for sale at the time. Those sellers were able to ask ridiculously high prices for their properties, and two houses actually sold for more than the asking prices! On the other hand, when the naval base closed and 2,000 civilian jobs were transferred to other parts of the country, it seemed like every other house in town was for sale. We were practically giving houses away to the few people who were buying."

> **Uniqueness** and **immobility** are the two characteristics of land that have the most impact on market value.

Supply and demand in the real estate market.   Two characteristics of real estate govern the way the market reacts to the pressures of supply and demand: *uniqueness* and *immobility* (see Chapter 2). *Uniqueness* means that, no matter how identical they may appear, no two parcels of real estate are ever exactly alike; each occupies its own unique geographic location. *Immobility* refers to the fact that property cannot be relocated to satisfy demand where supply is low. Nor can buyers always relocate to areas with greater supply. For these reasons, real estate markets are local markets. Each geographic area has different types of real estate and different conditions that drive prices. In these small, well-defined areas, real estate offices can keep track of both what type of property is in demand and what parcels are available.

IN PRACTICE Technological advances and market changes have widened the real estate professional's local market. No longer limited to a single small area, brokers and salespersons must track trends and conditions in a variety of different and sometimes distant local markets. Technological devices—personal digital assistants (PDAs), office computers, information networks, and laptop personal computers (PCs), cellular phones, fax machines, and a growing arsenal of other devices—help real estate practitioners stay on top of their wide-ranging markets.

Because of real estate's uniqueness and immobility, the market generally adjusts slowly to the forces of supply and demand. Though a home offered for sale can be withdrawn in response to low demand and high supply, it is much more likely that oversupply will result in lower prices. When supply is low, on the other hand, a high demand may not be met immediately because development and construction are lengthy processes. As a result, development tends to occur in uneven spurts of activity.

Even when supply and demand can be forecast with some accuracy, natural disasters such as hurricanes and earthquakes can disrupt market trends. Similarly, sudden changes in financial markets or local events such as plant relocations or environmental factors can dramatically disrupt a seemingly stable market.

Factors Affecting Supply

Factors that tend to affect the supply side of the real estate market's supply and demand balance include labor force availability, construction and material costs, and government controls and financial policies.

Labor force and construction and material costs A shortage of skilled labor or building materials or an increase in the cost of materials can decrease the amount of new construction. High transfer costs, such as taxes, and construction permit fees can also discourage development. Increased construction costs may be passed along to buyers and tenants in the form of higher prices and increased rents that can further slow the market.

Government controls and financial policies The government's monetary policy can have a substantial impact on the real estate market. The Federal Reserve Board (the Fed) establishes a *discount rate* of interest for the money it lends to commercial banks. That rate has a direct impact on the *interest rates* the banks in turn charge to borrowers. These interest rates play a significant part in people's ability to buy homes. Such government agencies as the Federal Housing Administration (FHA) and the Government National Mortgage Association (Ginnie Mae) can affect the amount of money available to lenders for mortgage loans. (See Chapter 16.) The Federal National Mortgage Association (Fannie Mae) and the Federal Home Loan Mortgage Corporation (Freddie Mac) are private companies under congressional charter that provide financial services and products that make it possible for low-income, moderate-income, and middle-income families to buy homes.

Factors affecting real estate supply are

- labor force,
- construction costs,
- government controls, and
- government financial policies.

Virtually any government action has some effect on the real estate market. For instance, federal environmental regulations may increase or decrease the supply and value of land in a local market. Real estate taxation is one of the primary sources of revenue for local governments. Policies on taxation of real estate can have either positive or negative effects. High taxes may deter investors. On the other hand, tax incentives can attract new businesses and industries. And, of course, along with these enterprises come increased employment and expanded residential real estate markets.

Local governments also can influence supply. Land-use controls, building codes, and zoning ordinances help shape the character of a community and control the use of land. Careful planning helps stabilize and even increase real estate values. The dedication of land to such amenities as forest preserves, schools, and parks also helps shape the market. Zoning and land-use controls are discussed in Chapter 20.

Factors Affecting Demand

Factors that tend to affect the demand side of the real estate market include population, demographics, and employment and wage levels.

> **Factors affecting real estate demand are**
>
> - population,
> - demographics, and
> - employment and wage levels.

Population   Because shelter is a basic human need, the demand for housing grows with the population. Although the total population of the country continues to rise, the demand for real estate increases faster in some areas than in others. In some locations, however, growth has ceased altogether or the population has declined. This may be due to economic changes (such as plant closings), social concerns (such as the quality of schools or a desire for more open space), or population changes (such as population shifts from colder to warmer climates). The result can be a drop in demand for real estate in one area, matched by an increased demand elsewhere.

Demographics   *Demographics* is the study and description of a population. The population of a community is a major factor in determining the quantity and type of housing in that community. Family size, the ratio of adults to children, the ages of children, the number of retirees, family income, lifestyle, and the growing number of single-parent and empty-nester households are all demographic factors that contribute to the amount and type of housing needed.

IN PRACTICE   *Niche marketing* is the phrase used to refer to the targeted marketing of specific demographic populations. For example, as baby boomers age and look for retirement housing, their need or demand is considered a niche market.

Employment and wage levels   Decisions about whether to buy or rent and how much to spend on housing are closely related to income. When job opportunities are scarce or wage levels low, demand for real estate usually drops. The market might, in fact, be affected drastically by a single major employer moving in or shutting down. Licensees must be aware of the business plans of local employers.

As we've seen, the real estate market depends on a variety of economic forces, such as interest rates and employment levels. To be successful, licensees must follow economic trends and anticipate where they will lead. How people use their income depends on consumer confidence. Consumer confidence is based not only on perceived job security but also on the availability of credit and the impact of inflation. General trends in the economy, such as the availability of mortgage money, interest rates, and the rate of inflation, will influence an individual's decision as to how to spend his or her income.

■ KEY POINT REVIEW

Real estate brokerage is the business of bringing people together in a real estate transaction conducted by

- a **broker** who is a person or company licensed to buy, sell, exchange, or lease real property for others for compensation and who may
    — be the agent of buyer, seller, or both, and
    — not be the agent of any party to the transaction, or
- a **salesperson** who conducts brokerage activities on behalf of the broker.

Appraisal is the process of estimating a property's value (typically, market value) that is based on established methods and an appraiser's professional judgment and is regulated by the following:

- Licensing or certification is required for many **federally related transactions.**
- Many states require licensing or certification for local transactions.

Property management is conducted by a **property manager,** a person or company hired to maintain and manage property on behalf of its owner whose

- scope of work depends on a **management agreement,** and
- basic responsibility is to protect the owner's investment while maximizing the owner's financial return.

In Georgia **Community association management** is conducted by a community association manager who oversees the association's daily operations.

- Scope of work depends on the management agreement.
- The basic responsibility is to protect the association's and the individual owners' financial position and the association's property.

Financing is the business of providing the funds that make real estate transactions possible through

- mortgage or deed of trust loans secured by the property, and
- commercial banks, savings associations, mortgage bankers, and mortgage brokerage companies.

Subdivision and development involves splitting a single property into smaller parcels (subdividing) and construction of improvements on the land (development).

Home inspection is a growing area of interest to both purchasers and homeowners, but note the following:

- A state **license** may be required of a home inspector
- An **inspection report** will show results of a thorough visual survey of a property

Real estate counseling involves independent advice based on sound professional judgment.

Types of real property include:

- **Residential**—single-family and multifamily
- **Commercial**—office space, shopping centers, stores, theaters, hotels, parking facilities
- **Industrial**—warehouses, factories, land in industrial districts, power plants
- **Agricultural**—farms, timberland, ranches, orchards
- **Special-purpose**—schools, places of worship, cemeteries, government-held property

The **real estate market** reflects principles of **supply and demand,** influenced by the **uniqueness** and **immobility** of parcels of real estate so that

- when the **supply increases** and demand remains stable, **prices go down,** and
- when **demand increases** and supply remains stable, **prices go up.**

The factors affecting the **supply** of real estate include

- **labor force** availability;
- **construction and material costs;**
- **government controls**—environmental, land-use, building codes, zoning; and
- **government financial policies** that impact interest rates and the money supply.

The factors affecting the **demand** for real estate include

- **population**—some areas grow faster than others; some decline;
- **demographics**—these include family size, lifestyles, and niche marketing; and
- **employment and wage levels**—these influence housing affordability.

■ RELATED WEB SITES

American Society of Home Inspectors: *www.ashi.org*
Appraisal Institute: *www.appraisalinstitute.org*
Building Owners and Managers Association International: *www.boma.org*
Commercial Investment Real Estate Institute: *www.ccim.com*
Counselors of Real Estate: *www.cre.org*
Empire Board of Realtists: *www.empireboard.com*
Fannie Mae: *www.fanniemae.com*

Federal Reserve Board: *www.federalreserve.gov*

Freddie Mac: *www.freddiemac.com*

Georgia Association of REALTORS®: *www.garealtor.com*

Georgia Real Estate Educators Association: *www.greea.org*

Ginnie Mae: *www.ginniemae.gov*

Institute of Real Estate Management: *www.irem.org/index2.html*

National Association of Exclusive Buyer Agents: *www.naeba.org*

National Association of Independent Fee Appraisers: *www.naifa.com*

National Association of Real Estate Brokers: *www.nareb.com*

National Association of REALTORS®: *www.realtor.org*

Real Estate Buyer's Agent Council: *www.rebac.net*

Real Estate Educators Association: *www.reea.org*

U.S. Department of Housing and Urban Development (HUD): *www.hud.gov*

CHAPTER 1 QUIZ

1. A professional estimate of a property's market value, based on established methods and using trained, professional judgment, is performed by a
    a. real estate broker.
    b. real estate appraiser.
    c. real estate counselor.
    d. home inspector.

2. In general, when the supply of a certain commodity increases,
    a. price tends to rise.
    b. price tends to drop.
    c. demand for it tends to rise.
    d. demand for it tends to drop.

3. Which of the following factors primarily affects supply in the real estate market?
    a. Population
    b. Demographics
    c. Employment
    d. Government financial policies

4. Which of the following factors is MOST likely to influence demand for real estate?
    a. The number of real estate brokers in the area
    b. The number of full-time real estate salespersons in the area
    c. The wage levels and employment opportunities
    d. The price of new homes being built in the area

5. Property management, appraisal, financing, and development are all examples of
    a. factors affecting demand.
    b. specializations within the real estate industry.
    c. non–real estate professions.
    d. activities requiring broker management and supervision.

6. A REALTOR® is BEST described as an individual who is
    a. a specially licensed real estate professional who acts as a point of contact between two or more people in negotiating the sale, purchase, or rental of property.
    b. any real estate broker or salesperson who assists buyers, sellers, landlords, or tenants in any real estate transaction.
    c. a member of the National Association of Real Estate Brokers who specializes in residential properties.
    d. a member of the National Association of REALTORS®.

7. A major manufacturer of automobiles announces that it will relocate one of its factories, along with 2,000 employees, to Smallville. What effect will this announcement MOST likely have on Smallville's housing market?
    a. Houses will be likely to become less expensive as a result of the announcement.
    b. Houses will likely become more expensive as a result of the announcement.
    c. Because the announcement involves an issue of demographics, not of supply and demand, housing prices will stay the same.
    d. The announcement involves an industrial property; residential housing will not be affected.

8. A licensee who has several years of experience in the industry decided to retire from actively marketing properties. Now she helps clients choose among the various alternatives involved in purchasing, using, or investing in property. What is her profession?
    a. Real estate counselor
    b. Real estate appraiser
    c. Real estate educator
    d. REALTOR®

9. The words broker and REALTOR® are
    a. interchangeable.
    b. different categories of membership in the National Association of REALTORS®.
    c. different titles offered by separate professional organizations.
    d. unrelated: A broker is a real estate licensee and a REALTOR® is a member of the National Association of REALTORS®.

10. Schools would be considered part of which real estate classification?
    a. Special purpose
    b. Industrial
    c. Commercial
    d. Government-held

11. An individual who manages the day-to-day operations of a mandatory, common interest property in a homeowners' association is a
    a. property counselor.
    b. property manager.
    c. financial asset manager.
    d. community association manager.

12. A community association manager performs everything EXCEPT
    a. negotiating leases for the owners of the common interest property.
    b. managing the affairs of owners with a common interest in a property.
    c. handling financial matters for the owners of common interest property.
    d. handling the day-to-day operations of common interest property.

CHAPTER 2

Real Property and the Law

- ■ **identify** the rights that convey with ownership of real property and the characteristics of real estate.

- ■ **describe** the difference between real and personal property and the various types of personalty.

- ■ **explain** the types of laws that affect real estate.

- ■ **distinguish** among the concepts of land, real estate, and real property.

- ■ **define** the following *key terms*:

accession	fixture	severance
air rights	heterogeneity	situs
annexation	improvement	subsurface rights
appurtenance	land	surface right
area preference	nonhomogeneity	trade fixture
bundle of legal rights	personal property	water rights
chattel	real estate	
emblements	real property	

■ LAND, REAL ESTATE, AND REAL PROPERTY

The words *land*, *real estate*, and *real property* are often used interchangeably. To most people, they mean the same thing. Strictly speaking, however, the terms refer to different aspects of the same idea. To fully understand the nature of real estate and the laws that affect it, licensees must be aware of the subtle yet important differences in meaning of these words.

Land

Land is defined as *the earth's surface extending downward to the center of the earth and upward to infinity, including permanent natural objects such as trees and water.* (See Figure 2.1.)

Land, then, includes not only the surface of the earth but also the underlying soil. It refers to things that are *naturally* attached to the land, such as boulders and plants. It includes the minerals and substances that lie far below the earth's surface. Land even includes the air above the earth, all the way up into space. These are known respectively as the *subsurface* and the *airspace*. Most of the surface of the earth, of course, is not land at all, but water. Special state and local laws govern the ownership of the wetter part of the earth, including lakes and rivers, as discussed in Chapter 7.

Real Estate

Real estate is defined as land *at, above, and below the earth's surface, plus all things permanently attached to it whether natural or artificial.* (See Figure 2.1.)

FIGURE 2.1

Land, Real Estate, and Real Property

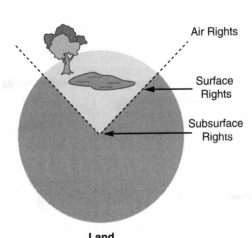

Land
Earth's surface to the center of the earth and the airspace above the land, including the trees and water

Real Estate
Land plus permanent human-made additions

Real Property
Real estate plus "bundle of legal rights"

The term *real estate* is similar to the term *land*, but it means much more. *Real estate* includes not only the natural components of the land but also all man-made improvements. An **improvement** is any artificial thing attached to the land, such as a building or a fence. The term *improvement*, as used in the real estate industry, refers to *any* addition to the land. The word is neutral. It doesn't matter whether the artificial attachment makes the property better-looking or more useful; the land is still said to be *improved*. Land also may be improved by streets, utilities, sewers, and other additions that make it suitable for building.

Real Property

The term *real property* is the broadest of all. It includes both land and real estate. **Real property** is defined as *the interests, benefits, and rights that are automatically included in the ownership of land and real estate*. (See Figure 2.1.)

Real property includes the surface, subsurface, and airspace, any improvements, and the legal rights of ownership that attach to ownership of a parcel of real estate.

Traditionally, ownership of real property is described as a **bundle of legal rights.** In other words, a purchaser of real estate actually buys the rights of ownership held by the seller. These rights include the

- right of *possession*;
- right to *control* the property within the framework of the law;
- right of *enjoyment* (that is, to use the property in any legal manner);
- right of *exclusion* (to keep others from entering or using the property); and
- right of *disposition* (to sell, will, transfer, or otherwise dispose of or encumber the property).

The concept of a bundle of rights comes from old English law. In the Middle Ages, a seller transferred property by giving the purchaser a handful of earth or a bundle of bound sticks from a tree on the property. The purchaser, who accepted the bundle, then owned the tree from which the sticks came and the land to which the tree was attached. Because the rights of ownership (like the sticks) can be separated and individually transferred, the sticks became symbolic of those rights. (See Figure 2.2.)

The word *title* to real property has two meanings: (1) the right to or ownership of the land as represented by the owner's bundle of rights and (2) evidence of that ownership by a deed. *Title* refers to ownership of real property, not to a printed document. The document by which the owner transfers title to the real property is the *deed*.

Real property is often coupled with the word *appurtenance*. An **appurtenance** is a right or privilege associated with the property, although not necessarily a part of it. Typical appurtenances include parking spaces in multiunit buildings, easements, water rights, and other improvements. An appurtenance is connected to the property, and ownership of the appurtenance normally conveys to the new owner when the property is sold.

FIGURE 2.2

The Bundle of Legal Rights

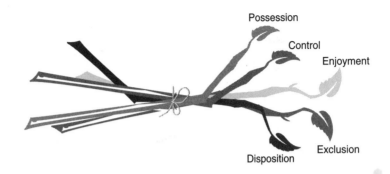

Possession

Control

Enjoyment

Exclusion

Disposition

IN PRACTICE When people talk about buying or selling homes, office buildings, and land, they usually call these things real estate. For all practical purposes, the term *real estate* is synonymous with *real property* as defined here. Thus, in everyday usage, real estate includes the legal rights of ownership specified in the definition of *real property*. Sometimes people use the term *realty* instead.

Subsurface, air, and water rights The right to use the surface of the earth is referred to as a **surface right.** However, real property ownership can also include **subsurface rights,** which are the rights to the natural resources lying below the earth's surface. Although it may be difficult to imagine, the two rights are distinct. An owner may transfer his or her surface rights without transferring the subsurface rights.

■ **FOR EXAMPLE** Anne sells the rights to any oil and gas found beneath her farm to an oil company. Later, Anne sells the remaining interests (the surface, air, and limited subsurface rights) to Bob, reserving the rights to any coal that may be found in the land. Bob sells the remaining land to Charles, but Bob retains the farmhouse, stable, and pasture. After these sales, four parties have ownership interests in the same real estate: (1) the oil company owns all the oil and gas; (2) Anne owns all the coal; (3) Bob owns the farmhouse, stable, and pasture; and (4) Charles owns the rights to the remaining real estate. (See Figure 2.3.)

The rights to use the air above the land, provided the rights have not been preempted by law, may be sold or leased independently. **Air rights** can be an important part of real estate, particularly in large cities, where air rights over railroads must be purchased to construct office buildings, such as the MetLife Building in New York City and the Prudential Building in Chicago. To construct such a building, the developer must purchase not only the air rights but also numerous small portions of the land's surface for the building's foundation supports.

Before air travel was common, a property's air rights were considered to be unlimited, extending upward into the farthest reaches of outer space. However, now that air travel is common, the courts and the U.S. Congress have put limits on air rights. Today, the courts permit reasonable interference with these rights, such as that necessary for aircraft (and presumably spacecraft), as long as the owner's right to use and occupy the land is not unduly lessened. Governments

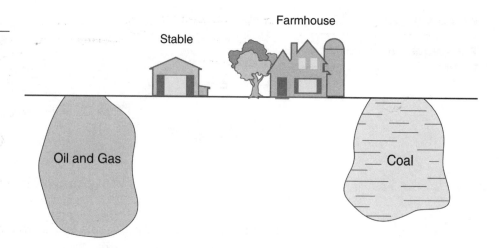

and airport authorities often purchase adjacent air rights to provide approach patterns for air traffic.

With the continuing development of solar power, air rights—and, more specifically, light or solar rights—are being closely examined by the courts. A new tall building that blocks sunlight from a smaller existing building may be held to be interfering with the smaller building's right to sunlight, particularly if systems in the smaller building are solar powered. Air and solar rights are established by laws and ordinances that vary widely from state to state and community to community.

Water rights are special common-law rights held by owners of land adjacent to rivers, lakes, or oceans and are restrictions on the rights of land ownership. Water rights are particularly important rights in drier western states, where water is a scarce and valuable public commodity. Water rights are discussed in Chapter 7.

■ REAL PROPERTY AND PERSONAL PROPERTY

Personal property, sometimes called *personalty,* is *all property that can be owned, that does not fit the definition of real property;* that is, if it's not real property, it's personal property.

An important distinction between the two is that personal property is *movable.* Items of personal property, also referred to as **chattels,** include such tangibles as chairs, tables, clothing, money, bonds, and bank accounts. Trade fixtures, discussed below, are included in this category.

Manufactured Housing

Manufactured housing is defined as *dwellings that are not constructed at the site but are built off-site and trucked to a building lot where they are installed or assembled.* Manufactured housing includes modular, panelized, precut, and mobile homes.

Generally, however, the term *mobile homes* is used to refer to factory-built housing constructed before 1976. Use of the term *mobile homes* was phased out with the passage of the National Manufactured Housing Construction and Safety Standards Act of 1976 when manufactured homes became federally regulated. Nevertheless, the term *mobile home* is still commonly used among licensees. Most states have agencies that administer and enforce the federal regulations for manufactured housing.

The distinction between real and personal property is not always obvious. Manufactured housing, for example, is generally considered personal property even though its mobility may be limited to a single trip to a park or development to be hooked up to utilities. Manufactured housing may, however, be considered real property if it becomes permanently affixed to the land. The distinction is generally one of state law. Whether manufactured housing is characterized as real or personal property may have an effect on how it is taxed. Real estate licensees should be familiar with local laws before attempting to sell manufactured housing. Some states permit only specially licensed dealers to sell such housing; other states require no special licensing.

In Georgia

Every retailer and retail broker who sells or offers for sale manufactured or mobile homes in Georgia must obtain a license. The license is valid from January 1 through December 31 of the year in which it was issued.

Under the Georgia Code (O.C.G.A. 8-2-183.1), there are conditions under which manufactured homes become real property. A manufactured home that has not been issued a certificate of title from the Georgia Real Estate Commission and that was sold on or after July 1, 2006, becomes real property if

1. the home is or is to be permanently affixed on real property and one or more persons with ownership interest in the home also has ownership interest in the real property; and
2. the owner of the home and the holders of all security interests execute and file a Certificate of Permanent Location in the county records where the property is located.

Once a Certificate of Permanent Location has been filed, the home becomes, for all legal purposes, a part of the real property on which it is located.

Plants

Trees and crops generally fall into one of two classes: (1) Trees, perennial shrubbery, and grasses that do not require annual cultivation, known as *fructus naturales*, are considered real estate; (2) annual plantings or crops of wheat, corn, vegetables, and fruit, known as **emblements** or *fructus industriales*, are generally considered personal property. As long as an annual crop is growing, it will be transferred as part of the real property unless other provisions are made in the sales contract. For example, a farmer won't have to dig up growing corn plants and haul them away unless the sales contract says so: The young corn remains on the land. The farmer may come back and harvest the corn when it's ready. The former owner or tenant is entitled to harvest the crops that result from his or her labor. Perennial crops, such as orchards or vineyards, are not personal property and so convey with the land.

An item of real property can become personal property by **severance.** For example, a growing tree is real estate until the owner cuts it down, literally severing it from the property. Similarly, an apple becomes personal property once it is picked from a tree.

It is also possible to change personal property into real property. If, for example, a landowner buys cement, stones, and sand, mixes them into concrete, and constructs a sidewalk across his or her land, the landowner has converted personal property (cement, stones, and sand) into real property (a sidewalk). This process is called **annexation.**

> The term used in the law for plants that do not require annual cultivation (such as trees and shrubbery) is *fructus naturales* (fruits of nature); **emblements** are known in the law as *fructus industriales* (fruits of industry).

Licensees need to know whether property is real or personal for many reasons. An important distinction arises, for instance, when the property is transferred from one owner to another. Real property is conveyed by deed, while personal property is conveyed by a bill of sale. Transfers of property are discussed in Chapter 12.

Classifications of Fixtures

In considering the differences between real and personal property, it is necessary to distinguish between a *fixture* and personal property.

Fixtures   A **fixture** is *personal property that has been so affixed to land or a building that, by law, it becomes part of the real property.* Examples of fixtures are heating systems, elevator equipment in highrise buildings, radiators, kitchen cabinets, light fixtures, and plumbing. Almost any item that has been added as a permanent part of a building is considered a fixture.

During the course of time, the same materials may be both real and personal property, depending on their use and location.

Legal tests of a fixture   The overall test that is used in determining whether an item is a fixture (real property) or personal property is a question of *intent*. (See Figure 2.4.) Did the person who installed the item intend it to remain permanently on the property or to be removable in the future? In determining intent, courts use the following three basic tests:

1. *Method of annexation:* How *permanent* is the method of attachment? Can the item be removed without causing damage to the surrounding property?
2. *Adaptation to real estate:* Is the item being *used* as real property or personal property? For example, a refrigerator is usually considered personal property. However, if a refrigerator has been adapted to match the kitchen cabinetry, it becomes a fixture.
3. *Agreement:* Have the parties *agreed* on whether the item is real or personal property in an offer to purchase?

Although these tests may seem simple, court decisions have been complex and inconsistent. Property that appears to be permanently affixed has sometimes

F I G U R E 2.4

Legal Tests of a Fixture

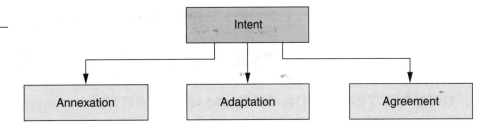

been ruled to be personal property, while property that seems removable has been ruled a fixture. It is important that an owner clarify what is to be sold with the real estate at the very beginning of the sales process.

IN PRACTICE At the time a property is listed, the seller and listing agent should discuss which items to include in the sale. The written sales contract between the buyer and the seller should specifically list all articles that are being included in the sale, particularly if any doubt exists as to whether they are personal property or fixtures (for instance, built-in bookcases, chandeliers, ceiling fans, or exotic shrubbery). This will avoid a misunderstanding between the parties that could result in the collapse of the transaction and expensive lawsuits. The most common disputed items between buyers and sellers are draperies, light fixtures, and appliances.

Trade fixtures A special category of fixtures includes property used in the course of business. An article owned by a tenant and attached to a rented space or building or used in conducting a business is a **trade fixture,** or a *chattel fixture*. Some examples of trade fixtures would be bowling alleys, store shelves, and barroom and restaurant equipment. Agricultural fixtures, such as chicken coops and toolsheds, are also included in this category. Trade fixtures must be removed on or before the last day the property is rented. The tenant is responsible for any damage caused by the removal of a fixture. Trade fixtures that are not removed become the real property of the landlord. Acquiring the property in this way is known as **accession** (this is related to the legal principle of *constructive annexation*).

■ **FOR EXAMPLE** Paul's Pizza leases space in a small shopping center. Paul bolted a large iron oven to the floor of the unit. When Paul's Pizza goes out of business or relocates, Paul will be able to take his pizza oven with him if he can repair the bolt holes in the floor; the oven is a trade fixture. On the other hand, if the pizza oven was brought into the restaurant in pieces, welded together, and set in concrete, Paul might not be able to remove it without causing structural damage. In that case, the oven might become a fixture.

Trade fixtures differ from other fixtures in the following ways:

■ Fixtures belong to the owner of the real estate, but trade fixtures are usually owned and installed by a tenant for the tenant's use.
■ Fixtures are considered a permanent part of a building, but trade fixtures are removable. Trade fixtures may be attached to a building so they appear to be fixtures.

Legally, fixtures are real property, so they are included in any sale or mortgage. Trade fixtures, however, are considered personal property and are not included in the sale or mortgage of real estate, except by special agreement.

■ CHARACTERISTICS OF REAL PROPERTY

Real property possesses seven basic characteristics that define its nature and affect its use. These characteristics fall into two broad categories—*economic* characteristics and *physical* characteristics.

Economic Characteristics

The four economic characteristics of land that affect its value as a product in the marketplace are scarcity, improvements, permanence of investment, and area preference.

Scarcity We usually do not consider land a rare commodity, but only about a quarter of the earth's surface is dry land; the rest is water. The total supply of land, then, is not limitless. While a considerable amount of land remains unused or uninhabited, the supply in a given location or of a particular quality is generally considered to be finite.

Improvements Building an improvement on one parcel of land can affect the land's value and use as well as that of neighboring tracts and whole communities. For example, constructing a new shopping center or selecting a site for a nuclear power plant or toxic waste dump can dramatically change the value of land in a large area.

Permanence of investment The capital and labor used to build an improvement represent a large fixed investment. Although even a well-built structure can be razed to make way for a newer building, improvements such as drainage, electricity, water, and sewerage remain. The return on such investments tends to be long term and relatively stable.

Location Most people are familiar with the popular saying that the three most important characteristics of a property are location, location, and location. Sometimes referred to as **area preference** or **situs**, this economic characteristic does not refer only to geography. Rather, it refers to people's preferences for one area over another, based on a number of factors. Area preference is based on such factors as history, reputation, convenience, and scenic beauty—as well as simple geography. It is the unique quality of these preferences that result in the different values for similar properties. Whatever it's called, however, remember: *Location is the single most important economic characteristic of land.*

■ **FOR EXAMPLE** A river runs through Bedford Falls, dividing the town more or less in half. On the north side of the river, known as North Town, houses sell for an average of $170,000. On the south side of the river, known as Southbank, identical houses sell for more than $200,000. The only difference is that homebuyers

---

Four Economic Characteristics of Real Estate
1. Scarcity
2. Improvements
3. Permanence of Investment
4. Location or Area Preference

think that Southbank is a better neighborhood, even though no obvious difference exists between the two equally pleasant sides of town.

Physical Characteristics

Land has three certain physical characteristics: immobility, indestructibility, and uniqueness.

Immobility   It is true that some of the substances of land are removable and that topography can be changed, but *the geographic location of any given parcel of land can never be changed. It is fixed, immobile*.

Indestructibility   Land is also *indestructible*. This permanence of land, coupled with the long-term nature of improvements, tends to stabilize investments in real property.

The fact that land is indestructible does not, however, change the fact that the improvements on land depreciate and can become obsolete, which may dramatically reduce the land's value. This gradual depreciation should not be confused with the knowledge that the *economic desirability* of a given location can change.

Uniqueness   No two parcels of land are ever exactly the same. Although they may be substantially similar, all parcels differ geographically because each parcel has its own location. The characteristics of each property, no matter how small, differ from those of every other. An individual parcel has no substitute because each is unique. The *uniqueness* of land is also referred to as its **heterogeneity** or **nonhomogeneity.**

Three Physical Characteristics of Real Estate

1. Immobility
2. Indestructibility
3. Uniqueness

■ LAWS AFFECTING REAL ESTATE

The unique nature of real estate has given rise to an equally unique set of laws and rights. Even the simplest real estate transaction involves a body of complex laws. Licensees must have a clear and accurate understanding of the laws that affect real estate.

The specific areas important to the real estate practitioner include the *law of contracts*, the *general property law*, the *law of agency*, and his or her state's *real estate license law*. All of these will be discussed in this text. Federal regulations, such as environmental laws, as well as federal, state, and local tax laws, also play an important role in real estate transactions. State and local land-use and zoning laws have a significant effect on the practice of real estate, too.

Obviously, a real estate practitioner can't be an expert in all areas of real estate law. However, licensees should know and understand some basic principles. Perhaps most important is the ability to recognize problems that should be referred to a competent attorney. Only attorneys are trained and licensed to prepare documents defining or transferring rights in property and to give advice on matters

Laws Affecting Real Estate

- Contract law
- General property law
- Agency law
- Real estate license law
- Federal regulations
- Federal, state, and local tax laws
- Zoning and land-use laws
- Federal, state, and local environmental regulations

of law. *Under no circumstances may a broker or salesperson act as an attorney unless he or she is also a licensed attorney representing a client in that capacity.*

All phases of a real estate transaction should be handled with extreme care. Carelessness in handling the negotiations and documents connected with a real estate sale can lead to disputes and expensive legal actions. The result can be a financial loss, a loss of goodwill in the community, a loss of business, or, in some cases, the loss or suspension of a real estate license.

Real estate license laws Because brokers and salespersons are involved with other people's real estate and money, the need for regulation of their activities has long been recognized. The purpose of real estate license laws is to protect the public from fraud, dishonesty and incompetence in real estate transactions. All 50 states, the District of Columbia, and all Canadian provinces have passed laws that require real estate brokers and salespersons to be licensed. Although state license laws are similar in many respects, they differ in some details, such as the amount and type of prelicense education required.

In Georgia | The practice of real estate in Georgia is governed by the Georgia Real Estate License Law, Title 43, Chapter 40 of the O.G.C.A. Other related laws can be found in the Georgia Code and the Rules and Regulations of the Georgia Real Estate Commission. Georgia license laws and rules are discussed in Chapter 14.

In all states, applicants must meet specific personal and educational qualifications. In addition, they must pass an examination to ensure at least a minimum level of competency. To qualify for license renewal, licensees must follow certain standards of business conduct. Many states also require that licensees complete continuing education courses.

It is extremely important that anyone planning to become a licensed real estate professional be fully aware of his or her state's specific license laws, licensure requirements, and rules and regulations governing the conduct of real estate agents in the state. When a licensee's practice is likely to extend into other states, he or she must be aware of these laws and regulations as well.

■ KEY POINT REVIEW

Land

- is the earth's **surface,** and where **water rights** are held by owners of land adjacent to rivers, lakes, or oceans;
- extends downward to the center of the earth, where **subsurface rights** include **mineral rights** and other natural resources, and those subsurface rights can be transferred separately from surface rights;
- stretches upward to infinity, and **air rights** can be sold separately from surface rights with some limitations to enable air travel;
- includes things **naturally attached** to the land, such as
  — **fructus naturales,** trees and crops not needing cultivation, and
  — **perennial crops,** orchards, and vineyards.

Real estate is

- land at, above, and below the earth's surface, plus
- all things **permanently attached** to the land, both
  - **natural** (trees, boulders) and
  - **artificial** (human-made improvements, such as buildings).

Real property is defined as the interests, benefits, and rights that are automatically included in the ownership of land and real estate. The **bundle of legal rights** includes the following:

- Right of **possession**
- Right to **control** the property
- Right of **enjoyment**
- Right of **exclusion**
- Right of **disposition**

In some states by law, and in common use, real estate and real property both refer to the land, improvements, and rights of ownership, and also may be referred to as **realty.**

Title to real property means the

- **right to ownership** of the land—bundle of rights, and
- **evidence of ownership** by written document, a **deed,** by which title is transferred.

An **appurtenance** is a right or privilege associated with real property in some way, such as a parking space in a multiunit building, an easement, or water rights, and is normally conveyed to the new owner when the property is sold.

Personal property (chattels) is all property that is not real property, is **movable,** and includes

- **emblements (fructus industriales),** annual plantings or crops of grains, vegetables, and fruit;
- items of real property that can become personal property by **severance** (removal);
- items of personal property that can become real property by **attachment** (construction materials); and
- **manufactured homes** that can be personal property unless **permanently affixed** to land.

In Georgia   In Georgia, once a Certificate of Permanent Location has been filed, a manufactured home becomes part of the real property.

A **fixture** is personal property that has been affixed to the land or to a building so that by law it becomes part of the real property. Legal tests for a fixture include the following:

- **Method of annexation**—not easily removable?
- **Adaptation to real estate**—ordinarily considered a permanent addition?

■ **Agreement of the parties**—stated as part of real estate in offer to purchase?

Trade fixtures (chattel fixtures) include property attached to the structure but used in the course of business such as

■ **personal property** if removed by tenant and the premises are returned to original condition before the lease expires; and
■ real property if left behind by tenant. The landlord can acquire this type of property by **accession,** an action related to the legal principle of **constructive annexation.**

The **characteristics of real estate** include the following:

■ Economic
   — Scarcity
   — Improvements
   — Permanence of investment
■ **Location**—most important
■ Physical
   — Immobility
   — Indestructibility
   — **Uniqueness—heterogeneity** or **nonhomogeneity**

The **laws** affecting real estate include the following:

■ State laws regarding **contracts, property, agency,** and **real estate licensing,** where **all** states require real estate brokers and salespersons to be licensed with requirements differing from state to state
■ State and local **land-use** and **zoning** laws
■ Federal and state **environmental** and **tax** laws

■ RELATED WEB SITES

Georgia Real Estate Commission, Real Estate License Law & Rules and
     Regulations: *www.grec.state.ga.us/about/relaw.html*
Manufactured Housing Institute: *www.manufacturedhousing.org*

CHAPTER 2 QUIZ

1. Real estate generally includes all the following *EXCEPT*
   a. trees.
   b. air rights.
   c. annual crops.
   d. mineral rights.

2. Harry owns a building in a commercial area of town. Tina rents space in the building and operates a bookstore. In Tina's bookstore, she has installed large reading tables fastened to the walls and bookshelves that create aisles from the front of the store to the back. These shelves are bolted to both the ceiling and the floor. Which of the following *BEST* characterizes the contents of Tina's bookstore?
   a. The shelves and tables are trade fixtures and will convey when Harry sells the building.
   b. The shelves and tables are trade fixtures and may properly be removed by Tina before her lease expires.
   c. Because Tina is a tenant, the shelves and tables are fixtures and may not be removed except with Harry's permission.
   d. Because the shelves and tables are attached to the building, they are treated the same as other fixtures.

3. The term *nonhomogeneity* refers to
   a. scarcity.
   b. immobility.
   c. uniqueness.
   d. indestructibility.

4. Another term for personal property is
   a. realty.
   b. fixtures.
   c. chattels.
   d. fructus naturales.

5. When an owner of real estate sells the property to someone else, which of the "sticks" in the bundle of legal rights is he or she using?
   a. Exclusion
   b. Legal enjoyment
   c. Control
   d. Disposition

6. Sam inherited Rolling Hills from his uncle. The first thing he did with the vacant property was to remove all the topsoil, which he sold to a landscaping company. Sam then removed a thick layer of limestone and sold it to a construction company. Finally, he dug 40 feet into the bedrock and sold it for gravel. When Sam died, he left Rolling Hills to his daughter, Pat. Which of the following statements is *TRUE*?
   a. Pat inherits nothing because Rolling Hills no longer exists.
   b. Pat inherits a large hole in the ground, but it is still Rolling Hills, down to the center of the earth.
   c. Pat owns the gravel, limestone, and topsoil, no matter where it is.
   d. Sam's estate must restore Rolling Hills to its original condition.

7. The buyer and the seller of a home are debating whether a certain item is real or personal property. The buyer says it is real property and should convey with the house; the seller says it is personal property and would not convey without a separate bill of sale. In determining whether an item is real or personal property, a court would *NOT* consider which of the following?
   a. The cost of the item when it was purchased
   b. Whether its removal would cause severe damage to the real estate
   c. Whether the item is clearly adapted to the real estate
   d. Any relevant agreement of the parties in their contract of sale

8. Which of the following is a physical characteristic of land?
   - a. Indestructibility
   - b. Improvements
   - c. Area preference
   - d. Scarcity

9. Which of the following describes the act by which real property can be converted into personal property?
   - a. Severance
   - b. Accession
   - c. Conversion
   - d. Separation

10. When moving into a newly purchased home, the buyer discovered that the seller had taken the electric lighting fixtures that had been installed over the vanity in the bathroom at the time of purchase. The seller had not indicated that the fixtures would be removed, and the contract did not address this issue. Which of the following is *TRUE*?
    - a. Lighting fixtures are normally considered to be real estate.
    - b. The lighting fixtures belong to the seller because he installed them.
    - c. These lighting fixtures are considered trade fixtures.
    - d. Original lighting fixtures are real property, but replacement fixtures would be personal property.

11. A buyer purchased a parcel of land and immediately sold the mineral rights to an oil company. The buyer gave up which of the following?
    - a. Air rights
    - b. Surface rights
    - c. Subsurface rights
    - d. Occupancy rights

12. Jerome is building a new enclosed front porch on his home. A truckload of lumber that he purchased has been left on his driveway for use in building the porch. At this point, the lumber is considered to be
    - a. real property because it will be permanently affixed to the existing structure.
    - b. personal property.
    - c. a chattel that is real property.
    - d. a trade or chattel fixture.

13. Method of annexation, adaptation to real estate, and agreement between the parties are the legal tests for determining whether an item is
    - a. a trade fixture or personal property.
    - b. real property or real estate.
    - c. a fixture or personal property.
    - d. an improvement.

14. Parking spaces in multiunit buildings, water rights, and similar things of value are classified as
    - a. covenants.
    - b. emblements.
    - c. chattels.
    - d. appurtenances.

15. A paint company purchases 100 acres of scenic forest land and builds several tin shacks there to store used turpentine, varnish, and similar chemical waste. Based on these facts alone, which of the following statements is *TRUE*?
    - a. The company's action constitutes improvement of the property.
    - b. The chemicals are considered appurtenances.
    - c. If the company is in the business of storing toxic substances, the tin shacks are considered trade fixtures.
    - d. Altering the property in order to store waste is not included in the bundle of legal rights.

CHAPTER 3

Concepts of Home Ownership

■ **identify** the various types of housing choices available to homebuyers.

■ **describe** the issues involved in making a home ownership decision.

■ **explain** the tax benefits of home ownership and the provisions of changes to the Tax Code.

■ **distinguish** the various types of homeowners' insurance policy coverage.

■ **define** the following *key terms:*

coinsurance clause	homeowners' insurance policy	liability coverage
equity		replacement cost

■ HOME OWNERSHIP

People buy their own homes for psychological as well as financial reasons. To many people, home ownership is a sign of financial stability. A home is an investment that can appreciate in value and provide federal income tax deductions. Home ownership also offers benefits that may be less tangible but are no less valuable, such as pride, security, and a sense of belonging to the community.

Types of Housing

As U.S. society evolves, the needs of its homebuyers become more specialized. The following paragraphs describe the types of housing currently available to meet these needs. Some housing types are not only innovative uses of real estate, but they also incorporate a variety of ownership concepts. These different forms of housing respond to the demands of a diverse marketplace.

Apartment complexes are groups of apartment buildings with any number of units in each building. The buildings may be lowrise or highrise, and the complexes may include parking, security, clubhouses, swimming pools, tennis courts, and even golf courses.

Condo = conventional
ownership
Co-op = proprietary lease

The *condominium* is a popular form of residential ownership, particularly for people who want the security of owning property without the care and maintenance that a house demands. It is also a popular ownership option in areas where property values make single-unit ownership inaccessible for many people. Condominium owners own their units individually and share ownership of common facilities (called *common elements*) such as halls, elevators, swimming pools, clubhouses, tennis courts, and surrounding grounds. Management and maintenance of building exteriors and common facilities are provided by the governing association and outside contractors, with expenses paid out of monthly assessments charged to owners. While condos are often apartment-style homes, this ownership form includes single-family and even commercial properties. The condominium form of ownership is discussed in Chapter 8.

A *cooperative* also has units that share common walls and facilities within a larger building. The owners, however, do not actually *own* the units. Instead, a corporation holds title to the real estate itself. The unit owners actually purchase shares of stock in the corporation, not their individual units. Owners receive *proprietary leases, not conventional deeds* that entitle them to occupy particular units. Like condominium unit owners, cooperative unit owners pay their share of the building's expenses. Cooperatives are discussed in Chapter 8.

Planned unit developments (PUDs), sometimes called *master-planned communities*, merge such diverse land uses as housing, recreation, and commercial units into one self-contained development. PUDs are planned under special zoning ordinances. These ordinances permit maximum use of open space by reducing lot sizes and street areas. Owners do not have direct ownership interest in the common areas. A community association is formed to maintain these areas, with fees collected from the owners. A PUD may be a small development of just a few homes or an entirely planned city.

Retirement communities, many of them in temperate climates, are often structured as PUDs. They may provide shopping, recreational opportunities, and health care facilities in addition to residential units. Security and convenience are major advantages offered by retirement communities to older homeowners.

Highrise developments, sometimes called *mixed-use developments* (MUDs), combine office space, stores, theaters, and apartment units in a single vertical community. MUDs usually are self-contained and offer laundry facilities, restaurants, food stores, valet shops, beauty parlors, barbershops, swimming pools, and other attractive and convenient features.

Converted-use properties are factories, warehouses, office buildings, hotels, schools, barns, churches, and other structures that have been converted to residential use. Developers often find renovation of such properties more aesthetically and economically appealing than demolishing a perfectly sound structure to build something new. An abandoned warehouse may be transformed into luxury loft condominium units; a closed hotel may reopen as an apartment building; and an old factory may be recycled into a profitable shopping mall.

Manufactured housing (also known as a *mobile home*) was once considered useful only as temporary residences. Now, however, mobile homes are more often permanent principal residences or stationary vacation homes. Relatively low cost, coupled with the increased living space available in the newer models, has made such homes an attractive option for many people. Increased sales have resulted in growing numbers of *housing parks* in some communities. These parks offer complete residential environments with permanent community facilities as well as semipermanent foundations and hookups for gas, water, and electricity.

Modular homes (also referred to as *prefabricated homes*) are also gaining popularity as the price of newly constructed "stick-built" homes rises. Each room in a modular home is preassembled at a factory, driven to the building site on a truck, then lowered onto its foundation by a crane. Later, workers finish the structure and connect plumbing and wiring. Entire developments can be built at a fraction of the time and cost of conventional stick-built construction.

Through *time-shares*, multiple purchasers share ownership of a single property, usually a vacation home. Each owner is entitled to use the property for a certain period of time each year, usually a specific week or month. In addition to the purchase price, each owner pays an annual maintenance fee.

■ HOUSING AFFORDABILITY

Congress, state legislatures, and local governments have been working to increase the affordability of housing for all people. In recent years, creative financing, low interest loans, and interest-only loans have helped make housing more affordable. As a result, according to the U.S. Bureau of the Census, by the end of year 2005, 68.88 percent of households were homeowners. However, real estate prices have risen, making it difficult for some buyers to save the down payment and closing costs needed to secure a conventional loan. Because more homeowners mean more business opportunities, real estate and related industry groups have a vital interest in ensuring affordable housing for all segments of the population.

Certainly, not everyone wants to own a home. Home ownership involves substantial commitment and responsibility. People whose work requires frequent moves or whose financial position is uncertain particularly benefit from renting. Renting also provides more leisure time by freeing tenants from management and maintenance.

Those who choose home ownership must evaluate many factors before they decide to purchase property. And the purchasing decision must be weighed carefully in light of each individual's financial circumstances. Renters can probably make a higher mortgage payment than their current rent payment, without requiring a pay increase, because of the tax savings realized by home ownership.

The decision to buy or to rent property involves considering

- how long a person wants to live in a particular area,
- a person's financial situation,
- housing affordability,
- current mortgage interest rates,
- tax consequences of owning versus renting property, and
- what may happen to home prices and tax laws in the future.

Mortgage Terms

Liberalized mortgage terms and payment plans offer many people the option of purchasing a home. Low down-payment mortgage loans are available under programs sponsored by the Federal Housing Administration (FHA) and the Department of Veterans Affairs (VA).

An increasing number of creative mortgage loan programs are being offered by various government agencies and private lenders. Adjustable-rate loans, whose lower initial interest rate makes it possible for many buyers to qualify for a mortgage loan, are now common. Specific programs may offer lower closing costs or deferred interest or principal payments for purchasers in targeted neighborhoods or for first-time buyers. Many innovative loans are tailored to suit the younger buyer, who may need a low interest rate to qualify but whose income is expected to increase in the coming years.

In recent years, the relaxed requirements for subprime loans have contributed to an increase in loan foreclosures.

Ownership Expenses and Ability to Pay

Home ownership involves many expenses, including utilities, such as electricity, natural gas, and water, trash removal, sewer charges, and maintenance and repairs. Owners also must pay real estate taxes and buy property insurance, and they must repay the mortgage loan with interest.

To determine whether a prospective buyer can afford a certain purchase, lenders mostly use automated underwriting and credit scoring. In the past, the formula for homebuyers who were able to provide at least 10 percent of the purchase price as a down payment was: The monthly cost of buying and maintaining a home—mortgage payments, both principal and interest, plus taxes and insurance impounds—could not exceed 28 percent of gross (i.e., pretax, monthly income). The payments on all debts—normally including long-term debt such as car payments, student loans, or other mortgages—could not exceed 36 percent of monthly income. Expenses such as insurance premiums, utilities, and routine medical care were not included in the 36 percent figure but were considered to be covered by the remaining 64 percent of the buyer's monthly income. These formulas may vary, however, depending on the type of loan program and the borrower's earnings, credit history, number of dependents, and other factors. But today, credit scores play a key role when lending institutions decide whether to lend money. (Note that these financial qualification ratios are true for most Fannie Mae and Freddie Mac conforming mortgages, but there are many loans available with ratios more liberal than these.)

■ **FOR EXAMPLE**   A prospective homebuyer wants to know how much house he or she can afford to buy. The buyer has a gross monthly income of $5,000. The buyer's allowable housing expense may be calculated as follows:

$5,000 gross monthly income × 28% = $1,400 total housing expense allowed

$5,000 gross monthly income × 36% = $1,800 total housing and other debt expense allowed

These formulas allow for other debts of 8 percent of gross monthly income—the difference between the 36 percent and 28 percent figures. If actual debts exceed the amount allowed and the borrower is unable to reduce them, the monthly payment would have to be lowered proportionately because the debts and housing payment combined cannot exceed 36 percent of gross monthly income. However, lower debts would not result in a higher allowable housing payment; rather, it would be considered a factor for approval.

> **Memory Tip**
> **Remember PITI**
>
> The basic costs of owning a home—mortgage Principal and Interest, Taxes, and Insurance, can be remembered by the acronym **PITI.**

Investment Considerations

Purchasing a home offers several financial advantages to a buyer. First, if the property's value increases, a sale could bring in more money than the owner paid—a long-term gain. Second, as the total mortgage debt is reduced through monthly payments, the owner's actual ownership interest in the property increases. This increasing ownership interest is called **equity** and represents the paid-off share of the property, held free of any mortgage. A tenant accumulates nothing except a good credit rating by paying the rent on time; a homeowner's mortgage payments build equity and so increase his or her net worth. Equity builds even further when the property's value rises. The third financial advantage of home ownership is the tax deduction available to homeowners but not to renters.

Tax Benefits

To encourage home ownership, the federal government allows homeowners certain income tax advantages. Homeowners may deduct from their income some or all of the mortgage interest paid, as well as real estate taxes and certain other expenses. Tax considerations may be an important part of any decision to purchase a home.

In the late 1990s, the federal government enacted several federal tax reforms that significantly changed the importance of tax considerations for most home-sellers. For instance, $500,000 is now excluded from capital gains tax for profits on the sale of a principal residence by married taxpayers who file jointly. Taxpayers who file singly are entitled to a $250,000 exclusion. The exemption may be used repeatedly, as long as the homeowners have both owned and occupied the property as their residence for at least two of the past five years. On investment real estate, the required period for a noncorporate taxpayer was changed from 18 months to 12 months for long-term capital gain.

> Current Market Value – Property Debt = **Equity**

First-time homebuyers may make penalty-free withdrawals from their tax-deferred individual retirement funds (IRAs) for down payments on their homes. However, these withdrawals are still subject to income tax. The limit on such withdrawals is $10,000 and must be spent entirely within 120 days on a down payment to avoid the 10 percent penalty.

In short, the changes in tax laws have generally benefited home ownership, which is good news for homeowners and real estate professionals.

Tax deductions Homeowners may deduct from their gross income

- mortgage *interest* payments on first and second homes (for mortgage balances below $1 million or $500,000 if married filing separately),
- real estate taxes (but *not* interest paid on overdue taxes),
- certain loan origination fees,
- loan discount points (whether paid by the buyer or the seller), and
- loan prepayment penalties.

IN PRACTICE Note that appraisal fees, notary fees, preparation costs, mortgage insurance premiums, and VA funding fees are not interest but are part of the cost of acquiring a home. When it is sold at a later date, these charges can be figured into the cost *basis*. Points are deductible in the year of a house purchase if certain criteria are met. Points are deducted over the life of the loan for a refinance. Note that real estate licensees should not provide tax advice and that homeowners should consult with accountants or attorneys about home ownership tax deductions. The rules are complicated and constantly changing.

■ HOMEOWNERS' INSURANCE

A home is frequently the biggest investment many people ever make. Most homeowners see the wisdom in protecting such an important investment by insuring it. Lenders usually require that a homeowner obtain insurance when the debt is secured by the property. While owners can purchase individual policies that insure against destruction of property by fire or windstorm, injury to others and theft of personal property, most buy a packaged **homeowners' insurance policy** to cover all these risks.

Coverage and Claims

The most common homeowner's policy is called a *basic form*. The basic form provides property coverage against

- fire and lightning,
- glass breakage,
- windstorm and hail,
- explosion,
- riot and civil commotion,
- damage by aircraft,
- damage from vehicles,
- damage from smoke,
- vandalism and malicious mischief,
- theft, and
- loss of property removed from the premises when it is endangered by fire or other perils.

A *broad-form* policy is also available. Broad-form homeowners' insurance covers

- falling objects;
- damage due to the weight of ice, snow, or sleet;
- collapse of all or part of the building;
- bursting, cracking, burning, or bulging of a steam or hot water heating system or of appliances used to heat water;
- accidental discharge, leakage, or overflow of water or steam from within a plumbing, a heating, or an air-conditioning system;
- freezing of plumbing, heating, and air-conditioning systems and domestic appliances; and
- injury to electrical appliances, devices, fixtures, and wiring from short circuits or other accidentally generated currents.

Further insurance is available from policies that cover almost all possible perils. Special apartment and condominium policies generally provide fire and windstorm, theft, and public **liability coverage** for injuries or losses sustained within the unit. However, they do not usually cover losses or damages to the structure. The basic structure is insured by either the landlord or the condominium owners' association.

Most homeowners' insurance policies contain a **coinsurance clause.** This provision usually requires that the owner maintain insurance equal to at least 80 percent of the **replacement cost** of the dwelling (not including the price of the land). An owner who has this type of policy may make a claim for the full cost of the repair or replacement of the damaged property without deduction for depreciation or annual wear and tear.

If the homeowner carries less than 80 percent of the full replacement cost, however, the claim will be handled in one of two ways. Either the loss will be settled for the *actual cash value* (replacement cost less depreciation) or it will be *prorated* by dividing the percentage of replacement cost actually covered by the policy by the minimum coverage requirement (usually 80 percent).

■ **FOR EXAMPLE** Tom's insurance policy is for 80 percent of the replacement cost of his home, or $80,000. His home is valued at $100,000, and the land is valued at $40,000. Tom sustains $30,000 in fire damage to his house. Tom can make a claim for the full cost of the repair or replacement of the damaged property, without deduction for depreciation. However, if Tom had insurance of only $70,000, his claim would be handled in one of two ways. He would receive either actual cash value (replacement cost of $30,000 less depreciation cost of say $3,000, or $27,000), or his claim would be prorated by dividing the percentage of replacement cost actually covered (0.70) by the policy minimum coverage requirement (0.80). So, 0.70 divided by 0.80 equals 0.875, and $30,000 multiplied by 0.875 equals $26,250.

Comprehensive Loss Underwriting Exchange

Comprehensive Loss Underwriting Exchange (CLUE) is a database of consumer claim history that enables insurance companies to access prior claim information in the underwriting and rating process. The database contains up to five years of personal property claim history. The reports include policy information such as name, date of birth, policy number, and claim information date (date and type of loss, amounts paid, and description of property covered).

IN PRACTICE Water-related problems have emerged in some properties over time. In particular, significant problems can occur with synthetic stucco exterior finishes and mold. The *exterior insulating finishing system* (EIFS) is a highly effective moisture barrier that also tends to *seal in* moisture—trapping water in the home's walls and resulting in massive wood rot. Frequently, the effects of the rotting cannot be seen until the damage is extensive and sometimes irreparable. If a homeowner suspects that EIFS was used on their home and is causing damage, the homeowner should have the property inspected. Some insurance companies refuse to cover homes with EIFS exteriors, and class action lawsuits have been brought against builders by distressed homeowners.

■ FEDERAL FLOOD INSURANCE PROGRAM

The National Flood Insurance Act of 1968 was enacted by Congress to help owners of property in flood-prone areas by subsidizing flood insurance and by taking land-use and land-control measures to improve future management for floodplain areas. The Federal Emergency Management Agency (FEMA) administers the flood program. The Army Corps of Engineers has prepared maps that identify specific flood-prone areas throughout the country. To finance property with federal or federally related mortgage loans, owners in flood-prone areas must obtain flood insurance. If they do not obtain the insurance, either they don't want it or they don't qualify. Because their communities may not have properly entered the program, they may not be eligible for this financial assistance.

In designated areas, flood insurance is required on all types of buildings—residential, commercial, industrial, and agricultural—for either the value of the property or the amount of the mortgage loan, subject to the maximum limits available. Policies are written annually and can be purchased from any licensed property insurance broker, the National Flood Insurance Program (NFIP), or the designated servicing companies in each state. However, if a borrower can produce a survey showing that the lowest part of the building is located above the 100-year flood mark, the borrower may be exempted from the flood insurance requirement, even if the property is in a flood-prone area.

IN PRACTICE   Massive losses in the NFIP due to the Mississippi floods in 1993 caused Congress to pass laws that greatly increase the number of properties that are required to be covered by the NFIP. This requirement not only results in higher expenses for the buyer but can also negatively affect property values. Agents should pay attention to what property is in a flood zone and communicate that to potential buyers.

■ KEY POINT REVIEW

The **types of housing** available incorporate a variety of **ownership concepts,** including the following:

- Single-family homes
- Apartment complexes
- Condominiums
- Cooperatives
- Planned unit developments (PUDs)
- Mixed-use developments (MUDs)
- Modular homes (prefabricated homes)
- Manufactured housing (mobile homes)
- Time-shares

Housing affordability has been aided by creative financing, low-interest loans, adjustable-rate loans, interest-only loans, and low-down-payment loans sponsored by the **Federal Housing Administration (FHA)** and the **Department of Veterans Affairs (VA)**.

The decision to rent or to buy is influenced by the following:

- Length of time individual will reside in area
- Individual's financial situation
- Housing **affordability**
- Current **mortgage interest rates**
- **Tax consequences** of owning versus renting property
- What may happen to home prices and tax laws in the future
- Ownership expenses and ability to pay the **PITI,** an acronym for the following:
  - <u>P</u>rincipal
  - <u>I</u>nterest
  - <u>T</u>axes
  - <u>I</u>nsurance
- Credit score
- **Investment** considerations for the homeowner include the following:
  - **Appreciation** in the value of the property
  - **Equity increase** with an **amortized** loan as the principal is paid
  - Tax deductions
  - **Capital gains taxation exclusion** of $250,000 or $500,000 profit on sale of principal residence, if owned and occupied at least two of the past five years

A first-time homeowner may make penalty-free withdrawals from an **individual retirement account (IRA)** for a down payment on a home within certain limits.

A **homeowners' insurance policy** is usually required by the lender, and the **basic policy** covers the following:

- Fire and lightning, windstorm and hail, glass breakage
- Explosion, riot, and civil commotion
- Damage by aircraft, vehicles, and smoke
- Vandalism, malicious mischief, and theft
- Loss of property removed from the premises when it is endangered by fire or other perils

The **homeowners' insurance broad-form policy** covers the following:

- Falling objects and damage due to weight of ice, snow, or sleet
- Collapse of all or part of the building
- Bursting, cracking, burning, or bulging of steam or hot water heating system or appliances used to heat water
- Accidental discharge, leakage, or overflow of water or steam from within a plumbing, heating, or air-conditioning system

- Freezing of plumbing, heating, and air-conditioning systems and domestic appliances
- Injury to electrical appliances, devices, fixtures, and wiring from short circuits or other accidentally generated currents

A **coinsurance clause** requires the homeowner to maintain insurance equal to at least 80 percent of replacement cost of the dwelling for full replacement on loss; if not, the loss will be settled for **actual cash value** or a **prorated amount.**

The **Comprehensive Loss Underwriting Exchange (CLUE)** is a database of consumer insurance claim history.

The **National Flood Insurance Act of 1968** subsidizes flood insurance and is administered by the **Federal Emergency Management Agency (FEMA).**

■ RELATED WEB SITES

Department of Housing and Urban Development (HUD):   *www.hud.gov*
Department of Veterans Affairs: *www.va.gov*
Federal Emergency Management Agency: *www.fema.gov*

CHAPTER 3 QUIZ

1. Which of the following are NOT costs or expenses of owning a home?
    a. Interest paid on borrowed capital
    b. Homeowners' insurance
    c. Maintenance and repairs
    d. Taxes on personal property

2. When a person buys a house using a mortgage loan, the difference between the amount owed on the property and its market value represents the homeowner's
    a. tax basis.
    b. equity.
    c. replacement cost.
    d. capital gain.

3. A building that is remodeled into residential units and is no longer used for the purpose for which it was originally built is an example of a(n)
    a. converted-use property.
    b. urban homesteading.
    c. planned unit development.
    d. modular home.

4. A highrise development that includes office space, stores, theaters, and apartment units is an example of which of the following?
    a. Planned unit development
    b. Mixed-use development
    c. Proprietary lease properties
    d. Special cluster zoning

5. Each room of Jan's house was preassembled at a factory, driven to the building site on a truck, and then lowered onto its foundation by a crane. Later, workers finished the structure and connected plumbing and wiring before Jan moved in. Which of the following terms BEST describes what type of home Jan owns?
    a. Mobile
    b. Modular
    c. Manufactured
    d. Converted

6. Five years ago, Marcia bought a home for $250,000. Home values in her area have improved, and the current market value of Marcia's house has increased by 15 percent. If Marcia has $95,875 left to pay on her mortgage loan, what is her current equity in her home?
    a. $138,712
    b. $154,125
    c. $191,625
    d. $250,000

7. For which of the following risks would a homeowner have to purchase a special policy in addition to a typical basic or broad-form homeowner's insurance policy?
    a. The cost of medical expenses for a person injured in the policyholder's home
    b. Theft
    c. Vandalism
    d. Flood damage

8. Peter wants to buy his first home but doesn't know how much he can afford to pay. He has a gross monthly income of $3,000. According to the traditional lender's rule of thumb formula, what is the total housing expense (principal, interest, taxes, and insurance) Peter can bear?
    a. $1,080
    b. $840
    c. $648
    d. $1,152

9. Marcia and Bob are a married couple who bought their house ten years ago for $150,000. Last week, they sold their home for $225,500. Based on these facts, how much capital gains tax will Marcia and Bob have to pay this year?
    a. None
    b. $7,550
    c. $11,325
    d. $75,500

10. Which of the following *BEST* expresses the concept of equity?

    a. Current Market Value minus Capital Gain
    b. Current Market Value minus Property Debt
    c. Current Market Value minus Cost of Land
    d. Replacement Cost minus Depreciation

11. Carol and her husband bought their house in 1968 (when they were 21) for $25,000 and have lived in it ever since. Today, the neighborhood has become very fashionable, and they sell the house for $450,000. How much of the gain is taxable on the couple's joint return this year?

    a. $25,000
    b. All
    c. None
    d. $637,000

12. Sam and Alice are a married couple who file a joint income tax return and have lived in their home for 20 years. Greg is a single homeowner who has lived in his home for five years. Mike and Cindy are father and daughter and bought their home together last year. Based on these facts, which of the following statements is *TRUE* if all three homes are sold today?

    a. All of these homeowners qualify for a $500,000 exclusion from capital gains taxation on the transactions.
    b. A $500,000 exclusion applies to Sam and Alice as well as to Mike and Cindy; a $250,000 exclusion applies to Greg.
    c. A $500,000 exclusion applies to Sam and Alice; a $250,000 exclusion applies to Greg; and no exclusion applies to Mike and Cindy.
    d. Only Sam and Alice qualify for any exclusion from capital gains taxation.

13. Theft, smoke damage, and damage from fire are covered under which type of homeowners' insurance policy?

    a. Basic form
    b. Broad form
    c. Coinsurance
    d. National Flood Insurance Program policies

14. A community that merges housing, recreation, and commercial units in one self-contained development is called a

    a. MUD.
    b. PUD.
    c. cooperative.
    d. condominium.

15. All of the following would be covered by a basic-form homeowners' insurance policy, *EXCEPT* damage caused by

    a. glass breakage.
    b. riot.
    c. frozen pipes.
    d. vandalism.

Agency

■ **LEARNING OBJECTIVES** *When you have finished reading this chapter, you should be able to:*

■ **identify** the various types of agency relationships common in the real estate profession and the characteristics of each.

■ **describe** the fiduciary duties involved in an agency relationship.

■ **explain** the process by which agency is created and terminated and the role of disclosure in agency relationships.

■ **distinguish** the duties owed by an agent to his or her client from those owed to customers.

■ **define** the following *key terms:*

agency	dual agency	listing agreement
agency coupled with an interest	express agency	negligent misrepresentation
agent	express agreement	principal
BRRETA	fraud	puffing
buyer's agents	general agent	special agent
client	implied agency	subagent
customer	implied agreement	universal agent
designated agent	law of agency	

■ INTRODUCTION TO REAL ESTATE AGENCY

The relationship between a real estate licensee and the parties involved in a real estate transaction is not a simple one. In addition to the parties' assumptions and expectations, the licensee is subject to a wide range of legal and ethical requirements designed to protect the seller, the buyer, and the transaction itself. **Agency** is the word used to describe that special relationship between a real estate licensee and the person he or she represents. Agency is governed by two kinds of law: *common law,* the rules of a society established by tradition and court decisions, and *statutory law,* the laws, rules, and regulations enacted by legislatures and other governing bodies.

The History of Agency

The basic framework of the law that governs the legal responsibilities of the broker to the people he or she represents is known as the *common-law law of agency.* The fundamentals of agency law have remained largely unchanged for hundreds of years. However, the *application* of the law has changed dramatically, particularly in residential transactions and especially in recent years. As states enact legislation that defines and governs the broker-client relationship, brokers are reevaluating their services. They must determine whether they will represent the seller, the buyer, or both (if that is permitted by state law) in a transaction. Where state laws permit, an increasing number of brokers are choosing to represent buyers exclusively. Brokers also must decide how they will cooperate with other brokers, depending on which party each broker represents. In short, the brokerage business is undergoing many changes as brokers focus on ways to enhance their services to buyers and sellers.

In Georgia	In Georgia, under O.C.G.A. 10-6A-12, a broker may act as a dual agent, but only with express written permission. Exclusive representation is also allowed in Georgia under O.C.G.A. 10-6A-13.

Even as the laws change, however, the underlying assumptions that govern the agency relationship remain intact. The principal-agent relationship evolved from the master-servant relationship under English common law. In that relationship, the servant owed absolute loyalty to the master. This loyalty replaced the servant's personal interests as well as any loyalty the servant might owe to others. In a modern-day agency relationship, the agent owes the principal similar loyalty. As masters used the services of servants to accomplish what they could not or did not want to do for themselves, principals use the services of agents. The agent is regarded as an expert on whom the principal can rely for specialized professional advice.

■ LAW OF AGENCY

The **law of agency** defines the rights and duties of the principal and the agent. It applies to a variety of business transactions. In real estate transactions, contract law and real estate licensing laws—in addition to the law of agency—interpret the relationship between licensees and their clients. The law of agency is a common-law concept (law from the judgments and decrees of courts as opposed to the legislature); it is being widely replaced by state statute.

In Georgia

In Georgia, the law of agency is governed by state statute, Title 10, Chapter 6A, "Brokerage Relationships in Real Estate Transactions," or **BRRETA.** The Georgia Code replaces the common law of agency.

Creation of Agency

An agency relationship may be based on a formal agreement between the parties, an **express agency,** or it may result from the parties' behavior, an **implied agency.**

Express agency   The principal and agent may enter into a contract, or an **express agreement,** in which the parties formally express their intention to establish an agency and state its terms and conditions. The agreement may be either oral or written. An agency relationship between a seller and a broker is generally created by a written employment contract, commonly referred to as a **listing agreement,** which authorizes the broker to find a buyer or tenant for the owner's property. Although a written listing agreement is usually preferred, some states consider an oral agreement binding. An express agency relationship between a buyer and a broker is created by a *buyer agency agreement.* Similar to a listing agreement, it stipulates the activities and responsibilities the buyer expects from the broker in finding the appropriate property for purchase or rent.

Implied agency   An agency may also be created by **implied agreement.** This occurs when the actions of the parties indicate that they have mutually consented to an agency. A person acts on behalf of another as agent; the other person, as principal, delegates the authority to act. Even though the parties may not have consciously planned to create an agency relationship, nonetheless, they can create one *unintentionally, inadvertently,* or *accidentally* by their actions.

In Georgia

Georgia recognizes implied agency.

■ **FOR EXAMPLE**   Nancy tells Betsy, a real estate broker, that she is thinking about selling her home. Betsy immediately contacts several prospective buyers. One of them makes an attractive offer without even seeing the property. Betsy goes to Nancy's house and presents the offer, which Nancy accepts. Although no formal agency agreement was entered into either orally or in writing, Betsy's actions *implied* to prospective buyers that Betsy was acting as Nancy's agent. If Betsy made any misrepresentations to the buyer, Nancy may be held liable. In addition, since Nancy accepted the offer, she may be obligated to pay a commission to Betsy.

Even though licensees may be required to disclose their agency status, it is often difficult for customers to understand the complexities of the law of agency. A buyer can easily assume that when he or she contacts a salesperson to show property to the buyer, the salesperson becomes his or her agent, even though, under a listing contract, the salesperson may *legally* represent the seller. An implied agency with the buyer can result if the words and conduct of the salesperson do not dispel this assumption. Otherwise, one agency relationship is created in conflict with another. *Dual representation*, which will be discussed in greater detail later in this chapter, may occur, even though it was not intended. Note that some state laws prohibit the creation of agency by implied actions or conduct.

`In Georgia` **Compensation** In Georgia, the *source of compensation does not determine agency* (O.C.G.A. 10-6A-11). An agent does not necessarily represent the person who pays his or her commission. In fact, agency can exist even if no fee is involved (called a *gratuitous agency*). For instance, a seller could agree to pay a commission to the buyer's agent, even though the agent is representing the buyer. The written agency agreement should state how the agent is being compensated and explain all the alternatives available.

Definitions

Real estate brokers and salespersons are commonly called **agents**. Legally, however, the term refers to strictly defined legal relationships. In the case of real estate, it is a relationship with buyers and sellers or with landlords and tenants.

`In Georgia` Under Georgia statute (O.C.G.A. 10-6A-3), the following terms have specific definitions:

- **Agency**—every relationship in which a real estate broker acts for or represents another as a client by the latter's written authority in a real property transaction.
- **Broker**—any individual or entity issued a broker's real estate license by the Georgia Real Estate Commission. The term "broker" includes the broker's affiliated licensees except where the context would otherwise indicate.
- **Brokerage engagement** (or listing or agency agreement)—a written contract where the seller, buyer, landlord, or tenant becomes the client of the broker and promises to pay the broker a valuable consideration or agrees that the broker may receive a valuable consideration from another in consideration of the broker producing a seller, buyer, tenant, or landlord ready, able, and willing to sell, buy, or rent or performing other brokerage services.
- **Brokerage relationship**—the agency and nonagency relationships that may be formed between the broker and the broker's clients and customers.
- **Client**—a person being represented by a broker in an agency capacity pursuant to a brokerage engagement.
- **Common source information companies**—any person, firm, or corporation that is a source, complier, or supplier of information regarding real estate for sale or lease and other data and includes, but is not limited to, multiple listing services.
- **Customer**—a person not being represented by a broker but for whom a broker may perform ministerial acts in a real estate transaction according to a verbal or written agreement.

- **Designated agent(s)**—one or more licensees affiliated with a broker who are assigned by the broker to represent solely one client to the exclusion of all other clients in the same transaction and to the exclusion of all other licensees affiliated with the broker.
- **Dual agent**—a broker who simultaneously has a client relationship with both seller and buyer or landlord and tenant in the same real estate transaction.
- **Material facts**—those facts that a party does not know, could not reasonably discover, and would reasonably want to know.
- **Ministerial acts**—acts as described in BRRETA and other acts that do not require the exercise of the broker's or the broker's affiliated licensees' professional judgment or skill, such as identifying property for sale and providing real estate statistics and information on property.
- **Transaction broker**—a broker who has not entered into a client relationship with any of the parties to a real estate transaction and who performs only ministerial acts on behalf of one or more of the parties, but who is paid valuable consideration by one or more parties to the transaction pursuant to a verbal or written agreement for performing brokerage services.

The discussion in this chapter is limited to the duties and obligations under BRRETA, which supersedes the principles governing traditional common-law agency relationships. Such common-law principles include duties of care, obedience, loyalty, disclosure, accounting, and confidentiality. While BRRETA lists duties and obligations to a client that include elements of common-law agency duties, the Georgia statute specifically states that it alone governs brokerage relationships in Georgia (O.C.G.A. 10-6A-4).

An agent works *for* the client and *with* the customer.

There is a distinction between the level of services an agent provides to a *client* and those services that the agent provides to a *customer*. The *client* is the **principal** to whom the agent gives advice and counsel. The agent is entrusted with certain *confidential information* and has *responsibilities* to the principal. In contrast, the *customer* is entitled to factual information and fair and honest dealings as a consumer but does not receive advice and counsel or confidential information about the principal. Any third party is a customer. The *agent works* **for** *the principal and* **with** *the customer*. Essentially, the agent supports and defends the principal's interests, not the customer's.

The relationship between the principal and agent must be *consensual*; that is, the principal *delegates* authority, and the agent *consents* to act. The parties must agree to form the relationship. An agent may be authorized by the principal to use the assistance of another, who may or may not, depending on local state law, become a **subagent** of the principal. The practice of subagency, while still legal in most states (including Georgia), is seldom practiced in most real estate markets due to the increased liability it entails for listing brokers.

Just as the agent owes certain duties to the principal, the principal has responsibilities toward the agent. The principal's primary duties are to comply with the agency agreement and cooperate with the agent; that is, the principal must not hinder the agent and must deal with the agent in good faith. The principal also must compensate the agent according to the terms of the agency agreement.

IN PRACTICE   Subagency is rapidly becoming the dinosaur of the real estate industry. In many areas, the multiple listing services (MLSs) or individual companies are refusing even to accept subagency.

Duties and Obligations

The agency agreement (or the "brokerage engagement" in Georgia) usually authorizes the broker to act for the principal. The agent's relationship of trust and confidence with the principal means that the broker owes the principal certain specific duties. These duties are not simply moral or ethical; they are the law under Georgia statute (O.C.G.A. 10-6A-5 through 10-6A-8).

`In Georgia`

`In Georgia`

10-6A-5: Duties and responsibilities of broker engaged by seller   A broker engaged by a seller must:

1. Perform the terms of the brokerage engagement made with the seller
2. Promote the interests of the seller by
   — seeking a sale at the price and terms as noted in the brokerage engagement or acceptable to the seller. The broker is not obligated to seek additional offers while the property is subject to a contract of sale, unless the brokerage engagement says otherwise;
   — promptly presenting all offers to and from the seller, even when the property is subject to a contract of sale;
   — disclosing material facts to the seller that the broker has actual knowledge of concerning the transaction;
   — advising the seller to obtain expert advice on matters beyond the broker's expertise; and
   — promptly accounting for all money and property received where the seller has or may have an interest.
3. Exercise reasonable skill and care in performing these duties under state statute, and performing any other duties the parties agree to in the brokerage engagement
4. Comply with all requirements of applicable statutes and regulations, including fair housing and civil rights laws
5. Maintain confidentiality for information received by the broker during the course of an engagement that is expressly requested by the seller unless the seller permits disclosure or disclosure is required by law. Disclosures between a broker and any of the broker's affiliated licensees assisting the broker in representing the seller do not breach the duty of confidentiality.

10-6A-7: Duties of broker engaged by buyer   A broker engaged by a buyer must:

1. Perform the terms of the brokerage engagement made with the buyer
2. Promote the interests of the buyer by
   — seeking a property at a price and terms acceptable to the buyer. However, a broker is not obligated to seek other properties for the buyer while the buyer is a party to a contract to purchase property, unless the brokerage engagement provides otherwise;

— presenting all offers to and from the buyer in a timely manner, even when the buyer is a party to a contract to purchase property;

— disclosing to the buyer adverse material facts about which the broker has actual knowledge concerning the transaction;

— advising the buyer to obtain expert advice regarding matters beyond the broker's expertise; and

— promptly accounting for all money and property received in which the buyer has or may have an interest.

3. Exercise ordinary skill and care in performing these duties and any other duties agreed to by the parties

4. Comply with all requirements of the state statutes and regulations, including fair housing and civil rights laws

5. Maintain confidentiality of all information received by a broker during the course of an engagement that is expressly requested by the buyer unless the buyer allows disclosure or it is required by law. However, disclosures between a broker and any of the broker's affiliated licensees assisting the broker in representing the buyer are not deemed to breach the duty of confidentiality.

Duties of broker engaged by landlord or tenant BRRETA, O.C.G.A. 10-6A-6, also lists the duties of a broker engaged by a landlord, including the duty to seek a tenant at the price and terms acceptable to the landlord and presenting all offers to and from the landlord. In O.C.G.A. 10-6A-8, BRRETA defines the duties of a broker engaged by a tenant, including the duty to seek a property to lease at a price and terms acceptable to the tenant and presenting all offers on behalf of the tenant in a timely manner. BRRETA clearly states that a broker may perform ministerial acts to the landlord while representing the tenant or to the tenant while representing the landlord without violating the terms of the brokerage engagement to the broker's principal.

Termination of Agency

In Georgia

Under Georgia statute (O.C.G.A. 10-6A-9), an agency commences at the time the client engages the broker, and may be terminated for any of the following reasons:

■ Completion of performance of the engagement; or

■ If completion of performance of the engagement is not applicable, the earlier of

— any date of expiration agreed upon by the parties in the brokerage engagement or in any amendments;

— any authorized termination of the relationship; or

— if no expiration is provided and no termination has occurred, then one year after initiation of the engagement.

After termination of the agency, the broker owes no further duties to the client, except a) to account for all moneys and property relating to the engagement; and b) to keep confidential all information received during the course of the engagement made confidential at the request of the client. Unless the client permits disclosure by subsequent work or conduct, disclosure is required by law, or the information becomes public from a source other than the broker.

Georgia law, O.C.G.A. 10-6A-9(c), is clear about what happens in the event a conflict arises between a broker's duty to keep the confidence of a client and the duty not to give customers false information. In this situation, the broker's duty to not give false information to customers prevails and governs the broker's actions.

An **agency coupled with an interest** is an agency relationship in which the agent is given an interest in the subject of the agency, such as the property being sold. An agency coupled with an interest cannot be revoked by the principal or be terminated upon the principal's death.

■ **FOR EXAMPLE** A broker agrees to provide the financing for a condominium building being constructed by a developer in exchange for the exclusive right to sell the units once the building is completed. The developer may not revoke the listing agreement once the broker has provided the financing because this is an agency coupled with an interest.

■ TYPES OF AGENCY RELATIONSHIPS

In Georgia

In Georgia, types of agency relationships are governed by the Brokerage Relationships in Real Estate Transactions Act (BRRETA), Title 10, Chapter 6A. Under O.C.G.A. 10-6A-4, a broker owes only the duties and obligations as set forth under statute, unless the parties expressly agree otherwise in writing signed by the parties.

BRRETA (O.C.G.A. 10-6A-10) requires all brokers to advise prospective clients of the types of agency relationships available through the broker. The broker must advise a prospective client of any brokerage relationship that would conflict with any interests of the client actually known by the broker, as well as the broker's compensation and whether the broker may share that compensation with other parties to the transaction. The broker must also advise the prospective client of the broker's obligations to keep information confidential.

A **universal agent** is a person empowered to do *anything* the principal could do personally. The universal agent's authority to act on behalf of the principal is virtually unlimited. A real estate broker typically does *not* have this scope of authority as an agent in a real estate transaction. This type of agency can be created by a general power of attorney, which makes the agent an attorney in fact.

A **general agent** may represent the principal in a broad range of matters related to a *particular business or activity*. The general agent may, for example, bind the principal to any contract within the scope of the agent's authority. A property manager typically is a general agent for the owner, and most sales agents are general agents of their broker.

A **general agent** represents the principal *generally*; a **special agent** represents the principal only for *special occasions*, such as the sale of a house.

A **special agent** or *limited agent* is authorized to represent the principal in *one specific act or business transaction only, under detailed instructions.* A real estate broker is usually a special agent. If hired by a seller, the broker is limited to finding a ready, willing, and able buyer for the property. A special agent for a buyer would have the limited responsibility of finding a property that fits the buyer's criteria. As a special agent, the broker may not bind the principal to any contract. A *special power of attorney* is another means of authorizing an agent to carry out only a specified act or acts.

■ **FOR EXAMPLE**   You are very busy with an important project, so you give your colleague $5 and ask him to buy your lunch. Your colleague is your *general agent:* You have limited his or her scope of activity to a particular business (buying your lunch) and established the amount that may be spent (up to $5). Still, he or she has broad discretion in selecting what you will eat and where he or she will buy it. However, if you had told your colleague, "Please buy me a Number 3 salad at Lettuce Eat Lettuce," you would have further limited his or her authority to a very specific task. Your colleague, therefore, would have been your *special agent*.

In Georgia

Finally, a **designated agent,** under Georgia law, means one or more licensees affiliated with a broker who are assigned by the broker to represent only one client to the exclusion of all other clients in the same transaction and to the exclusion of all other licensees affiliated with the broker.

Single Agency

In single agency, the agent represents only one party in any single transaction. In Georgia, the agent owes statutory duties exclusively to one principal, who may be *either* the buyer or the seller (or the landlord or tenant) in a transaction. The customer is the party not represented by the agent. (See Figure 4.1.)

In Georgia

While a single agency broker may represent both sellers and buyers, he or she cannot represent both in the same transaction and remain a single agent. This avoids conflicts and results in client-based service and loyalty to only one client. On the other hand, it traditionally rules out the sale of in-house listings to represented buyers, although in designated agency states this may be permitted. The broker must establish policies for the firm that define for whom the client services are performed.

FIGURE   4.1

Single Agency

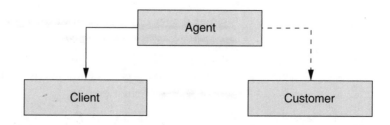

Subagency

A subagency is created when one broker, usually the seller's agent, appoints other brokers (with the seller's permission) to help perform client-based functions on the principal's behalf. These *cooperating brokers* have the same fiduciary obligation to the seller as does the listing broker, helping produce a ready, willing, and able buyer for the property. Subagency can expose the seller's broker (and agent) to liability for the actions of the subagent. This arrangement may be created through an offer of cooperation and compensation made in an MLS.

IN PRACTICE   Under the agency statutes of some states, real estate agents are specifically prohibited from making offers of subagency through an MLS. Licensees should be aware of their states' laws regarding subagency.

In Georgia   In Georgia, subagency is rarely used because of the liability issues and potential dual agency in MLS coop transactions.

Seller Representation

If a seller contracts with a broker to market the seller's real estate, the broker becomes an *agent* of the seller; the seller is the *principal*, the broker's *client*. In single agency, a buyer who contacts the broker to review properties listed with the broker's firm is the broker's *customer*. Though obligated to deal fairly with all parties to a transaction and to comply with all aspects of the license law, the broker is strictly accountable only to the principal—in this case, the seller. The customer (in this case, the buyer) represents himself or herself. However, more common today is the situation where the buyer is also represented.

The listing contract usually authorizes the broker to use licensees employed by the broker as well as the services of other cooperating brokers in marketing the seller's real estate. These cooperating brokers may assist the broker (agent) as subagents, buyer's agents, or nonagents, or they may be the agents for other parties.

The relationship of a salesperson or an associate broker to an employing broker is also an agency. These licensees are thus agents of the broker and owe the same duties as the broker to the principal.

Buyer Representation

When a buyer contracts with a broker to locate property and represent his or her interests in a transaction, the buyer is the *principal*—the broker's client. The broker, as *agent*, is strictly accountable to the buyer. The seller is the customer.

In the past, it was simple: Brokers always represented sellers, and buyers were expected to look out for themselves. With the widespread use of MLSs and subagency, a buyer often had the mistaken impression that the subagent was the buyer's agent, although the reality was that both agent and subagent represented the seller's interests.

Today, however, most residential brokers and salespersons are discovering the opportunities of buyer representation. Some brokers and salespersons have become specialists in the emerging field of buyer brokerage, representing buyers exclusively. Real estate commissions or boards across the country have developed rules and procedures to regulate such *buyer's brokers,* and local real estate associations develop agency representation forms and other materials for them to use. Professional organizations offer assistance, certification, training, and networking opportunities for **buyer's agents.**

A buyer agency relationship is established in the same way as any other agency relationship: by contract or agreement (see Figure 4.3). The buyer's agent may receive a flat fee or a share of the commission or both, depending on the terms of the agency agreement. Buyer brokerage and buyer agency agreements are discussed in Chapter 6.

IN PRACTICE   Many broker transactions use cooperative agents. When a broker puts a seller's house in an MLS, the broker is basically inviting other agents from other companies to cooperate with the broker in his or her representation of the seller. The broker is still the seller's agent, and the other agents are not the seller's agent. If a cooperative agent helps a broker sell a house, the broker pays the agent a co-op fee out of the broker's commission. The amount of the fee is noted in the MLS listing. For example, it might say, "CC:04," meaning the co-operative commission is 4 percent.

Participation in an MLS, by itself, does not necessarily create a subagency relationship. Because of widespread agency reforms, a co-operating broker cannot be presumed to be a subagent.

In Georgia

In Georgia, under O.C.G.A. 10-6A-15, a broker is not to be considered a subagent of any client of another broker solely because of membership or another affiliation by the broker in a common source information company, including but not limited to multiple listing services. In addition, a broker is not deemed to have an agency relationship with a common source information company, unless provided for in a written agreement between the parties.

Owner as Principal

An owner may employ a broker to market, lease, maintain, or manage the owner's property. Such an arrangement is known as *property management.* The broker is made the agent of the property owner through a property management agreement. As in any other agency relationship, the broker has a statutory responsibility to the client-owner. Sometimes, an owner may employ a broker for the sole purpose of marketing the property to prospective tenants. In this case, the broker's responsibility is limited to finding suitable tenants for the owner's property. Property management is discussed further in Chapter 18.

Dual Agency

In **dual agency**, the agent represents two principals in the same transaction. Dual agency requires equal loyalty to two separate principals at the same time. Because agency originates with the broker, dual agency arises when the broker is the agent of the buyer *and* either the agent or subagent of the seller. The salespersons, as agents of the broker, have fiduciary or statutory responsibilities to the same principals as well. The challenge is to fulfill the fiduciary or statutory obligations to one principal without compromising the interests of the other, especially when the parties' interests may not only be separate, but even opposite. While practical methods of ensuring fairness and equal representation may exist, it should be noted that a dual agent can never fully represent either party's interests. (See Figure 4.2.)

Because of the obvious risks inherent in dual agency—ranging from conflicts of interest to outright abuse of trust—the practice is illegal in some states. In those states where dual agency is permitted, however, all parties must consent to it, usually in writing.

■ **FOR EXAMPLE**   Mary, a real estate broker, is the agent for the owner of Roomy Manor, a large mansion. Jody, a prospective buyer, comes into Mary's office and asks Mary to represent her in her search for a modest home. After several weeks of activity, including two offers unsuccessfully negotiated by Mary, Jody spots the For Sale sign in front of Roomy Manor. She tells Mary she wants to make an offer and asks for Mary's advice on a likely price range. Mary is now in the difficult position of being a dual agent: Mary represents the seller, who naturally is interested in receiving the highest possible price, and the buyer, who is interested in making a successful low offer.

Disclosed dual agency   Real estate licensing laws may permit dual agency only if the buyer and seller are *informed* and *consent* to the broker's representation of both in the same transaction. Although the possibility of conflict of interest still exists, disclosure is intended to minimize the risk *for the broker* by ensuring that both principals are aware of the effect of dual agency on their respective interests. The disclosure alerts the principals that they may have to assume greater responsibility for protecting their interests than they would if they had independent representation. The broker must reconcile how, as agent, he or she will discharge the fiduciary duties on behalf of both principals, particularly providing loyalty and protecting confidential information. Because the duties of disclosure and confidentiality are limited by mutual agreement, they must be carefully explained to the parties in order to establish *informed consent*.

FIGURE   4.2

Dual Agency

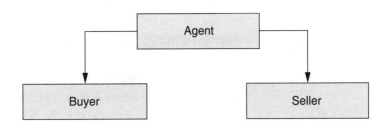

Georgia law (O.C.G.A. 10-6A-12) has specific requirements for a broker acting as a dual agent. A broker may act as a dual agent only with the written consent of all clients. The written consent must contain

- a description of the transaction(s) in which the broker will serve as a dual agent;
- a statement that the broker represents two clients whose interests are or at times could be different or even adverse;
- a statement that a dual agent will disclose all adverse material facts relevant to the transaction and actually known to the dual agent to all parties in the transaction, except for confidential information that is not allowed to be disclosed by Georgia law;
- a statement that the broker or the broker's affiliated licensees will disclose in a timely manner to each client in a real estate transaction the nature of any material relationship the broker and the broker's affiliated licensees have with the other clients in the transaction other than those incidental to the transaction (a material relationship means any known personal, familial, or business relationship between the broker or the broker's affiliated licensees and a client that would impair the ability of the broker or affiliated licensees to exercise fair and independent judgment with another client);
- a statement that the client does not have to consent to the dual agency; and
- a statement that consent was given voluntarily and that the engagement has been read and understood.

A broker may withdraw from representing a client who has not consented to a disclosed dual agency at any time prior to the existence of the dual agency and will not be held liable. When a withdrawal occurs, the broker may receive a referral fee for referring a client to a broker employed by a different real estate brokerage firm.

Every broker must develop and enforce an office brokerage relationship policy among affiliated licensees which either permits or rejects the practice of disclosed dual agency.

Dual agency has existed in everyday real estate practice in every state for more than a century. In small, mostly rural market areas, there was often only one broker available. Because of the limited population of the market, the broker knew most of the local properties and residents (and possibly their parents and grandparents) very well. In situations like this, it was virtually impossible to avoid dual agency. Of course, in such circumstances, there was usually no problem because the parties all knew and trusted each other. Such situations are rare today, having been complicated by changes in society and in the license laws.

Designated agency In some states, including Georgia, designated agency is legal. Under BRRETA (O.C.G.A. 10-6A-13), a designated agent has the same duties and responsibilities as a broker engaged by a seller, buyer, landlord, or tenant. If a broker appoints different designated agents, neither the broker, the broker's licensees, nor the brokerage firm is deemed to be dual agents.

When designated agents are appointed, the broker, the clients, and the designated agents are considered to possess only actual knowledge and information. No knowledge is imputed between and among the broker, designated agents, and the clients. Designated agents must not disclose, except to the designated agent's broker, confidential information. Confidential information is defined as any information the disclosure of which has not been consented to by the client that could harm the negotiating position of the client.

Undisclosed dual agency   A broker may not intend to create a dual agency. However, like any other agency, it may occur *unintentionally* or *inadvertently*. Sometimes the cause is carelessness. Other times a salesperson does not fully understand his or her fiduciary responsibilities. Some salespersons lose sight of other responsibilities when they focus intensely on bringing buyers and sellers together. For instance, a salesperson representing the seller might suggest to a buyer that the seller will accept less than the listing price. Or that same salesperson might promise to persuade the seller to accept an offer that is in the buyer's best interests. *Giving a buyer any specific advice on how much to offer can lead the buyer to believe that the salesperson represents the buyer's interests and is acting as the buyer's advocate.*

Any of these actions can create an *implied* agency with the buyer and violate the duties of loyalty and confidentiality to the principal-seller. Because neither party has been informed of the situation and been given the opportunity to seek separate representation, the interests of both are jeopardized. This undisclosed dual agency violates licensing laws. It can result in the rescission of the sales contract, forfeiture of a commission, a lawsuit for damages, and possible license problems.

■ **FOR EXAMPLE**   Using the previous Roomy Manor example, if Mary doesn't tell Jody that Mary represents the seller of the property, Mary will be an undisclosed dual agent. Mary has two options. First, knowing Jody's comfortable financial situation and intense desire for the property, Mary might choose not to tell Jody about the dual agency situation. Instead, Mary could tell her that Roomy Manor's owner will accept nothing less than the full asking price. While this will ensure that Mary receives the maximum possible commission, it will also subject Mary to severe penalties for violating the state's licensing laws. Alternatively, Mary may disclose her relationship with the seller and work out a dual agency agreement with both parties in which Mary legally represents both parties' interests.

A more common example of dual agency would be if Mary employed two salespersons, Ryan and Sally. Ryan is the listing salesperson for Roomy Manor, and Sally meets and begins representing the buyer, Jody. Because both Ryan and Sally are associated with Mary's real estate brokerage, Mary may be construed as a dual agent and will have to enter into a disclosed dual agency agreement with the parties.

Disclosure of Agency

Licensees are required to reveal for whom they provide client-based services. Understanding the scope of the service a party can expect from the agent allows a customer to make an informed decision about whether to seek his or her own representation.

Mandatory agency disclosure laws now exist in every state, including Georgia. These laws stipulate when, how, and to whom disclosures must be made. They may, for instance, dictate that a particular type of written form be used. The laws might state what information an agent must provide to gain informed consent where disclosed dual agency is permitted. The laws might even go so far as to require that all agency alternatives be explained, including the brokerage firm's policies regarding its services. Frequently, printed brochures outlining agency alternatives are available to a firm's clients and customers.

Whether or not the law requires it, licensees should explain to both buyers and sellers what agency alternatives exist, how client and customer services differ, and how these services affect the interests of each party. Once a client-based relationship is established, it is critical that customers understand how this affects their interests. If the broker represents two principals in the same transaction, the impact on both parties must be explained. A general rule of thumb is to make the disclosure before any confidential information is disclosed about an individual's motivation or financial situation.

In Georgia

In Georgia, under BRRETA (O.C.G.A. 10-6A-10), brokers have duties prior to entering into brokerage engagement relationships. The brokerage engagement must advise the prospective client of the types of agency relationships available through the broker; any brokerage relationships held by the broker with other parties that would conflict with the prospective client's interests, except when a broker is or may be representing other sellers and landlords in selling or leasing property; the broker's compensation; and the broker's obligation to keep information confidential.

Nonagency

A nonagent (also referred to as a *transactional broker, facilitator, coordinator,* or *contract broker*) is not an agent of either party. (Note Georgia's statutory definition of *transaction broker* at the beginning of this chapter.) A nonagent's job is simply to help both the buyer and the seller with the necessary paperwork and formalities involved in transferring ownership of real property. The buyer and the seller negotiate the sale without representation.

In Georgia

The nonagent is expected to treat all parties honestly and competently, to locate qualified buyers or suitable properties, to help the parties arrive at mutually acceptable terms, and to assist in the closing of the transaction. Nonagents are equally responsible to both parties and must disclose known defects in a property. However, they may not negotiate on behalf of either the buyer or the seller, and they must not disclose confidential information to either party. Nonagents are typically paid a commission. Nonagency is legal in only a few states, including Georgia.

■ CUSTOMER-LEVEL SERVICES

Even though an agent's primary responsibility is to the principal, the agent also has responsibilities to third parties. Any time a licensee works with a third party, or **customer,** the licensee is responsible for adhering to state and federal consumer protection laws as well as the ethical requirements imposed by professional associations and state regulators. In addition, the licensee's duties to the customer include

- reasonable care and skill in performance;
- honesty;
- disclosure of all facts that the licensee knows or should reasonably be expected to know that materially affect the value or desirability of the property; and
- accountability.

> An agent owes a **customer** the duties of *reasonable care and skill*; *honesty*; *disclosure of known facts* about the property (not the seller); and *accountability*.

As part of the recent trend for more consumer protection of purchasers, many states have enacted statutes requiring the disclosure of certain property conditions to prospective buyers. Generally, these apply to sellers of residential properties, often for one to four dwelling units. Prepurchase structural inspections, termite infestation reports, or other protective documentation may also be used. The actual disclosures that sellers are required to make vary according to each state's law.

Environmental Hazards

Disclosure of environmental health hazards, which can render properties unusable for the buyer's intended purpose, may be required. For instance, federal law requires the disclosure of lead-based paint hazards. Frequently, the buyer or the buyer's mortgage lender requests inspections or tests to determine the presence or level of risk.

IN PRACTICE   Licensees are urged to obtain advice from state and local authorities responsible for environmental regulation whenever the following conditions may be present: toxic waste dumping; underground storage tanks; contaminated soil or water; nearby chemical or nuclear facilities; and health hazards such as radon, asbestos, and lead paint.

Opinion versus Fact

Brokers, salespersons, and other staff members must always be careful about the statements they make. They must be sure that the customer understands whether the statement is an opinion or a fact. Statements of opinion are permissible only as long as they are offered as opinions and without any intention to deceive.

Statements of fact, however, must be accurate. Exaggeration of a property's benefits is called **puffing.** While puffing is legal, licensees must ensure that none of their statements can be interpreted as fraudulent. **Fraud** is the *intentional misrepresentation* of a material fact in such a way as to harm or take advantage of another person. That includes not only making false statements about a property but also intentionally concealing or failing to disclose important facts.

FIGURE 4.3

Exclusive Buyer Brokerage Agreement

EXCLUSIVE BUYER BROKERAGE AGREEMENT

Georgia
Association
of REALTORS®

2010 Printing

State law prohibits Broker from representing Buyer as a client without first entering into a written agreement with Buyer under O.C.G.A. § 10-6A-1 et. seq.

For and in consideration of the mutual promises contained herein and other good and valuable consideration; _____
_____ as buyer (hereinafter referred to as "Buyer"), and _____
as broker and its affiliated licensees (hereinafter collectively referred to as "Broker") do hereby enter into this Agreement, this date of
_____.

1. **Exclusive Agreement.** Buyer hereby agrees to hire Broker to act as Buyer's exclusive real estate broker and agent to assist Buyer in locating, and to the extent agreed upon elsewhere herein in negotiating, the purchase or exchange of real property. Buyer warrants that Buyer is not a party to any other current buyer brokerage engagement agreement, exclusive or non-exclusive and that any previous buyer brokerage agreement entered into between Buyer and any other real estate brokerage has either been terminated or has expired and not been renewed. Buyer further acknowledges that if another broker is found to be the procuring cause of the purchase of real property by Buyer, Broker shall not be entitled to a real estate commission in said transaction and Buyer shall be responsible for paying Broker's commission.

2. **Term.** The term of this Agreement shall begin on the date of _____ and shall continue through the date of _____, unless otherwise terminated in accordance with this Agreement.

3. **Broker's Duties to Buyer.** Broker's sole duties to Buyer shall be to:
    A. attempt to locate property suitable to Buyer for purchase;
    B. comply with all applicable laws in performing its duties hereunder including the Brokerage Relationships in Real Estate Transactions Act, O.C.G.A. § 10-6A-1 et. seq; and
    C. [Select one. The box not checked shall not be a part of this Agreement.]
        ☐ 1. Assist to the extent requested by Buyer in negotiating the terms of and filling out a pre-printed real estate purchase and sale agreement; or
        ☐ 2. Not assist in negotiating the terms of or filling out a pre-printed real estate purchase and sale agreement and/or counteroffer.

4. **Buyer's Duties.** Buyer agrees to:
    A. work only with Broker (and not with any other real estate broker, licensee or seller) in identifying, previewing, and seeing property for purchase by Buyer;
    B. be available to meet with Broker to see property;
    C. timely respond to communications from Broker;
    D. provide Broker with accurate information as requested by Broker (including financial information about Buyer's financial ability to complete the transaction and written authorization to obtain verification of funds);
    E. inspect and otherwise become familiar with any potentially adverse conditions relating to the physical condition of any property in which Buyer becomes interested, any improvements located on such property and the neighborhood surrounding such property; and
    F. become familiar with the terms of any purchase agreement and other documents which Buyer may sign and comply with the duties and deadlines contained therein.

5. **Retainer Fee.** In entering into this Agreement Buyer has paid Broker a Retainer Fee of $_____
    which shall be non-refundable except as follows. In the event Buyer purchases real property in a transaction in which Broker is paid a commission, the Retainer Fee shall be refunded to Buyer by Broker at the closing of the transaction. Otherwise, the Retainer Fee shall be retained by Broker to partially offset Broker's costs and compensate Broker for Broker's time in providing real estate brokerage services to Buyer.

6. **Commission.**
    A. **Custom in Georgia Is That the Seller Pays the Real Estate Commission.** Buyer acknowledges that the custom in Georgia is for the seller of property to pay the commissions of the real estate brokers. Normally, this obligation is created in a listing agreement in which the seller agrees to pay the listing broker a commission in certain circumstances including the sale of the property. In most cases, these agreements also require the listing broker to share the commission it receives with the broker, if any, working with or representing the Buyer in the transaction if that broker is the procuring cause of the sale (or exchange) of the property. This broker is commonly referred to as the selling broker and in this Agreement is also referred to as "Broker."
    B. **Broker Shall Seek to Be Paid Commission from Either the Listing Broker or Seller.** In all transactions in which Broker is entitled to a real estate commission hereunder, Broker shall seek to be paid its commission from either the listing broker, if the property is listed or from the seller directly if the property is not listed. In any purchase and sale (or exchange) transaction in which Broker is paid its sales commission from either the seller or listing broker, Buyer shall have no further obligation to pay Broker a commission relative to the purchase and sale (or exchange) of the property. Broker agrees to disclose to Buyer any properties in which the seller or listing broker thereof are not offering to pay the selling broker a real estate commission if the selling broker is the procuring cause of the sale.

F4, Exclusive Buyer Brokerage Agreement, Page 1 of 5, 01/01/10

F I G U R E 4.3 (CONTINUED)

Exclusive Buyer Brokerage Agreement

C. **Situations Where Buyer Agrees to Pay Commission.** In the event the prospective seller or listing broker does not pay Broker a sales commission, then Buyer shall pay Broker the following commission ("Commission") at closing on all real property which Buyer purchases, acquires through an exchange or contracts to purchase or exchange during the term of this Agreement (or during the Protected Period after the termination or expiration of this Agreement as discussed in greater detail below). *[Select one or more of the following sections below. The sections not marked shall not be a part of this Agreement]:*

☐ $_____;
☐ (Other)_____;
☐ _____ percent (%) of the sales price;

D. **Separate Commission on Lease.** In addition, if Buyer leases property or enters into a lease/purchase contract during this Agreement, Buyer shall also pay Broker a separate commission for the duration of the lease and any renewal or extension thereof in the amount of _____ and such commission shall be paid as follows: _____.

Notwithstanding any provision to the contrary contained herein, the payment of a leasing commission (including in lease purchase transactions) shall not relieve either Seller or Buyer from paying any sales commission they may owe in a purchase and sale transaction.

7. **Protected Period and Commission.** In the event that during the Protected Period, as that term is defined below, following termination or expiration of this Brokerage Agreement, Buyer purchases, contracts to purchase or exchange, leases or lease purchases any property which during the term of this Agreement was submitted to, identified or shown to Buyer by Broker or for which Broker provided information about to Buyer, then Buyer shall pay Broker at closing or the commencement of any lease, if applicable, the commission or commissions set forth above. The term "Protected Period" shall refer to the _____ day period following the earlier of either: (a) the expiration of this Agreement; or (b) the date that the Agreement is terminated upon the mutual, written consent of the Broker and Buyer. In addition, if this Agreement is terminated by Buyer without the express, written consent of Broker, the Protected Period shall be the time period referenced above plus the number of days remaining on the term of the Agreement at the time it was terminated early without the express written consent of Broker. In such event, the Protected Period shall commence from the date this Agreement was terminated early without the express, written consent of Broker. For the purposes of this Agreement, the term "Buyer" shall include Buyer, all members of the Buyer's immediate family, any legal entity in which Buyer or any member of Buyer's immediate family owns or controls, directly or indirectly, more than ten percent (10%) of the shares or interests therein, and any third party who is acting under the direction or control of any of the above parties. The commission rights and obligations set forth herein shall survive the termination or expiration of this Agreement.

8. **Default by Buyer.** Notwithstanding any provision to the contrary contained herein, in the event Buyer defaults under any contract (including an option contract) to purchase or exchange real property, Buyer agrees to immediately pay Broker a commission that is the greater of either: (a) the commission amount referenced in section 8C, Situations Where Buyer Agrees to Pay Commission above, or (b) the commission Broker would have received had the transaction closed pursuant to any agreement between Broker and either the seller or listing broker of said property. In addition, Buyer agrees to immediately pay the listing broker in said transaction the commission the listing broker would have received had the transaction closed. The listing broker in such transactions is expressly intended to be a third party beneficiary to this Agreement and may enforce its rights to a commission either jointly with Broker or separately.

9. **Limits on Broker's Authority and Responsibility.** Buyer acknowledges and agrees that Broker:
   A. may show property in which Buyer is interested to other prospective buyers;
   B. shall not be responsible to advise Buyer on any matter including but not limited to the following: any matter which could have been revealed through a survey, title search or inspection of the property; the condition of the property, any portion thereof, or any item therein; building products and construction techniques; the necessity or cost of any repairs to the property; mold; hazardous or toxic materials or substances; termites and other wood destroying organisms; the tax or legal consequences of this transaction; the availability and cost of utilities or community amenities; the appraised or future value of the property; any condition(s) existing off the property which may affect the property; the terms, conditions and availability of financing; and the uses and zoning of the property whether permitted or proposed. Buyer acknowledge that Brokers are not experts with respect to the above matters and that, if any of these matters or any other matters are of concern to them, they should seek independent expert advice relative thereto. Buyer acknowledges that Broker shall not be responsible to monitor or supervise any portion of any construction or repairs to property and that such tasks clearly fall outside the scope of real estate brokerage services;
   C. shall owe no duties to Buyer nor have any authority on behalf of Buyer other than what is set forth in this Agreement;
   D. shall make all disclosures required by law;
   E. shall not be responsible for insuring that Buyer complies with the duties and deadlines contained in any purchase agreement entered into by Buyer and that Buyer shall be solely responsible for the same; and
   F. shall, under no circumstances, have any liability greater than the amount of the real estate commission paid hereunder to Broker (excluding any commission amount paid to a cooperating real estate broker, if any) or, if no real estate commission is paid to Broker, than a sum not to exceed one hundred dollars; and
   G. shall be held harmless from any and all claims, causes of action, or damages arising out of or relating to:
      1. inaccurate and/or incomplete information provided by Broker to Buyer;
      2. earnest money handled by anyone other than Broker; or
      3. any injury to persons on the property and/or loss of or damage to the property or anything contained therein.

10. **Disclosures.**
   A. Broker agrees to keep confidential all information which Buyer asks to be kept confidential by express request or instruction unless the Buyer permits such disclosure by subsequent word or conduct or such disclosure is required by law. Buyer acknowledges, however, that Seller and Seller's broker may possibly not treat any offer made by Buyer (including its existence, terms and conditions) as confidential unless those parties have entered into a Confidentiality Agreement with Buyer.

F I G U R E 4.3 (CONTINUED)

Exclusive Buyer Brokerage Agreement

B. Broker may not knowingly give customers false information.

C. In the event of a conflict between Broker's duty not to give customers false information and the duty to keep the confidences of Buyer, the duty not to give customers false information shall prevail.

D. Unless specified below, Broker has no other known agency relationships with other parties that would conflict with any interests of Buyer (except that Broker may represent other buyers, sellers, tenants and landlords in buying, selling or leasing property.)

11. **Disclosure of Potentially Fraudulent Activities.**

A. To help prevent fraud in real estate transactions, Buyer does hereby give Broker permission to report any suspicious, unusual and/or potentially illegal or fraudulent activity (including but not limited to mortgage fraud) to:
    1. Governmental officials, agencies and/or authorities and/or
    2. Any mortgage lender, mortgage insurer, mortgage investor and/or title insurance company (and/or their agents and representatives) could potentially be harmed if the activity was in fact fraudulent or illegal.

B. Buyer acknowledges that Broker does not have special expertise with respect to detecting fraud in real estate transactions. Therefore, Buyer acknowledges that:
    1. Activities which are fraudulent or illegal may be undetected by Broker; and
    2. Activities which are lawful and/or routine may be reported by Broker as being suspicious, unusual or potentially illegal or fraudulent.

12. **Broker's Policy on Agency.** Unless Broker indicates below that Broker is not offering a specific agency relationship, the types of agency relationships offered by Broker are: seller agency, buyer agency, designated agency, dual agency, sub-agency, landlord agency, and tenant agency. The agency relationship(s), if any, not offered by Broker is/are the following: _____

_____

_____

13. **Dual Agency Disclosure.** *[Applicable only if Broker's agency policy is to practice dual agency]* If Buyer and a prospective seller are both being represented by the same Broker, Buyer is aware that Broker will be acting as a dual agent in that transaction and consents to the same. Buyer has been advised that:

A. In serving as a dual agent, Broker is representing two clients whose interests are or at times could be different or even adverse;

B. Broker will disclose all adverse, material facts relevant to the transaction and actually known to the dual agent to all parties in the transaction except for information made confidential by request or instructions from either client which is not otherwise required to be disclosed by law;

C. Buyer does not have to consent to dual agency and, the consent of Buyer to dual agency has been given voluntarily and Buyer has read and understands the brokerage engagement agreement.

D. Notwithstanding any provision to the contrary contained herein, Buyer hereby directs Broker, while acting as a dual agent, to keep confidential and not reveal to the other party any information which could materially and adversely affect Buyer's negotiating position.

E. Broker or Broker's affiliated licensees will timely disclose to each client the nature of any material relationship with other clients other than that incidental to the transaction. A material relationship shall mean any actually known personal, familial, or business relationship between Broker and a client which would impair the ability of Broker to exercise fair and independent judgment relative to another client. The other party whom Broker may represent in the event of dual agency may or may not be identified at the time Buyer enters into this Agreement. If any party is identified after the Agreement and has a material relationship with Broker, then Broker shall timely provide to Buyer a disclosure of the nature of such relationship.

14. **Designated Agency Disclosure.** *[Applicable only if Broker's agency policy is to practice designated agency]* Buyer does hereby consent to Broker acting in a designated agency capacity in transactions in which Broker is representing Buyer and a prospective seller. With designated agency, the Broker assigns one or more of its affiliated licensees exclusively to represent a prospective seller and one or more of its other affiliated licensees exclusively to represent Buyer.

15. **Independent Contractor Relationship.** This Agreement shall create an independent contractor relationship between Broker and Buyer. Broker shall at no time be considered an employee of Buyer. If there is an affiliated licensee of Broker directly assisting Broker in marketing and selling the Property, said licensee shall be an:
[Select all which apply. Any section not selected shall not be a part of this Agreement].
☐ Independent contractor of Broker
☐ Employee of Broker

16. **Extension.** If during the term of this Brokerage Agreement, Buyer and a prospective seller enter into a real estate sales contract which is not consummated for any reason whatsoever, then the original expiration date of this Agreement shall be extended for the number of days that the property was under contract.

17. **No Imputed Knowledge.** Buyer acknowledges and agrees that with regard to any property in which Buyer develops an interest, there shall be no knowledge imputed between Broker and Broker's licensees or between the different licenses of Broker. Broker and each of Broker's licensees shall be deemed to have only actual knowledge of such properties.

18. **Governing Law.** This Agreement may be signed in multiple counterparts and shall be governed by and interpreted pursuant to the laws of the State of Georgia.

19. **Entire Agreement.** This Agreement constitutes the sole and entire agreement between the parties. No representation, promise or inducement not included in this Agreement shall be binding upon any party hereto. This Agreement and the terms and conditions herein may not be amended, modified or waived except by the written agreement of Buyer. The failure of the parties to adhere strictly to the terms and conditions of this Agreement shall not constitute a waiver of the right of the parties later to insist on such strict adherence.

F I G U R E   4.3 (CONTINUED)

Exclusive Buyer Brokerage Agreement

20. GAR Forms. The Georgia Association of REALTORS®, Inc. ("GAR") makes certain standard real estate forms available to its members. These GAR forms are frequently provided to the parties in real estate transactions by the REALTORS® with whom they are working. No party is required to use any GAR form. Since these forms are generic and written with the interests of multiple parties in mind, they may need to be modified to meet the specific needs of the parties using them. If any party has any questions about his or her rights and obligations under any GAR form he or she should consult an attorney. The parties hereto agree that the GAR forms may only be used in accordance with the licensing agreement of GAR. While GAR forms may be modified by the parties, no GAR form may be reproduced with sections removed, altered or modified unless the changes are visible on the form itself or in a stipulation, addendum, exhibit or amendment thereto.

21. Notices.
    A. Communications Regarding Real Estate Transactions. Client acknowledges that many communications and notices in real estate transactions are of a time sensitive nature and that the failure to be available to receive such notices and communications can have adverse legal, business and financial consequences. During the term of this Agreement, Client agrees to remain reasonably available to receive communications from Broker.
    B. Notices between Broker and Client Regarding this Agreement. Client and Broker agree that communications and notices between them regarding the terms of this Agreement shall be in writing, signed by the party giving the notice, and may be delivered in person or to any address, e-mail address and/or facsimile number to the person to whom the communication or notice is being given specifically set forth in this Agreement. It is the intent of the parties that those means of transmitting notices for which a party has not provided an address or number shall not be used for receiving notices and communications. For example, if a party has not provided an e-mail address in this Agreement, it shall mean that the party is not accepting notices or communications sent by this means.
    C. Client Contact Information.
    The contact information of Client(s) is set forth below:

_____
Client Name

_____
Address for Receiving Notice

_____

_____

Business Telephone: _____
Home Telephone: _____
Cell Phone: _____
Facsimile Number: _____
E-mail Address: _____

_____
Client Name

_____
Address for Receiving Notice

_____

_____

Business Telephone: _____
Home Telephone: _____
Cell Phone: _____
Facsimile Number: _____
E-mail Address: _____

Client agrees to immediately update Broker of any changes to the above referenced information.

SPECIAL STIPULATIONS: The following Special Stipulations, if conflicting with any exhibit, addendum, or preceding paragraph, shall control:

F I G U R E 4.3 (CONTINUED)

Exclusive Buyer Brokerage Agreement

Additional Special Stipulations are ☐ or are ☐ not attached.

BY SIGNING THIS AGREEMENT, BUYER ACKNOWLEDGES THAT: (1) BUYER HAS READ ALL PROVISIONS AND DISCLOSURES MADE HEREIN; (2) BUYER UNDERSTANDS ALL SUCH PROVISIONS AND DISCLOSURES AND HAS ENTERED INTO THIS AGREEMENT VOLUNTARILY; AND (3) BUYER IS NOT SUBJECT TO A CURRENT BUYER BROKERAGE AGREEMENT WITH ANY OTHER BROKER.

RECEIPT OF A COPY OF THIS AGREEMENT IS HEREBY ACKNOWLEDGED BY BUYER.
The above Agreement is hereby accepted, _____ o'clock _____ .m., on the date of _____ .

Broker _____   Buyer's Signature _____

Address: _____

_____   Print or Type Name

_____   Buyer's Signature _____

MLS Office Code   Brokerage Firm License Number   Print or Type Name

Broker's Phone#_____ & FAX#_____

By: _____
Broker or Broker's Affiliated Licensee

_____
Print or Type Name

_____
Agent's Georgia Real Estate License Number

Email Address: _____

The misrepresentation or omission does not have to be intentional to result in broker liability. A **negligent misrepresentation** occurs when the broker *should have known* that a statement about a material fact was false. The fact that the broker may actually be ignorant about the issue is no excuse. If the buyer relies on the broker's statement, the broker is liable for any damages that result. Similarly, if a broker accidentally fails to perform some act—for instance, if he or she forgets to deliver a counteroffer—the broker may be liable for damages that result from such a negligent omission.

■ **FOR EXAMPLE**   While showing a potential buyer a very average-looking house, broker Dan described even its plainest features as "charming" and "beautiful." Because the statements were obviously Dan's personal opinions designed to encourage a positive feeling about the property (or puff it up), their truth or falsity is not an issue.

Broker Gil was asked by a potential buyer if a particular neighborhood was safe. Although Gil knew that the area was experiencing a skyrocketing rate of violent crime, Gil assured the buyer that no problem existed. Gil also neglected to inform the buyer that the lot next to the house the buyer was considering had been sold to a waste disposal company for use as a toxic dump. Both may be examples of fraudulent misrepresentation.

If a contract to purchase real estate is obtained as a result of fraudulent misstatements, the contract may be disaffirmed or renounced by the purchaser. In such a case, the broker not only loses a commission but can be liable for damages if either party suffers loss because of the misrepresentation. If the licensee's misstatements were based on the owner's own inaccurate statements and the licensee had no independent duty to investigate their accuracy, the broker may be entitled to a commission, even if the buyer rescinds the sales contract.

Property Conditions

Georgia law (O.C.G.A. 10-6A-5(b)) is specific about duties involving the disclosure of property conditions. For a broker engaged by a **seller**, the broker must disclose the following in a timely manner to all parties with whom the broker is working:

In Georgia

- All adverse material facts that pertain to the physical condition of the property and any improvements, including but not limited to material defects in the property, environmental contamination, and facts required by law to be disclosed that are known by the broker and that could not be discovered by a reasonably diligent inspection by the buyer
- All material facts that pertain to existing adverse physical conditions in the immediate neighborhood (one mile) of the property that are known to the broker and could not be discovered by the buyer upon a diligent inspection or through the review of reasonably available government materials (such as land-use maps and plans and zoning ordinances)

The state statute does not create a duty for a broker to discover or seek to discover adverse material facts of a property's condition or existing adverse conditions in the immediate neighborhood. A broker may not give prospective buyers false information. However, a broker is not liable for providing false information to a buyer if the broker did not have actual knowledge that the information was false, and discloses to the buyer the source of the information.

Georgia law makes it clear that it does not limit the obligation of a seller to disclose adverse material facts known by the seller to the prospective buyer, nor does it limit the obligation of prospective buyers to inspect and familiarize themselves with the physical condition of the property and the neighborhood in which it is located. Violations of this subsection (O.C.G.A. 10-6A-5(b)(2)) do not create liability on the part of the broker unless the broker has been found to have engaged in fraud.

■ **FOR EXAMPLE** In *Dasher v. Davis*, 274 Ga. App. 788, 618 S.E.2nd 728 (Ct. App. 2005), an agent listed a home for sale. In the disclosure statement, the sellers indicated the septic system had been professionally serviced. After the house was under contract but prior to closing, the sellers experienced a septic system problem and notified the agent that the septic tank had to be pumped. The agent faxed the information to the purchasers' REALTOR®, who signed it and returned it to the agent. After closing, the purchasers notified the agent that they were having problems with the septic system and the purchasers filed suit, alleging the agent concealed a defect in the home's septic system. The Georgia Court of Appeals found there was no evidence the agent knowingly concealed a material defect in the property or that he breached his obligations under BRRETA.

For a broker engaged by a buyer, (O.C.G.A. 10-6A-7) the broker must disclose in a timely manner to a prospective seller with whom the broker is working as a customer all material facts actually known by the broker concerning the buyer's financial ability to perform the terms of the sale, and in residential transactions, the buyer's intent to occupy the property as a principal residence.

Brokers must not knowingly give prospective sellers false information. However, a broker cannot be found liable for providing false information to the seller if the broker did not have actual knowledge that the information was false and discloses to the seller the source of the information. GAR Form F57, Broker's Information Disclosure, was created to provide such written disclosure. (See Figure 4.4.)

The prospective buyer is under obligation to disclose to the prospective seller all adverse material facts actually known by the buyer concerning the buyer's financial ability to perform the terms of the sale, and in residential transactions, the buyer's intent to occupy the property as a principal residence. Violations do not create liability on the part of the broker absent a finding of fraud on the part of the broker.

F I G U R E   4.4

Broker's Information Disclosure

BROKER'S INFORMATION DISCLOSURE

Georgia
Association
of REALTORS®

2010 Printing

This Information Disclosure pertains to that certain property located at _____

_____, and/or as described below:

_____

_____

_____

_____ ("Licensee") has been asked the following question by

_____ (fill in name of party)

Question:

In response to this question, Licensee has found out the following information:

Answer:

The source of the information to the above answer is as follows:

Source:

Additional pages are ☐ **or are** ☐ **not attached.**

The information in this Information Disclosure has been provided to the party indicated above by Licensee, this date of
_____. The information contained herein is not guaranteed to be accurate or complete.
The party receiving this information should independently verify all information contained herein.

Licensee's Signature: _____

Print or Type Name: _____

F57, Broker's Information Disclosure, 01/01/10

A broker engaged by a buyer in a real estate transaction may provide assistance to the seller by performing ministerial acts; this does not violate the broker's brokerage engagement with the buyer nor does performing ministerial acts for the seller constitute a brokerage engagement with the seller.

A broker engaged by a buyer does not breach any duty by showing properties in which the buyer is interested to other prospective buyers.

Stigmatized Properties

Stigmatized properties are those that society has branded as undesirable because of events that occurred there or because of a sexual offender who currently lives in an area. For example, under the federal Megan's Law, all states are required to release information to the public about known convicted sex offenders when necessary to protect the public's safety. The federal law does not mandate active notification; however, some state laws do. The residence of a known sexual offender can deem a property stigmatized because buyers may not want to live in that vicinity.

Perhaps the more common stigma is a criminal event, such as homicide, illegal drug manufacturing, gang-related activity, or a tragedy, such as suicide. Properties have even been stigmatized by rumors that they are haunted. Because of the potential liability to a licensee for inadequately researching and disclosing material facts concerning a property's condition, licensees should seek competent counsel when dealing with a stigmatized property.

In Georgia | Some states have laws regarding the disclosure of information about stigmatized properties. Georgia has a stigmatized property law (O.C.G.A. 44-1-16), which states that no owner of real property, broker, or affiliated licensee is liable for failing to disclose the fact or suspicion of property being occupied by someone with a virus or disease, or that it was the site of a homicide or death by accidental or natural causes. However, if questions are posed regarding stigmatized property, a broker must answer truthfully to the best of his or her knowledge unless the questions are prohibited or constitute a violation of federal or state law.

IN PRACTICE   A disclosure that a property's previous owner or occupant died of AIDS or was HIV-positive constitutes illegal discrimination against the handicapped under the federal Fair Housing Act, discussed in Chapter 21.

■ KEY POINT REVIEW

An **agent** represents a **principal** in dealings with a **third party.** Note the following:

- **Agency** is a relationship in which the agent is held in a position of special trust and confidence by the principal.
- A **subagent** is an agent of an agent.
- A **client** is the principal.

- A **customer** is the nonrepresented party for whom some level of service is provided and who is entitled to fairness and honesty.
- A **transactional broker** does not enter into a client relationship with any parties and performs ministerial acts on behalf of one or more of the parties.

Real estate agency relationships are governed by **common law,** which is established by tradition and court decisions, and **statutory law,** which is passed by state legislatures and other governing bodies.

In Georgia

In Georgia, real estate relationships are governed by statute (BRRETA).

- **Disclosure** by real estate brokers of agency relationship is required in every state.

Agency relationships encompass the following:

- **Express** agency is based on a formal agreement between the parties.
- **Implied** agency results from the behavior of the parties.
- The **compensation** source does not determine agency because
  — the agent may be compensated by someone other than the agent's client, and
  — agency can exist even if no compensation is involved—**gratuitous agency.**

In Georgia

An agent has duties of **trust and confidence** with the principal. Under BRRETA (Brokerage Relationships in Real Estate Transactions Act), a broker engaged by the seller has the following duties:

- Perform terms of brokerage engagement
- Promote interests of seller by seeking terms and sale price as noted in brokerage engagement or acceptable to seller; quickly presenting all offers to and from the seller; disclosing material facts of which broker has actual knowledge; advising seller to obtain expert advice on areas outside expertise; and promptly accounting for all money and property received
- Exercise reasonable care and skill in performing duties
- Comply with all state and federal laws
- Maintain confidentiality

A broker engaged by the buyer has the following duties:

- Perform terms of brokerage engagement
- Promote interests of buyer by seeking property at price and terms acceptable to buyer; quickly presenting all offers to and from the buyer; disclosing adverse material facts of which broker has actual knowledge; advising buyer to obtain expert advice on areas outside expertise; and promptly accounting for all money and property received
- Exercise ordinary skill and care in performing duties
- Comply with all state and federal laws
- Maintain confidentiality

Under Georgia law, **termination of agency** may be accomplished by the

- completion of performance of the engagement; or
- if completion is not applicable, earlier of a) any date agreed upon by the parties in engagement or its amendments; b) any authorized termination of relationship; or c) if no expiration is provided and no termination occurred, then one year after initiation of the engagement.

Agency coupled with an interest cannot be revoked by the principal or terminated upon the principal's death.

A **general agent** represents the principal in a broad range of matters.

A **special agent** (or **limited agent**) represents the principal in one specific act or business transaction only, under detailed instructions.

A **designated agent** (or **designated representative**) is authorized by the broker to act as the agent of a specific principal.

A **single agency** is one in which an agent represents only one party in a transaction.

A **dual agency** is one in which an agent represents two principals in the same transaction.

A **buyer's broker** represents a buyer as an agent to find property that meets the buyer's specifications, as set out in the **buyer-broker agreement.**

A **nonagent** (legal in only a few states, including Georgia) is an agent of neither party to a transaction but helps both buyer and seller with necessary paperwork and formalities.

Statements to clients and customers should be clearly identified as **opinion** or **fact.** Note the following distinctions:

- **Puffing** is legal exaggeration of a property's benefits.
- **Fraud** is the intentional misrepresentation of a material fact to harm or take advantage of another person.
- **Negligent misrepresentation** occurs when a broker **should have known** that a statement about a material fact was false.

In Georgia

In Georgia, a broker engaged by a seller must promptly disclose to all parties all adverse material facts pertaining to the physical condition of the property and existing adverse physical conditions in the immediate neighborhood known to broker. There is no statutory duty for the broker to discover adverse material facts of the property's condition or the neighborhood.

A broker engaged by a buyer must promptly disclose to a prospective seller all material facts actually known by the broker, including the buyer's financial ability to perform terms of the sale.

Stigmatized properties may require an agent to consult an attorney.

CHAPTER 4 QUIZ

1. The relationship between broker and seller is generally what type of agency?
   a. Special
   b. General
   c. Implied
   d. Universal

2. Which of the following statements is *TRUE* of a real estate broker acting as the agent of the seller?
   a. The broker is obligated to render loyalty to the seller.
   b. The broker can disclose confidential information about the seller to a buyer if it increases the likelihood of a sale.
   c. The broker can agree to a change in price without the seller's approval.
   d. The broker can accept a commission from the buyer without the seller's approval.

3. Alan, a real estate broker, lists Miranda's home for $189,500. Later that same day, Claude comes into Alan's office and asks for general information about homes for sale in the $130,000 to $140,000 price range but refuses representation by Alan's company at this time. Based on these facts, which of the following statements is *TRUE?*
   a. Both Miranda and Claude are Alan's customers.
   b. Miranda is Alan's client; Claude is a customer.
   c. Alan owes duties to both Miranda and Claude.
   d. If Claude later asks for buyer representation by Alan's firm, he cannot have it because of the firm's earlier agreement with Miranda.

4. In a dual agency situation, a broker may represent both the seller and the buyer if
   a. the broker informs either the buyer or the seller of this fact.
   b. the buyer and the seller are related by blood or marriage.
   c. both parties give their informed consent, usually in writing, to the dual agency.
   d. both parties are represented by attorneys.

5. Which of the following events will terminate an agency in a broker-seller relationship?
   a. The broker discovers that the market value of the property is such that he or she will not make an adequate commission.
   b. The owner declares personal bankruptcy.
   c. The owner abandons the property.
   d. The broker appoints other brokers to help sell the property.

6. Designated agency is *MOST* likely to occur when
   a. there is a client buyer and a customer seller.
   b. the seller and buyer are represented by different companies.
   c. both buyer and seller are customers.
   d. buyer and seller are represented by the same company.

7. A buyer who is a client of the broker wants to purchase a house that the broker has listed for sale. Which of the following statements is *TRUE?*
   a. The broker may proceed to write an offer on the property and submit it.
   b. The broker should refer the buyer to another broker to negotiate the sale.
   c. The seller and buyer must be informed of the situation and agree, in writing, to the broker's representing both of them.
   d. The buyer should not have been shown a house listed by the broker.

8. A broker helps a buyer and seller with paperwork but does not represent either party. This is
   a. dual agency.
   b. prohibited in all states as a broker must always represent one party.
   c. transactional brokerage.
   d. designated agency.

9. Broker Ben tells a prospective buyer, "This property has the most beautiful river view." In fact, the view includes the river and the back of a shopping center. Which of the following statements is *TRUE*?
   a. Broker Ben has committed fraud.
   b. Broker Ben is guilty of negligent misrepresentation.
   c. Broker Ben is guilty of intentional misrepresentation.
   d. Broker Ben is merely puffing.

In Georgia

10. In Georgia, a broker may act as a dual agent
    a. with the express verbal consent of all parties.
    b. with the express written consent of all parties.
    c. without the consent of the parties, as long as he or she discloses the dual agency in the sales contract.
    d. without restriction.

11. In Georgia, broker duties owed to a client
    a. are general fiduciary duties.
    b. are determined by the Georgia Real Estate Commission.
    c. are determined by a special statute (BRRETA).
    d. must be set forth in the engagement agreement.

12. Broker Smith has one licensee, Brown, who represents the seller in listing a house for sale. Another of Smith's licensees, Green, has a client who would like to see the house. Smith appoints Green to represent the buyer exclusively. Green's status is that of
    a. a dual agent.
    b. a designated agent.
    c. a transaction broker.
    d. none of the above.

13. Which is *NOT* a duty of a broker engaged by a buyer?
    a. Disclosing the fact that the seller's roof has leaks
    b. Advising the buyer to consult with a tax adviser regarding the tax consequences of owning a second home
    c. Giving the buyer an account of money that the seller gave to the broker to repair defects in the property
    d. Seeking other properties for the buyer after the buyer is a party to a contract of sale (unless the engagement agreement provides otherwise)

CHAPTER 5

Real Estate Brokerage

■ **LEARNING OBJECTIVES**   *When you have finished reading this chapter, you should be able to:*

■ **identify** the role of technologies, personnel, and license laws in the operation of a real estate business.

■ **describe** the various types of antitrust violations common in the real estate industry and the penalties involved with each.

■ **explain** how a broker's compensation is usually determined.

■ **distinguish** employees from independent contractors and explain why the distinction is important.

■ **define** the following *key terms:*

antitrust laws	employee	procuring cause
brokerage	independent contractor	ready, willing, and able
brokerage engagement	Internet advertising	buyers
CAN-SPAM Act of 2003	Internet Listing Display	Uniform Electronic
commission	Policy	Transactions Act
disclaimers	Junk Fax Prevention Act	(UETA)
electronic contracting	minimum level of service	Web site management
Electronic Signatures in	National Do Not Call	tools
Global and National	Registry	
Commerce Act (E-Sign)		

■ THE HISTORY OF BROKERAGE

The nature of real estate brokerage services, particularly those provided in residential sales transactions, has changed significantly in recent years. Through the 1950s, real estate brokerage firms were primarily one-office, minimally staffed, family-run operations. The broker listed an owner's property for sale and found a buyer without assistance from other brokerage companies. The sale was eventually negotiated and closed. It was relatively clear that the broker represented the seller's interests. The common-law doctrine of *caveat emptor* ("let the buyer beware") was the rule; buyers were pretty much on their own.

In the 1960s, however, the way buyers and sellers were brought together in real estate transactions began to change. Brokers started to share information about properties they listed, resulting in two brokers cooperating to sell a property. The brokers formalized this exchange of information by creating multiple listing services (MLSs). The MLS expedited sales by increasing a single property's exposure to a greater number of potential buyers. Because it resulted in more sales, the MLS quickly became a widely used industry service. But one thing stayed the same: Both brokers still represented the seller's interest.

While sellers benefited from this arrangement, buyers came to question whether their interests were being protected. They began to demand not only accurate, factual information but also objective advice, particularly in the face of increasingly complex real estate transactions. Buyers view the real estate licensee as the expert on whom they can rely for guidance. In short, buyers have begun to seek not only protection but representation as well. Almost all states recognize buyer agency today, and a large percentage of sales contracts are written by buyer agents.

■ REAL ESTATE LICENSE LAWS

All 50 states, the District of Columbia, and all Canadian provinces license and regulate the activities of real estate brokers and salespersons. While the laws share a common purpose, the details vary from state to state. Uniform policies and standards for administering and enforcing state license laws are promoted by an organization of state license law officials known as ARELLO, the Association of Real Estate License Law Officials.

In Georgia Real estate practice in Georgia is governed by the Georgia Real Estate License Law, Title 43, Chapter 40 of the O.G.C.A., Brokerage Relationships in Real Estate Transactions Act (BRRETA), and other regulations. These are discussed in Chapter 14.

Purpose of License Laws

Real estate license laws have been enacted to protect the public by ensuring a standard of competence and professionalism in the real estate industry. The laws achieve this goal by

- establishing basic requirements for obtaining a real estate license and, in many cases, requiring continuing education to keep a license;
- defining which activities require licensing;
- describing the acceptable standards of conduct and practice for licensees; and
- enforcing those standards through a disciplinary system.

The purpose of these laws is not merely to regulate the real estate industry. Their main objective is to make sure that the rights of purchasers, sellers, tenants, and owners are protected from unscrupulous or sloppy practices. *The laws are not intended to prevent licensees from conducting their businesses successfully or to interfere in legitimate transactions.* Laws cannot create an ethical or a moral marketplace. However, by establishing minimum levels of competency and the limits of permitted behavior, laws can make the marketplace safer and more honest.

Each state has a licensing authority—a commission, a department, a division, a board, or an agency—for real estate brokers and salespersons. This authority has the power to issue licenses, make real estate information available to licensees and the public, and enforce the statutory real estate law.

In Georgia	In Georgia, the licensing authority is the Georgia Real Estate Commission.

Each licensing authority has also adopted a set of administrative rules and regulations that further define the statutory law. The rules and regulations provide for administering the law and set operating guidelines for licensees. *The rules and regulations have the same force and effect as any law.* Both the law and the rules are usually enforced through fines and the denial, suspension, or revocation of licenses. Civil and criminal court actions can be brought against violators in some serious cases.

IN PRACTICE   Each state's real estate license laws and the rules and regulations of its real estate commission or board establish the framework for all of a licensee's activities. *It is vital that each licensee have a clear and comprehensive understanding of his or her state's laws and regulations, not only for purposes of the licensing examination, but to ensure that the licensee's practice of real estate is both legal and successful.* This is the case for licensees as well who hold licenses as a result of reciprocity, and who were granted a license in another state without the necessity of special courses or examinations.

■ REAL ESTATE BROKERAGE

Brokerage is simply the business of bringing parties together. Mortgage brokers match lenders with borrowers; stockbrokers bring together investors and corporations; customs brokers help importers navigate through complex customs procedures. A *real estate broker* is defined as a person licensed to buy, sell, exchange, or lease real property for others and to charge a fee for these services.

A brokerage business may take many forms. It may be a *sole proprietorship* (a single-owner company), a corporation, or a partnership with another broker. The office may be independent or part of a regional or national franchise. The business may consist of a single office or multiple branches. The broker's office may be located in a downtown highrise, a suburban shopping center, or the broker's home. A typical real estate brokerage may specialize in one kind of transaction or service or may offer an array of services.

No matter what form it takes, however, a real estate brokerage has the same demands, expenses, and rewards as any other small business. The real estate industry, after all, is made up of thousands of small businesses operating in defined local markets. A real estate broker faces the same challenges as an entrepreneur in any other industry. In addition to mastering the complexities of real estate transactions, the broker must be able to handle the day-to-day details of running a business. He or she must set effective policies for every aspect of the brokerage operation: maintaining space and equipment, hiring employees and salespersons, determining compensation, directing staff and sales activities, and implementing procedures to follow in carrying out agency duties. Each state's real estate license laws and regulations establish the business activities and methods of doing business that are permitted.

IN PRACTICE   A broker should advise parties to secure legal counsel to protect their interests. *Although real estate brokers and salespersons may bring buyers and sellers together, and in most states may fill in preprinted blank purchase agreement forms, only an attorney may offer legal advice or prepare legal documents. Licensees who are not attorneys are prohibited from practicing law.*

Broker-Salesperson Relationship

Although brokerage firms vary widely in size, few brokers today perform their duties without the assistance of salespersons. Consequently, much of the business's success hinges on the broker-salesperson relationship.

A *real estate salesperson* is any person licensed to perform real estate activities on behalf of a licensed real estate broker. The broker is fully responsible for the actions performed in the course of the real estate business by all persons licensed under the broker. In turn, all of a salesperson's activities must be performed in the name of the supervising broker. The salesperson can carry out *only* those responsibilities assigned by the broker with whom he or she is affiliated and can receive compensation *only* from that broker. As an agent of the broker, the salesperson has no authority to make contracts with or receive compensation from any other party. The broker is liable for the acts of the salesperson within the scope of the employment agreement.

IN PRACTICE   The salesperson must always be supervised by his or her broker. The broker cannot delegate office supervision of salespeople to a person not licensed as a broker.

Independent contractor versus employee   The employment agreement between a broker and a salesperson should define the nature, obligations, and responsibilities of the relationship. Essentially, the salesperson may be either an *employee* or an *independent contractor*. State license laws generally treat the salesperson as the employee of the affiliate broker, regardless of whether the salesperson is considered to be an employee or an independent contractor for income tax purposes. Whether a salesperson is treated as an employee or an independent contractor affects the structure of the salesperson's responsibilities and the broker's liability to pay and withhold taxes from the salesperson's earnings.

A broker can exercise certain *controls* over salespersons who are employees. The broker may require an **employee** to follow rules governing such matters as working hours, office routine, attendance at sales meetings, assignment of sales quotas, and adherence to dress codes. As an employer, a broker is required by the federal government to withhold Social Security tax and income tax from wages paid to employees. The broker is also required to pay unemployment compensation tax on wages paid to one or more employees, as defined by state and federal laws. In addition, employees might receive benefits such as health insurance, profit-sharing plans, and worker's compensation.

A broker's relationship with a salesperson who is an **independent contractor** is very different. As the name implies, an independent contractor operates more independently than an employee, and a broker may not exercise the same degree of control over the salesperson's activities. While the broker may control *what* the independent contractor does, the broker cannot dictate how to do it. The broker cannot *require* the independent contractor to keep specific office hours or attend sales meetings. Independent contractors are responsible for paying their own income and Social Security taxes and receive nothing from brokers that could be construed as an employee benefit, such as health insurance or paid vacation time. As a rule, independent contractors use their own materials and equipment.

The Internal Revenue Service often investigates the independent contractor-employee situation in real estate offices. Under the *qualified real estate agent* category in the Internal Revenue Code, meeting the following three requirements can establish an independent contractor status:

1. The individual must have a current real estate license.
2. He or she must have a written contract with the broker that specifies that the salesperson will not be treated as an employee for federal tax purposes.
3. At least 90 percent of the individual's income as a licensee must be based on sales production and not on the number of hours worked.

IN PRACTICE   A broker should have a standardized employment agreement drafted and reviewed by an attorney to ensure its compliance with federal law.

The broker should also be aware that written agreements carry little weight with an IRS auditor if the actions of the parties contradict the provisions of the contract. Specific legal and tax questions regarding independent contractors should be referred to a competent attorney or accountant.

Real Estate Assistants

A *real estate assistant* (also known as a *personal assistant* or *professional assistant*) is a combination office manager, marketer, organizer, and facilitator with a fundamental understanding of the real estate industry. An assistant may or may not have a real estate license, depending on state law. The extent to which the assistant can help the broker or salesperson with transactions is often determined by state license laws. Depending on state law, an assistant may perform duties ranging from clerical and secretarial functions to office management, telemarketing, market strategy development, and direct contact with clients and customers. A licensed assistant can set up and host open houses and assist in all aspects of a real estate transaction.

In Georgia, Rule 520-1-.07 sets forth guidelines for using unlicensed support personnel. The guidelines include:

- When a licensee who is affiliated with a broker engages support personnel to assist in real estate brokerage activities, both the firm and the licensee are responsible for the acts of the support personnel, assuring the support personnel comply with laws and regulations, and seeing that licensed support personnel are properly licensed with the firm. Unlicensed support personnel may only perform ministerial duties.
- Active licensees affiliated with one firm may not work as support personnel for a licensee in another firm. Inactive licensees may only perform activities not requiring licensure.
- Any real estate brokerage firm allowing a licensee to employ (or to use as an independent contractor) support personnel must enter into a written agreement authorizing the use of the support personnel and delineating duties.

The Commission has identified the following as tasks that unlicensed support personnel cannot perform:

- Making cold calls for the purpose of seeking prospects for listings, leasing, sales, exchanges, or property management
- Hosting open houses, kiosks, home show booths, or fairs
- Preparing promotional materials without the review and approval of the licensee and supervising broker
- Showing property
- Answering questions related to title, financing, or closings (other than time and place)
- Answering questions regarding a listing except for information on price and amenities expressly written by the licensee
- Discussing or explaining a contract, listing, lease, or agreement with anyone outside the firm
- Negotiating or agreeing to any commission on behalf of a licensee

- Discussing the attributes or amenities of a property, under any circumstances, with a prospective purchaser or lessee
- Discussing with a property owner the terms and conditions of the real property offered for sale or lease
- Collecting or holding deposit monies, rent or anything of value received from a property owner or a prospective purchaser or lessee
- Providing property owners or prospective purchasers or lessees with any advice on the sale, purchase, exchange, or lease of real property that is listed or to be listed
- Holding himself or herself out as being licensed or affiliated with a firm as a licensee

IN PRACTICE   On occasion, real estate teams are formed in brokerage firms in Georgia. When this occurs, the qualifying broker is responsible for the supervision and accountability of each team member.

Technology

In addition to assistants, a wide range of technologies is available to help a real estate licensee do his or her job more efficiently and effectively. The advances in technology and its effects on the practice of real estate brokerage are moving so fast that it can be difficult to keep abreast of the most recent changes. The National Association of REALTORS® (NAR) is a good resource for updates.

Computers and laptops   Computers are a necessary ingredient in any modern real estate brokerage. Licensees can find community, legal, licensing, and mortgage information on the Internet via many services. Multiple-listing and homefinder services are available to real estate professionals through their professional associations. Numerous software packages have been designed specifically for real estate professionals. Some of these programs help real estate brokers and salespersons with such office management tasks as billing, accounting, and timekeeping. Other software assists with developing Web-based descriptions of property for sale, marketing and advertising properties, and designing and producing flyers, business cards, pamphlets, and other promotional materials.

In some states, continuing education requirements can be met through the use of specially designed continuing education software. Real estate Web sites, home pages, and computer networks help licensees keep in touch, and some cable, digital, and satellite television channels are dedicated solely to real estate programming for both consumers and professionals.

Real estate brokers and salespersons can carry laptop computers that link them with their offices or the Web, an MLS, or a mortgage company from virtually anywhere.

In Georgia   The Rules and Regulations of the Georgia Real Estate Commission provide guidance on computer-based courses. A computer-based course is defined as one that is delivered through CD-ROM technology, floppy disks, or over the Internet.

The Georgia Real Estate Commission does not permit schools to offer videotapes or replays of approved courses for credit. A live educational setting is required with interaction between students and instructors. The rules that apply to in-class courses also apply to distance learning courses.

See *www.grec.state.ga.us* for the Rules and Regulations of the Georgia Real Estate Commission.

The Internet and Web sites   The Internet has brought tremendous change to the real estate industry. Real estate practitioners and consumers rely heavily on the Internet for a variety of services. The Internet is a powerful tool for consumers in finding information about properties, relocation services, and particular communities. Often, real estate Web site information is updated daily.

Most real estate agencies have Web sites that provide extraordinary databases for property and other searches. Keep in mind that the NAR has adopted a new **Internet Listing Display Policy** that replaces and consolidates the Virtual Office Web site (VOW) and the Internet Data Exchange (IDX) policies. The new NAR policy allows all MLS members to have equal rights to display MLS data, and it respects the rights of property owners and their listing brokers to market a property as they wish. All MLSs had until July 1, 2006, to adopt the policy. A *blanket opt-out* provision provides that those MLS participants interested in keeping their listings off of competitors' Web sites cannot then display other brokers' listings. However, brokers who have opted out of displaying their listings on competitors' Web sites can, at the direction of a seller, make an exception and display the seller's property on the Web sites of all other members of the MLS. See Related Web Sites at the end of this chapter for more information about the policy.

Many real estate Web sites have **disclaimers** that indicate the material on their site is solely for informational purposes and that no warranties or representations have been made.

Licensees can purchase **Web site management tools** to help with their marketing efforts. These tools help assess the effectiveness of Internet marketing by providing statistics on the number of page views, the number of people visiting the site, the most visited pages, the Web site page used to enter and exit, and the operating system and browser information of visitors, among other data.

E-mail   E-mail is yet another powerful tool making communication between real estate agents and consumers much more efficient. Gone are the days of playing phone tag. Instead, sending a quick e-mail message saves both agents and consumers valuable time. A real estate agent should be prepared for consumers who primarily want to communicate through the use of e-mail.

In communicating with clients or consumers via e-mail, the following are some suggestions: use the subject line in a useful and helpful manner; try to avoid spelling errors; respond promptly to all e-mail messages; don't overuse emoticons (smileys); be specific, to the point, and brief; and pay attention to the size of any attachments you send. Do not send unsolicited e-mails.

E-mail is an excellent opportunity for the ongoing marketing of your business. Make sure that all of your contact information is up-to-date in your signature line, and use automated signatures. If you do use a lot of e-mail in your business, setting up an auto-responder is helpful when you are away for a period of time.

Licensees who send commercial e-mails need to be aware of the requirements of the **CAN-SPAM Act of 2003** (Controlling the Assault of Non-Solicited Pornography and Marketing Act). Briefly, the act prohibits the following:

- Misleading or false header information ("from," "to" and routing information must be accurate and identify the person who initiated the e-mail)
- Deceptive subject lines

In addition, the act requires that e-mail recipients have an opt-out method and that commercial e-mail be identified as an advertisement that includes the sender's valid physical postal address.

Virtual communities   Even if you do not participate in virtual communities, it is good to be aware of how they are being used by consumers. Listservs®, e-mail lists, bulletin boards, and chat rooms are all popular virtual communities.

Cell phones   Cellular telephones give licensees the ability to communicate instantly with anyone in their real estate practice, from lenders to consumers. The technology in cell phones continues to advance, providing access to e-mail, the Internet, and text messaging, as well as built-in digital cameras and PDA (see below) features. Wireless communication is paramount in today's real estate practice.

Digital cameras   Digital cameras are an excellent technological tool for both real estate marketing and brokerage.

PDAs   Handheld personal digital assistants (PDAs) help licensees manage time, information, and client databases much more effectively. PDAs can serve many functions, including use as a portable database of an MLS listing and as a place for storing information on prospective buyer's comments on a home, which then can be forwarded to the seller. They may also provide quick access to e-mail, contact management, a calendar, and calculators. New and improved software is continually being developed for PDAs.

Other technology   Portable fax machines, pagers, and tablet personal computers (PCs) help make licensees available to their offices and clients 24 hours a day. Voice-mail systems can track caller response to advertisements and give callers information about specific properties when the broker or salesperson is unavailable. Yard signs are available that broadcast details about a property on an AM radio band, so drivers passing by can tune in for tempting information. Pen-based notebooks and portable digital voice recorders are other helpful devices.

Licensees need to be aware of the federal **Junk Fax Prevention Act,** which states that it is illegal to send an unsolicited commercial fax message without express consent or without an established business relationship with the recipient. If a state has a law regarding fax use, that state's law governs rather than the federal law.

Georgia does not have any laws regarding communication restrictions that supersede federal law.

Blogs are used by licensees to exchange information. The NAR maintains a blog in order to inform licensees of the latest technological trends in the industry and to provide a forum for asking questions.

Vlogs are also being used by licensees. *Vlogs* are the video version of a blog. They are often used with out-of-town consumers looking for a home. Visitors to a Vlog Web site download the video. Creating a Vlog can be costly because it requires a Web cam, camcorder, or digital camera with video capabilities, and video editing software.

Internet Advertising

State laws vary regarding **Internet advertising.** In Georgia, Rule 520-1-.09 of the Commission's Rules and Regulations defines Internet advertising as subject to the regulations governing all other advertising media.

- All advertising must be in the name of the real estate firm holding the licensee's license.
- An abbreviated form of the firm's name cannot be used.
- The advertisement must not be inaccurate or misleading in any material fact or in any way misrepresent terms, values, property, services, or policies.
- The advertisement must not be directed at or refer to persons of a particular color, race, religion, handicap, sex, national origin, or familial status.
- When a licensee advertises properties located outside of Georgia or offers brokerage services outside of Georgia, the licensee must have the proper license in that jurisdiction or otherwise be in full compliance with its laws.
- All Internet advertisements must be reviewed by the licensee's broker.

Security

As technology becomes more available and convenient, it brings security problems for both licensees and clients. Systems can be subject to attack by viruses, worms, adware, and spyware, placing personal information and databases at risk. Phishing e-mails may ask for personal information that should not be shared. It is important for a licensee to take security seriously to avoid placing one's firm and the information provided by clients at risk. Good security practices change as technology changes. Following are a few security measures to keep in mind:

- Place firewalls on servers and computers
- Keep virus and spyware protective software up to date
- Use passwords, changed with some frequency, and encryption, especially when using public hotspots to convey information

- Be reluctant to open e-mail and especially e-mail attachments from unknown sources
- Be aware that wireless environments, including those used by computers, phones, and PDAs may be subject to content viewing and listening in by others
- Stay attentive to phishing scams
- Keep current on software security patches
- Practice good back-up procedures and have off-site storage for back-up records
- Research carefully those companies a real estate firm outsources for its information technology (IT) and Web services
- Talk with your IT personnel about suspicious situations regarding the computer system or wireless environment

All this technology is a great boon to practitioners, but real estate brokers and salespersons must make careful decisions about which technologies best suit their needs. Furthermore, they must keep up with the rapidly changing world of high-tech real estate tools to remain competitive.

IN PRACTICE   Home listings are available to the general public on the Internet through real estate agency Web sites and other Web sites such as Cyber-Homes, at *www.cyberhomes.com,* and NAR, at *www.realtor.com.* By accessing these services, potential buyers can preview photographs of properties and narrow their searches by price range, number of bedrooms, amenities, neighborhood, school district, and so forth.

Electronic Contracting

Technology and the Internet have significantly changed the way in which real estate transactions are performed. As a result, **electronic contracting** is a growing field in real estate practice because it quickly and efficiently integrates information in a real estate transaction between clients, lenders, and title and closing agents. The transactions are conducted through e-mail, or fax, and can save a lot of time and money.

Two federal Acts govern electronic contracting: the **Uniform Electronic Transactions Act (UETA),** and the **Electronic Signatures in Global and National Commerce Act (E-Sign).**

The UETA sets forth basic rules for entering an enforceable contract using electronic means and has been enacted in most states. The primary purpose of the UETA is to remove barriers in electronic commerce that would otherwise prevent enforceability of contracts. The UETA validates and effectuates electronic records and signatures in a procedural manner. It is intended to complement any state's digital signature statute. The UETA does not in any way require parties to use electronic means. Following are UETA's four key provisions:

1. A contract cannot be denied its legal effect just because an electronic record was used.

2. A record or signature cannot be denied its legal effect just because it is in an electronic format.
3. If a state's law requires a signature on a contract, an electronic signature is sufficient.
4. If a state's law requires a written record, an electronic record is sufficient.

In Georgia

Contract forms, such as those provided by the GAR, may stipulate criteria for the use of electronic means for delivery and receipt and/or the validity of electronic signatures.

E-Sign functions as the electronic transactions law in states that have not enacted the UETA, and some sections of E-Sign apply to states that have enacted the UETA. The purpose of the E-Sign is to make contracts (including signatures) and records legally enforceable regardless of the medium in which they are created. For example, contracts formed using e-mail have the same legal significance as those formed on paper.

Both UETA and E-Sign address issues involving notices, contracts, notarization and acknowledgment, and transferable records. Some of the problems that have arisen in electronic contracting include legal barriers, issues of forgery and nonrepudiation, and lack of confidence in technology. Legal barriers have been diminished as electronic contracting is now governed by the two federal acts. Issues of forgery can occur but are rare. *Nonrepudiation* refers to the situation where someone denies having signed a document online. Again, this is a rare occurrence. Confidence in technology increases as improvements are made in the software and people become more accustomed to online transactions.

IN PRACTICE When entering a residential purchase sale agreement, it is important for the parties to feel comfortable with and clearly communicate the method chosen for transacting the agreement, whether by paper and ink or by e-mail.

Broker's Compensation

The broker's compensation is specified in the contract with the principal. In Georgia, the seller, buyer, landlord, or tenant enters into a contract with the broker that is referred to as a **brokerage engagement** (or agency agreement). The contract specifies that the seller, buyer, landlord, or tenant becomes the client of the broker and promises to pay the broker a valuable consideration or agrees that the broker may receive a valuable consideration from another in consideration of the broker producing a seller, buyer, tenant, or landlord ready, able, and willing to sell, buy, or rent the property or performing other brokerage services. Note that in Georgia under O.C.G.A. 10-6A-11, the payment or promise of payment of compensation to a broker does not determine whether a brokerage relationship has been created.

In Georgia

License laws may stipulate that a written agreement must establish the compensation to be paid. Compensation can be in the form of a **commission** or brokerage fee (computed as a percentage of the total sales price), a flat fee, or an hourly rate. *The amount of a broker's commission is negotiable in every case.* Attempting, however subtly, to impose uniform commission rates is a clear violation of state and federal antitrust laws (discussed later in this chapter). A *broker may, however, set the minimum rate acceptable for that broker's firm.* The important point is for broker and client to agree on a rate before the agency relationship is established. A commission may be any percentage of the sales price that the market will bear, and it is that amount agreed upon between the broker and client. Brokers in different parts of the country and in different kinds of real estate charge commissions ranging from less than 5 percent to more than 8 percent.

A commission is usually considered *earned* when the work for which the broker was hired has been accomplished. Most sales commissions are payable when the sale is consummated by *delivery of the seller's deed.* This provision is generally included in the listing agreement. When the sales or listing agreement specifies no time for the payment of the broker's commission, the commission is usually earned when

- a completed sales contract has been executed by a ready, willing, and able buyer;
- the contract has been accepted and executed by the seller; and
- copies of the contract are in the possession of all parties.

To be entitled to a sales commission, an individual must be

- a licensed broker,
- the procuring cause of the sale, and
- employed by the buyer or seller under a valid contract.

To be considered the **procuring cause** of a sale, the broker must have started or caused a chain of events that resulted in the sale. For example, activities such as conducting open houses, placing advertisements in the newspaper, and showing the house to the buyer are considered procuring cause. A broker who causes or completes such an action without a contract or without having been promised payment is a *volunteer* and may not legally claim compensation. Many other factors affect a broker's status as procuring cause. For instance, if the agent abandons the transaction, he or she may not be able to return and claim to have been the procuring cause. In all cases, the key is determining *who really sold the property.* Procuring cause disputes between brokers are usually settled through an arbitration hearing conducted by the local real estate board or association. Disputes between a broker and a client may go to court, however.

To be a **procuring cause**, the broker must have started a chain of events that resulted in a sale.

Once a seller accepts an offer from a ready, willing, and able buyer, the broker is entitled to a commission. A **ready, willing, and able buyer** is one *prepared to buy on the seller's terms and ready to take positive steps toward consummation of the transaction.* Courts may prevent the broker from receiving a commission if the broker knew the buyer was unable to perform. If the transaction is not consummated, the broker may still be entitled to a commission if the seller

- had a change of mind and refused to sell;
- has a spouse who refused to sign the deed;
- had a title with uncorrected defects;

- committed fraud with respect to the transaction;
- was unable to deliver possession within a reasonable time;
- insisted on terms not in the listing (for example, the right to restrict the use of the property); or
- had a mutual agreement with the buyer to cancel the transaction.

> A **ready, willing, and able buyer** is one prepared to buy on the seller's terms and ready to complete the transaction.

In general, then, a *broker is due a commission if a sale is not consummated because of the principal's default*.

In most states, it is illegal for a broker to pay a commission to anyone other than the salesperson licensed with the broker or to another broker. Fees, commissions, or other compensation cannot be paid to unlicensed persons for services that require a real estate license. *Other compensation* includes tangible gifts, such as a new television, or other premiums, such as a vacation. For example, a broker cannot provide a ski vacation trip to a buyer for making an offer on a house. This is not to be confused with referral fees paid between brokers for leads. Referral fees are legal as long as both individuals are licensed.

In Georgia

In Georgia, under O.C.G.A. 43-40-25(b)(17)(c), a broker may pay a commission to an unlicensed corporation or legal entity in which the affiliated license has 20 percent or more interest.

Salesperson's Compensation

The amount of compensation a salesperson receives is set by mutual agreement between the broker and the salesperson. A broker may agree to pay a fixed salary or a share of the commissions from transactions originated by a salesperson. In some cases, a salesperson may draw from an account against earned shares of commissions. Some brokers require salespersons to pay all or part of the expenses of advertising listed properties.

Some firms have adopted a *100 percent commission plan* in which salespersons pay a monthly service charge to their brokers to cover the costs of office space, telephones, and supervision in return for keeping 100 percent of the commissions from the sales they negotiate. The 100 percent commission salesperson pays all of his or her own expenses.

Other companies have *graduated commission splits* based on a salesperson's achieving specified production goals. For instance, a broker might agree to split commissions 50/50 up to a $25,000 salesperson's share; 60/40 for shares from $25,000 to $30,000; and so on. Commission splits as generous as 80/20 or 90/10 are possible, however, particularly for high producers.

However the salesperson's compensation is structured, only the employing broker can pay it. In cooperating transactions, the commission must first be received by the employing broker and then be paid to the salesperson, unless otherwise permitted by license laws and agreed to by the employing broker.

MATH CONCEPTS

SHARING COMMISSIONS

A commission might be shared by many people: The listing broker, the listing salesperson, the selling broker, and the selling salesperson. Drawing a diagram can help you determine which person is entitled to receive what amount of the total commission. For example, salesperson Ed, while working for broker Harry, took a listing on a $189,000 house at a 6 percent commission rate. Salesperson Tom, while working for broker Matt, found the buyer for the property. If the property sold for the listed price, the listing broker and the selling broker shared the commission equally, and the selling broker kept 45 percent of what he received, how much did salesperson Tom receive? (If the broker retained 45 percent of the total commission he received, his salesperson would receive the balance: 100% − 45% = 55%.)

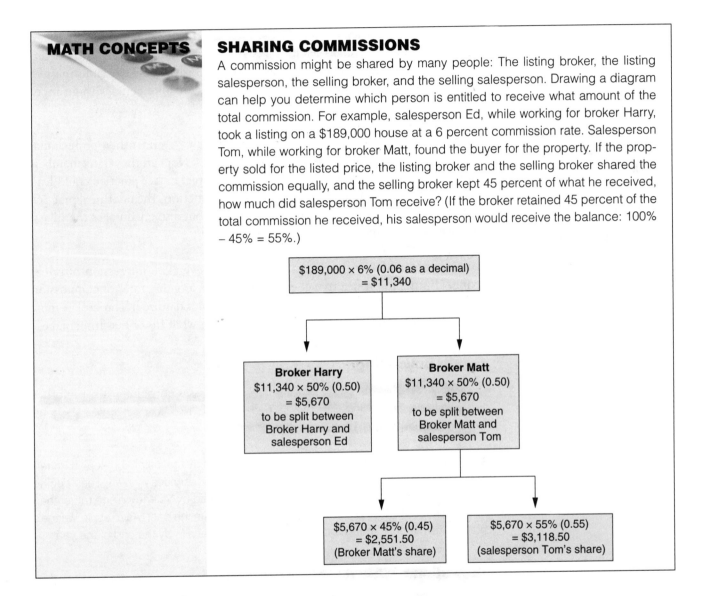

■ ANTITRUST LAWS

The real estate industry is subject to **antitrust laws.** At the federal level, the Sherman Antitrust Act provides specific penalties for a number of illegal business activities. Each state has its own antitrust laws as well. These laws prohibit monopolies and any contracts, combinations, and conspiracies that unreasonably restrain trade—that is, behaviors that interfere with the free flow of goods and services in a competitive marketplace. The most common antitrust violations are price-fixing, group boycotting, allocation of customers or markets, and tie-in agreements.

Price-Fixing

Price-fixing is the practice of setting prices for products or services rather than letting competition in the open market establish those prices. In real estate, price-fixing occurs when competing brokers agree to set sales commissions, fees, or management rates. *Price-fixing is illegal.* Brokers must independently determine commission rates or fees for their own firms only. These decisions must be based on a broker's business judgment and revenue requirements without input from other brokers.

Multiple-listing organizations, boards of REALTORS®, and other professional organizations may not set fees or commission splits. Nor can they deny membership to brokers based on the fees the brokers charge. Either practice could lead the public to believe that the industry not only sanctions the unethical practice of withholding cooperation from certain brokers but also encourages the illegal practice of restricting open-market competition.

The broker's, and agent's, challenge is to avoid even the impression of price-fixing. Hinting to prospective clients that there is a "going rate" of commission or a "normal" fee implies that rates are, in fact, standardized. The broker must make it clear to clients that the rate stated is only what his or her firm charges.

> **Antitrust violations include**
> - price-fixing,
> - group boycotting,
> - allocation of customers,
> - allocation of markets, and
> - tie-in agreements.

Group Boycotting

Group boycotting occurs when two or more businesses conspire against another business or agree to withhold their patronage to reduce competition. Group boycotting is illegal under the antitrust laws.

■ **FOR EXAMPLE** Valerie and Nick, the only real estate brokers in Potterville, agree that there are too many apartment-finder services in town. They decide to refer all prospective tenants to the service operated by Valerie's niece rather than handing out a list of all providers, as they have done in the past. As a result, Valerie's niece runs the only apartment-finder service in Potterville by the end of the year.

Allocation of Customers or Markets

Allocation of customers or markets involves an agreement between brokers to divide their markets and refrain from competing for each other's business. Allocations may be made on a geographic basis, with brokers agreeing to specific territories within which they will operate exclusively. The division may also occur by markets, such as by price range or category of housing. These agreements result in reduced competition.

Tie-in Agreements

Finally, *tie-in agreements* (also known as *tying agreements*) are agreements to sell one product only if the buyer purchases another product as well. The sale of the first (desired) product is *tied* to the purchase of a second (less desirable) product.

■ **FOR EXAMPLE**   Dan, a real estate broker, owns a vacant lot in a popular area of town. Bill, a builder, wants to buy the lot and build three new homes on it. Dan refuses to sell the lot to the builder unless Bill agrees to list the improved lot with Dan so that Dan can sell the homes. This sort of list-back arrangement violates antitrust laws.

In Georgia   Licensees should be aware of two Georgia statutes dealing with antitrust violations: the Fair Business Practices Act of 1975 (FBPA), of O.C.G.A 10-1-390 et seq., and the Uniform Deceptive Trade Practices Act (UDTPA), O.C.G.A. 10-1-370 et seq. The FBPA regulates advertising, and restricts activities encouraging public consumer transactions. A licensee who intentionally uses fraudulent or misleading information to encourage the sale of real property could violate the act. The act only applies when the activity is directed toward the public as a whole. The UDTPA provides virtually the same protections as the FBPA, except under the UDTPA, no actual consumer transaction has to take place for a violation to occur.

Penalties

The penalties for violating antitrust laws are severe. For instance, under the federal Sherman Antitrust Act, people who fix prices or allocate markets may be subject to a maximum $100,000 fine and three years in prison. For corporations, the penalty may be as high as $1 million. In a civil suit, a person who has suffered a loss because of the antitrust activities of a guilty party may recover triple the value of the actual damages plus attorney's fees and costs.

Fee-for-Services

The Internet has revolutionized the real estate profession in many ways. One of the more notable impacts of the Internet is that it has allowed buyers and sellers to have tremendous access to information about real estate, housing, financing, and law. The Internet has caused a radical shift in that the average consumer is now much more knowledgeable about real estate matters. With knowledge and information, a consumer is more innovative and independent. The advent of the Internet has also meant that the consumer is privy to information immediately. Consumers now want instant access to real estate information.

The successful licensee will understand and encourage consumers' innovation. In the process, it is critical for the licensee to identify what services he or she can provide and underscore the value of those services. While emphasizing the services that a licensee provides, it may be important for the licensee to think of himself or herself as a *consultant*. While consumers are more independent, real estate expertise is almost always needed.

It may be important for licensees to be more flexible and open to seeing their occupation as a *bundle of services* that can be unbundled. Note that unbundling fee-for-services is different from discounted real estate services. *Fee-for-services* is the arrangement where the consumer decides which services he or she needs and then works with and pays the licensee solely for those services. *Discounted real estate services* is the arrangement where a consumer receives all of the real estate services, but at a discounted price.

Unbundling services means offering services in a piecemeal fashion. For example, a consultant may want to offer a seller the following services:

- Helping the seller prepare the property for sale
- Performing a competitive market analysis (CMA) and pricing the property
- Assisting with marketing the property using the MLS and any Web sites
- Locating and screening a buyer
- Drafting a purchase sales agreement and helping with negotiations
- Assisting with the closing transaction

Other services include those for a buyer. For example, a consultant may offer a buyer the following services:

- Consulting on renting versus owning
- Helping a buyer with a mortgage preapproval
- Consulting on a buyer's desired location
- Visiting properties with a buyer and checking property information
- Drafting a purchase sales agreement and helping with negotiations

In Georgia

While some states allow a consultant to assist with the closing real estate transaction, in Georgia, the Supreme Court has issued a formal advisory opinion stating that the closing of a real estate transaction constitutes the practice of law, and, if performed by someone other than a duly licensed Georgia attorney, results in the prohibited unlicensed practice of law. Check with the State Bar of Georgia for current advice in this area (*www.gabar.org* or 404-527-8743).

Note the discussion that follows regarding minimum level of services and the problems that can occur when providing a limited service.

While licensees want to encourage consumers to use all of their services (*full-service*) for a commission rate, when it becomes apparent that a consumer wants help with one or several services only, then it would be helpful for the licensee to have in mind the best compensation model. Many licensees use either an hourly rate or a flat fee for particular services. In determining a flat fee, licensees consider the amount of hours it would take to do a particular task and multiply that by an hourly rate. In order to avoid a price-fixing claim, it is important that brokers independently establish their fees and do not develop their fees based on a "norm" in the industry.

Licensees may also want to develop their own lists of services for sellers and buyers, as well as a list of specific services to help those consumers selling their home on their own (FSBOs).

Communicating with consumers and identifying their real estate needs are key. Licensees provide an array of valuable services that consumers can pick and choose from. Knowledgeable and independent consumers can seem threatening to a licensee; however, the licensee has the opportunity to emphasize the value and variety of real estate services offered, for varying fees. Remember that it is ultimately the broker who decides whether an unbundling of services is good for the company.

■ **FOR EXAMPLE**   Chris wants to buy a house without contracting with a licensee but needs help writing an offer. Chris asks Sally, a broker friend of hers, to write an offer to purchase. Sally consults with Chris, writes the offer to purchase, and charges Chris a set fee for her service.

Minimum Level of Service

Problems have emerged with the growing number of brokerages offering *limited-service* listing agreements. These agreements stipulate that a listing broker offers no services other than that of placing a listing in the MLS. When a seller enters into this kind of agreement, the seller is essentially representing himself or herself. The seller may well be aware of this; however, when questions emerge involving the transaction, the seller sometimes turns to the buyer's representative for answers, putting the real estate professional in an ethical quandary. Seller questions and licensee answers of this type could lead to a claim of dual agency. However, if a licensee does not provide help, the transaction could be in jeopardy.

In response to this problem, some states have enacted legislation defining an *exclusive brokerage agreement*. Other states have proposed regulations that define the **minimum level of services** a consumer should expect from a licensee. For example, one state now requires all exclusive brokerage agreements specify that the broker—through one or more sponsored licensees—must provide, at a minimum, the following:

■ Accept delivery of and present offers and counteroffers to the client
■ Assist the client in developing, negotiating, and presenting offers and counteroffers
■ Answer the client's questions about offers, counteroffers, and contingencies

In Georgia   Under recent Georgia legislation, (Senate Bill 114), when a broker specifically says in a listing contract or brokerage agreement that he or she is not providing negotiation services to the client, a selling agent can present an offer directly to a seller. See Chapter 14, Unfair Trade Practices under O.C.G.A. 43-40-25(14), for further information.

National Do Not Call Registry

In 2003, federal *do-not-call* legislation was signed into law, and real estate professionals must comply with the provisions of the **National Do Not Call Registry.** The registry is managed by the Federal Trade Commission; it is a list of telephone numbers from consumers who have indicated their preference to limit the telemarketing calls they receive. The registry applies to any plan, program, or campaign to sell goods or services through interstate phone calls. The registry does not limit calls by political organizations, charities, or telephone surveyors.

A real estate professional may call a consumer with whom it has an established business relationship for up to 18 months after the consumer's last purchase, delivery, or payment, even if the consumer is listed on the National Do Not Call Registry. Also, a real estate professional may call a consumer for up to three months after the consumer makes an inquiry or submits an application. Note that if a consumer asks a company not to call even if there is an established business relationship, then the company must abide by the consumer wishes.

To access the National Do Not Call Registry, visit *www.telemarketing.donotcall.gov*. The only information accessible (for a fee) from the national registry is a registrant's telephone number. Starting in January, 2005, telemarketers and sellers are now required to search the registry at least once every 31 days and drop from their call lists registered consumer phone numbers.

Most states have do-not-call rules or regulations as well. It is important to keep up to date with your own state's laws regarding do-not-call policies, as well as the national law.

■ KEY POINT REVIEW

All 50 states, Canadian provinces, and the District of Columbia have **real estate license laws** and **rules with the force and effect of law** that

- establish basic requirements for obtaining a **real estate license;**
- may require **continuing education** for license renewal;
- define which **activities** require licensing;
- describe acceptable **standards of conduct and practice;** and
- enforce standards through a **disciplinary system.**

In Georgia   In Georgia, real estate practice is governed by the Georgia Real Estate License Law, Title 43, Chapter 40 of the O.C.G.A., BRRETA, and Rules and Regulations of the Georgia Real Estate Commission. The licensing authority is the Georgia Real Estate Commission.

A **real estate broker** is licensed to buy, sell, exchange, or lease real property for others for a fee, and may operate as a

- **sole proprietorship,**
- **partnership,** or
- corporation.

The real estate **brokerage** may be **independent** or part of a regional or national **franchise.**

Unless licensed as an attorney, a real estate broker is **not allowed to give legal advice** and should always advise parties to the transaction to secure **legal counsel** to protect their interests.

A **real estate salesperson** is licensed to perform real estate activities **only** on behalf of a licensed real estate broker.

A broker-employer is **liable** for actions of the salesperson within scope of the employment agreement.

When hired by an employing broker as an **independent contractor,** the salesperson

- usually receives a **commission**, with **no withholding** for Social Security, income tax, and other purposes;
- has the **freedom** to set hours and accomplish goals;
- does not relieve the broker of **liability** for related **work activities** of the salesperson; and
- must comply with **Internal Revenue Service (IRS)** requirements for a **qualified real estate agent.**

When a salesperson is hired by an employing broker as an **employee,** the

- salesperson may receive **salary** in lieu of or in addition to commission;
- salesperson may receive **benefits,** such as health insurance, profit-sharing, and workers' compensation;
- broker is required to **withhold** Social Security, income taxes, and other applicable federal and state taxes from earnings of the salesperson;
- broker sets **hours, duties,** and other specifics of day-to-day work; and
- broker has **liability** for related **work activities** of salesperson.

Real estate assistants (a.k.a., personal assistants or professional assistants) can perform administrative, marketing, and duties allowed by law in two ways:

- If **licensed** they must have an **employment agreement** with employing broker.
- If **unlicensed** they are limited in activities that they can performed.

In Georgia   Georgia Rule 520-1-.07 sets forth specific duties for unlicensed personnel support.

The **Internet** is invaluable for communication, research, and the marketing and advertising of a brokerage and properties because of the following:

- **E-mail** is accessible to most consumers and is fast and effective
- **Blogs** are used to communicate with other agents and clients
- **Vlogs** (video blogs) are becoming increasingly popular and helpful but tend to be expensive to produce
- **Multiple listing systems (MLSs)** may offer shared Web listings
- Brokerage and agent **Web pages** offer agent and property details
- **Realtor.com,** sponsored by the National Association of REALTORS®, and other popular Web sites pull in prospective buyers and sellers
- **Advertising** on the Internet can be effective, but it must comply with state and federal laws
- **Security** is generally trustworthy but requires continual upgrading of security measures and knowledgeable business practices to avoid phishing scams and other attempts at identity theft

Electronic contracting has sped up document transmission, made transactions more efficient for all parties, and has been clarified by two federal laws:

1. The **Uniform Electronic Transactions Act (UETA)** has been adopted in most states and does not require electronic communication, but if it is used, the
   — **contract** cannot be denied legal effect just because an electronic record was used, and
   — **record** or **signature** cannot be denied legal effect just because it is in electronic format.
2. **Electronic Signatures in Global and National Commerce Act (E-Sign)** function as **electronic transactions** law in states that have not enacted UETA and make **contracts** (including signatures) and **records** legally enforceable regardless of the medium in which they are created.

Broker's compensation must be agreed upon before agency relationship is established and can be a **commission** based on sales price, **flat fee,** or **hourly rate,** but note the following:

- **Fee for services** is based on charges for separate broker activities that the client desires (*unbundling of services*).
- Some states now require **minimum services** to be offered by the broker.

The broker may set a **minimum commission rate** acceptable for the firm, but any attempt to impose a **uniform commission rate** would be a violation of state and federal antitrust laws.

In Georgia	In Georgia, seller and buyer or landlord and tenant may enter into a contract called a *brokerage engagement* that promises to pay the broker valuable consideration.

To be entitled to compensation in a sales transaction, an individual must be

- a licensed **broker;**
- **employed** by the buyer or seller under a **valid contract;** and
- the **procuring cause** of the sale by starting or causing a chain of events that resulted in the sale.

The commission is earned when the seller accepts an offer from a **ready, willing, and able buyer** prepared to buy on the seller's terms and ready to take positive steps toward consummation of the transaction.

A **salesperson's compensation** is set by mutual agreement of the employing broker and the salesperson.

Antitrust laws are both state and federal (**Sherman Antitrust Act**) and prohibit

- **monopolies;** and
- contracts, combinations, and conspiracies that **unreasonably restrain trade,** including:
   — **price-fixing,**
   — **group boycotting,**

— **allocation of customers or markets,** and

— **tie-in agreements (tying agreements)** forcing customers to purchase a product when only another was wanted.

Penalties for antitrust violations include the following:

- Under the **Sherman Act,** violators face up to a **$350,000 fine** and **three years in prison,** with corporate fines as high as **$10 million.**
- In a **civil suit** the successful plaintiff may recover triple damages plus attorney's fees and costs.

Do-not-call legislation is found at federal and state levels:

- The **National Do Not Call Registry,** managed by the Federal Trade Commission,
  — lists **telephone numbers** of consumers who have asked to be registered; and
  — **prohibits interstate calls** to those numbers to sell goods or services.
- Many states provide their own do-not-call legislation for in-state calls.

■ RELATED WEB SITES

Association of Real Estate Licensing Law Officials: *www.arello.org*

Georgia Real Estate Commission: *www.grec.state.ga.us*

National Do Not Call Registry: *www.donotcall.gov/default.aspx*

Electronic Transactions Act: *www.nccusl.org/nccusl/desktopdefault.aspx*

Electronic Signature and Records Law: *www.fda.gov/ora/complianceref/part11/*

E-Sign Law: *www.findlaw.com/casecode/index.html*

State Bar of Georgia: *www.gabar.org*

U.S. Department of Internal Revenue: *www.irs.gov*

U.S. Department of Justice, Antitrust Division: *www.usdoj.gov/atr*

CHAPTER 5 QUIZ

1. Which of the following statements BEST explains the meaning of this sentence: "To recover a commission for brokerage services, a broker must *be employed* as the agent of the client"?
   a. The broker must work in a real estate office.
   b. The client must make an express or implied agreement to pay a commission to the broker.
   c. The broker must express an interest in representing the client.
   d. The broker must have a salesperson employed in the office.

2. A licensee who is paid in a lump sum and who is personally responsible for paying his or her own taxes is probably a(n)
   a. transactional broker.
   b. buyer's agent.
   c. independent contractor.
   d. employee.

3. Margot is a licensed real estate salesperson. Her written contract with broker George specifies that she is not an employee. In the last year, just less than half of Margot's income from real estate activity came from sales commissions. The remainder was based on an hourly wage paid by George. Using these facts, it is MOST likely that the IRS would classify Margot as which of the following for federal income tax purposes?
   a. Self-employed
   b. Employee
   c. Independent contractor
   d. Part-time real estate salesperson

4. When acting as an employee rather than an independent contractor, a salesperson may be obligated to
   a. list properties in his or her own name.
   b. work set hours.
   c. accept a commission from another broker.
   d. advertise property on his or her own behalf.

5. A real estate broker learns that her neighbor wishes to sell his house. The broker knows the property well and is able to persuade a customer-buyer to make an offer for the property. The broker then asks the neighbor if she can present an offer from the prospective buyer, and the neighbor agrees. At this point, which of the following statements is TRUE?
   a. The neighbor is not obligated to pay the broker a commission.
   b. The buyer is obligated to pay the broker for locating the property.
   c. The neighbor is obligated to pay the broker a commission for producing an offer to purchase.
   d. The broker may not be considered the procuring cause without a written contract.

6. A broker would have the right to dictate which of the following to an independent contractor?
   a. Number of hours the person would have to work
   b. Work schedule the person would have to follow
   c. Sales meetings the person would need to attend
   d. Compensation the person would receive

7. Licensees Fred and Rick were found guilty of conspiring with each other to allocate real estate brokerage markets. Lucy suffered a $90,000 loss because of their activities. If Lucy brings a civil suit against Fred and Rick, what can she expect to recover?
   a. Nothing, because a civil suit cannot be brought for damages resulting from antitrust activities
   b. Only $90,000—the amount of actual damages Lucy suffered
   c. Actual damages plus attorney's fees and costs
   d. $270,000 plus attorney's fees and costs

8. Jim and Ruth are both salespersons who work for NMN Realty. One afternoon, they agree to divide their town into a northern region and a southern region. Jim will handle listings in the northern region, and Ruth will handle listings in the southern region. Which of the following statements is *TRUE* regarding this agreement?

    a. The agreement between Jim and Ruth does not violate antitrust laws.

    b. The agreement between Jim and Ruth constitutes illegal price-fixing.

    c. Jim and Ruth have violated the Sherman Antitrust Act and are liable for triple damages.

    d. Jim and Ruth are guilty of group boycotting with regard to other salespersons in their office.

9. A state has recently updated its *Rules and Regulations for the Real Estate Profession*. Assuming this state is like all other states and provinces, which of the following statements is *TRUE* regarding this publication?

    a. The rules and regulations are state laws enacted by the legislature.

    b. The rules and regulations are a set of administrative rules adopted by the state real estate commission and do not have the same force and effect as the statutory license law.

    c. The rules and regulations are a set of administrative rules adopted by the state real estate commission that define the statutory license law and have the same force and effect as the license law itself.

    d. The rules and regulations create a suggested level of competence and behavior but are not enforceable against real estate licensees.

10. Louise is a skilled salesperson at Alpha Realty. After a particularly challenging transaction finally closes, the client gives her a check for $500 "for all your extra work." Which of the following statements is accurate?

    a. While such compensation is irregular, it is appropriate for Louise to accept the check.

    b. Louise may receive compensation only from her broker.

    c. Louise should accept the check and deposit it immediately in a special escrow account.

    d. Louise's broker is entitled to 80 percent of the check.

11. A broker has established the following office policy: "All listings taken by any salesperson associated with this real estate brokerage must include compensation based on a 7 percent commission. No lower commission rate is acceptable." If the broker attempts to impose this uniform commission requirement, which of the following statements is *TRUE?*

    a. A homeowner may sue the broker for violating the antitrust law's prohibition against price-fixing.

    b. The salespersons associated with the brokerage will not be bound by the requirement and may negotiate any commission rate they choose.

    c. The broker must present the uniform commission policy to the local professional association for approval.

    d. The broker may, as a matter of office policy, legally set the minimum commission rate acceptable for the firm.

12. GHI Realty has adopted a 100 percent commission plan. The monthly desk rent required of sales associates is $1,500, payable on the last day of the month. In August, a sales associate closed an $189,500 sale with a 6 percent commission and a $125,000 sale with a 5.5 percent commission. The salesperson's additional expenses for the month were $2,170. How much of her total monthly income did the salesperson keep?

    a. $14,575
    b. $16,075
    c. $16,745
    d. $18,245

13. Diana, a salesperson, took a listing on a house that sold for $329,985. The commission rate was 8 percent. Carol, a salesperson employed by another broker, found the buyer. Diana's broker received 60 percent of the commission on the sale; Carol's broker received 40 percent. If Diana's broker kept 30 percent, and paid Diana the remainder, how much did Diana earn on this sale?

    a. $3,167.86
    b. $7,391.66
    c. $11,087.50
    d. $15,839.28

14. On the sale of any property, a salesperson's compensation is based on the total commission paid to the broker. The salesperson receives 30 percent of the first $2,500, 40 percent of any amount between $2,500 and $7,500, and 50 percent of any amount exceeding $7,500. If a property sells for $234,500 and the broker's commission rate is 6.5 percent, what is the salesperson's total compensation?

    a. $5,847.00
    b. $6,621.25
    c. $6,871.25
    d. $7,621.25

15. The real estate licensing authority in Georgia is the

    a. Georgia Real Estate Commission.
    b. Georgia Secretary of State.
    c. Georgia Business License Division.
    d. Georgia legislature.

16. In Georgia, real estate closings can be conducted by

    a. real estate brokers.
    b. attorneys.
    c. real estate consultants.
    d. real estate salespersons.

Listing Agreements and Buyer Representation

■ **LEARNING OBJECTIVES**   *When you have finished reading this chapter, you should be able to:*

■ **identify** the different types of listing and buyer representation agreements and their terms.

■ **describe** the ways in which a listing may be terminated.

■ **explain** the listing process and the parts of the listing agreement.

■ **distinguish** among the characteristics of the various types of listing and buyer representation agreements.

■ **define** the following *key terms:*

brokerage engagement
buyer agency agreement
competitive market
   analysis (CMA)
exclusive-agency listing

exclusive-right-to-sell
   listing
market value
multiple listing service
   (MLS)

net listing
open listing
option listing

■ LISTING AGREEMENTS

A listing agreement is an employment contract rather than a real estate contract. It is a contract for the personal professional services of the broker, not for the transfer of real estate. A listing agreement may be either written or oral. Most states, however, either by their statutes of frauds or by specific rule from their real estate licensing authorities, require that the listing be in writing to be enforceable in court.

In Georgia

In Georgia, a **brokerage engagement** (also known as a listing or agency agreement) is a written contract in which the seller or buyer becomes the client of the broker and promises to pay the broker a valuable consideration or agrees that the broker may receive a valuable consideration from another for producing a ready, able, and willing prospective buyer or seller, or performing other brokerage services.

Under Georgia Rule 520-1-.06 each exclusive brokerage agreement must fully set forth its terms and an expiration date. At the time of securing a brokerage engagement, the licensee must furnish copies of the engagement to each person signing it.

As agent, the broker is authorized to represent the principal (and the principal's real estate) to third parties. That authorization includes obtaining and submitting offers for the property. The real estate salesperson's authority to provide brokerage services originates with his or her broker. Even though the real estate salesperson may perform most, if not all, of the listing services, the listing remains with the broker.

Under both the law of agency and most state license laws, only a broker can act as agent to list, sell, rent, or purchase another person's real estate and provide other services to a principal. This is true in Georgia as well. A salesperson who performs these acts does so only in the name and under the supervision of the broker (a salesperson is a general agent of the broker). Throughout this chapter, unless otherwise stated, the terms *broker, agent,* and *firm* are intended to include both the broker and a salesperson working for the broker. However, the parties to a listing contract are the seller and the broker.

Types of Listing Agreements

Several types of listing agreements exist. The type of contract determines the specific rights and obligations of the parties. (See Table 6.1.)

Exclusive-Right-to-Sell Listing

■ One authorized broker-agent receives a commission.
■ Seller pays broker-agent regardless of who sells property.

Exclusive-right-to-sell listing   In an **exclusive-right-to-sell listing,** one broker is appointed as the seller's sole agent. The broker is given the exclusive right, or *authorization,* to market the seller's property. If the property is sold while the listing is in effect, the seller must pay the broker a commission *regardless of who sells the property.* In other words, if the seller finds a buyer without the broker's assistance, the seller *still* must pay the broker a commission. Sellers benefit from this form of agreement because the broker feels freer to spend time and money

TABLE 6.1	Exclusive-Right-to-Sell	Exclusive-Agency	Open Listing
Types of Listing Agreements	One broker	One broker	Multiple brokers
	Broker is paid regardless of who sells the house.	Broker is paid only if he or she is procuring cause.	Only selling broker is paid.
		Seller retains the right to sell without obligation.	Seller retains the right to sell without obligation.

actively marketing the property, making a timely and profitable sale more likely. From the broker's perspective, an exclusive-right-to-sell listing offers the greatest opportunity to receive a commission.

Exclusive-agency listing   In an **exclusive-agency listing,** *one* broker is authorized to act as the exclusive agent of the principal. However, *the seller retains the right to sell the property without obligation to the broker.*

Open listing   In an **open listing** (also known in some areas as a *nonexclusive listing, general, or simple listing*), the seller retains the right to employ any number of brokers as agents. The brokers can act simultaneously, and the seller is obligated to pay a commission to only that broker who successfully produces a ready, willing, and able buyer. If the seller personally sells the property *without the aid of any of the brokers,* the seller is not obligated to pay a commission. A listing contract that does not specifically provide for an exclusive-right-to-sell listing or an exclusive-agency listing ordinarily creates an open listing.

The terms of even an open listing must be negotiated, however. These negotiated terms should be in writing to protect the agent's ability to collect an agreed-on fee from the seller. Written terms may be in the form of a listing agreement (if the agent represents the seller) or a fee agreement (if the agent represents the buyer or the seller does not wish to be represented).

Special Listing Provisions

Multiple listing   A *multiple listing clause* may be included in an exclusive listing. It is used by brokers who are members of a **multiple listing service (MLS).** As discussed in Chapter 4, an MLS is a marketing organization whose broker members make their own exclusive listings available through other brokers and gain access to other brokers' listed properties as well.

An MLS offers advantages to both brokers and sellers. Brokers develop a sizable inventory of properties to be sold and are assured a portion of the commission if they list property or participate in the sale of another broker's listing. Sellers gain because the property is exposed to a larger market.

The contractual obligations among the member brokers of an MLS vary widely. Most MLSs require that a broker turn over new listings to the service within a specific, fairly short period of time after the broker obtains the listing. The length of time during which the listing broker can offer a property exclusively without

Exclusive-Agency Listing

- There is one authorized agent.
- Broker receives a commission only if she or he is the procuring cause.
- Seller retains the right to sell without obligation.

Open Listing

- There are multiple agents.
- Only the selling agent is entitled to a commission.
- Seller retains the right to sell independently without obligation.

notifying the other member brokers varies. Some MLSs, however, permit a broker up to five days before he or she must submit the listing to the service.

Under the provisions of most MLSs, a participating broker makes a unilateral offer of cooperation and compensation to other member brokers. The broker must have the written consent of the seller to include the property in an MLS. All brokers must determine the appropriate way to proceed to protect their clients.

IN PRACTICE Technology has enhanced the benefits of MLS membership. In addition to providing instant access to information about the status of listed properties, MLSs often offer a broad range of other useful information about mortgage loans, real estate taxes and assessments, and municipalities and school districts. They are equally helpful to the licensee who needs to make a competitive market analysis to determine the value of a particular property before suggesting an appropriate range of listing prices. Computer-assisted searches also help buyers select properties that best meet their needs.

> In a **net listing**, the broker is entitled to any amount exceeding the seller's stated net; in an **option listing**, the broker has the right to purchase the property.

Net listing A **net listing** provision specifies that the seller will receive a net amount of money from any sale, with the excess going to the listing broker as commission. The broker is free to offer the property at any price greater than that net amount. Because a net listing can create a conflict of interest between the broker's fiduciary responsibility to the seller and the broker's profit motive, it is illegal in many states, including Georgia, and is discouraged in others.

■ **FOR EXAMPLE** A seller explained her situation to her broker: "I want to sell my house, but I don't want to be bothered with percentages and bargaining and offers and counteroffers. I just need to walk out of this deal with $150,000 in my pocket. You sell the place for any price you want and keep anything over $150,000." The broker knows that comparable homes in the area are selling for more than $200,000. What should the broker do about this offer of a net listing?

Option listing An **option listing** provision gives the broker the right, but not the obligation, to purchase the listed property within a certain period of time. If the option is not exercised within the specified time period, then the option expires. Use of an option listing may open the broker to charges of fraud unless the broker is scrupulous in fulfilling all obligations to the property owner. In some states, a broker who chooses to exercise such an option must first inform the property owner of the broker's profit in the transaction and secure *in writing* the owner's agreement to it. Note that an option listing is different from when a broker's firm *guarantees* to purchase property on specified terms and conditions if the property does not sell within a certain time. Also, an option listing differs from an option contract, which will be discussed in Chapter 11.

■ TERMINATION OF LISTINGS

A listing agreement is a personal service contract between a broker and a seller. Its success depends on the broker's personal, professional efforts. Because the broker's services are unique, he or she cannot turn over the listing to another broker without the principal's written consent. The property owner cannot force the broker to perform, but the broker's failure to work diligently toward fulfilling the contract's terms constitutes abandonment of the listing. In the event the listing is abandoned or revoked by the broker, the owner is entitled to sue the broker for damages.

Of course, the property owner might also fail to fulfill the terms of the agreement. A property owner who refuses to cooperate with the broker's reasonable requests, such as allowing the broker to show the property to prospective buyers, or who refuses to proceed with a complete sales contract, could be liable for damages to the broker. If either party cancels the contract, he or she may be liable for damages to the other.

A listing agreement may be terminated for the following reasons:

- When the agreement's purpose is fulfilled, such as when a buyer or tenant is produced
- When the agreement's term expires without a successful transfer
- If the property is destroyed or its use is changed by some force outside the owner's control, such as a zoning change or condemnation by eminent domain (see Chapter 20)
- If title to the property is transferred by operation of law, as in the case of the owner's bankruptcy
- If the broker and seller mutually agree to end the listing or if one party ends it unilaterally (in which case he or she may be liable to the other party for damages)
- If either party dies or becomes incapacitated
- If either the broker or seller breaches the contract, the agreement is terminated and the breaching or canceling party may be liable to the other for damages

Expiration of Listing Period

All exclusive listings should specify a definite period of time during which the broker is to be employed. *In most states, failing to specify a definite termination date in a listing is grounds for the suspension or revocation of a real estate license.*

In Georgia

Under Georgia Rule 520-1-.06(1)(a), the brokerage engagement must state a definite expiration date.

Courts have discouraged the use of *automatic extension clauses* in exclusive listings, such as a clause providing for a base period of 90 days that "continues thereafter until terminated by either party hereto by 30 days' notice in writing." Extension clauses are illegal in some states, and many listing contract forms specifically provide that there can be no automatic extensions of the agreement. Some courts have held that an extension clause actually creates an open listing rather than an exclusive-agency agreement.

Some listing contracts contain a *broker protection clause*. This clause provides that the property owner will pay the listing broker a commission if, within a specified number of days after the listing expires, the owner transfers the property to someone the broker originally introduced to the owner. This clause protects a broker who was the procuring cause from losing a commission because the transaction was completed after the listing expired. The time for such a clause usually parallels the terms of the listing agreement. A six-month listing may carry a broker protection clause of six months after the listing's expiration, for example. To protect the owner and prevent any liability of the owner for two separate commissions, most of these clauses stipulate that they cannot be enforced if the property is relisted under a new contract either with the original listing broker or with another broker.

■ THE LISTING PROCESS

Before signing a contract, the broker and seller must discuss a variety of issues. The seller's most critical concerns typically are the selling price of the property and the net amount the seller can expect to receive from the sale. The broker has several professional tools to provide information about a property's value and to calculate the proceeds from a sale.

Most sellers ask other questions as well: "How quickly will the property sell?" "What services will the broker provide during the listing period?" This is the broker's opportunity to explain the various types of listing agreements, the ramifications of different agency relationships, and the marketing services the broker provides. At the end of this process the seller should feel comfortable with his or her decision to list with the broker.

Similarly, before the listing agreement is finalized, the broker should be prepared to fulfill the duties and obligations the agreement imposes. The seller should have provided comprehensive information about both the property and his or her personal concerns. Based on this information, the broker can accept the listing with confidence that the seller's goals can be met in a profitable manner for both parties.

Pricing the Property

While it is the responsibility of the broker or salesperson to advise and assist, *it is the seller who must determine the listing price for the property*. Because the average seller does not have the resources needed to make an informed decision about a reasonable listing price, real estate agents must be prepared to offer their knowledge, information, and expertise.

A **competitive market analysis** is an analysis of market activity among comparable properties; it is not the same as a formal appraisal.

A salesperson can help the seller determine a listing price for the property by using a **competitive market analysis (CMA).** This is a comparison of the prices of properties recently sold, properties currently on the market, and properties that did not sell. The comparisons must be made with properties similar in location, size, age, style, and amenities to the seller's property. Although a CMA is not a formal appraisal, the salesperson uses many of the same methods and techniques an appraiser uses in arriving at a reasonable value range. (See Chapter 19.) If no adequate comparisons can be made, or if the property is unique in some way, the seller may prefer that a professional appraiser conduct a detailed, formal estimate of the property's value.

Market Value

The most probable price a property would bring in an arm's-length transaction under normal conditions on the open market is the **market value.**

Whether a CMA or a formal appraisal is used, the figure sought is the property's market value. **Market value,** discussed in Chapter 19, is the most probable price property would bring in an arm's-length transaction under normal conditions on the open market. A CMA estimates market value as likely to fall within a range of values (for instance, $175,000 to $180,000). A CMA, however, should not be confused with a formal appraisal, which will indicate a specific value rather than a range.

While it is the property owner's privilege to set whatever listing price he or she chooses, a broker should consider rejecting any listing in which the price is substantially exaggerated or severely out of line with the indications of the CMA or appraisal. These tools provide the best indications of what a buyer will likely pay for the property. An unrealistic listing price will make it difficult for the broker to properly market the seller's property within the agreed-upon listing period. Furthermore, a seller who is unreasonable about the property's value may prove uncooperative on other issues later on.

Seller's Return

The broker can easily calculate roughly how much the seller will net from a given sales price or what sales price will produce a desired net amount. The Math Concepts on the next page illustrate how the formulas are applied.

IN PRACTICE   When helping a seller determine an appropriate listing price, the broker must give an estimate of value that is reasonable, conservative, and as accurate as possible. Overpriced listings cost the broker time and money in wasted marketing and advertising and give sellers false hopes of riches to come. Ultimately, failing to move overpriced listings will cost the broker future business opportunities as well.

Information Needed for Listing Agreements

Obtaining as many facts as possible about the property ensures that most contingencies can be anticipated. This is particularly important when the listing will be shared with other brokers through an MLS and the other licensees must rely on the information taken by the lister.

The information needed for a listing agreement generally includes the

- names and relationship, if any, of the owners;
- street address and legal description of the property;
- size, type, age, and construction of improvements;
- number of rooms and their sizes;
- dimensions of the lot;
- existing loans, including such information as the name and address of each lender, the type of loan, the loan number, the loan balance, the interest rate, the monthly payment and what it includes (principal, interest, real estate tax impounds, hazard insurance impounds, mortgage insurance premiums), whether the loan may be assumed by the buyer and under what circumstances, and whether the loan may be prepaid without penalty;
- possibility of seller financing;
- amount of any outstanding special assessments and whether they will be paid by the seller or assumed by the buyer;
- zoning classification of the property;
- current (or most recent year's) property taxes;
- neighborhood amenities (for instance, schools, parks and recreational areas, churches, and public transportation);
- real property, if any, to be removed from the premises by the seller and any personal property to be included in the sale for the buyer (both the listing contract and the subsequent purchase contract should be explicit on these points);
- additional information, if any, that would make the property more appealing and marketable; and
- required disclosures, if any, concerning agency representation and property conditions.

Disclosures

Disclosures of agency relationships and property conditions are important consumer safeguards. As discussed in Chapter 4, most states, including Georgia, have enacted laws requiring that agents disclose whose interests they legally represent. It is important that the seller be informed of the company's policies regarding single agency, dual agency, and buyer agency. In addition, the seller should be informed about potential cooperation with subagents and buyer's agents.

Chapter 4 also mentioned that seller disclosure of property conditions is required by law in many states. These disclosures normally cover a wide range of structural, mechanical, and other conditions that a prospective purchaser should know about to make an informed decision. Frequently, the laws require that the seller complete a standardized form. It is the licensee's responsibility to see that the seller complies with these disclosures. Agents should caution sellers to make truthful disclosures to avoid litigation arising from fraudulent or careless misrepresentations.

In Georgia   In Georgia, seller disclosures are not required, although they are widely used.

MATH CONCEPTS

CALCULATING SALES PRICES, COMMISSIONS, AND NET TO SELLER

When a property sells, the sales price equals 100 percent of the money being transferred. Therefore, if a broker is to receive a 6 percent commission, 94 percent will remain for the seller's other expenses and equity. To calculate a commission using a sales price of $225,000 and a commission rate of 6 percent, multiply the sales price by the commission rate:

$$\$225,000 \times 6\% = \$225,000 \times 0.06 = \$13,500 \text{ commission}$$

To calculate a sales price using a commission of $13,500 and a commission rate of 7 percent, divide the commission by the commission rate:

$$\$13,500 \div 7\% = \$13,500 \div 0.07 = \$192,857 \text{ sales price}$$

To calculate a commission rate using a commission of $8,200 and a sales price of $164,000, divide the commission by the sales price:

$$\$8,200 \div \$164,000 = 0.05, \text{ or } 5\% \text{ commission rate}$$

To calculate the net to the seller using a sales price of $125,000 and a commission rate of 8 percent, multiply the sales price by 100 percent minus the commission rate:

$$\$125,000 \times (100\% - 8\%) = \$125,000 \times (92\%) = \$125,000 \times 0.92 = \$115,000$$

The same result could be achieved by calculating the commission ($125,000 × 0.08 = $10,000) and deducting it from the sales price ($125,000 – $10,000 = $115,000); however, this involves unnecessary extra calculations.

You may use this circle formula to help you with these calculations. If you know two of the figures, you can determine the third.

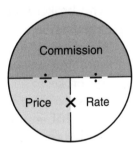

In Summary: Sales price × Commission rate = Commission
Commission ÷ Commission rate = Sales price
Commission ÷ Sales price = Commission rate
Sales price × (100% – Commission rate) = Net to seller

■ THE LISTING CONTRACT FORM

A wide variety of listing contract forms is available. Some brokers have attorneys draft form contracts for their firms, some use forms prepared by their multiple listing services, some use forms produced by their state real estate licensing authorities, and some are created by their state REALTOR® Associations. Some brokers use a separate *information sheet* (also known as a *profile* or *data sheet*) for recording property features. That sheet is wed to a second form containing the contractual obligations between the seller and the broker: listing price, duration of the agreement, signatures of the parties, and so forth. Other brokers use a single form. A sample Georgia Exclusive Seller Listing Agreement appears in Figure 6.1.

In Georgia

Listing Agreement Issues

Regardless of which standard form of listing agreement is used, the same considerations arise in most real estate transactions. This means that all listing contracts tend to require similar information. However, licensees should review the specific forms used in their areas and refer to their states' laws for any specific requirements. Some of the considerations covered in a typical contract are discussed in the following paragraphs.

The type of listing agreement   The contract may be an exclusive-right-to-sell listing (the most common type), an exclusive-agency listing, or an open listing. The type of listing agreement determines the extent of a broker's authority to act on the principal's behalf. Most MLSs do not permit open listings to be posted in the MLS system.

The broker's authority and responsibilities   The contract should specify whether the broker may place a sign on the property and advertise and market the property. Another major consideration is whether the broker is permitted to authorize subagents or buyer's brokers through an MLS. Will the contract allow the broker to show the property at reasonable times and on reasonable notice to the seller? May the broker accept earnest money deposits on behalf of the seller, and what are the broker's responsibilities in holding the funds? Without the written consent of the seller, the broker cannot undertake any of these or other important activities.

The names of all parties to the contract   Anyone who has an ownership interest in the property must be identified and should sign the listing to validate it. If the property is owned under one of the forms of co-ownership discussed in Chapter 8, that fact should be clearly established. If one or more of the owners is married, it is wise to obtain the spouse's consent and signature on the contract to release any marital rights. If the property is in the possession of a tenant, that should be disclosed (along with the terms of the tenancy), and instructions should be included on how the property is to be shown to a prospective buyer.

F I G U R E   6.1

Sample Listing Agreement

EXCLUSIVE SELLER LISTING AGREEMENT
(ALSO REFERRED TO AS EXCLUSIVE SELLER BROKERAGE AGREEMENT)

Georgia
Association
of REALTORS®

2010 Printing

State law prohibits Broker from representing Seller as a client without first entering into a written agreement with Seller under O.C.G.A. § 10-6A-1 et. seq.

For and in consideration of the mutual promises contained herein and other good and valuable consideration, _____
_____ as seller (hereinafter referred to as "Seller" or "Client"), and _____
_____ as broker and its affiliated licensees (hereinafter collectively referred to as "Broker") do
hereby enter into this Agreement, this date of _____.

1. **Exclusive Listing Agreement.** Seller hereby grants to Broker the exclusive right and privilege as the agent of the Seller to show and
   offer for sale the property located at _____,_____
   Georgia _____ TAXID/PIN # _____ and more particularly described in the Legal Description
   Paragraph below (all of which is hereinafter collectively referred to as "Property") as the real estate broker for Seller. The term of this
   Agreement shall begin on the date of _____ and shall continue through the date of _____
   _____ (hereinafter referred to as "Listing Period"), unless otherwise terminated in accordance with this Agreement.

2. **Legal Description.** The full legal description of the Property is:
   [Select A, B, C or D below. The sections not marked shall not be a part of this Agreement].

   ☐ **A.** attached as an exhibit hereto;

   ☐ **B.** identical to the legal description for the property contained in the deed recorded in Deed Book _____, Page _____,
   et. seq., _____ County, Georgia records;

   ☐ **C.** described below:
   Land Lot(s) _____ of the _____ District, _____ Section/ GMD,
   Lot _____, Block _____, Unit _____, Phase/Section_____ of
   _____ Subdivision/Development,
   _____ County, Georgia according to the plat recorded in
   Plat Book _____, Page _____, et. seq., _____ County, Georgia records.

   ☐ **D.** described below if Property is a condominium unit and a full unit legal description is to be used:
   Unit _____ of _____Condominium ("Condominium"), located
   in Land Lot _____ of the _____ District of _____ County, Georgia, together with its percentage
   of undivided interest in the common elements of the Condominium, and its interest in the limited common elements assigned to
   the unit ("Unit"). The Condominium was created pursuant to the Declaration of Condominium for any Condominium ("Declaration"),
   recorded in Deed Book _____, Page _____, et seq.,_____ County, Georgia records
   ("Declaration"), and shown and delineated on the plat of survey filed in Condominium Plat Book _____, Page
   _____ County, Georgia records, and on the floor plans filed in
   _____ Condominium Floor Plan Book _____, Page _____, _____ County, Georgia records.

3. **Broker's Duties to Seller.** Broker's sole duties to Seller shall be to:
   A. Use Broker's best efforts to procure a buyer ready, willing, and able to purchase Property at a sales price of at least
   $_____ (which amount includes the commission) or any other price acceptable to Seller;
   B. Comply with all applicable laws in performing its duties hereunder including the Brokerage Relationships in Real Estate Transaction
   Act, O.C.G.A. § 10-6A-1 et. seq.; and
   C. *[Select one. The box not checked shall not be a part of this Agreement.]*
   ☐ 1. Assist to the extent requested by Seller in negotiating the terms of and filling out a pre-printed real estate purchase and sale
   agreement; or
   ☐ 2. Not assist in negotiating the terms of or filling out a pre-printed real estate purchase and sale agreement and/or counteroffer.

4. **Seller's Duties.** Seller represents that Seller:
   A. presently has title to Property or has full authority to enter into this Agreement;
   B. will cooperate with Broker to sell Property to prospective buyers and will refer all inquiries concerning the sale of Property to the
   Broker during the term of this agreement;
   C. will make Property available for showing at reasonable times as requested by Broker;
   D. will provide Broker with accurate information regarding Property (including information concerning all adverse material facts pertaining
   to the physical condition of Property); and
   E. must fully comply with all state and federal laws.

F I G U R E 6.1 (CONTINUED)

Sample Listing Agreement

5. **Marketing.**

   A. **Generally:** If Seller desires to limit the manner or scope in which the Property is marketed Seller should check the appropriate box or boxes below. Any box not selected shall not be a part of this Agreement.

   ☐ Seller does not wish to have information about the Property displayed on the Internet.

   ☐ Seller does not wish to have the address of the Property identified on the Internet, but does wish to have all other information about the Property displayed on the Internet.

   ☐ Seller does not wish for third parties to be able to write comments or reviews regarding the listing or display a hyperlink to such reviews on an Internet web site of a broker or affiliated licensee of a broker.

   Other than the restrictions referenced above, Broker is authorized to market and advertise Property for sale in any media of Broker's choosing, including the Internet and multiple listing services, and attempt to procure buyers for the Property in cooperation with other real estate brokers and their affiliated licensees. Seller acknowledges that other members of multiple listing services will have the right to download, supplement and manipulate listing information regarding the Property placed on a multiple listing service by Broker. Seller grants Broker and Broker's agents and licensee's permission to use all available technology to create, record, store and/or retrieve images and recordings of the Property. Such images and recordings shall not belong to or be the property of Seller and may not be copied, reproduced or used by Seller or other third parties without the express written permission of the Broker or owner thereof. Seller agrees not to place any advertisements on the Property or to advertise the Property for sale in any media except with the prior written consent of Broker. Broker is also hereby authorized to place Broker's "For Sale" sign on Property. If the Property is sold or a contract for the sale or exchange of the Property is entered into during the term of this Agreement, the Broker may advertise the Property (including images thereof) in any media of Broker's choosing as being "under contract" while a sale is pending and as being "sold" upon the closing of the Property.

   B. **Multiple Listing Service(s):** Broker agrees to file this listing with the following multiple listing service(s) _____ _____. Broker agrees to file this listing with said Service(s) within 48 hours after Seller signs the same (excepting weekends, federal holidays and postal holidays). Seller acknowledges that the MLS(s) is/are not a party to this Agreement and is/are not responsible for errors or omissions on the part of Seller or Broker. Seller agrees to indemnify Service(s) from and against any and all claims, liabilities, damages or losses arising out of or related to the listing and sale of Property. Seller acknowledges that by virtue of listing the Property in MLS(s), all MLS(s) members and their affiliated licensees, will have access to Seller's listing information for the purpose of assisting Seller in the sale of the Property.

   C. **Consent of Seller to be Called:** If Seller is on a "Do Not Call List," Seller expressly consents to any of the above parties calling Seller for any purpose related to the sale of the Property. Seller further acknowledges and agrees that no MLS(s) member or any affiliated licensee of the MLS(s) member shall have any liability for calling the Seller after the expiration or termination of this Agreement. Such calls are hereby expressly consented to by Seller. This paragraph shall survive past the term of this Agreement.

   D. **Lockboxes:** A lockbox may be used in connection with the marketing of Property. There have been isolated instances of reported burglaries of homes on which lockboxes have been placed and for which the lockbox has been alleged to have been used to access the home. In order to minimize the risk of misuse of the lockbox, Broker recommends against the use of lockboxes on door handles that can be unscrewed from the outside or on other parts of the home from which the lockbox can be easily removed. Since others will have access to Property, Seller agrees to either remove all valuables or put them in a secure place.

6. **Retainer Fee.** In entering into this Agreement Seller has paid Broker a Retainer Fee of $_____ which shall be non-refundable except as follows. In the event Seller sells the Property in a transaction in which Broker is paid the full commission referenced herein, the Retainer Fee shall be refunded to Seller by Broker at the closing of the transaction. Otherwise, the retainer fee shall be retained by Broker to partially offset Broker's costs and compensate Broker for Broker's time in providing real estate brokerage services to Seller.

7. **Commission.**

   A. In the event that during the term of this Agreement Seller enters into a contract (including an option contract) for the sale or exchange of the Property, or any portion thereof, with any buyer, Seller agrees to pay Broker at closing (and regardless of whether the closing is during or after the term of this Agreement), the following commission: *[Select one or more of the following sections below. The sections not marked shall not be a part of this Agreement.]:*

   ☐ _____ percent (%) of the sales price;

   ☐ $_____ ;

   ☐ (Other)_____ .

   In addition, Seller agrees to immediately pay Broker the commission referenced above if during the term of this Agreement any of the following events occur:

   1. Seller defaults under any contract to sell or exchange the Property (including an option contract);
   2. Without the consent of Broker, Seller and a buyer mutually agree to terminate a contract for the purchase and sale or exchange of the Property (including an option contract) except where the mutual termination occurs subsequent to either: a) the failure of a contingency or condition precedent to which the contract was subject or b) the lawful and timely exercise by either Seller or a buyer of a unilateral right to terminate the contract; or
   3. Seller refuses to accept a lawful, bona fide, written offer to purchase the Property meeting the following terms and conditions at a time when the Property is not otherwise under contract:
      (a) The purchase price in the offer, after deducting all fees, costs and contributions to be paid by the Seller (other than the real estate brokerage commission to be paid by Seller and the Seller's payment of ad valorem property taxes through the date of closing) is for at least the full listing price set forth herein and is to be paid in cash or cash equivalent at the closing.
      (b) The offer is not subject to contingencies, conditions precedent, due diligence periods, or required terms other than those set forth herein;

Chapter 6   Listing Agreements and Buyer Representation   **109**

FIGURE 6.1 (CONTINUED)

Sample Listing Agreement

(c) The offer is not subject to Seller warranties or representations other than: (1) those warranties the Seller agrees to provide in any Seller's Property Disclosure Statement the Seller has filled out and made available to prospective buyers for inclusion in any offer, and (2) the Seller warranting to convey good and marketable title (which for all purposes herein shall have the same meaning as set forth in the GAR Purchase and Sale Agreement, Form F20) to the Property at closing by general warranty deed; and

(d) The date of closing in the offer is not less than thirty (30) days nor more than forty-five (45) days from the offer date. Notwithstanding the above, in the event there are multiple offers to purchase the Property, Seller shall not be in breach of this Agreement if the Seller first gives the prospective buyers a reasonable opportunity (not exceeding 10 days from the date of the first offer) to make their best offer to purchase the Property.

B. Broker shall share this commission with a cooperating broker, if any, who procures the buyer of Property by paying such cooperating broker at closing _____ percent (%) of the sales price of Property **OR $** _____. In addition, cooperating brokers are expressly intended to be third-party beneficiaries under this Agreement.

C. If Seller during the Protected Period, as that term is hereinafter defined, sells or contracts to sell or exchange Property to any buyer who made an offer on, was introduced to, visited, received information on, inquired about, or otherwise learned of the Property during the term of this Agreement, as a result of the efforts of the Broker, then Seller shall pay the commission referenced above to Broker at the closing of the sale or exchange of Property to said buyer. The term "Protected Period" shall refer to the _____ day period following the earlier of either: (a) the expiration of this Agreement; or (b) the date that the Agreement is terminated upon the mutual, written consent of the Broker and Seller. If this Agreement is terminated by Seller without the express, written consent of Broker, the Protected Period shall be the time period referenced above plus the number of days that remained on the term of this Agreement at the time it was terminated early without the express, written consent of Broker. In such event, the Protected Period shall commence on the date this Agreement was terminated early without the express written consent of Broker. For the purposes of this Agreement, the term "buyer" shall include buyer, all members of the buyer's immediate family, any legal entity in which buyer or any member of buyer's immediate family owns or controls, directly or indirectly, more than ten percent (10%) of the shares or interests therein, and any third party who is acting under the direction or control of any of the above parties. Notwithstanding the above, no listing commission shall be paid to Broker if this Agreement has either expired or been terminated upon the mutual, written consent of Broker and Seller and the Property is sold or contracted to be sold to a prospective buyer by or through another licensed broker with whom Seller has signed an exclusive right to sell listing agreement. The commission rights and obligations set forth herein shall survive the termination or expiration of this Agreement.

8. **Seller Default.** In the event Seller defaults under this Agreement, Seller shall, in addition to its other obligations set forth elsewhere herein, reimburse Broker for the out-of-pocket costs and expenses incurred by Broker and Broker's affiliated Licensees in seeking to market and sell the Property. Such costs and expenses shall include without limitation printing and copying charges, mileage at the highest rate allowed by the IRS as a business deduction and expenses to advertise the Property in various media. Seller shall also pay all costs, fees and charges for removing the listing from any multiple listing service. The payment of these costs, fees, charges and expenses by Seller shall not waive or limit Broker's right to assert any other claim, cause of action or suit (hereinafter collectively "Claims") against Seller for a real estate commission(s) and/or other damages and shall not release Seller from such Claims. Notwithstanding the above, the amount of such fees, charges, costs and expenses paid by Seller to Broker hereunder shall be an offset against any Claim of Broker for a real estate commission(s).

9. **Seller's Property Disclosure Statement.** Within _____ days of the date of this Agreement, Seller agrees to provide Broker with a current, fully executed Seller's Property Disclosure Statement. Broker is hereby authorized to distribute the same to prospective buyers interested in Property.

10. **Limits on Broker's Authority and Responsibility.** Seller acknowledges and agrees that Broker:
    A. may show other properties to prospective buyers who are interested in Property;
    B. shall not be responsible to advise Seller on any matter including but not limited to the following: any matter which could have been revealed through a survey, title search or inspection of Property; the condition of Property, any portion thereof, or any item therein; building products and construction techniques; the necessity or cost of any repairs to Property; mold; hazardous or toxic materials or substances; termites and other wood destroying organisms; the tax or legal consequences of this transaction; the availability and cost of utilities or community amenities; the appraised or future value of Property; any condition(s) existing off Property which may affect Property; the terms, conditions and availability of financing; and the uses and zoning of Property whether permitted or proposed. Seller acknowledges that Broker is not an expert with respect to the above matters and that, if any of these matters or any other matters are of concern to them, they should seek independent expert advice relative thereto. Seller acknowledge that Broker shall not be responsible to monitor or supervise any portion of any construction or repairs to Property and that such tasks clearly fall outside the scope of real estate brokerage services;
    C. shall owe no duties to Seller nor have any authority to act on behalf of Seller other than what is set forth in this Agreement;
    D. may make all disclosures required by law;
    E. may disclose all information about Property to others;
    F. shall, under no circumstances, have any liability greater than the amount of the real estate commission paid hereunder to Broker (excluding any commission amount paid to a cooperating real estate broker, if any) or, if no real estate commission is paid to Broker, than a sum not to exceed one hundred dollars; and
    G. shall be held harmless from any and all claims, causes of action, or damages arising out of or relating to:
       1. inaccurate and/or incomplete information provided by Broker to a prospective buyer;
       2. earnest money handled by anyone other than Broker; and/or
       3. any injury to persons on Property and/or loss of or damage to Property or anything contained therein.

Sample Listing Agreement

11. <u>Disclosures</u>.
   A. Broker agrees to keep confidential all information which Seller asks to be kept confidential by express request or instruction unless Seller permits such disclosure by subsequent word or conduct or such disclosure is required by law. Seller acknowledges, however, that Buyer and Buyer's broker may possibly not treat any offer made by Seller (including its existence, terms and conditions) as confidential unless those parties have entered into a Confidentiality Agreement with Seller.
   B. Broker may not knowingly give customers false information.
   C. In the event of a conflict between Broker's duty not to give customers false information and the duty to keep the confidences of Seller, the duty not to give customers false information shall prevail.
   D. Unless specified below, Broker has no other known agency relationships with other parties which would conflict with any interests of Seller (except that Broker may represent other buyers, sellers, landlords, and tenants in buying, selling or leasing property).
   E. In the event Seller has unilaterally terminated a Listing Agreement on the Property with a different broker, Seller acknowledges that in addition to Seller's commission obligations to Broker set forth herein, Seller may also owe a real estate commission to the previous broker in certain circumstances.

12. <u>Disclosure of Potentially Fraudulent Activities</u>.
   A. To help prevent fraud in real estate transactions, Seller does hereby give Broker permission to report any suspicious, unusual and/or potentially illegal or fraudulent activity (including but not limited to mortgage fraud) to:
      1. Governmental officials, agencies and/or authorities and/or
      2. Any mortgage lender, mortgage insurer, mortgage investor and/or title insurance company which could potentially be harmed if the activity was in fact fraudulent or illegal.
   B. Seller acknowledges that Broker does not have special expertise with respect to detecting fraud in real estate transactions. Therefore, Seller acknowledges that:
      1. Activities which are fraudulent or illegal may be undetected by Broker; and
      2. Activities which are lawful and/or routine may be reported by Broker as being suspicious, unusual or potentially illegal or fraudulent.

13. <u>Broker's Policy on Agency</u>. Unless Broker indicates below that Broker is not offering a specific agency relationship, the types of agency relationships offered by Broker are: seller agency, buyer agency, designated agency, dual agency, sub-agency, landlord agency, and tenant agency. The agency relationship(s), if any, not offered by Broker is/are the following: _____
   _____
   _____ .

14. <u>Dual Agency Disclosure</u>. *[Applicable only if Broker's agency policy is to practice dual agency]* If Seller and a prospective buyer are both being represented by the same Broker, Seller is aware that Broker is acting as a dual agent in this transaction and consents to the same. Seller has been advised that:
   A. In serving as a dual agent, Broker is representing two clients whose interests are or at times could be different or even adverse;
   B. Broker will disclose all adverse, material facts relevant to the transaction and actually known to the dual agent to all parties in the transaction except for information made confidential by request or instructions from either client which is not otherwise required to be disclosed by law;
   C. Seller does not have to consent to dual agency and, the consent of the Seller to dual agency has been given voluntarily and the Seller has read and understands the brokerage engagement agreement.
   D. Notwithstanding any provision to the contrary contained herein, Seller hereby directs Broker, while acting as a dual agent, to keep confidential and not reveal to the other party any information which could materially and adversely affect their negotiating position.
   E. Broker or Broker's affiliated licensees will timely disclose to each client the nature of any material relationship with other clients other than that incidental to the transaction. A material relationship shall mean any actually known personal, familial, or business relationship between Broker and a client which would impair the ability of Broker to exercise fair and independent judgment relative to another client. The other party whom Broker may represent in the event of dual agency may or may not be identified at the time Seller enters into this Agreement. If any party is identified after the Agreement and has a material relationship with Broker, then Broker shall timely provide to Seller a disclosure of the nature of such relationship.

15. <u>Designated Agency Disclosure</u>. *[Applicable only if Broker's agency policy is to practice designated agency]* Seller does hereby consent to Broker acting in a designated agency capacity in transactions in which Broker is representing Seller and a prospective buyer. With designated agency, Broker assigns one or more of its affiliated licensees exclusively to represent the Seller and one or more of its other affiliated licensees exclusively to represent the prospective buyer.

16. <u>Independent Contractor Relationship</u>. This Agreement shall create an independent contractor relationship between Broker and Seller. Broker shall at no time be considered an employee of Seller. If there is an affiliated licensee of Broker directly assisting Broker in marketing and selling the Property, said licensee shall be an: *[Select all which apply. Any section not selected shall not be a part of this Agreement]*.
   ☐ Independent contractor of Broker
   ☐ Employee of Broker

17. <u>Extension</u>. If during the term of this Agreement, Seller and a prospective buyer enter into a real estate sales contract or option to purchase contract which is not consummated for any reason whatsoever, then the original expiration date of this Agreement shall be automatically extended for the number of days that Property was under contract.

18. <u>No Imputed Knowledge</u>. Seller acknowledges and agrees that with regard to any property in which Seller intends to sell, there shall be no knowledge imputed between Broker and Broker's licensees or between the different licensees of Broker. Broker and each of Broker's licensees shall be deemed to have only actual knowledge of such properties.

F1, Exclusive Seller Listing Agreement, Page 4 of 6, 01/01/10

F I G U R E   6.1 (CONTINUED)

Sample Listing Agreement

19. <u>Governing Law</u>. This Agreement may be signed in multiple counterparts and shall be governed by and interpreted pursuant to the laws of the State of Georgia.

20. <u>Entire Agreement</u>. This Agreement constitutes the sole and entire agreement between the parties. No representation, promise or inducement not included in this Agreement shall be binding upon any party hereto. This Agreement and the terms and conditions herein may not be amended, modified or waived except by the written agreement of Seller. The failure of the parties to adhere strictly to the terms and conditions of this Agreement shall not constitute a waiver of the right of the parties later to insist on such strict adherence.

21. <u>GAR Forms</u>. The Georgia Association of REALTORS®, Inc. ("GAR") makes certain standard real estate forms available to its members. These GAR forms are frequently provided to the parties in real estate transactions by the REALTORS® with whom they are working. No party is required to use any GAR form. Since these forms are generic and written with the interests of multiple parties in mind, they may need to be modified to meet the specific needs of the parties using them. If any party has any questions about his or her rights and obligations under any GAR form he or she should consult an attorney. The parties hereto agree that the GAR forms may only be used in accordance with the licensing agreement of GAR. While GAR forms may be modified by the parties, no GAR form may be reproduced with sections removed, altered or modified unless the changes are visible on the form itself or in a stipulation, addendum, exhibit or amendment thereto.

22. <u>Notices</u>.
    A. Communications Regarding Real Estate Transactions. Client acknowledges that many communications and notices in real estate transactions are of a time sensitive nature and that the failure to be available to receive such notices and communications can have adverse legal, business and financial consequences. During the term of this Agreement, Client agrees to remain reasonably available to receive communications from Broker.
    B. Notices between Broker and Client Regarding this Agreement. Client and Broker agree that communications and notices between them regarding the terms of this Agreement shall be in writing, signed by the party giving the notice, and may be delivered in person or to any address, e-mail address and/or facsimile number to the person to whom the communication or notice is being given specifically set forth in this Agreement. It is the intent of the parties that those means of transmitting notices for which a party has not provided an address or number shall not be used for receiving notices and communications. For example, if a party has not provided an e-mail address in this Agreement, it shall mean that the party is not accepting notices or communications sent by this means.
    C. Client Contact Information.
    The contact information of Client(s) is set forth below:

_____	Business Telephone: _____
Client Name	Home Telephone: _____
_____	
Address for Receiving Notice	Cell Phone: _____
_____	
_____	Facsimile Number: _____
_____	E-mail Address: _____
_____	
_____	Business Telephone: _____
Client Name	Home Telephone: _____
_____	
Address for Receiving Notice	Cell Phone: _____
_____	
_____	Facsimile Number: _____
_____	E-mail Address: _____

Client agrees to immediately update Broker of any changes to the above referenced information.

SPECIAL STIPULATIONS: The following Special Stipulations, if conflicting with any exhibit, addendum, or preceding paragraph, shall control:

F I G U R E 6.1 (CONTINUED)

Sample Listing Agreement

Additional Special Stipulations are ☐ or are ☐ not attached.

BY SIGNING THIS AGREEMENT, SELLER ACKNOWLEDGES THAT: (1) SELLER HAS READ ALL PROVISIONS AND DISCLOSURES MADE HEREIN; (2) SELLER UNDERSTANDS ALL SUCH PROVISIONS AND DISCLOSURES AND HAS ENTERED INTO THIS AGREEMENT VOLUNTARILY; AND (3) SELLER IS NOT SUBJECT TO A CURRENT LISTING AGREEMENT WITH ANY OTHER BROKER.

RECEIPT OF A COPY OF THIS AGREEMENT IS HEREBY ACKNOWLEDGED BY SELLER.

The above Agreement is hereby accepted _____ o'clock _____ .m. on the date of _____ .

_____   _____
Broker   Seller's Signature

Address: _____   _____
                                                                       Print or Type Name

_____   _____
                                                                       Seller's Signature

_____   _____
MLS Office Code   Brokerage Firm License Number   Print or Type Name

Broker's Phone#_____ & FAX#_____

By: _____
       Broker or Broker's Affiliated Licensee

_____
Print or Type Name

_____
Agent's Georgia Real Estate License Number

Email Address: _____

F1, Exclusive Seller Listing Agreement, Page 6 of 6, 01/01/10

In Georgia In Georgia, there are no statutory marital rights by ownership (such as community property or tenancy by the entirety), only inchoate rights by divorce. Many brokers get both party signatures as a precaution.

The brokerage firm   The brokerage company name, the employing broker, and, if appropriate, the salesperson taking the listing must all be identified.

The listing price   This is the proposed gross sales price. The seller's proceeds will be reduced by unpaid real estate taxes, special assessments, mortgage and trust deed debts, and any other outstanding obligations.

Real property and personal property   Any personal property that will be left with the real estate when it is sold must be explicitly identified. Similarly, any items of real property that the seller expects to remove at the time of the sale must be specified as well. Some of these items may later become points of negotiation when a ready, willing, and able buyer is found for the property. Typical items to consider include major appliances, swimming pool and spa equipment, fireplace accessories, storage sheds, window treatments, stacked firewood, and stored heating oil.

Leased equipment   Will any leased equipment—security systems, cable television boxes, water softeners, special antennas—be left with the property? If so, the seller is responsible for notifying the equipment's lessor of the change of property ownership.

The description of the premises   In addition to the street address, the legal description, lot size, and tax parcel number may be required for future insertion into a purchase offer.

The proposed dates for the closing and the buyer's possession   These dates should be based on an anticipated sale date. The listing agreement should allow adequate time for the paperwork involved (including the buyer's qualification for any financing) and the physical moves to be arranged by the seller and the buyer.

The closing   Details of the closing—such as a closing attorney, title company, or escrow company—should be considered even at this early stage. Which designated party will complete the settlement statements, disburse the funds, and file the proper forms, such as documents to be recorded, documents to be sent to the Internal Revenue Service, and documents to be submitted for registering foreign owners? In some states, because the buyer designates the settlement agent, the seller must identify any special needs at the beginning of the process.

The evidence of ownership   The most commonly used proofs of title are a warranty deed and either a title insurance policy or an abstract and legal opinion.

Encumbrances   Which liens will be paid in full at the closing by the seller and which liens will be assumed by the buyer?

Home warranty program   In some situations, it may be advisable for a buyer or seller to purchase a home warranty with the property. Typically, a home warranty program covers such things as plumbing, electrical, and heating systems, hot water heaters, duct work, and major appliances. Some brokers offer this with every home they sell as a way of encouraging people to buy. In many states, a home warranty program can be provided in a listing contract or an offer to purchase. Coverages, deductibles, limitations, and exclusions in the contract should be read carefully.

The commission   The circumstances under which a commission will be paid must be specifically stated. Is payment earned only on the sale of the property or on any transfer of interest created by the broker? Will it be a percentage or a flat fee? When will it be paid? Will it be paid directly by the seller or by the party handling the closing?

The termination of the contract   A contract should provide some way for the parties to end it. Under what circumstances will the contract terminate? Can the seller arbitrarily refuse to sell or cooperate with the listing broker?

The broker protection clause   As previously discussed, brokers may be well advised to protect their interests against possible fraud or a reluctant buyer's change of heart. Under what circumstances will the broker be entitled to a commission after the agreement terminates? How long will the clause remain in effect?

Warranties by the owner   The owner is responsible for certain assurances and disclosures that are vital to the agent's ability to market the property successfully. Is the property suitable for its intended purpose? Does it comply with the appropriate zoning and building codes? Will it be transferred to the buyer in essentially the same condition as it was originally presented, considering repairs or alterations to be made as provided for in a purchase contract? Are there any known defects?

Indemnification (hold harmless) wording   The seller and the broker may agree to hold each other harmless (that is, not to sue one another) for any incorrect information supplied by one to the other. Indemnification may be offered regardless of whether the inaccuracies are intentional or unintentional.

Nondiscrimination (equal opportunity) wording   The seller must understand that the property will be shown and offered without regard to the race, color, religion, national origin, family status, sex, or handicap of the prospective buyer. Refer to other federal nondiscrimination laws, and state and local fair housing laws for a complete listing of protected classes in your area. Georgia prohibits discrimination in real estate practice and transactions. (See Chapter 21.)

In Georgia

Antitrust wording   The contract should indicate that all commissions have been negotiated between the seller and the broker. It is illegal for commissions to be set by any regulatory agency, trade association, or other industry organization.

The signatures of the parties   All parties identified in the contract must sign it, including all individuals who have a legal interest in the property.

The date the contract is signed   This date may differ from the date the contract actually becomes effective, particularly if a salesperson takes the listing, then must have his or her broker sign the contract to accept employment under its terms.

I N   P R A C T I C E   Anyone who takes a listing should use *only* the appropriate documents provided by the broker. Most brokers are conscientious enough to use only documents that have been carefully drafted or reviewed by an attorney so that their construction and legal language comply with the appropriate federal, state, and local laws. Such contracts should also give consideration to local customs, such as closing dates and the proration of income and expenses, with which most real estate attorneys are familiar.

■ BUYER AGENCY AGREEMENTS

Like a listing agreement, a **buyer agency agreement** is an employment contract. In this case, however, the broker is employed as the *buyer's* agent. The buyer, rather than the seller, is the principal. The purpose of the agreement is to find a suitable property. An agency agreement gives the buyer a degree of representation possible only in a fiduciary relationship. A buyer's broker must protect the buyer's interests at all points in the transaction.

In Georgia   In Georgia, buyer agency agreements are governed by BRRETA (Brokerage Relationships in Real Estate Transactions Act), O.C.G.A. 10-6A-1 et seq.

Types of Buyer Agreements

Three basic types of buyer agency agreements exist:

1. *Exclusive buyer agency agreement (or exclusive right to represent)*—This is a completely exclusive agency agreement. The buyer is legally bound to compensate the agent whenever the buyer purchases a property of the type described in the contract. The broker is entitled to payment regardless of whether he or she locates the property. Even if the buyer finds the property independently, the agent is entitled to payment.
2. *Exclusive-agency buyer agency agreement*—Like an exclusive buyer agency agreement, this is an exclusive contract between the buyer and the agent. However, this agreement limits the broker's right to payment. The broker is entitled to payment only if he or she locates the property the buyer ultimately purchases. The buyer is free to find a suitable property without obligation to pay the agent.

3. *Open buyer agency agreement*—This agreement is a nonexclusive agency contract between a broker and a buyer. It permits the buyer to enter into similar agreements with an unlimited number of brokers. The buyer is obligated to compensate only the broker who locates the property the buyer ultimately purchases.

Buyer Representation Issues

A number of issues must be discussed by a broker and a buyer before they sign a buyer agency agreement. For instance, the licensee should make the same disclosures to the buyer that the licensee would make to a seller in a listing agreement. The licensee should explain the forms of agency available and the parties' rights and responsibilities under each type. The specific services provided to a buyer-client should be clearly explained. Compensation issues need to be addressed as well. Buyer's agents may be compensated in the form of a flat fee for services, an hourly rate, or a percentage of the purchase price. The agent may require a *retainer fee* at the time the agreement is signed to cover initial expenses. The retainer may be applied as a credit toward any fees due at the closing. A buyer's agent also may be compensated by sharing the commission being paid by the seller.

As in any agency agreement, the source of compensation is not the factor that determines the relationship. A buyer's agent may be compensated by either the buyer or the seller. Issues of compensation are *always* negotiable.

Because the agency contract employs the agent to represent the buyer and locate a suitable property, the licensee must obtain detailed financial information from the buyer. In addition, the buyer's agent needs information about the buyer's specific requirements for a suitable property.

IN PRACTICE   Buyer agency, like any other kind of real estate agency, is increasingly subject to detailed provisions of state law. If a state has adopted an agency statute, it is highly likely that the rights, duties, and obligations of buyer's agents are specifically established.

■ KEY POINT REVIEW

A **listing agreement** is an **employment contract** for the professional services of the broker; it may be written or oral, though in most states the agreement must be in writing to be enforceable in court.

In Georgia   In Georgia, a listing agreement (also known as an agency agreement or a brokerage engagement) is a written contract in which a seller or buyer becomes the broker's client. All those who sign it must receive a copy.

As an **agent,** the **broker** is authorized to represent the **principal,** and the principal's real estate, to third parties. A real estate **salesperson** is a **general agent** of the broker and can carry out listing services only in the name and under the supervision of the broker.

The characteristics of an **exclusive-right-to-sell listing** include the following:

- **One broker** is appointed as seller's sole agent.
- If the property is sold while the listing is in effect, the broker is entitled to a commission no matter who sells the property, even the seller.

An **exclusive-agency listing**

- authorizes **one broker** to act as the sole agent of seller, but
- allows the **seller** to retain the right to sell the property without obligation to the broker.

In an **open listing** (also known as a **nonexclusive listing, general listing,** or **simple listing**) the

- seller retains the right to employ **any** number of brokers as agents;
- seller is obligated to pay a commission to **only** the broker who successfully produces a **ready, willing, and able buyer;**
- seller is not obligated to pay a commission if the seller personally sells the property without the aid of any broker; and
- open listing is the default relationship if the listing agreement does not specifically create an exclusive-right-to-sell listing or an exclusive-agency listing.

A **multiple listing clause** may be included in an exclusive listing agreement with the seller's consent, and it

- permits cooperation with other brokers in the **multiple listing service (MLS);**
- requires that the **MLS rules** for publication of a listing be followed;
- explains that **membership** in the MLS usually provides that a participating broker has to make a **unilateral** offer of cooperation and compensation to other member brokers; and
- requires that a **buyer's broker** who is member of MLS must notify the listing broker before any communication with the seller takes place.

A **net listing** has the following characteristics:

- The seller is to receive a net amount of money from any sale.
- The excess over the net from the sale will go to the listing broker as commission.
- The broker is free to offer the property at any price greater than the net amount.
- In Georgia Net listings may be prohibited by state law, and are prohibited in Georgia.

An **option listing** gives the broker the right, but not the obligation, to purchase the listed property within a certain period of time.

A **listing agreement** may be **terminated** when the

- agreement's **purpose** is fulfilled;
- agreement's term expires without a successful transfer;
- property is **destroyed** or its use changed by factors outside the owner's control;
- **title** to the property is transferred by operation of law;

- broker and seller **mutually agree** to end the listing;
- listing is **unilaterally** ended by one party, in which case the terminating party may be liable for damages;
- either party **dies** or become **incapacitated;** and
- either broker or seller **breaches** the contract.

The **broker protection clause** preserves a broker's commission if, within a certain number of days, the owner transfers the property to someone the broker introduced to them.

A **competitive market analysis (CMA)** should accomplish the following:

- Compare prices of properties similar to the seller's property that recently sold, those that are currently on the market, and those that did not sell
- Determine **market value**—the most probable price the property would bring in an **arm's length transaction** under normal conditions on the open market
- Derive a range of value

Disclosures of agency relationships and property condition are important consumer safeguards and may be required by state law.

Following are the three types of **agency agreement:**

1. **Exclusive buyer agency agreement (exclusive right to represent)** includes the following:
   — It is a completely **exclusive** agency agreement.
   — Buyer must compensate agent whenever buyer purchases a property of the type described in the agency agreement.
   — Broker is entitled to payment regardless of whether he or she locates the property.
   — Broker is entitled to payment even if buyer finds a property independently.
2. **Exclusive-agency buyer agency agreement** has the following characteristics:
   — It is an **exclusive** contract between buyer and agent.
   — Broker is entitled to payment only if broker locates the property the buyer ultimately purchases.
   — Buyer is free to find a suitable property without obligation to agent.
3. **Open agency agreement** has the following characteristics:
   — It is a **nonexclusive** agency contract between broker and buyer.
   — Buyer is permitted to enter into similar agreements with unlimited number of brokers.
   — Buyer is obligated to compensate only broker who locates the property the buyer ultimately purchases.

Buyer's broker's compensation may be a **flat fee** for services, an **hourly** rate, or a **percentage** of the purchase price, a **retainer** fee, or a **share of commission** being paid by the seller.

CHAPTER 6 QUIZ

1. A listing taken by a real estate salesperson is technically an employment agreement between the seller and the
   a. broker.
   b. local multiple listing service.
   c. salesperson.
   d. salesperson and broker together.

2. Which of the following is a similarity between an exclusive-agency listing and an exclusive-right-to-sell listing?
   a. Under each, the seller retains the right to sell the real estate without the broker's help and without paying the broker a commission.
   b. Under each, the seller authorizes only one particular salesperson to show the property.
   c. Both types of listings give the responsibility of representing the seller to one broker only.
   d. Both types of listings are open listings.

3. The listing agreement on a residential property states that it expires on May 2. Which of the following events would NOT terminate the listing?
   a. The agreement is not renewed prior to May 2.
   b. The owner dies on April 29.
   c. On April 15, the owner tells the listing broker that the owner is dissatisfied with the broker's marketing efforts.
   d. The house is destroyed by fire on April 25.

4. A seller has listed a property under an exclusive-agency listing with a broker. If the seller sells the property personally during the term of the listing to someone who learns about the property through the seller, the seller will owe the broker
   a. no commission.
   b. the full commission.
   c. a partial commission.
   d. only reimbursement for the broker's costs.

5. Under a listing agreement, the broker is entitled to sell the property for any price, as long as the seller receives $85,000. The broker may keep any amount over $85,000 as a commission. This type of listing is called a(n)
   a. exclusive-right-to-sell listing.
   b. exclusive-agency listing.
   c. open listing.
   d. net listing.

6. Which of the following is a similarity between an open listing and an exclusive-agency listing?
   a. Under each, the seller avoids paying the broker a commission if the seller sells the property to someone the broker did not procure.
   b. Each grants a commission to any broker who procures a buyer for the seller's property.
   c. Under each, the broker earns a commission regardless of who sells the property, as long as it is sold within the listing period.
   d. Each grants the exclusive right to sell to whatever broker procures a buyer for the seller's property.

7. The final decision on a property's listed price should be made by the
   a. listing agent.
   b. appraised value.
   c. seller.
   d. seller's attorney.

8. A seller hired Lana, a broker, under the terms of an open listing. While that listing was still in effect, the seller—without informing Lana—hired Frank under an exclusive-right-to-sell listing for the same property. If Lana produces a buyer for the property whose offer the seller accepts, then the seller must pay a
   a. full commission only to Lana.
   b. full commission only to Frank.
   c. full commission to both Lana and Frank.
   d. half commission to both Lana and Frank.

9. Gloria listed her residence with broker Dave. Dave brought an offer at full price and terms of the listing from buyers who are ready, willing, and able to pay cash for the property. However, Gloria changed her mind and rejected the buyers' offer. In this situation, Gloria

   a. must sell her property.
   b. owes a commission to Dave.
   c. is liable to the buyers for specific performance.
   d. is liable to the buyers for compensatory damages.

10. Which of the following is *TRUE* of an open buyer agency listing?

    a. The buyer may enter into agreements with multiple brokers and be obligated to pay only the broker who locates the property that the buyer ultimately purchases.
    b. While the buyer may enter into agreements with multiple brokers, he or she is under no obligation to pay the broker; the seller bears all brokerage expenses.
    c. Because multiple brokers may be involved, an open buyer agency agreement involves reduced fiduciary duties.
    d. The buyer may not look for or make offers on properties on his or her own.

11. Nancy, a broker, and Jim enter into an exclusive-agency buyer agency agreement. What does this mean?

    a. Jim is obligated to compensate Nancy, regardless of who locates the property ultimately purchased.
    b. Nancy is entitled to payment only if she or any broker acting under her authority locates the property Jim ultimately purchases.
    c. Jim may enter into similar agreements with any number of other brokers.
    d. If Jim finds the property without any help from Nancy, Jim must pay Nancy a reduced compensation.

12. Which of the following statements is *TRUE* of a competitive market analysis (CMA)?

    a. A CMA is the same as an appraisal.
    b. A CMA can help the seller price the property.
    c. By law in most states, a CMA must be completed for each listing taken.
    d. A CMA should not be retained in the property's listing file.

13. A property was listed with a broker who belonged to a multiple listing service and was sold by another member broker for $253,500. The total commission was 6 percent of the sales price. The selling broker received 60 percent of the commission, and the listing broker received the balance. What was the listing broker's commission?

    a. $5,475.60
    b. $6,084.00
    c. $7,605.00
    d. $9,126.00

14. Sue signs a listing agreement with broker Ken to sell her home. The agreement states that Ken will receive a 7 percent commission. The home sells for $220,000. What is the net amount that Sue will receive from the sale?

    a. $15,400
    b. $204,600
    c. $205,678
    d. $220,000

15. A seller has sold property to a neighbor without the services of a real estate broker. However, the seller still owes the broker a commission because the seller signed a(n)

    a. exclusive-agency listing.
    b. open listing.
    c. exclusive-right-to-sell listing.
    d. option listing.

16. Most states require that listing agreements contain a(n)

    a. multiple listing service (MLS) clause.
    b. definite contract termination date.
    c. automatic extension clause.
    d. broker protection clause.

17. A written agreement between a broker and a client includes the following language: "In return for the compensation agreed upon, Broker will assist Client in locating and purchasing a suitable property. Broker will receive the agreed compensation regardless of whether Broker, Client, or some other party locates the property ultimately purchased by Client." What kind of agreement is this?

    a. Exclusive-agency listing
    b. Exclusive-agency buyer agency agreement
    c. Exclusive buyer agency agreement
    d. Open buyer agency agreement

In Georgia

---

18. The contract by which a client hires a real estate broker in Georgia is known as a(n)

    a. option agreement.
    b. listing agreement.
    c. multiple listing.
    d. brokerage engagement.

19. A broker sold a house in Atlanta for $360,000 and received a commission of $23,400 according to the terms of the listing. What was the broker's commission rate?

    a. 5 percent
    b. 5.5 percent
    c. 6 percent
    d. 6.5 percent

20. A broker sold a house in Jonesboro, Georgia, and received a 5 percent commission. The broker gave the listing salesperson $5,400, which was 40 percent of the firm's commission. What was the selling price of the property?

    a. $260,000
    b. $270,000
    c. $290,000
    d. $310,000

CHAPTER

Interests in Real Estate

■ **LEARNING OBJECTIVES** *When you have finished reading this chapter, you should be able to:*

■ **identify** the kinds of limitations on ownership rights that are imposed by government action and the form of conveyance of property.

■ **describe** the various estates in land and the rights and limitations they convey.

■ **explain** concepts related to encumbrances and water rights.

■ **distinguish** the various types of governmental powers and how they are exercised.

■ **define** the following *key terms*:

accretion	encumbrance	license
appurtenant easement	erosion	lien
avulsion	escheat	life estate
condemnation	estate in land	littoral rights
deed restrictions	fee simple	party wall
easement	fee simple absolute	police power
easement by condemnation	fee simple defeasible	prior appropriation
easement by necessity	fee simple determinable	remainder interest
easement by prescription	freehold estate	reversionary interest
easement in gross	future interest	riparian rights
eminent domain	homestead	tacking
encroachment	leasehold estate	taxation
	legal life estate	year's support

■ LIMITATIONS ON THE RIGHTS OF OWNERSHIP

Ownership of real estate is not absolute, that is, a landowner's power to control his or her property is subject to other interests. Keep in mind that a landowner's power to control his or her property relates to the landowner having title of the property and the bundle of legal rights that accompanies the title. Even the most complete ownership the law allows is limited by public and private restrictions. These restrictions are intended to ensure that one owner's use or enjoyment of his or her property does not interfere with others' use or enjoyment of their property or with the welfare of the general public. Licensees should have a working knowledge of the restrictions that might limit current or future owners. A zoning ordinance that will not allow a doctor's office to coexist with a residence, a condo association bylaw prohibiting resale without board approval, or an easement allowing the neighbors to use the private beach may not only burden today's purchaser but also deter a future buyer.

This chapter puts the various interests in real estate in perspective—what rights they confer and how use of the ownership may be limited.

■ GOVERNMENT POWERS

Individual ownership rights are subject to certain powers, or rights, held by federal, state, and local governments. These limitations on the ownership of real estate are imposed for the general welfare of the community and, therefore, supersede the rights or interests of the individual. Government powers include police power, eminent domain, taxation, and escheat.

Police Power

Every state has the power to enact legislation to preserve order, protect the public health and safety, and promote the general welfare of its citizens. That authority is known as a state's **police power.** The state's authority is passed on to municipalities and counties through legislation called *enabling acts*.

Of course, what is identified as being *in the public interest* varies widely from state to state and region to region. Generally, however, a police power is used to enact environmental protection laws, zoning ordinances, and building codes. Regulations that govern the use, occupancy, size, location, and construction of real estate also fall within the police powers.

Police powers may be used to achieve a community's needs or goals. A city that deems growth to be desirable, for instance, may exercise its police powers to enact laws encouraging the purchase and improvement of land. On the other hand, an area that wishes to retain its current character may enact laws that discourage development and population growth.

**Memory Tip
Four Government
Powers**

The four government powers can be remembered by the acronym **PETE:** Police, Eminent domain, Taxation, and Escheat.

Like the rights of ownership, the state's power to regulate land use is not absolute. The laws must be uniform and nondiscriminatory; that is, they may not operate to the advantage or disadvantage of any one particular owner or owners. See Chapter 20 for more on police power.

Eminent Domain

Eminent domain is the right of the government to acquire privately owned real estate for public use. **Condemnation** is the process by which the government exercises this right, by either judicial or administrative proceedings. In the taking of property, just compensation is to be paid to the owner, and the rights of the property owner are to be protected by due process of law. Ideally, the public agency and the owner of the property in question agree on compensation through direct negotiation, and the government purchases the property for a price considered fair by the owner. In some cases, the owner may simply dedicate the property to the government as a site for a school, park, or another beneficial use. Sometimes, however, in cases where the owner's consent cannot be obtained, the government agency can initiate condemnation proceedings to acquire the property.

Eminent domain is the government's right to seize property; **condemnation** is the way the right is exercised.

Generally, states delegate their power of eminent domain to quasi-public bodies and publicly held companies responsible for various facets of public service. For instance, a public housing authority might take privately owned land to build low-income housing; the state's land-clearance commission or redevelopment authority could use the power of eminent domain to make way for urban renewal. If there were no other feasible way to do so, a railway, utility company, or state highway department might acquire farmland to extend a railroad track, bring electricity to a remote new development, or build a highway.

In the past, the proposed use for taking property was to be for the public good. However, in June 2005, the U.S. Supreme Court, in *Kelo v. City of New London*, significantly changed the definition of public use. The court held that local governments can condemn homes and businesses for private or economic development purposes.

In *Kelo v. City of New London*, a development agent, on behalf of the city, initiated condemnation proceedings on land owned by nine property owners who refused to have their property taken. The development plan involved land for commercial, residential, and recreational purposes. The court noted that the development plan was not going to benefit a particular class of identifiable individuals. Further, although the owners' properties were not blighted, the city determined that a program of economic rejuvenation was justified and entitled to deference. *Economic development* fit within the broad definition of *public purpose*. The court found that the city's proposed disposition of petitioners' properties qualified as a *public use* within the meaning of the Takings Clause of the 5th Amendment of the U.S. Constitution.

In this case, the city had invoked a state statute that authorized the use of eminent domain to promote economic development. The court decision leaves it to the states to establish rules that cities must follow when exercising eminent domain powers. In response to this court decision, many state legislators are drafting legislation to impose a narrow definition of *public use* in eminent domain proceedings to stop condemnations justified on purely economic grounds. (The Georgia legislature has passed such a statute.)

Taxation

Taxation is a charge on real estate to raise funds to meet the public needs of a government. Taxes on real estate include annual real estate taxes assessed by local and area governmental entities, including school districts; taxes on income realized by individuals and corporations on the sale of property; and special fees that may be levied for special projects. Nonpayment of taxes may give government the power to claim an interest in the property itself according to procedures outlined in Chapter 10.

Escheat

Although escheat is not actually a limitation on ownership, it is an avenue by which the state may acquire privately owned real or personal property. State laws provide for ownership to transfer, or **escheat,** to the state when an owner dies leaving no heirs (as defined by the law) and no will that directs how the real estate is to be distributed. In some states, real property escheats to the county where the land is located; in other states, it becomes the property of the state. Escheat is intended to prevent property from being ownerless or abandoned.

■ ESTATES IN LAND

An **estate in land** defines the degree, quantity, nature, and extent of an owner's interest in real property. Many types of estates exist. However, not all *interests* in real estate are *estates*. To be an estate in land, an interest must allow possession (either now or in the future) and must be measurable by duration. Lesser interests such as easements (discussed later in this chapter), which allow use but not possession, are not estates.

■ **FOR EXAMPLE** Bob owns a movie theater. Bob's ownership interest is an *estate* because Bob has the right to all the income from the theater, the right to change the theater into a restaurant, the right to tear down the theater and build something else on the land, and the right to sell the theater to someone else—in short, the theater belongs to Bob. When Matt buys a ticket and sits down to watch a movie in Bob's theater, Matt has an *interest* in the property, but it is *not* an estate. Matt's interest is limited to the temporary use of a limited part of the theater.

Historically, estates in land have been classified as freehold estates and leasehold estates. The two types of estates are distinguished primarily by their duration.

Freehold estates last for an indeterminable length of time, such as for a lifetime or forever. They include fee simple (also called an *indefeasible fee*), defeasible fee, and life estates. A fee simple estate continues for an indefinite period and may be passed along to the owner's heirs. A life estate is based on the lifetime of a person and ends when that individual dies. Freehold estates are illustrated in Figure 7.1. Various types of freehold estates will be highlighted in this chapter.

Leasehold estates last for a fixed period of time. They include estates for years and estates from period to period. Estates at will and estates at sufferance are also leaseholds, though by their operation they are not generally viewed as being for fixed terms. (See Chapter 17 for more information on leasehold estates.)

Fee Simple Estate

An estate in **fee simple** (or **fee simple absolute**) is the highest interest in real estate recognized by law. Fee simple ownership is absolute ownership: The holder is entitled to all rights to the property. It is limited only by public and private restrictions, such as zoning laws and restrictive covenants (discussed in Chapter 20). Because this estate is of unlimited duration, it is said to run forever. Upon the death of its owner, it passes to the owner's heirs or as provided by will. A fee simple estate is also referred to as an *estate of inheritance* or simply as *fee ownership*.

FIGURE 7.1

Freehold Estates

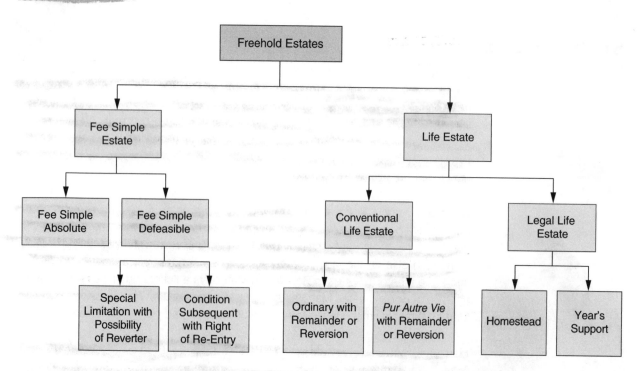

Fee simple defeasible   A **fee simple defeasible** (or *defeasible fee*) estate is a qualified estate, that is, it is subject to the occurrence or nonoccurrence of some specified event. Two types of defeasible estates exist: those subject to a condition subsequent and those qualified by a special limitation.

Fee simple *defeasible*:
"On the condition that"

Fee simple *determinable*:
"So long as"
"While"
"During"

A fee simple estate may be qualified by a *condition subsequent*, which means that the new owner must *not* perform some action or activity. The former owner retains a *right of reentry* so that if the condition is broken, the former owner can retake possession of the property through legal action. Conditions in a deed are different from restrictions or covenants because of the grantor's right to reclaim ownership, a right that does not exist under private restrictions.

■ **FOR EXAMPLE**   A grant of land *on the condition that* there be no consumption of alcohol on the premises is a fee simple subject to a condition subsequent. If alcohol is consumed on the property, the former owner has the right to reacquire full ownership. It will be necessary for the grantor (or the grantor's heirs or successors) to go to court to assert that right, however.

A fee simple estate also may be qualified by a *special limitation*. The estate ends *automatically* on the current owner's failure to comply with the limitation. The former owner retains a *possibility of reverter*. If the limitation is violated, the former owner (or his or her heirs or successors) reacquires full ownership, with no need to reenter the land or go to court. A fee simple with a special limitation is also called a **fee simple determinable** because it may end automatically. The language used to distinguish a special limitation—the words *so long as* or *while or during*—is the key to creating this estate.

The *right of entry* and *possibility of reverter* may never take effect. If they do, it will be only at some time in the future. Therefore, each of these rights is considered a **future interest.**

■ **FOR EXAMPLE**   A grant of land from an owner to her church *so long as the land is used only for religious purposes* is a fee simple with a special limitation. The church has the full bundle of rights possessed by a property owner, but one of the "sticks" in the bundle—the "control" stick, in this case—has a string attached. If the church ever decides to use the land for a nonreligious purpose, the original owner will, in effect, "yank the string," causing title to revert to him or her (or to his or her heirs or successors).

Life Estate

A **life estate** is a freehold estate limited in duration to the life of the owner or the life of some other designated person or persons. Unlike other freehold estates, a life estate is not inheritable and cannot be devised. It passes to future owners according to the provisions of the life estate.

A life tenant is entitled to the rights of ownership, that is, the life tenant can enjoy both possession and the ordinary use and profits arising from ownership, just as if the individual were a fee owner. The ownership may be sold, mortgaged, or leased, but it is always subject to the limitation of the life estate.

A life tenant's ownership rights, however, are not absolute. The life tenant may not injure the property, such as by destroying a building or allowing it to deteriorate. In legal terms, this injury is known as waste. Those who will eventually own the property could seek an injunction against the life tenant or sue for damages.

Because the ownership will terminate on the death of the person against whose life the estate is measured, a purchaser, lessee, or lender can be affected. The life tenant can sell, lease, or mortgage only his or her interest, that is, ownership for a lifetime. Because the interest is obviously less desirable than a fee simple estate, the life tenant's rights are limited.

Conventional life estate   A *conventional life* estate is created intentionally by the owner. It may be established either by deed at the time the ownership is transferred during the owner's life or by a provision of the owner's will after his or her death. The estate is conveyed to an individual who is called the *life tenant.* The life tenant has full enjoyment of the ownership for the duration of his or her life. When the life tenant dies, the estate ends and its ownership passes to another designated individual or returns to the previous owner.

■ **FOR EXAMPLE**   Alex, who has a fee simple estate in Blackacre, conveys a life estate to Peter for Peter's lifetime. Peter is the life tenant. On Peter's death, the life estate terminates, and Alex once again owns Blackacre. If Peter's life estate had been created by Alex's will, however, subsequent ownership of Blackacre would be determined by the provisions of the will.

Pur autre vie   A life estate also may be based on the lifetime of a person other than the life tenant. This is known as an estate *pur autre vie* ("for the life of another"). Although a life estate is not considered an estate of inheritance, a life estate pur autre vie provides for inheritance by the life tenant's heirs only until the death of the person against whose life the estate is measured. A life estate pur autre vie is often created for a physically or mentally incapacitated person in the hope of providing an incentive for someone to care for him or her.

■ **FOR EXAMPLE**   Alex conveys a life estate in Blackacre to Peter as the life tenant for the duration of the life of Dale, Alex's elderly relative. Peter is still the life tenant, but the measuring life is Dale's. On Dale's death, the life estate ends. If Peter should die while Dale is still alive, Peter's heirs may inherit the life estate. However, when Dale dies, the heirs' estate ends.

Remainder and reversion   The fee simple owner who creates a conventional life estate must plan for its future ownership. When the life estate ends, it is replaced by a fee simple estate. The future owner of the fee simple estate may be designated in one of two ways:

1. **Remainder interest:** The creator of the life estate may name a *remainderman* as the person to whom the property will pass when the life estate ends. (*Remainderman* is the legal term; neither the term *remainderperson* nor the term *remainderwoman* is used.) (See Figure 7.2.)

FIGURE 7.2

Remainder Interest

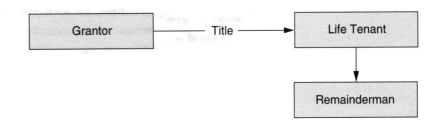

2. **Reversionary interest:** The creator of the life estate may choose not to name a remainderman. In that case, the creator will recapture ownership when the life estate ends. The ownership is said to revert to the original owner. (See Figure 7.3.)

■ **FOR EXAMPLE**   Alex conveys Blackacre to Peter for Peter's lifetime and designates Rick to be the remainderman. While Peter is still alive, Rick owns a *remainder* interest, which is a nonpossessory estate; that is, Rick does not possess the property but has an interest in it nonetheless. This is a *future interest* in the fee simple estate. When Peter dies, Rick automatically becomes the fee simple owner.

On the other hand, Alex may convey a life estate in Blackacre to Peter during Peter's life. On Peter's death, ownership of Blackacre reverts to Alex. Alex has retained a *reversionary* interest (also a nonpossessory estate). Alex has a *future interest* in the ownership and may reclaim the fee simple estate when Peter dies. If Alex dies before Peter, Alex's heirs (or other individuals specified in Alex's will) then will assume ownership of Blackacre when Peter dies.

Legal life estate   A legal life estate is not created voluntarily by an owner. Rather, it is a form of life estate established by state law. It becomes effective automatically when certain events occur. *Dower, curtesy,* and *homestead* are the legal life estates currently used in some states.

In Georgia   In Georgia, the term **year's support** has replaced dower and curtesy.

Dower and curtesy provide the nonowning spouse with a means of support after the death of the owning spouse. *Dower* is the life estate that a wife has in the real estate of her deceased husband. *Curtesy* is an identical interest that a husband has in the real estate of his deceased wife. (In some states, dower and curtesy are referred to collectively as either dower or curtesy.)

FIGURE 7.3

Reversionary Interest

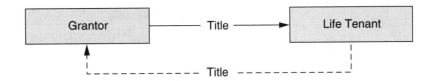

Dower and curtesy provide that the nonowning spouse has a right to a one-half or one-third interest in the real estate for the rest of his or her life, even if the owning spouse wills the estate to others. Because a nonowning spouse might claim an interest in the future, both spouses may have to sign the proper documents when real estate is conveyed. The signature of the nonowning spouse would be needed to release any *potential* common-law interests in the property being transferred.

Most states have abolished the common-law concepts of dower and curtesy in favor of the Uniform Probate Code (UPC). The UPC gives the surviving spouse a right to an elective share on the death of the other spouse. Community property states never used dower and curtesy. (Community property is discussed in Chapter 1.)

In Georgia Under year's support (O.C.G.A. 53-3-1 et seq.), a surviving spouse and/or minor children can petition the probate court to have real and/or personal property set aside from the estate to provide for 12 months' support from the date of the decedent's death. The petition must be made within 24 months of the death.

IN PRACTICE Year's support is virtually unique to Georgia. It is rare to have a law that allows the award of real property in a statutory proceeding.

A **homestead** is a legal life estate in real estate occupied as the family home. In effect, the home (or at least some part of it) is protected from creditors during the occupant's lifetime. In states that have homestead exemption laws, a portion of the area or value of the property occupied as the family home is exempt from certain judgments for debts such as charge accounts and personal loans. The homestead is not protected from real estate taxes levied against the property or a mortgage for the purchase or cost of improvements, that is, if the debt is secured by the property, the property cannot be exempt from a judgment on that debt.

In some states, all that is required to establish a homestead is for the head of a household (sometimes a single person) to own or lease the premises occupied by the family as a residence. In other states, the family is required by statute to file a notice. A family can have only one homestead at any given time.

How does the homestead exemption actually work? In most states, the homestead exemption merely reserves a certain amount of money for the family in the event of a court sale. In a few states, however, the entire homestead is protected from sale altogether. Once the sale occurs, any debts secured by the home (a mortgage, unpaid taxes, or mechanics' liens, for instance) will be paid from the proceeds. Then the family will receive the amount reserved by the homestead exemption. Finally, whatever remains will be applied to the family's unsecured debts.

In Georgia The Georgia homestead law provides for a partial exemption from ad valorem taxation and a partial exemption from levy and sale (O.C.G.A. 48-5-44).

■ **FOR EXAMPLE** Greenacre is Tim's homestead. In Tim's state, the homestead exemption is $25,000. At a court-ordered sale, the property is purchased for $80,000. First, Tim's remaining $35,000 mortgage balance is paid; then Tim receives $25,000. The remaining $20,000 is applied to Tim's unsecured debts.

Of course, no sale would be ordered if the court could determine that nothing would remain from the proceeds for the creditors. If Greenacre could not be expected to bring more than $40,000, the priority of the mortgage lien and homestead exemption would make a sale pointless.

■ ENCUMBRANCES

An **encumbrance** is a claim, charge, or liability that attaches to real estate. An encumbrance does not have a possessory interest in real property; it is not an estate. Simply put, an *encumbrance* is a right or an interest held by someone other than the fee owner of the property that affects title to real estate. An encumbrance may lessen the value or obstruct the use of the property, but it does not necessarily prevent a transfer of title.

Encumbrances may be divided into the following two general classifications:

1. *Liens* (usually monetary charges) and
2. *Encumbrances* such as restrictions, easements, and encroachments that affect the condition or use of the property.

Liens

A **lien** is a charge against property that provides security for a debt or an obligation of the property owner. If the obligation is not repaid, the lienholder is entitled to have the debt satisfied from the proceeds of a court-ordered or forced sale of the debtor's property. Real estate taxes, mortgages and trust deeds, judgments, and mechanics' liens all represent possible liens against an owner's real estate. Liens are discussed in detail in Chapter 10.

Deed Restrictions

Deed restrictions, also referred to as *covenants, conditions, and restrictions*, or *CC&Rs*, are private agreements that affect the use of land. They may be imposed by an owner of real estate and included in the seller's deed to the buyer. Typically, however, restrictive covenants are imposed by a developer or subdivider to maintain specific standards in a subdivision. Such restrictive covenants are listed in the original development plans for the subdivision filed in the public record. Deed restrictions are discussed in Chapter 20.

Easements

An **easement** is the right to use the land of another for a particular purpose. An easement may exist in any portion of the real estate, including the airspace above or a right-of-way across the land.

FIGURE 7.4

Easement Appurtenant

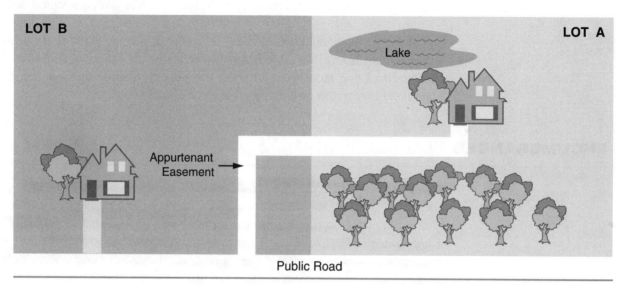

The owner of Lot A has an appurtenant easement across Lot B to gain access to his property from the paved road. Lot A is dominant, and Lot B is servient.

An **appurtenant easement** is annexed to the ownership of one parcel and allows this owner the use of a neighbor's land. For an appurtenant easement to exist, two adjacent parcels of land must be owned by two different parties. The parcel over which the easement runs is known as the servient tenement; the neighboring parcel that benefits is known as the dominant tenement. (See Figure 7.4 and Figure 7.5.)

An appurtenant easement is part of the dominant tenement, and if the dominant tenement is conveyed to another party, the easement transfers with the title. This type of easement is said to *run with the land*. It is an encumbrance on property and will transfer with the deed of the dominant tenement forever unless the holder of the dominant tenement somehow releases that right.

■ **FOR EXAMPLE** Kim and Larry own adjoining parcels of land near a lake. Kim's property borders the lake, and Larry's does not. Kim grants Larry an easement, established by a deed properly delivered, accepted, and recorded. The easement gives Larry the right to cross Kim's property to reach the lake. This is an easement appurtenant. When Kim sells the lakefront property to Mike, the easement is automatically included, even if Kim's deed fails to mention it. Larry's easement has become a limitation on the ownership rights of Kim's land.

An **easement in gross** is an *individual interest* in or right to use someone else's land. For instance, a railroad's right-of-way is an easement in gross. So is the right-of-way for a pipeline or high-tension power line (utility easements). Commercial easements in gross may be assigned, conveyed, and inherited. However,

FIGURE 7.5

Easement Appurtenant and Easement in Gross

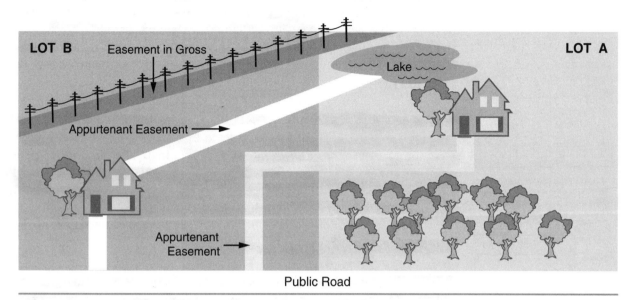

The owner of Lot B has an appurtenant easement across Lot A to gain access to the lake. Lot B is dominant and Lot A is servient. The utility company has an easement in gross across both parcels of land for its power lines. Note that Lot A also has an appurtenant easement across Lot B for its driveway. Lot A is dominant and Lot B is servient.

personal easements in gross usually are not assignable. Generally, a personal easement in gross terminates on the death of the easement owner. An easement in gross is often confused with the similar personal right of license, discussed later in this chapter.

Creating an easement   An easement is commonly created by a written agreement between the parties that establishes the easement right. It also may be created by the grantor in a deed of conveyance, where the grantor either *reserves* an easement over the sold land or *grants* the new owner an easement over the grantor's remaining land. An easement may be created by longtime *use*, as in an easement by prescription; by necessity; and by implication, that is, the situation or the parties' actions *imply* that they intend to create an easement.

The creation of an easement always involves two separate parties, one of whom is the owner of the land over which the easement runs. It is impossible for the owner of a parcel of property to have an easement over his or her own land.

Party wall easement   A **party wall** can be an exterior wall of a building that straddles the boundary line between two lots, or it can be a commonly shared partition wall between two connected properties. Each lot owner owns the half of the wall on his or her lot, and each has an appurtenant easement in the other half of the wall. A written party wall agreement must be used to create the easement rights. Expenses to build and maintain the wall are usually shared. A fence built on the lot line is treated the same as a wall. A party driveway shared by and partly on the land of adjoining owners must also be created by written agreement, specifying responsibility for expenses.

Easement by necessity   An appurtenant easement that arises when an owner sells part of his or her land that has no access to a street or public way except over the seller's remaining land is an **easement by necessity**. An easement by necessity is created by court order based on the principle that owners have the right to enter and exit their land (the right of *ingress* and *egress*)—they should not be landlocked. Remember, this form of easement is called an *easement by necessity*; it is not merely for convenience and is not imposed simply to validate a shortcut.

Easement by prescription   When the claimant has made use of another's land for a certain period of time as defined by state law, an **easement by prescription**, or a *prescriptive easement*, may be acquired. The prescriptive period may be from 10 to 21 years. The claimant's use must have been continuous, exclusive, and without the owner's approval. The use must be visible, open, and notorious, that is, the owner must have been able to learn of it.

In Georgia | In Georgia, the prescriptive period is 20 years.

The concept of **tacking** provides that successive periods of continuous occupation by different parties may be combined (tacked) to reach the required total number of years necessary to establish a claim for a prescriptive easement. To tack on one person's possession to that of another, the parties must have been *successors in interest*, such as an ancestor and his or her heir, a landlord and a tenant, or seller and buyer.

■ **FOR EXAMPLE**   Judy's property is located in Georgia, which has a prescriptive period of 20 years. For the past 22 years, Frank has driven his car across Judy's front yard several times a day to reach his garage from a more comfortable angle. Frank has an *easement by prescription*.

For 25 years, Lester has driven across Judy's front yard two or three times a year to reach his property when he's in a hurry. He does not have an easement by prescription because his use was not continuous.

For 15 years, Eric parked his car on Judy's property, next to Judy's garage. Six years ago, Eric sold his house to Nick, who continued to park his car next to Judy's garage. Last year, Nick acquired an *easement by prescription* through *tacking*.

Easement by condemnation   An **easement by condemnation** is acquired for a public purpose through the right of eminent domain. The owner of the servient tenement must be compensated for any loss in property value.

Terminating an easement   An easement may be ended

1. when the purpose for which the easement was created no longer exists;
2. when the owner of either the dominant or the servient tenement becomes the owner of both—the properties are merged under one legal description (also known as *termination by merger*);
3. by release of the right of easement to the owner of the servient tenement;

4. by abandonment of the easement (the intention of the parties is the determining factor);

5. by nonuse of a prescriptive easement;

6. by adverse possession by the owner of the servient tenement;

7. by destruction of the servient tenement (for instance, the demolition of a party wall);

8. by lawsuit (an *action to quiet title*) against someone claiming an easement; or

9. by excessive use, as when a residential use is converted to a commercial purpose.

Note that an easement may not *automatically* terminate for these reasons. Certain legal steps may be required.

Licenses

A **license** is a personal privilege to enter the land of another for a specific purpose. A license differs from an easement in that *it can be terminated or canceled by the licensor* (the person who granted the license). If a right to use another's property is given orally or informally, it generally is considered to be a license rather than a personal easement in gross. A license ends on the death of either party or the sale of the land by the licensor.

> **Physical Encumbrances**
> ■ Restrictions
> ■ Easements
> ■ Licenses

■ **FOR EXAMPLE**   Peter asks Harry for permission to park a boat in Harry's driveway. Harry says, "Sure, go ahead!" Peter has a *license*, but Harry may tell Peter to move the boat at any time. Similarly, a ticket to a theater or sporting event is a *license*: The holder is permitted to enter the facility and is entitled to a seat. But if the ticket holder becomes rowdy or abusive, he or she may be asked to leave.

Encroachments

An **encroachment** occurs when all or part of a structure, such as a building, fence, or driveway, illegally extends beyond the land of its owner or beyond the legal building lines. An encroachment usually is disclosed by either a physical inspection of the property or a spot survey. A *spot survey* shows the location of all improvements located on a property and whether they extend over the lot or building lines. As a rule, a spot survey is more accurate and reliable than a simple physical inspection. If a building encroaches on adjoining land, the neighbor may be able to either recover damages or secure removal of the portion of the building that encroaches. Encroachments that exceed a state's prescriptive period, however, may give rise to easements by prescription.

IN PRACTICE   Because an undisclosed encroachment could make a title unmarketable, an encroachment should be noted in a listing agreement and the sales contract. An encroachment is not disclosed by the usual title evidence provided in a real estate sale unless a survey is submitted while the title examination is being made.

■ WATER RIGHTS

Whether for agricultural, recreational, or other purposes, waterfront real estate has always been desirable. Each state has strict laws that govern the ownership and use of water as well as the adjacent land. The laws vary among the states, but all are closely linked to climactic and topographical conditions. Where water is plentiful, for instance, many states rely on the simple parameters set by the common-law doctrines of riparian and littoral rights. Where water is scarce, a state may control all but limited domestic use of water according to the doctrine of prior appropriation.

Riparian Rights

Riparian rights are common-law rights granted to owners of land along the course of a river, stream, or similar body of water. Although riparian rights are governed by laws that vary from state to state, they generally include the unrestricted right to use the water. As a rule, the only limitation on the owner's use is that it cannot interrupt or alter the flow of the water or contaminate it in any way. In addition, an owner of land that borders a nonnavigable waterway, (i.e., a body of water unsuitable for commercial boat traffic) owns the land under the water to the exact center of the waterway. Land adjoining commercially navigable rivers, on the other hand, is usually owned to the water's edge, with the state holding title to the submerged land. (See Figure 7.6.) Navigable waters are considered public highways in which the public has an easement or right to travel.

> **Water Rights**
> ■ **Riparian** refers to rivers, streams, and similar waterways.
> ■ **Littoral** refers to lakes, oceans, and similar bodies of water.

FIGURE 7.6

Riparian Rights

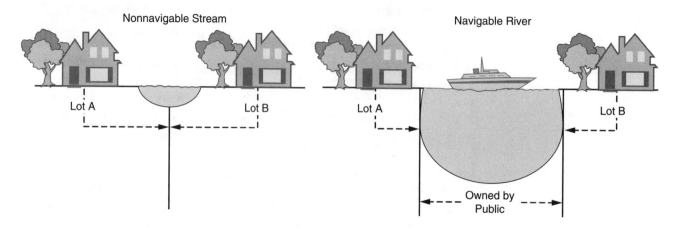

| In Georgia | Georgia is a riparian rights state. |

■ **FOR EXAMPLE**   Nick owns property that borders a nonnavigable, narrow river. The property directly across the river from Nick's property is owned by Jane who has decided not to build on her property. Nick owns far more property on his side of the river than does Jane. Because Jane is never on her property and Nick feels he owns more of the river than Jane, Nick wants to build a dock that borders Jane's property so he can dock his boat on the other side of the river. However, because Nick's riparian rights only go to the center of the river, he cannot build a dock on the other side of the river without Jane's permission.

Littoral Rights

Closely related to riparian rights are the **littoral rights** of owners whose land borders commercially navigable lakes, seas, and oceans. Owners with littoral rights enjoy unrestricted use of available waters but own the land adjacent to the water only up to the mean, that is, average high-water mark. (See Figure 7.7.) All land below this point is owned by the government.

Riparian and littoral rights are appurtenant (or attached) to the land and cannot be retained when the property is sold. The right to use the water belongs to whoever owns the bordering land and cannot be retained by a former owner after the land is sold.

Accretion, Erosion, and Avulsion

The amount of land an individual owns may be affected by the natural action of water. An owner is entitled to all land created through **accretion**—increases in

FIGURE 7.7

Littoral Rights

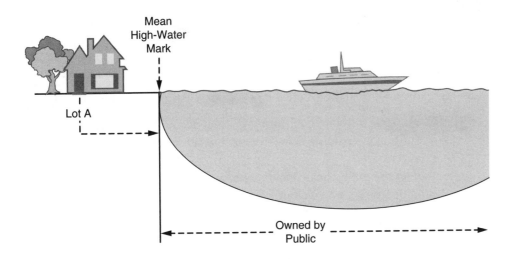

the land resulting from the deposit of soil by the water's action. (Such deposits are called *alluvion* or *alluvium*.) If water recedes, new land is acquired by *reliction*.

On the other hand, an owner may lose land through **erosion.** Erosion is the gradual and imperceptible wearing away of the land by natural forces, such as wind, rain, and flowing water. Fortunately, erosion usually takes hundreds or even thousands of years to have any noticeable effect on a person's property. Flash floods or heavy winds, however, can increase the speed of erosion.

If erosion is a slow natural process, avulsion is its opposite. **Avulsion** is the sudden removal of soil by an act of nature. It is an event that causes the loss of land much less subtly than does erosion. An earthquake or a mudslide, for instance, can cause an individual's landholding to become much smaller very quickly.

Doctrine of Prior Appropriation

In states where water is scarce, ownership and use of water are often determined by the doctrine of **prior appropriation.** Under this doctrine, the right to use any water, with the exception of limited domestic use, is controlled by the state rather than by the landowner adjacent to the water.

To secure water rights in prior appropriation states, a landowner must demonstrate to a state agency that he or she plans a *beneficial* use for the water, such as crop irrigation. If the state's requirements are met, the landowner receives a permit to use a specified amount of water for the limited purpose of the beneficial use. Although statutes governing prior appropriation vary from state to state, the priority of water rights is usually determined by the oldest recorded permit date.

Once granted, water rights attach to the land of the permit holder. The permit holder may sell a water right to another party.

Issuance of a water permit does not grant access to the water source. All access rights-of-way over the land of another (easements) must be obtained from the property owner.

■ KEY POINT REVIEW

Government powers can be recalled by **PETE,** an acronym for the following:

- **Police power** is the state's authority—passed down to municipalities and counties through **enabling acts**—to enact nondiscriminatory legislation to
  — preserve order,
  — protect the public health and safety, and
  — promote the general welfare of citizens.

- **Eminent domain** is the government's right to acquire, that is, **take** privately owned real estate for a public or economically beneficial use through
  - **condemnation,** which is a process that begins with a judicial or an administrative proceeding, or
  - **just compensation,** which must be paid to the property owner.
- **Taxation** is a charge on real estate to raise funds to meet public needs.
- **Escheat** of property to the state occurs when a deceased leave no will and no lawful heirs.

A **freehold estate** lasts for an indeterminable length of time and can fall into the following categories:

- Fee simple or fee simple absolute (indefeasible fee), which is the highest estate recognized by law.
- Defeasible fee—a qualified estate subject to occurrence or nonoccurrence of some specified event.
- Life estate, which is based on the lifetime of a person and ends when that person dies.

A **leasehold estate** lasts for a fixed period of time.

An **encumbrance** is a claim, charge, or liability that attaches to real estate and may be one of the following:

- **Liens** are charges against property that provide security for a debt or obligation of the property owner.
- **Deed restrictions (covenants, conditions, and restrictions, or CC&Rs)** are private agreements that affect the use of land.
- Restrictive covenants are listed in the subdivision development plan.

Easements are rights to use the land of another for a particular purpose, as follows:

- An **appurtenant easement** is said to **run with the land** because it will transfer when title to the land does.
- An easement in gross is an individual interest in or right to use land of another.
- An easement is usually created by **written agreement** between the parties.
- A **party wall** is a shared wall between two properties; each side owns one half and has appurtenant easement to the other half of the wall.
- An **easement by necessity** arises when land has no access to a street or public way.
- An **easement by prescription** is acquired when a claimant has used another's land for a period of time defined by state law; successive owners can **tack** their interests.

An easement is **terminated**

- when the purpose for which it was created no longer exists;
- when the owner of either dominant or servient tenement becomes owner of both (called **termination by merger**);
- when the owner of a servient tenement **releases** the right of easement;

- if the easement is **abandoned**;
- by **nonuse** of prescriptive easement;
- by **adverse possession** by the owner of the servient tenement;
- by **destruction** of the servient tenement;
- by lawsuit (**action to quiet title**) against someone claiming an easement; and
- by **excessive use**.

License is a personal privilege to enter the land of another for a specific purpose that can be terminated or canceled by the licensor (person granting license).

Encroachment occurs when all or part of a structure illegally extends beyond onto land of another or beyond legal building lines, as indicated by **spot survey**.

Water rights are determined by common law and statute, are attached to the land, and have the following characteristics:

- **Riparian rights** are common law rights granted to owners of land along river, stream, or similar body of water. (Georgia is a riparian rights state.)
- **Littoral rights** belong to owners of land that borders commercially navigable lakes, seas, and oceans.
- **Accretion** increases land by deposit of soil (**alluvion** or **alluvium**) brought about through action of water.
- **Erosion** is the gradual, imperceptible wearing away of land by natural forces.
- **Avulsion** is the sudden removal of soil by act of nature.
- The **doctrine of prior appropriation** in some states provides that water use, aside from limited domestic use, is controlled by the state rather than the landowner adjacent to the water; to use the water, the landowner must demonstrate **beneficial use** of the water, such as irrigation of crops.

■ RELATED WEB SITES

Eminent Domain: *www.realtor.org*
Interests in Real Estate: *www.law.cornell.edu/topics/real_property.html*

CHAPTER 7 QUIZ

1. The right of a government body to take ownership of real estate for public use is called
   a. escheat.
   b. eminent domain.
   c. condemnation.
   d. police power.

2. A purchaser of real estate learns that his ownership rights could continue forever and that no other person claims to be the owner or has any ownership control over the property. This person owns a
   a. fee simple interest.
   b. life estate.
   c. determinable fee.
   d. fee simple on condition subsequent.

3. Joan owned the fee simple title to a vacant lot adjacent to a hospital and was persuaded to make a gift of the lot. She wanted to have some control over its use, so her attorney prepared her deed to convey ownership of the lot to the hospital "so long as it is used for hospital purposes." After completion of the gift the hospital will own a
   a. fee simple absolute estate.
   b. license.
   c. fee simple determinable.
   d. leasehold estate.

4. After Dan had purchased his house and moved in, he discovered that his neighbor regularly used Dan's driveway to reach a garage located on the neighbor's property. Dan's attorney explained that ownership of the neighbor's real estate includes an easement over the driveway. Dan's property is properly called
   a. the dominant tenement.
   b. a freehold.
   c. a leasehold.
   d. the servient tenement.

5. A *license* is an example of a(n)
   a. appurtenant easement.
   b. encroachment.
   c. temporary use right.
   d. restriction.

6. Betsy is the owner of Blueacre. During her lifetime, Betsy conveys a life estate in Blueacre to Chuck. Under the terms of the grant, Chuck's life estate will terminate when Betsy's uncle dies and Betsy will regain the property. Which of the following is correct?
   a. Chuck possesses a life estate pur autre vie, measured by the life of Betsy's uncle.
   b. Chuck possesses a conventional life estate.
   c. Betsy may not grant any life estate while her uncle is alive.
   d. Betsy's uncle has a legal life estate.

7. An appurtenant easement
   a. terminates with the sale of the property.
   b. is a right-of-way for a utility company.
   c. is revocable.
   d. can be created only if adjacent properties have different owners.

8. If the owner of real estate does not take action against a trespasser before the statutory period has passed, the trespasser may acquire the legal authority to continue using the property through
   a. an easement by necessity.
   b. a license.
   c. title by eminent domain.
   d. an easement by prescription.

9. A property owner wants to use water from a river that runs through the property to irrigate a potato field. To do so, the owner is required by state law to submit an application to the Department of Water Resources describing in detail the beneficial use he plans for the water. If the department approves the owner's application, it will issue a permit allowing a limited amount of river water to be diverted onto the property. Based on these facts, it can be assumed that this property owner's state relies on which of the following rules of law?
   a. Common-law riparian rights
   b. Common-law littoral rights
   c. Doctrine of prior appropriation
   d. Doctrine of highest and best use

10. Which of the following is *NOT* an example of governmental power?
    a. Dedication
    b. Police power
    c. Eminent domain
    d. Taxation

11. Property deeded to a town "for recreational purposes only" conveys a
    a. fee simple absolute.
    b. fee simple on condition subsequent.
    c. leasehold interest.
    d. determinable fee.

12. A property owner who has the legal right to cross over a neighbor's land holds a(n)
    a. estate in land.
    b. easement.
    c. police power.
    d. encroachment.

13. James conveys ownership of his residence to his church but reserves for himself a life estate in the residence. The interest the church owns during James' lifetime is a
    a. pur autre vie.
    b. remainder.
    c. reversion.
    d. leasehold.

14. Kevin has fenced his property. By mistake, the fence extends one foot over Kevin's lot line onto a neighbor's property. The fence is an example of a(n)
    a. license.
    b. encroachment.
    c. easement by necessity.
    d. easement by prescription.

15. Katie has permission from Todd to hike on his property during the autumn months. Katie has
    a. an easement by necessity.
    b. an easement by condemnation.
    c. riparian rights.
    d. a license.

16. Which of the following statements about encumbrances on real estate is *TRUE*?
    a. Easements and encroachments are always encumbrances on the land that is subject to them.
    b. The presence of an encumbrance makes it impossible to sell the encumbered property.
    c. All encumbrances must be removed before the title can be transferred.
    d. An encumbrance is of no monetary value to its owner.

17. A tenant who rents an apartment from the owner of the property holds a(n)
    a. easement.
    b. license.
    c. freehold interest.
    d. leasehold interest.

18. Because a homeowner failed to pay her real estate taxes on time, the taxing authority imposed a claim against her property. This claim is known as a(n)
    a. deed restriction.
    b. lien.
    c. easement.
    d. reversionary interest.

19. The type of easement that is a right-of-way for a utility company's power lines is a(n)
    a. easement in gross.
    b. easement by necessity.
    c. easement by prescription.
    d. nonassignable easement.

20. Joe's property extends to the middle of the creek that borders his land under what type of water rights?
    a. Littoral rights
    b. Riparian rights
    c. Doctrine of prior appropriation
    d. Alluvion rights

21. John built a house on the river 10 years ago. Today the house sits 30 feet inland. The natural process of increasing land from the deposit of soil is called
    a. reliction.
    b. alluvion.
    c. erosion.
    d. accretion.

22. Mary has divided much of her land into smaller parcels and has recently sold a tract near a nature preserve that is landlocked and cannot be entered except through one of the other tracts. The buyer of that property will probably be granted what type of easement by court action?

    a. Easement by necessity
    b. Easement in gross
    c. Easement by prescription
    d. Easement by condemnation

23. All of the following will terminate an easement *EXCEPT*

    a. adverse possession by the owner of the servient tenement.
    b. nonuse of a prescriptive easement.
    c. abandonment of easement.
    d. release of the right of easement to the dominant tenement.

24. Lucy's husband, Fred, died last month in Conyers, Georgia, owning real property and personal property. He did not have a will. Lucy petitioned the probate court for an award of real and personal property from Fred's estate. Her right to this property is known as

    a. year's support.
    b. dower.
    c. curtesy.
    d. community property.

25. Larry owns a house in Decatur, Georgia, that he occupies as his principal residence. He receives a partial exemption from ad valorem taxes and a partial exemption from levy and sale. This exemption is known as

    a. dower.
    b. curtesy.
    c. homestead.
    d. year's support.

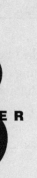

Forms of Real Estate Ownership

■ FORMS OF OWNERSHIP

Although the forms of ownership available are controlled by state laws, a fee simple estate may be held in three basic ways:

1. In *severalty*, where title is held by one individual
2. In *co-ownership*, where title is held by two or more individuals
3. In *trust*, where a third individual holds title for the benefit of another

■ OWNERSHIP IN SEVERALTY

When real estate is owned by one individual, that individual is said to own the property in **severalty.** The term comes from the fact that this sole owner is *severed* or *cut off* from other owners. The severalty owner has sole rights to the ownership and sole discretion to sell, will, lease or otherwise transfer part or all of the ownership rights to another person. A sole owner may be a single individual or an artificial person, such as a corporation. For example, a city park is owned in severalty because the city is incorporated. A corporation is an artificial person that may hold and convey title to property.

State laws may modify how ownership is held. For example, in a community property state, income and property secured during the marriage is shared equally, but property owned before marriage, or inherited after, is considered separate property.

| In Georgia | Georgia does not have community property and therefore property obtained during a marriage is the separate property of each spouse. |

■ CO-OWNERSHIP

When title to one parcel of real estate is held by two or more individuals, those parties are called *co-owners* or *concurrent owners*. Most states commonly recognize various forms of **co-ownership.** Individuals may co-own property as tenants in common, joint tenants, or tenants by the entirety, or they may co-own it as community property. During the lifetime of the co-owners, however, there is no apparent difference among the various types of ownership. Only when the property is conveyed or one of the owners dies do the differences become apparent.

| In Georgia | Tenancy by the entirety is not recognized in Georgia and neither is community property. |

Tenancy in Common

A parcel of real estate may be owned by two or more people as tenants in common. In a **tenancy in common,** each tenant holds an *undivided fractional interest* in the property. A tenant in common may hold, say, a one-half or one-third interest in a property. The physical property, however, is not divided into a

FIGURE 8.1

Tenancy in Common

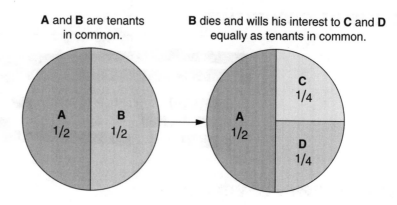

A and B are tenants in common.

B dies and wills his interest to C and D equally as tenants in common.

specific half or third. The co-owners have *unity of possession*, that is, they are entitled to possession of the whole property. It is the *ownership* interest, not the property, that is divided.

The deed creating a tenancy in common may or may not state the fractional interest held by each co-owner. If no fractions are stated, the tenants are presumed to hold equal shares. For example, if five people hold title, each would own an undivided one-fifth interest.

Because the co-owners own separate interests, each can sell, convey, mortgage, or transfer his or her interest without the consent of the other co-owners. However, no individual tenant may transfer the ownership of the entire property. When one co-owner dies, the tenant's undivided interest passes according to his or her will. (See Figure 8.1.)

Forms of Co-ownership

1. Tenancy in common
2. Joint tenancy
3. Tenancy by the entirety
4. Community property

(In Georgia, forms are tenancy in common and joint tenancy.)

TABLE 8.1

Remembering Legal Terminology: "OR" versus "EE"

Throughout this chapter and the rest of the book, we will be referring to people as *grantor* and *grantee, trustor* and *trustee, mortgagor* and *mortgagee,* and so on. Because the terminology can be confusing, we've included this table to help you remember who's who in a transaction. Refer back to this table when the terms come up in other chapters, too.

Product	Person Giving the Product	Person Receiving the Product
Devise	Devisor	Devisee
Grant	Grantor	Grantee
Legacy	Legator	Legatee
Lease	Lessor	Lessee
Mortgage*	Mortgagor	Mortgagee
Offer	Offeror	Offeree
Option	Optionor	Optionee
Sublease	Sublessor	Sublessee
Trust	Trustor	Trustee

*Note that a mortgage is a written agreement that pledges real estate as security for the payment of a debt. The mortgagor is the borrower. This person (the mortgagor) gives the mortgagee (the lender) a mortgage or deed of trust (property interest) on the property used to secure the loan.

When two or more people acquire title to real estate and the deed does not indicate the form of the tenancy, the new owners are usually determined to have acquired title as tenants in common.

In Georgia   In Georgia, if the deed is made to a husband and wife with no further explanation, there is an automatic assumption of tenancy in common.

Joint Tenancy

Most states, including Georgia, recognize some form of **joint tenancy** in property owned by two or more people.

The most distinguishing feature of joint tenancy is the **right of survivorship.** Upon the death of a joint tenant, his or her interest does not pass to heirs or according to a will. Rather, the entire ownership remains in the surviving joint tenant(s). Essentially, there is simply one less owner.

As each successive joint tenant dies, the surviving joint tenants acquire the deceased tenant's interest. The last survivor takes title in severalty and has all the rights of sole ownership, including the right to pass the property to his or her heirs. (See Figure 8.2.)

IN PRACTICE   The form under which title is to be taken by individuals or married partners should be discussed with an attorney. Remember that licensees may not give legal advice or engage in the practice of law.

FIGURE 8.2

Joint Tenancy with Right of Survivorship

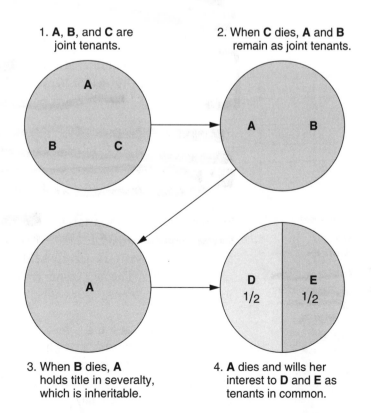

1. **A, B,** and **C** are joint tenants.

2. When **C** dies, **A** and **B** remain as joint tenants.

3. When **B** dies, **A** holds title in severalty, which is inheritable.

4. **A** dies and wills her interest to **D** and **E** as tenants in common.

Creating joint tenancies   A joint tenancy can be created only by the intentional act of conveying a deed or giving the property by will. It cannot be implied or created by operation of law. The deed must specifically state the parties' intention to create a joint tenancy, and the parties must be explicitly identified as joint tenants. Some states, however, have abolished the right of survivorship as the distinguishing characteristic of joint tenancy. In these states, the deed must explicitly indicate the intention to create the right of survivorship for that right to exist.

The following four *unities* are required to create a joint tenancy:

1. Unity of *possession*—all joint tenants holding an undivided right to possession
2. Unity of *interest*—all joint tenants holding equal ownership interests
3. Unity of *time*—all joint tenants acquiring their interests at the same time
4. Unity of *title*—all joint tenants acquiring their interests by the same document

The four unities are present when the following requirements are met:

- Title is acquired by one deed.
- The deed is executed, signed, and delivered at one time.
- The deed conveys equal interests to all of the parties.
- The parties hold undivided possession of the property as joint tenants.

> Special wording is required in a deed creating a joint tenancy, such as, *"To A and B as joint tenants with the right of survivorship."*

Because the unities must be satisfied, many states require the use of an intermediary when a sole owner wishes to create a joint tenancy between himself or herself and others. The owner conveys the property to a nominee, or *straw man*. Then the nominee conveys it back, naming all the parties as joint tenants in the deed. As a result, all the joint tenants acquire title at the same time by one deed.

Some states have eliminated this "legal fiction" and allow the sole owner to execute a deed to himself or herself and others "as joint tenants and not as tenants in common," thereby creating a valid joint tenancy.

> **In Georgia**

The Georgia Joint Tenancy Act of 1976 allows an individual or a couple holding property as tenants in common to convey property to themselves as joint tenants. This effectively abolishes the time requirement by statute and also means that there is no need in Georgia for a straw man.

Terminating joint tenancies   A joint tenancy is destroyed when any one of the four unities of joint tenancy is terminated. A joint tenant is free to convey his or her interest in the jointly held property, but doing so destroys the unities of time and title. The new owner cannot become a joint tenant. Rights of other joint tenants, however, are unaffected.

> **Memory Tip**
> **The Four Unities**
>
> The four unities necessary to create a joint tenancy may be remembered by the acronym **PITT**:
> 1. Possession
> 2. Interest
> 3. Time
> 4. Title

■ **FOR EXAMPLE**   Alva, Betty, and Cindy hold title to Blackacre as joint tenants. Alva conveys her interest to Doris. Doris now owns a fractional interest in Blackacre as a tenant in common with Betty and Cindy, who continue to own their undivided interest as joint tenants. (See Figure 8.3.) Doris is presumed to have a one-third interest, which may be reconveyed or left to Doris's heirs.

FIGURE 8.3

Combination of Tenancies

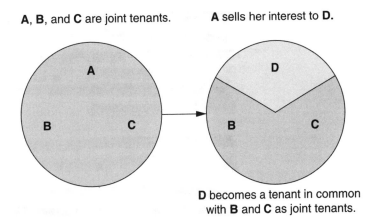

A, B, and C are joint tenants.

A sells her interest to D.

D becomes a tenant in common with B and C as joint tenants.

Termination of Co-ownership by Partition Suit

Cotenants who wish to terminate their co-ownership may file an action in court to **partition** the property. Partition is a legal way to dissolve the relationship when the parties do not voluntarily agree to its termination. If the court determines that the land cannot be divided physically into separate parcels without destroying its value, the court will order the real estate sold. The proceeds of the sale will then be divided among the co-owners according to their fractional interests.

Ownership by Married Couples

Tenancy by the entirety   Some states (but *not* Georgia), allow husbands and wives to use a special form of co-ownership called **tenancy by the entirety.** In this form of ownership, each spouse has an equal, undivided interest in the property. (The term *entirety* refers to the fact that the owners are considered one indivisible unit because early common law viewed a married couple as one legal person.) A husband and wife who are tenants by the entirety have rights of survivorship. During their lives, they can convey title *only by a deed signed by both parties*. One party cannot convey a one-half interest, and generally they have no right to partition or divide. On the death of one spouse, the surviving spouse automatically becomes sole owner.

A tenancy by the entirety may be terminated in the following ways:

- By the death of either spouse (the surviving spouse becomes sole owner in severalty)
- By agreement between both parties (through the execution of a new deed)
- By divorce (which leaves the parties as tenants in common)
- By a court-ordered sale of the property to satisfy a judgment against the husband and wife as joint debtors (the tenancy is dissolved so that the property can be sold to pay the judgment)

**Memory Tip
Remember J'S DAD**

The methods of terminating a tenancy by the entirety may be remembered by the acronym J'S DAD: Judgment Sale, Death, Agreement, or Divorce.

Community property rights Community property laws are based on the idea that a husband and wife, rather than merging into one entity, are equal partners in the marriage. Any property acquired during a marriage is considered to be obtained by mutual effort. The states' community property laws vary widely. Essentially, however, they all recognize two kinds of property: separate property and community property.

In Georgia | Georgia does not have community property. Property acquired during a marriage is considered separate property.

Separate property is real or personal property that was owned solely by either spouse before the marriage. It also includes property acquired by gift or inheritance during the marriage, as well as any property purchased with separate funds during the marriage. Any income earned from a person's separate property remains part of his or her separate property. Separate property can be mortgaged or conveyed by the owning spouse without the signature of the nonowning spouse.

Community property consists of all other property, both real and personal, acquired by either spouse during the marriage. Any conveyance or encumbrance of community property requires the signatures of *both* spouses. When one spouse dies, the survivor automatically owns one-half of the community property. The other half is distributed according to the deceased spouse's will. If the spouse dies without a will, the other half is inherited by the surviving spouse or by the decedent's other heirs, depending on state law. Community property does *not* provide an automatic right of survivorship as joint tenancy does.

TABLE 8.2

Forms of Co-ownership

	Property Held	Property Conveyed
Tenancy in Common	Each tenant holds a fractional undivided interest.	Each tenant can convey or devise his or her interest, but not entire interest.
Joint Tenancy	Unity of ownership. Created by intentional act; unities of possession, interest, time, title.	Right of survivorship; cannot be conveyed to heirs.
Tenants by the Entirety (not in Georgia)	Husband and wife have equal undivided interest in property.	Right of survivorship; convey by deed signed by both parties. One party can't convey one-half interest.
Community Property (not in Georgia)	Husband and wife are equal partners in marriage. Real or personal property acquired during marriage is community property.	Conveyance requires signature of both spouses. No right of survivorship; when spouse dies, survivor owns one-half of community property. Other one-half is distributed according to will or, if no will, according to state law.

■ TRUSTS

A **trust** is a device by which one person transfers ownership of property to someone else to hold or manage for the benefit of a third party. Perhaps a grandfather wishes to ensure the college education of his granddaughter, so he transfers his oil field to the grandchild's mother. He instructs the mother to use its income to pay for the grandchild's college tuition. In this case, the grandfather is the *trustor*—the person who creates the trust. The granddaughter is the *beneficiary*—the person who benefits from the trust. The mother is the *trustee*—the party who holds legal title to the property and is entrusted with carrying out the trustor's instructions regarding the purpose of the trust. The trustee is a *fiduciary*, who acts in confidence or trust and has a special legal relationship with the beneficiary. The trustee's power and authority are limited by the terms of the trust agreement, will, or deed in trust.

IN PRACTICE The legal and tax implications of setting up a trust are complex and vary widely from state to state. Attorneys and tax experts should always be consulted on the subject of trusts.

Most states allow real estate to be held in trust. Depending on the type of trust and its purpose, the trustor, trustee, and beneficiary can all be either people or legal entities, such as corporations. *Trust companies* are corporations set up for this specific purpose.

Real estate can be owned under living or testamentary trusts and land trusts. It can also be held by investors in a real estate investment trust (REIT).

Living and Testamentary Trusts

A property owner may provide for his or her own financial care or for that of the owner's family by establishing a trust. This trust may be created by agreement during the property owner's lifetime (a *living trust*) or established by will after the owner's death (a *testamentary trust*). (Note that neither of these are related to the so-called living will, which deals with the right to refuse medical treatment.)

The person who creates the trust conveys real or personal property to a trustee (usually a corporate trustee), with the understanding that the trustee will assume certain duties. These duties may include the care and investment of the trust assets to produce an income. After paying the trust's operating expenses and trustee's fees, the income is paid to or used for the benefit of the beneficiary. The trust may continue for the beneficiary's lifetime, or the assets may be distributed when the beneficiary reaches a certain age or when other conditions are met.

In recent years, living trusts have become a major estate planning tool used to minimize the time and costs of probate. In a living trust, the property owner (trustor, grantor, or settler) transfers ownership of real and personal property to a trustee. The trustee is often the trustor. In this way, the owner continues to control the assets of the trust. The trustee may transfer property into and out of the trust, subject to the trust agreement. Upon the death of the trustee, the property passes to the beneficiary or beneficiaries without the need for probate. In the case of community property, the husband and wife may transfer real and personal property into a trust and name themselves as joint trustees with rights of survivorship. Upon the death of the surviving trustee the estate is distributed to the beneficiary or beneficiaries.

Land Trusts

In the creation of *land trusts*, real estate is the only asset. As in all trusts, the title to the property is conveyed to a trustee, and the beneficial interest belongs to the beneficiary. In the case of land trusts, however, the beneficiary is usually also the trustor. While the beneficial interest is *personal property*, the beneficiary retains management and control of the real property and has the right of possession and the right to any income or proceeds from its sale. Land trusts are frequently created for the conservation of farmland, forests, coastal land, and scenic vistas.

One of the distinguishing characteristics of a land trust is that the *public records usually do not name the beneficiary*. A land trust may be used for secrecy when assembling separate parcels. There are other benefits as well. A beneficial interest can be transferred by assignment, making the formalities of a deed unnecessary. The beneficial interest in property can be pledged as security for a loan without having a mortgage recorded. Because the beneficiary's interest is personal, it passes at the beneficiary's death under the laws of the state in which the beneficiary lived. If the deceased owned property in several states, additional probate costs and inheritance taxes can be avoided.

A land trust ordinarily continues for a definite term, such as 20 years. If the beneficiary does not extend the trust term when it expires, the trustee is usually obligated to sell the real estate and return the net proceeds to the beneficiary.

IN PRACTICE   Licensees should exercise caution in using the term *trust deed*. It can mean both a *deed **in** trust* (which relates to the creation of a living, testamentary, or land trust) and a *deed **of** trust* (a financing document similar to a mortgage). Because these documents are not interchangeable, using an inaccurate term can cause serious misunderstandings.

■ OWNERSHIP OF REAL ESTATE BY BUSINESS ORGANIZATIONS

A business organization is a legal entity that exists independently of its members. Ownership by a business organization makes it possible for many people to hold an interest in the same parcel of real estate. Investors may be organized to finance a real estate project in various ways. Some provide for the real estate to be owned by the entity; others provide for direct ownership by the investors.

Partnership

A **partnership** is an association of two or more persons who carry on a business for profit as co-owners. In a **general partnership,** all the partners participate in the operation and management of the business and share full liability for business losses and obligations. A **limited partnership,** on the other hand, consists of one or more general partners as well as limited partners. The business is run by the general partner or partners. The limited partners are not legally permitted to participate, and each can be held liable for business losses only to the extent of his or her investment. The limited partnership is a popular method of organizing investors because it permits investors with small amounts of capital to participate in large real estate projects with a minimum of personal risk.

Most states have adopted the Uniform Partnership Act (UPA), which permits real estate to be held in the partnership name. The Uniform Limited Partnership Act (ULPA) also has been widely adopted. It establishes the legality of the limited partnership entity and provides that realty may be held in the limited partnership's name. Profits and losses are passed through the partnership to each partner, whose individual tax situation determines the tax consequences.

General partnerships are dissolved and must be reorganized if one partner dies, withdraws, or goes bankrupt. In a limited partnership, however, the partnership agreement may provide for the continuation of the organization following the death or withdrawal of one of the partners.

Corporations

A **corporation** is a legal entity—an artificial person—created under the authority of the laws of the state from which it receives its charter. A corporation is managed and operated by its *board of directors*. The charter sets forth the powers of the corporation, including its right to buy and sell real estate (based on a resolution by the board of directors). Because the corporation is a legal entity, it can own real estate in *severalty, or as a tenant in common.* Some corporations are permitted by their charters to purchase real estate for any purpose; others are limited to purchasing only the land necessary to fulfill the entities' corporate purposes.

| In Georgia | The creation and regulation of corporations in Georgia is governed by the Georgia Business Corporation Code (O.C.G.A. 14-2-202).

As a legal entity, a corporation continues to exist until it is formally dissolved. The death of one of the officers or directors does not affect title to property owned by the corporation.

Individuals participate, or invest, in a corporation by purchasing stock. Because stock is *personal property*, shareholders do not have direct ownership interest in the real estate owned by a corporation. Each shareholder's liability for the corporation's losses is usually limited to the amount of his or her investment.

One of the main disadvantages of corporate ownership of income property is that the profits are subject to *double taxation*. As a legal entity, a corporation must file an income tax return and pay tax on its profits. The portion of the remaining profits distributed to shareholders as dividends is taxed again as part of the shareholders' individual incomes.

An alternative form of business ownership that provides the benefit of a corporation as a legal entity but avoids double taxation is known as an S *corporation*. Profits of S corporations are taxed at the applicable rates of their shareholders, whether or not distributed to them as dividends. S corporations are generally small, closely held corporations that are not taxed directly. S corporations are subject to strict requirements regulating their structure, membership, and operation. If the Internal Revenue Service (IRS) determines that an S corporation has failed to comply with these detailed rules, the entity will be redefined as some other form of business organization, and its favorable tax treatment will be lost.

Syndicates and Joint Ventures

Generally speaking, a **syndicate** is two or more people or firms joined together to make and operate a real estate investment. A syndicate is not in itself a legal entity; however, it may be organized into a number of ownership forms, including co-ownership (tenancy in common, joint tenancy), partnership, trust, or corporation. A **joint venture** is a form of partnership in which two or more people or firms carry out a single business project. The joint venture is characterized by a time limitation resulting from the fact that the joint venturers do not intend to establish a permanent relationship.

Limited Liability Companies

The **limited liability company (LLC)** is a relatively recent form of business organization. An LLC combines the most attractive features of limited partnerships and corporations. The members of an LLC enjoy the limited liability offered by a corporate form of ownership and the tax advantages of a partnership. In addition, the LLC offers flexible management structures without the complicated requirements of S corporations or the restrictions of limited partnerships. The structure and methods of establishing a new LLC, or of converting an existing entity to the LLC form, vary from state to state.

■ CONDOMINIUMS, COOPERATIVES, TOWN HOUSES, AND TIME-SHARES

Home does not refer only to a brick bungalow on a grassy lawn surrounded by a white picket fence. A growing urban population, diverse lifestyles, changing family structures, and heightened mobility have created a demand for new forms of ownership. Condominiums, cooperatives, town houses, and time-share arrangements are four types of property ownership that have arisen in residential, commercial, and industrial markets to address our society's changing real estate needs.

See Table 8.3 for a comparison chart of these types of property ownership.

Condominium Ownership

The **condominium** form of ownership has become increasingly popular throughout the United States. Condominium laws, often called *horizontal property acts*, have been enacted in every state. Under these laws, the owner of each unit holds a *fee simple title* to the unit. The individual unit owners also own a specified share of the undivided interest in the remainder of the building and land, known as the **common elements.** Common elements typically include such items as land, courtyards, lobbies, the exterior structure, hallways, elevators, stairways, and the roof, as well as recreational facilities such as swimming pools, tennis courts, and

TABLE 8.3

Four Types of Property Ownership

Type	Condominium	Cooperative	Town House	Time-Share
Description	Single units are located in lowrise and highrise complexes.	Single units are located in lowrise and highrise complexes.	Two-floor units share common walls; units are usually clustered together.	Multiple purchasers buy interests in real estate—usually resort or hotel property. Each purchaser has right to use unit for set time each year.
Ownership	Owners have fee title to interior space of units and share title to common areas. In some cases a condo association may own the common areas.	Tenants own shares in a corporation, partnership, or trust that holds title to the building. Tenants have proprietary leases and the right to occupy their respective units.	Owners have fee title to dwelling unit and lot. They share title to common areas. Town houses are often organized as condominiums.	Time-share estate is a fee simple interest. Time-share use agreement is personal property that expires after a specified time period.
Transfer	Single units are conveyed by deed or will.	Shares are personal property. Shareholders may sell or transfer shares. Transfer of shares may be restricted by bylaws.	Single units conveyed by deed or will.	An interest in a time-share *estate* may be conveyed by deed or will by the owner. An interest in time-share *use* is personal property that may or may not be transferable according to the contract.
Governed by	Declaration of condominium and elected board of directors	Bylaws of the corporation and elected board of directors or trustees	Elected board of directors (condominiums) or homeowners' association	Developer

FIGURE 8.4

Condominium Ownership

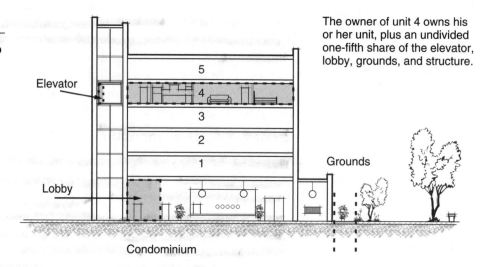

The owner of unit 4 owns his or her unit, plus an undivided one-fifth share of the elevator, lobby, grounds, and structure.

Elevator

5
4
3
2
1

Grounds

Lobby

Condominium

golf courses. (See Figure 8.4.) The individual unit owners own these common elements as *tenants in common*. State law usually provides, however, that unit owners do not have the same right to partition that other tenants in common have. Condominium ownership is not restricted to highrise buildings. Lowrises, town houses, and detached structures can all be condominiums.

In Georgia

Creation of a condominium   Georgia has not adopted the Uniform Condominium Act (UCA), and instead has the Georgia Condominium Act (O.C.G.A. 44-3-71 et seq.). Under its provisions, a condominium is created and established when the owner of an existing building (or the developer of unimproved property) executes and records a *declaration of condominium*. As described in O.C.G.A. 44-3-77, the declaration includes

- the name of the condominium, which must include the word "condominium";
- the county or counties in which the condominium is located;
- a metes-and-bounds legal description, including any horizontal upper and lower boundaries as well as the vertical lateral boundaries;
- a description of the boundaries of the units;
- a description of any limited common elements showing the unit(s) to which each is assigned;
- a description of all common elements that may subsequently be assigned as limited common elements together with a statement that they may be assigned and a description of the method of assignment;
- the allocation to each unit of an undivided interest in common elements;
- the allocation to each unit of a number of votes in the association;
- the allocation to each unit of a share of the liability for common expenses;
- any limitations or restrictions on the powers of the association and the board of directors;
- the name and address of the person who prepared the declaration; and
- a statement of any restrictions on the general use of the condominium or a statement that there are no restrictions.

If a condominium is expandable, convertible, or a leasehold, the Georgia Condominium Act has a number of additional requirements the declaration must contain, such as: detailed information about options to expand, a statement about the number of votes in the association, and liability for common expenses.

IN PRACTICE   If you are involved in a condominium real estate transaction, be sure to review the Georgia Condominium Act.

Owning a condominium   Once the property is established as a condominium, each unit becomes a separate parcel of real estate that is owned in fee simple and may be held by one or more persons in any type of ownership or tenancy recognized by state law. A condominium unit may be mortgaged like any other parcel of real estate. The unit can usually be sold or transferred to whomever the owner chooses, unless the condominium association provides for a *right of first refusal*. In this case, the owner is required to offer the unit at the same price to the other owners in the condominium or the association before accepting an outside purchase offer.

Real estate taxes are assessed and collected on each unit as an individual property. Default in the payment of taxes or a mortgage loan by one unit owner may result in a foreclosure sale of that owner's unit. An owner's default, however, does not affect the other unit owners.

IN PRACTICE   When someone buys a condominium, he or she should do as much background research as possible. Examining and understanding association fees and rules are critical so the buyer is aware of his or her responsibilities and is not surprised by a particular fee or rule. Most states require the disclosure of condominium documents to buyers; it's important that the buyer examine them.

Operation and administration   The condominium property is administered by an association of unit owners. The association may be governed by a board of directors or another official entity, and it may manage the property on its own or hire a property manager.

The association must enforce any rules it adopts regarding the operation and use of the property. The association is responsible for the maintenance, repair, cleaning, and sanitation of the common elements and structural portions of the property. It must also maintain fire, extended-coverage, and liability insurance.

The expenses of maintaining and operating the building are paid by the unit owners in the form of fees and assessments. Both fees and assessments are imposed and collected by the owners' association. Recurring fees (referred to as *condo fees*) are paid by each unit owner. The fees may be due monthly, quarterly, semiannually, or annually, depending on the provisions of the bylaws. The size of an individual owner's fee is generally determined by the size of his or her unit. For instance, the owner of a three-bedroom unit pays a larger share of the total expense than the owner of a one-bedroom unit. If the fees are not paid, the association may seek a court-ordered judgment to have the delinquent owner's unit sold to cover the outstanding amount or place a lien on the property.

Assessments are special payments required of unit owners to address some specific expense, such as a new roof. Assessments are structured like condo fees: Owners of larger units pay proportionately higher assessments than owners of smaller units.

Cooperative Ownership

In a **cooperative,** a corporation holds title to the land and building. The corporation then offers *shares of stock* to prospective tenants. The price the corporation sets for each apartment becomes the price of the stock. The purchaser becomes a shareholder in the corporation by virtue of stock ownership and receives a *proprietary lease* to the apartment for the life of the corporation. Because stock is personal property, the cooperative tenant-owners do not own real estate, as is the case with condominiums. Instead, they own an interest in a corporation that has only one asset: the building.

Operation and management   The operation and management of a cooperative are determined by the corporation's bylaws. Through their control of the corporation, the shareholders of a cooperative control the property and its operation. They elect officers and directors who are responsible for operating the corporation and its real estate assets. Individual shareholders are obligated to abide by the corporation's bylaws.

An important issue in most cooperatives is the method by which shares in the corporation may be transferred to new owners. For instance, the bylaws may require that the board of directors approve any prospective shareholders. In some cooperatives, a tenant-owner must sell the stock back to the corporation at the original purchase price so that the corporation realizes any profits when the shares are resold.

■ **FOR EXAMPLE**   In a highly publicized incident, former President Richard Nixon's attempt to move into a highly exclusive Manhattan cooperative apartment building was blocked by the cooperative's board. In refusing to allow the controversial ex-president to purchase shares, the board cited the unwanted publicity and media attention other celebrity tenants would suffer.

The corporation incurs costs in the operation and maintenance of the entire parcel, including both the common property and the individual apartments. These costs include real estate taxes and any mortgage payments the corporation may have. The corporation also budgets funds for such expenses as insurance, utilities, repairs and maintenance, janitorial and other services, replacement of equipment, and reserves for capital expenditures. Funds for the budget are assessed to individual shareholders, generally in the form of monthly fees similar to those charged by a homeowners' association in a condominium.

Unlike in a condominium association, which has the authority to impose a lien on the title owned by someone who defaults on maintenance payments, the burden of any defaulted payment in a cooperative falls on the remaining shareholders. Each shareholder is affected by the financial ability of the others. For this reason, approval of prospective tenants by the board of directors frequently involves financial evaluation. If the corporation is unable to make mortgage and tax payments because of shareholder defaults, the property might be sold by court order in a foreclosure suit. This would destroy the interests of all shareholders, including those who have paid their assessments.

Advantages   Cooperative ownership, despite its risks, has become more desirable in recent years for several reasons. Lending institutions view the shares of stock as acceptable collateral for financing. The availability of financing expands the transferability of shares beyond wealthy cash buyers. As a tenant-owner, rather than a tenant who pays rent to a landlord, the shareholder has some control over the property. Tenants in cooperatives also enjoy certain income tax advantages. The IRS treats cooperatives as it does fee simple interest in single homes or condominiums in regard to deductibility of loan interest, property taxes, and homesellers' tax exclusions. Finally, owners enjoy freedom from maintenance.

IN PRACTICE   The laws in some states may prohibit real estate licensees from listing or selling cooperative interests because the owners own only personal property. Individuals who participate in these transactions may need a securities license appropriate for the type of cooperative interest involved.

Town House Ownership

A popular form of housing in urban centers is the **town house.** *Town house* is a term often used to describe any type of housing connected by common walls. In fact, the town-house concept is a cross between single-family houses and apartments. Normally, each town house has two floors and is located on a small lot.

Most town house developments are planned unit developments (PUDs). Title to each unit and lot is vested in the individual owner. Each owner also has a fractional interest in the common areas. Common areas include open spaces, recreational facilities, driveways, and sidewalks. The owner may sell, lease, will, or otherwise transfer the dwelling unit. The rights to the use of common areas pass with title.

Time-Share Ownership

Time-share ownership permits multiple purchasers to buy interests in real estate, usually a resort property. Each purchaser receives the right to use the facilities for a certain period of time. A *time-share estate* includes a real property interest in condominium ownership; a *time-share use* is a contract right under which the developer owns the real estate.

In Georgia   In Georgia, the promotion or sale of all time-share units is regulated by Statute O.C.G.A. 44-3-162 et seq. A time-share estate is a real property estate having the character and incidents of a fee simple estate, or if a leasehold, an estate for years, unless changed by statute.

For time-share projects located outside the state of Georgia, project instruments must be recorded as required by the law of the jurisdiction in which the time-share is located.

Before the transfer of a time-share use (or interval), and no later than the date of any sales agreement, the developer must provide a copy of the public offering statement and any of its amendments or supplements. The sales agreement is voidable without penalty by the purchaser for seven days (Sundays and holidays excepted) after receiving the public offering statement or for seven days after signing any sales agreement, whichever is later. If cancelled, all payments made by the purchaser must be refunded within 30 days after receipt of the cancellation notice.

Developers can also cancel without penalty sales agreements up to seven days (Sundays and holidays excepted) after the signing of any sales agreement. The developer must return all payments made by the purchaser within 30 days after canceling the agreement and return all materials received in good condition, reasonable wear and tear excepted.

A time-share *estate* is a fee simple interest. The owner's occupancy and use of the property are limited to the contractual period purchased—for instance, the 17th complete week, Sunday through Saturday, of each calendar year. The owner is assessed for maintenance and common area expenses based on the ratio of the ownership period to the total number of ownership periods in the property. Time-share estates theoretically never end because they are real property interests. However, the physical life of the improvements is limited and must be looked at carefully when considering such a purchase.

The principal difference between a time-share *estate* and a time-share *use* lies in the interest transferred to an owner by the developer of the project. A time-share *use* consists of the right to occupy and use the facilities for a certain number of years. At the end of that time, the owner's rights in the property terminate. In effect, the developer has sold only a right of occupancy and use to the owner, not a fee simple interest.

In Georgia   Under the Georgia Code, a time-share use means any contractual right of exclusive occupancy that does not fall within the definition of time-share estate, including, without limitation, a vacation license, prepaid hotel reservation, club membership, limited partnership, or vacation bond. Time-share estate means an ownership or leasehold interest in real property divided into measurable chronological periods.

Each purchaser of a time-share interval must be given a public offering statement, and the statement must be signed by the purchaser to be valid and enforceable. The statement must disclose such items as the address of the time-share intervals; the developer's ownership interest; the nature of the interest being offered; a general description of the units; any budgetary information for the time-share intervals for one year after the date of the first transfer to a purchaser; anything affecting title; notice of any pending actions material to the time-share; insurance coverage; financial arrangements; any special closing costs; and conspicuous statements on the cover related to cancellation, legal questions, and the need for the purchaser to review the document before signing.

If there is any material change in the public offering statement, a developer must immediately amend the statement. If any person related to the sale and purchase of a time-share violates any provisions of the law or the project instruments, the person(s) affected by the violation has a claim for relief. Punitive damages may be awarded for a willful violation, and a court may award reasonable attorney's fees.

Some time-sharing programs specify certain months or weeks of the year during which the owner can use the property. Others provide a rotation system under which the owner can occupy the unit during different times of the year in different years. Some include a swapping privilege for transferring the ownership period to another property to provide some variety for the owner. Time-shared properties typically are used 50 weeks each year, with the remaining two weeks reserved for maintenance of the improvements.

Membership camping is similar to time-share use. The owner purchases the right to use the developer's facilities, which usually consist of an open area with minimal improvements (such as camper and trailer hookups and restrooms). Normally, the owner is not limited to a specific time for using the property; use is limited only by weather and access.

■ KEY POINT REVIEW

Ownership in severalty—title held by one individual—has the following characteristics:

- Sole rights to ownership
- Sole discretion to transfer part or all ownership rights to another person
- May be a single individual or an artificial person, such as a corporation

Co-ownership—title held by two or more individuals—may be one of four forms:

1. **Tenancy in common,** where
   — each tenant holds an **undivided fractional interest;**
   — **co-owners have unity of possession**—right to occupy entire property;
   — each interest can be sold, conveyed, mortgaged, or transferred; and
   — interest passes by will when a co-owner dies.
2. **Joint tenancy,** where tenants enjoy the four unities, **PITT,** an acronym for the following:
   — **Unity of possession**—all joint tenants have undivided right to possession.
   — **Unity of interest**—all joint tenants own an equal interest.

— **Unity of time**—all joint tenants acquire their interest at the same time.

— **Unity of title**—title conveyed to all joint tenants by the same document.

Joint tenants also enjoy the **right of survivorship**—on death of a joint tenant, that interest passes to the other joint tenant(s).

Termination of joint tenancy is by

— **death** of all but one joint tenant, who then owns the property in severalty;

— **conveyance** of a joint tenant's interest, but only as to that interest; or

— **partition suit,** which can be brought to force division or sale of property.

3. **Tenancy by the entirety,** recognized by some states but *not* Georgia, has the following traits:

— Only available to **husband and wife**

— Title conveyed only by **deed signed by both**

— Carries **right of survivorship**; survivor becomes owner in severalty

— **Terminated by**

- **death** of either spouse,
- **agreement** of spouses,
- **divorce,** or
- **court-ordered sale** to satisfy judgment against spouses as joint debtors

4. **Community property,** recognized by some states (but not Georgia), is generally property acquired during marriage that is not separate property. In Georgia, property obtained during a marriage is the separate property of each spouse.

Note the following:

— **Separate property** is property owned by one spouse before marriage (or in Georgia, during marriage), or by inheritance or gift to one spouse, or with proceeds of separate property.

— **Community property** requires signatures of both spouses to be conveyed.

— **Separate property** of one spouse requires only that spouse's signature to be conveyed.

— On **death** of one spouse, other spouse owns one-half of community property and other half is distributed according to deceased spouse's will or according to state law if deceased left no will.

A **trust** involves title being conveyed by a **trustor** (owner) to a **trustee** to be held for a beneficiary. Following are types of trusts:

■ A **living trust** is used to avoid probate by transferring property to beneficiary on death of trustor, who is usually also the trustee.

■ A **testamentary trust** is created by will to hold deceased's property and convey to beneficiary at some future time.

■ A **land trust** is used to convey real estate to a trustee, with a beneficiary usually also the trustor, but public records usually do not name the beneficiary.

A **partnership** is an association of two or more persons who carry on a business for profit as co-owners in general or limited partnership, as provided by state law.

■ In a **general partnership**
 — all partners **participate** in operation and management, and
 — partners share **full liability** for business losses and obligations.
■ A **limited partnership** has both general partners and limited partners.
■ **General partners** run the business.
■ **Limited partners** do not participate in running the business and are liable for business losses only to the extent of the individual's investment.

The Uniform Partnership Act (UPA) and **The Uniform Limited Partnership Act (ULPA)** have been adopted by most states and allow real estate to be held in a partnership's name or in a limited partnership's name.

A **corporation** is created according to state law (in Georgia, the Georgia Business Corporation Code) with the following characteristics:

■ The **charter** sets forth the powers of the corporation.
■ A corporation is managed and operated by a **board of directors**. Death of an officer or director does not affect title to property held by a corporation.
■ Stock in a corporation is owned by **shareholders**. Each shareholder's **liability** for a corporation's losses is usually limited to the amount of the shareholder's investment.
■ **Double taxation** results when a corporation pays income taxes and shareholders pay tax on dividends paid to them.
■ With an **S corporation**, corporate income is taxed at applicable rates of shareholders, whether or not distributed as dividends; strict IRS requirements must be met.

A **syndicate** is two or more people or companies coming together to make and operate a real estate investment. A syndicate is not itself a legal entity and may be set up as co-ownership (tenancy in common, joint tenancy), partnership, trust, or corporation.

A **joint venture** is a form of partnership in which two or more people or companies carry out a single business project.

A **limited liability** company (LLC) may be permitted by state law and offers its members the following benefits:

■ **Limited liability** offered by a corporate form of ownership
■ **Tax advantages** of a partnership (no double taxation)
■ **Flexible management structure** without S corporation requirements or restrictions on limited partnership

Condominium laws (**horizontal property acts**) of each state (in Georgia, the Georgia Condominium Act) define condominium but generally share the following similarities:

- Owner holds fee simple title to the interior of a unit as well as an undivided share in the remainder of the building and land, known as the common elements.
- **Common elements** are owned by condominium unit owners as tenants in common.
- Condominium is administered by **homeowners' association** of unit owners that may decide to hire an outside property management firm.
- **Maintenance** of common elements is funded by **fees** charged to each unit owner.
- Unit owners have no right to partition common elements.
- Condominium unit may be mortgaged; default on payment does not affect other unit owners.
- Extraordinary expenses, such as new landscaping, may be paid by an **assessment** of each unit owner, typically based on the size of the unit
- Condominium association may have a **right of first refusal** when unit owner wants to sell.
- The **Uniform Condominium Act (UCA)** has been adopted by many states (but not Georgia) and defines how condominium is created and owned.

In a cooperative, title to the land and building is held by a corporation, which sells shares of stock to prospective tenants.

- A purchaser of stock becomes a **shareholder** in the corporation and receives a **proprietary lease** to the apartment for the life of the corporation.
- Stock is owned as personal property and not real estate.
- **Lender** may accept stock as collateral for financing, which expands pool of potential owners.
- **IRS** treats cooperative same as houses or condominiums for tax purposes.

A **town house**, a form of development in which houses share common vertical walls, is noteworthy for the following:

- It is usually a **planned unit development (PUD)**.
- **Title** to individual unit includes a fractional interest in common areas.

A time-share permits the sale of a **leasehold interest (time-share use)** or **deeded ownership (time-share estate)** that allows occupancy during a specific period of time, typically weekly.

| In Georgia |

The **Model Real Estate Time-Share Act** deals with time-share management and protections for purchasers of units. In Georgia, time-share units are regulated by the Georgia Code on Time-Share Projects and Programs.

■ RELATED WEB SITES

Legal Information Institute: Uniform Condominium Act: *www.law.cornell.edu/uniform/vol7.html#condo*

Official Code of Georgia Annotated (O.C.G.A.):   *www.grec.state.ga.us*

Small Business Administration: *www.sba.gov*

CHAPTER 8 QUIZ

1. The four unities of possession, interest, time, and title are associated with which of the following?
   a. Community property
   b. Severalty ownership
   c. Tenants in common
   d. Joint tenancy

2. A parcel of property was purchased by two friends, Kevin and Zelda. The deed they received from the seller at closing conveyed the property "to Kevin and Zelda" without further explanation. Kevin and Zelda took title as which of the following?
   a. Joint tenants
   b. Tenants in common
   c. Tenants by the entirety
   d. Community property owners

3. Mary, Nick, and Oliver are joint tenants with rights of survivorship in a tract of land. Oliver conveys his interest to Violet. Which of the following statements is *TRUE*?
   a. Mary and Nick are still joint tenants.
   b. Mary, Nick, and Violet are joint tenants.
   c. Mary, Nick, and Violet are tenants in common.
   d. Violet now has severalty ownership.

4. Ann owns one of 20 town houses in the Luxor Lakes development in fee simple, along with a 5 percent ownership share in the parking facilities, recreation center, and grounds. What kind of property does Ann own?
   a. Cooperative
   b. Condominium
   c. Time-share
   d. Land trust

5. Paul conveys a vineyard in trust to Ruth, with the instruction that any income derived from the vineyard be used for Tanya's medical care. Which of the following statements MOST accurately describes the relationship of these parties?
   a. Paul is the trustee, Ruth is the trustor, and Tanya is the beneficiary.
   b. Paul is the trustor, Ruth is the trustee, and Tanya is the beneficiary.
   c. Paul is the beneficiary, Ruth is the trustor, and Tanya is the trustee.
   d. Paul is the trustor, Ruth is the beneficiary, and Tanya is the trustee.

6. Ed, Frank, and Gina were concurrent owners of a parcel of real estate. Frank died, and his interest passed according to his will to become part of his estate. Frank was a
   a. joint tenant.
   b. tenant in common.
   c. tenant by the entirety.
   d. severalty owner.

7. A legal arrangement under which the title to real property is held to protect the interests of a beneficiary is a
   a. trust.
   b. corporation.
   c. limited partnership.
   d. general partnership.

8. A condominium form of ownership is officially established when the
   a. construction of the improvements is completed.
   b. owner records a declaration in the public record.
   c. condominium owners' association is established.
   d. the unit owners all file their documents in the public record.

9. An owner purchased an interest in a house in Beachfront. The owner is entitled to the right of possession only between July 10 and August 4 of each year. Which of the following is MOST likely the type of ownership that has been purchased?

   a. Cooperative
   b. Condominium
   c. Time-share
   d. Trust

10. A corporation is a legal entity, a *person* in the eyes of the law. Property owned by the corporation is owned in

    a. trust.
    b. partnership.
    c. severalty.
    d. survivorship tenancy.

11. Which of the following refers to ownership by one person?

    a. Tenancy by the entirety
    b. Community property
    c. Tenancy in common
    d. Severalty

12. All of the following can be classified as real property EXCEPT

    a. ownership in severalty.
    b. cooperative unit ownership.
    c. condominium unit ownership.
    d. a tenancy in common.

13. Bleak House is owned by Fred, George, and Harry as tenants in common. If George dies without a will, to whom will his interest pass?

    a. Fred and Harry equally
    b. George's heirs
    c. The state, by the law of escheat
    d. Fred and Harry in joint tenancy

14. Which of the following is MOST likely evidence of ownership in a cooperative?

    a. Tax bill for an individual unit
    b. Existence of a reverter clause
    c. Shareholder's stock certificate
    d. Right of first refusal

15. Sandra lives in the elegant Howell Tower. Sandra's possessory interest is evidenced by a proprietary lease. What does Sandra own?

    a. Condominium unit
    b. Cooperative unit
    c. Time-share
    d. Leasehold

16. An owner has purchased a fee simple interest in a lakefront cottage along with 6 percent of the parking lot, laundry room, and boathouse. What kind of ownership interest has been bought?

    a. Membership camping interest
    b. Time-share estate
    c. Cooperative unit
    d. Condominium unit

17. If property is held by two or more owners as survivorship tenants, the interest of a deceased cotenant will be passed to the

    a. surviving owner or owners.
    b. heirs of the deceased.
    c. state under the law of escheat.
    d. trust under which the property was owned.

In Georgia

18. Georgia law allows which of the following form(s) of co-ownership?

    a. Tenancy by the entirety
    b. Community property
    c. Both a and b
    d. Neither a nor b

19. Steve is the developer of a time-share development in Tybee Island, Georgia. Brenda inspects one of the units, and Steve gives her a copy of the public offering statement for the time-share on March 1. On March 6, Brenda signs a sales agreement for the time-share and gives Steve a deposit check for $1,000. She changes her mind and delivers a letter to Steve on March 12 stating that she is voiding the sales agreement and demands the return of her deposit money. Steve refuses. Which statement is correct concerning this situation?

a. Brenda is not entitled to her deposit because she signed a binding sales agreement.

b. Brenda is not entitled to her deposit because she attempted to void the contract more that ten days after receiving the public offering statement.

c. Brenda is entitled to her deposit because she voided the contract within seven days after receiving the public offering statement or signing the sales agreement, whichever is later.

d. Brenda is entitled to her deposit because she can void a time-share sales agreement any time before closing.

20. Under the Georgia Condominium Act, which of the following must be in the condominium declaration?

a. The name of the condominium, which must contain the word "condominium"

b. A metes-and-bounds legal description

c. Neither a nor b

d. Both a and b

CHAPTER

Legal Descriptions

- **identify** the three methods used to describe real estate.

- **describe** how a survey is prepared.

- **explain** how to read a rectangular survey description.

- **distinguish** the various units of land measurement.

- **define** the following *key terms:*

air lots	land lots	monuments
benchmarks	legal description	plat map
datum	lot-and-block (recorded plat) system	point of beginning (POB)
districts		rectangular (government) survey system
Georgia Militia District	metes-and-bounds description	
headrights		section

■ DESCRIBING LAND

People often refer to real estate by its street address, such as "1234 Main Street." While that is usually enough for the average person to find a particular building, it is not precise enough to be used on documents affecting the ownership of land. Further, addresses can change as streets are renamed or rural roads become absorbed into growing communities. Sales contracts, deeds, mortgages, and trust deeds, for instance, require a much more specific (or *legally sufficient*) description of property to be binding.

Courts have stated that a description is *legally sufficient* if it allows a competent surveyor to *locate* the parcel. In this context, however, *locate* means the surveyor must be able to define the exact boundaries of the property. The street address "1234 Main Street" would not tell a surveyor how large the property is or where it begins and ends. Several alternative systems of identification have been developed that express a **legal description** of real estate: one that is sufficiently specific that an independent surveyor could locate the exact dimensions of the property being described.

In Georgia   A contract for the sale of real estate or a lease must have a complete legal description in Georgia. For this purpose a street address is insufficient. If the legal description is not present, the contract cannot be enforced. Obtaining an accurate legal description of the property therefore is an important first step in developing the materials for a sale or lease. Since property descriptions in Georgia can be complicated, it is wise to involve surveyors and attorneys to resolve any difficulties with the property description.

■ METHODS OF DESCRIBING REAL ESTATE

Three basic methods can be used to describe real estate:

1. Metes and bounds
2. Rectangular (or government) survey
3. Lot and block (recorded plat)

Although each method can be used independently, the methods may be combined in some situations. Some states use only one method; others use all three.

In Georgia   Georgia uses the metes-and-bounds and lot and block methods.

The *metes-and-bounds description* is the oldest type of legal description. Metes-and-bounds descriptions were used in the original thirteen colonies and in those states that were being settled while the rectangular survey system was being developed. Today, as technology allows for greater precision and expanded record keeping, there is greater integration of land description information. Currently, the Federal Bureau of Land Management and the USDA Forest Service are developing the National Integrated Land System (NILS) in cooperation with states, counties, and private industry. This new system of land description is designed to be compatible with both the metes-and-bounds description and the rectangular survey system. The NILS is using a common data model based on graphic information systems (GIS) technology and new software tools to provide survey data and information for land records.

Metes-and-Bounds Method

The **metes-and-bounds description** is the oldest type of legal description. *Metes* means distance, and *bounds* means compass directions or angles. The method relies on a property's physical features to determine the boundaries and measurements of the parcel. A metes-and-bounds description starts at a designated place on the parcel, called the **point of beginning (POB).** The POB is the same as the POE (point of ending), but often only a POB is used in describing a property. From there, the surveyor proceeds around the property's boundaries. The boundaries are recorded by referring to linear measurements, natural and artificial landmarks (called *monuments*), and directions. A metes-and-bounds description always ends back at the POB so that the tract being described is completely enclosed.

Monuments are fixed objects used to identify the POB, all corners of the parcel or ends of boundary segments, or the location of intersecting boundaries. In colonial times, a monument may have been a natural object, such as a stone, large tree, lake, or stream. It also may have been a human-made object, such as a street, highway, fence, canal, or markers. Today, monuments are iron pins or concrete posts placed by the U.S. Corps of Engineers, another governmental department, or trained private surveyors. Measurements often include the words *more or less* because the location of the monuments is more important than the distance stated in the wording. The actual distance between monuments takes precedence over any linear measurements in the description. However, monuments can be moved and surveyors in metes and bounds usually give their final reference in terms of bearings and distance but include the statement "to the point of beginning (POB)" to ensure closure and to remove questions if an error in footage prevents closure.

In metes-and-bounds descriptions, compass bearings involving degrees, minutes, and seconds are sometimes used along with directions. For example, "straight line from point A to point B runs 25 degrees, 10 minutes east of due south."

In Georgia | In Georgia, metes-and-bounds descriptions must contain the following: the state and county, district and land lot numbers; section or **Georgia Militia District** (GMD) designations; a beginning point, compass directions moving to a point of closure, and a possible address.

Legally, the street address does not have to be included, but when it is, it is usually included with language similar to the following: "Being known as 236 Sycamore Drive according to the present system of numbering land in Fulton County, Georgia."

FIGURE 9.1

Metes-and-Bounds Tract

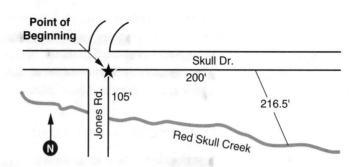

An example of an old, historical metes-and-bounds description of a parcel of land (pictured in Figure 9.1) follows:

> *A tract of land located in Red Skull, Boone County, Georgia, described as follows: Beginning at the intersection of the east line of Jones Road and the south line of Skull Drive; then east along the south line of Skull Drive 200 feet; then south 15° east 216.5 feet, more or less, to the center thread of Red Skull Creek then northwesterly along the center line of said creek to its intersection with the east line of Jones Road; then north 105 feet, more or less, along the east line of Jones Road to the point of beginning.*

When used to describe property within a town or city, a metes-and-bounds description may begin as follows:

> *Beginning at a point on the southerly side of Kent Street, 100 feet easterly from the corner formed by the intersection of the southerly side of Kent Street and the easterly side of Broadway; then . . .*

In this description, the POB is given by reference to the corner intersection. *Again, the description must close by returning to the POB.*

An example of a technically assisted metes-and-bounds description follows:

> *Beginning at a point (POB) on the North side of Newberry Street 100.50 feet East from the corner formed by the intersection of the East boundary of Peter Road and the North boundary of Newberry Street; then East 90 degrees, 15 minutes, 200.22 feet; then North 1 degree, 3 minutes, 2 seconds 300 feet; then West 89 degrees, 10 minutes, 3 seconds, 200.05 feet; then direct to the POB.*

Metes-and-bounds descriptions can be complex. When they include detailed compass directions or concave and convex lines, they can be difficult to understand. Sometimes the lines are curved on an arc or radius that becomes part of the description. Natural deterioration or destruction of the monuments in a description can make boundaries difficult to identify. For instance, "Raney's Oak" may have died long ago, and "Hunter's Rock" may no longer exist. Computer programs are available that convert the data of the compass directions and dimensions to a drawing that verifies that the description closes to the POB. Professional surveyors should be consulted for definitive interpretations of any legal description.

Technological advances, such as the use of computers, lasers, satellites, and global positioning systems, have meant a resurgence in property descriptions using points of reference or metes-and-bounds descriptions. Such technologically developed descriptions are used not only in the original metes-and-bounds areas, but also alongside the rectangular survey system. Given the technology, the metes-and-bounds system is the most accurate method.

Rectangular (Government) Survey System

The **rectangular survey system** (or the **government survey system**) is not used in Georgia. However, Georgia licensees may see property descriptions using this system when they work with clients who have holdings in other states or when they are assisting clients with relocation to or from Georgia.

In Georgia

The rectangular survey system was established by Congress in 1785 to standardize the legal description of land acquired by the newly formed federal government. The system uses a set of principal meridians (37 across the continental United States) running north and south and base lines running east and west, referenced by degrees of longitude and latitude.

The rectangles formed by these lines are further divided into townships, ranges, sections, and quarter-sections. Each township, for example, contains 36 sections. Since the meridians and base lines exist in theory, sometimes adjustments are made using a correction line. Undersized or oversized sections lead to fractional sections or government lots.

The following is an example of a property description using the rectangular survey method:

> The S1/2 of the NW1/4 of the SE1/4 of Section 11, Township 8 North, Range 6 West of the Fourth Principal Meridian.

Headrights, Georgia Militia Districts, and Sections

Legal descriptions in Georgia developed along with its history. Some of the earliest descriptions of property in Georgia in the eastern area use a **headrights** approach to define property along the coastal areas of the state. Since these descriptions were in place before the state was divided into districts and lots, these legal descriptions depend on natural boundaries and markers such as rocks and trees, and the parcels are irregular in shape.

In Georgia

In the older headright areas, sometimes a Georgia Militia District line designation is used to define a property. Early in its history, Georgia formed military districts to raise manpower for the common defense. These lines were used to define property and may be mentioned in legal descriptions. These lines are not related to county and other more contemporary lines. The initials GMD are sometimes used in these property descriptions.

In the northern part of Georgia, an additional grid **section** was also used in some counties that involved larger sections of land. These sections are generally larger, and may appear on property descriptions in the northern part of the state.

Districts and Land Lots

In Georgia, a survey was done in the 1800s that divided much of the state into the present description system of **districts** and **landlots.** For the most part, the grid lines divide the area into rectangles or squares. Large square areas are divided into districts. Land lots further divide each district into small sections.

Land lots will vary in size, with smaller lots usually in the north and larger lots in the central and southern parts of the state. In these property descriptions, a district and land lot number define the property's boundaries.

Lots-and-Block System

The third method of legal description is the **lot-and-block (recorded plat) system.** This system uses lot-and-block numbers referred to in a **plat map** filed in the public records of the county where the land is located. The lot-and-block system is often used to describe property in subdivisions.

A lot-and-block survey is performed in two steps. First, a large parcel of land is described either by the metes-and-bounds method or by rectangular survey. Once this large parcel is surveyed, it is broken into smaller parcels. As a result, a lot-and-block legal description always refers to a prior metes-and-bounds or rectangular survey description. For each parcel described under the lot-and-block system, the *lot* refers to the numerical designation of any particular parcel. The *block* refers to the name of the subdivision under which the map is recorded. The *block* reference is drawn from the early 1900s, when a city block was the most common type of subdivided property.

The lot-and-block system starts with the preparation of a *subdivision plat* by a licensed surveyor or an engineer. (See Figure 9.2.) On this plat, the land is divided into numbered or lettered lots and blocks, and streets or access roads for public use are indicated. Lot sizes and street details must be described completely and must comply with all local ordinances and requirements. When properly signed and approved, the subdivision plat is recorded in the county in which the land is located. The plat becomes part of the legal description. In describing a lot from a recorded subdivision plat, three identifiers are used:

1. Lot and block number
2. Name or number of the subdivision plat
3. Name of the county and state

FIGURE 9.2

Subdivision Plat Map of Block A

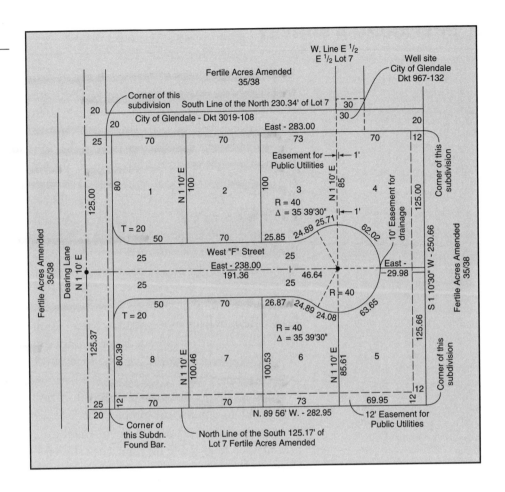

The following is an example of a lot-and-block description in Georgia:

> *Lot 71, Happy Valley Estates 2, located in Land Lot 237 of the 4th District of Fulton County, Georgia.*

In Georgia, lot-and-block descriptions may refer to the plat recording in the land records of the county. An example might read:

> *Being known and designated as Lot No. 15 on "Final Plat Section Two Waterford Subdivision" which plat is duly recorded among the land records of Fulton County in Plat Book No. 27, Folio 59.*

Some subdivided lands are further divided by a later resubdivision. In the following example, one developer (Western View) purchased a large parcel from a second developer (Homewood). Western View then resubdivided the property into different-sized parcels:

> *Lot 4, Western View Resubdivision of the Homewood Subdivision, located in a portion of west half of Section 19, Township 10 North, Range 13 East of the Black Hills Principal Meridian in Fulton County, Georgia.*

In working with descriptions of property, licensees may deal not only with plat maps, but also with plot surveys or plot maps, improvement surveys, or spot surveys that describe a piece of real estate showing its boundaries and features, such as roads, buildings, and fences.

■ PREPARING A SURVEY

Legal descriptions should not be altered or combined without adequate information from a surveyor or title attorney. A licensed surveyor is trained and authorized to locate and determine the legal description of any parcel of land. The surveyor does this by preparing two documents: a survey and a survey sketch. The *survey* states the property's legal description. The *survey sketch* shows the location and dimensions of the parcel. When a survey also shows the location, size, and shape of buildings on the lot, it is referred to as a *spot survey*.

IN PRACTICE Because legal descriptions, once recorded, affect title to real estate, they should be prepared only by a professional surveyor. Real estate licensees who attempt to draft legal descriptions create potential risks for themselves and their clients and customers.

Legal descriptions should be copied with extreme care. An incorrectly worded legal description in a sales contract may result in a conveyance of more or less land than the parties intended. For example, damages suffered from an incorrect description could be extensive if buildings and improvements need to be moved because the land is not owned upon which the improvements were made. Often, even punctuation is extremely critical. Title problems can arise for the buyer who seeks to convey the property at a future date. Even if the contract can be corrected before the sale is closed, the licensee risks losing a commission and may be held liable for damages suffered by an injured party because of an improperly worded legal description.

■ MEASURING ELEVATIONS

Just as surface rights must be identified, surveyed, and described, so must rights to the property above the earth's surface. Recall from Chapter 2 that *land* includes the space above the ground. In the same way land may be measured and divided into parcels, the air itself may be divided. An owner may subdivide the air above his or her land into **air lots.** Air lots are composed of the airspace within specific boundaries located over a parcel of land.

The *condominium laws* passed in all states (see Chapter 8) require that a registered land surveyor prepare a plat map that shows the elevations of floor and ceiling surfaces and the vertical boundaries of each unit with reference to an official *datum* (discussed later in this chapter). A unit's floor, for instance, might be 60 feet above the datum and its ceiling, 69 feet. Typically, a separate plat is prepared for each floor in the condominium building.

In Georgia

The following is an example of the legal description of a condominium apartment unit that includes a fractional share of the common elements of the building and land:

> UNIT____, Level ____, as delineated on a survey of all that tract or parcel of land lying and being in Land Lot 144 of the 8th District, 4th section of Elizabeth

(fictional) county of the state of Georgia, and more particularly described as follows: (here one would find a beginning point and bearings distances, which would outline the property in question.)

Subsurface rights can be legally described in the same manner as air rights. However, they are measured *below* the datum rather than above it. Subsurface rights are used not only for coal mining, petroleum drilling, and utility line location but also for multistory condominiums—both residential and commercial—that have several floors below ground level.

Datum

A **datum** is a point, line, or surface from which elevations are measured or indicated. For the purpose of the United States Geological Survey (USGS), *datum* is defined as the mean sea level at New York Harbor. A surveyor would use a datum in determining the height of a structure or establishing the grade of a street.

Benchmarks   Monuments are traditionally used to mark surface measurements between points. A monument could be a marker set in concrete, a piece of steel-reinforcing bar (rebar), a metal pipe driven into the soil, or simply a wooden stake stuck in the dirt. Because such items are subject to the whims of nature and vandals, their accuracy is sometimes suspect. As a result, surveyors rely most heavily on benchmarks to mark their work accurately and permanently.

Benchmarks are permanent reference points that have been established throughout the United States. They are usually embossed brass markers set into solid concrete or asphalt bases. While used to some degree for surface measurements, their principal reference use is for marking datums.

IN PRACTICE   All large cities have established a local official datum used in place of the USGS datum. For instance, the official datum for Chicago is known as the *Chicago City Datum*. It is a horizontal plane that corresponds to the low-water level of Lake Michigan in 1847 (the year in which the datum was established) and is considered to be at zero elevation. Although a surveyor's measurement of elevation based on the USGS datum will differ from one computed according to a local datum, it can be translated to an elevation based on the USGS.

■ LAND ACQUISITION COSTS

Cities with local datums also have designated official local benchmarks, which are assigned permanent identifying numbers. Local benchmarks simplify surveyors' work because the basic benchmarks may be miles away.

MATH CONCEPTS

LAND ACQUISITION COSTS

To calculate the cost of purchasing land, use the same unit in which the cost is given. Costs quoted per square foot must be multiplied by the proper number of square feet; costs quoted per acre must be multiplied by the proper number of acres; and so on.

To calculate the cost of a parcel of land of three acres at $1.10 per square foot, convert the acreage to square feet before multiplying:

43,560 square feet per acre × 3 acres = 130,680 square feet

130,680 square feet × $1.10 per square foot = $143,748

To calculate the cost of a parcel of land of 17,500 square feet at $60,000 per acre, convert the cost per acre into the cost per square foot before multiplying by the number of square feet in the parcel:

$60,000 per acre ÷ 43,560 square feet per acre = $1.38 (rounded) per square foot

17,500 square feet × $1.38 per square foot = $24,150

■ LAND UNITS AND MEASUREMENTS

It is important to understand land units and measurements because they are integral parts of legal descriptions. Some historically used measurements are listed in Table 9.1. Today, "rods," "cubic yards," and "chains" are often not used.

TABLE 9.1

Units of Land Measurement

Unit	Measurement
mile	5,280 feet; 1,760 yards; 320 rods
rod	16.5 feet; 5.50 yards
square mile	640 acres (5,280 × 5,280 = 27,878,400 ÷ 43,560)
acre	43,560 sq. feet
cubic yard	27 cubic feet
square yard	9 square feet
square foot	144 square inches
chain	66 feet; 4 rods; 100 links

■ KEY POINT REVIEW

To convey a parcel of land, its description must be **legally sufficient** (i.e., specific enough) for a competent **surveyor** to locate it. Three major methods of legal description of land are used in the United States, and more than one may be used for the same parcel.

The **metes-and-bounds method** of legal description of land is the oldest used in the United States and is the most accurate when used with **global positioning systems (GPSs)** and other modern technology. A metes-and-bounds description

■ measures distances (**metes**);
■ starts from a **point of beginning (POB)**;
■ follows compass directions or angles (**bounds**);
■ arrives at the **point of ending (POE)**, which must be the same as the POB;
■ uses **monuments** (fixed objects or markers) to identify the POB and corners or places where boundary lines change direction. Monuments may be **natural objects**, such as a tree, rock, or stream, or **iron pins or concrete posts** placed by the U.S. Army Corps of Engineers or a private surveyor;
■ requires the **actual distance** between monuments to take precedence over stated distance.

The **rectangular survey system (government survey system)**—established by Congress in 1785—is used in 37 states but *not* in Georgia, and it

■ divides land into **rectangles;**
■ **is measured from the intersection of one of 37 principal meridians (north/south line) and base lines (east/west line);**
■ **is referenced by degrees of longitude and latitude.**

In Georgia

Headrights

■ Early descriptions of property in Eastern Georgia use headrights
■ Depend on natural boundaries and markers
■ Parcels are irregular in shape

Georgia Militia Districts (GMD)

■ A Georgia Militia District line designation may define a property.
■ Georgia formed military districts to raise manpower for the common defense.
■ These lines are not related to county and other more contemporary lines.

Sections

■ In northern Georgia, an additional grid section is also used.
■ These sections are larger.

Districts and land lots

■ Sometimes property is described using a set of grid lines developed as part of an 1800s survey of the state.
■ The grid lines divide the area into rectangles or squares.

■ Large square or rectangular areas are divided into districts.
■ Land lots further divide each district into small sections.
■ In these property descriptions, a district and land lot number will define the property's boundaries.

A **lot and block (recorded plat) system** is often used to describe property in a subdivision and typically

■ starts with a **metes-and-bounds description** of a larger parcel;
■ divides it further into **block (subdivision)** and **lot (individual parcel) numbers**; and
■ references all data in a subdivision **plat map**, noting lot sizes, street names, and other required information that is
— **approved** by the governing body, and
— filed in **public records** of the county where the land is located.

Survey preparation includes both a **legal description** and a **survey sketch**. Legal description must be transcribed **exactly** as written to avoid future problems over incorrect boundaries.

Elevations must be measured if **air lots** above surface or **subsurface rights** are to be described and conveyed, with

■ distances noted as above or below **datum**, defined by U.S. Geological Survey (USGS) as **mean sea level at New York Harbor**, and making use of
— permanent **benchmarks** often based on a **local official datum**, and
— monuments marking surface measurements between points.

The most common units of **land measurement** include the

■ **mile** of 5,280 feet,
■ **acre** of 43,560 square feet (approximately 207 × 207 feet), and
■ **square mile** of 640 acres.

■ RELATED WEB SITE

U.S. Geological Survey: *www.usgs.gov*

CHAPTER 9 QUIZ

1. In describing real estate, the system that may use a property's physical features to determine boundaries and measurements is
   a. rectangular survey.
   b. metes and bounds.
   c. government survey.
   d. lot and block.

2. Which of the following terms does *NOT* involve the elevation of real estate?
   a. Benchmark
   b. Point of beginning
   c. Air lot
   d. Datum

3. Tom purchased 4.5 acres of land for $78,400. An adjoining owner wants to purchase a strip of Tom's land measuring 150 feet by 100 feet. What should this strip cost the adjoining owner if Tom sells it for the same price per square foot he originally paid for it?
   a. $3,000
   b. $6,000
   c. $7,800
   d. $9,400

4. Which of the following are *NOT* basic components of metes-and-bounds descriptions?
   a. Tangible and intangible monuments
   b. Base lines, principal meridians, and townships
   c. Degrees, minutes, and seconds
   d. Points of beginning

5. A property contains ten acres. How many lots of not less than 50 feet by 100 feet could be subdivided from the property if 26,000 square feet were dedicated for roads?
   a. 80
   b. 81
   c. 82
   d. 83

6. The *LEAST* specific method for identifying real property is
   a. rectangular survey.
   b. metes and bounds.
   c. street address.
   d. lot and block.

In Georgia

---

7. The squares or rectangles used in Georgia legal descriptions are known as
   a. townships and ranges.
   b. sections and meridians.
   c. landlots and districts.
   d. base lines and meridians.

8. The portions of counties used to identify property in the counties located in the headright area of the state are known as
   a. Georgia Militia Districts.
   b. sections.
   c. townships.
   d. ranges.

9. Which method(s) of legal descriptions are used in Georgia?
   a. Metes and bounds
   b. Rectangular (government) survey
   c. Lot and block
   d. Both a and c

181

Real Estate Taxes and Other Liens

When you have finished reading this chapter, you should be able to:

- **identify** the various classifications of liens.

- **describe** how real estate taxes are applied through assessments, tax liens, and the use of equalization ratios.

- **explain** how nontax liens, such as mechanics' liens, mortgage liens, and judgment liens are applied and enforced.

- **distinguish** the characteristics of voluntary, involuntary, statutory, and equitable liens.

- **define** the following *key terms:*

ad valorem tax	involuntary lien	special assessments
assessment	judgment	specific liens
attachment	lien	statutory lien
encumbrance	lis pendens	subordination agreements
equalization factor	Local Improvement	tax liens
equitable lien	District (LID)	tax sale
estate taxes	mechanic's lien	vendor's lien
general liens	mill	voluntary lien
general real estate tax	mortgage lien	
inheritance taxes	redemption	

■ LIENS

A **lien** is a charge or claim against a person's property, made to enforce the payment of money. Whenever someone borrows money, the lender generally requires some form of *security*. Security (also referred to as *collateral*) is something of value that the borrower promises to give the lender if the borrower fails to repay the debt. When the lender's security is in the form of real estate, the security is called a *lien*.

Liens are not limited to security for borrowed money (such as *mortgage liens*). Liens can be enforced against property by a government agency to recover taxes owed by the owner (**tax liens**). A lien can be used to compel the payment of an assessment or other special charge as well. A *mechanic's lien* represents an effort to recover payment for work performed. In all these ways, a person or an entity can use another's property to ensure payment for work performed, services rendered, or debts incurred. If a lien is not paid in the prescribed time, the lienholder may execute on the lien and this may force the sale of the property according to a particular state's statute.

> All liens are encumbrances, but not all encumbrances are liens.

A lien represents only an *interest* in ownership; it does not constitute actual ownership of the property. It is an encumbrance on the owner's title. An **encumbrance** is any charge or claim that attaches to real property and lessens its value or impairs its use. An encumbrance does not necessarily prevent the transfer or conveyance of the property, but because an encumbrance is *attached* to the property, it transfers or conveys along with it. Liens differ from other encumbrances, however, because they are financial or monetary in nature and attach to the property because of a debt. Other encumbrances may be physical in nature and may affect the owner's use of the property, such as easements or encroachments, which are discussed in Chapter 7.

Generally, a lienholder must institute a legal action to force the sale of the property or acquire title. The debt is then paid out of the proceeds.

> **Memory Tip**
> **Creating a Lien**
>
> The four ways of creating a lien may be remembered by the acronym **VISE:**
> 1. Voluntary
> 2. Involuntary
> 3. Statutory
> 4. Equitable

There are many different types of liens. (See Figure 10.1.) One way liens are classified is by *how* they are created. A **voluntary lien** is created *intentionally* by the property owner's action, such as when someone takes out a mortgage loan. An **involuntary lien**, on the other hand, is not a matter of choice: It is created by law. It may be either statutory or equitable. A **statutory lien** is created by statute. A real estate tax lien, for example, is an involuntary, statutory lien. It is created by statute without any action by the property owner. An **equitable lien** arises out of common law. It is created by a court based on fairness. A court-ordered judgment that requires a debtor to pay the balance on a delinquent charge account, for instance, would be an involuntary, equitable lien on the debtor's real estate.

Liens may be classified according to the type of property involved. **General liens** affect all the property, both real and personal, of a debtor. This includes judgments, estate and inheritance taxes, decedent's debts, corporate franchise taxes,

FIGURE 10.1

Types of Liens

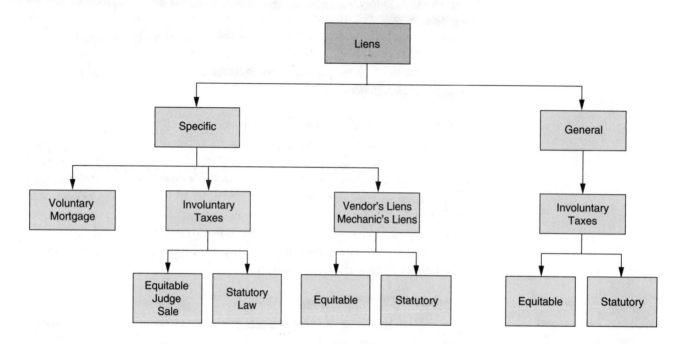

and Internal Revenue Service taxes. A lien on real estate differs from a lien on personal property. A lien attaches to real property *at the moment it is filed and recorded.* In contrast, a lien does not attach to personal property *until the personal property is seized.*

Specific liens are secured by specific property and affect only that particular property. Specific liens on real estate include vendor's liens, mechanics' liens, mortgage liens, real estate tax liens, and liens for special assessments and utilities. (Specific liens can also secure personal property, as when a lien is placed on a car to secure payment of a car loan.) A **vendor's lien** is a lien belonging to a vendor (or seller of a property) for the unpaid purchase price of the property, where the vendor or seller has not taken any other lien or security such as a mortgage beyond the personal obligation of the purchaser. Vendor's liens in real estate are uncommon and arise out of the use of owner financing to sell property.

In Georgia | In Georgia, a broker may place a lien against commercial property for unpaid commissions (O.C.G.A. 44-14-602).

Effects of Liens on Title

The existence of a lien does not necessarily prevent a property owner from conveying title to someone else. The lien might reduce the value of the real estate, however, because few buyers will take on the risk of a property that has a lien on it. Because the lien attaches to the property, not the property owner, a new owner could lose the property if the creditors take court action to enforce payment. Once properly established, a lien *runs with the land* and will bind all successive owners until the lien is paid and cleared.

IN PRACTICE   A buyer should insist on a title search before closing a real estate transaction so that any recorded liens are revealed. If liens are present, the buyer may decide to purchase at a lower price or at better terms, require the liens be paid, or refuse to purchase.

Priority of liens   *Priority of liens* refers to the order in which claims against the property will be paid off, that is, *satisfied*. In general, the rule for priority of liens is *first to record, first in right (priority)*. The priority of payment is from the date the liens are recorded in the public records of the county in which the property is located. A lien's priority is also in accordance with state law, which varies from state to state.

In Georgia

In Georgia, liens that are not regulated and fixed as to rank by title are ranked according to date of the liens, with the oldest having priority (O.C.G.A. 44-14-323).

There are some notable exceptions to this rule. For instance, real estate taxes and special assessments generally take priority over all other liens, regardless of the order in which the liens are recorded. This means that outstanding real estate taxes and special assessments are paid from the proceeds of a court-ordered sale *first*. For example, mechanics' liens (liens for performing labor or furnishing material in improving real property) would never take priority over tax and special assessment liens. The remainder of the proceeds is used to pay other outstanding liens *in the order of their priority*.

■ **FOR EXAMPLE**   Mottley Mansion is ordered sold by the court to satisfy Bob's debts. The property is subject to a $50,000 judgment lien, incurred as a result of a suit to recover a mechanic's lien for installing a new addition to the mansion. $295,000 in interest and principal remain to be paid on Mottley Mansion's mortgage. This year's unpaid real estate taxes amount to $5,000. The judgment lien was entered in the public record on February 7, 2006, and the mortgage lien was recorded January 22, 2004. If Mottley Mansion is sold at the tax sale for $375,000, the proceeds of the sale will be distributed in the following order:

1. $5,000 to the taxing bodies for this year's real estate taxes
2. $295,000 to the mortgage lender (the entire amount of the mortgage loan outstanding as of the date of sale)
3. $50,000 to the creditor named in the judgment lien
4. $25,000 to Bob (the proceeds remaining after paying the first three items)

However, if Mottley Mansion sold for $325,000, the proceeds would be distributed as follows:

1. $5,000 to the taxing bodies for this year's real estate taxes

2. $295,000 to the mortgage lender (the entire amount of the mortgage loan outstanding as of the date of sale)

3. $25,000 to the creditor named in the judgment lien

4. $0 to Bob

Although the creditor is not repaid in full, this outcome is considered fair for two reasons:

1. The creditor's interest arose later than the others, so the others' interests took priority.

2. The creditor knew (or should have known) about the creditors ahead of it when it extended credit to Bob, so it was aware (or should have been aware) of the risk involved.

Subordination agreements are written agreements between lienholders to change the priority of mortgage, judgment, and other liens. Under a subordination agreement, the holder of a superior or prior lien agrees to permit a junior lienholder's interest to move ahead of his or her lien. Priority and recording of liens are discussed in Chapter 16.

■ REAL ESTATE TAX LIENS

As discussed in Chapter 7, the ownership of real estate is subject to certain government powers. One of these is the right of state and local governments to impose (levy) taxes to pay for their functions. Because the location of real estate is permanently fixed, the government can levy taxes with a high degree of certainty that the taxes will be collected. The annual taxes levied on real estate usually have priority over previously recorded liens, so they may be enforced by a court-ordered sale.

There are two types of real estate taxes: general real estate taxes (also called *ad valorem taxes*) and special assessments or improvement taxes. Both are levied against specific parcels of property and automatically become liens on those properties.

General Tax (Ad Valorem Tax)

The **general real estate tax** is an **ad valorem tax.** *Ad valorem* is Latin for *according to value.* Ad valorem taxes are based on the *value of the property being taxed.* They are specific, involuntary, statutory liens. These are taxes levied by various government agencies and municipalities, including

- states;
- counties;
- cities, towns, boroughs, and villages;
- school districts (local elementary and high schools, publicly funded junior colleges, and community colleges);
- drainage districts;

- water districts;
- sanitary districts; and
- parks, forest preserves, and recreation districts.

Real estate property taxes are a favored source of revenue for local governments because real estate cannot be hidden and is relatively easy to value. Property taxes pay for a wide range of government services and programs.

Exemptions from general taxes   Most state laws exempt certain real estate from taxation. Such property must be used for tax-exempt purposes, as defined in the statutes. The most common exempt properties are owned by

- cities;
- various municipal organizations (such as schools, parks, and playgrounds);
- state and federal governments;
- religious and charitable organizations;
- hospitals; and
- educational institutions.

Many state laws also allow special exemptions to reduce real estate tax bills for certain property owners or land uses. For instance, senior citizens and veterans are frequently granted reductions in the assessed values of their homes. Some state and local governments offer real estate tax reductions to attract industries and sports franchises. Many states also offer tax reductions for agricultural land.

In Georgia   Properties in Georgia exempt from paying general real estate taxes include religious and charitable organizations and insurance companies that pay a tax upon premium income. For further information, see O.C.G.A. 48-7-25.

The homestead exemption is allowed in Georgia under O.C.G.A. 48-5-44 from all ad valorem taxes for state, county, and school purposes (but not for taxes levied by municipalities) and cannot exceed $2,000 of the value of the homestead.

In addition, there is a homestead exemption for individuals 62 or older with annual incomes not exceeding $30,000 (O.C.G.A. 48-5-47.1). For these purposes, a homestead means the primary residence and not more than five contiguous acres of land immediately surrounding the residence. In this situation, the homeowner is granted an exemption on the person's homestead from all ad valorem taxes in an amount equal to the amount of the assessed value of that homestead that exceeds the assessed value of the homestead for the immediately preceding taxable year. Note that the $30,000 income limit is a total for all those residing in the residence.

Assessment   Real estate is valued for tax purposes by county or township assessors or appraisers. This official valuation process is called **assessment.** A property's *assessed value* is generally based on the sales prices of comparable properties, although practices may vary. Land values may be assessed separately from buildings or other improvements, and different valuation methods may be used for different types of property. State laws may provide for property to be reassessed periodically.

In Georgia, the property tax assessment process focuses on the fair market value of the property. This is typically determined by the most recent sales price of the property. Then, by state mandate, the "assessed value" of the property is established as 40 percent of the market value.

Sometimes, a property owner may feel that an error was made in determining the assessed value of his or her property—usually that the assessment is too high in comparison with the assessments of neighboring properties. Such owners may present their objections to a local board of appeal or board of review. Protests or appeals regarding tax assessments may ultimately be taken to court.

Equalization   In some jurisdictions, when it is necessary to correct inequalities in statewide tax assessments, an **equalization factor** is used to achieve uniformity. An equalization factor may be applied to raise or lower assessments in a particular district or county. The assessed value of each property in the area is multiplied by the equalization factor, and the tax rate is then applied to the *equalized assessment*.

■ **FOR EXAMPLE**   The assessments in Laslo County are 20 percent lower than the average assessments throughout the rest of the state. This underassessment can be corrected by requiring the application of an equalization factor of 120 percent to each assessment in Laslo County. Therefore, a parcel of land assessed for tax purposes at $120,000 would be taxed on an equalized value of $144,000.

$$(\$120,000 \times 1.20 = \$144,000)$$

In Georgia, the State Board of Education is responsible for calculating the equalization rate for local school systems on an annual basis. State law (O.C.G.A. 20-2-165) specifies the process required for the equalization calculation.

Tax rates   The process of arriving at a real estate tax rate begins with the *adoption of a budget* by each taxing district. Each budget covers the financial requirements of the taxing body for the coming fiscal year. The fiscal year may be the January through December calendar year or some other 12-month period designated by statute. The budget must include an estimate of all expenditures for the year. In addition, the budget must indicate the amount of income expected from all fees, revenue sharing, and other sources. The net amount remaining to be raised from real estate taxes is then determined by the difference between these figures.

The next step is *appropriation*. Appropriation is the way a taxing body authorizes the expenditure of funds and provides for the sources of the funding. Appropriation generally involves the adoption of an ordinance or the passage of a law that states the specific terms of the proposed taxation.

The amount to be raised from the general real estate tax is then imposed on property owners through a *tax levy*. A *tax levy* is the formal action taken to impose the tax, usually a vote of the taxing district's governing body.

The *tax rate* for each taxing body is computed separately. To arrive at a tax rate, the total monies needed for the coming fiscal year are divided by the total assessments of all real estate located within the taxing body's jurisdiction.

■ **FOR EXAMPLE** A taxing district's budget indicates that $3.2 million must be raised from real estate tax revenues. The assessment roll (assessor's record) of all taxable real estate within the district equals $100 million. The tax rate is computed as follows:

$$\$3,200,000 \div \$100,000,000 = 0.032, \text{ or } 3.2\%$$

The *tax rate* may be stated in a number of ways. In many areas, it is expressed in mills. A **mill** is *1/1,000 of a dollar*, or *$0.001*. The tax rate may be expressed as a mill-per-dollar ratio, for instance, in dollars per hundred or in dollars per thousand. A tax rate of 0.032 or 3.2 percent could be expressed as 32 mills or $3.20 per $100 of assessed value or $32 per $1,000 of assessed value.

Tax bills A property owner's tax bill is computed by applying the tax rate to the assessed valuation of the property.

Generally, one tax bill that incorporates all real estate taxes levied by the various taxing districts is prepared for each property. In some areas, however, separate bills are prepared by each taxing body. Sometimes, the real estate taxing bodies may operate on different budget years so that the taxpayer receives separate bills for various taxes at different times during the year.

The calculation of the tax bill generally takes into account the various taxing bodies, any equalization factors used to achieve uniformity, and the tax rate that is then calculated on the equalized value.

■ **FOR EXAMPLE** If a property is assessed for tax purposes at $160,000, at a tax rate of 3 percent, or 30 mills, the tax will be $4,800: $160,000 × 0.03.

If an equalization factor is used, the computation with an equalization factor of 120 percent will be $5,760: $160,000 × 1.20 = $192,000, then $192,000 × 0.03 = $5,760.

The due dates for tax payments (also called the *penalty dates*) are set by statute. Taxes may be payable in two installments (semiannually), four installments (quarterly), or 12 installments (monthly). In some areas, taxes become due at the beginning of the current tax year and must be paid in advance (for example, the year 2006 taxes must be paid at the beginning of 2006). In other areas, taxes are payable during the year after the taxes are levied (2006 taxes are paid throughout 2006). In some states taxes are paid one year in reverse and you cannot pay any portion of the ad valorem taxes during the current year (for example, 2005 taxes could not be paid until the tax books open in 2006). And in still other areas, a partial payment is due in the year of the tax, with the balance due in the following year (2006 taxes are payable partly during 2006 and partly during 2007).

Some states offer discounts and monthly payment plans to encourage prompt payment of real estate taxes. Penalties, in the form of monthly interest charges on overdue taxes, are added to all taxes that are not paid when due. (See Table 10.1.)

Enforcement of tax liens   Real estate taxes must be valid to be enforceable. That means they must be levied properly, must be used for a legal purpose, and must be applied equitably, that is, fairly, to all property. Real estate taxes that have remained delinquent for the statutory period can be collected through a **tax sale.** While the methods and details of the various states' tax sale procedures differ substantially, the results are the same.

Generally, the delinquent taxpayer can redeem the property any time before the tax sale. The taxpayer exercises this *equitable right of redemption* by paying the delinquent taxes plus interest and charges (any court costs or attorney's fees). In those states that permit **redemption,** the bidding at a tax sale is based on the interest rate the defaulted taxpayer would have to pay to redeem the property, that is, the person who bids the lowest redemption interest rate (the one most beneficial for the taxpayer) becomes the successful bidder. That interest rate theoretically would be the easiest for the taxpayer to pay to redeem the property.

TABLE 10.1

Calculating Real Estate Taxes

Shown here is a summary example of calculating taxes on a home with a market value of $200,000 with a rate of 30 mill (doubled in the last row). Three different methods are used in calculating the taxes: (1) the rate per the assessed value; (2) an equalization factor to obtain assessments to fair market value; and (3) the tax rate or mill rate.

Calculating Tax Base	Tax Rate based on $100 increments, $3 per $100 (doubled in last row)	Tax Rate based on $1,000 increment or mill rate of 30, $30 per $1,000 (doubled in last row)
100 percent market value in the assessment.	$200,000 ÷ $100 × $3 = $6,000	$200,000 ÷ $1,000 × $30 = $6,000
Assessment is 20 percent lower than market value with a 125 percent equalization.	$160,000 × 1.25 ÷ $100 × $3 = $6,000	$160,000 × 1.25 ÷ $1,000 × $30 = $6,000
Assessed value is 50 percent of the market value. No equalization is used, but tax rate is doubled in this row.	$100,000 ÷ $100 × $6 = $6,000	$100,000 ÷ $1,000 × $60 = $6,000

A tax sale is usually held according to a published notice after a court has rendered a judgment for overdue taxes, penalties, and administrative costs, and has ordered that the property be sold. A tax sale is advertised in local newspapers and a notice of sale is posted on the affected property. The county sheriff or other public official then holds a public sale of the property. Because a specific amount of delinquent tax and penalty must be collected, the purchaser at a tax sale must pay at least that amount. A *certificate of sale* is usually given to the highest bidder when he or she pays the delinquent tax amount in cash. The certificate of sale gives the holder the right to take possession of the property.

In Georgia

In Georgia, a tax deed sale is advertised in a local paper that focuses on legal issues for the county. The auction sale price must cover at least the delinquent tax amount and all penalties, fees, and expenses associated with the delinquency. The final sales price is based on the competitive bidding process at the auction.

The holder of the certificate of sale may be required to wait for a while after the sale to receive the deed to the property. Some states grant a period of redemption *after the tax sale*. In this case, the defaulted owner (or the defaulted owner's creditors) may redeem the property by paying the amount collected at the tax sale plus interest and charges (including any taxes levied since the sale). This is known as a *statutory right of redemption*. (The right of redemption is discussed in Chapter 1.) If the property is not redeemed within the statutory period, the certificate holder can apply for a *tax deed (sheriff's deed)*. The quality of the title conveyed by a tax deed varies from state to state.

In Georgia

Georgia allows for the equitable right of redemption, but does not have a statutory right of redemption.

In some states, tax-delinquent land is sold or conveyed to the state or a taxing authority. At the expiration of the redemption period, the state or other taxing authority sells the property at auction and issues a tax deed to the highest bidder. The deed issued to the purchaser conveys good title because it is considered a conveyance by the state of state-owned land. In some jurisdictions, tax-delinquent land that is not sold at a tax sale due to lack of buyers is forfeited to the state. The state may then either use the land for its own purposes or sell it later.

Special Assessments and Local Improvement District Taxes

Special assessments are taxes levied on real estate to fund public improvements to the property. Property owners in the area of the improvements are required to pay for them because their properties benefit directly from the improvements. For example, the installation of paved streets, curbs, gutters, sidewalks, storm sewers, or street lighting increases the values of the affected properties. The owners, in effect, reimburse the levying authority. However, dollar-for-dollar increases in value are rarely the result.

Special assessments are always specific and statutory, but they can be either involuntary or voluntary liens. Improvements initiated by a public agency create involuntary liens. However, when property owners petition the local government to install a public improvement for which the owners agree to pay, such as a sidewalk or paved alley, the assessment lien is voluntary.

Whether the lien is voluntary or involuntary, each property in the improvement district is charged a prorated share of the total amount of the assessment. The share is determined either on a fractional basis (four houses may equally share the cost of one streetlight) or on a cost-per-front-foot basis (wider lots incur a greater cost than narrower lots for street paving and curb and sidewalk installation).

Special assessments are generally paid in equal annual installments over a period of years. The first installment is usually due during the year following the public authority's approval of the assessment. The first bill includes one year's interest on the property owner's share of the entire assessment. Subsequent bills include one year's interest on the unpaid balance. Property owners have the right to prepay any or all installments to avoid future interest charges.

For large scale improvement projects such as streets, sidewalks, and water or sewer construction, a **Local Improvement District (LID)** may be created. A LID is a specific geographical area formed by a group of property owners working together to fund needed capital improvements. LID taxation is simply a financing method available for the design and construction of public improvements.

Rules pertaining to the creation of LIDs vary according to state law, but typically a project is initiated by a petition of property owners or the city's manager of public works. The LID creation process allows for property owner objection, public hearings, and a city council vote for approval. If the LID is approved, the city undertakes all aspects of design, financing, and construction and sells bonds to provide funding for the project. Property owners in the LID repay bonds, plus interest, through special assessments over usually a 10-year to 20-year period.

In some parts of the country, strict subdivision regulations and LIDs have just about eliminated special assessments. Most items for which assessments have traditionally been levied are now required to be installed at the time of construction as a condition of a subdivision's approval.

Homeowner Tax Relief

The rapid increase in the value of homes in many parts of the United States has helped millions of homeowners. Many have cashed out part of this equity to pay for their children's college educations, buy investment property, or buy consumer goods and services. Others have sold out, moved to lower priced areas of the country, and invested their equity in a less expensive home and/or an investment property.

For those who cannot, or do not want to sell, there is a negative side to appreciation of values—increased property taxes and insurance. In some areas, the rapid pace of home appreciation is forcing many low-income and moderate-income homeowners to sell because they are unable to pay the higher taxes. To help alleviate this problem, several states have passed laws allowing homeowners to pay lower taxes than owners of other types of real estate. Some states, in an effort to avoid increased home foreclosures, subsidize low-income homeowners' tax bills.

■ OTHER LIENS ON REAL PROPERTY

In addition to real estate tax and special assessment liens, a variety of other liens may be charged against real property.

Mortgage Liens (Deed of Trust Liens)

A **mortgage lien,** or, as used in some states, a *deed of trust lien*, is a voluntary lien on real estate given to a lender by a borrower as security for a real estate loan. It becomes a lien on real property when the lender records the documents in the county where the property is located. Lenders generally require a preferred lien, referred to as a *first mortgage lien*. This means that no other liens against the property (aside from real estate taxes) would take priority over the mortgage lien. Subsequent liens are referred to as *junior liens*. (Mortgages and deeds of trust are discussed in detail in Chapter 15.)

In Georgia

Georgia uses a lien document called the security deed. It replaces the deed of trust used in some states and is discussed further in Chapter 14.

Mechanic's Liens

A **mechanic's lien** is a specific, involuntary lien that gives security to persons or companies that perform labor or furnish material to improve real property. A mechanic's lien is available to contractors, subcontractors, architects, equipment lessors, surveyors, laborers, and other providers. This type of lien is filed when the owner has not fully paid for the work or when the general contractor has been compensated but has not paid the subcontractors or suppliers of materials. However, statutes in some states prohibit subcontractors from placing liens directly on certain types of property, such as owner-occupied residences. While laws regarding mechanic's liens vary from state to state, there are many similarities.

To be entitled to a mechanic's lien, the person who did the work must have had a contract (express or implied) with the owner or the owner's authorized representative, such as a general contractor. A person claiming a mechanic's lien must file a notice of lien in the public record of the county where the property is located within a certain time after the work has been completed.

In Georgia

According to Georgia's mechanics' lien statute (O.C.G.A. 44-14-361), mechanics' liens are inferior to

■ liens for taxes;

- general and special liens of laborers;
- general liens of landlords for rent when a distress warrant is issued;
- claims for purchase money due persons who have only given bonds for titles; and
- general liens when actual notice has been communicated before the work was done.

Except for the previously listed liens, mechanics' liens are superior to all other liens. The aggregate amount of a mechanic's lien cannot exceed the contract price of improvements made or services rendered.

If improvements that were not ordered by the property owner have commenced, the property owner should execute a document called a *notice of nonresponsibility* to relieve himself or herself from possible mechanics' liens. By posting this notice in some conspicuous place on the property and recording a verified copy of it in the public record, the owner gives notice that he or she is not responsible for the work done. This may prevent the filing of mechanics' liens on the property.

IN PRACTICE In most states, a mechanic's lien takes priority from the time it attaches. Nonetheless, a claimant's notice of lien will not be filed in the public record until some time after that. A prospective purchaser of property that has been recently constructed, altered, or repaired should be cautious about possible unrecorded mechanics' liens against the property.

Judgments

A **judgment** is a decree issued by a court. When the decree establishes the amount a debtor owes and provides for money to be awarded, it is referred to as a *money judgment*. Judgments most often result from damages caused to one person by another person through wrongful act, breach of contract, or nonpayment of a debt.

A judgment is a general, involuntary, equitable lien on both real and personal property owned by the debtor. A judgment is not the same as a mortgage because no specific parcel of real estate was given as security at the time the debt was created. A lien usually covers only property located within the county in which the judgment is issued. As a result, a notice of the lien must be filed in any county to which a creditor wishes to extend the lien coverage. Judgments expire after a number of years, but in some states can be renewed indefinitely by the judgment creditor.

To enforce a judgment, the creditor must obtain a *writ of execution* from the court. A writ of execution directs the sheriff to seize and sell as much of the debtor's property as is necessary to pay both the debt and the expenses of the sale. A judgment does not become a lien against the personal property of a debtor until the creditor orders the sheriff to levy on the property and the levy is actually made.

A judgment lien's priority is established by one or a combination of the following (as provided by state law):

■ Date the judgment was entered by the court
■ Date the judgment was filed in the recorder's office
■ Date a writ of execution was issued

When real property is sold to satisfy a debt, the debtor should demand a legal document known as a *satisfaction of judgment* (or *satisfaction piece*), or, in those states using trust deeds, a deed of reconveyance, which must be filed with either the clerk of the court or, in some states, the recorder of deeds. Filing the satisfaction of judgment clears the record of the lien.

Lis pendens   There is often a considerable delay between the time a lawsuit is filed and the time final judgment is rendered. When any suit is filed that affects title to real estate, a special notice, known as a **lis pendens** (Latin for *litigation pending*), is recorded. A lis pendens is not itself a lien, but rather *notice of a possible future lien*. Recording a lis pendens notifies prospective purchasers and lenders that there is a potential claim against the property. It also establishes a priority for the later lien: The lien is backdated to the recording date of the lis pendens.

Attachments   To prevent a debtor from conveying title to such previously unsecured real estate while a court suit is being decided, a creditor may seek a writ of **attachment.** A writ of attachment is a court order against the property of another person that directs the sheriff or other officer of the court to seize or take control of a property. By this writ, the court retains custody of the property until the suit concludes. Most attachments arise from an action for payment of an unsecured debt. For example, a plaintiff in a lawsuit may attach a defendant's property to gain a security interest in order to foreclose the property, or to prevent the defendant from disposing of the property that may be needed to pay a judgment.

The writ of attachment is filed in the public records and creates an involuntary, specific lien. The plaintiff's lien priority may date to the filing of the lawsuit or to the filing of the judgment. Because the creditor may fail to gain a judgment, the creditor must post a *surety* bond or deposit with the court. The bond must be sufficient to cover any possible loss or damage the debtor may suffer while the court has custody of the property. In the event the judgment is not awarded to the creditor, the debtor will be reimbursed from the bond.

Estate and Inheritance Liens

Federal **estate taxes** and state **inheritance taxes** (as well as the debts of decedents) are general, statutory, involuntary liens that encumber a deceased person's real and personal property. These are normally paid or cleared in probate court proceedings. Probate and issues of inheritance are discussed in Chapter 12.

Liens for Municipal Utilities

Municipalities often have the right to impose a specific, equitable, involuntary lien on the property of an owner who refuses to pay bills for municipal utility services.

Bail Bond Lien

A real estate owner who is charged with a crime for which he or she must face trial may post bail in the form of real estate rather than cash. The execution and recording of such a bail bond creates a specific, statutory, voluntary lien against the owner's real estate. If the accused fails to appear in court, the lien may be enforced by the sheriff or another court officer.

Corporation Franchise Tax Lien

State governments generally levy a corporation franchise tax on corporations as a condition of allowing them to do business in the state. Such a tax is a general, statutory, involuntary lien on all real and personal property owned by the corporation.

IRS Tax Lien

A federal tax lien, or *Internal Revenue Service (IRS) tax lien*, results from a person's failure to pay any portion of federal taxes, such as income and withholding taxes. A federal tax lien is a general, statutory, involuntary lien on all real and personal property held by the delinquent taxpayer. Its priority, however, is based on the date of filing or recording; it does not supersede previously recorded liens. The same rules apply to most state income tax liens.

■ KEY POINT REVIEW

A **lien** is a claim of a creditor or taxing authority against the **real property** of a debtor that is used as **security** to ensure repayment of the debt. Note the following:

■ A lien is not an ownership interest in real estate but is an **encumbrance** that transfers or conveys with it (**runs with the land**) and lessens its value or impairs its use because it binds all successive owners until paid and cleared.

■ If debtor **defaults** in payment of debt, **lienholder** must bring legal action to
— force the **sale** of the property, or
— **acquire title.**

Creation of a lien may be **VISE,** an acronym for the following:

■ **Voluntary** if it is created by action of the property owner, such as a mortgage

■ **Involuntary** if it is created without the property owner's express permission

- **S**tatutory if it is created by statute
- **E**quitable if it is created by a court based on the common law

A lien is either of the following:

- **General**—affects all of debtor's property, both real and personal. General liens include judgments, estate and inheritance taxes, decedent's debts, corporate franchise taxes, and Internal Revenue Service taxes.
- **Specific**—affects only identified property. Specific liens include vendor's lien, mechanic's lien, mortgage lien, real estate tax lien, liens for special assessments and utilities.

`In Georgia`   In Georgia, specific liens also include liens against commercial property for unpaid commissions.

Priority of liens determines the order in which claims will be **satisfied** (paid off):

- Generally (and in Georgia), **first to record** is **first in right**.
- Real estate taxes and special assessments take **priority** over all other liens.
- A **subordination agreement** between lienholders can be used to change order of priority.

Real estate taxes include the following:

- **Ad valorem taxes**, based on value of property taxed, are
  — specific, involuntary, statutory liens; and
  — levied by states, counties, municipalities, school districts, utility districts, parks and recreation districts, and others.
- **Exemptions** may be available for schools, parks, hospitals, or property owned by municipal, state, or federal governments, or religious or charitable organizations.

  `In Georgia`
  — In Georgia, homestead exemptions are available from all ad valorem taxes for state, county, and schools, but not for taxes levied by municipalities. Individuals 62 or older with annual incomes not exceeding $30,000 have homestead exemptions.
- **Reductions** in tax may be made for certain homeowners including low-income homeowners, senior citizens, and veterans, or for property owned by industries, sports franchises, or farmers.
- Property **assessments** (valuations) are conducted by county or township tax assessors or appraisers.
  — **Assessed value** is generally based on sales prices of comparable properties. Land value may be assessed separately from building value and improvements, and different valuation methods may be used for different types of property.

  `In Georgia`
  — In Georgia, by state mandate, a property's assessed value is established as 40 percent of the market value.
  — **Equalization factor** may be applied to correct inequalities in statewide tax assessments. The State Board of Education of Georgia is responsible for calculating the equalization factor.
- **Tax rates** for each taxing body are computed separately (and may be expressed in mills [one mill is 1/1,000 of a dollar, or $0.001]). Mills may be shown as dollars per hundred or thousand dollars of assessed value.

Enforcement of tax liens is as follows:

- **Delinquent** taxes can be collected through a **tax sale**.
- Statutory **notice** requirements must be followed before tax sale.
- **Taxpayer** usually has **equitable right of redemption** any time before tax sale.
- **Bidder** at tax sale who bids lowest **redemption interest rate** receives **certificate of sale**.

In Georgia
- Some states (but not Georgia) allow **statutory right of redemption** following tax sale.
- If **no bidders** at tax sale, property may be forfeited to the state.

Levied on property that benefits from public improvements, **special assessments**

- are always specific and statutory,
- may be voluntary or involuntary, and
- are usually paid in annual installments over a period of years.

A **mortgage** or **deed of trust lien** is a voluntary lien given to a lender by a borrower as security for real estate loan.

In Georgia
Georgia uses a lien document called the security deed. The lien takes effect when the lender records documents in the county where the property located.

- A **first mortgage lien** on a property, when recorded, has **priority** over other liens (except for tax liens); subsequent liens are **junior liens**.

A **mechanic's lien** is a specific, involuntary lien that gives security to persons or companies that perform labor or furnish material to improve real property.

A mechanic's lien is **filed** when an **owner** has not fully paid for work, or the **general contractor** has been compensated but has not paid subcontractors or suppliers of materials.

- In some states, including Georgia, mechanics' liens have priority over some previously recorded liens such as mortgages.

A **judgment**, a decree issued by a court, is a general, involuntary, equitable lien on both real and personal property owned by a debtor that must be filed in **every county** in which the judgment debtor owns property.

- While lawsuit is pending,
  — **lis pendens** can be filed to give notice of possible future lien and establish priority of claimant, and
  — **writ of attachment** can be sought from the court to authorize the sheriff to seize the property that the debtor may attempt to convey.

Other liens include:

- **Estate and inheritance tax liens**
- **Lien for municipal utilities**
- **Corporation franchise tax lien**
- **IRS tax lien**

■ RELATED WEB SITE

U.S. Department of Internal Revenue Service: *www.irs.gov*

CHAPTER 10 QUIZ

1. Which of the following liens affects all real and personal property of a debtor?
   a. Specific
   b. Voluntary
   c. Involuntary
   d. General

2. Priority of liens refers to which of the following?
   a. Order in which a debtor assumes responsibility for payment of obligations
   b. Order in which liens will be paid if property is sold to satisfy a debt
   c. Dates liens are filed for record
   d. Fact that specific liens have greater priority than general liens

3. A lien on real estate made to secure payment for a specific municipal improvement project is which of the following?
   a. Mechanic's lien
   b. Special assessment
   c. Ad valorem
   d. Utility lien

4. Which of the following would be classified as a general lien?
   a. Mechanic's lien
   b. Bail bond lien
   c. Judgment
   d. Real estate taxes

5. Which of the following liens usually would be given highest priority in disbursing funds from a foreclosure sale?
   a. Mortgage dated last year
   b. Real estate taxes due
   c. Mechanic's lien for work started before the mortgage was made
   d. Judgment rendered the day before foreclosure

6. A specific parcel of real estate has a market value of $160,000 and is assessed for tax purposes at 75 percent of market value. The tax rate for the county in which the property is located is 40 mills. The tax bill will be
   a. $6,400.
   b. $5,000.
   c. $5,200.
   d. $4,800.

7. Which of the following taxes would target homeowners in particular?
   a. Personal property tax
   b. Sales tax
   c. Real property tax
   d. Luxury tax

8. A mechanic's lien claim arises when a contractor has performed work or provided material to improve a parcel of real estate on the owner's order and the work has not been paid for. Such a contractor has a right to
   a. tear out his or her work.
   b. record a notice of the lien.
   c. record a notice of the lien and file a court suit within the time required by state law.
   d. have personal property of the owner sold to satisfy the lien.

9. What is the annual real estate tax on a property valued at $135,000 and assessed for tax purposes at $47,250, with an equalization factor of 125 percent, when the tax rate is 25 mills?
   a. $945
   b. $1,181
   c. $1,418
   d. $1,477

10. Which of the following is a voluntary, specific lien?
    a. IRS tax lien
    b. Mechanic's lien
    c. Mortgage lien
    d. Seller's lien

11. A seller sold a buyer a parcel of real estate. Title has passed, but to date the buyer has not paid the purchase price in full, as originally agreed on. If the seller wants to force payment, which of the following remedies would the seller be entitled to seek?

    a. Attachment
    b. Mechanic's lien
    c. Lis pendens
    d. Judgment

12. A general contractor recently filed suit against a homeowner for nonpayment. The contractor now learns that the homeowner has listed the property for sale with a real estate broker. In this situation, which of the following will the contractor's attorney use to protect the contractor's interest?

    a. Seller's lien
    b. Buyer's lien
    c. Assessment
    d. Lis pendens

13. Which of the following statements MOST accurately describes special assessment liens?

    a. They are general liens.
    b. They are paid on a monthly basis.
    c. They take priority over mechanics' liens.
    d. They cannot be prepaid in full without penalty.

14. Which of the following creates a lien on real estate?

    a. Easement running with the land
    b. Unpaid mortgage loan
    c. License
    d. Encroachment

15. Which of the following statements is TRUE of both a mortgage lien and a judgment lien?

    a. They must be entered by the court.
    b. They involve a debtor-creditor relationship.
    c. They are general liens.
    d. They are involuntary liens.

16. The right of a defaulted taxpayer to recover property before its sale for unpaid taxes is the

    a. statutory right of reinstatement.
    b. equitable right of appeal.
    c. statutory right of assessment.
    d. equitable right of redemption.

17. Which of the following is a specific, involuntary, statutory lien?

    a. Real estate tax lien
    b. Income tax lien
    c. Estate tax lien
    d. Judgment lien

18. General real estate taxes levied for the operation of the government are called

    a. assessment taxes.
    b. ad valorem taxes.
    c. special taxes.
    d. improvement taxes.

In Georgia

19. In Georgia, which legal document pledges the property as collateral for the lender to receive a return of funds at a foreclosure sale?

    a. Deed of trust
    b. Mortgage
    c. Security deed
    d. Tax deed

20. All of the following exist in Georgia EXCEPT

    a. equitable right of redemption.
    b. statutory right of redemption.
    c. special assessments.
    d. ad valorem taxation.

11 CHAPTER

Real Estate Contracts

When you have finished reading this chapter, you should be able to:

- ■ **identify** the requirements for a valid contract.

- ■ **describe** the various types of contracts used in the real estate business.

- ■ **explain** how contracts may be discharged.

- ■ **distinguish** among bilateral and unilateral, executed and executory, and valid, void, and voidable contracts.

- ■ **define** the following *key terms:*

assignment	executed contract	reality of consent
bilateral contract	executory contract	rescission
breach of contract	express contract	statute of frauds
consideration	implied contract	suit for specific
contingencies	installment contract	performance
contract	land contract	time is of the essence
counteroffer	lease	unenforceable contract
disclosure	liquidated damages	unilateral contract
earnest money	novation	valid
equitable title	offer and acceptance	void
escrow contract	option	voidable

■ CONTRACT LAW

A **contract** is a voluntary agreement or promise between legally competent parties, supported by legal consideration, to perform (or refrain from performing) some legal act. That definition may be easier to understand if we consider its various parts separately.

A contract must be

- *voluntary*—no one may be forced into a contract;
- *an agreement or a promise*—a contract is essentially a promise or set of promises;
- made by *legally competent parties*—the parties must be viewed by the law as capable of making a legally binding promise;
- supported by *legal consideration*—a contract must be supported by some valuable thing that induces a party to enter into the contract and that must be legally sufficient to support a contract; and
- about a *legal act*—no one may make a legal contract to do something illegal.

> A **contract** is a voluntary, legally enforceable promise between two competent parties to *perform* (or *not perform*) some legal act in exchange for consideration.

Brokers and salespersons use many types of contracts and agreements to carry out their responsibilities to sellers, buyers, and the general public. The general body of law that governs such agreements is known as *contract law.*

IN PRACTICE   Real estate professionals are advised to use preprinted and preapproved forms provided by their associations or employing brokers. Also, remember that practitioners should be careful to not practice law without a license. Both the buyer and the seller have the option of selecting their own attorney.

Express and Implied Contracts

A contract may be *express* or *implied,* depending on how it is created. An **express contract** exists when the parties state the terms and show their intentions in *words.* An express contract may be either oral or written. The majority of real estate contracts are express contracts; they have been reduced to writing. Under the **statute of frauds,** certain types of contracts must be in writing to be enforceable in a court of law. (*Enforceable* means that the parties may be forced to comply with the contract's terms and conditions.) In an **implied contract,** the agreement of the parties is demonstrated by their *acts and conduct.*

■ FOR EXAMPLE   Fritz signs a contract to purchase Daisy's house for $450,000. Daisy signs the contract and agrees. This is an express contract.

The parties in a real estate transaction come to terms orally over lunch, and one party asks the other to send an e-mail confirming the terms of the agreement. If the other party agrees and sends an e-mail, then it can probably be determined that the parties have an implied agreement to conduct their real estate transaction electronically rather than in writing.

Bilateral and Unilateral Contracts

Contracts may be classified as either bilateral or unilateral. In a **bilateral contract,** both parties promise to do something; one promise is given in exchange for another. A listing agreement is a bilateral contract in which the broker promises to use his or her skills to produce a buyer and the seller promises to pay a commission or brokerage fee. A real estate sales contract is a bilateral contract because the seller promises to sell a parcel of real estate and convey title to the property to the buyer, who promises to pay a certain sum of money for the property. An exclusive-right-to-sell listing contract is a bilateral contract.

Bi means *two*—a **bilateral** contract must have two promises.

Uni means *one*—a **unilateral** contract has only one promise.

A **unilateral contract,** on the other hand, is a one-sided agreement. One party makes a promise to induce a second party to do something. The second party is not legally obligated to act. However, if the second party does comply, the first party is obligated to keep the promise. For instance, a law enforcement agency might offer a monetary payment to anyone who can aid in the capture of a criminal. Only if someone *does* aid in the capture is the reward paid. An option contract, which will be discussed later, is another example of a unilateral contract.

■ **FOR EXAMPLE**   Tim, a homeowner, offers to pay a commission to any broker who finds a buyer for his home. No broker is obliged to find a buyer, and Tim will be obligated to pay a commission only if a broker finds a buyer. This is a unilateral contract.

A real estate sales contract is a bilateral contract. In the contract, the buyer usually promises to pay money for the property and the seller promises to transfer title at closing.

Executed and Executory Contracts

A contract may be classified as either executed or executory, depending on whether the agreement is performed. An **executed contract** is one in which all parties have fulfilled their promises: The contract has been performed. *Executed* should not be confused with the word *execute*, which refers to the signing of a contract. An **executory contract** exists when one or both parties still have an act to perform. A sales contract is an executory contract from the time it is signed until closing: Ownership has not yet changed hands, and the seller has not received the sales price. At closing, the sales contract is executed.

Table 11.1 highlights the issues involved in the formation of a contract, which are talked about in detail in this chapter.

Essential Elements of a Valid Contract

A contract must meet certain minimum requirements to be considered legally valid. The following are the basic essential elements of a contract.

TABLE   11.1

Contract Formation Issues

There are preformation, formation, and postformation issues involved in a contract.

Preformation	Formation	Postformation
Essential Elements	Classification	Discharge
Offer, Acceptance, Consideration, Legal Purpose, Legal Capacity	Valid, Void, Voidable, Enforceable, Unenforceable, Express, Implied, Unilateral, Bilateral, Executory, Executed	Performance, Breach, Remedies (Damages, Specific Performance, Rescission)

Offer and acceptance   There must be an offer by one party that is accepted by the other. The person who makes the offer is the *offeror*. The person to whom an offer is made is the *offeree*. This requirement is also called *mutual assent*. It means that there must be a *meeting of the minds*, that is, there must be complete agreement between the parties about the purpose and terms of the contract. Courts look to the *objective intent of the parties* to determine whether they intended to enter into a binding agreement. In cases where the statute of frauds applies, the **offer and acceptance** must be in writing. The wording of the contract must express all the agreed-on terms and must be clearly understood by the parties.

An *offer* is a promise made by one party, requesting something in exchange for that promise. The offer is made with the intention that the offeror will be bound to the terms if the offer is accepted. The terms of the offer must be definite and specific and must be communicated to the offeree.

An *acceptance* is a promise by the offeree to be bound by the *exact* terms proposed by the offeror. The acceptance must be communicated to the offeror. Proposing any deviation from the terms of the offer constitutes a rejection of the original offer and becomes a new offer. This is known as a **counteroffer.** The counteroffer must be accepted by the original offering party for a contract to exist.

Besides being terminated by a counteroffer, an offer may be terminated by the offeree's outright rejection of it. Alternatively, an offeree may fail to accept the offer before it expires. The offeror may revoke the offer at any time before acceptance. This *revocation* must be communicated to the offeree by the offeror, either directly or through the parties' agents. The offer is also revoked if the offeree learns of the revocation and observes the offeror acting in a manner that indicates that the offer no longer exists.

Elements of a Contract

- Offer and acceptance
- Consideration
- Legally competent parties
- Consent
- Legal purpose

Consideration   The contract must be based on consideration. **Consideration** is something of legal value offered by one party and accepted by another as an inducement to perform or to refrain from performing some act. There must be a definite statement of consideration in a contract to show that something of value was given in exchange for the promise. Consideration is some interest or benefit accruing to one party, or some loss or responsibility by the other party.

Consideration must be *good and valuable* between the parties. The courts do not inquire into the adequacy of consideration. Adequate consideration ranges from as little as a promise of *love and affection* to a substantial sum of money. Anything that has been bargained for and exchanged is legally sufficient to satisfy the requirement for consideration. The only requirements are that the parties agree and that no undue influence or fraud has occurred.

Reality of consent   A contract that complies with all of the basic requirements may still be either void or voidable. This is because of the doctrine of **reality of consent.** A contract must be entered into as the free and voluntary act of each party. Each party must be able to make a prudent and knowledgeable decision without undue influence. A mistake, misrepresentation, fraud, undue influence, or duress would deprive a person of that ability. If any of these circumstances is present, the contract is voidable by the injured party. If the other party were to sue for breach, the injured party could use lack of voluntary assent as a defense.

Legal purpose   A contract must be for a legal purpose, that is, even with all the other elements (consent, competent parties, consideration, and offer and acceptance), if the contract is to do something illegal, it is not a valid contract. So when an adult entertainment center enters into a contract to buy property in an area zoned for solely residential purposes, the contract is invalid because of its illegal purpose.

Legally competent parties   All parties to the contract must have *legal capacity*, that is, they must be of legal age and have enough mental capacity to understand the nature or consequences of their actions in the contract. In most states, including Georgia, 18 is the age of contractual capacity. Under state law, an imprisoned felon or certain mentally ill persons may be legally incompetent to enter into a contract.

Validity of contracts   A contract can be described as valid, void, voidable, or unenforceable, depending on the circumstances.

A contract is **valid** when it meets all the essential elements that make it legally sufficient, or enforceable.

A contract is **void** when it has no legal force or effect because it lacks some or all of the essential elements of a contract. A contract that is void was never a contract in the eyes of the law. For example, the use of a forged name in a listing contract would make the contract void.

A contract that is **voidable** appears on the surface to be valid but may be rescinded or disaffirmed by one or both parties based on some legal principle. A voidable contract is considered by the courts to be valid if the party who has the option to disaffirm the agreement does not do so within a period of time prescribed by state law. A contract with a minor, for instance, is usually voidable. It is voidable because minors are generally permitted to *disaffirm* real estate contracts at any time while under age and for a certain period of time after reaching majority age.

A Contract May Be

- **valid**—has all legal elements: Fully enforceable;
- **void**—lacks one or all elements: No legal force or effect;
- **voidable**—has all legal elements: May be rescinded or disaffirmed; or
- **unenforceable**—has all legal elements: enforceable only between the parties.

By the same token, a minor may *affirm* a contract entered into when he or she was underage, in effect validating the contract after the fact. A contract entered into by a mentally ill person is usually voidable during the mental illness and for a reasonable period after the person is cured. On the other hand, a contract made by a person who has been adjudicated insane (that is, found to be insane by a court) is void on the theory that the judgment is a matter of public record.

IN PRACTICE   Mental capacity to enter into a contract is not the same as medical sanity. The test is whether the individual in question is capable of understanding what he or she is doing. A party may suffer from a mental illness but have a clear understanding of the significance of his or her actions. This is a thorny legal and psychological question that requires consultation with experts.

An **unenforceable contract** also seems on the surface to be valid; however, neither party can sue the other to force performance. For example, an oral agreement for the sale of a parcel of real estate would be unenforceable. Because the statute of frauds requires that real estate sales contracts be in writing, the defaulting party could not be taken to court and forced to perform. There is, however, a distinction between a suit to force performance and a suit for damages, which is permissible in an oral agreement. An unenforceable contract is said to be *valid as between the parties*. This means that once the agreement is fully executed and both parties are satisfied, neither has reason to initiate a lawsuit to force performance.

■ DISCHARGE OF CONTRACTS

A contract is *discharged* when the agreement is terminated. Obviously, the most desirable case is when a contract terminates because it has been completely performed, with all its terms carried out. However, a contract may be terminated for other reasons, such as a party's breach or default.

Performance of a Contract

Each party has certain rights and duties to fulfill. The question of *when* a contract must be performed is an important factor. Many contracts call for a specific time by which the agreed-on acts must be completely performed. In addition, some contracts provide that **"time is of the essence."** *Time is of the essence* means that the contract must be performed within the time limit specified. A party who fails to perform on time is liable for breach of contract.

IN PRACTICE   When a *time is of the essence* clause is used in a contract, the parties should consult with an attorney. The ramifications of a breach of a contract where *time is of the essence* is used can be significant. For example, a buyer could lose escrow funds, or the seller could lose the right to enforce the contract.

When a contract does not specify a date for performance, the acts it requires should be performed within a reasonable time. The interpretation of what constitutes a reasonable time depends on the situation. Generally, unless the parties agree otherwise, if the act can be done immediately, it should be performed immediately. Courts have sometimes declared contracts to be invalid because they did not contain a time or date for performance.

Assignment

Assignment is a transfer of rights or duties under a contract. Normally, rights may be assigned to a third party (called the *assignee*) unless the contract forbids it. Obligations may also be assigned (or *delegated*), but the original party remains primarily liable unless specifically released. An assignment may be made without the consent of the other party unless the contract includes a clause that permits or forbids assignment.

■ **FOR EXAMPLE**   Bill is widowed and in his 80s, looking to move closer to his children. Bill finds a house he wants to purchase, but because of a prescheduled surgery, he cannot be there for the closing. Bill assigns his contract rights to his son, Andrew, so that the property may be purchased in a real estate closing transaction without Bill being present or signing documents.

Novation

A contract may be performed by **novation,** that is, the substitution of a new contract in place of the original. The new agreement may be between the same parties, or a new party may be substituted for either (this is *novation of the parties*). The parties' intent must be to discharge the old obligation. For instance, when a real estate purchaser assumes the seller's existing mortgage loan, the lender may choose to release the seller and substitute the buyer as the party primarily liable for the mortgage debt. Or when there are many changes on a real estate contract and it is faxed several times, it may no longer be legible. Novation occurs when a new, clear contract with all of the accepted changes is signed by all of the parties. When a contract is performed by novation, both parties must consent to novation.

Breach of Contract

A contract may be terminated if it is breached by one of the parties. A **breach of contract** is a violation of any of the terms or conditions of a contract without legal excuse. For instance, a seller who fails to deliver title to the buyer breaches a sales contract. The breaching or defaulting party assumes certain burdens, and the nondefaulting party has certain remedies.

Assignment = substitution of parties
Novation = substitution of contracts

If the seller breaches a real estate sales contract, the buyer may sue for *specific performance* unless the contract specifically states otherwise. In a **suit for specific performance,** the buyer asks the court to force the seller to go through with the sale and convey the property as previously agreed. The buyer may choose to sue for *damages*, however, in which case he or she asks that the seller pay for any costs and hardships suffered by the buyer as a result of the seller's breach.

If the buyer defaults, the seller can sue for damages or sue for the purchase price. A suit for the purchase price is essentially a suit for specific performance: The seller tenders the deed and asks that the buyer be compelled to pay the agreed price.

The contract may limit the remedies available to the parties, however. A *liquidated damages* clause, in a real estate purchase contract, specifies the amount of money to which the seller is entitled if the buyer breaches the contract. In some real estate purchase contracts, the earnest money deposit is used as liquidated damages.

Statute of limitations   The law of every state limits the time within which parties to a contract may bring legal suit to enforce their rights. The *statute of limitations* varies for different legal actions, and any rights not enforced within the applicable time period are lost.

In Georgia   In Georgia, the statute of limitations for contracts not under seal is six years.

Other reasons for termination   Contracts may also be discharged or terminated when any of the following occurs:

- *Partial performance* of the terms, along with a written acceptance by the other party. For instance, if the parties agree that the work performed is *close enough* to complete, they can agree that the contract is discharged even if some minor elements remain unperformed.
- *Substantial performance,* in which one party has substantially performed on the contract but does not complete all the details exactly as the contract requires. (Such performance may be enough to force payment, with certain adjustments for any damages suffered by the other party.) For instance, where a newly constructed addition to a home is finished except for polishing the brass doorknobs, the contractor is entitled to the final payment.
- *Impossibility of performance,* in which an act required by the contract cannot be legally accomplished.
- *Mutual agreement* of the parties to cancel.
- *Operation of law*—such as in the voiding of a contract by a minor—as a result of fraud, due to the expiration of the statute of limitations, or because a contract was altered without the written consent of all parties involved.
- *Rescission*—one party may cancel or terminate the contract as if it had never been made. Cancellation terminates a contract without a return to the original position. **Rescission,** however, returns the parties to their original positions before the contract, so any monies that have been exchanged must be returned. Rescission is normally a contractual remedy for a breach, but a contract may also be rescinded by the mutual agreement of the parties.

■ CONTRACTS USED IN THE REAL ESTATE BUSINESS

The written agreements most commonly used by brokers and salespersons are

■ listing agreements and buyer agency agreements,
■ real estate sales contracts,
■ options,
■ land contracts or contracts for deed, and
■ leases and escrow agreements.

Many states have specific guidelines for when and how real estate licensees may prepare contracts for their clients and customers. These guidelines are created by state real estate officials, court decisions, or statutes. *A real estate licensee who is not a licensed attorney may not practice law.* The practice of law includes preparing legal documents, such as deeds and mortgages, and offering advice on legal matters. A broker or salesperson, however, may be permitted to fill in the blanks on certain approved preprinted documents, such as sales contracts and leases, as directed by the client. No separate fee may be charged for completing the forms.

Contract forms Because so many real estate transactions are very similar in nature, preprinted forms are available for most kinds of contracts. The use of preprinted forms raises three problems: (1) what to write in the blanks, (2) what words and phrases should be ruled out by drawing lines through them because they don't apply, and (3) what additional clauses or agreements (called *addenda* or *exhibits* in Georgia) should be added. All changes and additions are usually initialed in the margin or on the rider by both parties when a contract is signed.

IN PRACTICE It is essential that both parties to a contract understand exactly what they are agreeing to. Poorly drafted documents, especially those containing extensive legal language, may be subject to various interpretations and lead to litigation. The parties to a real estate transaction should be advised to have sales contracts and other legal documents examined by their lawyers before they sign them to ensure that the agreements accurately reflect their intentions. When preprinted forms do not sufficiently cover special provisions in a transaction, the parties should have an attorney draft an appropriate contract.

Listing and Buyer Agency Agreements

A *listing agreement* (also known in Georgia as a brokerage engagement) is an employment contract. It establishes the rights and obligations of the broker as agent and the seller as principal. A buyer agency contract establishes the relationship between a buyer and his or her agent. Refer to Chapter 6 for a complete discussion of the various types of listing agreements and buyer agency agreements and to Figure 6.1 for a sample contract.

Some states suggest or require the use of specific forms of listing contracts. Oral listing contracts for a period of less than one year are recognized in some states, while in other states only written listing contracts are recognized. However, in Georgia, there is no statutory required form of a listing contract.

IN PRACTICE If a contract contains any ambiguity, the courts generally interpret the agreement against the party who prepared it.

Sales Contracts

A real estate sales contract contains the complete agreement between a buyer of a parcel of real estate and the seller. Depending on the area, this agreement may be known as an *offer to purchase*, a *contract of purchase and sale*, or a *purchase agreement*.

Whatever the contract is called, it is an offer to purchase real estate as soon as it has been prepared and signed by the purchaser. If the document is accepted and signed by the seller, it becomes a contract of sale. This transformation is referred to as *ripening*.

The real estate sales contract is the most important document in the sale of real estate. It establishes the legal rights and obligations of the buyer and seller. In effect, it dictates the contents of the deed.

A sample Purchase and Sale Agreement is shown in Figure 11.1.

Several details frequently appear in a sales contract in addition to the essential elements of a contract. These include

- the sales price and terms;
- a legal description of the land;
- a statement of the kind and condition of the title, and the form of deed to be delivered by the seller;
- the kind of title evidence required, who will provide it, and how many defects in the title will be eliminated; and
- a statement of all the terms and conditions of the agreement between the parties, and any contingencies (discussed later in this chapter).

The following paragraphs discuss some of the issues that often arise as an offer to purchase develops into a contract of sale.

Offer A broker lists an owner's real estate for sale at whatever price and conditions the owner sets. When a prospective buyer is found, the broker helps him or her prepare an offer to purchase. The offer is signed by the prospective buyer and presented by the licensee to the seller. This is an offer. Both the buyer and seller may be represented by a broker.

Counteroffer As discussed earlier in this chapter, *any* change to the terms proposed by the buyer creates a *counteroffer*. The original offer ceases to exist because the seller has rejected it. The buyer may accept or reject the seller's counteroffer. If the buyer wishes, he or she may continue the process by making another counteroffer. Any change in the last offer may result in a counteroffer until either the parties reach agreement or one of them walks away.

A **counteroffer** is a *new* offer; it voids the original offer.

F I G U R E   11.1

Purchase and Sale Agreement

PURCHASE AND SALE AGREEMENT

Offer Date: _____

Georgia
Association
of REALTORS®

2010 Printing

1. **Purchase and Sale.** The undersigned buyer ("Buyer") agrees to buy and the undersigned seller ("Seller") agrees to sell the Property with the following address: _____,
City _____, County _____, Georgia, Zip Code_____
TAXID/PIN # _____ together with all fixtures, landscaping, improvements, and appurtenances (except those identified in any Seller's Property Disclosure Statement attached hereto as not remaining with the Property) and as more particularly described in the Legal Description Paragraph below (all of which is hereinafter collectively referred to as "Property").

2. **Legal Description.** The full legal description of the Property is:
   [Select A, B or C below. The sections not marked shall not be a part of this Agreement]
   ☐ **A.** attached as an exhibit hereto;
   ☐ **B.** identical to the legal description for the property contained in the deed recorded in Deed Book _____, Page _____, et. seq., _____ County, Georgia records;
   ☐ **C.** described below:
   Land Lot(s) _____ of the _____ District, _____ Section/
   GMD, Lot _____, Block _____, Unit _____, Phase/Section_____
   of _____ Subdivision/Development,
   _____ County, Georgia according to the plat recorded in
   Plat Book _____, Page _____, et. seq., _____ County, Georgia records.

3. **Purchase Price and Method of Payment.** At closing, Buyer agrees to pay Seller the purchase price of the Property of $_____ U.S. Dollars: cash, wire transfer of immediately available funds, or a cashier's check issued for the closing by a federally insured bank, savings bank, savings and loan association or credit union where the funds are immediately available. The above forms of payment shall be deemed to be the equivalent of Buyer paying all cash at closing which shall be the method of payment.

4. **Amount and Deposit of Earnest Money.** Buyer has paid to_____ ("Holder") earnest money of $_____ check, **OR** $_____ cash, which has been received by Holder. The earnest money shall be deposited in Holder's escrow/trust account (with Holder retaining the interest if the account is interest bearing) within five (5) banking days from the Binding Agreement Date. If Buyer writes a check for earnest money and the same is deposited into Holder's escrow/trust account, Holder shall not be required to return the earnest money until the check has cleared the account on which the check was written. In the event any earnest money check is dishonored by the bank upon which it is drawn, Holder shall promptly give notice of the same to Buyer and Seller. Buyer shall have three (3) banking days after receiving such notice to deliver good funds to Holder. In the event Buyer does not timely deliver good funds, Seller shall have the right to terminate this Agreement upon notice to Buyer.

5. **Closing Costs and Other Settlement Expenses.**
   A. Items Paid By Buyer at Closing. At closing, Buyer shall pay the following:
   1. Georgia property transfer tax;
   2. All costs, fees and charges to have the closing attorney search title and prepare: (a) the warranty deed; (b) owner's affidavit; (c) Buyer's powers of attorney; and (d) all promissory notes, deeds to secure debt and other loan documents required by any lender providing financing in the transaction;
   3. All closing costs, tax service charges, recording costs, courier fees, overnight delivery fees, document preparation fees, underwriting fees, delivery, copying and handling charges, and all other costs, fees, charges and amounts to close this transaction otherwise, except as they relate to the clearance of title encumbrances and/or defects necessary for Seller to be able to convey good and marketable title to the Property.
   B. Items Paid By Seller at Closing. At closing, Seller shall pay the following:
   1. The sum of $_____ to be used by Buyer as a contribution for the items in the paragraph above. In addition, Buyer may use the Seller's contribution to pay for, including but not limited to, survey costs, appraisals, insurance (including flood insurance, if applicable), inspections, termite treatment and/or repair guarantee and, if Buyer is obtaining mortgage financing, escrow establishment charges, loan discount points, costs to buy down a loan, and other similar costs (unless any of the same are prohibited by Buyer's mortgage lender). Unspent sums, if any, shall remain with the Seller.
   2. Except as provided above, all sums, costs, charges and fees necessary to clear title encumbrances and/or defects to allow Seller to be able to convey good and marketable title to the Property.
   3. Any extra costs, fees and charges resulting from Seller not being able to attend the closing in person.
   C. Prorated Amounts: Seller and Buyer agree to prorate the following: (1) real estate taxes and community association assessments, if any, for the calendar year in which the sale is closed, as of the date of closing; and (2) all utility bills, solid waste and other fees, as of the date of closing (or the day of possession of Property by Buyer, whichever is later) that are issued after closing and include service for any period of time Property was owned/occupied by Seller or Seller's invitees. In the event real estate taxes are paid at closing based upon an estimated tax bill or tax bill under appeal, Buyer and Seller upon the issuance of the actual tax bill or the appeal being resolved shall promptly make any financial adjustments between themselves as are necessary to prorate the tax bill correctly. This subparagraph shall survive the closing.

F20, Purchase and Sale Agreement, Page 1 of 7, 01/01/10

FIGURE 11.1 (CONTINUED)

Purchase and Sale Agreement

6. <u>Closing and Transfer of Possession.</u>
   A. **Closing:** This transaction shall be closed on _____ or on such other date as may be agreed to in writing by the parties. No later than at the conclusion of the closing, Seller shall provide the Buyer with all keys in Seller's possession or under Seller's control, to all locks that shall remain with the Property.
   B. **Right to Extend Unilaterally the Closing Date:** Buyer or Seller may unilaterally extend the closing date for seven (7) days upon notice to the other party given prior to or on the date of closing if: (1) Seller cannot satisfy valid title objections (except for liens, judgments, and deeds to secure debt that can be satisfied through the payment of money or by bonding off the same); or (2) Buyer's mortgage lender, if any, (including in "all cash" transactions) or the closing attorney cannot fulfill their respective obligations by the date of closing due to no fault of Buyer. In such event, Buyer and Seller consent to the closing attorney and/or any such mortgage lender disclosing to the parties and their Brokers the basis for the delay. The exercise of the right to extend unilaterally the closing date by either party shall cause the right to extend unilaterally the closing date to terminate and no longer be a part of this Agreement.
   C. **Possession:** Buyer agrees to allow Seller to retain possession of Property until and through:
   [Select one. The sections not marked shall not be a part of this Agreement.]
   ☐**1.** the closing; **OR** ☐**2.** _____ hours after the closing; **OR** ☐**3.** _____ days after the closing at _____ o'clock _____.m.

7. <u>Closing Attorney.</u> This transaction shall be closed by the law firm of _____.
   If Buyer is given the right to select a law firm from a mortgage lender's approved list of closing attorneys, Buyer agrees to select said law firm. If the law firm named above is not on the mortgage lender's approved list, and cannot be added in time to close this transaction, Buyer may select another law firm from lender's approved list to close this transaction. The closing attorney shall represent the mortgage lender in any transaction in which the Buyer obtains mortgage financing (including transactions where the method of payment referenced herein is "all cash"). In transactions where the Buyer does not obtain mortgage financing, the closing attorney shall represent the:
   ☐ Buyer **OR** ☐ Seller. If the closing attorney declines to represent the party selected, the party may select a different closing attorney.

8. <u>Title.</u>
   A. **Warranty:** Seller warrants that at the closing Seller will convey good and marketable title to said Property by general warranty deed subject only to: (1) zoning; (2) general utility, sewer, and drainage easements of record as of the Binding Agreement Date and upon which the improvements do not encroach; (3) declarations of condominium and declarations of covenants, conditions and restrictions of record on the Binding Agreement Date; and (4) leases and other encumbrances specified in this Agreement. Buyer agrees to assume Seller's responsibilities in any leases specified in this Agreement.
   B. **Examination:** Buyer may examine title and furnish Seller with a written statement of title objections at or prior to the closing. If Seller fails or is unable to satisfy valid title objections at or prior to the closing or any unilateral extension thereof, which would prevent the Seller from conveying good and marketable title to the Property, then Buyer, among its other remedies, may terminate the Agreement upon written notice to Seller. Good and marketable title as used herein shall mean title which a title insurance company licensed to do business in Georgia will insure at its regular rates, subject only to standard exceptions.
   C. **Survey:** A survey of Property is ☐ **OR** is not ☐ attached to this Agreement as an exhibit. Notwithstanding any other provision to the contrary contained herein, Buyer shall have the right to terminate this Agreement upon notice to Seller if a new survey performed by a surveyor licensed in Georgia is obtained which is materially different from any survey attached hereto as an exhibit with respect to Property. The term "materially different" shall not apply to any improvements constructed by Seller in their agreed-upon locations subsequent to Binding Date Agreement. Matters revealed in said survey shall not relieve the warranty of title obligations of Seller referenced above.

9. <u>Risk of Damage to Property.</u> Seller warrants that at the time of closing or upon the granting of possession, if at a time other than at closing, Property will be in substantially the same condition (including conditions disclosed in the Seller's Property Disclosure Statement) as on the Binding Agreement Date, except for normal wear and tear, and changes made to the condition of Property pursuant to the written agreement of Buyer and Seller. Seller shall deliver Property clean and free of trash and debris at time of possession. Notwithstanding the above, if the Property is destroyed or substantially damaged prior to closing, Seller shall promptly give notice to Buyer of the same and provide Buyer with whatever information Seller has regarding the availability of insurance and the disposition of any insurance claim. Buyer or Seller may terminate this Agreement not later than fourteen (14) days from receipt of the above notice, except that any party who causes the Property to be destroyed or substantially damaged as the result of that party's criminal conduct shall forfeit the right to terminate this Agreement and shall be in default hereunder. If Buyer or Seller does not terminate this Agreement, Seller shall cause Property to be restored to substantially the same condition as on the Binding Agreement Date. The date of closing shall be extended until the earlier of one year from the original date of closing, or seven (7) days from the date that Property has been restored to substantially the same condition as on the Binding Agreement Date and a new certificate of occupancy (if required) is issued.

10. <u>Inspection.</u>
    A. **Right of Buyer to Inspect Property:** Buyer and/or Buyer's representatives shall have the right to enter Property at Buyer's expense and at reasonable times (including immediately prior to closing) to inspect, examine, test and survey Property. Seller shall cause all utility services and any pool, hot tub and similar items to be operational so that Buyer may complete all inspections under this Agreement. Buyer agrees to hold Seller and all Brokers harmless from all claims, injuries, and damages arising out of or related to the exercise of these rights.
    B. **Duty of Buyer to Inspect Neighborhood:** Buyer acknowledges that: (1) in every neighborhood there are conditions which different buyers may find objectionable and (2) Buyer has had the full opportunity to become acquainted with all existing neighborhood conditions (and proposed changes thereto) which could affect the Property including without limitation land-fills, quarries, high-voltage power lines, cemeteries, airports, prisons, stadiums, odor and/or noise producing land uses, crime, schools serving the Property, political jurisdictional maps and land use and transportation maps and plans. It shall be Buyer's sole duty to become familiar with neighborhood conditions of concern to Buyer. **If Buyer is concerned about the possibility of a registered sex offender residing in a neighborhood in which Buyer is interested, Buyer should review the Georgia Violent Sex Offender Registry available on the Georgia Bureau of Investigation Website at www.gbi.georgia.gov.**

F20, Purchase and Sale Agreement, Page 2 of 7, 01/01/10

FIGURE 11.1 (CONTINUED)

Purchase and Sale Agreement

11. <u>Property Sold Subject to Due Diligence Period or "As-Is."</u>
[Select Section A. or B. below. The section not marked shall not be a part of this Agreement.]
☐ **A. Property Sold Subject to Due Diligence Period.**
   1. **Contract Is Option Contract.** For and in consideration of the additional payment of Ten Dollars ($10) by the Buyer to the Seller, the receipt and sufficiency of which is hereby acknowledged, Seller does hereby grant Buyer the option of terminating this Agreement, for any reason, for a _____ day period from the Binding Agreement Date ("Due Diligence Period"). This Agreement shall be an option contract until the Due Diligence Period has ended without Buyer terminating the same.
   2. **Purpose of Due Diligence Period.** During the Due Diligence Period, Buyer may, but shall not be required to: (a) arrange any loans Buyer needs to complete the purchase of the Property; and (b) conduct at Buyer's sole expense whatever evaluations, inspections, appraisals, examinations, surveys, and testing, if any, Buyer deems appropriate to determine whether Buyer's option to terminate this Agreement should be exercised. This shall include but not be limited to testing for lead-based paint and/or lead-based paint hazards, inspecting for active infestation of and/or damage from termites and other wood destroying organisms and determining if the Property or the improvements thereon are in a flood plain. During the Due Diligence Period, Buyer may also propose an amendment(s) to this Agreement to address any concerns of Buyer with the Property.
   3. **Right to Terminate.** If Buyer decides to exercise Buyer's option to terminate this Agreement, Buyer must give notice of the same to Seller prior to the end of the Due Diligence Period. If Buyer fails to give such notice in a timely manner, the Due Diligence Period shall terminate and Buyer shall be deemed to have accepted the Property "as-is." The expiration of the Due Diligence Period shall not terminate any other contingencies to which this Agreement may be subject.
   4. **Warranties of Buyer.** Buyer warrants that Buyer is ☐ **OR** is not ☐ currently under contract (including option contracts) to purchase other real property. Buyer warrants that during the Due Diligence Period Buyer shall ☐ have the right to enter into other such contracts **OR** ☐ not enter into any other such contracts. Buyer shall be in default of the Agreement if Buyer breaches Buyer's warranties in this subparagraph.
☐ **B. Property Sold "As Is."** All parties agree that Property is being sold "as is," with all faults including but not limited to damage from termites and other wood destroying organisms and lead-based paint and lead-based paint hazards. Seller shall have no obligation to make any repairs or replacements to Property.

12. <u>Return and Disbursement of Earnest Money.</u>
  A. Return of Earnest Money to Buyer: Subject to the Disbursement of Earnest Money paragraph below, Buyer shall be entitled to the earnest money upon the: (1) failure of the parties to enter into a binding agreement; (2) failure of any contingency or condition to which this Agreement is subject; (3) termination of this Agreement due to the default of Seller; or (4) termination of this Agreement in accordance with a specific right to terminate set forth in the Agreement. Otherwise, the earnest money shall be applied towards the purchase price of the Property at closing or if other funds are used to pay the purchase price then the earnest money shall be returned to Buyer.
  B. Disbursement of Earnest Money: Holder shall disburse the earnest money upon: (1) the closing of Property; (2) a subsequent written agreement of Buyer and Seller; (3) an order of a court or arbitrator having jurisdiction over any dispute involving the earnest money; or (4) the failure of the parties to enter into a binding agreement (where there is no dispute over the formation or enforceability of the Agreement). In addition, Holder may disburse the earnest money upon a reasonable interpretation of the Agreement, provided that Holder first gives all parties fifteen (15) days notice stating to whom and why the disbursement will be made. Any party may object to the proposed disbursement by giving written notice of the same to Holder within the fifteen (15) day notice period. Objections not timely made in writing shall be deemed waived. If Holder receives an objection and, after considering it, decides to disburse the earnest money as originally proposed, Holder may do so and send notice to the parties of Holder's action. If Holder decides to modify its proposed disbursement, Holder shall first send a new fifteen (15) day notice to the parties stating the rationale for the modification and to whom the disbursement will now be made.
  C. Interpleader: If there is a dispute over the earnest money which the parties cannot resolve after a reasonable period of time, and where Holder has a bona fide question as to who is entitled to the earnest money, Broker may interplead the earnest money into a court of competent jurisdiction. Holder shall be reimbursed for and may deduct from any funds interpleaded, its costs and expenses, including reasonable attorney's fees actually incurred. The prevailing defendant in the interpleader lawsuit shall be entitled to collect its attorney's fees and court costs and the amount deducted by Holder from the non-prevailing defendant.
  D. Hold Harmless: All parties hereby agree to indemnify and hold Holder harmless from and against all claims, causes of action, suits and damages arising out of or related to the performance by Holder of its duties hereunder. All parties further covenant and agree not to sue Holder for damages relating to any decision of Holder to disburse earnest money made in accordance with the requirements of this Agreement.

13. <u>Agency and Brokerage.</u>
  A. Agency Disclosure: In this Agreement, the term "Broker" shall mean a licensed Georgia real estate broker or brokerage firm and, where the context would indicate, the broker's affiliated licensees. No Broker in this transaction shall owe any duty to Buyer or Seller greater than what is set forth in their brokerage engagements and the Brokerage Relationships in Real Estate Transactions Act, O.C.G.A. § 10-6A-1 et. seq.;
   1. **No Agency Relationship.** Buyer and Seller acknowledge that, if they are not represented by a Broker, they are each solely responsible for protecting their own interests, and that Broker's role is limited to performing ministerial acts for that party.
   2. **Listing Broker.** Broker working with the Seller is identified on the signature page as the "Listing Broker"; and said Broker is ☐ **OR** is not ☐ representing Seller;
   3. **Selling Broker.** Broker working with Buyer (including in transactions where Broker is representing Seller) is identified on the signature page as "Selling Broker;" and said Broker is ☐ **OR** is not ☐ representing Buyer; and
   4. **Dual Agency or Designated Agency.** If Buyer and Seller are both being represented by the same Broker, a relationship of either designated agency ☐ **OR** dual agency ☐ shall exist.

       F20, Purchase and Sale Agreement, Page 3 of 7, 01/01/10

F I G U R E   11.1 (CONTINUED)

Purchase and Sale Agreement

        a. Dual Agency Disclosure. *[Applicable only if dual agency has been selected above.]*
        Buyer and Seller are aware that Broker is acting as a dual agent in this transaction and consent to the same. Buyer and Seller have been advised that:
        (1) In serving as a dual agent, Broker is representing two clients whose interests are or at times could be different or even adverse;
        (2) Broker will disclose all adverse, material facts relevant to the transaction and actually known to the dual agent to all parties in the transaction except for information made confidential by request or instructions from each client which is not otherwise required to be disclosed by law;
        (3) Buyer and Seller do not have to consent to dual agency and, the consent of Buyer and Seller to dual agency has been given voluntarily and the parties have read and understand their brokerage engagement agreements.
        (4) Notwithstanding any provision to the contrary contained herein, Buyer and Seller each hereby direct Broker, while acting as a dual agent, to keep confidential and not reveal to the other party any information which could materially and adversely affect their negotiating position.
        b. Designated Agency Assignment. *[Applicable only if the designated agency has been selected above.]*
        Broker has assigned _____ to work exclusively with Buyer as Buyer's designated agent and _____ to work exclusively with Seller as Seller's designated agent. Each designated agent shall exclusively represent the party to whom each has been assigned as a client and shall not represent in this transaction the client assigned to the other designated agent.

    B. Brokerage: Seller has agreed to pay Listing Broker(s) a real estate commission pursuant to that certain brokerage engagement agreement entered into between the parties and incorporated herein by reference ("Listing Agreement"). Pursuant to the terms of the Listing Agreement, the Listing Broker has agreed to share that commission with the Selling Broker.

    The closing attorney is hereby authorized and directed to pay the Broker(s) at closing, their respective commissions out of the proceeds of the sale. If the sale proceeds are insufficient to pay the full commission, the party owing the commission shall pay any shortfall at closing. If more than one Broker is involved in the transaction, the closing attorney is directed to pay each Broker its respective portion of said commission. The acceptance by the Broker(s) of a partial real estate commission at the closing shall not relieve the Seller of the obligation to pay the remainder thereof after the closing unless the Broker(s) have expressly and in writing agreed to accept the lesser amount in full satisfaction of the Broker(s) claim to a commission.

    C. Material Relationship Disclosure: Brokers and/or their affiliated licensees have the following material relationship(s) with either Buyer and/or Seller as follows: _____
_____.

14. **Disclaimer.** Buyer and Seller acknowledge that they have not relied upon any advice, representations or statements of Brokers other than what is expressly included in this Agreement and waive and shall not assert any claims against Brokers involving the same. Buyer and Seller agree that Brokers shall not be responsible to advise Buyer and Seller on any matter including but not limited to the following: any matter which could have been revealed through a survey, title search or inspection of Property; the condition of Property, any portion thereof, or any item therein; building products and construction techniques; the necessity or cost of any repairs to Property; mold; hazardous or toxic materials or substances; termites and other wood destroying organisms; the tax or legal consequences of this Agreement and transaction; the availability and cost of utilities or community amenities; the appraised or future value of Property; any condition(s) existing off Property which may affect Property; the terms, conditions and availability of financing; and the uses and zoning of Property whether permitted or proposed. Buyer and Seller acknowledge that Brokers are not experts with respect to the above matters and that, if any of these matters or any other matters are of concern to them, they should seek independent expert advice relative thereto. Buyer and Seller acknowledge that Brokers shall not be responsible to monitor or supervise any portion of any construction or repairs to Property and that such tasks clearly fall outside the scope of real estate brokerage services.

15. **Lead-Based Paint.** A portion of any residential dwelling on the Property was ☐ **OR** was not ☐ built prior to 1978. If any portion of a residential dwelling was built prior to 1978, the Lead-Based Paint Exhibit must be and is hereby attached as an exhibit to this Agreement by Seller. For the purposes of this paragraph, the term "residential dwelling" shall include any painted fixture, component or material used therein that was built or manufactured prior to 1978.

16. **Notices.**
    A. All Notices Must Be In Writing. All notices, including but not limited to offers, counteroffers, acceptances, amendments, demands, notices of termination and other notices, required or permitted hereunder shall be in writing, signed by the party giving the notice. It is the intent of the parties that the requirements of this Notice paragraph shall apply even prior to this Agreement becoming binding.
    B. Method of Delivery of Notice. Subject to limitations and conditions set forth herein, notices may only be delivered: (1) in person; (2) by an overnight delivery service, prepaid; (3) by facsimile transmission (FAX); (4) by registered or certified U. S. mail, prepaid, return receipt requested; or (5) by e-mail.
    C. When Notice Is Deemed Received. Except as may be provided herein, a notice shall not be deemed to be given, delivered or received until it is actually received by the party to whom the notice was intended or that person's authorized agent. Notwithstanding the above, a notice sent by FAX shall be deemed to be received by the party to whom it was sent as of the date and time it is transmitted to either the party or the party's authorized agent provided that the sending FAX produces a written confirmation showing the correct date and the time of the transmission and the telephone number referenced herein to which the notice should have been sent.
    D. When Notice to Broker Is Notice to Broker's Client. Except in transactions where the Broker is practicing designated agency, notice to the Broker or the affiliated licensee of Broker representing a party in the transaction shall for all purposes herein be deemed to be notice to that party. Said Broker and affiliated licensee shall be authorized agents of the party for the purpose of receiving notice. In any transaction where the Broker is practicing designated agency, only notice to the affiliated licensee designated by Broker to represent the party in the transaction shall be notice to that party. Personal delivery of notice may only be delivered to the party intended to receive the same or that party's authorized agent.

        F20, Purchase and Sale Agreement, Page 4 of 7, 01/01/10

FIGURE 11.1 (CONTINUED)

Purchase and Sale Agreement

E. Notice by Fax or E-Mail to a Broker or Affiliated Licensee of a Broker. Notices by fax or e-mail to a Broker or the affiliated licensee of a Broker may only be sent to the e-mail address or fax number, if any, of the Broker or the affiliated licensee of the Broker set forth in the Broker/Licensee Contact Information section of the signature page of this Agreement or subsequently provided by the Broker or the affiliated licensee of Broker following the notice procedures set forth herein. If no fax number or e-mail address is included in the Broker/Licensee Contact Information section of the signature page of this Agreement (or is subsequently provided by the Broker or the affiliated licensee of Broker following the notice procedures) then notice by the means of communication not provided shall not be valid for any purpose herein. Notice to a Broker or the affiliated licensee of Broker who is working with, but not representing a party, shall not be deemed to be notice to that party. Any party sending notice by FAX or email shall send an original copy of the notice if so requested by the other party. A faxed or emailed signature of a party shall constitute an original signature binding upon that party.

F. Notice to Unrepresented Party. A party who is not represented by a Broker in the transaction may receive notices by Fax or e-mail at the e-mail address or fax number, if any, of the party set forth below or at such other fax number or e-mail address as the party may provide following the notice procedures set forth herein. If no e-mail address or fax number is provided for below, or is subsequently provided by the party following the notice procedures set forth herein, then notice through the means of communication not provided shall not be valid for any purpose herein.

Unrepresented Buyer: _____   Unrepresented Seller: _____

Fax No._____   Fax No._____

E-Mail Address: _____   E-Mail Address: _____

17. **Default.**

In the event of a default of this Agreement by Buyer or Seller, the non-defaulting party may pursue any and all remedies available at law or in equity relative to the default. In the event this Agreement is terminated by Seller due to the default of Buyer, Holder shall offer the earnest money to Seller, by check, which if accepted and deposited by Seller, shall constitute liquidated damages in full settlement of all claims of Seller against Buyer. The parties agree that such liquidated damages shall not be a penalty but are instead a reasonable pre-estimate of Seller's actual damages, which damages are difficult to ascertain. Nothing herein shall prevent the Seller from declining any tender of the earnest money by the Holder. In such event, Holder may disburse the earnest money to Buyer upon a reasonable interpretation of the Agreement as set forth elsewhere herein.

Notwithstanding any other provision to the contrary contained in either this Agreement or in any brokerage engagement agreement entered into by Buyer or Seller with any real estate broker, in the event the sale is not closed because of the failure or refusal of Buyer or Seller to perform any of their respective obligations, the defaulting party shall pay the Broker(s) the full commission the Broker(s) would have been entitled to under the Listing Agreement (incorporated herein by reference) had the transaction closed. The Selling Broker and Listing Broker may jointly or independently pursue the defaulting party for their respective portions of the commission. If the defaulting party has not entered into a brokerage engagement agreement with either the Listing Broker or Selling Broker herein or such agreement is no longer in full force and effect as of the Binding Agreement Date, this Agreement shall create a separate cause of action on the part of the Brokers herein against the defaulting party. In the event the defaulting party has entered into a brokerage engagement agreement with either the Listing Broker or Selling Broker that is in full force and effect as of the Binding Agreement Date, this section of the Agreement shall serve to amend such brokerage engagement agreement and shall control over and supersede any conflicting or inconsistent provisions contained therein. The consideration for the rights granted herein to Broker(s) shall be the mutual promises set forth in this Agreement and other good and valuable consideration the receipt and sufficiency of which is acknowledged by Buyer and Seller. The rights granted herein to Broker(s) shall survive the termination of this Agreement. Notwithstanding the above, the payment to the Broker(s) by the defaulting party of the full commission(s) referenced above shall relieve the defaulting party of any other commission obligation owed to the Broker(s).

18. **Other Provisions.**

A. **Warranties Transfer:** Seller agrees to transfer to Buyer, at closing, subject to Buyer's acceptance thereof (and at Buyer's expense, if there is any cost associated with said transfer), Seller's interest in any existing manufacturer's warranties, service contracts, termite treatment and/or repair guarantee and/or other similar warranties which, by their terms, may be transferable to Buyer.

B. **Repairs:** All agreed upon repairs and replacements shall be performed in a good and workmanlike manner prior to closing.

C. **Binding Effect, Entire Agreement, Modification, Assignment:** This Agreement constitutes the sole and entire agreement between all of the parties, supersedes all of their prior written and verbal agreements and shall be binding upon the parties and their successors, heirs and permitted assigns. No representation, promise or inducement not included in this Agreement shall be binding upon any party hereto. This Agreement may not be amended, modified or waived except upon the written agreement of Buyer and Seller. This Agreement may not be assigned by Buyer except with the written agreement of Seller. Any assignee shall fulfill all the terms and conditions of this Agreement.

D. **Survival of Agreement:** The following shall survive the closing of this Agreement: (1) the obligation of a party to pay a real estate commission; (2) any warranty of title; and (3) any obligations which the parties herein agree shall survive the closing or may be performed or fulfilled after the closing.

E. **Governing Law and Interpretation:** This Agreement may be signed in multiple counterparts each of which shall be deemed to be an original and shall be interpreted in accordance with the laws of the State of Georgia. No provision herein, by virtue of the party who drafted it, shall be interpreted less favorably against one party than another. All references to time shall mean the time in Georgia.

F. **Time of Essence:** Time is of the essence of this Agreement.

G. **Terminology:** As the context may require in this Agreement: (1) the singular shall mean the plural and vice versa; and (2) all pronouns shall mean and include the person, entity, firm, or corporation to which they relate.

H. **Binding Agreement Date:** The Binding Agreement Date in this Agreement shall be the date when the party making the last offer, or the Broker (except in a designated agency transaction) or affiliated licensee of Broker representing that party as a client, receives notice that the offer has been accepted. This party (or the Broker or affiliated licensee representing this party as a client) shall fill in the Binding Agreement Date below and promptly give notice of this date to the other party. Filling in the Binding Agreement Date shall not be deemed to be a counteroffer.

F20, Purchase and Sale Agreement, Page 5 of 7, 01/01/10

F I G U R E   11.1 (CONTINUED)

Purchase and Sale Agreement

> **I. Responsibility to Cooperate:** All parties agree to take all actions and do all things reasonably necessary to fulfill the terms and conditions of this Agreement in good faith and in a timely manner. Buyer and Seller shall execute and deliver such certifications, affidavits, and statements as are required at closing to meet the requirements of any lender(s) and of federal and state law.
>
> **J. GAR Forms:** The Georgia Association of REALTORS®, Inc. ("GAR") makes certain standard real estate forms available to its members. These GAR forms are frequently provided to the parties in real estate transactions by the REALTORS® with whom they are working. No party is required to use any GAR form. Since these forms are generic and written with the interests of multiple parties in mind, they may need to be modified to meet the specific needs of the parties using them. If any party has any questions about his or her rights and obligations under any GAR form he or she should consult an attorney. The parties hereto agree that the GAR forms may only be used in accordance with the licensing agreement of GAR. While GAR forms may be modified by the parties, no GAR form may be reproduced with sections removed, altered or modified unless the changes are visible on the form itself or in a stipulation, addendum, exhibit or amendment thereto.
>
> **19. Exhibits and Addenda.** All exhibits and/or addenda attached hereto, listed below, or referenced herein are made a part of this Agreement. If any such exhibit or addendum conflicts with any preceding paragraph (including any changes thereto made by the parties), said exhibit or addendum shall control:
>
> ☐ Legal Description of the Property as Exhibit "_____"
>
> ☐ Financing Contingency as Exhibit "_____"
>
> ☐ The ☐ FHA Loan Exhibit **OR** ☐ VA Loan Exhibit as Exhibit "_____"
>
> ☐ A Survey of Property as Exhibit "_____"
>
> ☐ Appraisal Contingency as Exhibit "_____"
>
> ☐ Seller's Property Disclosure Statement as Exhibit "_____"
>
> ☐ Lead-Based Paint Exhibit as Exhibit "_____"
>
> ☐ Source of Buyer's Funds as Exhibit "_____"
>
> ☐ Sale or Lease of Buyer's Property Contingency as Exhibit "_____"
>
> ☐ Back-up Agreement Contingency as Exhibit "_____"
>
> ☐ Community Association Disclosure as Exhibit "_____"
>
> ☐ Other _____
>
> ☐ Other _____
>
> ☐ Other _____
>
> ☐ Other _____
>
> ☐ Other _____
>
> **SPECIAL STIPULATIONS:** The following Special Stipulations, if conflicting with any exhibit, addendum, or preceding paragraph (including any changes thereto made by the parties), shall control:

FIGURE 11.1 (CONTINUED)

Purchase and Sale Agreement

Additional Special Stipulations are ☐ **or are** ☐ **not attached.**

Time Limit of the Offer: The terms of this Agreement shall constitute an offer ("Offer") which shall expire at _____ o'clock _____.m. on the date of _____ unless prior to that time it is accepted in writing by the party to whom the offer was made and notice of the acceptance is delivered back to the party making the offer.

_____
Buyer's Signature

_____
Print or Type Name

_____
Buyer's Signature

_____
Print or Type Name

_____
Selling Broker

By: _____
    Broker or Broker's Affiliated Licensee

_____
Print or Type Name

_____   _____
MLS Office Code   Brokerage Firm License Number

Multiple Listing Number _____

Selling Broker/Licensee Contact Information:

Phone# _____

Fax# _____

E-Mail _____

_____
Selling Agent's Georgia Real Estate License Number

_____
Seller's Signature

_____
Print or Type Name

_____
Seller's Signature

_____
Print or Type Name

_____
Listing Broker

By: _____
    Broker or Broker's Affiliated Licensee

_____
Print or Type Name

_____   _____
MLS Office Code   Brokerage Firm License Number

Listing Broker/Licensee Contact Information:

Phone# _____

Fax# _____

E-Mail _____

_____
Listing Agent's Georgia Real Estate License Number

Binding Agreement Date: The Binding Agreement Date in this transaction is the date of _____ and has been filled in by _____.

An offer or counteroffer *may be revoked at any time before it has been accepted,* even if the person making the offer or counteroffer agreed to keep the offer open for a set period of time.

Acceptance   If the seller agrees to the original offer or a later counteroffer *exactly as it was made* and signs the document, the offer has been *accepted.* Acceptance of the offer means that a contract is *formed.* The licensee must advise the buyer of the seller's acceptance and obtain the approval of the parties' attorneys if the contract calls for it. A copy of the contract must be provided to each party.

An offer is not considered accepted until the person making the offer has been *notified of the other party's acceptance.* When the parties communicate through an agent or at a distance, questions may arise regarding whether an acceptance, a rejection, or a counteroffer has occurred. Current technologies make communication faster; a signed agreement that is faxed, for instance, would constitute adequate communication. The licensee must transmit all offers, acceptances, or other responses as soon as possible to avoid questions of proper communication.

In Georgia   In Georgia, the widely used GAR Purchase and Sale Agreement states that when the last offeror or offeror's agent receives an accepted offer, the Binding Agreement Date, the effective date of delivery, occurs. The time periods in the contract provisions commence on the Binding Agreement Date.

Earnest money deposits   It is customary (although not essential) for a purchaser to provide a deposit when making an offer to purchase real estate. This deposit, usually in the form of a check, is referred to as **earnest money.** The earnest money deposit is evidence of the buyer's intention to carry out the terms of the contract in good faith. The check is given to the broker, who holds it for the parties in a special account. In some areas, deposits may be held in escrow by the seller's attorney. If the offer is not accepted, the earnest money deposit is immediately returned to the would-be buyer.

The amount of the deposit is a matter to be agreed on by the parties. Under the terms of most listing agreements, a real estate broker is required to accept a *reasonable amount* as earnest money. As a rule, the deposit should be an amount sufficient to

- discourage the buyer from defaulting,
- compensate the seller for taking the property off the market, and
- cover any expenses the seller might incur if the buyer defaults.

Some contracts provide that the deposit becomes the seller's property as liquidated damages if the buyer defaults. The seller might also claim further damages, however, unless the contract limits recovery to the deposit alone.

Earnest money held by a broker must be held in a special *trust,* or *escrow,* account. This money cannot be mixed with a broker's own personal funds (called *commingling*). A broker may not use earnest money funds for his or her personal use (called *conversion*). A separate escrow account does not have to be opened for each earnest money deposit received; all deposits may be kept in one account. A broker must maintain full, complete, and accurate records of all earnest money deposits.

The special account may or may not pay interest, depending on state law. If the account bears interest, there must be some provision in the contract for how the interest earned will be distributed. The broker must provide the parties with an accounting of the amount and dates of interest payments. Often, a check for the interest amount is given to the buyer at closing. On the other hand, the contract may provide for the interest to be paid to the seller as part of the purchase price.

See Chapter 14 for the Georgia requirements on managing trust accounts and trust funds.

Equitable title   When a buyer signs a contract to purchase real estate, he or she does not receive title to the land. Title transfers only upon delivery and acceptance of a deed. However, after both buyer and seller have executed a sales contract, the buyer acquires an *interest* in the land. This interest is known as **equitable title.** A person who holds equitable title has rights that vary from state to state. Equitable title may give the buyer an insurable interest in the property.

Destruction of premises   In many states, including Georgia, once the sales contract is signed by both parties, the buyer bears the risk of any damage to the property that may occur before closing. Of course, the contract may provide otherwise. Furthermore, the laws and court decisions of a growing number of states have placed the risk of loss on the seller. Many of these states have adopted the Uniform Vendor and Purchaser Risk Act, which specifically provides that the seller bear any loss that occurs before the title passes or the buyer takes possession.

Liquidated damages   To avoid a lawsuit if one party breaches the contract, the parties may agree on a certain amount of money that will compensate the nonbreaching party. That money is called **liquidated damages.** If a sales contract specifies that the earnest money deposit is to serve as liquidated damages in case the buyer defaults, the seller will be entitled to keep the deposit if the buyer refuses to perform without good reason. The seller who keeps the deposit as liquidated damages may not sue for any further damages if the contract provides that the deposit is the seller's sole remedy.

Parts of a sales contract   All real estate sales contracts can be divided into a number of separate parts. Although each form of contract contains these divisions, their location within a particular contract may vary. Most sales contracts include the following information:

■   The purchaser's name and a statement of the purchaser's obligation to purchase the property, including how the purchaser intends to take title

- An adequate description of the property. A street address is *not* adequate for a legal description in either a contract or deed in Georgia. (See Chapter 14.)
- The seller's name and a statement of the type of deed a seller agrees to give, including any covenants, conditions, and restrictions
- The purchase price and how the purchaser intends to pay for the property, including earnest money deposits, additional cash from the purchaser, and the conditions of any mortgage financing
- The amount and form of the down payment or earnest money deposit and whether it will be in the form of a check or promissory note
- A provision for the closing of the transaction and the transfer of possession of the property to the purchaser by a specific date
- A provision for title evidence (abstract and legal opinion, certificate of title, Torrens certificate, or title insurance policy)
- The method by which real estate taxes, rents, fuel costs, and other expenses are to be prorated
- A provision for the completion of the contract should the property be damaged or destroyed between the time of signing and the closing date
- A liquidated damages clause, a right-to-sue provision, or another statement of remedies available in the event of default
- Contingency clauses (such as the buyer's obtaining financing or selling a currently owned property or the seller's acquisition of another desired property or clearing of the title; attorney approval and home inspection are other commonly included contingencies)
- The dated signatures of all parties. In some states, but *not* Georgia, the seller's nonowning spouse may be required to release potential marital or homestead rights. An agent may sign for a principal if the agent has been expressly authorized to do so by a power of attorney. When sellers are co-owners, all must sign if the entire ownership is being transferred.
- In most states, an agency disclosure statement

Additional provisions   Many sales contracts provide for the following:

- Any personal property to be left with the premises for the purchaser (such as major appliances or lawn and garden equipment)
- Any real property to be removed by the seller before the closing (such as a storage shed)
- The transfer of any applicable warranties on items such as heating and cooling systems or built-in appliances
- The identification of any leased equipment that must be transferred to the purchaser or returned to the lessor (such as security systems, cable television boxes, and water softeners)
- The appointment of a closing or settlement agent
- Closing or settlement instructions
- The transfer of any impound or escrow account funds
- The transfer or payment of any outstanding special assessments
- The purchaser's right to inspect the property shortly before the closing or settlement (often called the *walk-through*)
- The agreement as to what documents will be provided by each party and when and where they will be delivered

Contingencies Additional conditions that must be satisfied before a sales contract is fully enforceable are called **contingencies.** A contingency includes the following three elements:

1. The actions necessary to satisfy the contingency
2. The time frame within which the actions must be performed
3. Who is responsible for paying any costs involved

The most common contingencies include the following:

- *Mortgage contingency.* A mortgage contingency protects the buyer's earnest money until a lender commits the mortgage loan funds.
- *Inspection contingency.* A sales contract may be contingent on the buyer's obtaining certain inspections of the property. Inspections may include those for wood-boring insects, lead-based paint, structural and mechanical systems, sewage facilities, and radon or other toxic materials.
- *Property sale contingency.* A purchaser may make the sales contract contingent on the sale of his or her current home. This protects the buyer from owning two homes at the same time and also helps ensure the availability of cash for the purchase.

The seller may insist on an *escape clause*. An escape clause permits the seller to continue to market the property until all the buyer's contingencies have been satisfied or removed. The buyer may retain the right to eliminate the contingencies if the seller receives a more favorable offer. (Note that contingencies create a *voidable contract:* If the contingencies are rejected or not satisfied, the contract is void.)

Amendments, addendums, and exhibits An *amendment* is a change to the existing content of a contract. Any time words or provisions are *added to or deleted from the body of the contract*, the contract has been amended. For instance, a form contract's provision requiring closing in 90 days might be crossed out and replaced with a 60-day period. Amendments must be initialed by all parties.

On the other hand, an *addendum* is any provision added to an existing contract *without altering the content of the original*. An addendum is essentially a new contract between the parties that includes the original contract's provisions *by reference*, that is, the addendum mentions the original contract. An addendum must be signed by the parties. For example, an addendum might be an agreement to split the cost of repairing certain flaws discovered in a home inspection.

| In Georgia |

In Georgia, exhibits are information or provisions attached to the contract that either add to, change, or delete preprinted contract language.

Disclosures   As discussed in Chapter 4 and Chapter 6, many states have enacted mandatory **disclosure** laws. The purpose of these laws is to help consumers make informed decisions. Many brokers have instituted procedures for making disclosures and recommending technical experts to ensure that purchasers have accurate information about real estate. Disclosure of property conditions may be included as part of a sales contract, or it may be a separate form. Many states require separate forms for disclosing environmental problems. (See Chapter 22.) In addition, as discussed in Chapter 4, disclosure of the broker's agency relationship may also be required by state law.

Options

An **option** is a contract by which an *optionor* (generally an owner) gives an *optionee* (a prospective purchaser or lessee) the right to buy or lease the owner's property at a fixed price within a certain period of time. The optionee pays a fee (the agreed actual consideration) for this option right. The optionee has no other obligation until he or she decides to either exercise the option right or allow the option to expire. An option is enforceable by only one party (unilateral contract)—the optionee. Options must contain all the terms and provisions required for a valid contract.

A common application of an option is a lease that includes an option for the tenant to purchase the property. Options on commercial real estate frequently depend on some specific conditions being fulfilled, such as obtaining a zoning change or a building permit. The optionee may be obligated to exercise the option if the conditions are met. Similar terms could also be included in a sales contract.

Land Contracts

A real estate sale can be made under a **land contract.** A land contract is sometimes called a *contract for deed,* a *bond for title,* an **installment contract,** a *land sales contract,* or *articles of agreement for warranty deed.* Under a typical land contract, the seller (also known as the *vendor*) retains legal title. The buyer (called the vendee) takes possession and gets equitable title to the property. The buyer agrees to give the seller a down payment and pay regular monthly installments of principal and interest over a number of years. The buyer also agrees to pay real estate taxes, insurance premiums, repairs, and upkeep on the property. Although the buyer obtains possession under the contract, *the seller is not obligated to execute and deliver a deed to the buyer until the terms of the contract have been satisfied.* This frequently occurs when the buyer has made enough payments to obtain a mortgage loan and pay off the balance due on the contract. Although a land contract is usually assumable by subsequent purchasers, it generally must be approved by the seller.

Leases and escrow agreements   A **lease** is any agreement that gives rise to the relationship of landlord and tenant or lessor and lessee. A lease is a contract for exclusive possession of land, for a term of time, at will, usually for a specified rent or compensation. An **escrow contract** is an agreement between a buyer, seller, and escrow holder setting forth rights and responsibilities of each. In some states, but *not* Georgia, an escrow contract is entered into when earnest money is deposited in a broker's escrow account.

■ KEY POINT REVIEW

Following are characteristics of a **valid contract:**

- A **voluntary agreement** based on **reality of consent**
  - if a mistake, misrepresentation, fraud, undue influence, or duress occurs, it is **voidable** by the injured party.
- The agreement or promise is based on an **offer** by one party (**offeror**) that is **accepted** by the other (**offeree**).
  - **Mutual assent** or **meeting of the minds** exists.
  - **Acceptance** and **Revocation** must be **communicated by offeree to offeror.**
  - A **counteroffer** terminates the original offer and initiates a new offer.
- Made by **legally competent parties** between parties of **legal age** who are able to understand the nature or consequences of their actions.
  - A contract with a minor is **voidable.**
- Supported by **legal consideration**
  - something of legal value, which could be *love and affection*, and
  - free of **undue influence** or **fraud.**
- Concerned with a **legal act**

A contract may be

- **express** or **implied** by conduct of parties;
- required to be **in writing** to be **enforceable** in a court of law;
- **bilateral** (having obligations on both sides) or **unilateral** (a promise by one side that can be accepted or rejected by the other side);
- **executed** (all parties have fulfilled their promises) or **executory** (one or both parties still has an act to perform);
- **void** if one of the essential elements is missing; or
- **voidable** if it may be **rescinded** or **disaffirmed** by one or both parties.

Contracts may be **discharged** (completed) by the following:

- **Performance,** which completes the contract terms
- **Partial performance,** if agreeable to both parties
- **Substantial performance,** depending on circumstances
- **Impossibility of performance** (required acts cannot be legally accomplished)
- **Assignment** (transfer of rights to **assignee** or **delegation** of duties)
- **Novation** (substitutes a new contract or party for the original)
- **Breach** by one of the parties without legal excuse
  - **Liquidated damages clause** may specify amount seller will receive if buyer defaults.
- Failure to enforce contract within **statute of limitations** (in Georgia, the statute of limitations is six years)
- **Mutual agreement** of parties

- **Operation of law**, as when a contract is void from inception
- **Rescission (cancellation)** by one or both parties

Real estate contracts may be completed by real estate licensees if preprinted, standard contract forms are used. **Real estate licensees who are not licensed attorneys may not practice law**. Standard forms may include the following:

- **Listing agreement**
- **Buyer agency agreement**
- **Real estate sales contract**
  - Usually accompanied by **earnest money deposit** held in **trust** or **escrow account** to avoid **commingling** with broker's own funds.
  - **Contingencies** to the sale (such as mortgage, inspection, and property sale contingencies) must be stated in the contract.
  - May provide for purchaser's right to inspect the property.
  - **Disclosures** required by state law must be made.
- **Land contract—contract for deed, bond for title, installment contract, land sales contract, articles of agreement for warranty deed**
- **Lease** between **lessor (landlord)** and **lessee (tenant)**
- **Escrow agreement** between buyer, seller, and escrow holder

■ RELATED WEB SITE

FindLaw: Contract Law: *www.findlaw.com/01topics/07contracts*

CHAPTER 11 QUIZ

1. A legally enforceable agreement under which two parties promise to do something for each other is known as a(n)

   a. escrow agreement.
   b. legal pledge.
   c. valid contract.
   d. option agreement.

2. Dave approaches Bob and says, "I'd like to buy your house." Bob says, "Sure," and they agree on a price. What kind of contract is this?

   a. Implied
   b. Unenforceable
   c. Void
   d. There is no contract.

3. A contract is said to be *bilateral* if

   a. one of the parties is a minor.
   b. the contract has yet to be fully performed.
   c. only one party to the agreement is bound to act.
   d. all parties to the contract exchange binding promises.

4. During the period of time after a real estate sales contract is signed, but before title actually passes, the status of the contract is

   a. voidable.
   b. executory.
   c. unilateral.
   d. implied.

5. A contract for the sale of real estate that does not state the consideration to be paid for the property and is not signed by the parties is considered to be

   a. voidable.
   b. executory.
   c. void.
   d. enforceable.

6. Nick and Kelly sign a contract under which Nick will convey Raptor Manor to Kelly. Nick changes his mind, and Kelly sues for specific performance. What is Kelly seeking in this lawsuit?

   a. Money damages
   b. New contract
   c. Deficiency judgment
   d. Conveyance of the property

7. In a standard sales contract, several words were crossed out or inserted by the parties. To eliminate future controversy as to whether the changes were made before or after the contract was signed, the usual procedure is to

   a. write a letter to each party listing the changes.
   b. have each party write a letter to the other approving the changes.
   c. redraw the entire contract.
   d. have both parties initial or sign in the margin near each change.

8. Mark makes an offer on Yolanda's house, and Yolanda accepts. Both parties sign the sales contract. At this point, Mark has what type of title to the property?

   a. Equitable
   b. Voidable
   c. Escrow
   d. Contract

9. The sales contract says the buyer will purchase only if an attorney approves the sale by the following Saturday. The attorney's approval is a

   a. contingency.
   b. reservation.
   c. warranty.
   d. consideration.

10. A broker uses earnest money placed in the company trust account to pay for the rent owed on the broker's office. Using escrow funds for this purpose is
    a. commingling of funds and is illegal.
    b. legal if the trust account is reimbursed by the end of the calendar month.
    c. legal if the seller gives consent in writing.
    d. conversion of funds and is illegal.

11. An option to purchase binds which of the following parties?
    a. Buyer only
    b. Seller only
    c. Neither buyer nor seller
    d. Both buyer and seller

12. Carl and Hannah enter into a real estate sales contract. Under the contract's terms, Carl will pay Hannah $500 a month for ten years. Hannah will continue to hold legal title to Mandalay Mansion. Carl will live in Mandalay Mansion and pay all real estate taxes, insurance premiums, and regular upkeep costs. What kind of contract do Carl and Hannah have?
    a. Option contract
    b. Contract for mortgage
    c. Unilateral contract
    d. Land or installment contract

13. Under the statute of frauds, all contracts for the sale of real estate must be
    a. originated by a real estate broker.
    b. on preprinted forms.
    c. in writing to be enforceable.
    d. accompanied by earnest money deposits.

14. The Fitzgeralds offer in writing to purchase a house for $120,000, including its draperies, with the offer to expire on Saturday at noon. The Wonderlies reply in writing on Thursday, accepting the $120,000 offer, but excluding the draperies. On Friday, while the Fitzgeralds consider this counteroffer, the Wonderlies decide to accept the original offer, draperies included, and state that in writing. At this point, the Fitzgeralds
    a. are legally bound to buy the house although they have the right to insist that the draperies be included.
    b. are not bound to buy.
    c. must buy the house and are not entitled to the draperies.
    d. must buy the house but may deduct the value of the draperies from the $120,000.

15. A buyer makes an offer to purchase certain property listed with a broker and leaves a deposit with the broker to show good faith. The broker should
    a. immediately apply the deposit to the listing expenses.
    b. put the deposit in an account, as provided by state law.
    c. give the deposit to the seller when the offer is presented.
    d. put the deposit in the broker's personal checking account.

16. From June 5 through October 15, Madeline suffered from a mental illness that caused delusions, hallucinations, and loss of memory. On July 1, Madeline signed a contract to purchase Brown's Farm, with the closing set for October 31. On September 24, Madeline began psychiatric treatment. Madeline was declared completely cured by October 15. Which of the following statements regarding Madeline's contract to purchase Brown's Farm is TRUE?
    a. The contract is voidable.
    b. The contract is void.
    c. The contract lacks reality of consent.
    d. The contract is fully valid and enforceable.

17. A broker has found a buyer for a seller's home. The buyer has indicated in writing a willingness to buy the property for $1,000 less than the asking price and has deposited $5,000 in earnest money with the broker. The seller is out of town for the weekend, and the broker has been unable to inform the seller of the signed document. At this point, the buyer has signed a(n)

    a. voidable contract.
    b. offer.
    c. executory agreement.
    d. implied contract.

18. A buyer and seller agree to the purchase of a house for $200,000. The contract contains a clause stating that time is of the essence. Which of the following statements is *TRUE?*

    a. The closing must take place within a reasonable period before the stated date.
    b. A time-is-of-the-essence clause is not binding on either party.
    c. The closing date must be stated as a particular calendar date, and not simply as a formula, such as "two weeks after loan approval."
    d. If the closing date passes and no closing takes place, the contract may be rescinded by the party who was ready to settle on the scheduled date.

19. A buyer signs a contract to purchase an office building in Savannah. The contract is silent as to who bears the risk of loss prior to closing. After the contract is signed, but before the closing, the building burns to the ground. According to Georgia law,

    a. the buyer can void the contract for lack of consideration.
    b. the buyer can rescind the contract but forfeits the earnest money.
    c. the buyer must bear the risk of loss or damage before the closing.
    d. the parties must split the loss equitably.

20. In Georgia, the statute of limitations for bringing a legal action based on a real estate sales contract is

    a. two years.
    b. four years.
    c. six years.
    d. ten years.

CHAPTER

12

Transfer of Title

■ TITLE

The term **title** has two meanings. Title to real estate means *the right to or ownership of the land*; it represents the owner's bundle of rights, discussed in Chapter 8. *Title* also serves as *evidence* of that ownership. A person who holds the title, if challenged in court, would be able to recover or retain ownership or possession of a parcel of real estate. *Title* is just a way of referring to ownership; it is *not* an actual printed document. The document by which the owner transfers his or her title to another is the *deed*. The deed must be recorded to give public notice of the holder's ownership.

Real estate may be transferred *voluntarily* by sale or gift. Alternatively, it may be transferred *involuntarily* by operation of law. Real estate may be transferred while the owner lives or by will or descent after the owner dies. In any case, it is the title that is transferred as a symbol of ownership.

■ VOLUNTARY ALIENATION

A **grantor** conveys property to a grantee.

A **grantee** receives property from a grantor.

A **deed** is the instrument that conveys property from a grantor to a grantee.

Voluntary alienation is the legal term for the voluntary transfer of title. The owner may voluntarily transfer title by either making a gift or selling the property. To transfer during one's lifetime, the owner must use some form of deed of conveyance.

A **deed** is the written instrument by which an owner of real estate intentionally conveys the right, title, or interest in the parcel of real estate to someone else. The statute of frauds requires that all deeds be in writing. The owner who transfers the title is referred to as the **grantor**. The person who acquires the title is called the **grantee**. A deed is executed (that is, signed) only by the grantor. To be able to execute a valid deed, the grantor must have legal capacity.

The formal requirements for a deed are created by state law, and thus vary from state to state.

Requirements for a Valid Deed

Georgia law requires that a valid deed contain the following elements:

In Georgia

- ■ A written instrument purporting to convey title to land
- ■ Grantor who has the legal competency to execute (sign) the deed
- ■ Grantee named with reasonable certainty to be identified
- ■ Recital of consideration
- ■ Granting clause (words of conveyance)
- ■ Habendum clause (to define ownership taken by the grantee)
- ■ Accurate legal description of the property conveyed
- ■ Any relevant exceptions or reservations
- ■ Signature of the grantor, which in Georgia must be witnessed by two parties (a competent adult and an official witness such as a notary public)
- ■ Delivery of the deed and acceptance by the grantee to pass title

A deed also may include a description of any *limitations* on the conveyance of a full fee simple estate and a recital of any *exceptions and reservations* (also known as *"subject to" clauses*) that affect title to the property.

Grantor   A grantor must be of *lawful age*, usually at least 18 years old. A deed executed by a minor is generally voidable.

A grantor also must be of *sound mind*. Generally, any grantor who can understand the action is viewed as mentally capable of executing a valid deed. A deed executed by someone who was mentally impaired at the time is voidable, but it is not void. If, however, the grantor has been judged legally incompetent, the deed will be void. Real estate owned by someone who is legally incompetent can be conveyed only with a court's approval.

The grantor's name must be spelled correctly and consistently throughout the deed. If the grantor's name has been changed since the title was acquired, as when a person changes his or her name by marriage, both names should be shown—for example, "Mary Smith, formerly Mary Jones."

Grantee   To be valid, a deed must name a grantee. The grantee must be specifically named so that the person to whom the property is being conveyed can be readily identified from the deed itself.

■ **FOR EXAMPLE**   Olive wanted to convey Whiteacre to her nephew, Jack Jackson. In the deed, Olive wrote the following words of conveyance: "I, Olive Burbank, hereby convey to Jack all my interest in Whiteacre." The only problem was that Olive also had a son named Jack, a cousin Jack, and a neighbor Jack. The grantee's identity could not be discerned from the deed itself. Olive should have conveyed Whiteacre "to my nephew, Jack Jackson."

If more than one grantee is involved, the granting clause should specify their rights in the property. The clause might state, for instance, that the grantees will take title as joint tenants or tenants in common. This is especially important when specific wording is necessary to create a joint tenancy.

Consideration   A valid deed must contain a clause acknowledging that the grantor has received consideration. Generally, the amount of consideration is stated in dollars. When a deed conveys real estate as a gift to a relative, love and affection may be sufficient consideration. In most states, however, it is customary to recite a *nominal* consideration, such as "$10 and other good and valuable consideration."

Granting Clause (Words of Conveyance)

A deed must contain a **granting clause** that states the grantor's intention to convey the property. Depending on the type of deed and the obligations agreed to by the grantor, the wording would be similar to one of the following:

■ "I, *JKL*, convey and warrant . . ."
■ "I, *JKL*, remise, release, alienate, and convey . . ."

- "I, *JKL*, grant, bargain, and sell . . ."
- "I, *JKL*, remise, release, and quitclaim . . ."

A deed that conveys the grantor's entire fee simple interest usually contains wording such as "to *ABC* and to her heirs and assigns forever." If the grantor conveys less than his or her complete interest, such as a life estate, the wording must indicate this limitation—for example, "to *ABC* for the duration of her natural life."

In order to convey property, the grantor must have a **vested interest** in the property. A vested interest is a present right, interest, or title to property that gives the holder the right to convey it to another, even though the right might not be enjoyed until a future time. For example, Arlo deeds a property to Betty. Title to the property vests in Betty. Later, Betty deeds the title to her daughter, Carmen, for her lifetime. Upon Carmen's death, title is to pass to Carmen's son, Don. A remainder interest vests in Don. Don may not take possession of the property until his mother's death, but meanwhile he can sell or transfer his interest in the property.

Habendum clause   When it is necessary to define or explain the ownership to be enjoyed by the grantee, a **habendum clause** may follow the granting clause. The habendum clause begins with the words *to have and to hold*. Its provisions must agree with those stated in the granting clause. For example, if a grantor conveys a time-share interest or an interest less than fee simple absolute, the habendum clause would specify the owner's rights as well as how those rights are limited (a specific time frame or certain prohibited activities, for instance).

Legal description of real estate   To be valid, a deed must contain an accurate legal description of the real estate conveyed. Land is considered adequately described if its sufficiency can be established in court.

Exceptions and reservations   A valid deed must specifically note any encumbrances, reservations, or limitations that affect the title being conveyed. This might include such things as restrictions and easements that run with the land. In addition to citing existing encumbrances, a grantor may reserve some right in the land, such as an easement, for his or her own use. A grantor may also place certain restrictions on a grantee's use of the property. Developers often restrict the number of houses that may be built on each lot in a subdivision. Such private restrictions must be stated in the deed or contained in a previously recorded document, such as the subdivider's master deed, that is expressly referred to in the deed. Many of these deed restrictions have time limits and often include renewal clauses.

In Georgia | **Signature of grantor**   To be valid, a deed must be signed by all grantors named in the deed. Georgia requires witnesses to the grantor's signature, but only for purposes of recording. The deed is binding between grantor and grantee without witnesses.

In Georgia, an attorney-in-fact can sign for a grantor. (An attorney-in-fact is not necessarily an attorney-at-law.) The attorney-in-fact must act under a *power of attorney*—the specific written authority to execute and sign one or more legal instruments for another person. The power of attorney must be recorded in the county where the property is located. The power of attorney terminates when the person on whose behalf it is exercised dies. As a result, adequate evidence must be submitted that the grantor was alive at the time the attorney-in-fact signed the deed.

A grantor's spouse is not required to sign any deed of conveyance to waive any marital or homestead rights in Georgia. The spouse is required to sign if he or she is an owner of the property.

Many states, including Georgia, still require a *seal* (or simply the word *seal* or the initials *L.S.*) to be written or printed after an individual grantor's signature. The corporate seal may be required of a corporate grantor.

Acknowledgment   An **acknowledgment** is a formal declaration that the person who signs a written document does so *voluntarily* and that his or her signature is genuine. The declaration is made before a *notary public* or an authorized public officer, such as a judge, a justice of the peace, or some other person as prescribed by state law. An acknowledgment usually states that the person signing the deed or other document is known to the officer or has produced sufficient identification to prevent a forgery. An acknowledgment does not relieve the Georgia requirement of having two witnesses.

Delivery and acceptance   A title is not considered transferred until the deed is actually *delivered* to and *accepted* by the grantee. The grantor may deliver the deed to the grantee either personally or through a third party. The third party, commonly known as an *escrow agent* (or *settlement agent*), will deliver the deed to the grantee as soon as certain requirements have been satisfied. *Title is said to "pass" only when a deed is delivered and accepted.* The effective date of the transfer of title from the grantor to the grantee is the date of delivery of the deed itself. (However, under the Torrens system, as discussed in Chapter 13, title does not pass until the deed has been examined and accepted for registration.)

> Transfer of title requires both delivery and acceptance of the deed.

Execution of Corporate Deeds

The laws governing a corporation's right to convey real estate vary from state to state. However, two basic rules must be followed:

1. A corporation can convey real estate only by authority granted in its *bylaws* or on a proper resolution passed by its *board of directors*. If all or a substantial portion of a corporation's real estate is being conveyed, usually a resolution authorizing the sale must be secured from the *shareholders*.
2. Deeds to real estate can be signed *only by an authorized officer*.

Rules pertaining to religious corporations and not-for-profit corporations vary even more widely. Because the legal requirements must be followed exactly, an attorney should be consulted for all corporate conveyances.

Types of Deeds

A deed can take several forms, depending on the extent of the grantor's pledges to the grantee. Regardless of any guarantees the deed offers, however, the grantee will want additional assurance that the grantor has the right to offer what the deed conveys. To obtain this protection, grantees commonly seek evidence of title, discussed in Chapter 13.

In Georgia

The most common deed forms in Georgia are the

- general warranty deed,
- special warranty deed (limited warranty deed),
- quitclaim deed,
- deed to secure debt (security deed),
- trustee's deed, and
- deed executed pursuant to a court order.

Deed forms used in other states also include bargain and sale deed and reconveyance deed.

General Warranty Deed

Five covenants:
1. Covenant of seisin
2. Covenant against encumbrances
3. Covenant of quiet enjoyment
4. Covenant of further assurance (not in Georgia)
5. Covenant of warranty forever

General warranty deed   A **general warranty deed** provides the greatest protection to the buyer. It is called a *general warranty deed* because the grantor is legally bound by certain covenants or warranties. In most states, including Georgia, the warranties are implied by the use of certain words specified by statute. In some states, the grantor's warranties are expressly written into the deed itself. Each state law should be examined, but some of the specific words include *convey and warrant* or *warrant generally*. The basic warranties are as follows:

- *Covenant of seisin:* The grantor warrants that he or she owns the property and has the right to convey title to it. (*Seisin* simply means *possession.*) The grantee may recover damages up to the full purchase price if this covenant is broken.
- *Covenant against encumbrances:* The grantor warrants that the property is free from liens or encumbrances, except for any specifically stated in the deed. Encumbrances generally include mortgages, mechanics' liens, and easements. If this covenant is breached, the grantee may sue for the cost of removing the encumbrances.
- *Covenant of quiet enjoyment:* The grantor guarantees that the grantee's title will be good against third parties who might bring court actions to establish superior title to the property. If the grantee's title is found to be inferior, the grantor is liable for damages.

In Georgia
- *Covenant of further assurance:* The grantor promises to obtain and deliver any instrument needed to make the title good. Georgia does not recognize the covenant of further assurance.
- *Covenant of warranty forever:* The grantor promises to compensate the grantee for the loss sustained if the title fails at any time in the future.

These covenants in a general warranty deed are not limited to matters that occurred during the time the grantor owned the property; they extend back to its origins. The grantor defends the title against both himself or herself and *all those who previously held title*.

<table>
<tr><td>

Special Warranty Deed

Two warranties:
1. Warranty that grantor received title
2. Warranty that property was unencumbered by grantor

</td></tr>
</table>

Special warranty deed (or limited warranty deed) A special warranty deed (or **limited warranty deed**) contains two basic warranties:

1. That the grantor received title
2. That the property was not encumbered *during the time the grantor held title*, except as otherwise noted in the deed

In effect, the grantor defends the title against himself or herself. The granting clause generally contains the words: "Grantor remises, releases, alienates, and conveys." The grantor may include additional warranties, but they must be specifically stated in the deed. In areas where a special warranty deed is more commonly used, the purchase of title insurance is viewed as providing adequate protection to the grantee.

A special warranty deed may be used by trustees, executors, and corporations. A special warranty deed is appropriate because one lacks the authority to warrant against acts of *predecessors in title* (the former owners). One may hold title for a limited time without having a personal interest in the proceeds. Sometimes, a special warranty deed may be used by a grantor who has acquired title at a tax sale.

Quitclaim Deed

No express or implied covenants or warranties:
- Used primarily to convey less than fee simple or to cure a title defect

Quitclaim deed A **quitclaim deed** provides the grantee with the least protection of any deed. It carries *no covenants or warranties* and generally conveys only whatever interest the grantor may have when the deed is delivered. If the grantor has no interest, the grantee will acquire nothing. Nor will the grantee acquire any right of warranty claim against the grantor. A quitclaim deed can convey title as effectively as a warranty deed if the grantor has good title when he or she delivers the deed, but it provides none of the guarantees that a warranty deed does. Through a quitclaim deed, the grantor only "remises, releases, and quitclaims" his or her interest in the property, if any.

Usually, a quitclaim deed is the only type of deed that may be used to convey less than a fee simple estate. This is because a quitclaim deed conveys only the grantor's right, title, or interest.

A quitclaim deed is frequently used to cure a defect, called a *cloud on the title*. For example, if the name of the grantee is misspelled on a warranty deed filed in the public record, a quitclaim deed with the correct spelling may be executed to the grantee to perfect the title.

A quitclaim deed is also used when a grantor allegedly *inherits* property but is not certain that the decedent's title was valid. A warranty deed in such an instance could carry with it obligations of warranty, while a quitclaim deed would convey only the grantor's interest, whatever it may be.

One of the most common uses of the quitclaim deed, however, is a simple *transfer* of property from one family member to another.

In Georgia

Deed to secure debt   A **deed to secure debt** (also known as a *security deed*) is the most commonly used mortgage instrument in Georgia. The borrower conveys legal title to the property to the lender for the purpose of securing the mortgage loan. The borrower retains equitable title, which includes all the benefits of ownership. If the borrower fails to make the mortgage payments, the lender forecloses on the property.

Trustee's Deed
Conveyance from trustee to third party

Trustee's deed   A deed executed by a trustee is a **trustee's deed.** It is used when a trustee conveys real estate held in the trust to anyone *other than the trustor.* The trustee's deed must state that the trustee is executing the instrument in accordance with the powers and authority granted by the trust instrument.

Deed executed pursuant to a court order   Executors' and administrators' deeds, masters' deeds, sheriffs' deeds, and many other types are all *deeds executed pursuant to a court order.* These deeds are established by state statute and are used to convey title to property that is transferred by court order or by will. The form of such a deed must conform to the laws of the state in which the property is located.

One common characteristic of deeds executed pursuant to court order is that the *full consideration* is usually stated in the deed. Instead of "$10 and other valuable consideration," for example, the deed would list the actual sales price.

Transfer Tax

Many states have enacted laws providing for a state **transfer tax** (also referred to in some states as a *grantor's tax*) on conveyances of real estate. In these states, the tax is usually payable when the deed is recorded.

In Georgia

Georgia law (O.C.G.A. 48-6-1 et seq.) requires that a transfer tax on conveyances of real estate be payable when the deed is recorded. The deed cannot be recorded unless the tax has been paid. The tax rate is one dollar for the first $1,000 or fraction thereof of the sales price, and ten cents for each additional $100 or fraction thereof. The tax is imposed on the seller, but may be paid by the purchaser.

MATH CONCEPTS

CALCULATING TRANSFER TAXES

The sales price of house is $189,450. The tax may be calculated as $1 for every whole $1,000 and 10 cents for each $100 above the whole thousands. The $50 is a fraction of $100, so $450 counts as $500.

$$189 \times \$1.00 = \$189$$
$$5 \times 0.10 = 0.50$$

Total transfer tax is $189.50.

| In Georgia | Under Georgia law, O.C.G.A. 48-6-2, certain deeds and instruments are exempt from the Georgia transfer tax: |

- Deeds to secure debt
- Deeds of gift
- Deeds executed by the state of Georgia, the United States, or any political subdivision of them (such as counties)
- Any lease of lands or tenements
- Any transfer of real estate between a husband and wife in a divorce case
- Any order for year's support awarding an interest in real property
- Deeds issued in lieu of foreclosure if deed is for a purchase money deed to secure debt that has existed for 12 months prior to the recording of the deed
- Deed from debtor to the first transferee at a foreclosure sale
- Deed that seeks to return property sold at a tax sale back to a defendant
- Deed of assent or distribution by an executor or a deed used to carry out a power of appointment
- Quitclaim deeds in which no consideration passes
- Deeds that affect a division of real property among joint tenants or tenants in common
- Deeds through which real property is transferred to a corporation and owners of the property have a majority ownership in the corporation, and vice versa
- Sales at a price of less than $100

■ INVOLUNTARY ALIENATION

Title to property may be transferred without the owner's consent by **involuntary alienation.** (See Figure 12.1.) Adverse possession is discussed later in this chapter. For a discussion of escheat and eminent domain, see Chapter 7; for a discussion of foreclosure, see Chapter 15. Involuntary transfers are usually carried out by operation of law—such as by condemnation or a sale to satisfy delinquent tax or mortgage liens. When a person dies intestate and leaves no heirs, the title to the real estate passes to the state by the state's power of escheat. As discussed in Chapter 7, land may be acquired through the process of accretion or actually lost through erosion.

Other acts of nature, such as earthquakes, hurricanes, sinkholes, and mudslides, may create or eliminate a landowner's holdings.

Transfer by Adverse Possession

Adverse possession is another means of involuntary transfer. An individual who makes a claim to certain property, takes possession of it, and, most important, uses it, may take title away from an owner who fails to use or inspect the property for a period of years. The law recognizes that the use of land is an important function of its ownership.

Involuntary Alienation

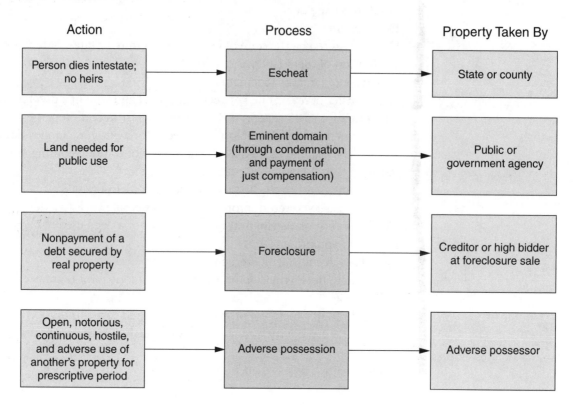

Usually, the possession by the claimant must be all of the following:

- *Open* (that is, obvious to anyone who looks)
- *Notorious* (that is, known by others)
- *Continuous* and uninterrupted
- *Hostile* (that is, without the true owner's consent)
- *Adverse* to the true owner's possession

In Georgia   In addition, in Georgia, possession must be

- accompanied by a claim of right in the possessor, and
- free of originating in fraud.

The necessary period of uninterrupted possession is a matter of state law. The statutory periods range from as few as five years in some states to as many as 30 years in others. Through the principle of *tacking* (discussed in Chapter 7), successive periods of different adverse possession by different adverse possessors can be combined, enabling a person who is not in possession for the entire required time to establish a claim.

In Georgia   Georgia has two different rules pertaining to adverse possession. If the possessor is in possession under a *claim of right*, the period of time for adverse possession to ripen into title is 20 years. If the possessor is in possession under *color of title* (such as a defective deed) the period is shortened to seven years.

In order to establish title by adverse possession, there must be proof of non-permissive use that is actual, open, notorious, exclusive, and adverse for the statutorily prescribed period. To claim title, the adverse possessor normally files an action in court to receive undisputed title. A claimant who does not receive title may acquire an easement by prescription.

IN PRACTICE   The right of adverse possession is a statutory right. State requirements must be followed carefully to ensure the successful transfer of title. The parties to a transaction that might involve adverse possession should seek legal counsel.

■ TRANSFER OF A DECEASED PERSON'S PROPERTY

A person who dies **testate** has prepared a will indicating how his or her property will be disposed of. In contrast, when a person dies **intestate** (without a will), real estate and personal property pass to the decedent's heirs according to the state's *statute of descent and distribution*. In effect, the state makes a will for an intestate decedent.

Legally, when a person dies, ownership of real estate immediately passes either to the heirs by descent or to the persons named in the will. Before these individuals can take full title and possession of the property, however, the estate must go through a judicial process called *probate,* and all claims against the estate must be satisfied.

Transfer of Title by Will

A **will** is an instrument made by an owner to convey title to real or personal property after the owner's death. A will is a testamentary instrument, that is, it takes effect only after death. This differs from a deed, which *must* be delivered during the lifetime of the grantor and which conveys a present interest in property. While the **testator,** the person who makes a will, is alive, any property included in the will still can be conveyed by the owner. The parties named in a will have no rights or interests as long as the party who made the will lives; they acquire interest or title only after the owner's death.

Only property owned by the testator at the time of his or her death may be transferred by will. The gift of real property by will is known as a **devise,** and a person who receives property by will is known as a *devisee.* The other two gifts by will are a bequest, which is a gift of personal property, and a legacy, which is a gift of money.

For title to pass to the devisees, state laws require that on the death of a testator, the will must be filed with the court and *probated.* Probate is a legal procedure for verifying the validity of a will and accounting for the decedent's assets. The process can take several months to complete.

| In Georgia | A will cannot supersede the Georgia law of year's support, which was enacted to protect the inheritance rights of a surviving spouse and minor children. When a will does not provide a spouse with a sufficient inheritance, he or she may demand it from the estate.

Legal requirements for making a will   A will must be executed and prepared according to the laws of the state in which the real estate is located. Only a valid and probated will can effectively convey title to real estate.

A testator must have legal capacity to make a will. There are no rigid tests to determine legal capacity. Usually, a person must be of *legal age* and of *sound mind.* Legal age varies from state to state. To demonstrate sound mind, the testator must have sufficient mental capacity to understand the nature and extent of the property he or she owns. A testator must understand the identity of his or her natural heirs and that the property will go to those persons named in the will. The drawing of a will must be a voluntary act, free of any undue influence by other people.

| In Georgia | In most states, including Georgia, a written will must be signed by its testator before two or more witnesses, who must also sign the document. The witnesses should not be individuals who are named as devisees in the will. Some states, including Georgia, do not permit real property to be conveyed by oral (*nuncupative*) wills or handwritten (*holographic*) wills.

A testator may alter a will any time before his or her death. Any modification, amendment, or addition to a previously executed will is contained in a separate document called a *codicil*.

Transfer of Title by Descent

| In Georgia | When a person dies intestate, title to his or her real estate and personal property passes to the decedent's heirs as determined by state law. Under Georgia's statute of descent and distribution, the primary **heirs** of the deceased are his or her spouse and close blood relatives (such as children, parents, brothers, sisters, aunts, uncles, and, in some cases, first and second cousins). The right to inherit under laws of descent varies from state to state, and intestate property is distributed according to the laws of the state in which the property is located. (See Table 12.1.)

Probate Proceedings

Probate is a formal judicial process that

- proves or confirms the validity of a will,
- determines the precise assets of the deceased person, and
- identifies the persons to whom the assets are to pass.

The purpose of probate is to see that the assets are distributed correctly. All assets must be accounted for, and the decedent's debts must be satisfied before any property is distributed to the heirs. In addition, estate taxes must be paid

TABLE 12.1

Sample Statutory Distributions

This table illustrates how a state's statute of descent and distribution might provide for an intestate's estate. The specific persons entitled to property, and the various percentages involved, vary from state to state. Remember: *Licensees should never try to determine descent or ownership status without consulting with legal counsel.*

Decedent Status	Family Status	How Property Passes
Married, surviving spouse[1]	No children No other relatives	100% to surviving spouse
	Children	50% to surviving spouse 50% shared by children or descendants of deceased child
Married, no surviving spouse	Children	Children share equally, with descendants of a deceased child taking their parent's share
Unmarried, no children	Relatives	100% to father or mother, brothers or sisters, or other relatives (such as grandparents or great-grandparents; uncles or aunts; nieces or nephews; first or second cousins) in order of priority
	No relatives or heirs as defined by state law	100% to state by escheat

[1]Some states allow the decedent's spouse the right to elect a life estate of dower or curtesy (as discussed in Chapter 7) in place of the share provided for in the law of descent. In Georgia, year's support takes the place of dower and curtesy.

before any distribution. The laws of each state govern the probate proceedings and the functions of the individuals appointed to administer the decedent's affairs.

Assets that are distributed through probate are those that do not otherwise distribute themselves. For instance, property held in joint tenancy or tenancy by the entirety passes immediately. Probate proceedings take place in the county *in which the decedent resided*. If the decedent owned real estate in another county, probate would occur in that county as well.

The person who has possession of the will—normally the person designated in the will as *executor*—presents it for filing with the Probate Court. The court is responsible for determining that the will meets the statutory requirements for its form and execution. If a codicil or more than one will exists, the court will decide how these documents should be probated.

The court must rule on a challenge if a will is contested. Once the will is upheld, the assets can be distributed according to its provisions. Probate courts distribute assets according to statute only when no other reasonable alternative exists.

When a person dies *intestate*, the court determines who inherits the assets by reviewing proof from relatives of the decedent and their entitlement under the statute of descent and distribution. Once the heirs have been determined, the court appoints an *administrator* or a *personal representative* to administer the affairs of the estate—the role usually taken by an executor.

Whether or not a will is involved, the administrator or executor is responsible for having the estate's assets appraised and for ensuring that all the decedent's debts are satisfied. He or she is also responsible for paying federal estate taxes and state inheritance taxes out of the assets. Once all obligations have been satisfied, the representative distributes the remaining property according to the terms of the will or the state's law of descent.

IN PRACTICE A broker entering into a listing agreement with the executor or administrator of an estate in probate should be aware that the amount of commission is approved by the court and that the commission is payable only from the proceeds of the sale. The broker will not be able to collect a commission unless the court approves the sale.

■ KEY POINT REVIEW

Title is **ownership,** or the right to ownership, of land, and **evidence** of that ownership.

Voluntary alienation, the voluntary transfer of title to real estate by **gift or sale** using some form of **deed.**

- **Grantor** (person who transfers title) must be of legal age and legally competent to execute (sign) deed. A deed executed by a **minor** is **voidable.**
  - **Mental impairment** at time of signing deed makes deed voidable.
  - If grantor has been declared **incompetent by a judge**, deed is **void.**
  - All names grantor has used should be provided.
- **Grantee** must be identifiable with sufficient certainty.
- **Consideration** (payment) of some form must be stated.
- **Granting clause** (words of conveyance) must be used.
- **Habendum clause** must define ownership interest taken by grantee; it specifies limits on ownership, such as with a time-share.
- **Legal description** of the property conveyed is essential.
- **Exceptions** or **reservations** of any relevance must be included.
- **Signature of the grantor(s)** must be **witnessed** by notary public or other official authorized and one unofficial witness in Georgia | In Georgia
- **Delivery** of the deed and **acceptance** by grantee is necessary.

Types of deeds include the following:

- **General warranty deed** provides greatest protection to grantee and includes:
  - **covenant of seisin:** warrants the grantor has the right to convey title;
  - **covenant against encumbrances:** warrants the property is free from liens or encumbrances, unless expressly stated;

- — **covenant of quiet enjoyment**: makes the grantor liable for damages if the grantee's title is found to be inferior;
- — **covenant of warranty forever**: the grantor's promise to compensate the grantee if title fails at any future time.

- ■ **Special warranty deed** (or **limited warranty deed**) includes the warranties that grantor received title and that property was not encumbered during the time the grantor held title, except as otherwise noted.
- ■ **Quitclaim deed** provides the least protection of any deed, carries no covenants or warranties, and conveys only whatever interest the grantor may have when deed is delivered.

In Georgia
- ■ **Deed to secure debt** is the Georgia form of mortgage instrument by which the borrower pledges real property as collateral for a debt.
- ■ **Trustee's deed** is used when trustee conveys property held in trust.
- ■ **Deed executed pursuant to court order** may be executors' and administrators' deeds, masters' deeds, sheriffs' deeds, and others; and usually states actual full consideration for deed.

In Georgia

In Georgia, transfer tax is required to be paid before recording deeds and conveyances.

Involuntary alienation (transfer) of title to property is usually by operation of law.

- ■ **Escheat**—property taken by state when deceased has no heirs
- ■ **Eminent domain**—property taken by public or government agency
- ■ **Foreclosure**—property taken by creditor for nonpayment of debt secured by real property
- ■ **Adverse possession**—property seizure occurring when someone who is not the lawful owner takes possession of property for the length of time specified by state law and usually in a way that is <u>O</u>pen, <u>N</u>otorious, <u>C</u>ontinuous, <u>H</u>ostile, <u>A</u>dverse, and in Georgia, under a claim of right, and not originating in fraud.

Transfer of title by will occurs when deceased dies **testate** (leaving a will), prepared as required by state law that generally includes the following:

- ■ Takes effect only after death and can be changed by **codicil** or revoked while **testator** is still alive.
- ■ **Devise** is gift of real property by will to the **devisee**.
- ■ **Bequest** is gift of personal property.
- ■ **Legacy** is gift of money.
- ■ To pass title to property on death, will must be **filed with court** and **probated**.
- ■ Will cannot supersede state laws protecting inheritance rights of surviving wife (**dower**) or husband (**curtesy**).

Transfer of title under a state's **statute of descent and distribution** occurs when a person dies **intestate** (without a will). **Probate** proceedings must be brought and an administrator appointed, and laws of the state where the real property is **located** govern property distribution.

CHAPTER 12 QUIZ

1. The basic requirements for a valid conveyance are governed by
   a. state law.
   b. local custom.
   c. national law.
   d. the law of descent.

2. Every deed must be signed by the
   a. grantor.
   b. grantee.
   c. grantor and grantee.
   d. devisee.

3. Henry, age 15, recently inherited many parcels of real estate from his late father and has decided to sell one of them. If Henry entered into a deed conveying his interest in the property to a purchaser, such a conveyance would be
   a. valid.
   b. void.
   c. invalid.
   d. voidable.

4. An instrument authorizing one person to act for another is called a(n)
   a. power of attorney.
   b. release deed.
   c. quitclaim deed.
   d. attorney-in-fact.

5. Under the covenant of quiet enjoyment, the grantor
   a. promises to obtain and deliver any instrument needed to make the title good.
   b. guarantees that if the title fails in the future, he or she will compensate the grantee.
   c. warrants that he or she is the owner and has the right to convey title to the property.
   d. assures that the title will be good against the title claims of third parties.

6. A deed includes the following statement: "The full consideration for this conveyance is $125,480." Which type of deed is this MOST likely to be?
   a. Gift deed
   b. Trustee's deed
   c. Deed in trust
   d. Deed executed pursuant to court order

7. Step 1: Doris decided to convey Blue House to John. Step 2: Doris signed a deed transferring title to John. Step 3: Doris gave the signed deed to John, who accepted it. Step 4: John took the deed to the county recorder's office and had it recorded. At which step did title to Blue House actually transfer or pass to John?
   a. Step 1
   b. Step 2
   c. Step 3
   d. Step 4

8. Luis conveys property to Ken by deed. The deed contains the following: (1) Ken's name, spelled out in full; (2) a statement that Luis has received $10 and Ken's love and affection; and (3) a statement that the property is for Ken "to have and to hold." Which of the following correctly identifies, in order, these three elements of the deed?
   a. Grantee; consideration; granting clause
   b. Grantee; consideration; habendum clause
   c. Grantor; habendum clause; legal description
   d. Grantee; acknowledgment; habendum clause

9. Wally signed a deed transferring ownership of his house to Luke. To provide evidence that his signature was genuine, Wally executed a declaration before a notary. This declaration is known as an
   a. affidavit.
   b. acknowledgment.
   c. affirmation.
   d. estoppel.

10. Rachel executes a deed to Peter as grantee, has it acknowledged, and receives payment from the buyer. Rachel holds the deed, however, and arranges to meet Peter the next morning at the courthouse to give the deed to him. At this point

    a. Peter owns the property because he has paid for it.

    b. legal title to the property will not officially pass until Peter has been given the deed the next morning.

    c. legal title to the property will not pass until Peter has received the deed and records it the next morning.

    d. Peter will own the property when he signs the deed the next morning.

11. Title to real estate may be transferred during a person's lifetime by

    a. devise.

    b. descent.

    c. involuntary alienation.

    d. escheat.

12. Ben bought acreage in a distant county, never went to see the acreage, and did not use the ground. Hilda moved her mobile home onto the land, had a water well drilled, and lived there for 22 years. Hilda may become the owner of the land if she has complied with the state law regarding

    a. requirements for a valid conveyance.

    b. adverse possession.

    c. avulsion.

    d. voluntary alienation.

13. Eminent domain and escheat are two examples of

    a. voluntary alienation.

    b. adverse possession.

    c. transfers of title by descent.

    d. involuntary alienation.

14. A house sells for $155,000; the buyer pays $50,000 in cash and gives the seller a mortgage for the balance. If the state has a transfer tax rate of 1 percent, what is the amount of state transfer tax that must be paid?

    a. $1,550

    b. $1,055

    c. $15,500

    d. $105,000

15. A person who has died without a will has died

    a. devisee.

    b. intestate.

    c. legatee.

    d. testator.

16. Title to real estate can be transferred at death by which of the following documents?

    a. Warranty deed

    b. Special warranty deed

    c. Trustee's deed

    d. Will

17. Jacob, a bachelor, died owning real estate that he devised by his will to his niece, Koralee. When will full title and possession pass to his niece?

    a. Immediately upon Jacob's death

    b. After his will has been probated

    c. After Koralee has paid all inheritance taxes

    d. When Koralee executes a new deed to the property

18. An owner of real estate was declared legally incompetent and was committed to a state mental institution. While institutionalized, the owner wrote and executed a will. The owner later died and was survived by a spouse and three children. The real estate will pass

    a. to the owner's spouse.

    b. to the heirs mentioned in the owner's will.

    c. according to the state laws of descent.

    d. to the state.

19. Generally, where does a probate proceeding involving real property take place?

   a. Only in the county in which the property is located

   b. Only in the county in which the decedent resided

   c. In both the county where the decedent resided and the county in which the property is located

   d. In the county in which the executor or the beneficiary resides

In Georgia

20. To be recorded in Georgia, the deed must be witnessed by

   a. an acknowledgment.

   b. one official witness and one unofficial witness.

   c. an acknowledgment and one unofficial witness.

   d. an acknowledgment and one official witness.

21. Which of the following is *NOT* a covenant of warranty in a Georgia general warranty deed?

   a. Covenant of seisin

   b. Covenant against encumbrances

   c. Covenant of quiet enjoyment

   d. Covenant of further assurance

22. In Georgia, when a borrower pledges a property as collateral for a real estate loan, the document most commonly used is called a

   a. mortgage.

   b. deed to secure debt.

   c. deed of trust.

   d. special warranty deed.

23. The Georgia real estate transfer tax rate is

   a. $1 for every $1,000 and $0.10 per $100 of transferred value.

   b. $1.50 for every $1,000 and $.015 per $100 of transferred value.

   c. $2 for every $1,000 and $0.20 per $100 of transferred value.

   d. $3 for every $10,000 or fraction thereof of transferred value.

24. Under Georgia law, to claim adverse possession, the claim must be

   a. accompanied by a claim of right.

   b. free of originating in fraud.

   c. both a and b.

   d. neither a nor b.

25. The period of time in Georgia in which adverse possession ripens is

   a. seven years under color of title.

   b. five years under a claim of right.

   c. both a and b.

   d. neither a nor b.

CHAPTER 13

Title Records

■ **identify** the various proofs of ownership.

■ **describe** recording, notice, and chain of title issues.

■ **explain** the process and purpose of a title search.

■ **distinguish** constructive and actual notice.

■ **define** the following *key terms:*

abstract of title	financing statement	subrogation
actual notice	inquiry notice	suit to quiet title
attorney's opinion of title	marketable title	title insurance
certificate of title	priority	title search
chain of title	recording	Torrens system
constructive notice	security agreement	Uniform Commercial Code (UCC)

■ PUBLIC RECORDS

Public records contain detailed information about each parcel of real estate in a city or county. These records are crucial in establishing ownership, giving notice of encumbrances, and establishing priority of liens. They protect the interests of real estate owners, taxing bodies, creditors, and the general public. The real estate recording system includes written documents that affect title, such as deeds and mortgages. Public records regarding taxes, judgments, probate, and marriage also may offer important information about the title to a particular property.

Public records are maintained by

- recorders of deeds,
- county clerks,
- county treasurers,
- city clerks,
- collectors, and
- clerks of court.

In Georgia   In Georgia, real estate records are kept by the Clerk of Superior Court of each county.

IN PRACTICE   Although we speak of prospective purchasers conducting title searches, the purchasers themselves rarely search the public records for evidence of title or encumbrances. Instead, *title companies* conduct searches before providing title insurance. An attorney also may search the title. Most lending institutions require title insurance as part of the mortgage loan commitment.

Recording

Recording is the act of placing documents in the public record. The specific rules for recording documents are a matter of state law. However, although the details may vary, all recording acts essentially provide that any written document that affects any estate, right, title, or interest in land *must be recorded in the county (in Georgia, it is by county) where the land is located* to serve as public notice. That way, anyone interested in the title to a parcel of property will know where to look to discover the various interests of all other parties. Recording acts also generally give legal priority to those interests recorded first (the *first in time, first in right* or *first come, first served* principle, discussed in Chapter 10).

In most states, written documents that affect land *must be recorded in the county where the land is located*.

To be *eligible for recording*, a document must be drawn and executed according to the recording acts of the state in which the real estate is located. For instance, a state may require that the parties' names be typed below their signatures or that the document be acknowledged before a notary public. In some states, the document must be witnessed. Others require that the name of the person who prepared the document appear on it. States may have specific rules about the size of documents and the color and quality of paper they are printed on. Electronic recording—using computers or fax machines, for instance—is permitted in a growing number of localities. Some states require a certificate of real estate value and the payment of current property taxes due for recording.

In Georgia

In Georgia, documents require two witnesses: an official witness (usually) a notary public) and an unofficial witness, a competent person above the age of maturity (18 years).

Notice

Anyone who has an interest in a parcel of real estate can take certain steps, called *giving notice*, to ensure that the interest is available to the public. This lets others know about the individual's interest. There are three basic types of notice: constructive notice, actual notice, and inquiry notice.

Constructive notice is the legal presumption that information may be obtained by an individual through diligent inquiry. Properly recording documents in the public record serves as constructive notice to the world of an individual's rights or interest. So does the physical possession of a property. Because the information or evidence is readily available to the world, a prospective purchaser or lender is responsible for discovering the interest.

Actual notice means that not only is the information available but someone has been given the information and actually knows it. An individual who has searched the public records and inspected the property has actual notice. Actual notice is also known as *direct knowledge*. If an individual can be proved to have had actual notice of information, he or she cannot use a lack of constructive notice (such as an unrecorded deed) to justify a claim.

Inquiry notice is notice that the law presumes a reasonable person would obtain by making further inquiry into a property. For example, if a customer is considering buying a rural lot of land and, upon inspecting it, sees a dirt road cutting across the land that is not mentioned in the public records, the customer is expected to make further inquiry into the dirt road.

Priority

Priority refers to the order of rights in time. Many complicated situations can affect the priority of rights in a parcel of real estate—who recorded first; which party was in possession first; who had actual or constructive notice. How the courts rule in any situation depends, of course, on the specific facts of the case. These are strictly legal questions that should be referred to the parties' attorneys.

■ **FOR EXAMPLE** In May, Betsy purchased Grayacre from Andy and received a deed. Betsy never recorded the deed but began farming operations on the property in June. In November, Andy (who was forgetful) again sold Grayacre, this time to Carrie. Carrie accepted the deed and promptly recorded it. However, because Carrie never inspected Grayacre to see whether someone was in possession, Betsy has the superior right to the property *even though Betsy never recorded the deed*. By taking possession, a purchaser gives constructive notice of his or her interest in the land.

Unrecorded Documents

Certain types of liens are not recorded. Real estate taxes and special assessments are liens on specific parcels of real estate and are not usually recorded until some time after the taxes or assessments are past due. Inheritance taxes and franchise taxes are statutory liens. They are placed against all real estate owned by a decedent at the time of death or by a corporation at the time the franchise taxes became a lien. Like real estate taxes, they are not recorded.

Notice of these liens must be gained from sources other than the recorder's office. Evidence of the payment of real estate taxes, special assessments, municipal utilities, and other taxes can be gathered from paid tax receipts and letters from municipalities. Creative measures are often required to get information about these *off the record* liens.

Chain of Title

Chain of title is the record of a property's ownership. Beginning with the earliest owner, title may pass to many individuals. Each owner is linked to the next so that a chain is formed. An unbroken chain of title can be traced through linking conveyances from the present owner back to the earliest recorded owner. Chain of title does not include liens and encumbrances or any other document not directly related to ownership.

If ownership cannot be traced through an unbroken chain, it is said that there is a gap in the chain. In these cases, the cloud on the title makes it necessary to establish ownership by a court action called a **suit to quiet title**. A suit might be required, for instance, when a grantor acquired title under one name and conveyed it under another name. Or there may be a forged deed in the chain, after which no subsequent grantee acquired legal title. All possible claimants are allowed to present evidence during a court proceeding; then the court's judgment is filed. Often, the simple procedure of obtaining any relevant quitclaim deeds (discussed in Chapter 12) is used to establish ownership.

Title Search and Abstract of Title

A **title search** is an examination of all of the public records to determine whether any defects exist in the chain of title. The records of the conveyances of ownership are examined, beginning with the present owner. Then the title is traced backward to its origin (or 40 years to 60 years, or some definite period of time depending on state statute; 50–60 years is common in Georgia). The time beyond which the title must be searched is limited in states that have adopted the Marketable Title Act. This law extinguishes certain interests and cures certain defects arising before the *root of the title*—the conveyance that establishes the source of the chain of title. Normally, the root is considered to be 40 years or more. Under most circumstances, then, it is necessary to search only from the current owner to the root.

Other public records are examined to identify wills, judicial proceedings, and other encumbrances that may affect title. These include a variety of taxes, special assessments, and other recorded liens.

Before providing money for a loan, a lender generally orders a title search to ensure that no lien is superior to its mortgage lien. In most cases, the cost of the title search is paid by the buyer, although this is negotiable between the parties.

An **abstract of title** is a summary report of what the title search found in the public record. A person who prepares this report is called an *abstractor*. The abstractor searches all the public records, and then summarizes the various events and proceedings that affected the title throughout its history. The report begins with the original grant (or root), then provides a chronological list of recorded instruments. All recorded liens and encumbrances are included, along with their current statuses. A list of all of the public records examined is also provided as evidence of the scope of the search.

IN PRACTICE An abstract of title is a condensed history of those items that can be found in public records. It does not reveal such items as encroachments or forgeries or any interests or conveyances that have not been recorded.

Marketable Title

Under the terms of the typical real estate sales contract, the seller is required to deliver **marketable title** to the buyer at the closing. To be marketable, a title must

- disclose no serious defects and not depend on doubtful questions of law or fact to prove its validity;
- not expose a purchaser to the hazard of litigation or threaten the quiet enjoyment of the property; and
- convince a reasonably well-informed and prudent purchaser, acting on business principles and with knowledge of the facts and their legal significance, that he or she could sell or mortgage the property at a later time.

Although a title that does not meet these requirements still could be transferred, it contains certain defects that may limit or restrict its ownership. A buyer cannot be forced to accept a conveyance that is materially different from the one bargained for in the sales contract. However, questions of marketable title must be raised by a buyer *before acceptance of the deed*. Once a buyer has accepted a deed with unmarketable title, the only available legal recourse is to sue the seller under any covenants of warranty contained in the deed.

In some states, a preliminary title search is conducted as soon as an offer to purchase has been accepted. In fact, it may be customary to include a contingency in the sales contract that gives the buyer the right to review and approve the title report before proceeding with the purchase. A preliminary title report also benefits the seller by giving him or her an early opportunity to cure title defects.

■ PROOF OF OWNERSHIP

Proof of ownership is evidence that title is marketable. A deed by itself is not considered sufficient evidence of ownership. Even though a warranty deed conveys the grantor's interest, it contains no proof of the condition of the grantor's title at the time of the conveyance. The grantee needs some assurance that he or she is actually acquiring ownership and that the title is marketable. A certificate of title or title insurance are commonly used to prove ownership. Less commonly used is the Torrens certificate (discussed in the following).

Certificate of Title

A **certificate of title** is a statement of opinion of the title's status on the date the certificate is issued. A *certificate of title is not a guarantee of ownership*. Rather, it certifies the condition of the title based on an examination of the public records—a title search. The certificate may be prepared by a title company, a licensed abstractor, or an attorney. An owner, a mortgage lender, or a buyer may request the certificate.

Although a certificate of title is used as evidence of ownership, it is not perfect. Unrecorded liens or rights of parties in possession cannot be discovered by a search of the public records. Hidden defects, such as transfers involving forged documents, incorrect marital information, incompetent parties, minors, or fraud, cannot be detected. A certificate offers no defense against these defects because they are unknown. The person who prepares the certificate is liable only for negligence in preparing the certificate.

IN PRACTICE   You may have heard the phrase under color of title. This phrase refers to a situation in which title is conveyed in a transaction by a written instrument (such as a deed or will) that is actually inadequate to legally transfer ownership, whether because it was incorrectly executed or because it was executed by someone who did not, in fact, hold title in the first place.

An abstract and **attorney's opinion of title** are used in some areas of the country as evidence of title. It is an opinion of the status of the title based on a review of the abstract. Similar to a certificate of title, the opinion of title does not protect against defects that cannot be discovered from the public records. Many buyers purchase title insurance to defend the title from these defects.

Title Insurance

Title insurance is a contract under which the policyholder is protected from losses arising from defects in the title. A title insurance company determines whether the title is insurable, based on a review of the public records. If so, a policy is issued. Unlike other insurance policies that insure against *future losses*, title insurance protects the insured from an event that occurred *before* the policy was issued. Title insurance is considered the best defense of title: The title insurance company will defend any lawsuit based on an insurable defect and pay claims if the title proves to be defective.

After examining the public records, the title company usually issues what may be called a *preliminary report of title* or a *commitment* to issue a title policy. This describes the type of policy that will be issued and includes

- the name of the insured party;
- the legal description of the real estate;
- the estate or interest covered;
- conditions and stipulations under which the policy is issued; and
- a schedule of all exceptions, including encumbrances and defects found in the public records and any known unrecorded defects.

The *premium* for the policy is paid once, at closing. The maximum loss for which the company may be liable cannot exceed the face amount of the policy (unless the amount of coverage has been extended by use of an *inflation rider*). When a title company makes a payment to settle a claim covered by a policy, the company generally acquires the right to any remedy or damages available to the insured. This right is called **subrogation.**

Coverage   Exactly which defects the title company will defend depends on the type of policy. (See Table 13.1.) A *standard coverage policy* normally insures the title as it is known from the public records. In addition, the standard policy insures against such hidden defects as forged documents, conveyances by incompetent grantors, incorrect marital statements, and improperly delivered deeds.

Extended coverage, as provided by an American Land Title Association (ALTA) policy, includes the protections of a standard policy plus additional protections. An extended policy protects a homeowner against defects that may be discovered by inspection of the property: rights of parties in possession, examination of a survey, and certain unrecorded liens.

Title insurance does not offer guaranteed protection against all defects. A title company will not insure a bad title or offer protection against defects that clearly appear in a title search. The policy generally names certain uninsurable losses, called *exclusions.* These exclusions include zoning ordinances, restrictive covenants, easements, certain water rights, and current taxes and special assessments.

T A B L E 13.1 **Owner's Title Insurance Policy**	Standard Coverage	Extended Coverage	Not Covered by Either Policy
	1. Defects found in public records 2. Forged documents 3. Incompetent grantors 4. Incorrect marital statements 5. Improperly delivered deeds	Standard coverage plus defects discoverable through the following: 1. Property inspection, including unrecorded rights of persons in possession 2. Examination of survey 3. Unrecorded liens not known of by policyholder	1. Defects and liens listed in policy 2. Defects known to buyer 3. Changes in land use brought about by zoning ordinances

Types of policies The different types of policies depend on who is named as the insured. An *owner's policy* is issued for the benefit of the owner (new buyer) and his or her heirs or devisees. A *lender's policy* is issued for the benefit of the mortgage company. The amount of the coverage depends on the amount of the mortgage loan. As the loan balance is reduced, the coverage decreases. Because only the lender's interest is insured, it is advisable for the owner to obtain a policy as well.

A lessee's interest can be insured with a *leasehold* policy. *Certificate of sale* policies are available to insure the title to property purchased in a court sale.

The Torrens System

The **Torrens system** is a legal registration system used to verify ownership and encumbrances. Registration in the Torrens system provides evidence of title without the need for an additional search of the public records. Under the Torrens system, an owner of real property submits a written application to register his or her title. The application is submitted to the court clerk of the county in which the real estate is located. If the applicant proves that he or she is the owner, the court enters an order to register the real estate. The registrar of titles is directed to issue a certificate of title. The original Torrens certificate of title in the registrar's office reveals the owner of the land and all mortgages, judgments, and similar liens. It does not, however, reveal federal or state taxes and some other items. The Torrens system of registration relies on the physical title document itself; a person acquires title only when it is registered.

IN PRACTICE The Torrens system is currently in use in fewer than ten states, and some of these states are in the process of phasing out Torrens registration altogether. Consult your state's law to determine whether the Torrens system is active in your area and whether new property transfers are subject to its procedures.

| In Georgia |

In Georgia, the Torrens registration is time-consuming and expensive, and although available, is rarely used.

■ UNIFORM COMMERCIAL CODE

The **Uniform Commercial Code (UCC)** is a commercial law statute that has been adopted, to some extent, in all 50 states. The UCC is concerned with personal property transactions; it does not apply to real estate. The UCC governs the documents when personal property is used as security for a loan.

For a lender to create a security interest in personal property, including personal property that will become fixtures, the UCC requires the borrower to sign a **security agreement**. The agreement must contain a complete description of the items against which the lien applies. A short notice of this agreement (called a financing statement or a UCC-1) must be filed. It identifies any real estate involved when personal property is made part of the real estate. Once the financing **statement** is recorded, subsequent purchasers and lenders are put on notice of the security interest in personal property and fixtures. Many lenders require that a security agreement be signed and a financing statement be filed when the real estate includes chattels or readily removable fixtures.

■ KEY POINT REVIEW

To serve as **public notice**, and with **priority** over subsequent documents, a **written document** is needed that

- affects an **estate, right, title,** or **interest** in **land** (such as deeds; mortgages, tax liens, and judgments; and marriage, probate, and other proceedings that may affect title;
- must be **drawn** and **executed** (signed);
- is written according to state law (**recording acts**); and
- is recorded in the **public records** that are maintained by the designated **official**, such as the recorder of deeds, county clerk, or city clerk, and held in the **county** (or city) in which the **property is located**.

Public records are typically **searched** by **title companies** that provide **title insurance** to prospective purchasers based on the findings of the search.

Constructive notice of a document is assumed when **due diligence** (such as a search of public records and inspection of the property) would reveal its existence. **Actual notice** means that an individual has **direct knowledge** of documents in the public records and facts revealed by an inspection of the property. **Inquiry notice** is imposed by law on an individual who discovers certain facts about a property that should warrant further investigation.

Unrecorded documents that may affect title, such as a tax lien, may not be recorded immediately, yet are still given priority by law and require search of tax records and other sources.

Chain of title is a record of property ownership, but it does not include liens and other encumbrances:

- A **gap** in chain or other dispute of ownership creates a **cloud on the title**, and
- a cloud on title is resolved by **suit to quiet title**.

The **time period** for which **title search** is conducted may be limited by state law.

An **abstract of title**, prepared by an **abstractor**, is a **summary** report of what title search reveals. It includes all **recorded liens** and **encumbrances** and lists **records searched**; but does **not** indicate forgeries and interests that are unrecorded or could be discovered by property inspection.

A **marketable title** is one that must

- **not have serious defects** nor rely on doubtful questions of law or fact to prove its validity;
- not expose purchaser to litigation or threaten **quiet enjoyment** of property; and
- convince a reasonably well-informed and prudent purchaser that the property could be sold or mortgaged at a later time.

Proof of ownership may be established by **certificate of title**, but it will not reveal unrecorded liens or rights of parties in possession.

Title insurance, issued as **owner's policy** or **lender's policy** under which the insured is protected from losses arising from defects in title, insures against hidden defects and identifies **exclusions** that include readily apparent title defects, zoning, and others.

The **Uniform Commercial Code (UCC)** has been adopted to some extent in all 50 states. It governs liens on **personal property** and specifies how a security interest may be created in personal property.

CHAPTER 13 QUIZ

1. A title search in the public records may be conducted by
    a. anyone.
    b. attorneys and abstractors only.
    c. attorneys, abstractors, and real estate licensees only.
    d. anyone who obtains a court order under the Freedom of Information Act.

2. Which of the following statements *BEST* explains why instruments affecting real estate are recorded?
    a. Recording gives constructive notice to the world of the rights and interests claimed by a party in a particular parcel of real estate.
    b. Failing to record will void the transfer.
    c. The instruments must be recorded to comply with the terms of the statute of frauds.
    d. Recording proves the execution of the instrument.

3. A purchaser went to the county building to check the recorder's records, which showed that the seller was the grantee in the last recorded deed and that no mortgage was on record against the property. The purchaser may assume which of the following?
    a. All taxes are paid, and no judgments are outstanding.
    b. The seller has good title.
    c. The seller did not mortgage the property.
    d. No one else is occupying the property.

4. The date and time a document was recorded help establish which of the following?
    a. Priority
    b. Abstract of title
    c. Subrogation
    d. Marketable title

5. Paul bought Linden's house, received a deed, and moved into the residence but neglected to record the document. One week later, Linden died, and his heirs in another city, unaware that the property had been sold, conveyed title to Mark, who recorded the deed. Who owns the property?
    a. Paul
    b. Mark
    c. Linden's heirs
    d. Both Paul and Mark

6. A property with encumbrances that will outlast the closing
    a. cannot be sold.
    b. can be sold only if title insurance is provided.
    c. cannot have a deed recorded without a survey.
    d. can be sold if a buyer agrees to take it subject to the encumbrances.

7. Which of the following would *NOT* be acceptable evidence of ownership?
    a. Attorney's opinion
    b. Title insurance policy
    c. Abstract
    d. Deed signed by the last seller

8. Chain of title is *MOST* accurately defined as a(n)
    a. summary or history of all documents and legal proceedings affecting a specific parcel of land.
    b. report of the contents of the public record regarding a particular property.
    c. instrument or document that protects the insured parties (subject to specific exceptions) against defects in the examination of the record and hidden risks such as forgeries, undisclosed heirs, errors in the public records, and so forth.
    d. record of a property's ownership.

9. A seller delivered title to a buyer at closing. A title search had disclosed no serious defects, and the title did not appear to be based on doubtful questions of law or fact or to expose the buyer to possible litigation. The seller's title did not appear to present a threat to the buyer's quiet enjoyment, and the title insurance policy provided was sufficient to convince a reasonably well-informed person that the property could be resold. The title conveyed would commonly be referred to as a(n)

    a. certificate of title.
    b. abstract of title.
    c. marketable title.
    d. attorney's opinion of title.

10. The person who prepares an abstract of title for a parcel of real estate

    a. searches the public records and then summarizes the events and proceedings that affect title.
    b. insures the condition of the title.
    c. inspects the property.
    d. issues title insurance.

11. Sally is frantic because she cannot find her deed and now wants to sell her property. She

    a. may need to sue for quiet title.
    b. must buy title insurance.
    c. does not need her original deed if it had been recorded.
    d. should execute a replacement deed to herself.

12. Mortgagee title policies protect which parties against loss?

    a. Buyers
    b. Sellers
    c. Lenders
    d. Buyers and lenders

13. Which of the following are traditionally covered by a standard title insurance policy?

    a. Unrecorded rights of persons in possession
    b. Improperly delivered deeds
    c. Changes in land use due to zoning ordinances
    d. Unrecorded liens not known to the policyholder

14. General Title Company settled a claim against its insured by making a substantial payment to the person who sued its client. General Title may now seek damages from the person who originally gave its insured a general warranty deed. Through what right can General Title recover the amount it paid out in the settlement?

    a. Escrow
    b. Encumbrance
    c. Subordination
    d. Subrogation

15. Which of the following is NOT covered by a standard title insurance policy?

    a. Forged documents
    b. Incorrect marital statements
    c. Unrecorded rights of parties in possession
    d. Incompetent grantors

16. Documents referred to as title evidence include

    a. policies of title insurance.
    b. general warranty deeds.
    c. security agreements.
    d. special warranty deeds.

17. Under the Uniform Commercial Code, a lender who wishes to give notice of its security interest in personal property used as security for a loan, must file a

    a. security agreement.
    b. financing statement.
    c. chattel agreement.
    d. quitclaim deed.

18. Kate sells a portion of her property to Lily. Lily promptly records the deed in the appropriate county office. If Kate tries to sell the same portion of her property to Mike, which of the following statements is *TRUE*?

a. Mike has been given constructive notice of the prior sale because Lily promptly recorded her deed.

b. Mike has been given actual notice of the prior sale because Lily promptly recorded her deed.

c. Because Mike's purchase of the portion of Kate's property is the more recent, it will have priority over Lily's interest, regardless of when Lily recorded the deed.

d. Because Mike purchased the property from its rightful owner, Mike is presumed by law to be aware of Lily's prior interest.

19. The real estate records in Georgia are maintained by the

a. Clerk of Probate Court.
b. Clerk of Superior Court.
c. Recorder of Deeds.
d. County Treasurer.

20. A title search in Georgia is typically traced backwards for a period

a. of 30 years.
b. back to the original deed to the first owner from the state of Georgia.
c. of 50 to 60 years.
d. of 100 years.

Georgia Real Estate License Law

■ **LEARNING OBJECTIVES** *When you have finished reading this chapter, you should be able to:*

- **identify** the four categories of licensure in Georgia.

- **describe** the requirements for managing trust accounts and trust funds.

- **explain** the unfair trade practices under the Georgia Real Estate License Law.

- **distinguish** nonresident licensure requirements.

- **define** the following *key terms*:

active license	Georgia Real Estate	Real Estate Education,
auctioneer	Commission	Research, and
broker	inactive license	Recovery Fund
broker's funds	investigation process	reinstatement of lapsed
community association	license by reciprocity	license
manager	license expiration	salesperson
continuing education	license renewal	trust accounts
criminal history report	nonresident license	trust funds
disciplinary provisions	postlicense education	unfair practices

The Georgia Real Estate License Law was adopted by the state legislature in 1925 and has undergone many revisions since that time. The law provides the standards by which licensees perform their duties and regulates the real estate industry for the protection of the public. It establishes the **Georgia Real Estate Commission** as the authoritative body over all real estate licensees.

The text of the law can be found at *http://www.grec.state.ga.us/*. Click on the link for Title 43, Chapter 40. This Web address also provides links to BRRETA (Title 10, Chapter 6A) and Rule 520, which contains the Commission's rules and regulations.

■ THE GEORGIA REAL ESTATE COMMISSION (TITLE 43, CHAPTER 40, SECTION 2)

The Georgia Real Estate Commission's role is to regulate the real estate brokerage industry through the licensing of practitioners with a goal of protecting the public interest. The commission is appointed by the governor and confirmed by the Georgia Senate. It is comprised of six members with five-year terms. Of the six members, five must be actively licensed and residents of Georgia for at least five years. The sixth member must have an interest in consumer affairs, and not have any interest in the real estate industry. Members serve until successors are appointed and qualified.

If a vacancy occurs, the governor fills the vacancy. A chairperson is appointed by the members. The Commission holds meetings at least once a month. A quorum consists of four members being present.

Members must recuse themselves from voting on any matters in which the member may have a conflict of interest, or when a contested case has been filed under the Georgia Administrative Procedure Act (Title 50, Chapter 13) because of the Commission's role in the case.

The governor has the authority to remove a Commission member for dishonesty, incompetence, neglect of duties, inability to perform the necessary duties, or being the subject of a disciplinary sanction, other than authorized by the Georgia Real Estate License Law (Title 43, Chapter 40), imposed by any professional licensing agency on the member's right to practice a trade or profession.

Real Estate Commissioner's Role (43-40-4 & 5)

The Real Estate Commissioner is appointed by the Commission to be the chief executive officer of the Commission and administers the policies adopted by the Commission. The commissioner's duties include hiring and overseeing staff in its daily activities. The commissioner may not hold an *active* real estate or related business license, nor can any other Real Estate Commission employee.

■ OBTAINING AND MAINTAINING A REAL ESTATE LICENSE

The License Law (Title 43, Chapter 40) and the Rules and Regulations of the Commission (Rule 520) determine who may obtain a real estate license, who is exempt from licensing requirements, and the types and requirements for real estate licenses in Georgia.

Who Needs to Be Licensed? (43-40-8, Rule 520-1-.04)

Anyone who engages, advertises, or holds themselves out as engaging as a licensee in a real estate transaction must first obtain a license from the Georgia Real Estate Commission, unless exempt under state statute.

Licenses are only granted to those who have a good reputation for honesty, trustworthiness, integrity, and competence to transact business in a way that safeguards the public's interest. In addition, applicants must provide satisfactory proof that licensing qualifications have been presented to the Commission.

Exempt Persons and Entities (43-40-29)

The requirement for holding a broker, salesperson, or community association manager license does not apply to the following:

- Owners or lessors or their regular employees who perform any real estate transaction act in the regular course of the management of property and the investment of anyone who manages residential apartment complexes under a contract approved by a federal agency for an organization exempt under 501(c)(3) of the Interval Revenue Code prior to January 1, 1989
- Attorneys-in-fact acting under duly executed power of attorney to convey real estate from owner or lessor
- Attorneys acting solely as an incident to the practice of law
- Any person acting as receiver, trustee in bankruptcy, administrator, executor, or guardian or acting under a will or trust
- Any officer or employee of government agency conducting official duties
- Any person employed by a public or private utility who performs any act on property owned, leased, or acquired in the regular course of, or incident to, the management of property
- Any person who as owner, employed full-time by the owner, or as owner of a management company provides property management services or community association management services
- Any person employed on a full-time basis by a community association for the purpose of providing community association management services
- Any person acting as a referral agent who is not involved in the performance of the real estate transaction (e.g., negotiations, execution of documents) that involves more than the mere referral of one person to another and who does not receive a fee and does not act as a referral agent in more than three transactions per year

- Any individual employed by a broker to assist in property management services on property where the broker has a written management agreement, provided that the individual's activities are authorized by the broker in a written agreement and that the activities are limited (e.g., delivering or receiving a lease application, showing a rental unit, providing information to a tenant about a security deposit or rent payment)
- Any person who provides property management services on properties available for less than 90 days' occupancy and meets certain conditions
- Any person who is a member of a community association and who provides community association management services only to one community association of which the person is a member
- Any person who performs solely physical maintenance on a property
- A licensed certified public accountant acting solely as an incident to the practice of public accounting

The exemptions do not apply to anyone who uses them to try to avoid becoming licensed.

Civil Penalty for the Unlicensed Practice of Real Estate (43-40-30, 43-40-31)

Anyone who acts as a licensee without a license or who violates provisions of the Georgia Real Estate License Law will be found guilty of a misdemeanor. The Commission may issue a cease and desist order prohibiting an individual from practicing as a real estate broker without a license. The cease and desist order is final ten days after it is issued unless a hearing is requested before the Commission. If the cease and desist order is violated, the Commission can impose a fine not to exceed $1,000 for each transaction constituting a violation of the order. Each day that an individual practices in violation of the law constitutes a separate violation.

■ LICENSE CATEGORIES AND REQUIREMENTS

Georgia has four types of real estate licenses: salesperson, associate broker, broker, and community association manager. Georgia law provides requirements and limitations specific to each type of license.

Salesperson's (or Sales Associate) License (43-40-8)

A **salesperson** acts on behalf of a broker and in this capacity may perform any real estate brokerage act that requires a real estate license in Georgia. In order to be active in real estate brokerage, a salesperson must be affiliated with a sole proprietorship, corporation, partnership, or limited liability company that is also licensed as a broker.

To obtain a salesperson license, the applicant must

- be at least 18 years of age to practice (can take the salesperson's examination at age 17, but cannot activate the license until age 18);

- be a resident of Georgia, unless the applicant has complied with nonresidency requirements;
- be a high school graduate or the holder of a certificate of equivalency;
- comply with statutory requirements regarding any criminal convictions;
- successfully complete at least 75 instructional hours in a salesperson's course of study approved by the Commission; and
- satisfactorily pass a real estate examination approved by the Commission.

To keep the salesperson's license in good standing, the applicant must

- take at least 25 instructional hours of coursework approved by the Commission in the first year of licensure (Failure to complete a postlicense course during the first year of being licensed will cause the license to lapse. The license may be reinstated by completing the coursework within six months of the lapse. As a condition of satisfactorily completing the course, the licensee must pass an exam that covers the subject matter in the course);
- obtain 24 instructional hours of **continuing education** seminars or courses every four years (the postlicense course taken during the first year of licensure only counts for six hours of this continuing education requirement);
- apply for licensure within 12 months of taking the exam; and
- pay the appropriate licensing fee: if within three months from taking the exam, $170; if more than three months but less than 12 months from taking the exam, $340.

There are no experience requirements for a salesperson's license.

Broker's (and Associate Broker's) License (43-40-8)

A **broker** may perform any real estate brokerage act that requires a real estate license in Georgia. Both individuals and firms may be licensed as brokers. In order to be active in real estate brokerage, a licensed broker must be affiliated with a sole proprietorship, corporation, partnership, or limited liability company that is also licensed as a broker.

The associate broker acts on behalf of a broker and may perform any real estate brokerage act that requires a real estate license in Georgia. The broker and the associate broker must meet the same educational requirements and conditions. Failure to meet any of these requirements is grounds for the Commission to deny a license without a hearing.

To obtain an associate broker or a broker license, the salesperson must

- be at least 21 years of age to practice (can take the salesperson's examination at age 20, but cannot activate the license until age 21);
- be a resident of Georgia, unless the salesperson has complied with nonresidency requirements;
- be a high school graduate or the holder of a certificate of equivalency;
- comply with statutory requirements regarding any criminal convictions;
- maintain a license in active status for at least three of the five years immediately prior to filing an application to become a broker;

- furnish evidence of completing 60 instructional hours in a broker's course of study approved by the Commission, provided that if licensed as a community association manager, the applicant furnishes evidence of completing an additional 75 instructional hours in courses of study approved by the Commission; and
- pass the real estate examination approved by the Commission after serving at least two years of active licensure.

The Commission's rules require a broker or an associate broker to complete 24 instructional hours of continuing education within the four-year renewal period for a license.

Community Association Manager (43-40-8)

A **community association manager** acts on behalf of a broker to manage one or more community associations. Community associations include condominium associations and homeowners' associations. In order to be active in community association management, a community association manager must be affiliated with a sole proprietorship, corporation, partnership, or limited liability company that is also licensed as a broker.

In order to qualify for a community association manager's license, an applicant must

- be at least 18 years old;
- be a resident of the state of Georgia, unless has complied with nonresidency requirements;
- be a high school graduate or the holder of a certificate of equivalency;
- comply with statutory requirements regarding any criminal convictions;
- furnish evidence of completion of at least 25 instructional hours in a community association manager's course or course of study approved by the Commission; and
- pass a real estate examination approved by the Commission, covering those matters confronting brokers who provide community association management services.

The Commission's rules require a community association manager complete 24 hours of continuing education within the four-year renewal period for a license.

Auctioneer's License

In addition to the four licenses mentioned, in Georgia, **auctioneers** of any commodity or property need an auctioneer's license. If the auctioneer is selling real estate, a salesperson's or a broker's license is also required.

Broker Firm Requirements (43-40-10)

The requirements for a firm to be granted a broker's license include: the firm designates an individual licensed as a broker as its qualifying broker who is responsible for assuring the firm and its licensees comply with all laws and regulations;

and the firm authorizes its qualifying broker to commit the firm to any settlement of a contested lawsuit before the commission. In addition, a broker's license is only granted to a firm when every person who acts as a licensee for the firm holds a real estate license.

Corporations, Limited Liability Companies, and Partnerships (43-40-18)

In Georgia, the requirements for licensure of sole proprietorships, corporations, partnerships, and limited liability companies include the following:

- A firm that operates as a sole proprietorship must be owned entirely by a licensed broker.
- The qualifying broker for a firm that operates as a corporation must be an officer of the corporation.
- The qualifying broker for a firm operating as a partnership must be a partner. If all partners of a partnership are corporations, the qualifying broker of the partnership must be one of the partner corporation's officers whose actions are binding on the corporation and partnership.
- The qualifying broker for a firm operating as a limited partnership must be the general partner. If the general partner of a limited partnership is a corporation, the qualifying broker must be one of that corporation's officers whose actions are binding on the corporation and general partner.
- The qualifying broker for a firm operating as a limited liability company must be a member or, if the articles of the organization or an agreement vests management in a manager, a manager may serve as the qualifying broker.

The Commission may deny a license to a corporation, limited liability company, or partnership if a stockholder, member, or partner who owns more than a 20 percent interest and does not bear a good reputation for honesty, trustworthiness, and integrity; has been convicted of any felonies; or has been sanctioned by a regulatory agency for violating a law in the sale of real estate.

■ THE LICENSING EXAMINATION (RULE 520-1-.04)

Candidates for licensure must pass a Commission-approved examination administered by Applied Measurement Professionals, Inc. (AMP). See Sample Georgia Real Estate Licensing Examination at the back of this book for detailed information on the content and structure of the licensing examinations.

Candidates who are disabled veterans may be eligible for preference points that are added to the examination grade. For further information about eligibility and points, see Rule 520-1-.04(3) and O.C.G.A. 43-1-9.

A candidate for licensure who has moved to Georgia from another state (other than Florida or a province in Canada) or is a candidate for nonresident licensure may be granted a license without further examination or education. (See "Nonresidents and License by Reciprocity" later in this chapter.)

The Commission has discretion to accept an electronic form of certified data from other states instead of written certification. However, if a candidate does not comply with the Commission's directions, the candidate must take and pass the qualifying exam for the Georgia license.

Under a special agreement between Georgia and Florida, if a candidate is a resident of Florida and has a current real estate license, the candidate can submit a certification of license history (not more than one year old) from the Florida Real Estate Commission along with the Georgia exam registration form. The candidate only has to pass the state content areas of the Georgia exam to be eligible for a Georgia real estate license. However, if the candidate is a Georgia resident and has a current real estate license from Florida, the requirements for one who has moved to Georgia from another state apply. (See "Nonresidents and License by Reciprocity" later in this chapter.)

■ THE REAL ESTATE LICENSE

Applications (520-1-.04)

After successfully passing the state examination, a formal application for licensure must be made to the state of Georgia. Applications for licensure, renewal of license, transfer of license, any change in the status of a license, and any change in a firm's name, must be on current Commission-approved forms. (See *www.grec.state.ga.us/forms.*) Changes in other information must be filed with the Commission, such as address changes, trust accounts, and individuals' names, may be done by letter.

An applicant must supply all information requested. Failure to supply all information may make the application incomplete.

Applicants who were previously active licensees outside Georgia must present an original certification of licensure from the outside state. If the applicant was a broker in another state, the applicant must present an original certification of licensure of the firm(s) the applicant served as broker. The certification of licensure must have been issued no more than 12 months prior to the application.

Criminal History Report (520-1-.04(7))

No more than 60 days prior to submitting an application, each applicant must submit the following:

1. A certified **criminal history report** issued by the Georgia Crime Information Center of the Georgia Bureau of Investigation, indicating whether the applicant has any record of a criminal past
2. For applicants who have not lived in Georgia, a certified criminal history report from their resident state, province or territory that is equivalent to the report required in (1)

If the report indicates that an applicant has a criminal record in another state, or if the Commission is unable to obtain a criminal history report, the applicant must (at his or her expense) provide any necessary fingerprints, fees, authorization, or other requirements in order for the Commission to obtain a Federal Crime Information Center Report from the Federal Bureau of Investigation.

Preliminary Decisions on Convictions or Sanctions (43-40-15 and 520-1-.04(11))

The Commission may deny a license to an applicant who has a prior criminal conviction or disciplinary sanction imposed by an occupational licensing body.

Recent Georgia Legislation (Senate Bill 114) provides that no person who has a criminal conviction is eligible to become an applicant for a real estate license unless the person has successfully completed all terms and conditions of any sentence imposed for the conviction. If the person has multiple convictions, at least five years must have passed after satisfying all the terms of the conviction before applying for licensure; if the person has a single conviction, at least two years must have passed.

If any of the following criminal charges are pending, one cannot apply for licensure: forgery, embezzlement, obtaining money under false pretenses, theft, extortion, conspiracy to defraud, a felony, a sex offense, a probation violation, or a crime involving moral turpitude. An applicant for licensure as a broker or associate broker who has been convicted of any of these offenses may be licensed only if at least ten years have passed since the conviction, sentence, or release from incarceration, whichever is later; no criminal charges are pending against the applicant; and the applicant presents proof of bearing a good reputation for honesty, trustworthiness, and integrity.

Because of the time and expense involved in becoming an applicant for licensure, an applicant can request the Commission make a preliminary decision on the conviction or sanction before taking the required education and examination. The preliminary decision is advisory and not binding.

Hearing after Denial of Application (520-1-.04(12))

If the Commission denies an application for licensure or reinstatement and the applicant has met all age, education, and exam requirements and paid the required fees, he or she may request a formal hearing. The hearing request must be made in writing within 60 days of the Commission's mailing notice regarding the application denial. If the hearing is granted and the application is again denied, the applicant may not make another application for a license without again passing a qualified exam and paying required fees.

Active or Inactive License (43-40-12 and 520-1-.05)

Active Georgia associate brokers, salespersons, and community association managers must be licensed under one active Georgia broker at a time. After making an original application for licensure, a salesperson or community association manager cannot commence work in real estate brokerage activities until the broker has received the licensee's wall certificate of licensure.

When a licensee is released by a broker, the licensee must not engage in the activities of a real estate broker until the licensee

1. affiliates his or her license with a new broker and mails a Change Application to the Commission; or
2. receives a wall certificate of licensure from the Commission authorizing the licensee to serve as the broker of a sole proprietorship or the qualifying broker of a corporation, limited liability company, or partnership.

An active Georgia associate broker, salesperson, or community association manager may also affiliate with a license issued by another state's real estate licensing regulatory body with a broker in that state, provided

1. that state's laws allow for affiliations in both states; and
2. the Georgia associate broker, salesperson, or community association manager has written permission to affiliate with a broker in another state and the permission clearly states the duties the licensee can undertake for each broker and that the licensee may not undertake brokerage activity on property located in Georgia except in behalf of the active Georgia broker.

Those who have a license that has been on **inactive** status for two years or longer must attend Commission approved course(s) of study totaling at least six instructional hours for each year the license was inactive. The course(s) must be taken no more than one year prior to the date of the reactivation of the license. However, this requirement does not apply to an inactive licensee who can furnish evidence of meeting the continuing education requirement for each renewal period during license inactivity.

A real estate broker who does not want to be actively engaged in brokerage business or any licensee who is temporarily not actively engaged on behalf of a broker may continue a license by making a written request to the Commission that the license be placed on inactive status. This must be done within 30 days of ceasing work. A licensee whose license is on inactive status may not engage in real estate brokerage business except in connection with property owned by the licensee.

Renewals (520-1-.05)

Renewal fees are required, and if not paid, licenses lapse according to the following schedule: for an individual license, it lapses on the last day of the month of the birthday of the individual licensee; and for a firm licensed as a broker, it lapses on the last day of the month of the fourth anniversary of its original licensure.

Reinstatement of Lapsed Licenses (43-40-12 and 520-1-.05)

A licensee whose license lapses because of nonpayment of fees or failing to satisfactorily complete all educational requirements, cannot engage in real estate brokerage activities until the license is **reinstated**. Upon lapsing, the wall certificate of licensure and pocket card must be forwarded by the licensee's broker to the Commission.

A licensee who did not have to meet continuing education requirements and whose license lapsed for more than one year, and who reinstates it by paying the required fees, is thereafter subject to continuing education requirements.

Any licensee who fails to pay a renewal fee and allows an inactive license to lapse may reinstate that license to *inactive status* within two years of the date of lapsing by paying the required fees. To reinstate an *inactive* license, a licensee other than a broker must obtain the signature of the broker for whom the licensee acts, and a broker must submit an application to the Commission prior to resuming brokerage activity. Any licensee who wants to activate a license that has been on inactive status must first meet the continuing education requirements for active licensure, unless the licensee has maintained an active license in another state that has continuing education requirements while the licensee's license was on inactive status in Georgia.

A licensee who fails to pay a renewal fee and allows an inactive license to lapse may reinstate the license to *active status* within two years of the date of its lapsing by paying the fees, provided the licensee has completed

1. an approved course totaling at least six instructional hours for each year or portion of year of continuing education due prior to the licensee's going on inactive status; and
2. an approved course totaling at least six instructional hours for each year or portion of year since the date the license was placed on inactive status.

A licensee who fails to pay a renewal fee and allows a license to lapse and does not choose to reinstate the license in accordance with the requirements may reinstate the license by furnishing proof of completion of any required prelicense education and by taking and passing a qualifying exam. A licensee who elects this option of becoming relicensed must take the national portion of the exam as well as the state portion.

A licensee who has passed a licensure exam and allows a license to lapse for more than two years but less than five years because of failing to pay a renewal fee may reinstate the license by paying all fees due and successfully completing any educational course the Commission may require.

Any licensee whose license has lapsed for more than five years because of failing to pay the renewal fee and wants to reinstate his or her license must meet the education and examination requirements for licensure.

Nonresidents and License by Reciprocity (43-40-9 and 520-1-.05(6))

A **nonresident** who holds a license issued on or before July 1, 1991, is not required to meet the requirements of the Georgia license law in order to continue to hold a Georgia license unless the nonresident allows the license to lapse or applies for a different type of license. The Commission may grant a Georgia license to a nonresident who is not licensed in his or her state of residence if the person meets the age, education, and examination requirements under the Georgia license law.

To be licensed in Georgia, nonresidents who are licensed in another state must

- show proof of current licensure in the applicant's state of residence and copies of records of any disciplinary actions taken;
- pay any required fees;
- sign a statement saying they have read the Georgia license law and its rules and regulations, and agree to follow them;
- affiliate with a broker if they are a community association manager, salesperson, or associate broker;
- file with the Commission a written statement that appoints the real estate commissioner to act as the licensee's agent, upon whom all judicial and legal notices are to be served; and
- agree in writing to cooperate with any investigation initiated by the Commission.

Georgia and Florida reciprocity   As noted earlier, Georgia and Florida have a special **reciprocity** agreement. If a licensee is a Florida resident, the licensee can submit both the Florida licensure certification and an exam registration form and pass only the Georgia portion of the exam in order to practice in Georgia. If the licensee is a Georgia resident but licensed in Florida, the above requirements for nonresidency licensure must be met.

Reciprocity by written agreement   A licensed broker of another state may enter into a written agreement with a Georgia broker to conduct real estate brokerage in Georgia without first obtaining a Georgia license. Under the written agreement, the Georgia broker is responsible for all real estate brokerage acts of the out-of-state broker and provides assurance that the out-of-state broker has an active license in his or her state. The Georgia broker must maintain a copy of the written agreement for at least three years after its expiration. The agreement must provide

- procedures to be followed when the out-of-state broker performs any acts of a broker on real property in Georgia;
- how the brokers will divide any earned commissions;
- that any listing or property management agreement for Georgia real property in which the out-of-state broker will participate will be in the name of the Georgia broker;
- that the out-of-state broker will conduct negotiations with any client of a Georgia broker only with the express permission of the Georgia broker;

- that any advertisement of Georgia real property will identify the listing Georgia broker;
- that any contracts, agreements, or offers on Georgia real property will identify the Georgia and out-of-state brokers and indicate that the out-of-state broker is not licensed in Georgia; that the agreement will be construed under Georgia law; and that the superior courts of Georgia will have jurisdiction over any actions brought against either broker;
- that any trust funds obtained in any transaction involving real property in Georgia by an out-of-state broker will be held in the Georgia broker's trust account unless otherwise agreed in writing by the parties involved; and
- any other matters as the Commission may require by rule or regulation.

Under a written agreement, if an out-of-state broker violates any provision of the Georgia law, the Commission can only suspend or revoke the Georgia broker's right to enter into written agreements with out-of-state brokers, unless the Georgia broker participated in the violation or failed to include in the agreement the provisions listed previously.

The Commission may enter into written agreements with similar licensing authorities of other states to allow licensees in those states to conduct real estate brokerage business in Georgia without obtaining a license in Georgia, provided that the other states afford the same opportunities to Georgia licensees.

■ LICENSE FEES (43-40-12 & 520-1-.04)

Applicants for real estate licenses are subject to appropriate fees in addition to the testing fee paid to AMP for the examination. Licensee fees are established by the Georgia Real Estate Commission. At the time an application for an examination is submitted, the commission collects a fee for the examination and an investigation fee if necessary.

Original License Fee

The activation fee for an original licensure as an individual broker, associate broker, salesperson, or community association manager is $45. The activation fee for a firm is $75. Both fees include $20 for the **Real Estate Education, Research, and Recovery Fund.**

Expiration and Renewal of Licenses

The renewal fee for the four-year renewal period for both individual licensees and firms is $125. If filed online, the fee is $100. In addition to the renewal fee, reinstatement fees after **license expiration** due to nonpayment of fees have a separate fee structure.

Returned Check and Other Penalty Fees

If a check is returned unpaid or for disputing a charge to a credit card, the applicant's account is charged $100. Under several circumstances, the Commission may charge a $25 fee, such as when a licensee fails to notify the Commission in writing within 30 days of a change of address or the opening or closing of a designated trust account.

■ CONTINUING EDUCATION

All individuals licensed after January 1, 1980, must furnish the Commission evidence of satisfactorily completing a continuing education course(s) approved by the Commission before renewing a license. The length of the course(s) must be at least six instructional hours for each year of the renewal period. There is no examination requirement. Individuals on active duty in the armed forces of the United States or in the Georgia General Assembly may choose to not meet this requirement while on active duty or during their terms of office, but must complete the course(s) within six months of the conclusion of active duty or term of office.

Postlicense Education (43-40-8 & 520-1-.05)

Within one year of receiving a license, a salesperson must satisfactorily complete a postlicense education course of study of at least 25 instructional hours (other than the Salespersons Prelicense Course or Broker's Prelicense Course) approved by the Commission. The course must be completed no earlier than one year before the date of issuance of the original salesperson's license, or no later than either a) one year after the date of issuance of an original salesperson's license or b) 18 months after the date of issuance of an original salesperson's license if the salesperson qualifies for a six-month extension.

If the salesperson is a nonresident and has successfully completed in his or her state of residence a postlicense course substantially similar to Georgia's Salespersons Postlicense Course prior to the issuance of a Georgia's salesperson's license (or in the first year after being issued such a license), the course will meet the statutory requirements.

■ YOUR REAL ESTATE BUSINESS AND THE GEORGIA LICENSE LAW (43-40-18, 43-40-30.1)

The brokerage activities of a firm are under the direct management and supervision of a broker. The Georgia Real Estate License Law provides rules for brokers in managing their firms and affiliated licensees.

The broker is responsible for establishing, implementing, and updating procedures for the sound operation of the firm, such as reviewing advertisements, contracts, and offers (review must take place within 30 days of the date of the offer or contract), the firm's trust accounting practices, and providing good safe-keeping for all records, policies and procedures for at least three years.

A broker will be held responsible for any affiliated licensee's violation of the Georgia Real Estate License law, unless the broker

- had reasonable procedures in place for supervising the affiliate's actions;
- did not participate in the violation; and
- did not ratify the violation.

As noted in Chapter 5, on occasion, real estate teams are created in brokerage firms. When this happens, the qualifying broker is responsible for the supervision and accountability of each team member. Real estate assistants are required to be licensed with their employing agent's broker and a signed agreement is required between the agent/broker/assistant. See Chapter 5 for information on rules pertaining to unlicensed support personnel.

Change of Address, Name, or Business Information (43-40-19)

If a broker changes the address of his or place of business, he or she must notify the Commission in writing within 30 days of the change.

When an affiliated licensee leaves a broker, the broker must immediately forward the licensee's license either to the Commission or to the new broker for whom the licensee will act. When a licensee's license is released by a broker, the licensee cannot engage in real estate activities until the licensee

- personally delivers to the Commission an approved application to transfer the license to a new broker or mails the application through the postal service; or
- receives a wall certificate from the Commission.

A licensee transferring to a new broker may continue to act as a licensee for the former broker on transactions begun prior to the transfer, provided

- both brokers agree in writing to the licensee's actions on behalf of the former broker, including enumerating which transactions the broker will be working on;
- the former broker agrees in writing to assume full responsibility for the licensee's activities in the agreement; and
- the agreement expresses the terms of compensation.

Georgia license law does not in any way establish an employer-employee or broker-independent contractor relationship between licensees. If such relationships are established, they are at the discretion of the licensees.

Managing Trust Accounts and Trust Funds (43-40-20 and 520-1-.08)

In a real estate brokerage transaction, any broker who accepts down payments, earnest money deposits, security deposits, rents, association fees, or other **trust funds** or whose affiliated licensees accept trust funds must maintain a separate, federally-insured bank checking account in Georgia designated as a trust or escrow for the deposit of these funds. A broker must notify the Commission the name of the bank where the account is maintained and the account number or the name of the account on the bank's form within one month of opening an account.

Each deposit in a **trust** or escrow **account** must include the following:

- Names of buyer and seller, tenant and landlord, member and community association, or broker
- Amount and date of deposit
- Identification of property involved
- Amount, payee, and date of each check drawn on escrow account in connection with the deposit

If a broker elects to deposit any funds into an interest-bearing account, the broker must obtain a written agreement by the parties prior to depositing the funds indicating to whom any earned interest is to be paid.

The Commission may examine a trust account at any time upon reasonable cause, and will examine an account during each renewal period. In lieu of an examination, the Commission may decide to accept a written report of the account from a certified public accountant. Also, in lieu of the renewal period examination, a data summary may be provided on a Commission form, so long as the data is complete and does not contain irregularities.

A broker may maintain more than one trust account but must notify the Commission of the additional accounts.

Affiliated Licensee Trust Accounts

When an affiliated licensee owns a trust or escrow account, the licensee must provide his or her broker a written reconciliation statement comparing the licensee's total trust liability with the reconciled bank balance of the licensee's trust account on at least a quarterly basis. The broker must notify the Real Estate Commission when an affiliated licensee owns his/her own trust account. Licensees' trust accounts must comply with Georgia Real Estate Commission trust account rules and regulations.

Broker's Funds and Trust Account

A broker may maintain the **broker's** own **funds** in a trust or escrow account only when they are clearly identified as the broker's deposit and for the following purposes:

1. If the bank requires a minimum balance be maintained to keep the account open, the broker can maintain that amount designated as the broker's funds.
2. If the bank requires a service charge on the account, the broker may maintain in his or her name a reasonable amount to cover the service charge or other related bank costs.
3. A broker may allow commissions due the broker that are being paid from funds of others held in the broker's designated trust or escrow account to remain in the account provided: a) the broker's accounting system

designates those commissions as the broker's funds and properly accounts for them; and b) each month the broker removes from the account any of the broker's funds that exceed the minimum necessary to comply with the above.

Only checks made payable to the broker may be used to withdraw monies designated as the broker's funds from the designated trust or escrow account.

A broker is not entitled to any part of the earnest money, security deposit, or other trust funds paid to the broker in connection with a real estate transaction as the broker's commission or fee until the transaction has been consummated or terminated.

Disbursal of Funds

A broker who disburses trust funds under the following circumstances is deemed to have properly fulfilled his or her duty to account for and remit money:

1. Upon the rejection or withdrawal of an offer to buy, sell, rent, lease, exchange, or option real estate
2. At the closing of the transaction
3. Upon securing a written agreement signed by all interested parties and separate from the contract that directs the broker to hold the funds
4. Upon the filing of an interpleader action in a court of law
5. Upon the order of a court of law
6. Upon a reasonable interpretation of the contract that directed the broker to deposit the funds

A broker must not disburse funds from a trust account without reasonable assurance that the bank has credited the funds to the broker's trust account. When a broker disburses funds to all parties of a contract where the parties do not expressly agree, the broker must immediately notify all parties of the disbursal in writing.

A broker who disburses trust funds from the trust or escrow account contrary to terms of a contract for sale or rental of real estate, or other contract creating the escrow, or who fails to disburse trust funds according to the terms of a contract, is considered by the Commission to have demonstrated incompetence to act as a real estate broker in a way that safeguards the public interest.

Nonresident Broker's Trust Funds

The Commission may allow a nonresident broker who accepts trust funds to maintain the trust account in a bank of the nonresident broker's state of residence, provided the Commission may examine the account.

Broker Managing Property or Community Association

A broker who manages real property or community associations may maintain a designated rental or assessment trust account separate from his or her other trust accounts. There must be enough funds credited and deposited to the owner's or association's account to cover the association's bills. Security deposits must be clearly identified and credited to the tenant and there must always be a balance in the account equal to the total of security deposits. A licensee who manages and owns rental property must maintain security deposits in designated trust accounts and may not post bond in lieu of maintaining security deposits.

IN PRACTICE   One of the most common public complaints to the Georgia Real Estate Commission relates to how licensees handle earnest money, often on property with which licensees have a personal involvement. Licensees must comply with Georgia laws and rules for the handling of earnest money whether or not the licensee is personally involved in the property.

Trust Fund Abandonment

When a licensee believes a person who placed trust funds in his or her care has abandoned those funds, the licensee may not disburse the funds unless

- there is written authorization by the licensee for disbursal of funds;
- the licensee has complied with the requirements of the Disposition of Unretained Property Act (44-12-191 et seq.); or
- the licensee has complied with state law or a court order.

Licensee Acting as Principal (520-1-.11(1))

When listing, selling, buying, exchanging, renting, leasing, or optioning real estate in a licensee's own name, the licensee must advise his or her broker in writing. Licensees must not advertise in a manner indicating that such advertising is made by a private party not licensed by the Commission. All advertising by a licensee must be under the name of the broker who holds his or her license, unless the broker has been notified of the specific property to be advertised and gives permission for such advertisement. A licensee must disclose that he or she is acting as a principal in the transaction by including one of the following legends in the advertisement:

1. "... seller/buyer/landlord holds a real estate license"
2. "... Georgia Real Estate License #_____"
3. "... G.A.R.E. Lic. #_____"

■ DISCIPLINARY PROVISIONS AND LOSS OF LICENSE

The Georgia Real Estate License Law prohibits certain trade practices in order to protect the public's interest. The Commission has authority to respond at its discretion to any unfair trade practice.

Unfair Practices (43-40-25)

Under the Georgia Real Estate License Law, there are 35 real estate trade practices considered **unfair** and subject to **disciplinary provisions**.

1. Because of race, color, religion, sex, disability, familial status, or national origin, refusing to sell or rent after making a bona fide offer; refusing to negotiate or otherwise making unavailable real estate to any person; discriminating against any person in the terms, conditions, or privileges of sale or rental of real estate or in the provision of services or facilities; making, printing, or publishing any notice, statement, or advertisement regarding the sale or rental of real estate that indicates any preference, limitation, or discrimination; representing to any person that real estate is not available for inspection, sale, or rental when such property is in fact available; or representing that a change has or will or may occur in a neighborhood to induce or discourage the listing, purchasing, selling, or renting of real estate

2. Intentionally advertising material that is misleading or inaccurate, or in any way misrepresenting property, terms, values, policies, or services

3. Failing to account for and remit money coming into the licensee's possession that belongs to others

4. Commingling the money or other property of the licensee's principals with the licensee's own

5. Failing to maintain and deposit in a separate, federally insured checking account all money received by an acting broker, or as escrow agent or the temporary custodian of funds of others, in a real estate transaction unless all parties have agreed otherwise in writing

6. Accepting, giving, or charging any undisclosed commission, rebate, or direct profit on expenditures made for a principal or for procuring a loan or insurance or conducting a property inspection

7. Representing or attempting to represent a real estate broker, other than the broker holding the licensee's license, without the express consent of the broker holding the licensee's license

8. Accepting a commission or other consideration by a licensee from anyone other than the broker holding that licensee's license without that broker's consent

9. Acting in a dual capacity of agent and undisclosed principal in any transaction

10. Guaranteeing or authorizing any person to guarantee future profits that may result from the resale of property

11. Placing a sign on any property offering it for sale or rent without the owner's written consent and failing to remove the sign within ten days after the expiration of a listing

12. Offering real estate for sale or lease without the owner's consent or on terms other than those authorized by the owner

13. Inducing any party to a contract of sale or lease or a brokerage agreement to break the contract or agreement for the purpose of substituting a contract with another principal

14. Negotiating a sale, exchange, or lease of real estate directly with an owner, lessor, purchaser, or tenant if the licensee knows the owner or if lessor has

a written outstanding listing contract in connection with the property granting an exclusive agency or exclusive right to sell to another broker or if a purchaser or tenant has a written outstanding brokerage agreement with another broker, unless the outstanding listing or brokerage agreement provides that the licensee holding the agreement will not provide negotiation services to the client

15. Indicating that an *opinion* given to a potential seller, purchaser, landlord, or tenant regarding a listing, lease, rental, or purchase price is an *appraisal* unless the licensee holds an appraiser classification under the statute

16. Performing or attempting to perform real estate activities on property located in another state without first properly obtaining licensure in that state

17. Paying a commission or compensation to any person for performing the services of licensee who has not first secured the appropriate license or is not cooperating as a nonresident licensed in a nonresident's state

18. Failing to include a fixed date of expiration in a written listing agreement and failing to give a copy of the agreement to the principal

19. Failing to deliver, within a reasonable time, a copy of a purchase agreement to the purchaser and seller

20. Failure by a broker to deliver to the seller, at the time a real estate transaction is consummated, a closing statement or failure to deliver to the buyer a statement showing all money received in the transaction and how it was disbursed (the broker must retain copies of these statements in the broker's files)

21. Making any substantial misrepresentations

22. Acting for more than one party in a transaction without the express written consent of all parties

23. Failure of an associate broker, salesperson, or community association manager to place, as soon after receipt as is practicably possible, in the broker's custody holding the licensee's license any deposit money or other funds entrusted to the licensee

24. Filing a listing contract or any document that creates a lien based on a listing contract for the purpose of casting a cloud on the title when no valid claim under the listing contract exists

25. Having demonstrated incompetency to act as a licensee to safeguard the public's interest or any other conduct that constitutes dishonest dealing

26. Obtaining a brokerage agreement, sales contract, or lease from an owner, purchaser, or tenant while knowing or having reason to believe that another broker has an exclusive brokerage agreement with this owner, purchaser, or tenant, unless the licensee has written permission from the broker; provided, however, that a licensee is allowed to present a bid for community association management if requested in writing from a community association board of directors

27. Failing to keep copies of all sales contracts, closing statements, offers, or other documents relating to the deposit of trust funds, accounting records related to the maintenance of trust accounts, and other documents related to closings for three years

28. Being or becoming a party to any falsification of a contract or other document in a real estate transaction

29. Failing to obtain the written agreement of the parties indicating to whom the broker must pay interest earned on deposited trust funds
30. Failing to disclose in a timely manner to all parties any agency relationship the licensee may have with any of the parties
31. Attempting to perform an act of a broker, associate broker, or salesperson when licensed as a community association manager
32. Attempting to sell, lease, or exchange the property of any member of a community association to which a licensee is providing community association management services without the express written consent of the association
33. Failure to deliver to a community association terminating a management contract within 30 days of the termination, or within such other time period as the management contract provides a record of all transactions and funds handled during the contract and not previously accounted for; all records received from the association or owner on its behalf; and any funds held on behalf of the association or owner
34. Inducing any person to alter, modify, or change another licensee's fee or commission without that licensee's prior written consent
35. Failing to obtain a person's agreement to refer that person to another licensee and informing the person whether the licensee will receive a valuable consideration for the referral

IN PRACTICE Georgia Senate Bill 114, O.C.G.A. 43-40-25(14) has been amended to allow selling agents to present offers directly to sellers when the listing agreement or brokerage engagement involved states in which the listing broker is not providing negotiation services to the client.

A license cannot be obtained by false or fraudulent representation. When a licensee has been found guilty of violating the Georgia Real Estate License Law or the Commission's Rules and Regulations, the Commission has the power to do any of the following:

- Refuse to grant or renew a license
- Administer a reprimand
- Suspend a license or an approval for any period of time
- Revoke any license or approval
- Revoke the license of a broker, qualifying broker, or associate broker and simultaneously issue such licensee a salesperson's license
- Impose on a licensee monetary assessments to reimburse the Commission for costs and expenses incurred in conducting any proceeding under the statute
- Impose a fine not to exceed $1,000 for each violation with fines for multiple violations limited to $5,000 in any one disciplinary proceeding or another amount agreed to by the parties
- Require completion of a course of study in real estate brokerage
- Require the filing of periodic reports by an independent accountant on a broker's trust account
- Limit or restrict any license or approval as the Commission deems necessary to protect the public

Investigation Process (43-40-27, 43-40-25.2, 43-40-26, 43-40-29)

The **investigation process** of any applicant for licensure or any licensee may be initiated under two circumstances: the Commission on its own motion or a written request to the Commission. In the course of an investigation, the Commission may issue subpoenas to compel the production of materials. The results of all investigations are reported only to the Commission or the commissioner, and the records of the investigation are not subject to subpoena in civil actions.

The investigative report includes a conclusion as to whether a possible violation has occurred. If no violation is found, the matter is closed. If evidence is found of a violation, the Commission has the authority to impose a sanction and issue a citation. Before the Commission censures a licensee, or revokes or suspends a license, it provides an opportunity for a hearing in the county of the Commission's domicile. After receiving a hearing notice, a licensee has the right to obtain a copy of the investigative record. At this point, a licensee may choose to hire an attorney. After hearing the evidence, the hearing officer reports the hearing's findings to the Commission, which then decides what disciplinary action should be taken.

For a more serious matter, the case is referred to the Attorney General. The Attorney General may file an injunctive action to prevent the licensee from performing further violations.

For violations involving real estate trust or escrow accounts or if a broker refuses to submit records to an inspector, the Commission concludes the trust account is unsafe. The Commission immediately submits a report to the Attorney General. A legal action may be brought by the state of Georgia preventing the broker from engaging in further violations.

Any person who has exhausted all administrative remedies and who is aggrieved by the Commission's final decision is entitled to a judicial review in the superior court of the county of the Commission's domicile.

Whenever the Commission revokes or suspends a license or when a licensee surrenders a license, the Commission may publish the licensee's name on its Web site or in any official publication of the agency.

Visit *www.grec.state.ga.us/about/resanctions.html* for a list of those with current sanctions and disciplinary actions since January 1, 1995.

■ THE REAL ESTATE EDUCATION, RESEARCH, AND RECOVERY FUND (43-40-22)

The Commission maintains a real estate education, research, and recovery fund with the primary purpose of compensating consumers who suffer damages from a licensee and are not able to recover through normal legal channels.

Collection from the Recovery Fund

Any person aggrieved by an act, representation, transaction, or conduct of a licensee in violation of the real estate licensing law or the rules and regulations of the Commission may recover actual or compensatory damages, not including interests and costs sustained, in the amount of not more than $15,000 per transaction regardless of the number of persons aggrieved or parcels of real estate involved in the transaction. In addition:

1. The liability of the fund for the acts of a licensee ends when a court order is issued authorizing judgment payments from the fund, or any unsatisfied portion of judgments, in an aggregate amount of $45,000 on behalf of the licensee.
2. A licensee acting as a principal or agent in a real estate transaction has no claim against the fund.

When an aggrieved person begins an action, he or she must notify the Commission in writing at the time of the start of the action. The Commission has the right to intervene and defend the action.

When an aggrieved person recovers a valid judgment against a licensee for an act that occurred on or after July 1, 1973, the aggrieved person may, upon termination of all proceedings, file a claim in the court in which the judgment was entered and, upon ten days' written notice to the Commission, may apply to the court for an order directing payment out of the recovery fund of the amount unpaid toward the judgment.

The court makes an order directing the Commission to pay from the recovery fund the sum it finds to be payable on the claim if the court is satisfied the aggrieved person has fully exhausted all remedies available for recovering the amount awarded by the court judgment.

Effect on Licensee

A licensee's license is automatically revoked if the Commission pays a settlement for a judgment against a licensee from the recovery fund. If the judgment is against a firm, the broker's license is revoked. A licensee is not eligible to receive a new license until the licensee has repaid in full, plus interest, the amount paid from the recovery fund. If a licensee receives a discharge in bankruptcy from repaying the recovery fund, this does not relieve the licensee from the penalties provided in the statute.

Statute of Limitations

A lawsuit that may ultimately result in collection from the fund must be commenced within two years after the date the alleged violation occurred.

Financing the Education, Research, and Recovery Fund

When applying for an original license, licensees pay a fee that is deposited in the recovery fund. At its discretion, the Commission can assess each licensee, only upon license renewal, an amount not to exceed $30 per year. If at any time the balance in the recovery fund is not sufficient to pay a claim, when there is sufficient money, the aggrieved person must be paid the ordered amount plus interest at the rate of four percent a year.

The Commission may use funds from the recovery fund to help underwrite costs of developing courses, conducting seminars or research, or other education for the benefit of licensees and the public. However, use of funds for these purposes cannot cause the recovery fund balance to go below $1 million.

■ KEY POINT REVIEW

Georgia Real Estate Commission is authoritative body over all real estate licensees. **Georgia Real Estate License Law** (Title 43, Chapter 40) and the Georgia Real Estate Commission's Rules and Regulations (Rule 520) regulate real estate industry.

The Commission has **six members** with five-year terms. A real estate commissioner, appointed by the Commission, **administers policies** adopted by the Commission.

Licenses are **required** for anyone who engages, advertises, or holds themselves out as engaging as a licensee in a real estate transaction, unless exempt under Georgia statute. Anyone who acts without a license or violates the law will be found guilty of a misdemeanor.

Georgia has four types of real estate license:

1. **Salesperson** (or sales associate) license applicant requirements:
   - Be at least 18 years of age
   - Be a resident of Georgia, unless nonresidency requirements are met
   - Be a high school graduate or hold certificate of equivalency
   - Comply with statutory requirements regarding any criminal convictions
   - Successfully complete required 75 instructional hours in a salesperson's course at approved school
   - Satisfactorily pass real estate examination

2. To keep the salesperson license, applicant must
   - take 25 instructional hours of postlicense courses at an approved school in first year of licensure;
   - obtain 24 instructional hours of continuing education every four years;
   - apply for licensure within 12 months of taking the exam; and
   - pay the appropriate license fee.

3. **Broker's** (and **associate broker's**) license applicant requirements:
   - Be at least 21 years of age
   - Be a resident of Georgia, unless nonresidency requirements are met
   - Be a high school graduate or hold certificate of equivalency

- Comply with statutory requirements regarding any criminal convictions
- Successfully complete at least 60 instructional hours in a broker's course of study, provided that if licensed as a community association manager, applicant completes additional 75 instructional hours of courses
- Satisfactorily pass real estate examination after serving two years of active licensure
- Broker or associate broker must complete **24 instructional hours of continuing education** within the four-year renewal period.

4. **Community association manager** applicant requirements:
- Be at least 18 years of age
- Be a resident of Georgia, unless nonresidency requirements are met
- Be a high school graduate or hold certificate of equivalency
- Comply with statutory requirements regarding any criminal convictions
- Complete at least 25 instructional hours in approved course work
- Satisfactorily pass real estate examination

Licensing exam: candidates for licensure must take a Commission-approved exam and obtain a passing score.

Real estate license: after passing the state exam, a formal application for licensure must be made. The applicant must attach a criminal history report no more than 60 days prior to submitting the application. After submitting the application, the applicant cannot commence real estate work until the broker has received the licensee's wall certificate of licensure from the Commission.

Nonresidents and license by reciprocity: a nonresident who holds a license issued before or on July 1, 1991, is not required to meet Georgia license law requirements unless the license had lapsed. The Commission may grant a license to a nonresident not licensed in the nonresident's state if he or she meets age, education, and exam requirements of Georgia. Nonresident licensees may apply for Georgia license if they

- show proof of licensure in their state of residence and supply any records of disciplinary actions taken;
- pay any fees;
- sign a statement saying they have read Georgia license law and agree to follow it;
- affiliate with a broker if they are not a broker;
- file a statement that allows the real estate commissioner to act as the licensee's agent; and
- agree in writing to cooperate with any commission investigation.

Managing trust accounts and trust funds: any broker who accepts down payments, earnest money deposits, security deposits, rents, or other trust funds must maintain a separate, federally insured bank checking account in Georgia designated as a trust for these funds. A broker is not entitled to any part of earnest or other money until the real estate transaction has been consummated or terminated.

Under Georgia license law, there are **35 real estate trade practices** considered unfair.

The Commission investigates any allegations of **licensee wrongdoing** and issues a report concluding whether a possible violation occurred. If no violation is found, the matter is closed. If a violation is found, Commission can issue a sanction and a citation and a hearing process begins.

Real Estate Education, Research, and Recovery Fund compensates consumers who suffer damages from licensees and are not able to recover through legal channels. The fund is also used to underwrite costs of education and research.

Licensees are encouraged to stay current on important information from the Georgia Real Estate Commission by subscribing to the GREC periodic newsletter, published online at *www.greab.state.ga.us*.

■ RELATED WEB SITES

Georgia Real Estate Commission: *www.greab.state.ga.us*
Georgia Real Estate Commission-approved forms: *www.grec.state.ga.us/forms*
Georgia Real Estate Commission disciplinary actions: *www.grec.state.ga.us/about/resanctions.html*
Georgia Real Estate License Law: *www.greab.state.ga.us/about/relaw.html*

CHAPTER 14 QUIZ

1. A person seeking a Georgia sales associate license must meet each of the following criteria *EXCEPT*
   a. be 18 years old.
   b. be a resident of Georgia.
   c. be a high school graduate.
   d. successfully complete a 75-hour prelicensing course.

2. Which statement is *FALSE* regarding requirements to obtain and keep a Georgia sales associate license?
   a. An individual must have a good reputation for honesty, trustworthiness, integrity, and competence to conduct business to safeguard the public's interest.
   b. An individual must take 24 hours of continuing education in the four-year renewal period.
   c. An individual must take at least ten quarter hours or six semester hours of college courses in real estate.
   d. An individual must take a 25-hour salespersons' post-licensing course.

3. Which statement is *TRUE* about the owner of a three-unit apartment building who rents out the units to tenants?
   a. He or she must have a sales associate's license.
   b. He or she must have a property manager's license.
   c. He or she may need a broker's license if the property is larger than 50 units.
   d. He or she does not need any license.

4. Which individual must have a sales associate's license even when he or she is representing the interests of the property owner?
   a. Accountant
   b. Administrator of a will or trust
   c. Attorney
   d. Auctioneer selling real estate

5. For a sales associate each of the following is considered an unfair practice under Georgia license law *EXCEPT*
   a. accepting an undisclosed commission for procuring a loan.
   b. accepting an undisclosed commission from a broker other than the broker holding the sales associate's license.
   c. acting for more than one party in a transaction even with the written consent of all parties.
   d. acting in a dual capacity of agent and undisclosed principal in a transaction.

6. A person seeking a Georgia broker's license must meet each criterion *EXCEPT*
   a. be 21 years of age.
   b. have five years' experience as a sales associate.
   c. be a high school graduate.
   d. successfully complete a 60-hour broker's prelicensing course.

7. For a salesperson, each of the following is considered an unfair practice under Georgia license law *EXCEPT*
   a. indicating a fixed date of expiration in a listing agreement.
   b. indicating that your sales price estimate is a valid appraisal.
   c. making false statements about the property.
   d. making changes in the commission structure without the consent of other interested licensees.

8. Maria is an employee of Judy Polk, a Georgia real estate broker. Judy has a written property management agreement with Atlanta Apartments, Inc., a company that owns several apartment complexes. Judy has a written agreement with Maria authorizing Maria to show apartments to potential renters and receive lease applications. Maria lives in a condominium and manages the condominium, providing limited services to the homeowners' association. What type/types of license(s) is Maria required to have?

    a. Real estate license only
    b. Community association manager's license only
    c. Both a real estate license and a community association manager's license
    d. Neither a real estate license nor community association manager's license

9. Sarah, an Alabama-licensed real estate broker, enters into a verbal agreement with a Georgia broker to conduct real estate brokerage business in Georgia. Sarah does not have a Georgia real estate license. Which statement is *TRUE* about Sarah's situation?

    a. Sarah cannot conduct real estate brokerage business in Georgia without being licensed.
    b. Sarah can conduct real estate brokerage business in Georgia, but she must have a written agreement with the Georgia broker.
    c. Sarah can conduct brokerage business under the supervision of a Georgia real estate broker if she obtains a 60-day temporary brokerage license.
    d. Sarah can conduct real estate brokerage business in Georgia without an agreement with a Georgia broker if she conducts three or fewer transactions in any calendar year.

10. Within one year of the issuance of an original salesperson's license, the salesperson must complete an approved postlicensing course of at least

    a. 6 instructional hours.
    b. 15 instructional hours.
    c. 25 instructional hours.
    d. 40 instructional hours.

11. A broker is responsible if an affiliated licensee violates any provisions of the Georgia Real Estate License Law unless the broker is able to demonstrate

    a. that the licensee is covered by a current errors and omissions insurance policy.
    b. that the broker did not participate in or ratify the violation.
    c. both a and b.
    d. neither a nor b.

12. When is a broker *NOT* allowed to disburse funds from his or her escrow account?

    a. At the closing of the transaction
    b. Upon the filing of an interpleader action in a court of law
    c. Upon notification by the broker's client that the other party to the transaction has breached the contract
    d. Upon the rejection of an offer to buy, sell, rent, lease, exchange, or option real estate

13. Georgia real estate broker Dan keeps $500 of his own money in his designated broker trust account because the bank requires $500 as a minimum deposit. Dan's water heater in his residence springs a leak and he uses an escrow account check in the amount of $240 to pay the plumber. The next day Dan makes a deposit of $240 of his own money to cover the check. Has Dan committed a violation?

    a. No, he can pay the plumber with an escrow check since he has more than $250 of his own funds in the account.
    b. No, he can write a check in any amount from his escrow account for personal expenses as long as he covers the check before it is taken from client funds.
    c. Yes, a broker can never personally use funds from a designated escrow account.
    d. Yes, a broker may only withdraw monies designated as the broker's funds by a check made payable to the broker.

14. When a salesperson is selling real estate in the salesperson's own name, he or she must
    a. notify his or her broker of the sale.
    b. not advertise in a manner indicating that such advertising is made by a private party, not licensed by the commission.
    c. disclose that he or she is acting as a principal in the transaction.
    d. do all of the above.

15. Georgia real estate broker Cheryl rents a storage unit for the files from real estate closings in which her firm acted as a real estate broker. The storage unit was getting full, so she disposed of the files that were four or more years old. In another action later the same week, Cheryl obtained an earnest money check from a buyer for a house that Cheryl had listed. The sales contract did not specify that Cheryl's firm would pay interest to the buyer or seller on the earnest money. Cheryl deposited the check in a designated escrow account at the bank that paid the interest to Cheryl. Has Cheryl committed a violation of the Georgia law?
    a. Yes, regarding disposing of the files only
    b. Yes, regarding the action on interest-bearing escrow only
    c. Yes, regarding both the disposing of files and the action on the interest-bearing escrow account
    d. No violation has been committed.

16. When a licensee has been found guilty of violating the Georgia Real Estate License Law or the Commission's Rules and Regulations, the commission has the power to
    a. revoke any other Georgia licenses that the licensee holds, such as a license to practice law.
    b. impose a fine not to exceed $5,000 for each violation with fines for multiple violations limited to $25,000.
    c. both a and b.
    d. neither a nor b.

17. Julia, a Georgia real estate licensee, acted as a principal in the sale of a small office building that she owned. Steve, a licensed Georgia real estate broker, acted as the listing broker for Julia's property. Steve deposited a $50,000 earnest money check from the purchaser in his escrow account, but stole the money prior to closing. Julia received $50,000 less than she was entitled to at the closing. She sued Steve and obtained a $50,000 judgment, which is uncollectible because Steve has left the country and his whereabouts are unknown. Julia applied to the Georgia Real Estate Commission for recovery of the $25,000 from the Real Estate Education, Research, and Recovery Fund. What can Julia recover in this situation?
    a. Julia can recover the full $50,000.
    b. Julia's recovery is limited to $45,000.
    c. Julia's recovery is limited to $15,000.
    d. Julia may not recover anything because she is a licensee acting as a principal in the transaction.

18. Susan is a licensed real estate salesperson in Tennessee and resides in Chattanooga. Susan applies to be licensed as a salesperson in Georgia. Susan must
    a. file with the Georgia Real Estate Commission a written statement that appoints the Real Estate Commissioner to act as the licensee's agent, upon whom all judicial and legal notices are directed when being served.
    b. post a bond with the Georgia Real Estate Commission in the amount of $10.000.
    c. both a and b.
    d. neither a nor b.

19. Sam has been a Georgia licensed salesperson for four years. When Sam's license is renewed, he must furnish the Commission with evidence of completing approved continuing education courses totaling at least how many hours for each year of the renewal period?
    a. 4
    b. 6
    c. 7
    d. 12

20. Sally, a Georgia-licensed real estate broker, acts as agent for buyers and sellers in real estate transactions. She also manages an apartment building for an investor. She has two escrow trust accounts, one for the transactions and the other for the rental property. Is this a violation of Georgia license law?

a. Yes, because a broker can have only one escrow account.

b. No, because two is the maximum number of escrow accounts for any one broker.

c. No, because a broker may maintain more than one trust account, but must notify the Commission of the additional accounts.

d. No, because a broker is required to maintain separate escrow accounts for transaction activities and rental activities.

CHAPTER

15

Real Estate Financing: Principles

■ **LEARNING OBJECTIVES**   *When you have finished reading this chapter, you should be able to:*

- ■ **identify** the basic provisions of security and debt instruments: promissory notes, mortgage documents, deeds of trust, and land contracts.

- ■ **describe** the effect of discount points on yield.

- ■ **explain** the procedures involved in a foreclosure.

- ■ **distinguish** between lien and title theories.

- ■ **explain** the three methods of foreclosure.

- ■ **define** the following *key terms:*

acceleration clause	foreclosure	note
alienation clause	hypothecation	novation
assume	interest	owner financing
beneficiary	intermediate theory	prepayment penalty
deed in lieu of foreclosure	lien theory	promissory note
deed to secure debt	loan origination fee	satisfaction
defeasance clause	mortgage	security deed
deficiency judgment	mortgagee	subject to
discount points	mortgagor	title theory
equitable right of redemption	negotiable instrument	usury

IN PRACTICE   Although it is best for licensees to refer customers and clients to a lender to be preapproved for a loan prior to writing a real estate sales contract, it is important for the licensee to be knowledgeable about real estate financing programs and products in order to provide quality service, especially when serving as buyer agents.

■ MORTGAGE LAW

The *mortgagor* is the *borrower.*

The *mortgagee* is the *lender.*

A **mortgage** is a lien or charge on the property of a debtor, called a mortgagor. The borrower, or **mortgagor,** receives a loan and in return gives a note and mortgage to the lender, called the **mortgagee.** When the loan is paid in full, the mortgagee issues a satisfaction of mortgage. The mortgage is a voluntary, specific lien. If the debtor defaults, the lender can sue on the note and foreclose on the mortgage.

Mortgage law is complex, since its origins date back to early Anglo-Saxon law and application varies from state to state. To complicate matters, many states have adopted deed of trust laws. In some states, deeds of trust have largely replaced the use of mortgages.

In Georgia

In Georgia, the voluntary, specific lien discussed in previous paragraphs as a "mortgage" is called the **security deed** or **deed to secure debt.** It is based on Anglo-Saxon law and it serves the same purpose as the mortgage and the deed of trust used in other states. The security deed pledges the real property as the collateral for the repayment of the loan specified in the promissory note. The security deed is given to the lender by the borrower. In the security deed, the lender is the grantee and the borrower is the grantor.

In **title theory** states, the mortgagor actually gives *legal title* to the mortgagee (or some other designated individual) and retains *equitable title.* Legal title is returned to the mortgagor only when the debt is paid in full (or some other obligation is performed). In theory, the lender actually owns the property until the debt is paid. The lender allows the borrower all the usual rights of ownership, such as possession and use. In effect, because the lender actually holds legal title, the lender has the right to immediate possession of the real estate and rents from the mortgaged property if the mortgagor defaults.

In **lien theory** states, the mortgagor retains both legal and equitable title. The mortgagee simply has a lien on the property as security for the mortgage debt. The mortgage, or deed of trust, is nothing more than collateral for the loan. If the mortgagor defaults, the mortgagee must go through a formal foreclosure proceeding to obtain legal title. The property is offered for sale at public auction, and the funds from the sale are used to pay the balance of the remaining debt. In some states, a defaulting mortgagor may *redeem* (buy back) the property during a certain period *after the sale.* A borrower who fails to redeem the property during that time loses the property irrevocably.

A number of states have adopted an **intermediate theory** that is based on the principles of title theory but requires that the mortgagee foreclose to obtain legal title.

| In Georgia | Georgia is an intermediate theory state. The security deed passes title to the lender (grantee) until the loan is paid in full. When payment is made in full, title is given to the borrower (grantor) who is the owner of the property. Upon a default of the loan by the borrower, the title is passed to the lender, with the lender receiving "power of sale" which means the lender can sell the property at public auction after meeting the legal requirement of advertising the property. There is no requirement to go to court; the public sale is a nonjudicial sale handled by the lender's attorney. |

IN PRACTICE   In reality, the differences between the parties' rights in a lien theory state and those in a title theory state are more technical than actual. Regardless of the theory practiced in any particular state, all borrowers and lenders observe the same general requirements to protect themselves in a loan transaction. Real estate loans are formal contracts that need to be in writing and include a description of the property pledged as collateral and a complete statement describing how the loan will be repaid. As with any contract, the parties must be legally competent, their signatures valid and attested, and adequate consideration exchanged.

■ SECURITY AND DEBT

A basic principle of property law is that no one can convey more than he or she actually owns. This principle also applies to mortgages. The owner of a fee simple estate can mortgage the fee. The owner of a leasehold or subleasehold can mortgage that leasehold interest. The owner of a condominium unit can mortgage the fee interest in the condominium. Even the owner of a cooperative interest may be able to offer that personal property interest as collateral for a loan.

A mortgage loan, like all loans, creates a relationship between a debtor and creditor. In the relationship, the creditor loans the debtor money for some purpose, and the debtor agrees to pay or pledge to pay the principal and interest according to an agreed-upon schedule. The debtor agrees to offer some property or collateral to the creditor if the loan is not repaid, although sometimes property is not pledged for this purpose or the loan is unsecured.

Mortgage loans are secured loans. There are two parts to a mortgage loan: the debt itself and the security for the debt. When a property is mortgaged, the owner must *execute* (sign) two separate instruments—a promissory note stating the amount owed, and a security document specifying the collateral used to secure the loan.

Hypothecation   In mortgage lending practice, a borrower is required to pledge specific real property as security (collateral) for the loan. The debtor retains the right of possession and control, while the creditor receives an underlying equitable right in the pledged property. This type of pledging is termed **hypothecation.** The right to foreclose on the pledged property in the event a borrower defaults is contained in a security agreement, such as a mortgage or a deed of trust.

■ PROMISSORY NOTES

The **promissory note,** referred to as the *note* or *financing instrument,* is the borrower's personal promise to repay a debt according to agreed-upon terms. The note exposes all of the borrower's assets to claims by secured creditors. The mortgagor executes one or more promissory notes to total the amount of the debt.

A promissory note executed by a borrower (known as the *maker* or *payor*) is a contract complete in itself. It generally states the amount of the debt, the time and method of payment, and the rate of interest. When signed by the borrowers and other necessary parties, the note becomes a legally enforceable and fully negotiable instrument of debt. When the terms of the note are satisfied, the debt is discharged. If the terms of the note are not met, the lender may choose to sue to collect on the note or to foreclose.

A note need not be tied to a mortgage or security deed. A note used as a debt instrument without any related collateral is called an *unsecured note.* Unsecured notes are used by banks and other lenders to extend short-term personal loans.

A **note** is a **negotiable instrument** like a check or bank draft. The lender who holds the note is referred to as the *payee* and may transfer the right to receive payment to a third party in one of two ways:

1. By signing the instrument over (that is, by *assigning* it) to the third party
2. By delivering the instrument to the third party

IN PRACTICE   All notes should be clearly dated. Accurate dates are essential because *time is of the essence* in every real estate contract. Also, the dates of the notes may be necessary to determine the chronological order of priority rights.

Interest

Interest is a charge for using money. Interest may be due at either the end or the beginning of each payment period. When payments are made at the end of a period, it is known as payment *in arrears*. This payment method is the general practice, and mortgages often call for end-of-period payments due on the first of the following month. Payments may also be made at the beginning of each period, however, when it is known as payment *in advance*. Whether interest is charged in arrears or in advance is specified in the note. This distinction is important if the property is sold before the debt is repaid in full.

Usury   To protect consumers from unscrupulous lenders, many states have enacted laws limiting the interest rate that may be charged on loans. In some states, the legal maximum rate is a fixed amount. In others, it is a floating interest rate, which is adjusted up or down at specific intervals based on a certain economic standard, such as the prime lending rate or the rate of return on government bonds.

Whichever approach is taken, charging interest in excess of the maximum rate is called **usury,** and lenders are penalized for making usurious loans. In some states, a lender that makes a usurious loan is permitted to collect the borrowed money, but only at the legal rate of interest. In others, a usurious lender may lose the right to collect any interest or may lose the entire amount of the loan in addition to the interest.

In Georgia

In Georgia, as of the date of this publication, the legal rate of interest is 7 percent. However, on loans below $3,000 the usury limit is 16 percent. On loans above $3,000, the limit is 5 percent per month or 60 percent per annum. For loans below $250,000 the interest rate must be specified in simple interest and evidenced in writing.

Loan origination fee   The processing of a mortgage application is known as *loan origination.* When a mortgage loan is originated, a **loan origination fee,** or transfer fee, is charged by most lenders to cover the expenses involved in generating the loan. These expenses include the loan officer's salary and paperwork, and the lender's other costs of doing business. A loan origination fee is not prepaid interest; rather, it is a charge that must be paid to the lender. The typical loan origination fee is 1 percent of the loan amount, although origination fees may range from one to three points (a *point* equals 1 percent of the loan amount).

IN PRACTICE   Because many real estate loans are made by private loan companies that may not be covered by federal regulations, it is important that borrowers insist on receiving a statement in advance from their lender that clearly states the total amount of the loan closing costs and the effective interest rate to avoid unpleasant surprises at closing. This *good-faith estimate* is required by the Real Estate Settlement Procedures Act (RESPA). The good-faith estimate is discussed in Chapter 23.

A **point** is 1 percent of the *amount being borrowed;* it is *not* 1 percent of the purchase price.

Discount points   A lender may sell a mortgage to investors (as discussed later in this chapter). However, the interest rate that a lender charges for a loan might be less than the *yield* (true rate of return) an investor demands. To make up the difference, the lender charges the borrower **discount points.** The number of points charged depends on two factors:

1. The difference between the loan's stated interest rate and the yield required by the investor.
2. How long the lender expects it will take the borrower to pay off the loan.

For the borrowers, one discount point equals 1 percent of the loan amount and is charged as prepaid interest at the closing. For instance, three discount points charged on a $100,000 loan would be $3,000 ($100,000 × 3%, or 0.03). If a house sells for $100,000 and the borrower seeks an $80,000 loan, each point would be $800, *not* $1,000. In some cases, however, the points in a new acquisition may be paid in cash at closing by the buyer (or, of course, by the seller on the buyer's behalf) rather than being financed as part of the total loan amount.

To figure how many points are charged on a loan, divide the total dollar amount of the points by the amount of the loan. For example, if the loan amount is $350,000 and the charge for points is $9,275, how many points are being charged?

$$\$9,275 \div \$350,000 = 0.0265 \text{ or } 2.65\% \text{ or } 2.65 \text{ points}$$

Prepayment penalty   Most mortgage loans are paid in installments over a long period of time. As a result, the total interest paid by the borrower may add up to more than the principal amount of the loan. That does not come as a surprise to the lender; the total amount of accrued interest is carefully calculated during the origination phase to determine the profitability of each loan. If the borrower repays the loan before the end of the term, the lender collects less than the anticipated interest. For this reason, some mortgage notes contain a *prepayment clause*. This clause requires that the borrower pay a **prepayment penalty** against the unearned portion of the interest for any payments made ahead of schedule.

The penalty may be as little as 1 percent of the balance due at the time of prepayment or as much as all the interest due for the first ten years of the loan. Some lenders allow the borrower to pay off a certain percentage of the original loan without paying a penalty. However, if the loan is paid in full, the borrower may be charged a percentage of the principal paid in excess of that allowance. *Lenders may not charge prepayment penalties on mortgage loans insured or guaranteed by the federal government or on those loans that have been sold to Fannie Mae or Freddie Mac.*

IN PRACTICE   Some states limit the amount of prepayment penalty lenders may impose, while others prohibit lenders from charging any penalty at all on prepaid residential mortgage or deed of trust loans. Some states allow lenders to charge a prepayment penalty *only* if the loan is paid off with funds borrowed from another source.

MATH CONCEPTS

DISCOUNT POINTS AND INVESTOR YIELD

Depending on the interest rate and loan term, it takes between six and ten discount points to increase the interest rate 1 percent on a 30-year loan. For example, eight points will increase a 25-year 8 percent loan to 9 percent. From the borrower's standpoint, one discount point equals 1 percent of the loan amount.

To calculate the net amount of a $150,000 loan after a three-point discount is taken, multiply the loan amount by 100 percent minus the discount:

$$\$150,000 \times (100\% - 3\%)$$
$$\$150,000 \times 97\%$$
$$\$150,000 \times 0.97 = \$145,500$$

Or deduct the dollar amount of the discount from the loan:

$$\$150,000 - (\$150,000 \times 3\%)$$
$$\$150,000 - (\$150,000 \times 0.03)$$
$$\$150,000 - \$4,500 = \$145,500$$

The borrower may receive a $150,000 loan, but the lender only loaned $145,500 of its own funds. The seller or someone else paid the difference. The lender will collect the full $150,000, plus interest, thus increasing its profit or yield.

■ MORTGAGES

A mortgage must clearly establish that the property is security for a debt, identify the lender and the borrower, and include an accurate legal description of the property. The mortgage incorporates the terms of the note by reference. It should be signed by all parties who have an interest in the real estate. Common provisions are discussed in the following.

Duties of the Mortgagor

The borrower is required to fulfill certain obligations. These usually include the following:

- Payment of the debt in accordance with the terms of the note
- Payment of all real estate taxes on the property given as security
- Maintenance of adequate insurance to protect the lender if the property is destroyed or damaged by fire, windstorm, or other hazard
- Maintenance of the property in good repair at all times
- Receipt of lender authorization before making any major alterations on the property

Failure to meet any of these obligations can result in a borrower's default. The loan documents may, however, provide for a grace period (such as 30 days) during which the borrower can meet the obligation and cure the default. If the borrower does not do so, the lender has the right to foreclose the mortgage and collect on the note.

Provisions for Default

The mortgage typically includes an **acceleration clause** to assist the lender in foreclosure. If a borrower defaults, the lender has the right to accelerate the maturity of the debt. This means the lender may declare the *entire* debt due and payable *immediately*. Without an acceleration clause, the lender would have to sue the borrower every time a payment was overdue.

Other clauses in a mortgage enable the lender to take care of the property in the event of the borrower's negligence or default. If the borrower does not pay taxes or insurance premiums or fails to make necessary repairs on the property, the lender may step in and do so. The lender has the power to protect the security (the real estate). Any money advanced by the lender to cure a default may be either added to the unpaid debt or declared immediately due from the borrower.

IN PRACTICE   In financing real estate sales, lenders seldom accept unsecured promissory notes because there would be no security for the loans. If borrowers defaulted, the lender would be forced to sue for a money judgment. In the meantime, the debtor might dispose of property and hide his or her assets. In some states, a money judgment cannot be used to foreclose on a debtor's personal residence. Because of these, and other reasons, lenders prefer a security interest in real property. The mortgage is known as the security instrument. The security instrument creates the lien on the property. The mortgage allows the lender to sue for foreclosure in the event the borrower defaults.

Georgia Residential Mortgage Fraud Act (O.C.G.A.16-8-100 et seq.)

In Georgia

In 2005, the Georgia General Assembly enacted the Georgia Residential Mortgage Fraud Act. The General Assembly found that fraud involving residential mortgages was at an all-time high, and that lending institutions and borrowers had lost hundreds of millions of dollars due to the fraud. Neighborhoods plagued by mortgage fraud had deteriorated. Property values that were fraudulently inflated had resulted in substantial increases in property taxes. As a result, the General Assembly passed the first mortgage fraud legislation of its kind in the country.

The statute makes it easier to prosecute mortgage fraud and provides for criminal penalties and civil forfeitures of property. Specifically, the statute says that a person commits the offense of residential mortgage fraud when, with the intent to defraud, the person

1. knowingly makes a deliberate misstatement, misrepresentation, or omission during the mortgage-lending process with the intent that it be relied on by a mortgage lender, borrower, or any other party to the mortgage lending process;
2. knowingly uses or facilitates the use of any deliberate misstatement, misrepresentation, or omission, knowing it contains such during the mortgage-lending process with the intent that it be relied on by a mortgage lender, borrower, or any other party to the mortgage-lending process;

3. receives any proceeds or other funds in connection with a residential mortgage closing that a person knew resulted from a violation of (1) or (2) above; or

4. files or causes to be filed with the official registrar of deeds of any Georgia county a document the person knows to contain a deliberate misstatement, misrepresentation, or omission.

A person found in violation of the statute is guilty of a felony, and upon conviction, is punished by imprisonment of not less than one year nor more than ten years, by a fine not to exceed $5,000, or both. However, if the violation involves engaging or participating in a pattern of mortgage fraud or a conspiracy or endeavor to engage in mortgage fraud, imprisonment is for not less than three years nor more than 20 years, by a fine not to exceed $100,000, or both.

Importantly, each residential property transaction subject to a violation of the statute constitutes a separate offense and does not merge with any other crimes under the statute.

IN PRACTICE   Licensees who discover potentially fraudulent activities during a transaction or at a closing are advised to contact their broker, law enforcement crime units, or the Georgia State Attorney General's office. Receiving a commission from a fraudulent transaction is illegal in Georgia.

Assignment of the Mortgage

As mentioned previously, without changing the provisions of a contract, a note may be sold to a third party, such as an investor or another mortgage company. The original mortgagee endorses the note to the third party and executes an *assignment of mortgage*. The assignee becomes the new owner of the debt and security instrument. When the debt is paid in full (or satisfied), the assignee is required to execute the satisfaction (or release) of the security instrument.

Release of the Mortgage Lien

When all loan payments have been made and the note has been paid in full, the borrower will want the public record to show that the debt has been satisfied and that the lender is divested of all rights conveyed under the mortgage. By the provisions of the **defeasance clause** in the document, the lender is required to execute a **satisfaction** (also known as a *release* or *discharge*) when the note has been fully paid. This document returns to the borrower all interest in the real estate originally conveyed to the lender. Entering this release in the public record shows that the debt has been removed from the property.

If the original lender has assigned the mortgage to another lender or investor by a recorded assignment, the release must be executed and recorded by the assignee or mortgagee.

Tax and Insurance Reserves

Many lenders require that borrowers provide a reserve fund to meet future real estate taxes and property insurance premiums. This fund is called an *impound*, a *trust*, or an *escrow account*. When the mortgage loan is made, the borrower starts the reserve by depositing funds to cover the amount of unpaid real estate taxes. If a new insurance policy has just been purchased, the insurance premium reserve will be started with the deposit of one-twelfth of the insurance premium liability. The borrower's monthly loan payments will include principal, interest, tax, and insurance reserves, and sometimes other costs, such as flood insurance or homeowners' association dues. The federal Real Estate Settlement Procedures Act (RESPA), which is discussed in Chapter 16, limits the total amount of reserves that a lender may require.

> The basic recurring components of a borrower's monthly loan payment may be remembered as **PITI: Principal, Interest, Taxes, and Insurance.**

Flood insurance reserves   The National Flood Insurance Reform Act of 1994 imposes certain mandatory obligations on lenders and loan servicers to set aside (*escrow*) funds for flood insurance on new loans for property in flood-prone areas. This means that if a lender or servicer discovers that a secured property is in a flood hazard area, it must notify the borrower. The borrower then has 45 days to purchase flood insurance. If the borrower fails to procure flood insurance, the lender must purchase the insurance on the borrower's behalf. The cost of the insurance may be charged back to the borrower.

Assignment of Rents

If the property involved includes rental units, the borrower may provide for rents to be assigned to the lender in the event of the borrower's default. The assignment may be included in the mortgage, or it may be a separate document. The assignment should clearly indicate that the borrower intends to *assign* the rents, not merely pledge them as security for the loan. In title theory states, lenders are automatically entitled to any rents if the borrower defaults.

Buying Subject to, Assuming, or Novating a Seller's Mortgage

When a person purchases real estate that has an outstanding mortgage, the buyer may take the property in one of two ways. The property may be purchased **subject to** the mortgage, or the buyer may **assume** the mortgage and agree to pay the debt. This technical distinction becomes important if the buyer defaults and the mortgage is foreclosed.

When the property is sold *subject to* the mortgage, the buyer is not personally obligated to pay the debt in full. The buyer takes title to the real estate knowing that he or she must make payments on the existing loan. Upon default, the lender forecloses and the property is sold by court order to pay the debt. If the sale does not pay off the entire debt, the purchaser is not liable for the difference. In some circumstances, however, the original seller might continue to be liable.

■ **FOR EXAMPLE** Robert owns an investment rental property that is mortgaged. For health reasons, he wants to sell the property to Janet, who has been managing the property and who also wants to use the rental property as an investment. Robert sells the property to Janet *subject to* the mortgage. In the sale, Janet takes title and assumes responsibilities for the loan, but after two months she can no longer make payments on the loan. There is a foreclosure sale and because Robert sold the property *subject to* the mortgage, Robert (not Janet) is personally liable if proceeds from the foreclosure sale do not meet the obligations.

In contrast, a buyer who purchases the property and *assumes* the seller's debt becomes *personally* obligated for the payment of the *entire debt*. If the debt is foreclosed and the court sale does not bring enough money to pay the debt in full, a *deficiency judgment* against the assumer and the original borrower may be obtained for the unpaid balance of the note.

■ **FOR EXAMPLE** When Judy bought her house a short time ago, interest rates were very low. Now, Judy has been unexpectedly transferred out of the country and needs to sell the house quickly. Because interest rates have risen dramatically since the time of Judy's loan, buyers may be attracted by the prospect of assuming Judy's mortgage. Clearly, if a buyer were to take out a mortgage now, the rate would be higher and the cost of home ownership would be increased. By assuming an existing loan with a more favorable interest rate, a buyer can save money.

Often, a seller wants to be completely free of the original mortgage loan. To accomplish this, the seller(s), buyer(s), and lender must execute a **novation** agreement in writing. The novation makes the buyer (assumer) solely responsible for any default on the loan. The original borrower (seller) is freed of any liability for the loan.

The existence of a lien does not prevent the transfer of property; however, when a secured loan is assumed, the mortgagee or **beneficiary** must approve the assumption and any release of liability of the original mortgagor. Because a loan may not be assumed without lender approval, the lending institution would require the assumer to qualify financially, and many lending institutions charge a transfer fee to cover the costs of changing the records. This charge usually is paid by the purchaser.

Alienation clause The lender may want to prevent a future purchaser of the property from being able to assume the loan, particularly if the original interest rate is low. For this reason, most lenders include an **alienation clause** (also known as a *resale clause*, *due-on-sale clause*, or *call clause*) in the note. An alienation clause provides that when the property is sold, the lender may either declare the entire debt due immediately or permit the buyer to assume the loan at an interest rate acceptable to the lender. Land contracts that involve a due-on-sale clause also limit the assumption of the contract.

Recording a Mortgage

The mortgage document must be recorded in the recorder's office of the county in which the real estate is located. Recording gives constructive notice to the world of the borrower's obligations. Recording also establishes the lien's priority, as discussed in Chapter 10. If the property is registered in the Torrens system, notice of the lien must be entered on the original Torrens certificate.

Priority of a Mortgage or Deed of Trust

Priority of mortgages and other liens normally is determined by the order in which they were recorded. A mortgage on land that has no prior mortgage lien is a *first mortgage*. If the owner later executes another loan for additional funds, the new loan becomes a *second mortgage* when it is recorded. The second lien is subject to the first lien; the first has prior claim to the value of the land pledged as security. Because second loans represent greater risk to the lender, they are usually issued at higher interest rates.

The priority of mortgage may be changed by a *subordination agreement*, in which the first lender subordinates its lien to that of the second lender. To be valid, such an agreement must be signed by both lenders.

■ PROVISIONS OF LAND CONTRACTS AND OWNER FINANCING

As discussed in Chapter 11, real estate can be purchased under a land contract, also known as a *contract for deed* or an *installment contract*. Real estate is usually sold on contract for specific **owner financing** reasons. For instance, mortgage financing may be unavailable to a borrower for some reason. High interest rates may make borrowing too expensive. Or the purchaser may not have a sufficient down payment to cover the difference between a mortgage loan and the selling price.

Under a land contract, the buyer (called the *vendee*) agrees to make a down payment and a monthly loan payment that includes interest and principal. The payment also may include real estate tax and insurance reserves. The seller (called the *vendor*) retains legal title to the property during the contract term, and the buyer is granted equitable title and possession. At the end of the loan term, the seller delivers clear title. The contract usually permits the seller to evict the buyer in the event of default. In that case, the seller may keep any money the buyer has already paid, which is construed as rent. Many states now offer some legal protection to a defaulting buyer under a land contract.

In Georgia

In Georgia, land contracts were at one time illegal because sellers took advantage of unknowing buyers. As a result, while land contracts are legal, they are not used as a general practice.

■ FORECLOSURE

When a borrower defaults on the payments or fails to fulfill any of the other obligations set forth in the mortgage, the lender's rights can be enforced through foreclosure. **Foreclosure** is a legal procedure in which property pledged as security is sold to satisfy the debt. The foreclosure procedure brings the rights of the parties and all junior lienholders to a conclusion. It passes title to either the person holding the mortgage document or to a third party who purchases the realty at a *foreclosure sale*. The purchaser could be the mortgagee. The property is sold *free of the foreclosing mortgage and all junior liens*.

Methods of Foreclosure

There are three general types of foreclosure proceedings—judicial, nonjudicial, and strict foreclosure. One, two, or all three may be available. The specific provisions and procedures for each vary from state to state.

Judicial foreclosure Judicial foreclosure allows the property to be sold by court order after the mortgagee has given sufficient public notice. When a borrower defaults, the lender may *accelerate* the due date of the remaining principal balance along with all overdue monthly payments and interest, penalties, and administrative costs. The lender's attorney can then file a suit to foreclose the lien. After presentation of the facts in court, the property is ordered sold. A public sale is advertised and held, and the real estate is sold to the highest bidder.

Nonjudicial foreclosure Some states allow nonjudicial foreclosure procedures to be used when the security instrument contains a *power-of-sale clause*. In nonjudicial foreclosure, no court action is required. In those states that recognize deed of trust loans, the trustee is generally given the power of sale. Some states allow a similar power of sale to be used with a mortgage loan.

To institute a nonjudicial foreclosure, the trustee or mortgagee may be required to record a notice of default at the county recorder's office. The default must be recorded within a designated time period to give notice to the public of the intended auction. The notice is generally provided by newspaper advertisements that state the total amount due and the date of the public sale. After selling the property, the mortgagee may be required to file a copy of a notice of sale or an affidavit of foreclosure.

| In Georgia | The "power of sale" provision in the security deed in Georgia is a nonjudicial foreclosure proceeding.

Strict foreclosure Although judicial foreclosure is the prevalent practice, it is still possible in some states for a lender to acquire mortgaged property through a *strict foreclosure* process. First, appropriate notice must be given to the delinquent borrower. Once the proper papers have been prepared and recorded, the court establishes a deadline by which time the balance of the defaulted debt must be paid in full. If the borrower does not pay off the loan by that date, the court simply awards full legal title to the lender. No sale takes place.

Deed in Lieu of Foreclosure

As an alternative to foreclosure, a lender may accept a **deed in lieu of foreclosure** from the borrower. This is sometimes known as a *friendly foreclosure* because it is carried out by mutual agreement rather than by lawsuit. The major disadvantage of the deed in lieu is that the mortgagee takes the real estate subject to all junior liens. In a foreclosure action, all junior liens are eliminated. Also, by accepting a deed in lieu of foreclosure, the lender usually loses any rights pertaining to FHA or private mortgage insurance or VA guarantees. Finally, it should be pointed out that a deed in lieu of foreclosure is still considered an adverse element in the borrower's credit history.

Redemption

Most states give defaulting borrowers a chance to redeem their property through the **equitable right of redemption.** (See Chapter 10.) If, after default *but before the foreclosure sale*, the borrower (or any other person who has an interest in the real estate, such as another creditor) pays the lender the amount in default, plus costs, the debt will be reinstated. In some cases, the person who redeems may be required to repay the accelerated loan in full. If some person other than the mortgagor or trustor redeems the real estate, the borrower becomes responsible to that person for the amount of the redemption.

Certain states also allow defaulted borrowers a period in which to redeem their real estate *after the sale*. During this period (which may be as long as one year), the borrower has a *right of redemption*. The mortgagor who can raise the necessary funds to redeem the property within the statutory period pays the redemption money to the court. Because the debt was paid from the proceeds of the sale, the borrower can take possession free and clear of the former defaulted loan. The court may appoint a receiver to take charge of the property, collect rents, and pay operating expenses during the redemption period. Redemption is illustrated in Figure 15.1.

In Georgia   Georgia does not have statutory redemption for the defaulted borrower.

Deed to Purchaser at Sale

If redemption is not made or if state law does not provide for a redemption period, the successful bidder at the sale receives a deed to the real estate. A sheriff or master-in-chancery executes this deed to the purchaser to *convey whatever*

F I G U R E   15.1

Redemption

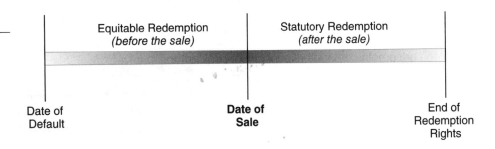

title the borrower had. The deed contains no warranties. Title passes as is but is free of the former defaulted debt.

Deficiency Judgment

The foreclosure sale may not produce enough cash to pay the loan balance in full after deducting expenses and accrued unpaid interest. In this case, the mortgagee may be entitled to a *personal judgment* against the borrower for the unpaid balance. Such a judgment is a **deficiency judgment.** It may also be obtained against any endorsers or guarantors of the note and against any owners of the mortgaged property who assumed the debt by written agreement. However, if any money remains from the foreclosure sale after paying the debt and any other liens (such as a second mortgage or mechanic's lien), expenses, and interest, these proceeds are paid to the borrower.

■ KEY POINT REVIEW

In a **mortgage,** the **mortgagor** (i.e., the real estate owner) borrows money from the **mortgagee** (lender), and the real estate is used as **security** for the debt.

The term **mortgage** refers to any **financing instrument** by which real estate is used as **security** for a debt. The mortgage can take the form of either a **mortgage lien** or a **deed of trust.**

In Georgia

To define mortgage, Georgia uses the terms "security deed" or "deed to secure debt," but not "deed of trust."

A **mortgage lien** on property is the old common-law form of mortgage with the following characteristics:

- **Lien-theory** states have specific requirements that must be met.
- A **mortgage document** is executed by the borrower and **recorded** in the county in which property is located.
- When a loan is paid in full, a **defeasance clause** requires the lender to execute a **satisfaction (release** or **discharge)** that is **recorded** to clear title.
- If the borrower **defaults,** the lender can **accelerate** the due date of the remaining principal balance and all other payments and costs.
- If the borrower continues in default, the lender can bring court action called **judicial foreclosure** where
  — the **judge** orders property sold;
  — the **public sale** is advertised and real estate is sold to **highest bidder;**
  — the borrower has **equitable right of redemption** within the time period (before and/or after sale) allowed by law;
  — no court action is necessary to begin the sale process if the mortgage has a **power-of-sale clause;**
  — the mortgagee may have the right to **personal judgment (deficiency judgment)** against the borrower for the unpaid balance, **when allowed by state law,** if the sale proceeds are less than the amount owed;

— the court can **award title** to the **lender** and no sale occurs if it is a **strict foreclosure**; and

— the lender may accept a **deed in lieu of foreclosure** from a defaulting borrower, but title is **subject to junior liens** that are eliminated in a foreclosure.

| In Georgia | Georgia uses an intermediate theory based on title theory but requires that the mortgagee foreclose to obtain legal title.

Also, the security deed's "power of sale" is a nonjudicial foreclosure proceeding.

The Georgia Residential Mortgage Fraud Act, enacted in 2005, makes it easier to prosecute a mortgage fraud and provides for criminal penalties and civil forfeitures of property.

Priority of mortgages and other liens is determined by the order in which they were recorded. **Priority** may be changed by **subordination agreement**.

An impound (trust or escrow) account may be required to create a reserve fund to ensure that future tax, property insurance, and other payments are made.

- **Borrower** funds the account through an increase in loan payment that can be remembered as **PITI**: Principal, Interest, Taxes, Insurance.
- Lender makes tax, insurance, and other payments on borrower's behalf.
- The **Real Estate Settlement Procedures Act (RESPA)** limits total amount of reserves that a lender may require.
- The **National Flood Insurance Reform Act of 1994** imposes obligations on lenders and loan servicers to set aside escrow funds for flood insurance on new loans for property in flood-prone areas.

When property with an **outstanding mortgage** is conveyed, the new owner may take title in one of two ways, if allowed by the loan document:

1. **Subject to** the existing mortgage, where the **new owner** makes payments on existing loans but is **not personally liable** if property is sold on default and proceeds of sale do not satisfy debt.

2. **Assuming** the existing mortgage or deed of trust, and agreeing to pay the debt, where the **new owner** takes personal responsibility for existing loans and is subject to a **deficiency judgment** if the property is sold on default and proceeds of sale do not satisfy debt.

A **novation** agreement may be used to release the seller from any future liability on loans secured by the real estate.

An **alienation clause (resale clause, due-on-sale clause, or call clause)** in a loan document will prevent future purchaser of the property from assuming the loan.

■ RELATED WEB SITES

Georgia Real Estate Commission pamphlet on how to prevent mortgage fraud, prepared by Georgia Real Estate Fraud Prevention and Awareness Coalition: *www.grec.state.ga.us*

Legal Information Institute: Mortgages: *www.law.cornell.edu/topics/mortgages.html*

CHAPTER 15 QUIZ

1. A charge of three discount points on a $120,000 loan equals
   a. $450.
   b. $3,600.
   c. $4,500.
   d. $116,400.

2. A prospective buyer needs to borrow money to buy a house. The buyer applies for and obtains a real estate loan from the VGY Company. Then the buyer signs a note and a mortgage. In this example, the buyer is referred to as the
   a. mortgagor.
   b. beneficiary.
   c. mortgagee.
   d. vendor.

3. In the previous question, VGY Company is the
   a. mortgagor.
   b. beneficiary.
   c. mortgagee.
   d. vendor.

4. In a land contract the vendee
   a. is not responsible for the real estate taxes on the property.
   b. does not pay interest and principal.
   c. has possession during the term of the contract.
   d. obtains legal title at closing.

5. A state law provides that lenders cannot charge more than 24 percent interest on any loan. This kind of law is called
   a. a Truth-in-Lending law.
   b. a usury law.
   c. the statute of frauds.
   d. RESPA.

6. Which of the following clauses would give a lender the right to have all future installments become due on default?
   a. Escalation
   b. Defeasance
   c. Alienation
   d. Acceleration

7. Under a typical land contract, when does the vendor give the deed to the vendee?
   a. When the contract is fulfilled and all payments have been made
   b. At the closing
   c. When the contract for deed is approved by the parties
   d. After the first year's real estate taxes are paid

8. If a borrower must pay a discount fee of $4,500 for points on a $90,000 loan, how many points is the lender charging for this loan?
   a. 2
   b. 3
   c. 5
   d. 6

9. When a seller is freed of any future liability for a loan assumed by a buyer, the seller has signed a(n)
   a. alienation clause.
   b. acceleration clause.
   c. release of contract.
   d. novation agreement.

10. Which of the following allows a mortgagee to proceed to a foreclosure sale without having to go to court first?
    a. Waiver of redemption right
    b. Power of sale
    c. Alienation clause
    d. Hypothecation

11. Pledging property for a loan without giving up possession is referred to as
    a. hypothecation.
    b. defeasance.
    c. alienation.
    d. novation.

12. Discount points on a mortgage are computed as a percentage of the
    a. selling price.
    b. amount borrowed.
    c. closing costs.
    d. down payment.

13. With the help of a mortgage loan from Pleasant Lenders, Tom bought a house at 123 Charming Street. Pleasant Lenders promptly recorded the mortgage. Three years later, Tom needs additional cash, so he places a second mortgage with Best Bank. Based on these facts, which of the following statements is *TRUE*?

   a. Because it is older, the loan from Pleasant Lenders is subject to the loan from Best Bank, which assumes priority in time.

   b. The loan from Best Bank is referred to as a *subordination loan*.

   c. The loan from Pleasant Lenders has priority over the loan from Best Bank.

   d. Best Bank cannot hold a security interest in the property already held as collateral by another lender.

14. A junior lien may become first in priority if the original lender agrees to execute a

   a. deed of trust.
   b. subordination agreement.
   c. second mortgage agreement.
   d. call clause.

15. A buyer purchased a home under an agreement that made the buyer personally obligated to continue making payments under the seller's existing mortgage. If the buyer defaults and the court sale of the property does not satisfy the debt, the buyer will be liable for making up the difference. The buyer has

   a. purchased the home subject to the seller's mortgage.
   b. assumed the seller's mortgage.
   c. benefited from the alienation clause in the seller's mortgage.
   d. benefited from the defeasance clause in the seller's mortgage.

16. Georgia uses which of the following theories of mortgage?

   a. Equitable theory
   b. Title theory
   c. Lien theory
   d. Intermediate theory

17. In Georgia, the legal document that pledges the property as collateral for the repayment of the loan is the

   a. note.
   b. security deed.
   c. tax deed.
   d. contract for deed.

18. When a lender wants to prevent a future purchaser of the property from being able to assume the loan, she places one of the following clauses into the security deed in Georgia. What is the name of that clause?

   a. Acceleration
   b. Assignment
   c. Alienation
   d. Assumption

Real Estate Financing: Practice

■ **LEARNING OBJECTIVES** *When you have finished reading this chapter, you should be able to:*

■ **identify** the types of institutions in the primary and secondary mortgage markets.

■ **describe** the various types of financing techniques available to real estate purchasers and the role of government financing regulations.

■ **explain** the requirements and qualifications for conventional, FHA, and VA loan programs.

■ **distinguish** among the different types of *creative* financing techniques that address borrowers' different needs.

■ **review** legislation affecting real estate financing.

■ **define** the following *key terms:*

adjustable-rate mortgage (ARM)
amortized loan
balloon payment
blanket loan
buydown
Community Reinvestment Act of 1977 (CRA)
computerized loan origination (CLO)
construction loan
conventional loan
Equal Credit Opportunity Act (ECOA)

Fannie Mae
Farm Credit System (Farm Credit)
Farm Service Agency (FSA)
Farmer Mac
Federal Deposit Insurance Corporation (FDIC)
federal funds rate
Federal Reserve System (the Fed)
FHA loan
Freddie Mac
Ginnie Mae

growing-equity mortgage (GEM)
home equity loan
index
interest-only mortgage
loan-to-value ratios
margin
Office of Thrift Supervision (OTS)
open-end loan
package loan
primary mortgage market
private mortgage insurance (PMI)

purchase-money mortgage (PMM)
Regulation Z
reverse-annuity mortgage (RAM)
sale-and-leaseback
secondary mortgage market
straight loan
trigger terms
Truth-in-Lending Act
VA loan
wraparound loan

■ INTRODUCTION TO THE REAL ESTATE FINANCING MARKET

The real estate financing market has the following three basic components:

1. Government influences, primarily the Federal Reserve System, but also the Home Loan Bank System and the Office of Thrift Supervision
2. The primary mortgage market
3. The secondary mortgage market

Under the umbrella of the financial policies set by the Federal Reserve System, the primary mortgage market originates loans that are bought, sold, and traded in the secondary mortgage market. Before turning to the specific types of mortgage options available to consumers, it is important to have a clear understanding of the bigger picture: the market in which those mortgages exist.

The Federal Reserve System

The role of the **Federal Reserve System (the Fed,** as it is commonly known) is to maintain sound credit conditions, help counteract inflationary and deflationary trends, and create a favorable economic climate. The Federal Reserve System divides the country into 12 federal reserve districts, each served by a federal reserve bank. All nationally chartered banks must join the Fed and purchase stock in its district reserve banks.

The Federal Reserve System regulates the flow of money and interest rates in the marketplace through its member banks by controlling their *reserve requirements* and *discount rates*. The Fed also can regulate the money supply through the Federal Open Market Committee (FOMC), which buys and sells U.S. government securities on the open market. When the FOMC sells securities, it effectively removes the money paid by buyers from circulation. When it buys them, it infuses its own reserves back into the general supply.

Reserve requirements   The Federal Reserve System requires that each member bank keep a certain amount of assets on hand as reserve funds. These reserves are unavailable for loans or any other use. This requirement not only protects customer deposits, but it also provides a means of manipulating the flow of cash in the money market.

By increasing its reserve requirements, the Federal Reserve in effect limits the amount of money that member banks can use to make loans. When the amount of money available for lending decreases, interest rates (the amount lenders charge for the use of their money) rise. By causing interest rates to rise, the government can slow down an overactive economy by limiting the number of loans that would have been directed toward major purchases of goods and services. The opposite is also true: By decreasing the reserve requirements, the Fed can encourage more lending. Increased lending causes the amount of money circulated in the marketplace to rise, while simultaneously causing interest rates to drop.

Discount rates Federal Reserve member banks are permitted to borrow money from the district reserve banks to expand their lending operations. The *discount rate* is the rate charged by the Federal Reserve when it lends to its member banks. The **federal funds rate** is the rate recommended by the Federal Reserve for the member banks to charge each other on short-term loans. These rates form the basis on which the banks determine the percentage rate of interest they will charge their loan customers. The *prime rate*, the short-term interest rate charged to a bank's largest, most creditworthy customers, is strongly influenced by the Fed's discount rate. In turn, the prime rate is often the basis for determining a bank's interest rate on other loans, including mortgages. These rates are usually higher than the prime rate. In theory, when the Federal Reserve discount rate is high, bank interest rates are high. When bank interest rates are high, fewer loans are made and less money circulates in the marketplace. On the other hand, a lower discount rate results in lower overall interest rates, more bank loans, and more money in circulation.

The Primary Mortgage Market

The **primary mortgage market** is made up of the lenders that originate mortgage loans. These lenders make money available directly to borrowers. From a borrower's point of view, a loan is a means of financing an expenditure; from a lender's point of view, a loan is an investment. All investors look for profitable returns on their investments. For a lender, a loan must generate enough income to be attractive as an investment. Income on the loan is realized from the following two sources:

1. *Finance charges* collected at closing, such as loan origination fees and discount points
2. *Recurring income*, that is, the interest collected during the term of the loan

An increasing number of lenders look at the income generated from the fees charged in originating loans as their primary investment objective. Once the loans are made, they are sold to investors. By selling loans to investors in the secondary mortgage market, lenders generate funds with which to originate additional loans.

In addition to the income directly related to loans, some lenders derive income from servicing loans for other mortgage lenders or investors who have purchased the loans. Servicing involves such activities as

- collecting payments (including insurance and taxes),
- accounting,
- bookkeeping,
- preparing insurance and tax records,
- processing payments of taxes and insurance, and
- following up on loan payment and delinquency.

The terms of the servicing agreement stipulate the responsibilities and fees for the service.

Some of the major lenders in the primary market include the following:

- *Thrifts, savings associations, and commercial banks.* These institutions are known as *fiduciary lenders* because of their fiduciary obligations to protect and preserve their depositors' funds. *Thrifts* is a generic term for the savings associations. Mortgage loans are perceived as secure investments for generating income and enable these institutions to pay interest to their depositors. Fiduciary lenders are subject to standards and regulations established by government agencies such as the **Federal Deposit Insurance Corporation (FDIC)** and the **Office of Thrift Supervision (OTS).** These agencies govern the practices of fiduciary lenders. The various government regulations (which include reserve fund, reporting, and insurance requirements) are intended to protect depositors against the reckless lending that characterized the savings and loan industry in the 1980s.

- *Insurance companies.* Insurance companies accumulate large sums of money from the premiums paid by their policyholders. While part of this money is held in reserve to satisfy claims and cover operating expenses, much of it is free to be invested in profit-earning enterprises, such as long-term real estate loans. Although insurance companies are considered primary lenders, they tend to invest their money in large, long-term loans that finance commercial, industrial, and larger multifamily properties rather than single-family home mortgages.

- *Credit unions.* Credit unions are cooperative organizations whose members place money in savings accounts. In the past, credit unions made only short-term consumer and home improvement loans. Recently, however, they have branched out to originating longer-term first and second mortgage and deed of trust loans.

- *Pension funds.* Pension funds usually have large amounts of money available for investment. Because of the comparatively high yields and low risks offered by mortgages, pension funds have begun to participate actively in financing real estate projects. Most real estate activity for pension funds is handled through mortgage bankers and mortgage brokers.

- *Endowment funds.* Many commercial banks and mortgage bankers handle investments for endowment funds. The endowments of hospitals, universities, colleges, charitable foundations, and other institutions provide a good source of financing for low-risk commercial and industrial properties.

- *Investment group financing.* Large real estate projects, such as highrise apartment buildings, office complexes, and shopping centers, are often financed as joint ventures through group financing arrangements like syndicates, limited partnerships, and real estate investment trusts.

- *Mortgage banking companies.* Mortgage banking companies originate mortgage loans with money belonging to insurance companies, pension funds, and individuals, and with funds of their own. They make real estate loans with the intention of selling them to investors and receiving a fee for servicing the loans. Mortgage banking companies are generally organized as stock companies. As a source of real estate financing, they are subject to fewer lending restrictions than are commercial banks or savings associations. Mortgage banking companies often are involved in all types of real estate loan activities and often serve as intermediaries between investors and borrowers. They are *not* mortgage brokers.

Primary Mortgage Market

- Trusts
- Savings associations
- Commercial banks
- Insurance companies
- Credit unions
- Pension funds
- Endowment funds
- Investment group financing
- Mortgage banking

■ *Mortgage brokers.* Mortgage brokers are not lenders. They are intermediaries who bring borrowers and lenders together. Mortgage brokers locate potential borrowers, process preliminary loan applications, and submit the applications to lenders for final approval. Frequently, they work with or for mortgage banking companies. They do not service loans once the loans are made. Mortgage brokers also may be real estate brokers who offer these financing services in addition to their regular real estate brokerage activities. Many state governments are establishing separate licensure requirements for mortgage brokers to regulate their activities.

IN PRACTICE   A growing number of consumers apply for mortgage loans via the Internet. Many major lenders have Web sites that offer information to potential borrowers regarding their current loan programs and requirements. In addition, online brokerage or matchmaking organizations link lenders with potential borrowers. Some borrowers prefer the Internet for its convenience in shopping for the best rates and terms, accessing a wide variety of loan programs, and speeding up the loan approval process.

Information on the Internet regarding lenders and their programs is constantly changing. Consider using a search engine such as *www.google.com* or *www.yahoo.com* to search for terms such as *real estate, financing, lending programs,* and *home mortgages.*

The Secondary Mortgage Market

In addition to the primary mortgage market, where loans are originated, there is a **secondary mortgage market.** In the secondary mortgage market, loans are bought and sold only after they have been funded. Lenders routinely sell loans to avoid interest rate risks and to realize profits on the sales. This secondary market activity helps lenders raise capital to continue making mortgage loans. Secondary market activity is especially desirable when money is in short supply; it stimulates both the housing construction market and the mortgage market by expanding the types of loans available. Growth in the use of secondary markets has greatly increased the standardization of loans.

When a loan is sold, the original lender may continue to collect the payments from the borrower. The lender then passes the payments along to the investor who purchased the loan. The investor is charged a fee for servicing of the loan.

In the secondary mortgage market, various agencies purchase a number of mortgage loans and assemble them into packages (called *pools*). These agencies purchase the mortgages from banks and savings associations. Securities that represent shares in these pooled mortgages are then sold to investors or other agencies. Loans are eligible for sale to the secondary market only when the collateral, borrower, and documentation meet certain requirements to provide a degree of safety for the investors. The major warehousing agencies are discussed in the following paragraphs. (See Table 16.1.)

TABLE 16.1	Institution	Secondary Market Function	Entity
Secondary Mortgage Market	Fannie Mae	Conventional, VA, FHA Loans	Privately Owned Corporation
	Ginnie Mae	Special Assistance Loans	Government Agency in HUD
	Freddie Mac	Mostly Conventional Loans	Privately Owned Corporation

Fannie Mae   Fannie Mae (formerly the Federal National Mortgage Association) is a government-sponsored enterprise. It is organized as a privately owned corporation that issues its own common stock and provides a secondary market for mortgage loans. Fannie Mae deals in conventional and Federal Housing Administration (FHA) and Department of Veterans Affairs (VA) loans. Fannie Mae buys from a lender a *block* or *pool* of mortgages that may then be used as collateral for *mortgage-backed securities (MBSs)* that are sold on the global market.

Ginnie Mae   Unlike Fannie Mae, **Ginnie Mae** (formerly the Government National Mortgage Association) is entirely a governmental agency. Ginnie Mae is a division of the Department of Housing and Urban Development (HUD), organized as a corporation without capital stock. Ginnie Mae administers special-assistance programs and guarantees MBSs using FHA and VA loans as collateral.

Ginnie Mae guarantees investment securities issued by private offerors (such as banks, mortgage companies, and savings and loan associations) and backed by pools of FHA and VA mortgage loans. The *Ginnie Mae pass-through certificate* is a security interest in a pool of mortgages that provides for a monthly pass-through of principal and interest payments directly to the certificate holder. Such certificates are guaranteed by Ginnie Mae.

Freddie Mac   Freddie Mac (formerly the Federal Home Loan Mortgage Corporation) is a government-sponsored enterprise, similar to Fannie Mae, that provides a secondary market for mortgage loans, primarily conventional loans. Freddie Mac has the authority to purchase mortgages, pool them, and sell bonds in the open market with the mortgages as security. However, Freddie Mac does not guarantee payment of Freddie Mac mortgages.

Many lenders use the standardized forms and follow the guidelines issued by Fannie Mae and Freddie Mac. In fact, the use of such forms is mandatory for lenders that wish to sell mortgages in the agencies' secondary mortgage market. The standardized documents include loan applications, credit reports, and appraisal forms.

IN PRACTICE   Because Fannie Mae and Freddie Mac are the largest sources of housing finance in the United States, many underwriting guidelines are written to comply with their regulations. Bank statements, tax returns, verifications of employment and child support—most of the paperwork a potential borrower must deal with—may be tied to Fannie Mae and Freddie Mac requirements.

■ FINANCING TECHNIQUES

Now that you understand *where* real estate financing comes from, we'll turn to the *what*: the types of financing available. Real estate financing comes in a wide variety of forms. While the payment plans described in the following sections are commonly referred to as *mortgages*, they are really *loans* secured by either a mortgage or a deed of trust.

Straight Loans

A **straight loan** (also known as a *term loan*) essentially divides the loan into two amounts, to be paid off separately. The borrower makes periodic payments of interest only, followed by the payment of the principal *in full at the end of the term*. Straight loans were once the only form of mortgage available. Today, they are generally used for home improvements and second mortgages rather than for residential first mortgage loans.

Interest-Only Mortgage

An **interest-only mortgage** is a mortgage that requires the payment of interest only for a stated period of time with the principal balance due at the end of the term. In the past, interest-only mortgages have been used for short-term financing. But today, interest-only mortgages have become a popular option, not only for home improvements and second mortgages, but also for long-term first mortgages. The InterestFirst™ mortgage requires payment of interest only for 10 years or 15 years, with the principal balance plus interest recalculated over the remaining years of the loan.

Balloon Payment Loan

When the periodic payments are not enough to fully amortize the loan by the time the final payment is due, the final payment is larger than the others. The final payment is called a **balloon payment.** It is a *partially amortized loan* because principal is still owed at the end of the term. It is frequently assumed that if payments are made promptly, the lender will extend the balloon payment for another limited term. The lender, however, is not legally obligated to grant this extension and can require payment in full when the note is due.

Amortized Loans

The word *amortize* literally means to kill off slowly, over time. Most mortgage and deed of trust loans are amortized loans. That is, they are paid off slowly, over time, in equal payments. Regular periodic payments are made over a term of years. The most common periods are 15 years or 30 years, although 20-year mortgages are also available. Unlike a straight loan payment, the payment in an **amortized loan** partially pays off both principal and interest. Each payment is applied first to the interest owed; the balance of the payment is then applied to the principal amount.

At the end of the term, the full amount of the principal and all interest due is reduced to zero. Such loans are also called *direct reduction loans*. Most amortized mortgage and deed of trust loans are paid in monthly installments. However, some are payable quarterly (four times a year) or semiannually (twice a year).

Different payment plans tend alternately to gain and lose favor with lenders and borrowers as the cost and availability of mortgage money fluctuate. The most frequently used plan is the *fully amortized loan*, or *level-payment loan*. The mortgagor pays a *constant amount*, usually monthly. The lender credits each payment first to the interest due, then to the principal amount of the loan. As a result, while each payment remains the same, the portion applied to repayment of the principal grows and the interest due declines as the unpaid balance of the loan is reduced. If the borrower pays additional amounts that are applied directly to the principal, the loan will amortize more quickly. This benefits the borrower because he or she will pay less interest if the loan is paid off before the end of its term. Of course, lenders are aware of this, too, and may guard against unprofitable loans by including penalties for early payment.

The amount of the constant payment of an amortizing loan is determined from a prepared mortgage payment book or a mortgage factor chart. (See Table 16.2.) The mortgage factor chart indicates the amount of monthly payment per $1,000 of loan, depending on the term and interest rate. This factor is multiplied by the number of thousands (and fractions of thousands) of the amount borrowed.

IN PRACTICE   Of course, there are relatively inexpensive calculators that will accurately perform most of the standard mortgage lending calculations. Also, most commercial lenders provide mortgage calculators on their Web sites. Nonetheless, it's valuable both to know what the calculator is doing and to be able to perform the calculations manually if the calculator breaks or no calculator is available.

Adjustable-Rate Mortgages (ARMs)

An **adjustable-rate mortgage (ARM)** is generally originated at one rate of interest. That rate then fluctuates up or down during the loan term, based on some objective economic indicator. Because the interest rate may change, the mortgagor's loan repayments also may change. Details of how and when the interest rate will change are included in the note. Common components of an ARM include the following:

- The interest rate is tied to the movement of an objective economic indicator called an **index.** Most indexes are tied to U.S. Treasury securities.
- Usually, the interest rate is the index rate plus a premium, called the *margin*. The **margin** represents the lender's cost of doing business. For example, the loan rate may be 2 percent over the U.S. Treasury bill rate.
- *Rate caps* limit the amount the interest rate may change. Most ARMs have two types of rate caps—periodic and life-of-the-loan (or aggregate). A periodic rate cap limits the amount the rate may increase at any one time. An aggregate rate cap limits the amount the rate may increase over the entire life of the loan.

TABLE 16.2

Mortgage Factor Chart

How To Use This Chart

To use this chart, start by finding the appropriate interest rate. Then follow that row over to the column for the appropriate loan term. This number is the *interest rate factor* required each month to amortize a $1,000 loan. To calculate the principal and interest (PI) payment, multiply the interest rate factor by the number of 1,000s in the total loan.

For example, if the interest rate is 8 percent for a term of 30 years, the interest rate factor is 7.34. If the total loan is $100,000, the loan contains 100 1,000s. Therefore, 100 × 7.34 = $734 PI only.

Rate	Term 10 Years	Term 15 Years	Term 20 Years	Term 25 Years	Term 30 Years
6	11.10	8.44	7.16	6.44	6.00
6⅛	11.16	8.51	7.24	6.52	6.08
6¼	11.23	8.57	7.31	6.60	6.16
6⅜	11.29	8.64	7.38	6.67	6.24
6½	11.35	8.71	7.46	6.75	6.32
6⅝	11.42	8.78	7.53	6.83	6.40
6¾	11.48	8.85	7.60	6.91	6.49
6⅞	11.55	8.92	7.68	6.99	6.57
7	11.61	8.98	7.75	7.06	6.65
7⅛	11.68	9.06	7.83	7.15	6.74
7¼	11.74	9.12	7.90	7.22	6.82
7⅜	11.81	9.20	7.98	7.31	6.91
7½	11.87	9.27	8.05	7.38	6.99
7⅝	11.94	9.34	8.13	7.47	7.08
7¾	12.00	9.41	8.20	7.55	7.16
7⅞	12.07	9.48	8.29	7.64	7.25
8	12.14	9.56	8.37	7.72	7.34
8⅛	12.20	9.63	8.45	7.81	7.43
8¼	12.27	9.71	8.53	7.89	7.52
8⅜	12.34	9.78	8.60	7.97	7.61
8½	12.40	9.85	8.68	8.06	7.69
8⅝	12.47	9.93	8.76	8.14	7.78
8¾	12.54	10.00	8.84	8.23	7.87
8⅞	12.61	10.07	8.92	8.31	7.96
9	12.67	10.15	9.00	8.40	8.05

- The mortgagor is protected from unaffordable individual payments by the *payment cap*. The payment cap sets a maximum amount for payments. With a payment cap, a rate increase could result in *negative amortization*, that is, an increase in the loan balance.
- The *adjustment period* establishes how often the rate may be changed. For instance, the adjustment period may be monthly, quarterly, or annually.
- Lenders may offer a *conversion option* that permits the mortgagor to convert from an adjustable-rate to a fixed-rate loan at certain intervals during the life of the mortgage. The option is subject to certain terms and conditions for the conversion.

Figure 16.1 illustrates the effect interest rate fluctuations and periodic caps have on an adjustable-rate mortgage. Obviously, without rate caps and payment caps, a single mortgage's interest rate could fluctuate wildly over several adjustment periods, depending on the behavior of the index to which it is tied. In

FIGURE 16.1

Adjustable-Rate Mortgage

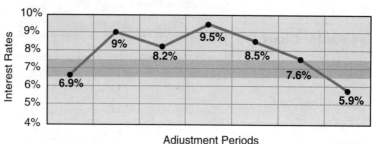

Figure 16.1, the borrower's rate changes from a low of 5.9 percent to a high of 9.5 percent. Such unpredictability makes personal financial planning difficult. On the other hand, if the loan had a rate cap of 7.5 percent, the borrower's rate would never go above that level, regardless of the index's behavior. Similarly, a lender would want a floor to keep the rate from falling below a certain rate (here, 6.5 percent). The shaded area in the figure shows how caps and floors protect against dramatic changes in interest rates.

Growing-Equity Mortgage (GEM)

A **growing-equity mortgage (GEM)** is also known as a *rapid-payoff mortgage*. The GEM uses a fixed interest rate, but payments of principal are increased according to an index or a schedule. Thus, the total payment increases, and the loan is paid off more quickly. A GEM is most frequently used when the borrower's income is expected to keep pace with the increasing loan payments.

Reverse-Annuity Mortgage (RAM)

A **reverse-annuity mortgage (RAM)** is one in which payments are made by the lender to the borrower. The payments, which may be made as regular monthly payments, in one lump sum, or as a line of credit to be drawn against, are based on the equity the homeowner has invested in the property given as security for the loan. This loan allows senior citizens on fixed incomes to realize, or use, the equity they have built up in their homes without having to sell. The borrower is charged a fixed rate of interest, and the loan is eventually repaid from the sale of the property or from the borrower's estate on his or her death.

■ LOAN PROGRAMS

Mortgage loans are generally classified based on their **loan-to-value ratios,** or LTVs. The *LTV* is the ratio of debt to value of the property. Value is the sale price or the appraisal value, whichever is less. The *lower* the ratio of debt to value, the *higher* the down payment by the borrower. For the lender, the higher down payment means a more secure loan, which minimizes the lender's risk.

Conventional Loans

Conventional loans are viewed as the most secure loans because their loan-to-value ratios are often lowest. Traditionally, the ratio is 80 percent of the value of the property or less because the borrower makes a down payment of at least 20 percent (although conventional loans with LTVs up to nearly 100 percent of the value of the property may be available). The security for the loan is provided solely by the mortgage; the payment of the debt rests on the ability of the borrower to pay. In making such a loan, the lender relies primarily on its appraisal of the security (the real estate). Information from credit reports that indicate the reliability of the prospective borrower is also important. Usually with a 20 percent down payment and a conventional loan, no additional insurance or guarantee on the loan is necessary to protect the lender's interest. A conventional loan is not government-insured or guaranteed, in contrast to FHA-insured and VA-guaranteed loans.

MATH CONCEPTS

THE MORTGAGE AMORTIZATION TRIANGLE

If you know what the monthly payment and interest rate are, you can easily track how much of each month's payment is being applied toward principal and how much is applied toward interest.

Always begin at the shaded box and follow the direction of the arrows to perform the calculations described in each box for each month's calculation. Your result will show how much of a given month's mortgage payment goes to pay principal, and what portion pays interest on the loan to the lender. For instance, if you wanted to see how much the loan principal would be reduced after three months, you would "go around the triangle" three times.

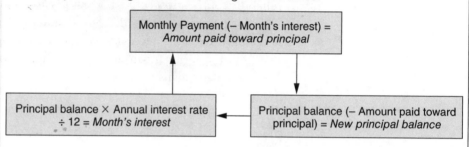

For example, assume a 30-year mortgage loan for $150,000 at a 7.75% annual interest rate and a monthly payment of $1,074 ($150,000 × 7.16 = $1,074). You can see how the triangle can help you determine the amount of principal and interest in each payment for the first two months of the loan (shown in each box as "1" and "2").

The principal balance on the loan at the end of the second month (the beginning of the third month) is $149,788.84.

What is the principal balance on this loan at the end of the third month?

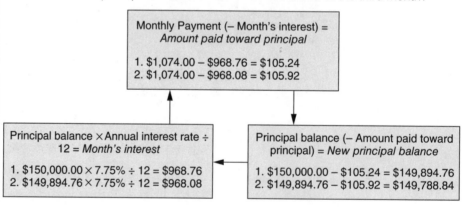

Solution

Step one:	$149,788.84 × 7.75% ÷ 12	= $967.38
Step two:	$1,074.00 − 967.38	= $106.62
Step three:	$149,788.84 − $106.62	= $149,682.22

Principal balance at the end of the third month is $149,682.22.

Lenders can set criteria by which a borrower and the collateral are evaluated to qualify for a loan. However, in recent years the secondary mortgage market has had a significant impact on the borrower qualifications, standards for the collateral, and documentation procedures followed by lenders. Loans must meet strict criteria to be sold to Fannie Mae and Freddie Mac. Lenders still can be flexible in their lending decisions, but they may not be able to sell unusual loans in the secondary market.

To qualify for a conventional loan under Fannie Mae guidelines, for instance, the borrower's monthly housing expenses, including PITI, must not exceed 28 percent of total monthly gross income. Also, the borrower's total monthly obligations, including housing costs plus other regular monthly payments, must not exceed 36 percent of his or her total monthly gross income (33 percent in the case of 95 percent LTV loans). Loans that meet these criteria are called *conforming loans*, and are eligible to be sold in the secondary market.

IN PRACTICE   On January 1, 2006, the Fannie Mae and Freddie Mac conforming loan limit rose to $417,000 from $365,650, which was the largest increase in 25 years. Fannie Mae and Freddie Mac conforming loans typically allow homebuyers to cut a quarter of a percent off their mortgage rate. On a $417,000 loan, the quarter percentage reduction could save a homeowner $24,000 over the life of the loan.

Loans that exceed the limits are referred to as *nonconforming loans* and are not marketable, but they must be held in the lender's investment portfolio.

Conforming loans with larger ratios may be available in certain situations. Both Fannie Mae and Freddie Mac currently have a variety of conforming affordable loan products with qualifying ratios of 33 percent for housing expense and up to 38 percent for total debt. These loans require only a 3 percent down payment but are subject to certain income limitations and may require the borrowers to attend home ownership classes.

■ **FOR EXAMPLE**   Following is the qualifying math for a $160,000 loan at 7.5 percent interest for 30 years with payments of $1,200 per month in principal and interest:

Combined Monthly Gross Income	$8,000
Monthly Housing Expenses:	
Principal and Interest	1,200
Property Taxes	400
Hazard Insurance	50
PMI Insurance	90
Homeowner Association Dues	+ 30
Total Housing Expense	$1,770

$1,770 ÷ 8,000 = 22%

Debt Expense:	
Installment Payments	$200
Revolving Charges	80
Auto Loan	250
Child Care	300
Other	+ 200
Total Debt Expense	$1,030
Plus Housing	+ $1,770
Grand Total	$2,800

$$\$2,800 \div 8,000 = 35\%$$

These borrowers will qualify for this loan under conventional loan guidelines of 28 percent and 36 percent.

> *Low* LTV = *High* down payment
>
> *High* down payment = *Low* lender risk

Private Mortgage Insurance

One way a borrower can obtain a mortgage loan with a lower down payment is by obtaining **private mortgage insurance (PMI).** In a PMI program, the buyer purchases an insurance policy that provides the lender with funds in the event that the lendee defaults on the loan. This allows the lender to assume more risk so that the loan-to-value ratio is higher than for other conventional loans. The borrower purchases insurance from a private mortgage insurance company as additional security to insure the lender against borrower default. Currently, LTVs of up to 97 percent of the appraised value of the property are possible with mortgage insurance, although these percentages may change.

PMI protects the top portion of a loan, usually 25 percent to 30 percent, against borrower default. The borrower pays a monthly premium or fee while the insurance is in force. Other methods of payment are available, however: The premium may be financed. When a borrower has limited funds available for an initial investment, these alternative methods of reducing closing costs are very important. Because only a portion of the loan is insured, once the loan is repaid to a certain level, the lender may agree to allow the borrower to terminate the PMI coverage. Practices for termination vary from lender to lender.

IN PRACTICE Effective on new loans originating after July 1999, a federal law requires that PMI automatically terminates if a borrower has accumulated at least 22 percent equity in the home *and* is current on mortgage payments.

The 22 percent of equity is based on the purchase price of the home and no credit is given for appreciation of the property. However, there may be some easing of this requirement.

Under the law, a borrower with a good payment history may request that PMI be canceled when he or she has built up equity equal to 22 percent of the purchase price. Lenders are required by the law to inform borrowers of their right to cancel PMI. Before this law was enacted, lenders could (and often did) continue to require monthly PMI payments long after borrowers had built up substantial equity in their homes and the lender no longer risked a loss from the borrower's default. Fannie Mae and Freddie Mac have extended this option to all loans that are in good standing and that have no additional financing added to the original loan.

MATH CONCEPTS

BALLOON PAYMENT LOAN

Consider a loan with the following terms: $130,000 at 6 percent interest, with interest only payable monthly and the loan fully repayable in 15 years. The following is how to calculate the amount of the final balloon payment:

$130,000 × 0.06 = $7,800 annual interest
$7,800 annual interest ÷ 12 months = $650 monthly interest payment
$130,000 principal payment + $650 final month's interest
= $130,650 final balloon payment

FHA-Insured Loans

The Federal Housing Administration (FHA), which operates under HUD, neither builds homes nor lends money itself. The common term **"FHA loan"** refers to a loan that is *insured* by the agency. These loans must be made by FHA-approved lending institutions. The FHA insurance provides security to the lender in addition to the real estate. As with private mortgage insurance, the FHA insures lenders against loss from borrower default.

The most popular FHA program is Title II, Section 203(b), fixed-interest rate loans for 10 years to 30 years on one-family to four-family residences. Rates are competitive with other types of loans, even though they are high-LTV loans. Certain technical requirements must be met before the FHA will insure the loans. These requirements include the following:

- The borrower is charged a percentage of the loan as a premium for the FHA insurance. The *up-front premium* is paid at closing by the borrower or some other party. It also may be financed along with the total loan amount. The up-front premium is charged on all loans except those for the purchase of a condominium. All FHA loans will have the monthly premium charged. Insurance premiums vary for new loans, refinancing, and condominiums.
- FHA regulations set standards for type and construction of buildings, quality of neighborhood, and credit requirements for borrowers.
- The mortgaged real estate must be appraised by an *approved FHA appraiser*. The loan amount generally cannot exceed either of the following:
  1. 98.75 percent for loans over $50,000 with 1.25 percent down (for loans less than $50,000, the buyer must contribute 3 percent of the sales price to the down payment and closing costs).
  2. 97.75 percent of the sales price or appraised value for loans over $50,000 with 2.25 percent down.

If the purchase price exceeds the FHA-appraised value, the buyer may pay the difference in cash as part of the down payment. In addition, the FHA has set maximum loan amounts for various regions of the country. In all cases, the purchaser must contribute 3 percent of the sales price to the transaction, either in down payment or closing costs.

Other types of FHA loans are available, including one-year adjustable-rate mortgages, home improvement and rehabilitation loans, and loans for the purchase of condominiums. Specific standards for condominium complexes and the ratio of owner-occupants to renters must be met for a loan on a condominium unit to be financed through the FHA insurance programs.

Although lenders can charge interest until the next payment due date on an FHA payoff, lenders may not deny the assumption of the mortgage by a qualified buyer even if the interest rates have skyrocketed.

MATH CONCEPTS

DETERMINING LTV

If a property has an appraised value of $200,000, secured by an $180,000 loan, the LTV is 90 percent:

$$\$180,000 \div \$200,000 = 90\%$$

IN PRACTICE The FHA sets lending limits for single-unit and multiple-unit properties. The limits vary significantly, depending on the average cost of housing in different regions of the country. In addition, the FHA changes its regulations for various programs from time to time. Contact your local FHA office or mortgage lender for loan amounts in your area and for specific loan requirements, or visit *www.hud. gov/offices/hsg/index.cfm.*

Prepayment privileges A borrower may repay an FHA-insured loan on a one-family to four-family residence without penalty. For loans made *before* August 2, 1985, the borrower must give the lender written notice of intention to exercise the prepayment privilege at least 30 days before prepayment. If the borrower fails to provide the required notice, the lender has the option of charging up to 30 days' interest. For loans initiated *after* August 2, 1985, no written notice of prepayment is required.

Assumption rules The assumption rules for FHA-insured loans vary, depending on the dates the loans were originated, as follows:

- FHA loans originating before December 1986 generally have no restrictions on their assumptions.
- For an FHA loan originating between December 1, 1986, and December 15, 1989, a creditworthiness review of the prospective assumer is required. If the original loan was for the purchase of a principal residence, this review is required during the first 12 months of the loan's existence. If the original loan was for the purchase of an investment property, the review is required during the first 24 months of the loan.
- For FHA loans originating on December 15, 1989, and later, no assumptions are permitted without complete buyer qualification.

Discount points The lender of an FHA-insured loan may charge discount points in addition to a loan origination fee. The payment of points is a matter of negotiation between the seller and the buyer. However, if the seller pays more than 6 percent of the costs normally paid by the buyer (such as discount points, the loan origination fee, the mortgage insurance premium, buydown fees, prepaid items, and impound or escrow amounts), the lender will treat the payments as a reduction in sales price and recalculate the mortgage amount accordingly.

VA-Guaranteed Loans

The Department of Veterans Affairs (usually referred to simply as VA) is authorized to guarantee loans to purchase or construct homes for eligible veterans and their spouses (including unremarried spouses of veterans whose deaths were service-related). The VA also guarantees loans to purchase mobile homes and plots on which to place them. A veteran who meets any of the following time-in-service criteria is eligible for a VA loan:

- 90 days of active service for veterans of World War II, the Korean War, the Vietnam conflict, and the Persian Gulf War
- A minimum of 181 days of active service during interconflict periods between July 26, 1947, and September 6, 1980
- Two full years of service during any peacetime period since 1980 for enlisted, and since 1981 for officers
- Six or more years of continuous duty as a reservist in the Army, Navy, Air Force, Marine Corps, or Coast Guard, or as a member of the Army or Air National Guard

The VA assists veterans in financing the purchase of homes with little or no down payments at market interest rates. The VA issues rules and regulations that set forth the qualifications, limitations, and conditions under which a loan may be guaranteed.

Like the term *FHA loan,* **VA loan** is something of a misnomer. The VA does not normally lend money; it guarantees loans made by lending institutions approved by the agency. The term *VA loan* refers to a loan that is not made by the agency but is guaranteed by it.

There is no VA dollar limit on the amount of the loan a veteran can obtain; this limit is determined by the lender and qualification of the buyer. The VA limits the amount of the loan it will guarantee.

IN PRACTICE   The VA loan guarantee is tied to the current conforming loan limit for Fannie Mae and Freddie Mac. Typically, lenders will loan four times the guarantee (for example, a conforming loan of $417,000 ÷ 4 = $104,250 VA guarantee).

To determine what portion of a mortgage loan the VA will guarantee, the veteran must apply for a *certificate of eligibility.* This certificate does not mean that the veteran automatically receives a mortgage. It merely sets forth the maximum guarantee to which the veteran is entitled. For individuals with full eligibility, no down payment is required for a loan up to the maximum guarantee limit.

The VA also issues a *certificate of reasonable value* (CRV) for the property being purchased. The CRV states the property's current market value based on a VA-approved appraisal. The CRV places a ceiling on the amount of a VA loan allowed for the property. If the purchase price is greater than the amount cited in the CRV, the veteran may pay the difference in cash. The CRV is based on an appraisal. New VA regulations allow only one active VA loan at a time, and a veteran may own only two properties acquired using VA loan benefits. However, a veteran may use his or her VA benefits as many times as he or she chooses, as long as the previous benefit use has been paid.

The VA borrower pays a loan origination fee to the lender, as well as a funding fee (2 percent to 3 percent, depending on the down payment amount) to the Department of Veterans Affairs. The funding fee depends on whether it is first time use (2 percent) or a subsequent use (3 percent). Reservists and National Guard veterans pay higher funding fees. Reasonable discount points may be charged on a VA-guaranteed loan, and either the veteran or the seller may pay them.

Prepayment privileges   As with an FHA loan, the borrower under a VA loan can prepay the debt at any time without penalty.

Assumption rules   VA loans made before March 1, 1988, are freely assumable, although an assumption processing fee will be charged. The fee is usually $500. For loans made on or after March 1, 1988, the VA must approve the buyer and assumption agreement. The original veteran borrower remains personally liable for the repayment of the loan unless the VA approves a *release of liability*. The release of liability will be issued by the VA only if

■   the buyer assumes all of the veteran's liabilities on the loan, and
■   the VA or the lender approves both the buyer and the assumption agreement.

A release also would be possible if another veteran used his or her own entitlement in assuming the loan.

IN PRACTICE   A release of liability issued by the VA does not release the veteran's liability to the lender. This must be obtained separately from the lender. Real estate licensees should contact their local mortgage lenders for specific requirements for obtaining or assuming VA-insured loans. The programs change from time to time.

Agricultural Loan Programs

The **Farm Service Agency (FSA)**, formerly the Farmers Home Administration, is a federal agency of the Department of Agriculture. The FSA offers programs to help families purchase or operate family farms. Through the Rural Housing and Community Development Service (RHCDS), it also provides loans to help families purchase or improve single-family homes in rural areas (generally areas with populations of fewer than 10,000 people). Loans are made to low-income and moderate-income families, and the interest rate charged can be as low as

1 percent, depending on the borrower's income. The FSA provides assistance to rural and agricultural businesses and industry through the Rural Business and Cooperative Development Service (RBCDS).

FSA loan programs fall into two categories:

1. Guaranteed loans, made and serviced by private lenders and guaranteed for a specific percentage by the FSA
2. Loans made directly by the FSA

The **Farm Credit System (Farm Credit)** provides loans to more than 500,000 borrowers, including farmers, ranchers, rural homeowners, agricultural cooperatives, rural utility systems, and agribusinesses. Unlike commercial banks, Farm Credit System banks and associations do not take deposits. Instead, loanable funds are raised through the system-wide sale of bonds and notes in the nation's capital markets.

Farmer Mac (formerly the Federal Agricultural Mortgage Corporation, or FAMC), is another government-sponsored enterprise (GSE) that operates similarly to Fannie Mae and Freddie Mac but in a context of agricultural loans. It was created to improve the availability of long-term credit at stable interest rates to America's farmers, and ranchers, and rural homeowners, businesses, and communities. Farmer Mac pools or bundles agricultural loans from lenders for sale as mortgage-backed securities.

IN PRACTICE   There have been many changes in all of the agricultural lending programs. Since 1994, the Farmer's Home Administration, the Rural Development Administration, the Rural Electrification Administration, and the Agricultural Cooperative Service have been combined into the USDA Rural Development Agency.

■ OTHER FINANCING TECHNIQUES

Because borrowers often have different needs, a variety of other financing techniques have been created. Other techniques apply to various types of collateral. The following pages consider some of the loans that do not fit into the categories previously discussed.

Purchase-Money Mortgages (PMMs)

A **purchase-money mortgage (PMM)** is a note and mortgage that is created at the time of purchase. The PMM's purpose is to make the sale possible. The term is used in two ways. First, it may refer to any security instrument that originates at the time of sale. Second, and more often, it refers to the instrument given by the purchaser to a seller who takes back a note for part or all of the purchase price. The mortgage may be a first or a junior lien, depending on whether prior mortgage liens exist.

■ **FOR EXAMPLE**   Ben wants to buy Brownacre for $200,000. Ben has a $40,000 down payment and agrees to assume an existing mortgage of $80,000. Because Ben might not qualify for a new mortgage under the circumstances, the owner agrees to take back a purchase-money second mortgage in the amount of $80,000. At the closing, Ben will execute a mortgage and note in favor of the owner, who will convey title to Ben.

Package Loans

A **package loan** includes not only the real estate but also all personal property and appliances installed on the premises. In recent years, this kind of loan has been used extensively to finance furnished condominium units. Package loans usually include furniture, drapes, carpets, and the kitchen range, refrigerator, dishwasher, garbage disposal, washer, dryer, food freezer, and other appliances as part of the sales price of the home.

Blanket Loans

A **blanket loan** covers more than one parcel or lot. It is usually used to finance subdivision developments. However, it can finance the purchase of improved properties or consolidate loans as well. A blanket loan usually includes a provision known as a *partial release clause*. This clause permits the borrower to obtain the release of any one lot or parcel from the blanket lien by repaying a certain amount of the loan. The lender issues a partial release for each parcel released from the mortgage lien. The release form includes a provision that the lien will continue to cover all other unreleased lots.

Wraparound Loans

A **wraparound loan** enables a borrower with an existing mortgage or deed of trust loan to obtain additional financing from a second lender without paying off the first loan. The second lender gives the borrower a new, increased loan at a higher interest rate and assumes payment of the existing loan. The total amount of the new loan includes the existing loan as well as the additional funds needed by the borrower. The borrower makes payments to the new lender on the larger loan. The new lender makes payments on the original loan out of the borrower's payments.

A wraparound mortgage can be used to refinance real property or to finance the purchase of real property when an existing mortgage cannot be prepaid. The buyer executes a wraparound mortgage to the seller or lender, who collects payments on the new loan and continues to make payments on the old loan. It also can finance the sale of real estate when the buyer wishes to invest a minimum amount of initial cash. A wraparound loan is possible only if the original loan permits it. For instance, an acceleration and alienation or a due-on-sale clause in the original loan documents may prevent a sale under a wraparound loan.

IN PRACTICE   To protect themselves against a seller's default on a previous loan, buyers should require that protective clauses be included in any wraparound document to grant buyers the right to make payments directly to the original lender.

Open-End Loans

An **open-end loan** secures a *note* executed by the borrower to the lender. It also secures any future *advances* of funds made by the lender to the borrower. The interest rate on the initial amount borrowed is fixed, but interest on future advances may be charged at the market rate in effect. An open-end loan is often a less costly alternative to a home improvement loan. It allows the borrower to *open* the mortgage or deed of trust to increase the debt to its original amount, or the amount stated in the note, after the debt has been reduced by payments over a period of time. The mortgage usually states the maximum amount that can be secured, the terms and conditions under which the loan can be opened, and the provisions for repayment.

Construction Loans

A **construction loan** is made to finance the construction of improvements on real estate such as homes, apartments, and office buildings. The lender commits to the full amount of the loan but disburses the funds in payments during construction. These payments are also known as *draws*. Draws are made to the general contractor or the owner for that part of the construction work that has been completed since the previous payment. Before each payment, the lender inspects the work. The general contractor must provide the lender with adequate waivers that release all mechanics' lien rights for the work covered by the payment.

A construction loan generally bears a higher-than-market interest rate because of the risks assumed by the lender. These risks include the inadequate releasing of mechanics' liens, possible delays in completing the construction, or the financial failure of the contractor or subcontractors. Construction loans are generally *short-term* or *interim financing*. The borrower pays interest only on the monies that have actually been disbursed. The borrower is expected to arrange for a permanent loan, also known as an *end loan* or *take-out loan*, that will repay or *take out* the construction financing lender when the work is completed. Some lenders now offer construction-to-permanent loans that become fixed mortgages upon completion. *Participation financing* is when a lender demands an equity position in the project as a requirement for the loan.

Sale-and-Leaseback

Sale-and-leaseback arrangements are used to finance large commercial or industrial properties. The land and building, usually used by the seller for business purposes, are sold to an investor. The real estate then is leased back by the investor to the seller, who continues to conduct business on the property as a tenant. The buyer becomes the lessor, and the original owner becomes the lessee. This enables a business to free money tied up in real estate to be used as working capital.

Sale-and-leaseback arrangements involve complicated legal procedures, and their success is usually related to the effects the transaction has on the firm's tax situation. Legal and tax experts should be involved in this type of transaction.

Buydowns

A **buydown** is a way to temporarily (or permanently) lower the interest rate on a mortgage or deed of trust loan. Perhaps a homebuilder wishes to stimulate sales by offering a lower-than-market rate. Or a first-time residential buyer may have trouble qualifying for a loan at the prevailing rates; relatives or the sellers might want to help the buyer qualify. In any case, a lump sum is paid in cash to the lender at the closing. The payment offsets (and so reduces) the interest rate and monthly payments during the mortgage's first few years. Typical buydown arrangements reduce the interest rate by 1 percent to 2 percent over the first one to two years of the loan term. After that, the rate rises. The assumption is that the borrower's income will also increase and that the borrower will be more able to absorb the increased monthly payments. In a permanent buydown, a larger upfront payment reduces the effective interest rate for the life of the loan.

Home Equity Loans

Using the equity buildup in a home to finance purchases is an alternative to refinancing. **Home equity loans** are a source of funds for homeowners to use for a variety of financial needs, including the following:

- To finance the purchase of expensive items
- To consolidate existing installment loans or credit card debt
- To pay medical, education, home improvement, or other expenses

The original mortgage loan remains in place; the home equity loan is junior to the original lien. If the homeowner completely refinances, the original mortgage loan and the home equity loan are paid off and replaced by a new loan. (This strategy is an alternative way to borrow the equity and is not really a home equity loan.)

A home equity loan can be taken out as a fixed loan amount or as an equity line of credit. With the *home equity line of credit*, referred to as a *HELOC*, the lender extends a line of credit that the borrower can use whenever he or she wants. The borrower receives the money by a check sent to him or her, by deposits made in a checking or savings account, or by a book of drafts the borrower can use up to his or her credit limit.

IN PRACTICE   The homeowner must consider a number of factors before deciding on a home equity loan, including

- the costs involved in obtaining a new mortgage loan or a home equity loan,
- current interest rates,
- total monthly payments, and
- income tax consequences.

Once the loan process has reached the point at which the borrowers' financial capability has been approved, the collateral's appraisal value is acceptable, and the legal title is clear, the loan is approved. At closing, a statement is prepared allocating credits and charges to the appropriate parties. Included in the prorations are loan interest, property taxes, insurance premiums, and rents and special assessments if applicable. Costs include points, placement fees, impound funds (escrows), mortgage insurance premium, credit report, appraisal fee, and escrow charges. After the final documents are signed and recorded, the monies are paid completing the process. (See Chapter 23.)

■ FINANCING LEGISLATION

The federal government regulates the lending practices of mortgage lenders through the Truth-in-Lending Act, the Equal Credit Opportunity Act, the Community Reinvestment Act of 1977, and the Real Estate Settlement Procedures Act.

Purchase-Money Truth-in-Lending Act and Regulation Z

Regulation Z, which was promulgated pursuant to the **Truth-in-Lending Act** by the Federal Trade Commission (FTC), requires that credit institutions inform borrowers of the true cost of obtaining credit. With proper disclosures, borrowers can compare the costs of various lenders to avoid the uninformed use of credit. Regulation Z applies when credit for $25,000 or less is extended to individuals for personal, familial, or household uses. Regardless of the amount, however, *Regulation Z generally applies when a credit transaction is secured by a residence*. The regulation does *not* apply to business or commercial loans or to agricultural loans of any amount. (So if an investor purchased a residential property for commercial purposes, Regulation Z would not apply.)

Under the Truth-in-Lending Act, a consumer must be fully informed of all finance charges and the true interest rate before a transaction is completed. The finance charge disclosure must include any loan fees, finder's fees, service charges and points, as well as interest. In the case of a mortgage loan made to finance the purchase of a dwelling, the lender must compute and disclose the *annual percentage rate (APR)*. However, the lender does not have to indicate the total interest payable during the term of the loan. Also, the lender does not have to include actual costs such as title fees, legal fees, appraisal fees, credit reports, survey fees, and closing expenses as part of the finance charge. (See Chapter 23.)

Creditor   A *creditor*, for purposes of Regulation Z, is any person who extends consumer credit more than 25 times each year or more than five times each year if the transactions involve dwellings as security. The credit must be subject to a finance charge or payable in more than four installments by written agreement.

Three-day right of rescission   In the case of most consumer credit transactions covered by Regulation Z, the borrower has three days in which to rescind the transaction by merely notifying the lender. *This right of rescission does not apply to owner-occupied residential purchase-money or first mortgage or deed of trust loans.* It does, however, apply to refinancing a home mortgage or to a home equity loan. In an emergency, the right to rescind may be waived in writing to prevent a delay in funding.

Advertising   Regulation Z provides strict regulation of real estate advertisements (in all media, including newspapers, flyers, signs, billboards, Web sites, radio or television ads, and direct mailings) that refer to mortgage financing terms. General phrases like "liberal terms available" may be used, but if details are given, they must comply with the act. The APR—which is calculated based on all charges rather than the interest rate alone—must be stated.

Advertisements for buydowns or reduced-interest rate mortgages must show both the limited term to which the interest rate applies and the annual percentage rate. If a variable-rate mortgage is advertised, the advertisement must include

- the number and timing of payments,
- the amount of the largest and smallest payments, and
- a statement of the fact that the actual payments will vary between these two extremes.

Specific credit terms, such as down payment, monthly payment, dollar amount of the finance charge, or term of the loan, are referred to as **trigger terms**, and may not be advertised unless the advertisement includes the following information:

- Cash price
- Required down payment
- Number, amounts, and due dates of all payments
- Annual percentage rate
- Total of all payments to be made over the term of the mortgage (unless the advertised credit refers to a first mortgage or deed of trust to finance the acquisition of a dwelling)

Penalties   Regulation Z provides penalties for noncompliance. The penalty for violation of an administrative order enforcing Regulation Z is $10,000 for each day the violation continues. A fine of up to $10,000 may be imposed for engaging in an unfair or a deceptive practice. In addition, a creditor may be liable to a consumer for twice the amount of the finance charge, for a minimum of $100 and a maximum of $1,000, plus court costs, attorney's fees, and any actual damages. Willful violation is a misdemeanor punishable by a fine of up to $5,000, one year's imprisonment, or both.

Equal Credit Opportunity Act

The federal **Equal Credit Opportunity Act (ECOA)** prohibits lenders and others who grant or arrange credit to consumers from discriminating against credit applicants on the basis of

- race,
- color,
- religion,
- national origin,
- sex,
- marital status,
- age (provided the applicant is of legal age), or
- dependence on public assistance.

In addition, lenders and other creditors must inform all rejected credit applicants of the principal reasons for the denial or termination of credit. The notice must be provided in writing, within 30 days. The federal ECOA also provides that a borrower is entitled to a copy of the appraisal report if the borrower paid for the appraisal.

Community Reinvestment Act of 1977 (CRA)

Community reinvestment refers to the responsibility of financial institutions to help meet their communities' needs for low-income and moderate-income housing. In 1977, Congress passed the **Community Reinvestment Act of 1977 (CRA)**. Under the CRA, financial institutions are expected to meet the deposit and credit needs of their communities; participate and invest in local community development and rehabilitation projects; and participate in loan programs for housing, small businesses, and small farms.

The law requires any federally supervised financial institution to prepare a statement containing

- a definition of the geographic boundaries of its community;
- an identification of the types of community reinvestment credit offered, such as residential housing loans, housing rehabilitation loans, small-business loans, commercial loans, and consumer loans; and
- comments from the public about the institution's performance in meeting its community's needs.

Financial institutions are periodically reviewed by one of four federal financial supervisory agencies: the Comptroller of the Currency, the Federal Reserve's Board of Governors, the Federal Deposit Insurance Corporation, or the Office of Thrift Supervision. The institutions must post a public notice that their community reinvestment activities are subject to federal review, and they must make the results of these reviews public.

Real Estate Settlement Procedures Act

The federal Real Estate Settlement Procedures Act (RESPA) applies to any residential real estate transaction involving a new first mortgage loan. RESPA is designed to ensure that buyer and seller are both fully informed of all settlement costs. This important federal law is discussed in detail in Chapter 23.

■ COMPUTERIZED LOAN ORIGINATION AND AUTOMATED UNDERWRITING

A **computerized loan origination (CLO)** system is an electronic network for handling loan applications through remote computer terminals linked to several lenders' computers. With a CLO system, a real estate broker or salesperson can call up a menu of mortgage lenders, interest rates, and loan terms, and then help a buyer select a lender and apply for a loan right from the brokerage office.

The licensee may assist the applicant in answering the on-screen questions and in understanding the services offered. The broker in whose office the terminal is located may earn fees of up to one half point of the loan amount. The *borrower*, not the mortgage broker or lender, *must pay the fee*. The fee amount may be financed, however. While multiple lenders may be represented on an office's CLO computer, consumers must be informed that other lenders are available. An applicant's ability to comparison shop for a loan may be enhanced by a CLO system; the range of options may not be limited. One-stop shopping real estate services and federal regulation pertaining to CLOs are discussed in Chapter 23.

On the lenders' side, new automated underwriting procedures can shorten loan approvals from weeks to minutes. Automated underwriting also tends to lower the cost of loan application and approval by reducing lenders' time spent on the approval process by as much as 60 percent. Freddie Mac uses a system called *Loan Prospector*. Fannie Mae has a system called *Desktop Underwriter* that reduces approval time to minutes, based on the borrower's credit report, a paycheck stub, and a drive-by appraisal of the property. Complex or difficult mortgages can be processed in less than 72 hours. Through automated underwriting, one of a borrower's biggest headaches in buying a home—waiting for loan approval—is eliminated. In addition, a prospective buyer can strengthen his or her purchase offer by including proof of loan approval.

Scoring and automated underwriting Lenders have been using credit scoring systems to predict prospective borrowers' likelihood of default for many years. When used as a part of traditional *manual* evaluation of applicants, credit scoring provides a useful objective standard against which to balance the loan officer's more subjective professional judgment. When used in automated underwriting systems, however, the application of credit scores has become somewhat controversial. Critics of scoring are concerned that they may not be accurate or fair, and, in the absence of human discretion, they could result in making it more difficult for low-income and minority borrowers to obtain mortgages.

Freddie Mac has the following to say about automated underwriting:

> *Whether using traditional or automated methods, underwriters must consider all three areas of underwriting—collateral, credit reputation, and capacity. When*

reviewing collateral, underwriters look at house value, down payment, and property type. Income, debt, cash reserves, and product type are considered when underwriters are looking at capacity. Credit scores are simply one consideration when underwriters are reviewing credit reputation. Even lenders who use an automated underwriting system, such as Loan Prospector, still rely on human judgment when the scoring system indicates that the loan application is a higher risk.

■ KEY POINT REVIEW

The **Federal Reserve System (the Fed)** consists of 12 federal reserve district banks.

The **primary mortgage market** consists of lenders that originate mortgage loans, dealing directly with borrowers and realizing income based on

- **finance charges** collected at loan closing, including
  - **loan origination fees** and
  - **discount points**;
- **recurring income**—interest collected during term of loan, if kept;
- funds generated by **sale of loans** on **secondary mortgage market**; and
- fees for **loan servicing** for other mortgage lenders or investors who have purchased the loans.

The **primary mortgage market lenders** include the following:

- **Fiduciary lenders**—thrifts, savings associations, commercial banks—subject to the
  - **Federal Deposit Insurance Corporation (FDIC)**
  - Office of Thrift Supervision (OTS)
- **Insurance companies**—generally investing in long-term commercial, industrial, and large multifamily properties
- Credit unions
- Pension funds
- **Endowment funds** of universities, colleges, and other institutions
- **Investment group financing**—joint ventures, syndicates, limited partnerships, real estate investment trusts (REITs)
- **Mortgage banking companies**
- **Mortgage brokers**

The **secondary mortgage** market, where loans are bought and sold after being funded, does the following:

- Provides **additional income** to lender and **frees up funds** to make more loans, with lender often retaining servicing functions for a fee.
- Purchases mortgage loans through agencies, assembles them into packages called **pools**, and sells them as **shares (securitized)** to investors or other agencies.

Fannie Mae (formerly the **Federal National Mortgage Association**) is a government-sponsored but privately owned corporation that issues its own common stock and

- creates **mortgage-backed securities** using pool of mortgages as collateral, and
- deals in conventional, FHA, and VA loans.

Ginnie Mae (formerly the **Government National Mortgage Association**) is entirely a government agency, a division of the **Department of Housing and Urban Development (HUD)**, organized as a corporation but without corporate stock that

- administers **special-assistance programs,**
- guarantees **mortgage-backed securities (MBSs)** using FHA and VA loans as collateral, and
- guarantees a **pass-through certificate.**

Freddie Mac (formerly the **Federal Home Loan Mortgage Corporation**) is a government-sponsored enterprise that

- has authority to purchase mortgages, pool them, and use them as security for bonds sold on the open market, but does not guarantee payment of mortgages.

Following are **types of financing**:

- **Straight loan (term loan)**—requiring periodic payments of interest only for the life of the loan, with payment of principal in full at the end of the loan term
- **Interest-only mortgage**—secured by real estate and generally short-term, with periodic payments of interest only and payment of principal in full at end of loan term
- **Balloon payment (partially amortized) loan**—situation where periodic payments of interest and principal are not great enough to pay down entire amount borrowed by end of loan term, resulting in larger final payment
- **Amortized (direct reduction, fully amortized, level payment) loan**—where equal periodic payments of interest and principal result in complete payment of amount borrowed over the term of the loan
- **Adjustable-rate mortgage (ARM)**—originated at a rate of interest that may change over the life of the loan based on a specified index, usually tied to U.S. Treasury securities

Growing equity (rapid-payoff) mortgage (GEM)—fixed interest rate but payments of principal increased according to an index or schedule so that loan is paid off more quickly.

- **Reverse-annuity mortgage (RAM)**—payments made by lender to borrower, at regular intervals (such as monthly), in a lump sum, or as a line of credit to be drawn against, allowing borrower to remain in home while receiving income.

Conventional loans are the most secure loans. Note the following:

- **The loan-to-value ratio (LTV)** is often lowest for these loans—traditionally 80 percent—meaning the down payment is 20 percent; but the LTV may be as high as 100 percent.
- Conventional loans are **not** government-insured or guaranteed.
- Conventional loans meet all the requirements of the secondary market, set by Fannie Mae and Freddie Mac, for **conforming loans**, including the following:
  — The borrower's **monthly housing expenses**, including PITI, should be no more than 28 percent of total monthly gross income (33 percent for certain affordable loan products designed for low-income borrowers).
  — The borrower's **total monthly obligations**, including housing costs and other regular monthly payments, must not exceed 36 percent of the total monthly gross income (33 percent in the case of 95 percent LTV loans and up to 38 percent for affordable loans).
- **Nonconforming loans** must be retained in the lender's investment portfolio.
- **Private mortgage insurance (PMI)** may be required for LTVs higher than 80 percent (that is, down payments of less than 20 percent) Note the following PMI conditions:
  — On loans originated after July, 1999, federal law required PMI **automatically** terminate if borrower has accumulated 22 percent equity in the home (based on purchase price) *and* is current on mortgage payments.
  — **Fannie Mae** and **Freddie Mac** have extended the automatic termination option to all loans that are in good standing and that have had no additional financing added to the original loan.

FHA-insured loans are backed by the **Federal Housing Administration (FHA)**, which is part of HUD. FHA does not make loans but insures loans made by an FHA-approved lending institution.

VA-guaranteed loans are backed by the **Department of Veterans Affairs** and are available to eligible veterans and spouses.

The Farm Service Agency (FSA), formerly **Farmers Home Administration**, is part of the Department of Agriculture and has the following programs to help families purchase or operate family farms:

- Rural Housing and Community Development Service (RHCDS)
- **Farm Credit System (Farm Credit)**
- **Farmer Mac** (formerly **Federal Agricultural Mortgage Corporation**)

Other types of loans include the following:

- A **purchase money mortgage (PMM)** is a note and mortgage created at the time of purchase.
- The **package loan** includes all personal property and appliances as well as real estate.

- A **blanket loan** covers more than one parcel or lot, and a **partial release clause** allows borrower to pay off part of loan to remove liens from one parcel or lot at a time.
- **Wraparound loans** allow the borrower to obtain additional financing, retaining the first loan on the property.
- An **open-end loan** secures the current loan to the borrower and future advances made by the lender to the borrower.
- **Construction loans** finance construction of property improvements.
- **Sale-and-leaseback loans** are used to finance large commercial or industrial properties.
- A **buydown** is a payment made at closing to reduce the interest rate on the loan.
- A **home equity loan (home equity line of credit)** is junior to the original lien.

The **Truth-in-Lending Act, Regulation Z** of the **Federal Trade Commission (FTC)**, requires that, when a loan is secured by a residence, lenders inform borrowers of the true cost of obtaining credit, within the following rules:

- The borrower has **three-day right of rescission**.
- **Advertising** is strictly regulated.
- There is a **$10,000 penalty** for each day the violation continues.

The **Equal Credit Opportunity Act (ECOA)** prohibits **discrimination** in granting or arranging credit on basis of race, color, religion, national origin, sex, marital status, age (as long as applicant is not a minor), or dependence on public assistance.

The **Community Reinvestment Act of 1977 (CRA)** requires information from lending institutions on the business area and the lender's efforts to respond to community's needs.

Computerized loan origination (CLO) allows real estate brokers and salespersons to assist loan applicants in surveying lenders and providing information.

Automated underwriting (loan processing) programs include Fannie Mae's Desktop Underwriter and Freddie Mac's Loan Prospector.

A **credit score** may be used as part of a loan application evaluation process.

■ RELATED WEB SITES

Fannie Mae: *www.fanniemae.com*
Farm Credit System: *www.farmcredit.com*
Federal Reserve Board: *www.federalreserve.gov*
Freddie Mac: *www.freddiemac.com*
Ginnie Mae: *www.ginniemae.gov*
Mortgage Banker's Association of America: *www.mbaa.org*
National Association of Mortgage Bankers: *www.namb.org*
National Reverse Mortgage Lenders Association: *www.reversemortgage.org*
U.S. Department of Agriculture Rural Development Agency:
   www.rurdev.usda.gov
U.S. Department of Housing and Urban Development (HUD):   *www.hud.gov*
U.S. Department of Veterans Affairs (VA):   *www.va.gov*
U.S. Farm Service Agency: *www.fsa.usda.gov*

CHAPTER 16 QUIZ

1. The buyers purchased a residence for $195,000. They made a down payment of $25,000 and agreed to assume the seller's existing mortgage, which had a current balance of $123,000. The buyers financed the remaining $47,000 of the purchase price by executing a mortgage and note to the seller. This type of loan, by which the seller becomes the mortgagee, is called a
   a. wraparound mortgage.
   b. package mortgage.
   c. balloon note.
   d. purchase-money mortgage.

2. A buyer purchased a new residence for $175,000. The buyer made a down payment of $15,000 and obtained a $160,000 mortgage loan. The builder of the house paid the lender 3 percent of the loan balance for the first year and 2 percent for the second year. This represented a total savings for the buyer of $8,000. What type of mortgage arrangement is this?
   a. Wraparound
   b. Package
   c. Blanket
   d. Buydown

3. Which of the following is NOT a participant in the secondary market?
   a. Fannie Mae
   b. Ginnie Mae
   c. Credit union
   d. Freddie Mac

4. Fran purchased her home for cash 30 years ago. Today Fran receives monthly checks from a mortgage lender that supplement her retirement income. Fran MOST likely has obtained a(n)
   a. shared-appreciation mortgage.
   b. adjustable-rate mortgage.
   c. reverse-annuity mortgage.
   d. overriding deed of trust.

5. If buyers seek a mortgage on a single-family house, they would be LEAST likely to obtain the mortgage from a
   a. mutual savings bank.
   b. life insurance company.
   c. credit union.
   d. commercial bank.

6. Which of the following characteristics of a fixed-rate home loan that is amortized according to the original payment schedule is TRUE?
   a. The amount of interest to be paid is predetermined.
   b. The loan cannot be sold in the secondary market.
   c. The monthly payment amount will fluctuate each month.
   d. The interest rate change may be based on an index.

7. When the Federal Reserve Board raises its discount rate, all of the following are likely to happen EXCEPT
   a. buyer's points will increase.
   b. interest rates will fall.
   c. mortgage money will become scarce.
   d. the percentage of ARMs will increase.

8. In a loan that requires periodic payments that do not fully amortize the loan balance by the final payment, what term BEST describes the final payment?
   a. Adjustment
   b. Acceleration
   c. Balloon
   d. Variable

9. A developer received a loan that covers five parcels of real estate and provides for the release of the mortgage lien on each parcel when certain payments are made on the loan. This type of loan arrangement is called a
   a. purchase-money loan.
   b. blanket loan.
   c. package loan.
   d. wraparound loan.

10. Funds for Federal Housing Administration (FHA) loans are usually provided by

   a. the FHA.
   b. the Federal Reserve.
   c. qualified lenders.
   d. the seller.

11. The provisions of the Truth-in-Lending Act (Regulation Z) require all of the following to be disclosed to a residential buyer *EXCEPT*

   a. discount points.
   b. the real estate brokerage commission.
   c. a loan origination fee.
   d. the loan interest rate.

12. A home is purchased using a fixed-rate, fully amortized mortgage loan. Which of the following statements regarding this mortgage is *TRUE?*

   a. A balloon payment will be made at the end of the loan.
   b. Each mortgage payment amount is the same.
   c. Each mortgage payment reduces the principal by the same amount.
   d. The principal amount in each payment is greater than the interest amount.

13. Which of the following *BEST* describes participants in the secondary market?

   a. Lenders who deal exclusively in second mortgages
   b. Institutional investors who buy and sell loans
   c. The major lender of residential mortgages and deeds of trust
   d. Institutional investors who supply money for FHA and VA loans

14. Which of the following is a correct statement about interest on a fully amortized mortgage or deed of trust loan?

   a. Interest may be paid in arrears, that is, at the end of each period for which it is earned.
   b. The interest portion of each payment increases throughout the term of the loan.
   c. Only interest is paid each period.
   d. The final interest payment will be determined after the last payment is made.

15. The primary activity of Freddie Mac is to

   a. guarantee mortgages with the full faith and credit of the federal government.
   b. buy and pool blocks of conventional mortgages and sell bonds that use them as security.
   c. act in tandem with GNMA to provide special assistance in times of tight money.
   d. buy and sell VA and FHA mortgages.

16. The federal Equal Credit Opportunity Act allows lenders to discriminate against potential borrowers on the basis of

   a. race.
   b. sex.
   c. dependence on public assistance.
   d. amount of income.

17. A borrower obtains a $100,000 mortgage loan for 30 years at 6 percent interest. If the monthly payments of $575 are credited first to interest and then to principal, what will be the balance of the principal after the borrower makes the first payment?

   a. $99,425
   b. $99,925
   c. $99,500
   d. $100,000

18. Using Table 16.2 on page 297, what is the monthly interest rate factor required to amortize a loan at 6½ percent over a term of 25 years?

   a. 6.91
   b. 6.75
   c. 7.46
   d. 6.67

19. Using Table 16.2 on page 297, calculate the principal and interest payment necessary to amortize a loan of $135,000 at 7¾ percent interest over 15 years.

   a. $1,111.85
   b. $1,270.35
   c. $1,279.80
   d. $1,639.16

20. Hal borrowed $85,000, to be repaid in monthly installments of $530.20 at 7 percent annual interest. How much of Hal's first month's payment was applied to reducing the principal amount of the loan?
    a. $40.00
    b. $34.37
    c. $530.20
    d. $495.83

21. If a lender agrees to make a loan based on an 80 percent LTV, what is the amount of the loan if the property appraises for $114,500 and the sales price is $116,900?
    a. $83,200
    b. $91,300
    c. $91,600
    d. $92,900

22. For a lender, income on the loan is realized from loan origination fees, discount points, and which of the following?
    a. Recurring interest income
    b. Investment groups
    c. The discount rate
    d. Amortization

23. In which of the following types of loans is the loan amount divided into two parts, to be paid off separately by periodic interest payments followed by payment of the principal in full at the end of the term?
    a. Amortized
    b. Straight
    c. ARM
    d. GEM

24. In an adjustable-rate mortgage, the interest rate is tied to an objective economic indicator called a(n)
    a. mortgage factor.
    b. discount rate.
    c. index.
    d. reserve requirement.

25. Which law requires that all advertising that references mortgage financing terms contain certain disclosures?
    a. Equal Credit Opportunity Act
    b. Fair Housing Act
    c. Community Reinvestment Act
    d. Truth-in-Lending Act (Regulation Z)

CHAPTER 17

Leases

■ LEASING REAL ESTATE

A **lease** is a contract between an owner of real estate (the **lessor**) and a tenant (the **lessee**). A lease is a contract to transfer the lessor's rights to exclusive possession and use of the property to the tenant for a specified period of time. The lease establishes the length of time the contract is to run and the amount the lessee is to pay for use of the property. Other rights and obligations of the parties are set forth as well.

In effect, the lease agreement combines two contracts. A lease is (1) a conveyance of an interest in the real estate and (2) a contract to pay rent and assume other obligations. The lessor grants the lessee the right to occupy the real estate and use it for purposes stated in the lease. In return, the landlord receives payment for use of the premises and retains a **reversionary right** to possession after the lease term expires. The lessor's interest is called a *leased fee estate plus reversionary right*.

The statute of frauds in most states requires lease agreements for more than one year to be in writing to be enforceable. If the lease cannot be performed within one year of being entered into, the statute of frauds also requires a written document. In general, oral leases for one year or less that can be performed within a year of their making are enforceable. Written leases should be signed by both the lessor and lessee.

IN PRACTICE Even though an oral lease may be enforceable, such as a lease for one year commencing on the day of agreement, it is always better practice to put lease agreements in writing. A written lease provides concrete evidence of the terms and conditions to which the parties have agreed. Any written agreement should be signed by both the landlord and tenant.

■ LEASEHOLD ESTATES

A tenant's right to possess real estate for the term of the lease is called a **leasehold (less-than-freehold) estate**. A leasehold is generally considered personal property. When the tenant assumes many of the landowner's obligations under a lease for life or for more than 99 years, certain states give the tenant some of the benefits and privileges of ownership.

Just as there are several types of freehold (ownership) estates, there are different kinds of leasehold estates. (See Figure 17.1.)

Estate for Years

An **estate** (tenancy) **for years** is a leasehold estate that continues for a definite period of time. That period may be years, months, weeks, or even days. An estate for years (sometimes referred to as an *estate for term*) always has specific starting and ending dates. When the estate expires, the lessee is required to vacate the

FIGURE   17.1

Leasehold Estates

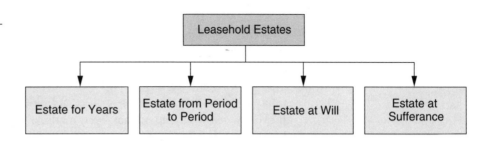

premises and surrender possession to the lessor. *No notice is required to terminate the estate for years* because the lease agreement states a specific expiration date. When the date comes, the lease expires, and the tenant's rights are extinguished.

If both parties agree, the lease for years may be terminated before the expiration date. Otherwise, neither party may terminate without showing that the lease agreement has been breached. Any extension of the tenancy requires that a new contract be negotiated.

As is characteristic of all leases, a tenancy for years gives the lessee the right to occupy and use the leased property according to the terms and covenants contained in the lease agreement. Remember that a lessee has the right to use the premises for the entire lease term. That right is unaffected by the original lessor's death or the sale of the property, unless the lease states otherwise. If the original lease provides for an option to renew, no further negotiation is required; the tenant merely exercises his or her option.

> **Estate (tenancy) for years**
> = *Any definite period*

Estate from Period to Period

An **estate from period to period,** or *periodic tenancy,* is created when the landlord and tenant enter into an agreement for an indefinite time, that is, the lease does not contain a specific expiration date. Such a tenancy is created initially to run for a definite amount of time—for instance, month to month, week to week, or year to year—but the tenancy continues indefinitely until proper notice of termination is given. Rent is payable at definite intervals. A periodic tenancy is characterized by *continuity* because it is automatically renewable under the original terms of the agreement until one of the parties gives notice to terminate. In effect, the payment and acceptance of rent extend the lease for another period. A **month-to-month tenancy,** for example, is created when a tenant takes possession with no definite termination date and pays monthly rent. Periodic tenancy is commonly used in residential leases.

■ **FOR EXAMPLE**   Landlord Larry and tenant Tim have agreed that Tim can rent an apartment by the month without specifying the number of months the lease will run. The lease simply continues until Larry or Tim gives proper notice to terminate.

Estate from period to period (periodic tenancy) = *Indefinite term; automatically renewing*

If the original agreement provides for the conversion from an estate for years to a periodic tenancy, no negotiations are necessary; the tenant simply exercises his or her option.

An estate from period to period also might be created when a tenant with an estate for years remains in possession, or holds over, after the lease term expires. If no new lease agreement has been made, a **holdover tenancy** is created. The landlord may evict the tenant or treat the holdover tenant as one who holds a periodic tenancy. The landlord's acceptance of rent usually is considered conclusive proof of acceptance of the periodic tenancy. The courts customarily rule that a tenant who holds over can do so for a term equal to the term of the original lease, provided the period is for one year or less. For example, a tenant with a lease for six months would be entitled to a new six-month tenancy. However, if the original lease were for five years, the holdover tenancy could not exceed one year. Some leases stipulate that in the absence of a renewal agreement, a tenant who holds over does so as a month-to-month tenant. In some states, a holdover tenancy is considered a tenancy at will (discussed below).

To *terminate a periodic estate, either the landlord or the tenant must give proper notice.* The form and timing of the notice are usually established by state statute. Normally, the notice must be given *one period in advance*, that is, to terminate an estate from week to week, one week's notice is required; to terminate an estate from month to month, one month's notice is required. For an estate from year to year, however, the notice requirements vary from two months to six months.

Estate at Will

An **estate (tenancy) at will** gives the tenant the right to possess property with the landlord's consent for an unspecified or uncertain term. An estate at will is a tenancy of indefinite duration; it continues until it is terminated by either party giving proper notice. No definite initial period is specified, as is the case in a periodic tenancy. An estate at will is automatically terminated by the death of either the landlord or the tenant. It may be created by express agreement or by operation of law. During the existence of a tenancy at will, the tenant has all the rights and obligations of a lessor-lessee relationship, including the duty to pay rent at regular intervals.

Estate (tenancy) at will = *Indefinite term; possession with landlord's consent*

■ **FOR EXAMPLE** Landlord Larry tells tenant Tim at the end of the lease that Larry's friend, Frances, will be moving into the apartment where Tim is currently leasing as soon as Frances gets into town. Larry tells Tim that he has the option of continuing to rent the apartment until Frances is ready to move in. If Tim agrees, a tenancy at will is created.

As a practical matter, tenancy at will is rarely used in a written agreement and is viewed skeptically by the courts. It is usually interpreted as a periodic tenancy, with the period being defined by the interval of rental payments.

Estate at Sufferance

An **estate** (tenancy) **at sufferance** arises when a tenant who lawfully possessed real property continues in possession of the premises *without the landlord's consent* after the rights expire. This estate can arise when a tenant for years fails to surrender possession at the lease's expiration. A tenancy at sufferance can also occur by operation of law when a borrower continues in possession after a foreclosure sale and beyond the redemption period's expiration.

When a tenant fails to surrender possession, or *holds over*, the tenant is responsible for the payment of monthly rent at existing terms and rate. If a lease contains a holdover clause, that lease governs the rights of both the landlord and tenant. If a lease does not contain such a clause, then a state's law governs and typically offers three options. The first possibility is that the landlord accepts rent offered by the tenant, creating a new tenancy under conditions of the original lease, and is called a *holdover tenancy*. If the original lease term was greater than one year, generally the new tenancy is limited to one year. The second possibility is that the landlord can treat the tenant as a *tenant in sufferance* by either objecting to the tenant holding over or informing the tenant of such treatment. This creates a month-to-month or periodic tenancy. The landlord receives rent, and both parties have to provide notice within a certain time period of terminating the arrangement. The third possibility is that the landlord can treat the tenant as a trespasser and proceed with an eviction and damages action. Under this situation, the landlord must comply with the *notice to quit* requirements in the lease and the landlord's state's laws regarding the landlord-tenant relationship.

> **Estate (tenancy) at sufferance** = *Tenant's previously lawful possession continued without landlord's consent*

■ LEASE AGREEMENTS

Most states require no special wording to establish the landlord-tenant relationship. The lease may be written, oral, or implied, depending on the circumstances and the requirements of the statute of frauds. The law of the state where the real estate is located must be followed to ensure the validity of the lease.

Requirements of a Valid Lease

A lease is a form of contract. To be valid, a lease must meet the following requirements, which are essentially the same as in any other contract:

- *Capacity to contract*. The parties must have the legal capacity to contract.
- *Legal objectives*. The objectives of the lease must be legal.
- *Offer and acceptance*. The parties must reach a mutual agreement on all the terms of the contract.
- *Consideration*. The lease must be supported by valid consideration. Rent is the normal consideration given for the right to occupy the leased premises. However, the payment of rent is not essential as long as consideration was granted in creating the lease itself. Sometimes, for instance, this consideration is labor performed on the property. Because a lease is a contract, it is not subject to subsequent changes in the rent or other terms unless these changes are in writing and executed in the same manner as the original lease.

> **Memory Tip**
>
> The elements of a valid lease can be remembered by the acronym **CLOAC**: **C**apacity, **L**egal objectives, **O**ffer and **A**cceptance, and **C**onsideration.

| In Georgia |

In Georgia, in addition to the four requirements listed previously,

- the lease must contain a legal description for the property, not just a mailing address, when the entire property is the subject of the lease; and
- a lease must be in writing if it is longer than one year in order for it to be enforceable in a legal proceeding.

The leased premises should be clearly described. The legal description of the real estate should be used if the lease covers land, such as a ground lease. If the lease is for a part of a building, such as an apartment, the space itself or the apartment designation should be described specifically. If supplemental space is to be included, the lease should clearly identify it.

IN PRACTICE Preprinted lease agreements are usually better suited to residential leases. Commercial leases are generally more complex, have different legal requirements, and may include complicated calculations of rent and maintenance costs. Drafting a commercial lease—or even a complex residential lease, for that matter—may constitute the practice of law. Unless the real estate licensee is also an attorney, legal counsel should be sought.

Possession of Premises

The lessor, as the owner of the real estate, is usually bound by the implied covenant of quiet enjoyment. Quiet enjoyment does not have anything to do with barking dogs or late-night motorcycles. The *covenant of quiet enjoyment* is a presumed promise by the lessor that the lessee may take possession of the premises. The landlord further guarantees that he or she will not interfere in the tenant's possession or use of the property.

The lease may allow the landlord to enter the property to perform maintenance, to make repairs, or for other stated purposes. The tenant's permission is usually required and may be stipulated in the lease.

| In Georgia |

Two legal principles can underlie the issue of possession of the premises. State law can impose "actual possession" in which the landlord is responsible to give the tenant the vacant space at the beginning of the lease. The other principle is "the right of possession" in which the landlord only gives the tenant the right to possess the space at the beginning of the lease. The tenant has the responsibility to remove (dispossess) the prior tenant. If the space is not vacant and the new tenant must remove the prior tenant (holdover tenant) with no legal claim to the space, the new tenant can withhold rent. Georgia lease law is based on the "right of possession" principle.

Use of Premises

A lessor may restrict a lessee's use of the premises through provisions included in the lease. Use restrictions are particularly common in leases for stores or commercial space. For example, a lease may provide that the leased premises are to be used only as a real estate office *and for no other purpose*. In the absence of such clear limitations, a lessee may use the premises for any *lawful* purpose.

Term of Lease

The term of a lease is the period for which the lease will run. It should be stated precisely, including the beginning and ending dates, together with a statement of the total period of the lease. For instance, a lease might run "for a term of 30 years beginning June 1, 2007, and end May 31, 2037." A perpetual lease for an inordinate amount of time or an indefinite term usually will be ruled invalid. However, if the language of the lease and the surrounding circumstances clearly indicate that the parties intended such a term, the lease will be binding on the parties. Some states prohibit leases that run for 100 years or more.

Security Deposit

Most leases require that the tenant provide some form of **security deposit** to be held by the landlord during the lease term. If the tenant defaults on payment of rent or destroys the premises, the lessor may keep all or part of the deposit to compensate for the loss. Some state laws set maximum amounts for security deposits and specify how they must be handled. Some prohibit security deposits from being used for both nonpayment of rent and property damage. Some require that lessees receive annual interest on their security deposits.

Other safeguards against nonpayment of rent may include advancing the rental payment, contracting for a lien on the tenant's property, or requiring the tenant to have a third person guarantee payment.

IN PRACTICE   A lease should specify whether a payment is a security deposit or an advance rental. If it is a security deposit, the tenant is usually not entitled to apply it to the final month's rent. If it is an advance rental, the landlord must treat it as income for tax purposes.

| In Georgia |

Georgia law (O.C.G.A. 44-7-31 et seq.) lists provisions relating to security deposits. Security deposits must be deposited in an escrow account established only for that purpose. Tenants must be informed in writing of the location and account number of the escrow account. In the alternative, landlords can post a surety bond with the clerk of court where the dwelling is located. The amount of the bond is the total amount of security deposits the landlord holds on behalf of the tenants or $50,000, whichever is less.

Prior to tendering a security deposit, the tenant must be given a list of existing damage to the premises. The tenant has the right to inspect the premises prior to taking occupancy. Both the landlord and tenant sign the list, which is conclusive evidence of its accuracy, though not the accuracy of any latent defects.

Within three business days after the occupancy is terminated, the landlord must inspect the premises and compile a list of any damage. The tenant has the right to inspect the premises within five business days after terminating occupancy in order to ascertain the accuracy of the list. The landlord and tenant sign this list. If the tenant refuses to sign the list, the tenant must sign a statement of dissent and note the items of dissent. A tenant who disputes the accuracy of a damages list may bring an action to recover any portion of the security deposit the tenant believes is being wrongfully withheld.

Within one month after the termination of a residential lease or surrender with acceptance of the condition of the premises, whichever occurs last, a landlord must return the full security deposit to the tenant. No security deposit can be retained by the landlord to cover ordinary wear and tear, provided there was no negligence, carelessness, accident, or abuse of the premises. In the event there is actual cause for retaining a portion of the security deposit, the landlord must provide the tenant with a written statement of the reasons for retention.

Improvements

Neither the landlord nor the tenant is required to make any improvements to the leased property. The tenant may, however, make improvements with the landlord's permission. Any alterations generally become the landlord's property; that is, they become fixtures. However, the lease may give the tenant the right to install trade fixtures. Trade fixtures may be removed before the lease expires, provided the tenant restores the premises to their previous condition, with allowance for the wear and tear of normal use.

Accessibility   The federal Fair Housing Act (discussed in Chapter 21) makes it illegal to discriminate against prospective tenants on the basis of physical disability. Tenants with disabilities must be permitted to make reasonable modifications to a property at their own expense. However, if the modifications would interfere with a future tenant's use, the landlord may require that the premises be restored to their original condition at the end of the lease term.

IN PRACTICE   The *Americans with Disabilities Act (ADA)* applies to commercial, nonresidential property in which public goods or services are provided. The ADA requires that such properties either be free of architectural barriers or provide reasonable accommodations for people with disabilities.

Maintenance of Premises

Most states require a residential lessor to maintain dwelling units in a habitable condition. Landlords must make any necessary repairs to common areas, such as hallways, stairs, and elevators, and maintain safety features, such as fire sprinklers and smoke alarms. The tenant does not have to make any repairs but must return the premises in the same condition they were received, with allowances for ordinary wear and tear.

Destruction of Premises

In leases involving agricultural land, the courts have held that when improvements are damaged or destroyed, the tenant is obligated to pay rent to the end of the term. The tenant's liability does not depend on whether the damage was his or her fault. This ruling has been extended in most states to include *ground leases* for land on which the tenant has constructed a building. In many instances, it also includes leases that give possession of an entire building to the tenant. In this case, the tenant leases the land on which that building is located, as well as the structure itself. Insurance is available to cover such contingencies.

A tenant who leases only part of a building, such as office or commercial space or a residential apartment, however, is *not* required to continue to pay rent after the leased premises are destroyed. In some states, if the property was destroyed as a result of the landlord's negligence, the tenant can even recover damages.

Assignment and Subleasing

When a tenant transfers all of his or her leasehold interests to another person, the lease has been assigned. The new tenant is legally obligated for all the promises the original tenant made in the lease.

When a tenant transfers less than all the leasehold interests by leasing them to a new tenant, he or she has *subleased* (or sublet) the property. The original tenant remains responsible for rent being paid by the new tenant and for any damage done to the rental during the lease term. The new tenant is responsible only to the original tenant to pay the rent due.

Assignment and subleasing are only allowed when a lease specifically permits them. In both assignments and subleases, details of the new arrangements should be in writing. In most cases, the **sublease** or **assignment** of a lease does not relieve the original lessee of the obligation to pay rent. The landlord may, however, agree to waive the former tenant's liability.

In Georgia | In Georgia, the typical preprinted residential lease contains a clause that explicitly prohibits the tenant from assignment and subletting of the space.

Recording a Lease

Possession of leased premises is considered constructive notice to the world of the lessee's leasehold interests. Anyone who inspects the property receives actual notice. For these reasons, it is usually considered unnecessary to record a lease. However, most states do allow a lease to be recorded in the county in which the property is located. Furthermore, leases of three years or longer often are recorded as a matter of course. Some states *require* that long-term leases be recorded, especially when the lessees intend to mortgage the leasehold interests.

In some states, only a memorandum of lease is filed. A memorandum of lease gives notice of the interest, but does not disclose the terms of the lease. Only the names of the parties and a description of the property are included.

Nondisturbance Clause

A **nondisturbance clause** is a mortgage clause that states the mortgagee agrees not to terminate the tenancies of lessees who pay their rent in the event the mortgagee forecloses on the mortgagor-lessor's building. This clause is often used in commercial leases.

Options

A lease may contain a clause that grants the lessee the privilege of renewing the lease (called a **renewal option**). The lessee must, however, give notice of his or her intention to exercise the option. Some leases grant the lessee the option to purchase the leased premises (called a **lease option**). This option normally allows the tenant the right to purchase the property at a predetermined price within a certain time period, possibly the lease term. The lease could also contain a **right of first refusal** clause allowing the tenant the opportunity to buy the property before the owner accepts an offer from another party. Although it is not required, the owner may give the tenant credit toward the purchase price for some percentage of the rent paid. The lease agreement is a primary contract over the option to purchase.

IN PRACTICE   All the general statements concerning provisions of a lease are controlled largely by the terms of the agreement and state law. Landlord-tenant laws also vary from state to state. Great care must be exercised in reading the entire lease document before signing it because every clause in the lease has an economic and a legal impact on either the landlord or the tenant. While preprinted lease forms are available, there is no such thing as a standard lease. When complicated lease situations arise, legal counsel should be sought.

■ TYPES OF LEASES

The manner in which rent is determined indicates the type of lease that exists. (See Table 17.1.) The different types of leases are described in the following.

Gross Lease

In a **gross lease**, the tenant pays a fixed rental, and the landlord pays all taxes, insurance, repairs, utilities, and the like connected with the property (usually called *property charges* or *operating expenses*). This is typically the type of rent structure involved in residential leasing.

TABLE 17.1

Types of Leases

Type of Lease	Lessee	Lessor
Gross lease	Pays basic rent	Pays property charges (taxes, repairs, insurance, etc.)
Net lease	Pays basic rent plus all or most property charges	May pay some property charges
Percentage lease (commercial and industrial)	Pays basic rent plus percent of gross sales (may pay property costs)	

Net Lease

In a **net lease,** the tenant pays all or some of the property charges in addition to the rent. The monthly rental is net income for the landlord after operating costs have been paid. Leases for entire commercial or industrial buildings and the land on which they are located, ground leases, and long-term leases are usually net leases.

In a *triple-net lease,* or *net-net-net lease,* the tenant pays all operating and other expenses in addition to a periodic rent. These expenses include taxes, insurance, assessments, maintenance, utilities, and other charges related to the premises.

Percentage Lease

Either a gross lease or a net lease may be **a percentage lease.** The rent is based on a minimum fixed rental fee plus a percentage of the gross income received by the tenant doing business on the leased property. This type of lease is usually used for retail businesses. The percentage charged is negotiable and varies depending on the nature of the business, the location of the property, and the general economic conditions.

Other Types of Leases

Variable lease   Several types of leases allow for increases in the rental charges during the lease periods. One of the more common is the graduated lease. A *graduated lease* provides for specified rent increases at set future dates. Another is the *index lease* that allows rent to be increased or decreased periodically based on changes in the consumer price index or some other indicator.

Ground lease   When a landowner leases unimproved land to a tenant who agrees to erect a building on the land, the lease is usually referred to as a **ground lease.** Ground leases usually involve separate ownership of the land and buildings. These leases must be for a long enough term to make the transaction desirable to the tenant investing in the building. They often run for terms of 50 years up to 99 years. Ground leases are generally *net leases:* The lessee must pay rent on the ground as well as real estate taxes, insurance, upkeep, and repairs.

Oil and gas lease   When an oil company leases land to explore for oil and gas, a special lease agreement must be negotiated. Usually, the landowner receives a cash payment for executing the lease. If no well is drilled within the period stated in the lease, the lease expires. However, most oil and gas leases permit the oil company to continue its rights for another year by paying another flat rental fee. Such rentals may be paid annually until a well is produced. If oil or gas is found, the landowner usually receives a percentage of its value as a royalty. As long as oil or gas is obtained in significant quantities, the lease continues indefinitely.

A **lease purchase** is used when a tenant wants to purchase the property but is unable to do so. Perhaps the tenant cannot obtain favorable financing or clear title, or the tax consequences of a current purchase would be unfavorable. In this arrangement, the purchase agreement is the primary consideration, and the lease is secondary. Part of the periodic rent is applied toward the purchase price of the property until it is reduced to an amount for which the tenant can obtain financing or purchase the property outright, depending on the terms of the lease purchase agreement.

A **sale and leaseback** is the arrangement when an owner of property sells the property and then leases it back again for an agreed period and rental. A sale and leaseback is often used when extra capital is needed on a construction project. The challenging aspects of a sale and leaseback are that the lessee can act more as an owner than a tenant, and any increase in land value inures to the new owner.

Agricultural landowners often lease their land to tenant farmers, who provide the labor to produce and bring in the crop. An owner can be paid by a tenant in one of two ways: (1) as an agreed-on rental amount in cash in advance—**cash rent,** or (2) as a percentage of the profits from the sale of the crop when it is sold—**sharecropping.**

■ DISCHARGE OF LEASES

As with any contract, a lease is discharged when the contract terminates. Termination can occur when all parties have fully performed their obligations under the agreement. In addition, the parties may agree to cancel the lease. If the tenant, for instance, offers to surrender the leasehold interest, and if the landlord accepts the tenant's offer, the lease is terminated. A tenant who simply abandons leased property, however, remains liable for the terms of the lease—including the rent. The terms of the lease will usually indicate whether the landlord is obligated to try to rerent the space. If the landlord intends to sue for unpaid rent, however, most states require an attempt to mitigate damages by rerenting the premises to limit the amount owed.

The lease does not terminate if the parties die or if the property is sold. There are two exceptions to this general rule. First, a lease from the owner of a life estate ends when the measuring life ends. The death of either party terminates a tenancy at will. Second, in all other cases, the heirs of a deceased landlord are bound by the terms of existing valid leases.

If leased real estate is sold or otherwise conveyed, the new landlord takes the property subject to the rights of the tenants. A lease agreement may, however, contain language that permits a new landlord to terminate existing leases. The clause, commonly known as a *sale clause*, requires that the tenants be given some period of notice before the termination. Because the new owner has taken title subject to the rights of the tenants, the sale clause enables the new landlord to claim possession and negotiate new leases under his or her own terms and conditions.

A tenancy may also be terminated by operation of law, as in a bankruptcy or condemnation proceeding.

Breach of Lease

When a tenant breaches any lease provision, the landlord may sue the tenant to obtain a judgment to cover past-due rent, damages to the premises, or other defaults. Likewise, when a landlord breaches any lease provision, the tenant is entitled to certain remedies. The rights and responsibilities of the landlord-tenant relationship are governed by state law.

Suit for possession—actual eviction   When a tenant breaches a lease or improperly retains leased premises, the landlord may regain possession through a legal process known as **actual eviction**. The landlord must serve notice on the tenant before commencing the lawsuit. Most lease terms require at least a ten-day notice in the case of default. In many states, however, only a five-day notice is necessary when the tenant defaults in the payment of rent. When a court issues a judgment for possession to a landlord, the tenant must vacate the property. If the tenant fails to leave, the landlord can have the judgment enforced by a court officer, who forcibly removes the tenant and the tenant's possessions. The landlord then has the right to re-enter and regain possession of the property.

In Georgia | In Georgia, the landlord's eviction of a tenant is generally known as **dispossession** (O.C.G.A. 44-7-50 et seq.). The process follows the following steps:

1. The landlord demands that the tenant leave the space (give up possession and vacate) and gives the tenant a reasonable time to respond (three to ten days).
2. If the tenant refuses to give up possession, the landlord or the landlord's agent or attorney goes to the magistrate court and files a "dispossessory affidavit" under oath. The affidavit contains the following:
   — Landlord's name
   — Tenant's name
   — Reasons for the eviction
   — Landlord's demand for possession of the property and the tenant's refusal
   — The amount of rent or other money owed
3. The magistrate court issues a summons to the sheriff requiring the tenant to answer (orally or in writing) within seven days from the date the summons is served.
4. If the tenant fails to respond at the end of the seventh day, the lawsuit is in default. The court can grant the landlord a writ of possession and the sheriff can remove the tenant immediately.
5. If the tenant answers the summons, a trial is held (typically in magistrate's court if the sum is less than $15,000). The tenant is allowed to remain in possession of the premises. The landlord may request that the court order the tenant to pay rent during this time.

In some states, in cases of nonpayment of rent, a landlord also has the right to *distrain*, that is, seize the tenant's property for rent in arrears, generally by changing the locks and giving notice. Most states require a court order for **distraint**.

In Georgia, a landlord who has a tenant who has not paid the rent and is removing personal property from the property can file an affidavit for distraint. The judge or magistrate receiving the affidavit issues a summons to the sheriff of the county for delivery to the tenant. The tenant is required to appear at a hearing set five to seven days in the future.

Tenants' remedies—constructive eviction If a landlord breaches any clause of a lease agreement, the tenant has the right to sue and recover damages against the landlord. If the leased premises become unusable for the purpose stated in the lease, the tenant may have the right to abandon them. This action, called **constructive eviction**, terminates the lease agreement. The tenant must prove that the premises have become unusable because of the conscious neglect of the landlord. To claim constructive eviction, the tenant must leave the premises while the conditions that made the premises uninhabitable exist.

■ **FOR EXAMPLE** Tim's lease requires that the landlord furnish heat. The landlord fails to repair a defective furnace, and no heat is provided to Tim's apartment during the winter months. Tim is forced to abandon the apartment. Because the lack of heat was due to the landlord's negligence, Tim has been constructively evicted.

Fran's lease requires that the landlord furnish water. Although the landlord carefully maintains the building's plumbing system, the pipes develop a leak, and Fran's apartment is without water for several weeks while the problem is being repaired. Fran abandons the apartment. Because the lack of water was not due to the landlord's negligence, however, Fran has not been constructively evicted.

Harry owns a nightclub and a neighboring apartment building. Ben leased an apartment from Harry. The noise from the nightclub in the late evening and early morning was intense, and Ben complained about it to Harry. Harry posted a sign in the nightclub that said, "Shhh: We Have Neighbors!" but the noise continued. Finally, Ben abandoned the apartment, and Harry sued to recover rent. The court held that Ben had been constructively evicted because of the loud noise.

Pro-Tenant Legislation

For the most part, leases are drawn up primarily for the benefit of the landlord. However, due to tenant's rights movements and increased consumer awareness, several states have adopted some variation of the Uniform Residential Landlord and Tenant Act. This model law addresses the need for both parties to a lease to fulfill certain basic obligations. The act addresses such issues as

■ the landlord's right of entry,
■ maintenance of the premises,

- the tenant's protection against retaliation by the landlord for complaints, and
- the disclosure of the property owners' names and addresses to the tenants.

The act further establishes the specific remedies available to both the landlord and the tenant if a breach of the lease agreement occurs.

| In Georgia | See Chapter 4 for a discussion of broker duties for landlords and tenants under Georgia law. |

■ FAIR HOUSING AND CIVIL RIGHTS LAWS

The fair housing laws affect landlords and tenants just as they do sellers and purchasers. All persons must have access to housing of their choice without any differentiation in the terms and conditions because of their race, color, religion, national origin, sex, handicap, or familial status. State and local municipalities may have their own fair housing laws that add protected classes such as age and sexual orientation. Withholding an apartment that is available for rent, segregating certain persons in separate sections of an apartment complex or parts of a building, and charging persons in the protected classes different amounts for rent or security deposits all constitute violations of the law. The fair housing laws are discussed in Chapter 21.

It is important that landlords realize that changes in the laws stemming from the federal Fair Housing Amendments Act of 1988 significantly alter past practices, particularly as they affect individuals with disabilities and families with children. The fair housing laws require that the same tenant criteria be applied to families with children that are applied to adults. A landlord cannot charge a different amount of rent or security deposit because one of the tenants is a child. While landlords have historically argued that children are noisy and destructive, the fact is that many adults are noisy and destructive as well.

■ KEY POINT REVIEW

A **lease** is a contract between the **lessor** (the owner of real estate) and the **lessee** that transfers **possession and use** of the property, lasts for a **specified period** of time, and is made in return for **consideration** (payment).

The **statute of frauds** in most states requires a lease to be **in writing** if termination will be more than one year from date of signing by lessor and lessee, or the lease is for a term longer than one year.

The lessor **(landlord)** has a **leased fee estate** and **reversionary right** to possession of property when lease expires.

The lessee (**tenant**) has a **leasehold** estate that can be an

- **estate for years (tenancy for years)**: continues for a definite period.
- **estate from period to period (periodic tenancy)**: has no specific expiration date, but rent is payable at definite intervals.
  — Has continuity because it automatically **renews**.
  — **Month-to-month tenancy**—a common form of residential lease.
- **holdover tenancy**—may be created when tenant with estate for years stays on after lease term expires and landlord accepts rent payment.
- **estate at will (tenancy at will)**: has no specified initial term; it is created by **express agreement** or **operation of law**; and can be **terminated** by the landlord or the tenant at any time on proper notice.
- **estate at sufferance (tenancy at sufferance)**: created when the tenant stays on without the landlord's consent after termination:
  — Landlord's acceptance of rent creates **holdover tenancy**
  — Landlord can treat tenant as a **trespasser** and begin eviction proceeding and action for damages under state laws

A **valid lease** requires parties with **CLOAC** (**C**apacity to contract, **L**egal objectives, **O**ffer and **A**cceptance, and valid **C**onsideration) and includes:

- **Description** of leased premises
- Implied **covenant of quiet enjoyment**
- Limitations on tenant's use of the property and the **Term** (length) of the lease

In Georgia
  — Georgia lease law is based on the right of possession where the landlord only gives the tenant the right to possess at the beginning of the lease.
- **Security deposit**, which must comply with state law
- Whether **improvements** may be made by the tenant:
  — Fixtures generally become the landlord's property, although **trade fixtures** may be removed by the tenant
  — **Federal Fair Housing Act** requires that the landlord allow a tenant with a physical disability to make reasonable modifications
  — **Americans with Disabilities Act (ADA)** requires that commercial nonresidential property be free of barriers or that reasonable accommodations be provided
- **Maintenance** of premises by landlord in compliance with state law
- **Destruction** of premises, and whether tenant is liable to pay rent
- **Assignment** of lease that relieves tenant of further obligation
- **Sublease** provisions
- **Recording** of lease that may be required by state law
- **Nondisturbance** clause
- **Option** that may give the tenant the **right to renew** the lease, **right to purchase property**, or **right of first refusal** before landlord can sell the property

In Georgia
In Georgia, a valid lease also requires a legal description and it must be in writing if longer than one year.

A **gross lease** requires the tenant to pay basic rent and the landlord to pay expenses of ownership.

A **net lease** requires the tenant to pay basic rent plus all or most property expenses and the landlord to pay some property expenses.

In a **percentage lease**, the tenant pays basic rent plus a percentage of gross sales and may pay property expenses.

A **variable lease** allows an increase in rent during the lease period. A **graduated lease** states specific rent increases. An **index lease** allows rent changes (up or down) based on the consumer price index or other indicator.

A **ground lease** involves separate ownership of the land and buildings.

An **oil and gas lease** allows exploration for and removal of oil and gas.

In a **lease purchase**, part of the rent typically is applied to the purchase price.

A **sale and leaseback** allows the original owner to use the property while freeing up capital for other business purposes.

In an **agricultural land lease**, rent is paid in advance (**cash rent**) or when the crop is sold (**sharecropping**).

The remedies for **breach** of a lease are governed by state law and include the following:

- Landlord may bring **suit for possession (actual eviction)**.
- Tenant may claim **constructive eviction** if premises are unusable.

| In Georgia | In Georgia, a landlord's eviction of a tenant is known as **dispossession**.

The **Uniform Residential Landlord and Tenant Act** has been adopted by some states.

| In Georgia | In Georgia, brokers owe duties under BRRETA when engaged by a tenant or landlord.

The **Fair Housing Amendments Act of 1988** prohibits discrimination on basis of race, color, religion, national origin, sex, handicap, or familial status. State and local governments may add more protected groups.

■ RELATED WEB SITE

Legal Information Institute: Landlord-Tenant Law:
www.law.cornell.edu/topics/landlord_tenant.html

CHAPTER 17 QUIZ

1. Which of the following transactions would *BEST* be described as involving a ground lease?
   a. A landowner agrees to let a tenant drill for oil on a property for 75 years.
   b. A tenant agrees to pay proportionate, increased rental based on annual appraisals of the rented property.
   c. A landlord charges a commercial tenant separate amounts for the rented land and for the leased building.
   d. A tenant pays a base amount for the property plus a percentage of business-generated income.

2. A tenant enters into a commercial lease that requires a monthly rent of a minimum fixed amount, plus an additional amount determined by the tenant's gross receipts exceeding $5,000. This type of lease is called a
   a. standard lease.
   b. gross lease.
   c. percentage lease.
   d. net lease.

3. If a tenant moved out of a rented store building because access to the building was blocked as a result of the landlord's negligence, the
   a. tenant would have no legal recourse against the landlord.
   b. landlord would be liable for the rent until the expiration date of the lease.
   c. landlord would have to provide substitute space.
   d. tenant would be entitled to recover damages from the landlord.

4. A tenant moves a pet into an apartment community that has a no-pets policy. The landlord wishes to remove the tenant due to the breach. The legal process to remove a tenant is known as
   a. constructive eviction.
   b. eminent domain.
   c. actual eviction.
   d. partial eviction.

5. Kevin still has five months remaining on a one-year apartment lease. When Kevin moves to another city, he transfers possession of the apartment to Linda for the entire remaining term of the lease. Linda pays rent directly to Kevin. In this situation, Kevin has become a(n)
   a. assignor.
   b. sublessor.
   c. sublessee.
   d. lessor.

6. Which of the following is *TRUE* about a hold-over tenant?
   a. The landlord must accept additional rent if the tenant remains on the premises.
   b. The tenant must give the landlord a 30-day notice to vacate.
   c. The tenant may continue to occupy the premises without permission of the landlord.
   d. The landlord may evict the tenant.

7. A tenant's tenancy for years will expire in two weeks. The tenant plans to move to a larger apartment across town when the current tenancy expires. In order to terminate this agreement, the tenant must
   a. give the landlord immediate notice or the lease will automatically renew.
   b. give the landlord one week's prior notice or the lease will automatically renew.
   c. do nothing because the agreement will terminate automatically at the end of the current term.
   d. sign a lease for the new apartment, which will automatically terminate the existing lease.

8. Under the negotiated terms of a certain residential lease, the landlord is required to maintain the water heater. If the tenant is unable to get hot water because of a faulty water heater that the landlord has failed to repair after repeated notification, the tenant could do all *EXCEPT*

    a. sue the landlord for damages.

    b. sue the landlord for breach of the covenant of seisin.

    c. abandon the premises claiming constructive eviction.

    d. terminate the lease agreement.

9. Jody has a one-year leasehold interest in Harbor House. The interest automatically renews itself at the end of each year. Jody's interest is referred to as a tenancy

    a. for years.

    b. from period to period.

    c. at will.

    d. at sufferance.

10. Mary has assigned her apartment lease to Ben, and the landlord has agreed to the assignment. Who is liable for payment of the rent?

    a. Ben is liable to Mary; Mary is liable to the landlord.

    b. Both Ben and Mary are liable to the landlord.

    c. Only Mary is liable.

    d. Only Ben is liable.

11. Which of the following would automatically terminate a residential lease?

    a. Total destruction of the property

    b. Sale of the property

    c. Failure of the tenant to pay rent

    d. Death of the tenant

12. Which of the following describes a net lease?

    a. An agreement in which the tenant pays a fixed rent and the landlord pays all taxes, insurance, and expenses related to the property

    b. A lease in which the tenant pays rent, plus some—or all—of the operating expenses related to the property

    c. A lease in which the tenant pays the landlord a percentage of the monthly income derived from the property

    d. An agreement granting an individual a leasehold interest in fishing rights for shoreline properties

13. A tenancy in which the tenant continues in possession after the lease has expired, without the landlord's permission, is a

    a. tenancy for years.

    b. periodic tenancy.

    c. tenancy at will.

    d. tenancy at sufferance.

14. A commercial lease calls for a minimum rent of $1,200 per month plus additional annual rent of 4 percent of the year's gross business exceeding $150,000. If the total rent paid at the end of one year was $19,200, how much business did the tenant do during the year?

    a. $159,800

    b. $250,200

    c. $270,000

    d. $279,200

15. Which of the following describes a gross lease?

    a. An agreement in which the tenant pays a fixed rent and the landlord pays all taxes, insurance, and expenses related to the property

    b. A lease in which the tenant pays rent plus some of the operating expenses related to the property

    c. A lease in which the tenant pays the landlord a percentage of the monthly income derived from the property

    d. An agreement allowing the tenant to terminate the lease if certain conditions near the premises become unbearable

16. A tenant signs a lease that includes a schedule of rent increases on specific dates over the course of the lease term. What kind of lease has this tenant signed?
    a. Percentage
    b. Net
    c. Graduated
    d. Index

17. The death of either the landlord or the tenant will terminate the lease and the parties' heirs will NOT be bound by its terms under which of the following tenancies?
    a. Tenancy for years
    b. Periodic tenancy
    c. Tenancy at will
    d. Tenancy at sufferance

18. In Georgia, the landlord's eviction of a tenant is generally known as a(n)
    a. actual eviction.
    b. constructive eviction.
    c. dispossession.
    d. sufferance.

19. If a landlord has a tenant who has not paid rent and is removing personal belongings from the property, the landlord can file an affidavit for
    a. distraint.
    b. disturbance.
    c. eviction.
    d. recapture.

20. According to Georgia law, security deposits must be
    a. promptly deposited in the building's assessment fee account.
    b. deposited in an earnest money account.
    c. deposited by the property manager in a damage deposit account.
    d. deposited in an escrow account established only for that purpose.

18

CHAPTER

Property Management

◼ OVERVIEW OF THE PROPERTY MANAGEMENT PROFESSION

Property management as a specialized field involves the leasing, managing, marketing, and overall maintenance of real estate owned by others, usually rental property. Property managers are used in residential real estate (condominiums, cooperatives, apartment buildings, town houses), industrial real estate (warehouses, factories, industrial parks), and commercial real estate (hotels, shopping malls, office buildings).

◼ THE PROPERTY MANAGER

The role of the **property manager** is complex, requiring the manager to wear many hats all at the same time. It isn't uncommon for a property manager to be a market analyst, salesperson, accountant, advertising specialist, and maintenance person all in the same day. In addition, the property manager frequently interacts with people in various professions, including lawyers, environmental engineers, and accountants. The three principal responsibilities of the property manager are to

A **property manager** must
1. achieve the goals of the owners,
2. generate income for the owners, and
3. preserve and increase the value of the property.

1. achieve the objectives of the property owners,
2. generate income for the owners, and
3. preserve and/or increase the value of the investment property.

The property manager carries out the goals of the property owners. In the process, the property manager is responsible for maintaining the owner's investment and making sure the property earns income. These goals can be accomplished in several ways. The physical property must be maintained in good condition. Suitable tenants must be found, rent must be collected, and employees must be hired and supervised. The property manager is responsible for budgeting and controlling expenses, keeping proper accounts, and making periodic reports to the owner. In all of these activities, the manager's primary goal is to operate and maintain the physical property in such a way as to preserve and enhance the owner's capital investment.

Some property managers work for property management companies. These firms manage properties for a number of owners under management agreements (discussed later in this chapter). Other property managers are independent. The property manager has an agency relationship with the owner, a relationship that involves greater authority and discretion over management decisions than an employee would have. A property manager or an owner may employ building managers to supervise the daily operations of a building. In some cases, these individuals may be residents of the building.

IN PRACTICE   In most states, licensed real estate brokers are permitted to manage properties for others. Some states have instituted separate property management licenses. Under certain conditions, such as being employed by the owner, some states permit nonlicensed individuals to manage properties. While some states require licensing in order to manage condominium or cooperative homeowners' associations, other states do not.

In Georgia

In Georgia, an individual who serves as the property manager with responsibilities for leasing space in the property and/or selling the property for a client must have a salesperson or broker license. The relationship between the property manager and the owner of the property is an agency relationship in which the property manager is the agent and the property owner is the principal.

Securing Management Business

Possible sources of property management business include

- corporate owners,
- apartment buildings,
- owners of small rental residential properties,
- homeowners' associations,
- investment syndicates,
- trusts, and
- owners of office buildings.

When a property manager secures business from any of these sources, a good reputation is often the manager's best advertising. A manager who consistently demonstrates the ability to increase property income over previous levels should have little difficulty finding new business.

A growing trend for the management of associations and planned unit developments is for a **community association management** to provide a team of property managers, accounting staff, office staff, and property consultants for property management. The prevalence of homeowners' and condominium associations combined with complex planning and development codes have placed new demands on property managers. Working as part of a team, property managers assist in providing a comprehensive array of services.

Before contracting to manage any property, however, the professional property manager should be certain that the building owner has realistic income expectations. Necessary maintenance, unexpected repairs, and effective marketing all take time and money. In addition, most states have landlord-tenant laws that require the landlord-owner to keep the property repaired and make sure it complies with building codes. Through the agency relationship with the owner, the property manager becomes responsible for repairs and the building's condition.

New Opportunities

There are many new management opportunities for property managers. For example, with the baby boom population needing senior housing in the coming years, there are many property management opportunities involved in managing housing for the elderly. Much of elderly housing consists of federally assisted housing programs. Property managers are responsible for the operations of the facility, as well as housekeeping, meal service, social event planning, medical emergency planning, and marketing. Also, when subsidized housing is involved, property managers need to be familiar with state and federal rules pertaining to eligibility requirements and income verification.

Multitenant properties are growing in popularity and need the services of a property manager. The key to successful property management in a multitenant property is the balancing of the owner's objectives with the varied needs of the tenants. Marketing and maintaining the appropriate mix of tenants is also important.

Resort housing property is another new opportunity for property managers. Aside from the traditional property management operations, a property manager becomes involved in the managing of short-term leases.

Property managers may also choose to provide a myriad of services, from concierge to leasing agent services. A new area for property managers to specialize in is the training and managing of concierge staff for office buildings and other settings. Concierge staff is responsible for anything from arranging for taxi rides to assisting with visual aids equipment for a conference.

Another new area of specialty within the property management field is asset management services. Similar to financial asset management, real property asset management involves helping to decide

- in what type of real estate to invest—commercial or residential;
- which property is best to purchase;
- the best financial sources for a real estate purchase; and
- when to dispose of property.

The asset manager monitors the portfolio of properties similar to a securities portfolio by analyzing the performance of the properties and making recommendations to the owners of the properties.

Corporate property managers manage properties for corporations that invest in real estate. Because these corporations do not usually deal in real estate, they are not necessarily knowledgeable about property management. Hiring a corporate property manager allows a corporation to invest in real estate and increase its capital without needing the specialized knowledge of property management. Typically, corporate property managers are employees of the corporation and not independent contractors.

Lastly, large property management companies are using the skills of leasing agents to help lease property to help decrease vacancy rates. Leasing agents are usually independent contractors working on a commission basis. They are in high demand because of their skills in securing lessees.

Professional Associations

Most metropolitan areas have local associations of building and property owners and managers that are affiliates of regional and national associations. The Institute of Real Estate Management (IREM) is one of the affiliates of the National Association of REALTORS®. It awards the Certified Property Manager (CPM) designation. The Building Owners and Managers Association International (BOMA) is a federation of local associations of building owners and managers.

The Building Owners and Managers Institute International (BOMI), an independent institute affiliated with BOMA, offers training courses leading to several designations: Real Property Administrator (RPA), Systems Maintenance Administrator (SMA), and Facilities Management Administrator (FMA). Other associations include the National Apartment Association (NAA) and the National Association of Residential Property Managers (NARPM). In addition, many specialized professional organizations provide information and contacts for condominium association managers, shopping center managers, and others.

■ THE MANAGEMENT PLAN AND AGREEMENT

The Management Plan

Property management begins with a **management plan.** A property manager prepares a management plan that includes the owner's objectives of the property. The plan is highly detailed and discusses what the manager hopes to accomplish, how, and when. In preparing a management plan, a property manager analyzes three factors: the owner's objectives, the regional and neighborhood market, and the specific property. The plan also includes a budgetary section on sources of revenue and anticipated expenses. Occupancy and absorption rates, as well as new starts, are critical indicators. While the management plan is a document for the present, it is forward-looking in determining the feasibility of a property owner's goals with a specific property.

The Management Agreement

The first step in taking over the management of any property is to enter into a *management agreement* (or *management contract*). The agreement is signed by the manager and the owner, and it defines the relationship between the parties. It is also a guide used in operating the property, as well as a document to be referred to in case of any future disputes.

The **management agreement** creates an agency relationship between the owner and the property manager. The property manager usually is considered to be a *general agent*. As an agent, the property manager is charged with the fiduciary responsibilities of care, obedience, accounting, loyalty, and disclosure, which can be remembered by the acronym COALD. After entering into an agreement with a property owner, a manager handles the property the same way the owner would. In all activities, the manager's first responsibility is to realize the highest return on the property in a manner consistent with the owner's instructions.

| In Georgia | As in any other contract involving real estate, the management agreement should be in writing, and under Rule 520-1-.06 of the Georgia Real Estate Commission, the management agreement must do the following:

■ Identify the property to be managed
■ Contain all the terms and conditions under which the property is to be managed

- Specify the terms and conditions on which the broker will remit property income to the owner and on which the broker will provide periodic written statements of property income and expenses to the owner, provided that periodic written statements are submitted to the owner on at least an annual basis
- Specify which payments of property-related expenses are to be made by the broker to third parties and how such payments are to be funded
- State the amount of fee or commission to be paid and when it will be paid
- Specify whether security deposits, prepaid rents, and fees or commissions will be held by the broker or owner
- Contain the effective date of the agreement and its termination date
- Provide the terms and conditions for termination of the property management agreement by the broker or property owner
- Contain signatures of broker and owner or their authorized agent

MATH CONCEPTS

RENTAL COMMISSIONS

Residential property managers often earn commissions when they find tenants for a property. Rental commissions are usually based on the annual rent from a property. For example, if an apartment unit rents for $1,200 per month and the commission payable is 8 percent, the commission is calculated as follows:

$$\$1,200 \text{ per month} \times 12 \text{ months} = \$14,400$$
$$\$14,400 \times 0.08 \ (8\%) = \$1,152$$

■ THE PROPERTY MANAGER'S RESPONSIBILITIES

A property manager's specific responsibilities are determined by the management agreement. Certain duties, however, are found in most agreements. These duties include creating financial reports, renting property, selecting tenants, maintaining good relations with tenants, marketing, and maintaining the property.

Financial Reports

One of the primary responsibilities of a property manager is maintaining financial reports, including an operating budget, cash flow report, profit and loss statement, and budget comparison statement. While there are no standard formats for these reports, there is some similarity among the reports and it is important for the property manager to adapt a report to meet an owner's needs.

Operating budget   An **operating budget** gives an owner a sense of the profit to expect during a certain period of time. For the property manager, the operating budget is a guide for the property's financial performance in the present and future.

Operating budgets are developed before attempting to rent property. They are based on anticipated revenues and expenses. Once a property manager has managed a property for a length of time, an operating budget is developed based on the results of the profit and loss statement in comparison to the original budget (actual versus projected). After making the comparison, a new operating budget is prepared for a new time period in the future.

Cash flow report   A **cash flow report** is a monthly statement that details the financial status of the property. Sources of income and expenses are noted, as well as net operating income and net cash flow. The cash flow report is the most important financial report because it provides a picture of current financial status of a property.

Income   In the income column of the cash flow report, items such as gross rentals collected, delinquent rental payments, utilities, vending contracts, and storage charges are noted. Any losses from uncollected rental payments or evictions are deducted from the total gross revenue. This gives you the total adjusted income.

In some properties, there is space that is not income producing, such as the property manager's office. The rental value of the property that is not producing income is subtracted from the gross rental income to equal the gross collectible, or billable, rental income.

Expenses   Typically, there are fixed and variable expenses involved with property management: administrative costs (including building personnel); operating expenses; and maintenance costs. The fixed expenses remain constant and do not change. These fixed expenses include employee wages, utilities, and other basic operating costs. The variable expenses can be recurring or nonrecurring, and can include capital improvements, building repairs, and landscaping.

The formula for arriving at Cash Flow is as follows:

Gross Rental Income + Other Income − Losses Incurred = Total Income

Total Income − Operating Expenses = Net Operating Income Before Debt Service (e.g., mortgage payments)

Net Operating Income Before Debt Service − Debt Service − Reserves = Cash Flow

Profit and loss statement   A **profit and loss statement** is prepared monthly, quarterly, semiannually, or annually. This statement provides a general financial picture based on the monthly cash flow reports and does not include itemized information. A formula for a profit and loss statement looks like this:

Gross Receipts − Operating Expenses − Total Mortgage Payment + Mortgage Loan Principal = Net Profit

Budget comparison statement   The **budget comparison statement** compares the actual results with the original budget, often giving either percentages or a numerical variance of actual versus projected income and expenses. Budget comparisons are especially helpful with future budgetary planning.

Renting the Property

Effective rental of the property is essential. However, the role of the property manager in managing a property should not be confused with that of a broker who acts as a leasing agent. The manager must be concerned with the long-term financial health of the property; the broker is concerned solely with renting space. The property manager may use the services of a leasing agent, but that agent does not undertake the full responsibility of maintaining and managing the property.

Setting rental rates Rental rates are influenced primarily by supply and demand. The property manager should conduct a detailed survey of the competitive space available in the neighborhood, emphasizing similar properties. In establishing rental rates, the property manager has the following four long-term considerations:

1. The rental income must be sufficient to cover the property's fixed charges and operating expenses.
2. The rental income must provide a fair return on the owner's investment.
3. The rental rate should be in line with prevailing rates in comparable buildings; it may be slightly higher or slightly lower, depending on the strength of the property.
4. The current vacancy rate in the property is a good indicator of how much of a rent increase is advisable. A building with a low vacancy rate (that is, few vacant units) is a better candidate for an increase than one with a high vacancy rate.

A rental rate for residential space is usually stated as the monthly rate *per unit*. Commercial leases—including office, retail, and industrial space rentals—are usually stated according to either annual or monthly rates *per square foot*.

If the vacancy level is high, the manager should attempt to determine why. An elevated level of vacancy does not necessarily indicate that rents are too high. Instead, the problem may be poor management or a defective or an undesirable property. The manager should attempt to identify and correct the problems first rather than immediately lower rents. On the other hand, a high occupancy rate may mean that rental rates are too low. Whenever the occupancy level of an apartment house or office building exceeds 95 percent, serious consideration should be given to raising rents. First, however, the manager should investigate the rental market to determine whether a rent increase is warranted.

Marketing

One of the primary responsibilities of a property manager is to ensure that a property generates income. To attract the best tenants, a property manager must have a firm marketing strategy in place. It is important that the property manager knows and understands the property before undertaking any marketing activities. In addition, researching supply and demand for the area where the property is located is essential as is knowing how much money is available for advertising.

Advertising   In all advertising and promotional activities, the material must comply with nondiscriminatory federal, state, and local laws. The content cannot market to one protected class, such as race, color, religion, sex, national origin, family status, or physical disabilities.

Advertising methods are numerous and include advertising in newspapers, brochures, and direct-mail pieces, and on Web sites, radio, television, and billboards. Deciding which method of advertising to use is usually based on budgetary factors as well as on market analysis.

Management activities   Because property management firms are often known by reputation, it is important for a firm to maintain good public relations. One way to foster good public relations is through community involvement and charitable giving.

Firms also have the capacity to write and issue public service announcements (PSAs or press releases) regarding special projects. These announcements can garner the attention of the media and, ultimately, prospective tenants.

Marketing costs   A cost-benefit analysis helps a property manager assess whether a particular advertising method worked to attract and secure tenants. Property marketing expenses are usually figured on a cost-per-prospect-per-lease basis. For example, if a three-bedroom apartment rents for $1,500 and is typically viewed by 10 prospects before it is leased, an $800 newspaper advertisement would cost $80 per prospect.

The Internet has significantly expanded a property manager's ability to reach consumers. Online apartment vacancy listing sites include *www.craigslist.com*; *www.apartmentfinder.com*; *www.forrent.com*; *www.apartmentguide.com*; and the Yahoo! Online Vacancy Listing.

Selecting Tenants

A building manager's success depends on establishing and maintaining sound, long-term relationships with his or her tenants. The first and most important step is selection. The manager should be sure that the premises are suitable for a tenant in size, location, and amenities. Most important, the manager should be sure that the tenant is able to pay for the space.

A commercial tenant's business should be compatible with the building and the other tenants. The manager must consider the business interests of his or her current tenants as well as the interests of the potential tenant. The types of businesses or services should be complementary, and the introduction of competitors into the same property should be undertaken with care. This not only pleases existing tenants but helps diversify the owner's investment and makes profitability more likely. Some commercial leases bar the introduction of similar businesses.

If a commercial tenant is likely to expand in the future, the manager should consider the property's potential for expansion.

The residential property manager must be sure to comply with all federal, state, and local fair housing laws in selecting tenants (see Chapter 17 and Chapter 21). Although fair housing laws do not apply to commercial properties, commercial property managers need to be aware of federal, state, and local antidiscrimination and equal opportunity laws that may govern industrial or retail properties.

Collecting rents   A property manager should accept only those tenants who can be expected to meet their financial obligations. The manager should investigate financial references, check with local credit bureaus, and, when possible, interview a prospective tenant's former landlord.

MATH CONCEPTS

CALCULATING MONTHLY RENT PER SQUARE FOOT (COMMERCIAL)

1. Determine the total square footage of the rental premises (generally floor space only).

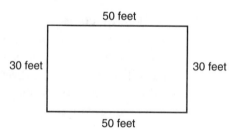

50 feet × 30 feet = 1,500 square feet

2. Find the total annual rent.

    $2,500 per month × 12 months = $30,000 per year

3. Divide the total annual rent by the total square feet to determine the annual rate per square foot.

    $30,000 ÷ 1,500 square feet = $20 per square foot

4. Convert the annual rate to a monthly rate.

    $20 ÷ 12 months = $1.67 per square foot

The terms of rental payment should be spelled out in the lease agreement, including

- time and place of payment,
- provisions and penalties for late payment and bounced checks, and
- provisions for cancellation and damages in case of nonpayment.

The property manager should establish a firm and consistent *collection plan*. The plan should include a system of notices and records that complies with state and local law.

Every attempt must be made to collect rent without resorting to legal action. Legal action is costly and time-consuming and does not contribute to good tenant relations. In some cases, however, legal action is unavoidable. In these instances, a property manager must be prepared to initiate and follow through with the necessary legal steps. Obviously, legal action must be taken in cooperation with the property owner's or management firm's legal counsel.

Maintaining Good Relations with Tenants

The ultimate success of a property manager depends on the ability to maintain good relations with tenants. Dissatisfied tenants eventually vacate the property. A high tenant turnover rate results in greater expenses for advertising and redecorating. It also means less profit for the owner due to uncollected rents.

An effective property manager establishes a good communication system with tenants. Regular newsletters or posted memoranda help keep tenants informed and involved. Maintenance and service requests must be attended to promptly, and all lease terms and building rules must be enforced consistently and fairly. If a manager fails to treat all tenants the same in terms of rent collection and enforcement of lease terms or rules and regulations, the manager could be violating fair housing laws. A good manager is tactful and decisive and acts to the benefit of both owner and occupants.

The property manager must be able to handle residents who do not pay their rents on time or who violate building regulations. When one tenant fails to follow the rules, the other tenants often become frustrated and dissatisfied. Careful record keeping shows whether rent is remitted promptly and in the proper amount. Records of all lease renewal dates should be kept so that the manager can anticipate expiration and retain good tenants who might otherwise move when their leases end.

Maintaining the Property

One of the most important functions of a property manager is the supervision of property maintenance. A manager must learn to balance the services provided with their costs, that is, to satisfy tenants' needs while minimizing operating expenses.

Four Types of Maintenance

1. Preventive
2. Repair or corrective
3. Routine
4. Construction

To maintain the property efficiently, the manager must be able to assess the building's needs and how best to meet them. Because staffing and scheduling requirements vary with the type, size, and geographic location of the property, the owner and manager usually agree in advance on maintenance objectives. In some cases, the best plan may be to operate a low-rental property, with minimal expenditures for services and maintenance. Another property may be more lucrative if kept in top condition and operated with all possible tenant services. A well-maintained, high-service property can command premium rental rates.

A primary maintenance objective is to *protect the physical integrity of the property over the long term*. For example, preserving the property by repainting the exterior or replacing the heating system helps decrease long-term maintenance costs. Keeping the property in good condition involves the following four types of maintenance:

1. Preventive
2. Repair or corrective
3. Routine
4. Construction

Preventive maintenance helps prevent problems and expenses.

Corrective maintenance corrects problems after they've occurred.

Preventive maintenance includes regularly scheduled activities such as painting and seasonal servicing of appliances and systems. Preventive maintenance preserves the long-range value and physical integrity of the building. This is both the most critical and the most neglected maintenance responsibility. Failure to perform preventive maintenance invariably leads to greater expense in other areas of maintenance.

Repair or **corrective maintenance** involves the actual repairs that keep the building's equipment, utilities, and amenities functioning. Repairing a boiler, fixing a leaky faucet, and mending a broken air-conditioning unit are acts of corrective maintenance.

A property manager also must supervise the **routine maintenance** of the building. Routine maintenance includes such day-to-day duties as cleaning common areas, performing minor carpentry and plumbing adjustments, and providing regularly scheduled upkeep of heating, air-conditioning, and landscaping. Good routine maintenance is similar to good preventive maintenance. Both head off problems before they become expensive.

IN PRACTICE One of the major decisions a property manager faces is whether to contract for maintenance services from an outside firm or hire on-site employees to perform such tasks. The property manager will make the decision on what is most cost-effective for the owner. This decision should be based on a number of factors, including the

- size of the building,
- complexity of the tenants' requirements,
- time and expense involved, and
- availability of suitable labor.

A commercial or an industrial property manager often is called on to make **tenant improvements** (*or build-outs*). These are **construction** alterations to the interior of the building to meet a tenant's particular space needs. Such alterations range from simply repainting or recarpeting to completely gutting the interior and redesigning the space by erecting new walls, partitions, and electrical systems. Tenant improvements are especially important when renting new buildings. In new construction, the interiors are usually left incomplete so that they can be adapted to the needs of individual tenants. One matter that must be clarified is which improvements will be considered trade fixtures (personal property belonging to the tenant) and which will belong to the owner of the real estate. Trade fixtures are discussed in Chapter 2.

Construction involves making a property meet a tenant's needs.

Modernization or renovation of buildings that have become functionally obsolete and thus unsuited to today's building needs is also important. (See Chapter 19 for a definition of *functional obsolescence*.) The renovation of a building often enhances the building's marketability and increases its potential income.

■ FEDERAL LAWS AFFECTING PROPERTY MANAGEMENT

Several federal laws affect the property management profession. The Americans with Disabilities Act, the Equal Credit Opportunity Act, and the Fair Housing Act all help to ensure that consumer rights are not violated, whether those rights involve the need to make accommodations for those with disabilities or the need to treat all housing applicants the same.

The Americans with Disabilities Act

The Americans with Disabilities Act (ADA) has had a significant impact on the responsibilities of the property manager, both in building amenities and in employment issues.

Title I of the ADA provides for the employment of qualified job applicants regardless of their disability. Any employer with 15 or more employees must adopt nondiscriminatory employment procedures. In addition, employers must make reasonable accommodations to enable individuals with disabilities to perform essential job functions.

Property managers also must be familiar with Title III of the ADA, which prohibits discrimination in commercial properties and public accommodations. The ADA requires that managers ensure that people with disabilities have full and equal access to facilities and services.

■ **FOR EXAMPLE** A prospective tenant is visually impaired. The property manager should be prepared to provide a lease agreement that is in enlarged, easy-to-read type or that is printed in braille.

The property manager typically is responsible for determining whether a building meets the ADA's accessibility requirements. The property manager also must prepare a plan for retrofitting a building that is not in compliance when removal of existing barriers is *readily achievable*, that is, can be performed without much difficulty or expense. Some tax advantages are available to help offset the expense of ADA compliance. ADA experts may be consulted, as may architectural designers who specialize in accessibility issues.

To protect owners of existing structures from the massive expense of extensively remodeling, the ADA recommends *reasonably achievable accommodations* to provide access to the facilities and services. New construction and remodeling, however, must meet higher standards of accessibility and usability because it costs less to incorporate accessible features in the design than to retrofit. Though the law intends to provide for people with disabilities, many of the accessible design features and accommodations benefit everyone.

IN PRACTICE The U.S. Department of Justice has ADA specialists available to answer general information questions about compliance issues. The ADA Information Line can be found at 800-514-0301 (TDD: 800-514-0383).

Existing barriers must be removed when this can be accomplished in a *readily achievable* manner—that is, with little difficulty and at low cost. (See Figure 18.1.) The following are typical examples of readily achievable modifications:

- Ramping or removing an obstacle from an otherwise accessible entrance
- Lowering wall-mounted public telephones
- Adding raised letters and braille markings on elevator buttons
- Installing auditory signals in elevators
- Reversing the direction in which doors open

Alternative methods can be used to provide reasonable accommodations if extensive restructuring is impractical or if retrofitting is unduly expensive. For instance, installing a cup dispenser at a water fountain, which is too high for an individual in a wheelchair, may be more practical than installing a lower water fountain.

IN PRACTICE Federal, state, and local laws may provide additional requirements for accommodating people with disabilities. Licensees should be aware of the full range of laws to ensure that their practices are in compliance.

Equal Credit Opportunity Act

The Equal Credit Opportunity Act (ECOA) prohibits a lender from denying a loan based on a person's race, color, religion, national origin, sex, marital status, age, and receipt of public assistance. The ECOA affects the property manager in several ways. A manager should use the same lease application for every applicant. Also, if a manager requires a credit report from one applicant, the manager should require credit reports from all applicants. The manager should be consistent in evaluating the income and debt of applicants and in determining whether to rent to an applicant.

> Guiding principle: what you do for one, do for all.

Fair Housing Act

The federal Fair Housing Act and its amendments (see Chapter 21) prohibit discrimination in the sale, rental, or financing of housing based on race, color, religion, national origin, sex, familial status, or handicap. Property managers need to ensure that their practices of attracting tenants do not violate fair housing laws. For example, blockbusting and steering are prohibited. *Blockbusting*

Reasonable Modifications to Public Facilities or Services

Provide doors with automatic opening mechanisms

Provide menus (and real estate listings) in a large-print or braille format

Install an intercom so customers can contact a second-floor business in a building without an elevator

Lower public telephones

Add grab bars to public restroom stalls

Permit guide dogs to accompany customers

Provide a shopper's assistant to help disabled customers

Provide ramps in addition to entry stairs

is encouraging people to rent or to sell a property by claiming that the entry of a protected class of people will have a negative impact on property values. *Steering* is the channeling of protected class members to certain buildings or neighborhoods.

I N   P R A C T I C E   Many of the fair housing complaints are related to property management issues.

■ RISK MANAGEMENT AND ENVIRONMENTAL ISSUES RELATED TO PROPERTY MANAGEMENT

Enormous monetary losses can result from certain unexpected or catastrophic events. As a result, one of the most critical areas of responsibility for a property manager is **risk management.**

Security of Tenants

The physical safety of tenants of the leased premises is an important issue for property managers and owners. Recent court decisions in several parts of the country have held owners and their agents responsible for physical harm that was inflicted on tenants by intruders. These decisions have prompted property managers and owners to think about how to protect tenants and secure apartments from intruders. There is also the concern of wrongdoing or criminal behavior inflicted by tenants on other tenants in the building. Many leases now have a crime-free provision that makes criminal activity, such as drug use or assault, a ground for eviction.

Risk Management Techniques

Risk management involves answering the question, "What happens if something goes wrong?" The perils of any risk must be evaluated in terms of options. In considering the possibility of a loss, the property manager must decide whether it is better to

> **Memory Tip**
>
> The four alternative risk management techniques may be remembered by the acronym **ACTOR**: **A**void, **C**ontrol, **T**ransfer, or **R**etain.

- *avoid it*, by removing the source of risk (for instance, a swimming pool may pose an unacceptable risk if a day-care center is located in the building);
- *control it*, by preparing for an emergency before it happens (by installing sprinklers, fire doors, and security systems, for example);
- *transfer it*, by shifting the risk onto another party (that is, by taking out an insurance policy); or
- *retain it*, by deciding that the chances of the event occurring are too small to justify the expense of any other response (an alternative might be to take out an insurance policy with a large *deductible*, which usually is considerably less expensive).

Types of Insurance

Insurance is one way to protect against losses. (See Chapter 3.) Many types of insurance, described in the following, are available.

Tenant's insurance   The property manager should notify tenants that in order to protect personal belongings, they must obtain renter's insurance. Business tenants can obtain their own business or commercial policy. Residential tenants need an HO-4 or renter's policy to insure the tenant's personal property. They are offered through the personal lines marketplace.

Commercial insurance   An *insurance audit* should be performed by a competent, reliable insurance agent who is familiar with insurance issues for the type of property involved. The audit will indicate areas in which greater or lesser coverage is recommended and will highlight particular risks. The final decision, however, must be made by the property owner.

Some common types of coverage available to income property owners and managers follow:

- *Fire and hazard*. Fire insurance policies provide coverage against direct loss or damage to property from a fire on the premises. Standard fire coverage can be extended to include other hazards such as windstorm, hail, smoke damage, or civil insurrection.

- *Flood.* Flood insurance is always a separate policy from home, rental, or building insurance policies. A flood insurance policy is available to any property located in a community participating in the National Flood Insurance Program (NFIP). It covers flooding caused by heavy rains, melting snow, inadequate drainage systems, or failed levees or dams. Consult *www.app1.fema.gov/nfip*.
- *Consequential loss, use, and occupancy.* Also known as *loss of rent* or *business interruption insurance*, consequential loss insurance covers the results, or consequences, of a disaster. Consequential loss can include the loss of rent or revenue to a business that occurs if the business's property cannot be used.
- *Contents and personal property.* This type of insurance covers building contents and personal property during periods when they are not actually located on the business premises.
- *Liability.* Public liability insurance covers the risks an owner assumes whenever the public enters the building. A claim paid under this coverage is used for medical expenses by a person who is injured in the building as a result of the owner's negligence. Claims for medical or hospital payments for injuries sustained by building employees hurt in the course of their employment are covered by state laws known as **workers' compensation acts.** These laws require that a building owner who is an employer obtain a workers' compensation policy from a private insurance company.
- *Casualty.* Casualty insurance policies include coverage against theft, burglary, vandalism, and machinery damage as well as health and accident insurance. Casualty policies are usually written on specific risks, such as theft, rather than being all-inclusive.
- *Surety bonds.* **Surety bonds** cover an owner against financial losses resulting from an employee's criminal acts or negligence while performing assigned duties.

Many insurance companies offer **multiperil policies** for apartment and commercial buildings. Such a policy offers the property manager an insurance package that includes standard types of commercial coverage, such as fire, hazard, public liability, and casualty. Special coverage for terrorism, earthquakes, and floods is also available.

Condominium associations carry insurance on all the *common elements*, and cooperatives carry insurance on the building. However, condominium owners and proprietary lease owners must carry their own casualty and liability insurance. In addition, if a condominium owner rents out space to a tenant, that tenant must carry their own insurance.

The property manager may also want to carry his or her own insurance to cover the office and contents of the office and to cover any professional malpractice problems. For example, a property manager may want to consider purchasing errors and omissions (E&O) insurance to protect against any financial management mistakes.

Claims

Two possible methods can be used to determine the amount of a claim under an insurance policy. One is the depreciated or actual cash value of the damaged property, that is, the property is not insured for what it would cost to replace it, but rather for what it was originally worth, less the depreciation in value that results from use and the passage of time. The other method is *current replacement cost*. In this sort of policy, the building or property is insured for what it would cost to rebuild or replace it today. When purchasing insurance, a manager must decide whether a property should be insured at full replacement cost or at a depreciated cost. Full replacement cost coverage is generally more expensive than depreciated cost. As with the homeowners' insurance policies discussed in Chapter 3, commercial policies include *coinsurance clauses* that require the insured to carry fire coverage, usually in an amount equal to 80 percent of a building's replacement value.

Property managers can encounter legal issues with insurance claims. For example, if the property owner is not present in order to file an insurance claim, the property manager must have proper authorization, such as a power of attorney.

Handling Environmental Concerns

The environment is an increasingly important property management issue. A variety of environmental issues, from waste disposal to air quality, must be addressed by the property manager. Tenant concerns, as well as federal, state, and local regulations, determine the extent of the manager's environmental responsibilities. While property managers are not expected to be experts in all of the disciplines necessary to operate a property, they are expected to be knowledgeable in many diverse subjects, most of which are technical in nature. Environmental concerns are one such subject.

The property manager must be able to respond to a variety of environmental problems. He or she may manage structures containing asbestos or radon or be called on to arrange an environmental audit of a property. Managers must see that any hazardous wastes produced by their employers or tenants are properly disposed of. Even the normally nonhazardous waste of an office building must be controlled to avoid violation of laws requiring segregation and recycling of types of wastes. Of course, a property manager may want to provide recycling facilities for tenants even if he or she is not required by law to do so. On-site recycling creates an image of good citizenship that enhances the reputation, and value, of a commercial or residential property.

Residential property managers of buildings constructed before 1978 must provide lead-based paint disclosure forms to all new tenants.

Air quality issues are a key concern for those involved in property management and design. Building-related illness (BRI) and sick building syndrome (SBS) are illnesses due to air quality problems. BRI is caused by toxic substances or pathogens and is a clinically diagnosed condition. Symptoms include asthma, hypersensitivity, and some allergies. SBS is more typical in an office building, and symptoms include fatigue, nausea, dizziness, headache, and sensitivity to odors. BRI and SBS are more prevalent today because of energy-efficiency standards used in building construction that make buildings more airtight with less ventilation. Often, increasing ventilation or replacing interior features such as carpeting can solve air quality problems.

■ GEORGIA COMMUNITY ASSOCIATION MANAGEMENT

In Georgia   The Georgia Property Owners' Association Act of 1994 (O.C.G.A. 44-3-220 et seq.) provides laws regarding community associations. A community association is an association of homeowners in a planned development, subdivision, condominium complex, town house development, or cooperative. The association is organized to preserve and maintain properties located within the development. (Community associations are also discussed in Chapter 1.)

Definitions

Community association management means the provision, for a valuable consideration, to others of management or administrative services on, in, or to the operation of the affairs of a community association. Community association management services include, but are not limited to: collecting, controlling, or disbursing the funds; obtaining insurance; arranging for and coordinating maintenance; and overseeing the daily operations. A community association manager is a person who acts on behalf of a real estate broker in providing only community association management services. (Chapters 1 and 14 discuss the separate license and education program for the community association manager.)

As distinguished from community association management services, property management services include the provision, for a valuable consideration, to another of marketing, including referring prospective tenants; leasing; physical, administrative, or financial maintenance; overall management of real property; or supervision of the foregoing activities for another pursuant to a property management agreement.

Community Association Structure and Powers

A community association has a board of directors responsible for operating and conducting the business affairs of the association on behalf of the owners. They operate under a set of bylaws, and typically have a president, vice president, secretary, and treasurer. The community association manager works closely with contractors, employees, board members, and volunteers, and interacts with the owners.

A community association has the power to

■ employ, retain, dismiss, and replace agents and employees;
■ make improvements on the common area;

- grant or withhold approval of any action by one or more lot owners or other persons entitled to occupancy of any lot if the action would change the exterior appearance or elect or provide for the appointment of an architectural control committee to grant or withhold such approval;
- grant easements, leases, and licenses for the common area;
- accept easements, leases, and licenses benefiting the development;
- acquire or lease property in the name of the association;
- borrow money; and
- amend association bylaws and articles of incorporation to conform to state law.

Some of the community association manager's duties may include the following:

- Maintaining financial records
- Preparing budgets
- Paying association expenses
- Sending meeting notices and attending board meetings
- Hiring and supervising staff
- Enforcing association rules
- Consulting with attorneys or accountants on legal or financial matters
- Arranging for such services as security, pest control, garbage

Fidelity Bond or Insurance 43-40-22.1 and Rule 520-1-.06)

`In Georgia`

The Georgia Real Estate Commission requires each broker who provides community association management services and who collects, controls, has access to, or disburses community association funds totaling more than $60,000 must at all times be covered by a **fidelity bond,** or fidelity insurance coverage, which protects the community association against loss of funds being held by the broker. The Commission establishes the criteria for fidelity bonds or insurance. Each broker providing community association management services must keep a copy of the fidelity bond or insurance policy, including current coverage amounts, for the community association.

Each broker must maintain a separate fidelity bond or insurance policy for each community association for which the broker provides community association management services.

■ KEY POINT REVIEW

A **property manager,** whether an individual or a company, acts as **general agent** of the investment property owner and has **fiduciary duties** to the owner of **care, obedience, accounting, loyalty,** and **disclosure (COALD)** in administering the property to accomplish the following:

- Achieve the **objectives** of the owner.
- Generate **income** for the owner.
- Preserve and increase the property's **value.**

Property management functions may require a real estate broker's or property manager's **license,** as provided by state law.

In Georgia

In Georgia, a property manager who leases space or sells property must have a salesperson's or broker's license.

Property managers may undertake **asset management** by helping the owner to decide the

- **type** of real estate in which to invest—residential or commercial;
- **best** property to purchase;
- **financial resources** to fund the purchase; and
- best time to **dispose** of the property

A **leasing agent** is usually a state-licensed real estate broker working as an **independent contractor** or property manager on a commission basis.

A **corporate property manager** is usually an **employee** of the corporation.

In Georgia

A **management plan** and **management agreement** under Georgia law should do the following:

- Identify property
- State terms and conditions for managing property
- Specify terms for broker remitting property income to owner
- Specify how expenses are to be paid by broker to third parties and how funded
- Provide amount of fee or commission and when is paid
- State whether security deposits or prepaid rents are held by broker or owner
- Contain agreement effective and termination dates
- Provide terms for termination
- Contain broker and owner signatures

The building manager **sets rents** that are

- sufficient to cover fixed charges and operating expenses and a **fair return** on owner's investment;
- in line with the **prevailing rates** in comparable buildings;
- a reflection of the current **vacancy rate** of the property;
- determined at a **monthly rate per unit** for residential property; and
- calculated at a **monthly rate per square foot** for commercial property.

A building manager **selects tenants** within certain parameters, while complying with all applicable federal, state, and local fair housing, antidiscrimination, and equal opportunity laws.

Commercial tenant considerations typically include the following:

- **Suitability** of the building in size, location, and amenities
- **Compatibility** with the building and other tenants
- **Availability** of space for expansion, if necessary

The building manager should establish a firm and consistent **collection plan** for rents. Lease agreement should spell out the

- **time and place** of payment;
- **penalties** for late payment and bounced checks; and
- **cancellation** procedures and **damages** in case of nonpayment.

Building managers maintain **good relations with tenants** with tact and uniformity through good **communication;** fair and consistent **enforcement** of rules; prompt attention to **maintenance and service** requests; and careful **record keeping** with attention to lease renewal dates.

To find and retain reliable tenants, a building manager must devise an **effective marketing strategy.**

Following are the federal laws affecting property management:

- **Americans with Disabilities Act (ADA),** which includes
  - **Title I,** which applies to **employers** with 15 or more employees and provides for employment of qualified job applicants regardless of disability, with reasonable accommodations; and
  - **Title III,** which prohibits discrimination in **commercial properties and public accommodations;** and requires that access to facilities and services be provided when reasonably achievable in existing buildings, with a higher standard for new construction or remodeling.
- **Equal Credit Opportunity Act (ECOA)** prohibits lender from denying loan based on person's race, color, religion, national origin, sex, marital status, age, and receipt of public assistance; additional protections may be added by state or local laws.
- **Fair Housing Act** and amendments prohibit discrimination in sale, rental, or financing of housing based on race, color, religion, national origin, sex, familial status, or handicap; additional protected individuals may be added by state or local laws.

Risk management includes treatment of risk by deciding whether to **a**void it, **c**ontrol it, **t**ransfer it, **or** **r**etain it (ACTOR) and focuses on tenant security and types of insurance available.

The **environmental concerns** that require attention of the property manager include the following:

- Structures containing **asbestos or radon**
- Environmental audits
- Disposal of **hazardous wastes**
- Recycling
- **Lead-based paint disclosure** for residential property constructed before 1978
- **Air quality** issues

In Georgia   The Georgia Property Owners' Association Act of 1994 provides laws regarding community management associations. A community association consists of homeowners in a planned development. The community association manager acts on behalf of a broker in providing community association management services.

Georgia law requires that each broker who provides community association management services (collecting, maintaining, disbursing, or having access to more than $60,000) must be covered by a fidelity bond or fidelity insurance.

■ RELATED WEB SITES

American Management Association: *www.amanet.org*
Building Owners and Managers Association: *www.boma.org*
Building Owners and Managers Institute: *www.bomi-edu.org*
Institute of Real Estate Management: *www.irem.org/home.cfm*
National Association of Home Builders: *www.nahb.com*
National Association of Residential Property Managers: *www.narpm.org*
U.S. Department of Justice: *www.usdoj.gov/crt/drs/drshome.htm*

CHAPTER 18 QUIZ

1. Which of the following types of insurance coverage insures an employer against MOST claims for job-related injuries?
   a. Consequential loss
   b. Workers' compensation
   c. Casualty
   d. Surety bond

2. Avoid, control, transfer, or retain are the four alternative techniques of
   a. tenant relations.
   b. acquiring insurance.
   c. risk management.
   d. property management.

3. From a management point of view, apartment building occupancy that reaches as high as 98 percent would tend to indicate that
   a. the building is poorly managed.
   b. the building has reached its maximum potential.
   c. building similar sites would not be profitable.
   d. rents could be raised.

4. A guest slips on an icy apartment building stair and is hospitalized. A claim against the building owner for medical expenses may be paid under which of the following policies held by the owner?
   a. Workers' compensation
   b. Casualty
   c. Liability
   d. Fire and hazard

5. Asbestos, SBS, and lead paint are all examples of
   a. issues beyond the scope of a property manager's job description.
   b. problems faced only by newly constructed properties.
   c. issues that arise under the ADA.
   d. environmental concerns that a property manager may have to address.

6. In the case of commercial or industrial properties, tenant improvements are
   a. tenant-owned fixtures.
   b. adaptations of space to suit tenants' needs.
   c. illegal unless authorized.
   d. landlord obligations.

7. Which of the following would be considered a variable expense when a manager develops an operating budget?
   a. Employee wages
   b. Utilities
   c. Building repairs
   d. Basic operating costs

8. In MOST market areas, rents are determined by
   a. supply and demand factors.
   b. the local apartment owners' association.
   c. HUD.
   d. a tenants' union.

9. Whittaker Towers, a highrise apartment building, burns to the ground. What type of insurance covers the landlord against the resulting loss of rent?
   a. Fire and hazard
   b. Liability
   c. Consequential loss, use, and occupancy
   d. Casualty

10. A property manager hires a full-time maintenance person. While repairing a faucet in one of the apartments, the maintenance person steals a television set, and the tenant sues the owner. The property manager could protect the owner against this type of loss by purchasing
    a. liability insurance.
    b. workers' compensation insurance.
    c. a surety bond.
    d. casualty insurance.

11. Commercial leases are usually expressed as a(n)
    a. monthly rate per unit.
    b. percentage of total space available.
    c. annual or monthly rate per square foot.
    d. annual rate per room.

12. A property manager repairs a malfunctioning boiler. This is classified as which type of maintenance?

    a. Preventive

    b. Corrective

    c. Routine

    d. Construction

13. A property manager who enters into a management agreement with an owner is usually a(n)

    a. special agent.

    b. general agent.

    c. universal agent.

    d. designated agent.

14. A semiannual statement sent to an owner that does not reflect the entire debt service as an expense is called a(n)

    a. cash flow report.

    b. profit and loss statement.

    c. budget comparison statement.

    d. operating budget statement.

15. An insurance policy package that includes standard commercial property coverage such as fire, hazard, public liability, and casualty is referred to as what kind of policy?

    a. Coinsurance

    b. Multiperil

    c. Universal

    d. Surety

16. Removing existing barriers when readily achievable in public buildings, such as adding braille markings to elevator buttons, is a requirement of which law?

    a. Fair Housing Act

    b. Equal Credit Opportunity Act

    c. Americans with Disabilities Act

    d. Regulation Z

17. Title III of the Americans with Disabilities Act (ADA) impacts which type of property?

    a. Residential

    b. Industrial

    c. Commercial and public accommodations

    d. Privately owned

18. In evaluating rental applications, it is important for the property manager to establish consistent criteria for acceptable debt and income ratios to be in compliance with

    a. federal antitrust laws.

    b. the Americans with Disabilities Act.

    c. Regulation Z.

    d. the Equal Credit Opportunity Act.

In Georgia

19. In Georgia, each of the following individuals needs a sales associate's license to lease space in a property EXCEPT a

    a. community association manager.

    b. property manager.

    c. property owner.

    d. sales manager.

20. A tenant signs a lease for the space in two small one-story buildings on the same site in Americus, Georgia, for $20,000 per year. The first building is a 25-by-30-foot rectangle, and the second building is a 40-by-20-foot rectangle. What is the annual per square foot cost for this space?

    a. $1.08

    b. $7.75

    c. $12.90

    d. $25.80

19 CHAPTER

Real Estate Appraisal

anticipation
appraisal
appraisal report
appraiser
assemblage
broker's price opinion (BPO)
capitalization rate
change
competitive market analysis (CMA)
competition
conformity
contribution
cost approach

depreciation
economic life
external obsolescence
functional obsolescence
gross income multiplier (GIM)
gross rent multiplier (GRM)
highest and best use (HABU)
income approach
index method
law of diminishing returns
law of increasing returns

market data approach
market value
physical deterioration
plottage
progression
quantity-survey method
reconciliation
regression
replacement cost new
reproduction cost
sales comparison approach
sales price
square-foot method

state-certified general real property appraiser
state-certified residential real property appraiser
state-licensed real property appraiser
state-registered real property appraiser
straight-line method
substitution
supply and demand
Uniform Standards of Professional Appraisal Practice (USPAP)
unit-in-place method
value

■ APPRAISING

An **appraisal** is an estimate or opinion of value based on supportable evidence and approved methods. An **appraisal report** is an opinion of market value on a property given to a lender or client with detailed and accurate information. An **appraiser** is an independent professional trained to provide an *unbiased* estimate of value in an impartial and objective manner, and according to the appraisal process. Appraising is a professional service performed for a fee.

Regulation of Appraisal Activities

Title XI of the Financial Institutions Reform, Recovery, and Enforcement Act of 1989 (FIRREA) requires that any appraisal used in connection with a federally related transaction must be performed by a competent individual whose professional conduct is subject to supervision and regulation. Appraisers must be licensed or certified according to state law. Each state adopts its own appraiser regulations. These laws must conform to the federal requirements that in turn follow the criteria for certification established by the Appraiser Qualifications Board of the Appraisal Foundation. Effective in January 2008, the requirements to become a state licensed or certified real property appraiser will significantly increase, according to the Appraisal Foundation. The Appraisal Foundation is a national body composed of representatives of the major appraisal and related organizations. Appraisers are also expected to follow the Uniform Standards of Professional Appraisal Practice (USPAP) established by the foundation's Appraisal Standards Board.

Effective in January 2008, the requirements to become a state-licensed or state-certified real property appraiser will significantly increase, as stipulated by the Appraisal Foundation.

A *federally related transaction* is any real estate-related financial transaction in which a federal financial institution or regulatory agency engages. These transactions involve the sale, lease, purchase, investment, or exchange of real property. They also include the financing, refinancing, or use of real property as security for a loan or an investment, including mortgage-backed securities. Appraisals of residential property valued at $250,000 or less are exempt and need not be performed by licensed or certified appraisers. Nonresidential properties valued at above $250,000 require a certified appraiser.

Competitive Market Analysis

Not all estimates of value are made by professional appraisers. As discussed in Chapter 6, a salesperson often must help a seller arrive at a listing price or a buyer determine an offering price for property without the aid of a formal appraisal report. In such a case, the salesperson prepares a report compiled from research of the marketplace, primarily similar properties that have been sold, known as a **competitive market analysis (CMA)**. The salesperson must be knowledgeable about the fundamentals of valuation to compile the *market data*. The competitive market analysis is not as comprehensive or technical as an appraisal and may be biased by a salesperson's anticipated agency relationship. A competitive market analysis should *not* be represented as an appraisal.

| In Georgia | Under Georgia law (O.C.G.A. 43-40-25), it is an unfair practice to indicate an opinion given to a seller, purchaser, landlord, or tenant regarding a listing, lease, rental, or purchase price is an appraisal unless the licensee holds an appraiser classification under statute. |

A **broker's price opinion (BPO)** is similar to a CMA but different. A BPO is commissioned by a bank or an attorney handling a divorce or estate matter. But if the matter involves a federally related transaction and/or it occurs in a mandatory licensing state, an appraiser is required and what a broker does cannot be referred to as an appraisal unless the broker is licensed or certified. In performing a BPO, the broker simply drives by the property, takes a picture, and fills out a BPO form to return to the bank or attorney. Brokers are paid for performing BPOs.

■ THE APPRAISAL PROCESS

Although appraising is not an exact or a precise science, the key to an accurate appraisal lies in the methodical collection and analysis of data. The appraisal process is an orderly set of procedures used to collect and analyze data to arrive at an ultimate value conclusion. The data are divided into two basic classes:

1. *General data*, covering the nation, region, city, and neighborhood. Of particular importance is the neighborhood, where an appraiser finds the physical, economic, social, and political influences that directly affect the value and potential of the subject property.
2. *Specific data*, covering details of the subject property as well as comparative data relating to costs, sales, income, and expenses of properties similar to and competitive with the subject property.

Figure 19.1 outlines the steps an appraiser takes in carrying out an appraisal assignment.

Once the approaches have been reconciled and an opinion of value has been reached, the appraiser prepares a report for the client. The report should

■ identify the real estate and real property interest being appraised;
■ state the purpose and intended use of the appraisal;
■ define the value to be estimated;
■ state the effective date of the value and the date of the report;
■ state the extent of the process of collecting, confirming, and reporting the data;
■ list all assumptions and limiting conditions that affect the analysis, opinion, and conclusions of value;
■ describe the information considered, the appraisal procedures followed, and the reasoning that supports the report's conclusions (if an approach was excluded, the report should explain why);

FIGURE   19.1

The Appraisal Process

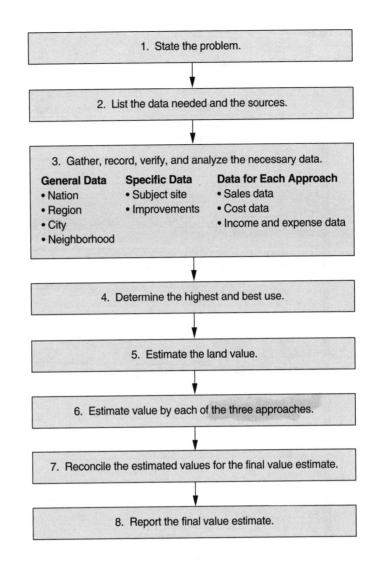

1. State the problem.

2. List the data needed and the sources.

3. Gather, record, verify, and analyze the necessary data.

General Data	**Specific Data**	**Data for Each Approach**
• Nation	• Subject site	• Sales data
• Region	• Improvements	• Cost data
• City		• Income and expense data
• Neighborhood		

4. Determine the highest and best use.

5. Estimate the land value.

6. Estimate value by each of the three approaches.

7. Reconcile the estimated values for the final value estimate.

8. Report the final value estimate.

- describe the appraiser's opinion of the highest and best use of the real estate;
- describe any additional information that may be appropriate to show compliance with the specific guidelines established in the **Uniform Standards of Professional Appraisal Practice (USPAP)** or to clearly identify and explain any departures from these guidelines; and
- include a signed certification, as required by the Uniform Standards.

Figure 19.2 shows the Uniform Residential Appraisal Report, the form required by many government agencies. It illustrates the types of detailed information required of an appraisal of residential property.

FIGURE 19.2

Uniform Residential Appraisal Report

Uniform Residential Appraisal Report   File

The purpose of this summary appraisal report is to provide the lender/client with an accurate, and adequately supported, opinion of the market value of the subject property.

SUBJECT

| Property Address | | City | | State | Zip Code |

Borrower — Owner of Public Record — County

Legal Description

Assessor's Parcel # — Tax Year — R.E. Taxes $

Neighborhood Name — Map Reference — Census Tract

Occupant ☐ Owner ☐ Tenant ☐ Vacant — Special Assessments $ — ☐ PUD — HOA $ ☐ per year ☐ per month

Property Rights Appraised ☐ Fee Simple ☐ Leasehold ☐ Other (describe)

Assignment Type ☐ Purchase Transaction ☐ Refinance Transaction ☐ Other (describe)

Lender/Client — Address

Is the subject property currently offered for sale or has it been offered for sale in the twelve months prior to the effective date of this appraisal? ☐ Yes ☐ No

Report data source(s) used, offering price(s), and date(s).

CONTRACT

I ☐ did ☐ did not analyze the contract for sale for the subject purchase transaction. Explain the results of the analysis of the contract for sale or why the analysis was not performed.

Contract Price $ — Date of Contract — Is the property seller the owner of public record? ☐ Yes ☐ No Data Source(s)

Is there any financial assistance (loan charges, sale concessions, gift or downpayment assistance, etc.) to be paid by any party on behalf of the borrower? ☐ Yes ☐ No
If Yes, report the total dollar amount and describe the items to be paid.

NEIGHBORHOOD

Note: Race and the racial composition of the neighborhood are not appraisal factors.

Neighborhood Characteristics	One-Unit Housing Trends	One-Unit Housing	Present Land Use %
Location ☐ Urban ☐ Suburban ☐ Rural	Property Values ☐ Increasing ☐ Stable ☐ Declining	PRICE AGE	One-Unit %
Built-Up ☐ Over 75% ☐ 25–75% ☐ Under 25%	Demand/Supply ☐ Shortage ☐ In Balance ☐ Over Supply	$ (000) (yrs)	2-4 Unit %
Growth ☐ Rapid ☐ Stable ☐ Slow	Marketing Time ☐ Under 3 mths ☐ 3–6 mths ☐ Over 6 mths	Low	Multi-Family %
Neighborhood Boundaries		High	Commercial %
		Pred.	Other %

Neighborhood Description

Market Conditions (including support for the above conclusions)

SITE

Dimensions — Area — Shape — View

Specific Zoning Classification — Zoning Description

Zoning Compliance ☐ Legal ☐ Legal Nonconforming (Grandfathered Use) ☐ No Zoning ☐ Illegal (describe)

Is the highest and best use of the subject property as improved (or as proposed per plans and specifications) the present use? ☐ Yes ☐ No If No, describe

Utilities	Public	Other (describe)		Public	Other (describe)	Off-site Improvements—Type	Public	Private
Electricity	☐	☐	Water	☐	☐	Street	☐	☐
Gas	☐	☐	Sanitary Sewer	☐	☐	Alley	☐	☐

FEMA Special Flood Hazard Area ☐ Yes ☐ No FEMA Flood Zone — FEMA Map # — FEMA Map Date

Are the utilities and off-site improvements typical for the market area? ☐ Yes ☐ No If No, describe

Are there any adverse site conditions or external factors (easements, encroachments, environmental conditions, land uses, etc.)? ☐ Yes ☐ No If Yes, describe

IMPROVEMENTS

General Description	Foundation	Exterior Description materials/condition	Interior materials/condition
Units ☐ One ☐ One with Accessory Unit	☐ Concrete Slab ☐ Crawl Space	Foundation Walls	Floors
# of Stories	☐ Full Basement ☐ Partial Basement	Exterior Walls	Walls
Type ☐ Det. ☐ Att. ☐ S-Det/End Unit	Basement Area sq. ft.	Roof Surface	Trim/Finish
☐ Existing ☐ Proposed ☐ Under Const.	Basement Finish %	Gutters & Downspouts	Bath Floor
Design (Style)	☐ Outside Entry/Exit ☐ Sump Pump	Window Type	Bath Wainscot
Year Built	Evidence of ☐ Infestation	Storm Sash/Insulated	Car Storage ☐ None
Effective Age (Yrs)	☐ Dampness ☐ Settlement	Screens	☐ Driveway # of Cars
Attic ☐ None	Heating ☐ FWA ☐ HWBB ☐ Radiant	Amenities ☐ Woodstove(s) #	Driveway Surface
☐ Drop Stair ☐ Stairs	☐ Other Fuel	☐ Fireplace(s) # ☐ Fence	☐ Garage # of Cars
☐ Floor ☐ Scuttle	Cooling ☐ Central Air Conditioning	☐ Patio/Deck ☐ Porch	☐ Carport # of Cars
☐ Finished ☐ Heated	☐ Individual ☐ Other	☐ Pool ☐ Other	☐ Att. ☐ Det. ☐ Built-in

Appliances ☐ Refrigerator ☐ Range/Oven ☐ Dishwasher ☐ Disposal ☐ Microwave ☐ Washer/Dryer ☐ Other (describe)

Finished area **above** grade contains: Rooms Bedrooms Bath(s) Square Feet of Gross Living Area Above Grade

Additional features (special energy efficient items, etc.)

Describe the condition of the property (including needed repairs, deterioration, renovations, remodeling, etc.).

Are there any physical deficiencies or adverse conditions that affect the livability, soundness, or structural integrity of the property? ☐ Yes ☐ No If Yes, describe

Does the property generally conform to the neighborhood (functional utility, style, condition, use, construction, etc.)? ☐ Yes ☐ No If No, describe

FIGURE 19.2 (CONTINUED)

Uniform Residential Appraisal Report

Uniform Residential Appraisal Report   File

| There are | comparable properties currently offered for sale in the subject neighborhood ranging in price from $ | | | | to $ | | | |
| There are | comparable sales in the subject neighborhood within the past twelve months ranging in sale price from $ | | | | to $ | | | |

FEATURE	SUBJECT	COMPARABLE SALE # 1		COMPARABLE SALE # 2		COMPARABLE SALE # 3	
Address							
Proximity to Subject							
Sale Price	$		$		$		$
Sale Price/Gross Liv. Area	$ sq. ft.	$ sq. ft.		$ sq. ft.		$ sq. ft.	
Data Source(s)							
Verification Source(s)							
VALUE ADJUSTMENTS	DESCRIPTION	DESCRIPTION	+(-) $ Adjustment	DESCRIPTION	+(-) $ Adjustment	DESCRIPTION	+(-) $ Adjustment
Sale or Financing Concessions							
Date of Sale/Time							
Location							
Leasehold/Fee Simple							
Site							
View							
Design (Style)							
Quality of Construction							
Actual Age							
Condition							
Above Grade	Total Bdrms. Baths	Total Bdrms. Baths		Total Bdrms. Baths		Total Bdrms. Baths	
Room Count							
Gross Living Area	sq. ft.	sq. ft.		sq. ft.		sq. ft.	
Basement & Finished Rooms Below Grade							
Functional Utility							
Heating/Cooling							
Energy Efficient Items							
Garage/Carport							
Porch/Patio/Deck							
Net Adjustment (Total)		☐ + ☐ -	$	☐ + ☐ -	$	☐ + ☐ -	$
Adjusted Sale Price of Comparables		Net Adj. % Gross Adj. %	$	Net Adj. % Gross Adj. %	$	Net Adj. % Gross Adj. %	$

I ☐ did ☐ did not research the sale or transfer history of the subject property and comparable sales. If not, explain

My research ☐ did ☐ did not reveal any prior sales or transfers of the subject property for the three years prior to the effective date of this appraisal.

Data source(s)

My research ☐ did ☐ did not reveal any prior sales or transfers of the comparable sales for the year prior to the date of sale of the comparable sale.

Data source(s)

Report the results of the research and analysis of the prior sale or transfer history of the subject property and comparable sales (report additional prior sales on page 3).

ITEM	SUBJECT	COMPARABLE SALE # 1	COMPARABLE SALE # 2	COMPARABLE SALE # 3
Date of Prior Sale/Transfer				
Price of Prior Sale/Transfer				
Data Source(s)				
Effective Date of Data Source(s)				

Analysis of prior sale or transfer history of the subject property and comparable sales

Summary of Sales Comparison Approach

Indicated Value by Sales Comparison Approach $

Indicated Value by: Sales Comparison Approach $ Cost Approach (if developed) $ Income Approach (if developed) $

This appraisal is made ☐ "as is", ☐ subject to completion per plans and specifications on the basis of a hypothetical condition that the improvements have been completed, ☐ subject to the following repairs or alterations on the basis of a hypothetical condition that the repairs or alterations have been completed, or ☐ subject to the following required inspection based on the extraordinary assumption that the condition or deficiency does not require alteration or repair:

Based on a complete visual inspection of the interior and exterior areas of the subject property, defined scope of work, statement of assumptions and limiting conditions, and appraiser's certification, my (our) opinion of the market value, as defined, of the real property that is the subject of this report is
$, as of   , which is the date of inspection and the effective date of this appraisal.

FIGURE 19.2 (CONTINUED)

Uniform Residential Appraisal Report

Uniform Residential Appraisal Report   File #

ADDITIONAL COMMENTS

COST APPROACH TO VALUE (not required by Fannie Mae)

Provide adequate information for the lender/client to replicate the below cost figures and calculations.

Support for the opinion of site value (summary of comparable land sales or other methods for estimating site value)

ESTIMATED ☐ REPRODUCTION OR ☐ REPLACEMENT COST NEW	OPINION OF SITE VALUE .... = $	
Source of cost data	Dwelling Sq. Ft. @ $	.... =$
Quality rating from cost service Effective date of cost data	Sq. Ft. @ $	.... =$
Comments on Cost Approach (gross living area calculations, depreciation, etc.)		
	Garage/Carport Sq. Ft. @ $	.... =$
	Total Estimate of Cost-New	.... = $
	Less Physical Functional External	
	Depreciation	=$( )
	Depreciated Cost of Improvements......................................	.... =$
	"As-is" Value of Site Improvements......................................	.... =$

Estimated Remaining Economic Life (HUD and VA only)   Years   Indicated Value By Cost Approach .... =$

INCOME APPROACH TO VALUE (not required by Fannie Mae)

Estimated Monthly Market Rent $ X Gross Rent Multiplier   = $ Indicated Value by Income Approach

Summary of Income Approach (including support for market rent and GRM)

PROJECT INFORMATION FOR PUDs (if applicable)

Is the developer/builder in control of the Homeowners' Association (HOA)? ☐ Yes ☐ No   Unit type(s) ☐ Detached ☐ Attached

Provide the following information for PUDs ONLY if the developer/builder is in control of the HOA and the subject property is an attached dwelling unit.

Legal name of project

Total number of phases   Total number of units   Total number of units sold

Total number of units rented   Total number of units for sale   Data source(s)

Was the project created by the conversion of an existing building(s) into a PUD? ☐ Yes ☐ No If Yes, date of conversion

Does the project contain any multi-dwelling units? ☐ Yes ☐ No Data source(s)

Are the units, common elements, and recreation facilities complete? ☐ Yes ☐ No If No, describe the status of completion.

Are the common elements leased to or by the Homeowners' Association? ☐ Yes ☐ No If Yes, describe the rental terms and options.

Describe common elements and recreational facilities

FIGURE 19.2 (CONTINUED)

Uniform Residential Appraisal Report

Uniform Residential Appraisal Report   File

This report form is designed to report an appraisal of a one-unit property or a one-unit property with an accessory unit; including a unit in a planned unit development (PUD). This report form is not designed to report an appraisal of a manufactured home or a unit in a condominium or cooperative project.

This appraisal report is subject to the following scope of work, intended use, intended user, definition of market value, statement of assumptions and limiting conditions, and certifications. Modifications, additions, or deletions to the intended use, intended user, definition of market value, or assumptions and limiting conditions are not permitted. The appraiser may expand the scope of work to include any additional research or analysis necessary based on the complexity of this appraisal assignment. Modifications or deletions to the certifications are also not permitted. However, additional certifications that do not constitute material alterations to this appraisal report, such as those required by law or those related to the appraiser's continuing education or membership in an appraisal organization, are permitted.

SCOPE OF WORK: The scope of work for this appraisal is defined by the complexity of this appraisal assignment and the reporting requirements of this appraisal report form, including the following definition of market value, statement of assumptions and limiting conditions, and certifications. The appraiser must, at a minimum: (1) perform a complete visual inspection of the interior and exterior areas of the subject property, (2) inspect the neighborhood, (3) inspect each of the comparable sales from at least the street, (4) research, verify, and analyze data from reliable public and/or private sources, and (5) report his or her analysis, opinions, and conclusions in this appraisal report.

INTENDED USE: The intended use of this appraisal report is for the lender/client to evaluate the property that is the subject of this appraisal for a mortgage finance transaction.

INTENDED USER: The intended user of this appraisal report is the lender/client.

DEFINITION OF MARKET VALUE: The most probable price which a property should bring in a competitive and open market under all conditions requisite to a fair sale, the buyer and seller, each acting prudently, knowledgeably and assuming the price is not affected by undue stimulus. Implicit in this definition is the consummation of a sale as of a specified date and the passing of title from seller to buyer under conditions whereby: (1) buyer and seller are typically motivated; (2) both parties are well informed or well advised, and each acting in what he or she considers his or her own best interest; (3) a reasonable time is allowed for exposure in the open market; (4) payment is made in terms of cash in U. S. dollars or in terms of financial arrangements comparable thereto; and (5) the price represents the normal consideration for the property sold unaffected by special or creative financing or sales concessions* granted by anyone associated with the sale.

*Adjustments to the comparables must be made for special or creative financing or sales concessions. No adjustments are necessary for those costs which are normally paid by sellers as a result of tradition or law in a market area; these costs are readily identifiable since the seller pays these costs in virtually all sales transactions. Special or creative financing adjustments can be made to the comparable property by comparisons to financing terms offered by a third party institutional lender that is not already involved in the property or transaction. Any adjustment should not be calculated on a mechanical dollar for dollar cost of the financing or concession but the dollar amount of any adjustment should approximate the market's reaction to the financing or concessions based on the appraiser's judgment.

STATEMENT OF ASSUMPTIONS AND LIMITING CONDITIONS: The appraiser's certification in this report is subject to the following assumptions and limiting conditions:

1. The appraiser will not be responsible for matters of a legal nature that affect either the property being appraised or the title to it, except for information that he or she became aware of during the research involved in performing this appraisal. The appraiser assumes that the title is good and marketable and will not render any opinions about the title.

2. The appraiser has provided a sketch in this appraisal report to show the approximate dimensions of the improvements. The sketch is included only to assist the reader in visualizing the property and understanding the appraiser's determination of its size.

3. The appraiser has examined the available flood maps that are provided by the Federal Emergency Management Agency (or other data sources) and has noted in this appraisal report whether any portion of the subject site is located in an identified Special Flood Hazard Area. Because the appraiser is not a surveyor, he or she makes no guarantees, express or implied, regarding this determination.

4. The appraiser will not give testimony or appear in court because he or she made an appraisal of the property in question, unless specific arrangements to do so have been made beforehand, or as otherwise required by law.

5. The appraiser has noted in this appraisal report any adverse conditions (such as needed repairs, deterioration, the presence of hazardous wastes, toxic substances, etc.) observed during the inspection of the subject property or that he or she became aware of during the research involved in performing this appraisal. Unless otherwise stated in this appraisal report, the appraiser has no knowledge of any hidden or unapparent physical deficiencies or adverse conditions of the property (such as, but not limited to, needed repairs, deterioration, the presence of hazardous wastes, toxic substances, adverse environmental conditions, etc.) that would make the property less valuable, and has assumed that there are no such conditions and makes no guarantees or warranties, express or implied. The appraiser will not be responsible for any such conditions that do exist or for any engineering or testing that might be required to discover whether such conditions exist. Because the appraiser is not an expert in the field of environmental hazards, this appraisal report must not be considered as an environmental assessment of the property.

6. The appraiser has based his or her appraisal report and valuation conclusion for an appraisal that is subject to satisfactory completion, repairs, or alterations on the assumption that the completion, repairs, or alterations of the subject property will be performed in a professional manner.

F I G U R E 19.2 (CONTINUED)

Uniform Residential Appraisal Report

Uniform Residential Appraisal Report

File #

APPRAISER'S CERTIFICATION: The Appraiser certifies and agrees that:

1. I have, at a minimum, developed and reported this appraisal in accordance with the scope of work requirements stated in this appraisal report.

2. I performed a complete visual inspection of the interior and exterior areas of the subject property. I reported the condition of the improvements in factual, specific terms. I identified and reported the physical deficiencies that could affect the livability, soundness, or structural integrity of the property.

3. I performed this appraisal in accordance with the requirements of the Uniform Standards of Professional Appraisal Practice that were adopted and promulgated by the Appraisal Standards Board of The Appraisal Foundation and that were in place at the time this appraisal report was prepared.

4. I developed my opinion of the market value of the real property that is the subject of this report based on the sales comparison approach to value. I have adequate comparable market data to develop a reliable sales comparison approach for this appraisal assignment. I further certify that I considered the cost and income approaches to value but did not develop them, unless otherwise indicated in this report.

5. I researched, verified, analyzed, and reported on any current agreement for sale for the subject property, any offering for sale of the subject property in the twelve months prior to the effective date of this appraisal, and the prior sales of the subject property for a minimum of three years prior to the effective date of this appraisal, unless otherwise indicated in this report.

6. I researched, verified, analyzed, and reported on the prior sales of the comparable sales for a minimum of one year prior to the date of sale of the comparable sale, unless otherwise indicated in this report.

7. I selected and used comparable sales that are locationally, physically, and functionally the most similar to the subject property.

8. I have not used comparable sales that were the result of combining a land sale with the contract purchase price of a home that has been built or will be built on the land.

9. I have reported adjustments to the comparable sales that reflect the market's reaction to the differences between the subject property and the comparable sales.

10. I verified, from a disinterested source, all information in this report that was provided by parties who have a financial interest in the sale or financing of the subject property.

11. I have knowledge and experience in appraising this type of property in this market area.

12. I am aware of, and have access to, the necessary and appropriate public and private data sources, such as multiple listing services, tax assessment records, public land records and other such data sources for the area in which the property is located.

13. I obtained the information, estimates, and opinions furnished by other parties and expressed in this appraisal report from reliable sources that I believe to be true and correct.

14. I have taken into consideration the factors that have an impact on value with respect to the subject neighborhood, subject property, and the proximity of the subject property to adverse influences in the development of my opinion of market value. I have noted in this appraisal report any adverse conditions (such as, but not limited to, needed repairs, deterioration, the presence of hazardous wastes, toxic substances, adverse environmental conditions, etc.) observed during the inspection of the subject property or that I became aware of during the research involved in performing this appraisal. I have considered these adverse conditions in my analysis of the property value, and have reported on the effect of the conditions on the value and marketability of the subject property.

15. I have not knowingly withheld any significant information from this appraisal report and, to the best of my knowledge, all statements and information in this appraisal report are true and correct.

16. I stated in this appraisal report my own personal, unbiased, and professional analysis, opinions, and conclusions, which are subject only to the assumptions and limiting conditions in this appraisal report.

17. I have no present or prospective interest in the property that is the subject of this report, and I have no present or prospective personal interest or bias with respect to the participants in the transaction. I did not base, either partially or completely, my analysis and/or opinion of market value in this appraisal report on the race, color, religion, sex, age, marital status, handicap, familial status, or national origin of either the prospective owners or occupants of the subject property or of the present owners or occupants of the properties in the vicinity of the subject property or on any other basis prohibited by law.

18. My employment and/or compensation for performing this appraisal or any future or anticipated appraisals was not conditioned on any agreement or understanding, written or otherwise, that I would report (or present analysis supporting) a predetermined specific value, a predetermined minimum value, a range or direction in value, a value that favors the cause of any party, or the attainment of a specific result or occurrence of a specific subsequent event (such as approval of a pending mortgage loan application).

19. I personally prepared all conclusions and opinions about the real estate that were set forth in this appraisal report. If I relied on significant real property appraisal assistance from any individual or individuals in the performance of this appraisal or the preparation of this appraisal report, I have named such individual(s) and disclosed the specific tasks performed in this appraisal report. I certify that any individual so named is qualified to perform the tasks. I have not authorized anyone to make a change to any item in this appraisal report; therefore, any change made to this appraisal is unauthorized and I will take no responsibility for it.

20. I identified the lender/client in this appraisal report who is the individual, organization, or agent for the organization that ordered and will receive this appraisal report.

Freddie Mac Form 70 March 2005   Page 5 of 6   Fannie Mae Form 1004 March 2005

F I G U R E   19.2 (CONTINUED)

Uniform Residential Appraisal Report

Uniform Residential Appraisal Report   File

21. The lender/client may disclose or distribute this appraisal report to: the borrower; another lender at the request of the borrower; the mortgagee or its successors and assigns; mortgage insurers; government sponsored enterprises; other secondary market participants; data collection or reporting services; professional appraisal organizations; any department, agency, or instrumentality of the United States; and any state, the District of Columbia, or other jurisdictions; without having to obtain the appraiser's or supervisory appraiser's (if applicable) consent. Such consent must be obtained before this appraisal report may be disclosed or distributed to any other party (including, but not limited to, the public through advertising, public relations, news, sales, or other media).

22. I am aware that any disclosure or distribution of this appraisal report by me or the lender/client may be subject to certain laws and regulations. Further, I am also subject to the provisions of the Uniform Standards of Professional Appraisal Practice that pertain to disclosure or distribution by me.

23. The borrower, another lender at the request of the borrower, the mortgagee or its successors and assigns, mortgage insurers, government sponsored enterprises, and other secondary market participants may rely on this appraisal report as part of any mortgage finance transaction that involves any one or more of these parties.

24. If this appraisal report was transmitted as an "electronic record" containing my "electronic signature," as those terms are defined in applicable federal and/or state laws (excluding audio and video recordings), or a facsimile transmission of this appraisal report containing a copy or representation of my signature, the appraisal report shall be as effective, enforceable and valid as if a paper version of this appraisal report were delivered containing my original hand written signature.

25. Any intentional or negligent misrepresentation(s) contained in this appraisal report may result in civil liability and/or criminal penalties including, but not limited to, fine or imprisonment or both under the provisions of Title 18, United States Code, Section 1001, et seq., or similar state laws.

SUPERVISORY APPRAISER'S CERTIFICATION: The Supervisory Appraiser certifies and agrees that:

1. I directly supervised the appraiser for this appraisal assignment, have read the appraisal report, and agree with the appraiser's analysis, opinions, statements, conclusions, and the appraiser's certification.

2. I accept full responsibility for the contents of this appraisal report including, but not limited to, the appraiser's analysis, opinions, statements, conclusions, and the appraiser's certification.

3. The appraiser identified in this appraisal report is either a sub-contractor or an employee of the supervisory appraiser (or the appraisal firm), is qualified to perform this appraisal, and is acceptable to perform this appraisal under the applicable state law.

4. This appraisal report complies with the Uniform Standards of Professional Appraisal Practice that were adopted and promulgated by the Appraisal Standards Board of The Appraisal Foundation and that were in place at the time this appraisal report was prepared.

5. If this appraisal report was transmitted as an "electronic record" containing my "electronic signature," as those terms are defined in applicable federal and/or state laws (excluding audio and video recordings), or a facsimile transmission of this appraisal report containing a copy or representation of my signature, the appraisal report shall be as effective, enforceable and valid as if a paper version of this appraisal report were delivered containing my original hand written signature.

APPRAISER

Signature_____
Name _____
Company Name _____
Company Address_____
_____
Telephone Number _____
Email Address_____
Date of Signature and Report_____
Effective Date of Appraisal _____
State Certification # _____
or State License # _____
or Other (describe) _____ State # _____
State _____
Expiration Date of Certification or License _____

ADDRESS OF PROPERTY APPRAISED

_____
_____

APPRAISED VALUE OF SUBJECT PROPERTY $ _____
LENDER/CLIENT
Name _____
Company Name _____
Company Address_____
_____
Email Address_____

SUPERVISORY APPRAISER (ONLY IF REQUIRED)

Signature _____
Name_____
Company Name _____
Company Address_____
_____
Telephone Number _____
Email Address_____
Date of Signature _____
State Certification # _____
or State License # _____
State _____
Expiration Date of Certification or License _____

SUBJECT PROPERTY

☐ Did not inspect subject property
☐ Did inspect exterior of subject property from street
    Date of Inspection _____
☐ Did inspect interior and exterior of subject property
    Date of Inspection _____

COMPARABLE SALES

☐ Did not inspect exterior of comparable sales from street
☐ Did inspect exterior of comparable sales from street
    Date of Inspection _____

IN PRACTICE The role of an appraiser is not to determine value. Rather, an appraiser develops a supportable and objective report about the value of the subject property. The appraiser relies on experience and expertise in valuation theories to evaluate market data. The appraiser does not establish the property's worth; instead, he or she verifies what the market indicates. This *verification* task is important to remember, particularly when dealing with a property owner who may lack objectivity about the realistic value of his or her property. The lack of objectivity also can complicate a salesperson's ability to list the property within the most probable range of market value. However, there are inherent conflicts between the appraiser's role and the real estate agent's and seller's roles. The agent and seller are seeking maximum value while looking ahead to the future. The appraiser analyzes current events and evaluates known future events, such as annexation or rezoning.

■ VALUE

> **Memory Tip**
> **Remember DUST**
>
> The four characteristics of value may be remembered by the acronym **DUST**: Demand, Utility, Scarcity, and Transferability.

To have **value** in the real estate market—that is, to have monetary worth based on desirability—a property must have the following characteristics:

- *Demand*—the need or desire for possession or ownership backed by the financial means to satisfy that need
- *Utility*—the property's usefulness for its intended purposes
- *Scarcity*—a finite supply
- *Transferability*—the relative ease with which ownership rights are transferred from one person to another

Market Value

Generally, the goal of an appraiser is to estimate or express an opinion of market value. The **market value** of real estate is the most probable price that a property should bring in a fair sale. This definition makes three assumptions. First, it presumes a competitive and open market. Second, the buyer and seller are both assumed to be acting prudently and knowledgeably. Third, market value depends on the price not being affected by unusual circumstances.

The following are essential to determining market value:

- The *most probable* price is not the average or highest price.
- The buyer and seller must be unrelated and acting without *undue pressure*.
- Both buyer and seller must be *well informed* about the property's use and potential, including both its defects and its advantages.
- A *reasonable time* must be allowed for exposure in the open market.
- Payment must be made in cash or its equivalent.
- The price must represent a normal consideration for the property sold, unaffected by special financing amounts or terms, services, fees, costs, or credits incurred in the market transaction.

> *Market value* is a reasonable opinion of a property's worth; *market price* is the actual selling price of a property; *cost* may not equal either market value or market price.

Market value versus market price   *Market value* is an opinion of value based on an analysis of data. The data may include not only an analysis of comparable sales but also an analysis of potential income, expenses, and replacement costs (less any depreciation). *Market price*, on the other hand, is what a property *actually* sells for—its sales price. In theory, market price should be the same as market value. Market price can be taken as accurate evidence of current market value, however, *only* if the conditions essential to market value exist. Sometimes, property may be sold below market value—for instance, when the seller is forced to sell quickly or when a sale is arranged between relatives.

Market value versus cost   An important distinction can be made between market value and *cost*. One of the most common misconceptions about valuing property is that cost represents market value. Cost and market value *may* be the same. In fact, when the improvements on a property are new, cost and value are likely to be equal. But more often, cost does *not* equal market value. For example, a homeowner may install a swimming pool for $20,000; however, the cost of the improvement may not add $20,000 to the value of the property.

Basic Principles of Value

A number of economic principles can affect the value of real estate. The most important are defined in the text that follows.

Anticipation   According to the principle of **anticipation,** value is created by the *expectation* that certain events will occur. Value can increase or decrease in anticipation of some future benefit or detriment. For instance, the value of a house may be affected if rumors circulate that an adjacent property may be converted to commercial use in the near future. If the property has been a vacant eyesore, it is possible that the neighboring home's value will increase. On the other hand, if the vacant property had been perceived as a park or playlot that added to the neighborhood's quiet atmosphere, the news of its replacement might cause the house's value to decline. The principle of anticipation is the foundation on which the income approach to value is based.

Change   No physical or economic condition remains constant. This is the principle of **change.** Real estate is subject to natural phenomena such as tornadoes, fires, and routine wear and tear. The real estate business is subject to market demands, like any other business. An appraiser must be knowledgeable about both the past and, the predictable future effects of natural phenomena and the behavior of the marketplace.

Competition   **Competition** is the interaction of supply and demand. Excess profits tend to attract competition. For example, the success of a retail store may cause investors to open similar stores in the area. This tends to mean less profit for all stores concerned unless the purchasing power in the area increases substantially.

Conformity The principle of **conformity** says that value is created when a property is in harmony with its surroundings. Maximum value is realized if the use of land conforms to existing neighborhood standards. In single-family residential neighborhoods, for instance, buildings should be similar in design, construction, size, and age.

Contribution Under the principle of **contribution,** the value of any part of a property is measured by its effect on the value of the whole. Installing a swimming pool, greenhouse, or private bowling alley may not add value to the property equal to the cost. On the other hand, remodeling an outdated kitchen or bathroom probably would.

Highest and best use The most profitable single use to which a property may be put, or the use that is most likely to be in demand in the near future, is the property's **highest and best use (HABU).** The use (known by the acronym PLEM) must be

- physically possible,
- legally permitted,
- economically or financially feasible, and
- most profitable or maximally productive.

The highest and best use of a site can change with social, political, and economic forces. For instance, a parking lot in a busy downtown area may not maximize the land's profitability to the same extent an office building might.

Increasing and diminishing returns The addition of improvements to land and structures increases value only to the assets' maximum value. Beyond that point, additional improvements no longer affect a property's value. As long as money spent on improvements produces an increase in income or value, the **law of increasing returns** applies. At the point where additional improvements do not increase income or value, the **law of diminishing returns** applies. No matter how much money is spent on the property, the property's value does not keep pace with the expenditures. For instance, a remodeled kitchen or bathroom might increase the value of a house; adding restaurant-quality appliances and gold faucets, however, would be a cost that the owner probably would not be able to recover.

Plottage The principle of **plottage** holds that merging or consolidating adjacent lots into a single larger one produces a greater total land value than the sum of the two sites valued separately. For example, two adjacent lots valued at $35,000 each might have a combined value of $90,000 if consolidated. The process of merging two separately owned lots under one owner is known as **assemblage.** *Plottage* is the amount value is increased by successful assemblage.

Regression and progression In general, the worth of a better-quality property is adversely affected by the presence of a lesser-quality property. This is known as the principle of **regression.** Thus, in a neighborhood of modest homes, a structure that is larger, better maintained, or more luxurious would tend to be valued in the same range as the less lavish homes. Conversely, under

---

Memory Tip
Remember HABU and PLEM

The order in which **highest and best use (HABU)** is analyzed can be remembered by using the acronym **PLEM:**
- Physically possible
- Legally permitted
- Economically feasible
- Most profitable

Plottage: The individual value of two adjacent properties may be greater if they are combined than if each is sold separately.

Regression is the lowering of a property's value owing to its neighbors.

Progression is the increasing of a property's value owing to its neighbors.

the principle of **progression,** the value of a modest home would be higher if it were located among larger, fancier properties.

Substitution   The principle of **substitution** says that the maximum value of a property tends to be set by how much it would cost to purchase an equally desirable and valuable substitute property. Substitution is the foundation of the sales comparison approach.

Supply and demand   The principle of **supply and demand** says that the value of a property depends on the number of properties available in the marketplace—the supply of the product. Other factors include the prices of other properties, the number of prospective purchasers, and the price buyers will pay.

■ THE THREE APPROACHES TO VALUE

To arrive at an accurate estimate of value, appraisers traditionally use three basic valuation techniques: the sales comparison approach, the cost approach, and the income approach. The three methods serve as checks against each other. Using them narrows the range within which the final estimate of value falls. Each method is generally considered most reliable for specific types of property.

The Sales Comparison Approach

In the **sales comparison approach** (also known as the **market data approach**), an estimate of value is obtained by comparing the property being appraised, the *subject property,* with recently sold *comparable properties,* that is, properties similar to the subject. Because no two parcels of real estate are exactly alike, each comparable property must be analyzed for differences and similarities between it and the subject property. This approach is a good example of the principle of substitution, discussed above. The **sales prices** of the comparables must be adjusted for any dissimilarities. The elements of comparison for which adjustments must be made include the following:

- *Property rights.* An adjustment must be made when less than fee simple, the full legal bundle of rights, is involved. This includes land leases, ground rents, life estates, easements, deed restrictions, and encroachments.
- *Financing concessions.* The financing terms must be considered, including adjustments for differences such as mortgage loan terms and owner financing or buydowns by a builder-developer.
- *Market conditions.* Interest rates, supply and demand, and other economic indicators must be analyzed.
- *Conditions of sale.* Adjustments must be made for motivational factors that would affect the sale, such as foreclosure, a sale between family members, or some nonmonetary incentive.
- *Market conditions since the date of sale.* An adjustment must be made if economic changes occur between the date of sale of the comparable property and the date of the appraisal.

■ *Location.* Similar properties might differ in price from neighborhood to neighborhood or even between locations within the same neighborhood.
■ *Physical features and amenities.* Physical features, such as the structure's age, size, and condition, may require adjustments.

The sales comparison approach is normally considered the most reliable of the three approaches in appraising single-family homes, where the intangible benefits may be difficult to measure otherwise. Most appraisals include a minimum of three comparable sales reflective of the subject property. An example of the sales comparison approach is shown in Table 19.1.

TABLE 19.1

Sales Comparison Approach to Value

	Subject Property: 155 Potter Drive	Comparables		
		A	B	C
Sales price		$260,000	$252,000	$265,000
Financing concessions	none	none	none	none
Date of sale		current	current	current
Location	good	same	poorer +6,500	same
Age	6 years	same	same	same
Size of lot	60' × 135'	same	same	larger –5,000
Landscaping	good	same	same	same
Construction	brick	same	same	same
Style	ranch	same	same	same
No. of rooms	6	same	same	same
No. of bedrooms	3	same	poorer +500	same
No. of baths	1½	same	same	better –500
Sq. ft. of living space	1,500	same	same	better –1,000
Other space (basement)	full basement	same	same	same
Condition—exterior	average	better –1,500	poorer +1,000	better –1,500
Condition—interior	good	same	same	better –500
Garage	2-car attached	same	same	same
Other improvements	none	none	none	none
Net adjustments		–1,500	+8,000	–8,500
Adjusted value		$258,500	$260,000	$256,500

Note: The value of a feature that is present in the subject but not in the comparable property is *added* to the sales price of the comparable. Likewise, the value of a feature that is present in the comparable but not in the subject property is *subtracted*. A good way to remember this is: CBS stands for "comp better subtract"; and CPA stands for "comp poor add." The adjusted sales prices of the comparables represent the probable range of value of the subject property. From this range, a single market value estimate can be selected.

The Cost Approach

The **cost approach** to value also is based on the principle of substitution. The cost approach consists of five steps:

1. Estimate the *value of the land* as if it were vacant and available to be put to its highest and best use. (Note that the value of the land is not subject to depreciation.)
2. Estimate the *current cost* of constructing buildings and improvements.
3. Estimate the *amount of accrued depreciation* resulting from the property's physical deterioration, external depreciation, and functional obsolescence.
4. *Deduct* the accrued depreciation (Step 3) from the construction cost (Step 2).
5. *Add* the estimated land value (Step 1) to the depreciated cost of the building and site improvements (Step 4) to arrive at the total property value.

■ **FOR EXAMPLE**

Value of the land	=	$50,000
Current cost of construction	=	$180,000
Accrued depreciation	=	$20,000
$180,000 – $20,000	=	$160,000
$50,000 + $160,000	=	$210,000

In this example, the *total property value* is $210,000.

There are two ways to look at the construction cost of a building for appraisal purposes: reproduction cost and replacement cost. **Reproduction cost** is the construction cost at current prices of an exact duplicate of the subject improvement, including both the benefits and the drawbacks of the property. **Replacement cost new** is the cost to construct an improvement similar to the subject property using current construction methods and materials, but not necessarily an exact duplicate. Replacement cost new is more frequently used in appraising older structures because it eliminates obsolete features and takes advantage of current construction materials and techniques.

An example of the cost approach to value, applied to the same property as in Table 19.1, is shown in Table 19.2.

Determining reproduction or replacement cost new   An appraiser using the cost approach computes the reproduction or replacement cost of a building using one of the following four methods:

1. **Square-foot method.** The cost per square foot of a recently built comparable structure is multiplied by the number of square feet (using exterior dimensions) in the subject building. The **square-foot method** is the most common and easiest method of cost estimation. Table 19.2 uses the square-foot method, which is also referred to as the *comparison method*. For some, usually nonresidential, properties such as warehouse space the cost per cubic foot of a recently built comparable structure is multiplied by the number of cubic feet in the subject structure.

TABLE 19.2

Cost Approach to Value

Subject Property: 155 Potter Drive		
Land Valuation: Size 60' × 135' @ $450 per front foot	=	$27,000
Plus site improvements: driveway, walks, landscaping, etc.	=	8,000
Total		$35,000
Building Valuation: Replacement Cost		
1,500 sq. ft. @ $85 per sq. ft. =	$127,500	
Less Depreciation:		
Physical depreciation		
Curable		
(items of deferred maintenance)		
exterior painting	$4,000	
Incurable (structural deterioration)	9,750	
Functional obsolescence	2,000	
External obsolescence	0	
Total Depreciation	$15,750	
Depreciated Value of Building		$111,750
Indicated Value by Cost Approach		$146,750

2. **Unit-in-place method.** In the **unit-in-place method,** the replacement cost of a structure is estimated based on the construction cost per unit of measure of individual building components, including material, labor, overhead, and builder's profit. Most components are measured in square feet, although items such as plumbing fixtures are estimated by cost. The sum of the components is the cost of the new structure.

3. **Quantity-survey method.** The quantity and quality of all materials (such as lumber, brick, and plaster) and the labor are estimated on a unit cost basis. These factors are added to indirect costs (for example, building permit, survey, payroll, taxes, and builder's profit) to arrive at the total cost of the structure.

   Because it is so detailed and time consuming, the **quantity-survey method** is usually used only in appraising historical properties. It is, however, the most accurate method of appraising new construction.

4. **Index method.** A factor representing the percentage increase of construction costs up to the present time is applied to the original cost of the subject property. Because it fails to take into account individual property variables, the **index method** is useful only as a check of the estimate reached by one of the other methods.

Depreciation In a real estate appraisal, **depreciation** is a loss in value due to all causes. It refers to a condition that adversely affects the value of an improvement to real property. Remember: Land does not depreciate—it retains its value indefinitely, except in such rare cases as downzoned urban parcels, improperly developed land, or misused farmland.

Depreciation is considered to be *curable* or *incurable,* depending on the contribution of the expenditure to the value of the property. For appraisal purposes (as opposed to depreciation for tax purposes) depreciation is divided into three classes, according to its cause:

1. **Physical deterioration.** A *curable* item is one in need of repair, such as painting (deferred maintenance), that is economically feasible and would result in an increase in value equal to or exceeding the cost. An item is *incurable* if it is a defect caused by physical wear and tear and its correction would not be economically feasible or contribute a comparable value to the building, such as a crack in the foundation. The cost of a major repair may not warrant the financial investment.

2. **Functional obsolescence.** *Obsolescence* means a loss in value from the *market's response* to the item. Outmoded or unacceptable physical or design features that are no longer considered desirable by purchasers are *curable*. Such features could be replaced or redesigned at a cost that would be offset by the anticipated increase in ultimate value. Outmoded plumbing, for instance, is usually easily replaced. Room function may be redefined at no cost if the basic room layout allows for it. A bedroom adjacent to a kitchen, for example, may be converted to a family room. But, currently undesirable physical or design features that could not be easily remedied because the cost of cure would be greater than its resulting increase in value are considered *incurable*. An office building that cannot be economically air-conditioned, for example, suffers from incurable functional obsolescence if the cost of adding air-conditioning is greater than its contribution to the building's value.

3. **External obsolescence.** If caused by negative factors not on the subject property, such as environmental, social, or economic forces, the depreciation is always *incurable*. The loss in value cannot be reversed by spending money on the property. For example, proximity to a nuisance, such as a polluting factory or a deteriorating neighborhood, is one factor that could not be cured by the owner of the subject property.

The easiest but least precise way to determine depreciation is the **straight-line method,** also called the *economic age-life method.* Depreciation is assumed to occur at an even rate over a structure's **economic life,** the period during which it is expected to remain useful for its original intended purpose. The property's cost is divided by the number of years of its expected economic life to derive the amount of annual depreciation.

For instance, a $420,000 property may have a land value of $240,000 and an improvement value of $180,000. If the improvement is expected to last 60 years, the annual straight-line depreciation would be $3,000 ($180,000 divided by 60 years). Such depreciation can be calculated as an annual dollar amount or as a percentage of a property's improvements.

The cost approach is most helpful in the appraisal of newer or special-purpose buildings such as schools, churches, and public buildings. Such properties are difficult to appraise using other methods because there are seldom enough local sales to use as comparables and because the properties do not ordinarily generate income.

Much of the functional obsolescence and all of the external obsolescence can be evaluated only by considering the actions of buyers in the marketplace.

The Income Approach

The **income approach** to value is based on the present value of the rights to future income. It assumes that the income generated by a property will determine the property's value. The income approach is used for valuation of income-producing properties such as apartment buildings, office buildings, and shopping centers and is based on anticipation. In estimating value using the income approach, an appraiser must take the following five steps:

1. Estimate annual *potential gross income*. An estimate of economic rental income must be made based on market studies. Current rental income may not reflect the current market rental rates, especially in the case of short-term leases or leases about to terminate. Potential income includes other income to the property from such sources as vending machines, parking fees, and laundry machines.

2. Deduct an appropriate allowance for vacancy and rent loss, based on the appraiser's experience, and arrive at the *effective gross income*.

3. Deduct the annual *operating expenses*, enumerated in Table 19.3, from the effective gross income to arrive at the annual *net operating income (NOI)*. Management costs are always included, even if the current owner manages the property. Mortgage payments (principal and interest) are *debt service* and are not considered operating expenses. Also, capital expenditures are not considered expenses; however, an allowance can be calculated representing the annual usage of each major capital item.

4. Estimate the price a typical investor would pay for the income produced by this particular type and class of property. This is done by estimating the rate of return (or yield) that an investor will demand for the investment of capital in this type of building. This rate of return is called the **capitalization rate** (or "cap" rate) and is determined by comparing the relationship of net operating income with the sales prices of similar properties that have sold in the current market. For example, a comparable property that is producing an annual net income of $15,000 is sold for $187,500. The capitalization rate is $15,000 divided by $187,500, or 8 percent. If other comparable properties sold at prices that yielded substantially the same rate, it may be concluded that 8 percent is the rate that the appraiser should apply to the subject property.

5. Apply the capitalization rate to the property's annual net operating income to arrive at the estimate of the property's value.

With the appropriate capitalization rate and the projected annual net operating income, the appraiser can obtain an indication of value by the income approach.

This formula and its variations are important in dealing with income property:

Income ÷ Rate = Value
Income ÷ Value = Rate
Value × Rate = Income

These formulas may be illustrated graphically as

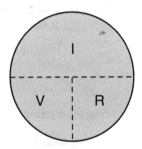

Net Operating Income ÷ Capitalization Rate = Value
Example: $18,000 income ÷ 9% cap rate = $200,000 value or $18,000
income ÷ 8% cap rate = $225,000 value

Note the relationship between the rate and value. As the rate goes down, the value increases.

A very simplified version of the computations used in applying the income approach is illustrated in Table 19.3.

T A B L E 19.3		
Income Capitalization Approach to Value		

Potential Gross Annual Income		$60,000
Market rent (100% capacity)		
Income from other sources (vending machines and pay phones)	+600	
	$60,600	
Less vacancy and collection losses (estimated) @4%		−2,424
Effective Gross Income		$58,176
Expenses:		
Real estate taxes	$9,000	
Insurance	1,000	
Heat	2,500	
Maintenance	6,400	
Utilities, electricity, water, gas	800	
Repairs	1,200	
Decorating	1,400	
Replacement of equipment	800	
Legal and accounting	600	
Advertising	300	
Management	3,000	
Total		$27,000
Annual Net Operating Income		$31,176
Capitalization rate = 10% (overall rate)		

Capitalization of annual net income: $31,176 ÷ 0.10 = $311,760
Income Value by Income Approach = $311,760

Gross rent or gross income multipliers Certain properties, such as single-family homes and two-unit buildings, are not purchased primarily for income. As a substitute for a more elaborate income capitalization analysis, the **gross rent multiplier (GRM)** and **gross income multiplier (GIM)** are often used in the appraisal process. Each relates the sales price of a property to its rental income.

Because single-family residences usually produce only rental incomes, the gross rent multiplier is used. This relates a sales price to monthly rental income. However, commercial and industrial properties generate income from many other sources (rent, concessions, escalator clause income, and so forth), and they are valued using their annual income from all sources.

The formulas are as follows:

1. For five or more residential units, and commercial or industrial property:

   Sales Price ÷ Gross Income = Gross Income Multiplier (GIM)
   or
2. For one to four residential units:

   Sales Price ÷ Gross Rent = Gross Rent Multiplier (GRM)

For example, if a home recently sold for $155,000 and its monthly rental income was $1,250, the GRM for the property would be computed

   $155,000 ÷ $1,250 = 124 GRM

To establish an accurate GRM, an appraiser must have recent sales and rental data from at least four properties that are similar to the subject property. The resulting GRM can then be applied to the estimated fair market rental of the subject property to arrive at its market value. The formula would be

   Rental Income × GRM = Estimated Market Value

Table 19.4 shows some examples of GRM comparisons.

Reconciliation

When the three approaches to value are applied to the same property, they normally produce three separate indications of value. (For instance, compare Table 19.1 with Table 19.2.) **Reconciliation** is the art of analyzing and

TABLE 19.4	Comparable No.	Sales Price ÷	Monthly Rent =	GRM
Gross Rent Multiplier	1	$280,000	$1,800	155.55
	2	243,000	1,350	180
	3	287,000	2,000	143.50
	4	262,500	1,675	156.72
	Subject	?	1,750	?

Note: Based on an analysis of these comparisons, a GRM of 156.72 seems reasonable for homes in this area. In the opinion of an appraiser, then, the estimated value of the subject property would be $1,750 × 156.72, or $274,260.

effectively weighing the findings from the three approaches. In reconciliation, an appraiser not only explains the appropriateness of each approach, but also the relative reliability of the data within each approach in line with the type of value sought. The appraiser should also explain how the data reflects the market functions.

The process of reconciliation is *not* simply taking the average of the three estimates of value. An *average* implies that the data and logic applied in each of the approaches are equally valid and reliable and should therefore be given equal weight. In fact, however, certain approaches are more valid and reliable with some kinds of properties than with others.

For example, in appraising a home, the income approach is rarely valid, and the cost approach is of limited value unless the home is relatively new. Therefore, the sales comparison approach is usually given greatest weight in valuing single-family residences. In the appraisal of income or investment property, the income approach normally is given the greatest weight. In the appraisal of churches, libraries, museums, schools, and other special-use properties, where little or no income or sales revenue is generated, the cost approach usually is assigned the greatest weight. From this analysis, or reconciliation, a single estimate of market value is produced.

■ GEORGIA APPRAISER CLASSIFICATIONS

In Georgia

Georgia issues four appraiser classifications. The first classification, the state-registered real property appraiser, has the simplest set of requirements. The other three classifications have the same general framework of requirements but the magnitude of the requirements increases as the individual chooses to move up to a higher certification.

State-Registered Real Property Appraiser

A registered appraiser may perform appraisals on any type of property except when the purpose of the appraisal is for use in a federally related financial transaction.

If an applicant has never held a classification, the applicant begins as a **state-registered real property appraiser.** Then the applicant may become a licensed or certified appraiser.

In order to qualify to become an applicant for an appraiser classification or approval, an applicant must

- be at least 18 years old;
- be a resident of Georgia, unless the applicant has complied with nonresidency provisions;
- have attained the level of education according to the Georgia Real Estate Appraisers Board's rule and regulations;

- have complied with statutory requirements regarding any criminal convictions;
- furnish evidence of completing instructional hours in any course the Board requires; and
- satisfactorily pass an examination approved by the Board.

Failure to meet any of these requirements can be sufficient grounds for denying a classification or approval without a hearing.

State-Licensed Real Property Appraiser (SLRPA)

A **state-licensed real property appraiser** may perform any appraisal that is not to be used in a federally related financial transaction and may perform appraisals for use in a federally related financial transaction in the following categories:

1. Non-complex one- to four-unit residential properties where the value of the financial transaction does not exceed $1,000,000
2. Any type of property where the transaction value is less than $250,000

In federally related transactions, licensed appraisers may not appraise real estate where a development analysis/appraisal is necessary and utilized.

State-Certified Residential Real Property Appraiser (SCRRPA)

A **state-certified residential real property appraiser** may perform any appraisal that is not to be used in a federally related financial transaction and may perform appraisals for use in a federally related financial transaction in the following categories:

1. One to four residential units without regard to transaction value or complexity
2. Any type of property where the transaction value is less than $250,000

State-Certified Residential Real Property Appraiser (SCRRPA)

A **state-certified general real property appraiser** may appraise any type of property for any purpose.

For a Summary of Permitted Appraisal Activity prepared by the Georgia Real Estate Appraisers Board, see *www.grec.state.ga.us/PDFS/Appraiser/ApprActivity. pdf*.

■ KEY POINT REVIEW

Appraisal is an estimate or opinion of **value** based on supportable evidence and appraisal methods;

■ defined by **Uniform Standards of Appraisal Practice (USPAP)** set by the **Appraisal Standards Board** of the **Appraisal Foundation.**

An **appraiser** must be state-licensed or certified for an appraisal performed as part of a **federally related transaction.**

A **competitive market analysis (CMA)** is a report by a real estate salesperson of market statistics, but it is not an appraisal.

A **broker's price opinion (BPO)** may be used in a non-federally related transaction.

Value is created by <u>d</u>emand, <u>u</u>tility, <u>s</u>carcity, <u>t</u>ransferability of property **(DUST). Market value** is the most probable price property should bring in a fair sale, but not necessarily the same as **price** paid, or **cost.**

A **sales comparison approach (market data approach)** makes use of sales of properties comparable (referred to as **comps**) to the property that is the subject of the appraisal by adding or subtracting value of a feature present or absent in the subject property versus the comp.

The **cost approach** estimates current **reproduction** or **replacement cost** of constructing building and other property improvements using the square-foot method, the unit-in-place method, the quantity-survey method, or the index method;

■ and estimates **accrued depreciation** using the **straight line method (economic age-life method)** *or* by estimating items of **physical deterioration, functional obsolescence,** or **external obsolescence.**

The **income approach** is based on present value of right to future income and uses the following five steps:

1. Estimate annual potential **gross income.**
2. Deduct allowance for vacancy and rent loss to find **effective gross income.**
3. Deduct annual operating expenses to find **net operating income (NOI).**
4. Estimate **rate of return (capitalization rate** or **cap rate)** for subject by analyzing cap rates of similar properties.
5. Derive estimate of subject's market value by applying cap rate to annual NOI using the formula **Income ÷ Rate = Value.**

Reconciliation is the process by which the validity and reliability of the results of the approaches to value are weighed objectively to determine the appraiser's **final opinion of value.**

In Georgia In Georgia, there are four appraiser classifications:

1. State-registered real property appraiser
   — Appraise any type of property, except one that involves a federally related financial transaction
   — Begin appraising in this classification
   — Requirements include: be 18 and a resident of Georgia, unless non-residency requirements are met; attain education at level required by Board; comply with statutory provisions regarding any criminal convictions; furnish evidence of completing required education; and pass exam
   — The Georgia Appraiser Board requires active appraisers complete 14 classroom hours during each renewal period

2. State-licensed real property appraiser (SLRPA)
   — Appraise any type of property, including federally related financial transactions for non-complex one- to four-unit residential properties where value of transaction is less than one million dollars, and any type of property where the transaction value is less than $250,000
   — When development analysis/appraisal is necessary, appraiser may not appraise federally related transaction

3. State-certified residential real property appraiser (SCRRPA)
   — Appraise any type of property, including federally related financial transactions for one to four residential units without regard to transaction value or complexity, and any type of property where transaction value is less than $250,000

4. State-certified general real property appraiser (SCGRPA)
   — Appraise any type of property for any purpose

■ RELATED WEB SITES

American Society of Appraisers: *www.appraisers.org*
American Society of Farm Managers and Rural Appraisers: *www.asfmra.org*
Appraisal Foundation: *www.appraisalfoundation.org*
Appraisal Institute: *www.appraisalinstitute.org*
Georgia Real Estate Appraisers Board, Summary of Permitted Appraisal
      Activity: *www.grec.state.ga.us/PDFS/Appraiser/ApprActivity.pdf*
Georgia Real Estate Commission and Appraisers Board:
      www.grec.state.ga.us/greab/appraisers.html
International Right of Way Association: *www.irwaonline.org*
National Association of Independent Fee Appraisers: *www.naifa.com*
National Association of Master Appraisers: *www.masterappraisers.org*

CHAPTER 19 QUIZ

1. Which of the following appraisal methods uses a rate of investment return?
   a. Sales comparison approach
   b. Cost approach
   c. Income approach
   d. Gross income multiplier method

2. The characteristics of value include which of the following?
   a. Competition
   b. Scarcity
   c. Anticipation
   d. Balance

3. 457 and 459 Tarpepper Street are adjacent vacant lots, each worth approximately $50,000. If their owner sells them as a single lot, however, the combined parcel will be worth $120,000. What principle does this illustrate?
   a. Substitution
   b. Plottage
   c. Regression
   d. Progression

4. The amount of money a property commands in the marketplace is its
   a. intrinsic value.
   b. market price.
   c. subjective value.
   d. book value.

5. A homeowner constructs an eight-bedroom brick house with a tennis court, a greenhouse, and an indoor pool in a neighborhood of modest two-bedroom and three-bedroom frame houses on narrow lots. The value of this house is MOST likely to be affected by what principle?
   a. Progression
   b. Assemblage
   c. Change
   d. Regression

6. In Question 5, the owners of the lesser-valued houses in the neighborhood may find that the values of their homes are affected by what principle?
   a. Progression
   b. Increasing returns
   c. Competition
   d. Regression

7. For appraisal purposes, accrued depreciation is NOT caused by
   a. functional obsolescence.
   b. physical deterioration.
   c. external obsolescence.
   d. accelerated depreciation.

8. The term *reconciliation* refers to which of the following?
   a. Loss of value due to any cause
   b. Separating the value of the land from the total value of the property to compute depreciation
   c. Analyzing the results obtained by the different approaches to value to estimate a final estimate of value
   d. The process by which an appraiser determines the highest and best use for a parcel of land

9. One method an appraiser can use to estimate a building's cost as new construction involves the estimated cost of the materials needed to build the structure, plus labor and indirect costs. This is called the
   a. square-foot method.
   b. quantity-survey method.
   c. cubic-foot method.
   d. unit-in-place method.

10. If a property's annual net income is $24,000 and it is valued at $300,000, what is its capitalization rate?
    a. 8 percent
    b. 10.5 percent
    c. 12 percent
    d. 15 percent

11. Which of the following is NOT used by an appraiser using the income approach to value?
    a. Annual net operating income
    b. Capitalization rate
    c. Accrued depreciation
    d. Annual gross income

12. An appraiser asked to estimate the value of an existing strip shopping center would probably give the MOST weight to which one of the following approaches to value?
    a. Cost approach
    b. Sales comparison approach
    c. Income approach
    d. Index method

13. The market value of a parcel of real estate is
    a. an estimate of its future benefits.
    b. the amount of money paid for the property.
    c. an estimate of the most probable price it should bring.
    d. its value without improvements.

14. Capitalization is the process by which annual net operating income is used to
    a. determine cost.
    b. estimate value.
    c. establish depreciation.
    d. determine potential tax value.

15. From the reproduction or replacement cost of a building, the appraiser deducts depreciation, which represents
    a. the remaining economic life of the building.
    b. remodeling costs to increase rentals.
    c. loss of value due to any cause.
    d. costs to modernize the building.

16. All of the following factors would be important in comparing properties under the sales comparison approach to value EXCEPT
    a. differences in dates of sale.
    b. differences in financing terms.
    c. differences in appearance and condition.
    d. differences in original cost.

17. An appraiser estimates that it would require 4,000 cubic feet of concrete, 10,000 feet of lumber, and $15,000 worth of copper pipe to replace a structure. The appraiser also estimates other factors, such as material, labor, overhead, and builder's profit. Which method of determining reproduction or replacement cost is this appraiser using?
    a. Square-foot method
    b. Quantity-survey method
    c. Index method
    d. Unit-in-place method

18. Which principle of value indicates that a developer's very profitable real estate project will attract others to engage in similar activity in the same area and thus drive down profits?
    a. Anticipation
    b. Competition
    c. Value
    d. Progression

19. Change, contribution, plottage, and substitution are some of the basic principles that affect what aspect of real estate?
    a. Demand
    b. Depreciation
    c. Value
    d. Supply

20. Gaslight fixtures in every unit of an apartment building would result in depreciation due to which of the following?
    a. Curable physical deterioration
    b. Curable functional obsolescence
    c. Incurable external obsolescence
    d. Incurable functional obsolescence

21. Which of the following methods of estimating reproduction or replacement cost new is generally used primarily as a check on the result reached using another method?
    a. Square-foot method
    b. Quantity-survey method
    c. Index method
    d. Unit-in-place method

22. What is the beginning appraisal classification one must start with in Georgia?
    a. State-classified real property appraiser
    b. State-licensed real property appraiser
    c. State-certified real property appraiser
    d. State-registered real property appraiser

23. A rental property in Decatur, Georgia, with four units (a quadraplex) has a monthly rent of $900 per unit, a net operating income of $20,000, and a current market value of $220,000. What is the GRM for this property?
    a. 0.016
    b. 0.091
    c. 11.0
    d. 61.1

24. Which of the following constitutes an unfair trade practice in Georgia?
    a. A licensee who holds an appraiser's license gives his appraisal opinion to a landlord.
    b. A state-licensed real property appraiser provides an appraisal on HUD property valued at $190,000.
    c. A real estate salesperson gives Tom, his friend, an appraisal opinion of his cabin.
    d. A state-certified residential real property appraiser gives an appraisal on commercial property valued at $2.5 million.

25. If a rental property in Buford, Georgia, with four units has a monthly rent of $900 per unit, a net operating income of $20,000 and a current market value of $220,000, the capitalization rate for this property is
    a. 0.016.
    b. 0.091.
    c. 11.0.
    d. 61.1.

Land-Use Controls and Property Development

■ **LEARNING OBJECTIVES** *When you have finished reading this chapter, you should be able to:*

■ **identify** the various types of public and private land-use controls.

■ **describe** how a comprehensive plan influences local real estate development.

■ **explain** the various issues involved in subdivision.

■ **distinguish** the function and characteristics of building codes and zoning ordinances.

■ **define** the following *key terms:*

buffer zone	developer	planned unit development
building code	enabling acts	(PUD)
certificate of occupancy	Georgia Land Sales Act	plat
clustering	gridiron	restrictive covenants
comprehensive plan	impact fees	subdivider
conditional-use permit	Interstate Land Sales Full	subdivision
curvilinear	Disclosure Act	taking
deed restriction	nonconforming use	variance
density zoning		zoning ordinances

■ LAND-USE CONTROLS

Land use is controlled and regulated through public and private restrictions and through the direct ownership of land by federal, state, and local governments. Over the years, the government's policy has been to encourage private ownership of land.

Home ownership is often referred to as the *American Dream*. It is necessary, however, for a certain amount of land to be owned by the government for such uses as municipal buildings, state legislative houses, schools, and military stations. Government ownership may also serve the public interest through urban renewal efforts, public housing, and streets and highways. Often, the only way to ensure that enough land is set aside for recreational and conservation purposes is through direct government ownership in the form of national and state parks and forest preserves. Beyond this sort of direct ownership of land, however, most government controls on property occur at the local level.

The states' *police power* is their inherent authority to create regulations needed to protect the public health, safety, and welfare. The states delegate to counties and local municipalities the authority to enact ordinances in keeping with general laws. The increasing demands placed on finite natural resources have made it necessary for cities, towns, and villages to increase their limitations on the private use of real estate. There are now controls over noise, air, and water pollution as well as population density.

■ THE COMPREHENSIVE PLAN

Local governments establish development goals by creating a **comprehensive plan**. This is also referred to as a *master plan*. Municipalities and counties develop plans to control growth and development. Each plan includes the municipality's, or another government body's, objectives for the future and the strategies and timing for those objectives to be implemented. For instance, a community may want to ensure that social and economic needs are balanced with environmental and aesthetic concerns. The comprehensive plan usually includes the following basic elements:

- *Land use,* that is, a determination of how much land may be proposed for residence, industry, business, agriculture, traffic and transit facilities, utilities, community facilities, parks and recreational facilities, floodplains, and areas of special hazards
- *Housing needs* of present and anticipated residents, including rehabilitation of declining neighborhoods as well as new residential developments
- *Movement of people and goods,* including highways and public transit, parking facilities, and pedestrian and bikeway systems
- *Community facilities and utilities* such as schools, libraries, hospitals, recreational facilities, fire and police stations, water resources, sewerage, waste treatment and disposal, storm drainage, and flood management

■ *Energy conservation* to reduce energy consumption and promote the use of renewable energy sources

The preparation of a comprehensive plan involves surveys, studies, and analyses of housing, demographic, and economic characteristics and trends. The municipality's planning activities may be coordinated with other government bodies and private interests to achieve orderly growth and development.

■ **FOR EXAMPLE** After the Great Chicago Fire of 1871 reduced most of the city's downtown to rubble and ash, the city engaged planner Daniel Burnham to lay out a design for Chicago's future. The resulting Burnham Plan of orderly boulevards linking a park along Lake Michigan with other large parks and public spaces throughout the city established an ideal urban space. The plan is still being implemented today.

■ ZONING

Zoning regulates and controls how land is used. **Zoning ordinances** are local laws that implement the comprehensive plan and regulate and control the use of land and structures within designated land-use districts. If the comprehensive plan is the big picture, zoning is the details. Zoning affects such things as

■ permitted uses of each parcel of land,
■ lot sizes,
■ types of structures,
■ building heights,
■ setbacks (the minimum distance away from streets or sidewalks that structures may be built),
■ style and appearance of structures,
■ density (the ratio of land area to structure area), and
■ protection of natural resources.

Zoning ordinances cannot be static; they must remain flexible to meet the changing needs of society.

■ **FOR EXAMPLE** In many large cities, factories and warehouses sit empty. Some cities have begun changing the zoning ordinances for such properties to permit new residential or commercial developments in areas once zoned strictly for heavy industrial use. Coupled with tax incentives, the changes lure developers back into the cities. The resulting housing is modern, conveniently located, and affordable. Simple zoning changes can help revitalize whole neighborhoods in big cities.

No nationwide or statewide zoning ordinances exist. Rather, zoning powers are conferred on municipal governments by state **enabling acts**. State and federal governments may, however, regulate land use through special legislation such as scenic easement, coastal management, and environmental laws.

Zoning Classifications

Land is divided into zones. The zones are identified by a coding system that outlines how the land may be used according to the code. Common zoning classifications include C for commercial, R for residential, and A for agriculture. There are subcategories in the classifications, and some land may be zoned for mixed use.

A **planned unit development** (PUD) is a development where land is set aside for mixed use purposes, such as residential, commercial, and public areas. Zoning regulations may be modified for PUDs.

Zoning Ordinances

Zoning ordinances have traditionally classified land use into residential, commercial, industrial, and agricultural. These land-use areas are further divided into subclasses. For example, residential areas may be subdivided to provide for detached single-family dwellings, semidetached structures containing not more than four dwelling units, walkup apartments, highrise apartments, and so forth.

To meet both the growing demand for a variety of housing types and the need for innovative residential and nonresidential development, municipalities are adopting ordinances for subdivisions and planned residential developments. Some municipalities also use **buffer zones**, such as landscaped parks and playgrounds, to screen residential areas from nonresidential zones. Certain types of zoning that focus on special land-use objectives are used in some areas. These include

- *bulk zoning* to control density and avoid overcrowding by imposing restrictions such as setbacks, building heights, and percentage of open area or by restricting new construction projects;
- *aesthetic zoning* to specify certain types of architecture for new buildings; and
- *incentive zoning* to ensure that certain uses are incorporated into developments, such as requiring the street floor of an office building to house retail establishments.

Constitutional issues and zoning ordinances Zoning can be a highly controversial issue. Among other things, it often raises questions of constitutional law. The preamble of the U.S. Constitution provides for the promotion of the general welfare, but the Fourteenth Amendment prevents the states from depriving "any person of life, liberty, or property, without due process of law." How is a local government to enact zoning ordinances that protect public safety and welfare without violating the constitutional rights of property owners?

Any land-use legislation that is destructive, unreasonable, arbitrary, or confiscatory usually is considered void. Furthermore, zoning ordinances must not violate the various provisions of the constitution of the state in which the real estate is located. Tests commonly applied in determining the validity of ordinances require that the

- power be exercised in a *reasonable manner;*
- provisions be *clear and specific;*
- ordinances be *nondiscriminatory;*
- ordinances promote *public health, safety, and general welfare* under the *police power* concept; and
- ordinances *apply to all property* in a *similar manner.*

Taking   The concept of **taking** comes from the *takings clause* of the Fifth Amendment to the U.S. Constitution. The clause reads, "nor shall private property be taken for public use, without just compensation." This means that when land is taken for public use through the government's power of eminent domain or condemnation, the owner must be compensated. In general, no land is exempt from government seizure. The rule, however, is that the government cannot seize land without paying for it. This payment is referred to as *just compensation*—compensation that is just, or fair.

Inverse condemnation is an action brought by a property owner seeking just compensation for land taken for a public use where it appears that the taker of the property does not intend to bring eminent domain proceedings. The property is condemned because its use and value have been diminished due to an adjacent property's public use, such as an airport or highway. For example, property along a newly constructed highway may be inversely condemned. While the property itself was not used in constructing the highway, the property value may be significantly diminished due to the construction of the highway close to the property. The property owner may bring an inverse condemnation action to be compensated for the loss. See Chapter 7 for further discussion of eminent domain.

It is sometimes very difficult to determine what level of compensation is fair in any particular situation. The compensation may be negotiated between the owner and the government, or the owner may seek a court judgment setting the amount.

IN PRACTICE   One method used to determine just compensation is the *before-and-after method.* This method is used primarily where a portion of an owner's property is seized for public use. The value of the owner's remaining property after the taking is subtracted from the value of the whole parcel before the taking. The result is the total amount of compensation due to the owner.

Zoning Permits

Zoning laws are generally enforced through the use of permits. Compliance with zoning can be monitored by requiring that property owners obtain permits before they begin any development. A permit will not be issued unless a proposed development conforms to the permitted zoning, among other requirements. Zoning permits are usually required before building permits can be issued.

Zoning hearing board   Zoning hearing boards (or zoning boards of appeal) have been established in most communities to hear testimony (positive and negative) about the effects a zoning ordinance may have on specific parcels of property. Petitions for variances or exceptions to the zoning law may be presented to an appeal board.

Impact fees   Many communities are now charging **impact fees** to developers to pay for capital improvements necessitated by increased population, such as schools, roads, utilities, and public safety.

Nonconforming use   Frequently, a lot or an improvement does not conform to the zoning use because it existed before the enactment or amendment of the zoning ordinance. Such a **nonconforming use** may be allowed to continue legally as long as it complies with the regulations governing nonconformities in the local ordinance, or until the improvement is destroyed or torn down, or until the current use is abandoned. If the nonconforming use is allowed to continue indefinitely, it is considered to be *grandfathered* into the new zoning.

■ **F O R   E X A M P L E**   Under Pleasantville's old zoning ordinances, the C&E Store was well within a commercial zone. When the zoning map was changed to accommodate an increased need for residential housing in Pleasantville, C&E was grandfathered into the new zoning; that is, it was allowed to continue its successful operations, even though it did not fit the new zoning rules.

> **Conditional-use permits** allow nonconforming but related land uses.
>
> **Variances** permit prohibited land uses to avoid undue hardship.

Variances and conditional-use permits   Each time a plan or zoning ordinance is enacted, some property owners are inconvenienced and want to change the use of their property. Generally, these owners may appeal for either a **conditional-use permit** or a **variance** to allow a use that does not meet current zoning requirements.

A *conditional-use permit* (also known as a *special-use permit*) usually is granted to a property owner to allow a special use of property that is defined as an *allowable conditional use within that zone*, such as a house of worship or day-care center in a residential district. For a conditional-use permit to be appropriate, the intended use must meet certain standards set by the municipality. Historic preservation districts often require specific use permits.

A *variance*, on the other hand, permits a landowner to use his or her property in a manner that is strictly prohibited by the existing zoning. Variances provide relief if zoning regulations deprive an owner of the reasonable use of his or her property. To qualify for a variance, the owner must demonstrate the unique circumstances that make the variance necessary. In addition, the owner must prove that he or she is harmed and burdened by the regulations. A variance might also be sought to provide relief if existing zoning regulations create a physical hardship for the development of a specific property. For example, if an owner's lot is level next to a road, but slopes steeply 30 feet away from the road, the zoning board may allow a variance so the owner can build closer to the road than the setback allows.

In Georgia | In Georgia, conditional-use permits are issued by zoning boards only after public hearings. The neighbors of a proposed use must be given an opportunity to voice their opinions. Variances may be issued administratively or after a public hearing.

A property owner also can seek a change in the zoning classification of a parcel of real estate by obtaining an *amendment* to the district map or a zoning ordinance for that area; that is, the owner can attempt to have the zoning changed to accommodate his or her intended use of the property. The proposed amendment must be brought before a public hearing on the matter and approved by the governing body of the community.

■ BUILDING CODES AND CERTIFICATES OF OCCUPANCY

Most municipalities have enacted ordinances to specify construction standards that must be met when repairing or erecting buildings. These are called **building codes,** and they set the requirements for kinds of materials and standards of workmanship, sanitary equipment, electrical wiring, fire prevention, and the like.

A property owner who wants to build a structure or alter or repair an existing building usually must obtain a building permit. Through the permit requirement, municipal officials are made aware of new construction or alterations and can verify compliance with building codes and zoning ordinances. Inspectors will closely examine the plans and conduct periodic inspections of the work. Once the completed structure has been inspected and found satisfactory, the municipal inspector issues a **certificate of occupancy** or *occupancy permit*.

If the construction of a building or an alteration violates a *deed restriction* (discussed later in this chapter), the issuance of a building permit will not cure this violation. A building permit is merely evidence of the applicant's compliance with municipal regulations.

Similarly, communities with historic districts, or those that are interested in maintaining a particular *look* or character, may have *aesthetic ordinances*. These laws require that all new construction or restorations be approved by a special board. The board ensures that the new structures will blend in with existing building styles. Owners of existing properties may need to obtain approval to have their homes painted or remodeled.

IN PRACTICE   The subject of planning, zoning, and restricting the use of real estate is extremely technical, and the interpretation of the law is not always clear. Questions concerning any of these subjects in relation to real estate transactions should be referred to legal counsel. Furthermore, the landowner should be aware of the costs for various permits.

■ SUBDIVISION

Most communities have adopted **subdivision** and *land development ordinances* as part of their comprehensive plans. An ordinance includes provisions for submitting and processing subdivision plats. A major advantage of subdivision ordinances is that they encourage flexibility, economy, and ingenuity in the use of land. A **subdivider** is a person who buys undeveloped acreage and divides it into smaller lots for sale to individuals or developers or for the subdivider's own use. A **developer,** who may also be a subdivider, improves the land, constructs homes or other buildings on the lots, and sells them. Developing is generally a much more extensive activity than subdividing.

Regulation of Land Development

Just as no national zoning ordinance exists, no uniform planning and land development legislation affects the entire country. Laws governing subdividing and land planning are controlled by the state and local governing bodies where the land is located. Rules and regulations developed by government agencies have, however, provided certain minimum standards. Many local governments have established standards that are higher than the minimum standards.

Subdividers split up land into parcels.

Developers construct improvements on the subdivided parcels.

Land development plan   Before the actual subdividing can begin, the subdivider must go through the process of *land planning*. The resulting land development plan must comply with the municipality's comprehensive plan. Although comprehensive plans and zoning ordinances are not necessarily inflexible, a plan that requires them to be changed must undergo long, expensive, and frequently complicated hearings.

Plats   From the land development and subdivision plans, the subdivider draws plats. A **plat** is a detailed map that illustrates the geographic boundaries of individual lots. It also shows the blocks, sections, streets, public easements, and monuments in the prospective subdivision. A plat also may include engineering data and restrictive covenants. The plats must be approved by the municipality before they can be recorded. (See Figure 9.10 in Chapter 9 for an example of a subdivision plat map.) Once a plat is properly recorded, it may be used as an adequate description of real property. A developer is often required to submit an *environmental impact report* with the application for subdivision approval. This report explains what effect the proposed development will have on the surrounding area.

Subdivision Plans

In plotting out a subdivision according to local planning and zoning controls, a subdivider usually determines the size as well as the location of the individual lots. The maximum or minimum size of a lot is generally regulated by local ordinances and must be considered carefully.

The land itself must be studied, usually in cooperation with a surveyor, so that the subdivision takes advantage of natural drainage and land contours. A subdivider should provide for *utility easements* as well as easements for water and sewer mains.

Most subdivisions are laid out by use of *lots and blocks*. An area of land is designated as a block, and the area making up this block is divided into lots.

One negative aspect of subdivision development is the potential for increased tax burdens on all residents, both inside and outside the subdivision. To protect local taxpayers against the costs of a heightened demand for public services, many local governments strictly regulate nearly all aspects of subdivision development.

Subdivision Density

Zoning ordinances control land use. Such control often includes minimum lot sizes and population density requirements for subdivisions and land developments. For example, a typical zoning restriction may set the minimum lot area on which a subdivider can build a single-family housing unit at 10,000 square feet. This means that the subdivider can build four houses per acre. Many zoning authorities now establish special **density zoning** standards for certain subdivisions. Density zoning ordinances restrict the average maximum number of houses per acre that may be built within a particular subdivision. If the area is density zoned at an average maximum of four houses per acre, for instance, the subdivider may choose to *cluster* building lots to achieve an open effect. Regardless of lot size or number of units, the subdivider will be consistent with the ordinance as long as the average number of units in the development remains at or below the maximum density. This average is called *gross density*.

Street patterns   By varying street patterns and **clustering** housing units, a subdivider can dramatically influence the amount of open or recreational space in a development. Two of these patterns are the **gridiron** and **curvilinear** patterns. (See Figure 20.1.)

The *gridiron* pattern evolved out of the government **rectangular** survey system. This pattern features large lots, wide streets, and limited-use service alleys. Sidewalks are usually adjacent to the streets or separated from them by narrow grassy

F I G U R E   20.1

Street Patterns

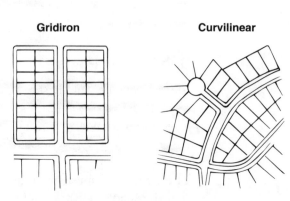

Gridiron   Curvilinear

areas. While the gridiron pattern provides for little open space and many lots may front on busy streets, it is an easy system to navigate.

The *curvilinear* system integrates major arteries of travel with smaller secondary and cul-de-sac streets carrying minor traffic. Curvilinear developments avoid the uniformity of the gridiron but often lack service alleys. The absence of straight-line travel and the lack of easy access tend to make curvilinear developments quieter and more secure. However, getting from place to place may be more challenging.

Clustering for open space   By slightly reducing lot sizes and clustering them around varying street patterns, a subdivider can house as many people in the same area as could be done using traditional subdividing plans but with substantially increased tracts of open space.

For example, compare the two subdivisions illustrated in Figure 20.2. Conventional Gardens is a conventionally designed subdivision containing 368 housing units. It uses 23,200 linear feet of street and leaves only 1.6 acres open for parkland. Contrast this with Cluster Estates. Both subdivisions are equal in size and terrain. But when lots are reduced in size and clustered around limited-access cul-de-sacs, the number of housing units remains nearly the same (366), with less street area (17,700 linear feet), and dramatically increased open space (23.5 acres). In addition, with modern building designs, this clustered plan could be modified to accommodate more than 1,000 town houses while retaining the attractive open spaces.

F I G U R E 20.2

Subdivision Styles

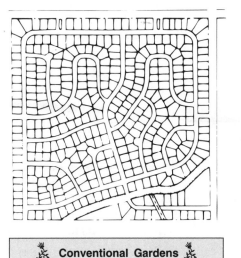

Conventional Gardens	Cluster Estates
12,500-square-foot lots	7,500-square-foot lots
368 housing units	366 housing units
1.6 acres of parkland	23.5 acres of parkland
23,200 linear feet of street	17,700 linear feet of street

■ PRIVATE LAND-USE CONTROLS

Not all restrictions on the use of land are imposed by government bodies. Certain restrictions to control and to maintain the desirable quality and character of a property or subdivision may be created by private entities, including the property owners themselves. These restrictions are separate from and in addition to the land-use controls exercised by the government. No private restriction can violate a local, state, or federal law.

Restrictive covenants   Restrictive covenants set standards for all the parcels within a defined subdivision. They usually govern the type, height, and size of buildings that individual owners can erect, as well as land use, architectural style, construction methods, setbacks, and square footage. The deed conveying a particular lot in the subdivision will refer to the plat or declaration of restrictions, thus limiting the title conveyed and binding all grantees. This is known as a **deed restriction.** Restrictions may have *time limitations*. A restriction might state that it is "effective for a period of 25 years from this date." After this time, it becomes inoperative. A time-limited covenant, however, may be extended by agreement.

In Georgia   In Georgia, restrictive covenants are also known as covenants, conditions, and restrictions, or "CCRs."

Restrictive covenants are usually considered valid if they are reasonable restraints that benefit all property owners in the subdivision—for instance, to protect property values or safety. If, however, the terms of the restrictions are too broad, they will be construed as preventing the free transfer of property. If any restrictive covenant or condition is judged unenforceable by a court, the estate will stand free from the invalid covenant or condition. Restrictive covenants cannot be for illegal purposes, such as for the exclusion of members of certain races, nationalities, or religions.

Private land-use controls may be more restrictive of an owner's use than the local zoning ordinances. The rule is that the more restrictive of the two takes precedence.

Private restrictions can be enforced in court when one lot owner applies to the court for an *injunction* to prevent a neighboring lot owner from violating the recorded restrictions. The court injunction will direct the violator to stop or remove the violation. The court retains the power to punish the violator for failing to obey. If adjoining lot owners stand idly by while a violation is committed, they can lose the right to an injunction by their inaction. The court might claim their right was lost through *laches*, that is, the legal principle that a right may be lost through undue delay or failure to assert it.

In Georgia   Under many modern CCRs, the restrictions may be enforced by a homeowners' association.

■ REGULATION OF LAND SALES

Just as the sale and use of property within a state are controlled by state and local governments, the sale of property in one state to buyers in another is subject to strict federal and state regulations.

Interstate Land Sales Full Disclosure Act

The federal **Interstate Land Sales Full Disclosure Act** regulates the interstate sale of unimproved lots. The act is administered by the Secretary of Housing and Urban Development (HUD), through the office of Interstate Land Sales registration. It is designed to prevent fraudulent marketing schemes that may arise when land is sold without being seen by the purchasers. (You may be familiar with stories about gullible buyers whose land purchases were based on glossy brochures shown by smooth-talking salespersons. When the buyers finally went to visit the "little pieces of paradise" they'd bought, they frequently found worthless swampland or barren desert.)

The act requires that developers file statements of record with HUD before they can offer unimproved lots in interstate commerce by telephone or through the mail. The statements of record must contain numerous disclosures about the properties.

Developers are also required to provide each purchaser or lessee of property with a printed report before the purchaser or lessee signs a purchase contract or lease. The report must disclose specific information about the land, including the

■ type of title being transferred to the buyer,
■ number of homes currently occupied on the site,
■ availability of recreation facilities,
■ distance to nearby communities,
■ utility services and charges, and
■ soil conditions and foundation or construction problems.

If the purchaser or lessee does not receive a copy of the report before signing the purchase contract or lease, he or she may have grounds to void the contract.

The act provides a number of exemptions. For instance, it does not apply to subdivisions consisting of fewer than 25 lots or to those in which the lots are of 20 acres or more. Lots offered for sale solely to developers also are exempt from the act's requirements, as are lots on which buildings exist or where a seller is obligated to construct a building within two years.

State Subdivided-Land Sales Laws

Many state legislatures have enacted their own subdivided-land sales laws. Some affect only the sale of land located outside the state to state residents. Other states' laws regulate sales of land located both inside and outside the states. These state land sales laws tend to be stricter and more detailed than the federal law. Licensees should be aware of the laws in their states and how they compare with federal law.

In Georgia

In Georgia, the **Georgia Land Sales Act** (O.C.G.A. 44-3-1 et seq.) regulates subdivided land located inside and outside the state. The act applies to subdivided land that is divided or proposed into 50 or more lots, parcels, units, or interests.

■ KEY POINT REVIEW

Land use is controlled and regulated through

- **public restrictions**—planning, zoning, building codes, subdivision plans;
- **private restrictions** imposed by deed; and
- **direct ownership** of land by federal, state, and local governments.

The **police power** of the state is its authority to create regulations to protect the **public health, safety, and welfare.** State **enabling acts** allow the power to enact laws authorized by the state's police power to be passed down to municipalities and other local governing authorities. Such regulations must be

- exercised in a **reasonable** manner;
- **clear and specific;**
- **nondiscriminatory;** and
- applicable to **all property** in a similar manner.

Land may be taken for public use through the government's **power of eminent domain** or **condemnation**, with the following limits:

- When a **taking** of property occurs, the Fifth Amendment to the U.S. Constitution requires that the owner be given **just (fair) compensation**.
- A property owner may claim compensation under **inverse condemnation** if an adjacent public land use diminishes the value of the owner's property, but the property has not been condemned for public use.

A **comprehensive plan (master plan)** created by a local government usually covers **land use, housing needs, movement of people and goods, community facilities** and **utilities,** and **energy conservation.**

Zoning ordinances are local laws implementing the land uses designated in the comprehensive plan and typically cover items such as **permitted uses,** lot sizes, types of structures, building heights, setbacks, **style and appearance** of structures, **density,** and protection of **natural resources**.

Zoning classifies property by uses and types, such as commercial, industrial, residential, agricultural, and **planned unit developments (PUDs).**

Other ways in which zoning is used include

- **buffer zones** screening residential from nonresidential areas;
- **bulk zoning** to control density;
- **aesthetic zoning** to specify certain types of architecture for new buildings; and
- **incentive zoning** to require certain uses in developments.

Zoning is enforced through the use of **permits,** and an individual case may be considered by a **zoning hearing board (or zoning board of appeals)** that may decide to

- allow a **nonconforming use** to continue;
- grant a **variance** from a zoning ordinance to permit a prohibited land use to avoid undue hardship; or
- grant a **conditional-use permit (special use permit).**

Building codes require **permits** for **new** construction and **remodeling** of or **additions** to existing construction. A **certificate of occupancy (occupancy permit)** is issued upon satisfactory completion of work for which the permit was issued.

Impact fees are charged to developers to subsidize the increased cost of services created by the development.

Subdivision and land development ordinances may be created by the state or may be made part of a local government's comprehensive plan. Subdivision and development usually include the following:

- **Subdivider** buys undeveloped acreage and divides it into smaller lots for sale to individuals or developers.
- **Developer** improves the land, constructs homes or other buildings, and sells them.
- **Plat map (subdivision map)** shows geographic boundaries of separate land parcels, usually by showing **blocks** of land divided into individual **lots.**
- **Subdivision plan** describes subdivision features and compliance with zoning and other laws, including **utility** easements, **density** zoning, **clustering,** and use of **gridiron** and **curvilinear** street patterns.
- **Private** land-use controls such as **restrictive covenants (deed restrictions)** placed in deeds to all property owners in a subdivision cannot impose an **illegal covenant or condition** and may be enforced by **injunction** against property owner in violation of covenant or restriction.
- If in conflict with local zoning, the **more restrictive** controls apply.

The **Federal Interstate Land Sales Full Disclosure Act** regulates the interstate sale of unimproved lots in subdivisions of 25 or more lots of less than 20 acres each. The law does not apply to subdivisions sold solely to developers. **State subdivision laws** may also apply to sales within the state of subdivisions located either inside or outside the state.

| In Georgia |

The Georgia Land Sales Act regulates subdivided land inside and outside the state.

■ RELATED WEB SITES

U.S. Department of Housing and Urban Development: Office of Housing: *www.hud.gov/offices/hsg/index.cfm*

U.S. Department of Housing and Urban Development: Housing Discrimination Complaints: *www.hud.gov/complaints/landsales.cfm*

CHAPTER 20 QUIZ

1. A subdivision declaration reads, "No property within this subdivision may be further subdivided for sale or otherwise, and no property may be used for other than single-family housing." This is an example of
    a. a restrictive covenant.
    b. an illegal reverter clause.
    c. R-1 zoning.
    d. a conditional-use clause.

2. A landowner who wants to use property in a manner that is prohibited by a local zoning ordinance but that would benefit the community can apply for which of the following?
    a. Conditional-use permit
    b. Prescriptive easement
    c. Occupancy permit
    d. Property dedication

3. What is *NOT* included in public land-use controls?
    a. Subdivision regulations
    b. Restrictive covenants
    c. Environmental protection laws
    d. Comprehensive plan specifications

4. Under its police powers, a municipality may regulate all of the following about housing in a development *EXCEPT*
    a. lot sizes.
    b. building heights.
    c. identity of ownership.
    d. type of structure.

5. The purpose of a building permit is to
    a. assert a deed's restrictive covenant.
    b. maintain municipal control over the volume of building.
    c. provide evidence of compliance with municipal regulations.
    d. show compliance with restrictive covenants.

6. Zoning powers are conferred on municipal governments in which of the following ways?
    a. By state enabling acts
    b. Through the master plan
    c. By popular local vote
    d. Through city charters

7. The town of East Westchester enacts a new zoning code. Under the new code, commercial buildings are not permitted within 1,000 feet of Lake Westchester. A commercial building that is permitted to continue in its former use even though it is built on the lakeshore is an example of
    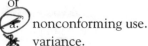
    a. nonconforming use.
    b. variance.
    c. special use.
    d. adverse possession.

8. To determine whether a location can be put to future use as a retail store, one would examine the
    a. building code.
    b. list of permitted nonconforming uses.
    c. housing code.
    d. zoning ordinance.

9. All of the following are legal deed restrictions *EXCEPT*
    a. types of buildings that may be constructed.
    b. allowable ethnic origins of purchasers.
    c. activities that are not to be conducted at the site.
    d. minimum size of buildings to be constructed.

10. A restriction in a seller's deed may be enforced by which of the following?
    a. Court injunction
    b. Zoning board of appeal
    c. City building commission
    d. State legislature

11. Glenda owns a large tract of land. After an adequate study of all the relevant facts, Glenda legally divides the land into 30 lots suitable for the construction of residences. In this situation, Glenda is acting as a(n)

    a. subdivider.
    b. developer.
    c. land planner.
    d. urban planner.

12. A map illustrating the sizes and locations of streets and lots in a subdivision is called a

    a. gridiron plan.
    b. survey.
    c. plat of subdivision.
    d. property report.

13. In the city of Glendale, developers are limited by law to constructing no more than an average of three houses per acre in any subdivision. What does this restriction regulate?

    a. Clustering
    b. Gross density
    c. Out-lots
    d. Covenants

14. The city of Northbend is laid out in a pattern of intersecting streets and avenues. All streets run north and south; all avenues run east and west. Northbend is an example of which street pattern style?

    a. Block plan
    b. Gridiron system
    c. Radial streets plan
    d. Intersecting system

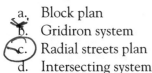

15. Permitted land uses and set-asides, housing projections, transportation issues, and objectives for implementing future controlled development would all be found in a community's

    a. zoning ordinance.
    b. comprehensive plan.
    c. enabling act.
    d. land-control law.

16. Which of the following items would usually NOT be shown on the plat for a new subdivision?

    a. Easements for sewer and water mains
    b. Land to be used for streets
    c. Numbered lots and blocks
    d. Prices of residential and commercial lots

17. Acorn Acres is a subdivision featuring spacious homes grouped on large cul-de-sac blocks connected to a central, winding road and surrounded by large, landscaped common areas. This is an example of which type of subdivision plan?

    a. Cluster plan
    b. Curvilinear system
    c. Rectangular street system
    d. Gridiron system

18. A subdivider can increase the amount of open or recreational space in a development by

    a. varying street patterns.
    b. meeting local housing standards.
    c. scattering housing units.
    d. eliminating multistory dwellings.

19. To protect the public from fraudulent interstate land sales, a developer involved in interstate land sales of 25 or more lots must

    a. provide each purchaser with a printed report disclosing details of the property.
    b. pay the prospective buyer's expenses to see the property involved.
    c. provide preferential financing.
    d. allow a 30-day cancellation period.

In Georgia

20. In Georgia, zoning variances may be issued

    a. administratively.
    b. after a public hearing.
    c. Both a and b
    d. Neither a nor b

Fair Housing and Ethical Practices

■ **LEARNING OBJECTIVES** *When you have finished reading this chapter, you should be able to:*

- ■ **identify** the classes of people who are protected against discrimination in housing by various federal laws.

- ■ **describe** how the Fair Housing Act is enforced.

- ■ **list** the exemptions allowed in the Fair Housing Act.

- ■ **explain** how fair housing laws address a variety of discriminatory practices and regulate real estate advertising.

- ■ **distinguish** the protections offered by the Fair Housing Act, the Housing and Community Development Act, the Fair Housing Amendments Act, the Equal Credit Opportunity Act, and the Americans with Disabilities Act.

- ■ **define** the following *key terms:*

Americans with Disabilities Act (ADA)	ethics	Title VIII of the Civil Rights Act of 1968
blockbusting	Fair Housing Act	U.S. Department of Housing and Urban Development (HUD)
Civil Rights Act of 1866	Fair Housing Amendments Act	
code of ethics	Georgia Fair Housing Law	
Equal Credit Opportunity Act (ECOA)	redlining	
	steering	

■ EQUAL OPPORTUNITY IN HOUSING

The purpose of civil rights laws that affect the real estate industry is to create a marketplace in which all persons of similar financial means have a similar range of housing choices. The goal is to ensure that everyone has the opportunity to live where he or she chooses. Owners, real estate licensees, apartment management companies, real estate organizations, lending agencies, builders, and developers must all take a part in creating this single housing market. Federal, state, and local fair housing or equal opportunity laws affect every phase of a real estate transaction, from listing to closing.

"All citizens of the United States shall have the same right in every state and territory as is enjoyed by white citizens thereof to inherit, purchase, lease, sell, hold, and convey real and personal property."

—Civil Rights Act of 1866

The U.S. Congress and the U.S. Supreme Court have created a legal framework that preserves the constitutional rights of all citizens. However, while the passage of laws may establish a code for public conduct, centuries of discriminatory practices and attitudes are not so easily changed. Real estate licensees cannot allow their own prejudices to interfere with the ethical and legal conduct of their profession. Similarly, the discriminatory attitudes of property owners or property seekers must not be allowed to affect compliance with the fair housing laws. Complying with fair housing laws is not always easy, and the pressure to avoid offending the person who pays the real estate commission or flat fee can be intense. However, just remember: *Failure to comply with fair housing laws is both a civil and criminal violation and constitutes grounds for disciplinary action against a licensee.*

In Georgia

The **Georgia Fair Housing Law** is substantially equivalent to federal fair housing laws. (See O.C.G.A. 8-3-200 et seq.)

IN PRACTICE Licensees must have a thorough knowledge of both state and federal fair housing laws. State laws may be stricter than the federal requirements and may provide protections for more classes of persons. State rules may provide for fines as well as the suspension or revocation of an offender's license.

The federal government's effort to guarantee equal housing opportunities to all U.S. citizens began with the passage of the **Civil Rights Act of 1866.** This law prohibits any type of discrimination based on race.

The U.S. Supreme Court's 1896 decision in *Plessy v. Ferguson* established the *separate but equal* doctrine of legalized racial segregation. A series of court decisions and federal laws in the 20 years between 1948 and 1968 attempted to address the inequities in housing that were the results of *Plessy.* Those efforts, however, tended to address only certain aspects of the housing market (such as federally funded housing programs). As a result, their impact was limited. Title VIII of the Civil Rights Act of 1968, however, prohibited specific discriminatory practices throughout the real estate industry.

■ FAIR HOUSING ACT

Title VIII of the Civil Rights Act of 1968 (called the federal Fair Housing Act) prohibited discrimination in housing based on race, color, religion, or national origin. In 1974, the Housing and Community Development Act added sex to the list of protected classes. In 1988, the Fair Housing Amendments Act included disability and familial status (that is, the presence of children). Today, these laws are known as the federal Fair Housing Act. (See Figure 21.1.) The **Fair Housing Act** prohibits discrimination on the basis of race, color, religion, sex, handicap, familial status, or national origin.

The act also prohibits discrimination against individuals because of their *association* with persons in the protected classes. This law is administered by the **U.S. Department of Housing and Urban Development (HUD).** HUD has established rules and regulations that further interpret the practices affected by the law. In addition, HUD distributes an equal housing opportunity poster. (See Figure 21.2.) The poster declares that the office in which it is displayed promises to adhere to the Fair Housing Act and pledges support for affirmative marketing and advertising programs.

In 1988, Congress passed the **Fair Housing Amendments Act** that expanded federal civil rights protections. In addition to race, color, religion, and national origin being protected classes, the act extended coverage to include families with children and those with physical or mental disabilities. The act also changed the penalties, making them more severe, and added damages, such as

FIGURE 21.1

Federal Fair Housing Laws

Legislation	Race	Color	Religion	National Origin	Sex	Age	Marital Status	Disability	Familial Status	Public Assistance Income
Civil Rights Act of 1866	●									
Fair Housing Act of 1968 (Title VIII)	●	●	●	●						
Housing and Community Development Act of 1974					●			●		
Fair Housing Amendments Act of 1988								●	●	
Equal Credit Opportunity Act of 1974 (lending)	●	●	●	●	●	●	●			●

FIGURE 21.2

Equal Opportunity Housing Poster

U.S. Department of Housing and Urban Development

EQUAL HOUSING
OPPORTUNITY

We Do Business in Accordance With the Federal Fair Housing Law

(The Fair Housing Amendments Act of 1988)

It is Illegal to Discriminate Against Any Person Because of Race, Color, Religion, Sex, Handicap, Familial Status, or National Origin

■ In the sale or rental of housing or residential lots

■ In advertising the sale or rental of housing

■ In the financing of housing

■ In the provision of real estate brokerage services

■ In the appraisal of housing

■ Blockbusting is also illegal

Anyone who feels he or she has been discriminated against may file a complaint of housing discrimination:
  1-800-669-9777 (Toll Free)
  1-800-927-9275 (TDD)

U.S. Department of Housing and Urban Development
Assistant Secretary for Fair Housing and Equal Opportunity
Washington, D.C. 20410

Previous editions are obsolete

form HUD-928.1A (2/2003)

those for noneconomic injuries (humiliation, embarrassment, inconvenience, mental anguish).

Later in 1995, another amendment was added to the act that repealed the facilities and services requirements designed to help older persons with physical and social needs. It also prohibits awarding monetary damages against those who reasonably relied, in good faith, on property being exempt from familial status provisions of the Fair Housing Act as housing for older persons.

IN PRACTICE   When HUD investigates a broker for discriminatory practices, it may consider failure to prominently display the equal housing opportunity poster in the broker's place of business as evidence of discrimination.

Table 21.1 describes the activities prohibited by the Fair Housing Act.

TABLE 21.1

Fair Housing Act Restrictions

Prohibited by Federal Fair Housing Act	Example
Refusing to sell, rent, or negotiate the sale or rental of housing	K owns an apartment building with several vacant units. When an Asian family asks to see one of the units, K tells them to go away.
Changing terms, conditions, or services for different individuals as a means of discriminating	S, a Roman Catholic, calls on a duplex and the landlord tells her the rent is $400 per month. When she talks to the other tenants, she learns that all the Lutherans in the complex pay only $325 per month.
Advertising any discriminatory preference or limitation in housing or making any inquiry or reference that is discriminatory in nature	A real estate agent places the following advertisement in a newspaper: "Just Listed! Perfect home for white family, near excellent parochial school!" A developer places this ad in an urban newspaper: "Sunset River Hollow–Dream Homes Just For You!" The ad is accompanied by a photo of several African American families.
Representing that a property is not available for sale or rent when in fact it is	J, who uses a wheelchair, is told that the house J wants to rent is no longer available. The next day, however, the For Rent sign is still in the window.
Profiting by inducing property owners to sell or rent on the basis of the prospective entry into the neighborhood of persons of a protected class	N, a real estate agent, sends brochures to homeowners in the predominantly white Ridgewood neighborhood. The brochures, which feature N's past success selling homes, include photos of racial minorities, population statistics, and the caption, "The Changing Face of Ridgewood."
Altering the terms or conditions of a home loan, or denying a loan, as a means of discrimination	A lender requires M, a divorced mother of two young children, to pay for a credit report. In addition, her father must cosign her application. After talking to a single male friend, M learns that he was not required to do either of those things, despite his lower income and poor credit history.
Denying membership or participation in a multiple listing service, a real estate organization, or another facility related to the sale or rental of housing as a means of discrimination	The Topper County Real Estate Practitioners' Association meets every week to discuss available properties and buyers. None of Topper County's black or female agents is allowed to be a member of the association.

Definitions

HUD's regulations provide specific definitions that clarify the scope of the Fair Housing Act.

Housing   The regulations define *housing* as a *dwelling* that includes any building or part of a building designed for occupancy as a residence by one or more families. This includes a single-family house, a condominium, a cooperative, or manufactured housing, as well as vacant land on which any of these structures will be built.

> The **Fair Housing Act prohibits discrimination** based on
> - race,
> - color,
> - religion,
> - sex,
> - handicap,
> - familial status, and
> - national origin.

Familial status   *Familial status* refers to the presence of one or more individuals who have not reached the age of 18 and who live with either a parent or guardian. The term includes a woman who is pregnant. In effect, it means that the Fair Housing Act's protections extend to families with children. Unless a property qualifies as housing for older persons, all properties must be made available to families with children under the same terms and conditions as to anyone else. It is illegal to advertise properties as being for adults only or to indicate a preference for a certain number of children. The number of persons permitted to reside in a property (the occupancy standards) must be based on objective factors such as sanitation or safety. Landlords cannot restrict the number of occupants to eliminate families with children.

■ **FOR EXAMPLE**   Gary owned an apartment building. One of his elderly tenants, Pam, was terminally ill. Pam requested that no children be allowed in the vacant apartment next door because the noise would be difficult for Pam to bear. Gary agreed and refused to rent to families with children. Even though Gary only wanted to make things easier for a dying tenant, Gary was nonetheless found to have violated the Fair Housing Act by discriminating on the basis of familial status.

Disability   A *disability* is a physical or mental impairment. The term includes having a history of, or being regarded as having, an impairment that substantially limits one or more of an individual's major life activities. Persons who have AIDS are protected by the fair housing laws under this classification.

IN PRACTICE   The federal fair housing law's protection of disabled persons does not include those who are current users of illegal or controlled substances. Nor are individuals who have been convicted of the illegal manufacture or distribution of a controlled substance protected under this law. However, the law does prohibit discrimination against those who are participating in addiction recovery programs. For instance, a landlord could lawfully discriminate against a cocaine addict but not against a member of Alcoholics Anonymous.

It is unlawful to discriminate against prospective buyers or tenants on the basis of disability. Landlords must make reasonable accommodations to existing policies, practices, or services to permit persons with disabilities to have equal enjoyment of the premises. For instance, it would be reasonable for a landlord to permit support animals (such as guide dogs) in a normally no-pets building or to provide a designated handicapped parking space in a generally unreserved lot.

People with disabilities must be permitted to make reasonable modifications to the premises at their own expense. Such modifications might include lowering door handles or installing bath rails to accommodate a person in a wheelchair. Failure to permit reasonable modification constitutes discrimination.

However, the law recognizes that some reasonable modifications might make a rental property undesirable to the general population. In such a case, the landlord is allowed to require that the property be restored to its previous condition when the lease period ends, reasonable wear and tear excepted. Where it is necessary to ensure with reasonable certainty that funds will be available to pay for the restorations at the end of the tenancy, the landlord may negotiate as part of a restoration agreement a provision requiring the tenant pay into an interest-bearing escrow account, over a reasonable period, a reasonable amount of money not to exceed the cost of the restorations. The interest in the account accrues to the benefit of the tenant. A landlord may not increase for handicapped persons any customarily required security deposit.

The law does not prohibit restricting occupancy exclusively to persons with handicaps in dwellings that are designed specifically for their accommodation.

For new construction of certain multifamily properties, a number of accessibility and usability requirements must be met under federal law. Access is specified for public and common-use portions of the buildings, and adaptive and accessible design must be implemented for the interior of the dwelling units. Some states have their own laws as well.

Racial discrimination. *Jones v. Mayer* In 1968, the Supreme Court heard the case of *Jones v. Alfred H. Mayer Company*, 392 U.S. 409 (1968). In its decision, the court upheld the Civil Rights Act of 1866. This decision is important because although the federal Fair Housing Act exempts individual homeowners and certain groups, the 1866 law prohibits all racial discrimination without exception. Where race is involved, no exceptions apply. This decision is also important because it prohibited racial discrimination in the sale or rental of privately held property.

The U.S. Supreme Court has expanded the definition of the term *race* to include ancestral and ethnic characteristics, including certain physical, cultural, or linguistic characteristics that are shared by a group with a common national origin. These rulings are significant because discrimination on the basis of race, as it is now defined, affords due process of complaints under the provisions of the Civil Rights Act of 1866.

IN PRACTICE A real estate agent or broker is not obligated to provide ethnic-diversity information to homebuyers. In a 2001 case from Ohio, *Hannah v. Sibcy Cline Realtors*, the issues were whether an agent or broker had the fiduciary duty to (1) inform a client whether a neighborhood was ethnically diverse, or (2) direct the client to resources that provided such information. The court concluded that while an agent or broker might choose to provide such information to a client or direct a client to resources about the ethnic diversity of a particular area, the agent or broker does so at his or her own risk, and there is no fiduciary duty to do so.

Exemptions to the Fair Housing Act

The federal Fair Housing Act covers most housing. However, in some circumstances, it provides for certain exemptions. The Fair Housing Act exempts

- owner-occupied buildings with no more than four units,
- single-family housing sold or rented without the use of a broker, and
- housing operated by organizations and private clubs that limit occupancy to members.

The sale or rental of a single-family home is exempt when

- the home is owned by an individual who does not own more than three such homes at one time (and who does not sell more than one every two years);
- a real estate broker or salesperson is *not* involved in the transaction; and
- discriminatory advertising is not used.

The rental of rooms or units is exempted in an owner-occupied one-family to four-family dwelling.

Note that dwelling units owned by religious organizations may be restricted to people of the same religion if membership in the organization is not restricted on the basis of race, color, or national origin. A private club that is not open to the public may restrict the rental or occupancy of lodgings that it owns to its members as long as the lodgings are not operated commercially. Membership in a private club must be open to people of all races, colors, and national origins.

The Fair Housing Act does not require that housing be made available to any individual whose tenancy would constitute a direct threat to the health or safety of other individuals or that would result in substantial physical damage to the property of others.

Housing for older persons   While the Fair Housing Act protects families with children, certain properties can be restricted to occupancy by elderly persons. Housing intended for persons age 62 or older or housing occupied by at least one person 55 years of age or older per unit (where 80 percent of the units are occupied by individuals 55 or older) is exempt from the familial status protection.

■ GEORGIA FAIR HOUSING LAW (O.C.G.A. 8-3-200 ET SEQ. AND RULES AND REGULATIONS 520-1-.13)

In Georgia   As noted early in this chapter, the Georgia Fair Housing Law is substantially similar to the Fair Housing Amendments Act of 1988. If the two are in conflict in any way, the federal law controls. The purposes of the Georgia Fair Housing Law are to

- provide for fair housing throughout Georgia;
- execute the policies embodied in Title VIII of the Civil Rights Act of 1968, as amended by the Fair Housing Amendments Act of 1988;

- safeguard all individuals from discrimination and promote the elimination of discrimination in any aspect relating to the sale, rental, or financing of dwellings or in the provision of brokerage services or facilities in connection with the sale or rental of a dwelling because of that individual's race, color, religion, sex, disability or handicap, familial status, or national origin; and
- promote the protection of each individual's interest in personal dignity and freedom from humiliation and the individual's freedom to take up residence wherever he or she chooses; to secure the state against domestic strife and unrest, which would menace its democratic institutions; to preserve the public safety, health, and general welfare; and to further the interests, rights, and privileges of individuals within the state.

In addition, under the Georgia Fair Housing Law, it is unlawful to

- refuse to sell or rent after a bona fide offer has been made, refuse to negotiate for the sale or rental of, or otherwise make unavailable or deny a dwelling because of race, color, religion, sex, disability, familial status, or national origin;
- make, print, or publish any notice, statement, or advertisement with respect to the sale or rental of a dwelling that indicates any preference, limitation, or discrimination based on race, color, religion, sex, disability, familial status, or national origin;
- represent to any person because of race, color, religion, sex, disability, familial status, or national origin that a dwelling is not available for inspection, sale, or rental when the dwelling is available; and
- induce (or attempt to) for profit any person to sell or rent a dwelling by representations regarding the entry or prospective entry into the neighborhood of a person of a particular race, color, religion, sex, familial status, or national origin or with a disability.

Nothing in the Georgia statute requires a dwelling be made available for rental or lease to an individual whose tenancy would constitute a direct threat to the health or safety of other individuals or whose tenancy would result in substantial physical damage to the property of others.

■ OTHER FEDERAL LAWS

Megan's Law

Federal legislation, known as Megan's Law, promotes the establishment of state registration systems to maintain residential information on every person who kidnaps children, commits sexual crimes against children, or commits sexually violent crimes. Upon release from prison, an offender must register his or her name with state authorities and indicate where he or she will be residing. Local law enforcement agencies may release relevant information about such an offender upon request if they deem it necessary for the protection of the public.

The **Equal Credit Opportunity Act prohibits discrimination in granting credit** based on
- race,
- color,
- religion,
- national origin,
- sex,
- marital status,
- age, and
- public assistance.

Megan's Law affects a licensee's duty of disclosure. In accordance with state law, a licensee may need to request that a customer sign a form indicating where the customer may obtain information about the sex offender registry. An index to sex offender registries in all 50 states can be found at *www.prevent-abuse-now.com/register.htm*. Typically, a licensee may be required to disclose information regarding a released offender if the licensee is aware that officials have informed individuals, groups, or the public that a sex offender resides in a particular area. (Megan's Law, in effect, creates another category of stigmatized property. See Chapter 4 for more information on stigmatized property.)

Equal Credit Opportunity Act

The federal **Equal Credit Opportunity Act (ECOA)** prohibits discrimination based on race, color, religion, national origin, sex, marital status, or age in the granting of credit. Note that the ECOA protects more classes of persons than the Fair Housing Act. The ECOA bars discrimination on the basis of marital status and age. For example, when deciding to give credit, a creditor may not consider your age, unless you're too young to sign contracts (generally 18 years of age), or your age is used in determining other factors important in creditworthiness, such as retirement. It also prevents lenders from discriminating against recipients of public assistance programs such as food stamps and Social Security. The ECOA is the only federal law that grants protection on age, marital status, and receipt of public assistance. As in the Fair Housing Act, the ECOA requires that credit applications be considered only on the bases of income, net worth, job stability, and credit rating.

Americans with Disabilities Act

Although the **Americans with Disabilities Act (ADA)** is not a housing or credit law, it still has a significant effect on the real estate industry. The ADA is important to licensees because it addresses the rights of individuals with disabilities in employment and public accommodations. Real estate brokers are often employers, and real estate brokerage offices are public spaces. The ADA's goal is to enable individuals with disabilities to become part of the economic and social mainstream of society. The ADA is discussed in Chapter 18.

Title I of the ADA requires that employers, including real estate licensees, make *reasonable accommodations* that enable an individual with a disability to perform essential job functions. Reasonable accommodations include making the work site accessible, restructuring a job, providing part-time or flexible work schedules, and modifying equipment that is used on the job. The provisions of the ADA apply to any employer with 15 or more employees.

IN PRACTICE   In 1999, the U.S. Supreme Court strictly limited the definition of *persons with disabilities* protected by the ADA. The decision excludes individuals whose disability, such as nearsightedness, can be corrected. In 2002, the U.S. Supreme Court narrowed the definition even further by stating that in determining whether a person is disabled, you need to ask whether the impairment(s) prevented or restricted the person from performing tasks that are of central importance to most people's daily lives.

Title III of the ADA provides for accessibility to goods and services for individuals with disabilities. While the federal civil rights laws have traditionally been viewed in the real estate industry as housing-related, the practices of licensees who deal with nonresidential property are significantly affected by the ADA. Because people with disabilities have the right to full and equal access to businesses and public services under the ADA, building owners and managers must ensure that any obstacle restricting this right is eliminated. The Americans with Disabilities Act Accessibility Guidelines (ADAAG) contain detailed specifications for designing parking spaces, curb ramps, elevators, drinking fountains, toilet facilities, and directional signs to ensure maximum accessibility. These requirements are discussed in Chapter 18.

The Americans with Disabilities Act requires reasonable accommodations in employment and access to goods, services, and public buildings.

ADA and the Fair Housing Act   The ADA exempts the following two types of property from its requirements:

1. Property that is covered by the Fair Housing Act
2. Property that is exempt from coverage by the Fair Housing Act

Some properties, however, are subject to both laws. For example, in an apartment complex, the rental office is a *place of public accommodation*. As such, it is covered by the ADA and must be accessible to persons with disabilities at the owner's expense. Individual rental units would be covered by the Fair Housing Act. If a tenant wished to modify the unit to make it accessible, he or she would be responsible for the cost.

Issues of housing and disability discrimination are often litigated in the courts. For example, in a 2005 case, *Wells v. State Manufactured Homes*, the landlord ordered the owner of a manufactured housing unit to move from the community because he claimed she violated the no-pets provision of her rental agreement. The landlord refused to make a reasonable accommodation for the owner's emotional disability by not permitting her to keep a dog. She filed suit under the ADA and Fair Housing Act. The court held that there was no violation of the Fair Housing Act or the ADA. The court said she failed to establish that her mental impairment substantially limited a major life activity and said that she was not disabled under the ADA.

IN PRACTICE   Real estate agents need a general knowledge of the ADA's provisions. It is necessary for a broker's workplace and employment policies to comply with the law. Amendments to the ADA are periodically introduced in the U.S. Congress, and it is important to be aware of changes in the law. Also, licensees who are building managers must ensure that the properties are legally accessible. However, ADA compliance questions may arise with regard to a client's property, too. Unless the agent is a qualified ADA expert, it is best to advise commercial clients to seek the services of an attorney, an architect, or a consultant who specializes in ADA issues. It is possible that an appraiser may be liable for failing to identify and account for a property's noncompliance.

■ FAIR HOUSING PRACTICES

For the civil rights laws to accomplish their goal of eliminating discrimination, licensees must apply them routinely. Of course, compliance also means that licensees avoid violating both the laws and the ethical standards of the profession. The following discussion examines the ethical and legal issues that confront real estate licensees.

Blockbusting

Blockbusting: Encouraging the sale or renting of property by claiming that the entry of a protected class of people into the neighborhood will negatively affect property values.

Blockbusting is the act of encouraging people to sell or rent their homes by claiming that the entry of a protected class of people into the neighborhood will have some sort of negative impact on property values. Blockbusting was a common practice during the 1950s and 1960s, as unscrupulous real estate agents profited by fueling "white flight" from cities to suburbs. Any message, however subtle, that property should be sold or rented because the neighborhood is "undergoing changes" is considered blockbusting. It is illegal to assert that the presence of certain persons will cause property values to decline, crime or antisocial behavior to increase, and the quality of schools to suffer.

A critical element in blockbusting, according to HUD, is the profit motive. A property owner may be intimidated into selling his or her property at a depressed price to the blockbuster, who in turn sells the property to another person at a higher price. Another term for this activity is *panic selling*. To avoid accusations of blockbusting, licensees should use good judgment when choosing locations and methods for marketing their services and soliciting listings.

Steering

Steering: Channeling home seekers toward or away from particular neighborhoods based on race, religion, national origin, or some other consideration.

Steering is the channeling of home seekers to particular neighborhoods. It also includes discouraging potential buyers from considering some areas. In either case, it is an illegal limitation of a purchaser's options.

Steering may be done either to preserve the character of a neighborhood or to change its character intentionally. Many cases of steering are subtle, motivated by assumptions or perceptions about a home seeker's preferences, based on some stereotype. Assumptions are not only dangerous—they are often *wrong*. The licensee cannot *assume* that a prospective home seeker expects to be directed to certain neighborhoods or properties. Steering anyone is illegal.

The number of immigrants in the United States continues to increase. According to the Joint Center for Housing Studies at Harvard University, immigrants have accounted for more than one-third of household growth in the United States since the 1990s, and will create a 39 percent increase in share of total homes owned by minorities by 2010. Any person involved in the real estate profession should learn to work and communicate well with buyers and sellers of different nationalities and cultures.

FIGURE 21.3

HUD's Advertising Guidelines

Category	Rule	Permitted	Not Permitted
Race Color National Origin	No discriminatory limitation/preference may be expressed	"master bedroom" "good neighborhood"	"white neighborhood" "no French"
Religion	No religious preference/limitation	"chapel on premises" "kosher meals available" "Merry Christmas"	"no Muslims" "nice Christian family" "near great Catholic school"
Sex	No explicit preference based on sex	"mother-in-law suite" "master bedroom" "female roommate sought"	"great house for a man" "wife's dream kitchen"
Handicap	No exclusions or limitations based on handicap	"wheelchair ramp" "walk to shopping"	"no wheelchairs" "able-bodied tenants only"
Familial Status	No preference or limitation based on family size or nature	"two-bedroom" "family room" "quiet neighborhood"	"married couple only" "no more than two children" "retiree's dream house"
Photographs or Illustrations of People	People should be clearly representative and nonexclusive	Illustrations showing ethnic races, family groups, singles, etc.	Illustrations showing only singles, African American families, elderly white adults, etc.

Advertising

No advertisement of property for sale or rent may include language indicating a preference or limitation. No exception to this rule exists, regardless of how subtle the choice of words. HUD's regulations cite examples that are considered discriminatory. (See Figure 21.3.) Note, however, that an advertisement that is gender specific, such as "female roommate sought," is allowed as long as the advertiser seeks to share living quarters with someone of the same gender. The media used for promoting property or real estate services cannot target one population to the exclusion of others. The selective use of media, whether by language or geography, may have discriminatory impact. For instance, advertising property only in a Korean-language newspaper tends to discriminate against non-Koreans. Similarly, limiting advertising to a cable television channel available only to white suburbanites may be construed as a discriminatory act. However, if an advertisement appears in general-circulation media as well, it may be legal.

IN PRACTICE The Fair Housing Council of Oregon filed a complaint against a local multiple listing service (MLS), charging that the phrase "adults only over 40" was included in the "Remarks" section of a condominium listing. While the condominium association's bylaws actually did contain the age restriction, the Fair Housing Council argued that including the phrase in the listing constituted discrimination against families with children in violation of the Fair Housing Act. The MLS paid $30,000 to settle with HUD, $20,000 of which went to support the antidiscrimination efforts of the Fair Housing Council of Oregon. The MLS also agreed to conduct regular computerized searches of its database for 67 different discriminatory words and phrases.

Appraising

Those who prepare appraisals or any statements of valuation, whether they are formal or informal, oral or written (including a competitive market analysis), may consider any factors that affect value. However, race, color, religion, national origin, sex, handicap, and familial status are not factors that may be considered.

Redlining

The practice of refusing to make mortgage loans or issue insurance policies in specific areas for reasons other than the economic qualifications of the applicants is known as **redlining.** Redlining refers to literally drawing a line around particular areas. This practice is often a major contributor to the deterioration of older neighborhoods. Redlining is frequently based on racial grounds rather than on any real objection to an applicant's creditworthiness; that is, the lender makes a policy decision that no property in a certain area is qualified for a loan, no matter who wants to buy it, because of the neighborhood's ethnic character. The federal Fair Housing Act prohibits discrimination in mortgage lending and covers not only the actions of primary lenders but also activities in the secondary mortgage market. A lending institution, however, can refuse a loan solely on sound economic grounds.

The Home Mortgage Disclosure Act requires all institutional mortgage lenders with assets in excess of $10 million and one or more offices in a given geographic area to make annual reports. The reports must detail all mortgage loans the institution has made or purchased, broken down by census tract. This law enables the government to detect patterns of lending behavior that might constitute redlining.

Intent and Effect

If an owner or real estate licensee *purposely* sets out to engage in blockbusting, steering, or other unfair activities, the intent to discriminate is *obvious*. However, owners and licensees must examine their activities and policies carefully to determine whether they have unintentional discriminatory *effects*. Whenever policies or practices result in unequal treatment of persons in the protected classes, they are considered discriminatory regardless of any innocent intent. This *effects test* is applied by regulatory agencies to determine whether an individual has been discriminated against.

Response to Concerns of Terrorism

In response to the concern of future terrorist attacks, landlords and property managers have been developing new security procedures. These procedures have focused on protecting buildings and residents. Landlords and property managers are also educating residents on signs of possible terrorist activity and how and where to report it. At the same time, landlords and property managers need to ensure that their procedures and education do not infringe on the fair housing rights of others.

For screening and rental procedures, it is unlawful to screen housing applicants on the basis of race, color, religion, sex, national origin, disability, or familial status. According to HUD, landlords and property managers have been inquiring about whether they can screen applicants on the basis of citizenship status. The Fair Housing Act does not specifically prohibit discrimination based solely on a person's citizenship status. Therefore, asking applicants for citizenship documentation or immigration status papers during the screening process does not violate the Fair Housing Act. For many years, the federal government has itself been asking for these documents in screening applicants for federally assisted housing. There is, however, a specific procedure for collecting and verifying citizenship papers provided by HUD.

■ **FOR EXAMPLE** Anita mentions in an interview with a landlord, Lester, that she left her native country to study at the local university. Lester is concerned about Anita's visa and whether it will expire during the lease term. Lester asks Anita for documentation to determine how long she is legally in the United States. Lester asks for this information, regardless of her race or national origin. Lester has not violated the Fair Housing Act.

Is it important that landlords and property managers apply and enforce all rules and procedures in a nondiscriminatory manner, treating all persons the same.

■ ENFORCEMENT OF THE FAIR HOUSING ACT

The federal Fair Housing Act is administered by the Office of Fair Housing and Equal Opportunity (OFHEO) under the direction of the secretary of HUD. Any aggrieved person who believes illegal discrimination has occurred may file a complaint with HUD within one year of the alleged act. HUD also may initiate its own complaint. Complaints may be reported to the Office of Fair Housing and Equal Opportunity, Department of Housing and Urban Development, Washington, DC 20410 or to the Office of Fair Housing and Equal Opportunity in care of the nearest HUD regional office. Complaints may also be submitted directly to HUD using an online form available on the HUD Web site.

Upon receiving a complaint, HUD initiates an investigation. Within 100 days of the filing of the complaint, HUD either determines that reasonable cause exists to bring a charge of illegal discrimination or dismisses the complaint. During this investigation period, HUD can attempt to resolve the dispute informally through conciliation. *Conciliation* is the resolution of a complaint by obtaining assurance that the person against whom the complaint was filed (the respondent) will remedy any violation that may have occurred. The respondent further agrees to take steps to eliminate or prevent discriminatory practices in the future. If necessary, these agreements can be enforced through civil action.

The aggrieved person has the right to seek relief through administrative proceedings. Administrative proceedings are hearings held before *administrative law judges (ALJs)*. An ALJ has the authority to award actual damages to the aggrieved person or persons and, if it is believed the public interest will be served, to impose monetary penalties. The penalties range from up to $11,000 for the first offense to $27,500 for a second violation within five years and $55,000 for further violations within seven years. The ALJ also has the authority to issue an injunction to order the offender to either do something (such as rent an apartment to the complaining party) or refrain from doing something (such as acting in a discriminatory manner).

The parties may elect civil action in federal court at any time within two years of the discriminatory act. For cases heard in federal court, unlimited punitive damages can be awarded in addition to actual damages. The court can also issue injunctions. As noted in Chapter 5, errors and omissions insurance carried by licensees normally does not pay for violations of the fair housing laws.

Whenever the attorney general has reasonable cause to believe that any person or group is engaged in a pattern or practice of resistance to the full enjoyment of any of the rights granted by the federal fair housing laws, he or she may file a civil action in any federal district court. Civil penalties may result in an amount not to exceed $50,000 for a first violation and an amount not to exceed $100,000 for second and subsequent violations.

Complaints brought under the Civil Rights Act of 1866 are taken directly to federal courts. The only time limit for action is a state's statute of limitations for *torts*—injuries one individual inflicts on another.

State and Local Enforcement Agencies

Many states and municipalities have their own fair housing laws. If a state or local law is *substantially equivalent* to the federal law, all complaints filed with HUD are referred to the local enforcement agencies. To be considered substantially equivalent, the local law and its related regulations must contain prohibitions comparable to those in the federal law. In addition, the state or locality must show that its local enforcement agency takes sufficient affirmative action in processing and investigating complaints and in finding remedies for discriminatory practices. It is important for all licensees to be aware of their states' fair housing laws, as well as applicable local ordinances.

In Georgia   If a violation of the fair housing law occurs in Georgia, the aggrieved party should contact one of the following agencies:

- Georgia Commission on Equal Opportunity, Fair Housing Division, 710 Cain Tower, 229 Peachtree Street, NE, Atlanta, GA 30303 (404-656-7708 or 800-473-OPEN)
- U.S. Department of HUD, Fair Housing and Equal Opportunity, 75 Spring Street, SW, Atlanta, GA 30303 (800-669-9777)

■ Atlanta Metro Fair Housing Services, 1083 Austin Ave. NE, P.O. Box 5467, Atlanta, GA 30307 (404-221-0147)

An aggrieved party can file a request for investigation on the Georgia Real Estate Commission's Web site, *www.grec.state.ga.us/PDFS/Other/ReqFor Investigation.pdf*.

Threats or Acts of Violence

Being a real estate agent is not generally considered a dangerous occupation. However, some licensees may find themselves the targets of threats or violence merely for complying with fair housing laws. The federal Fair Housing Act of 1968 protects the rights of those who seek the benefits of the open housing law. It also protects owners, brokers, and salespersons who aid or encourage the enjoyment of open housing rights. Threats, coercion, and intimidation are punishable by criminal action. In such a case, the victim should report the incident immediately to the local police and to the nearest office of the Federal Bureau of Investigation.

■ IMPLICATIONS FOR BROKERS AND SALESPEOPLE

The real estate industry is largely responsible for creating and maintaining an open housing market. Brokers and salespersons are a community's real estate experts. Along with the privilege of profiting from real estate transactions come the social and legal responsibilities to ensure that everyone's civil rights are protected. The reputation of the industry cannot afford *any* appearance that its licensees are not committed to the principles of fair housing. Licensees and the industry must be publicly conspicuous in their equal opportunity efforts. Establishing relationships with community and fair housing groups to discuss common concerns and develop solutions to problems is a constructive activity. What's more, a licensee who is active in helping to improve his or her community will earn a reputation for being a concerned citizen that may well translate into a larger client base.

Fair housing *is* the law. The consequences for anyone who violates the law are serious. In addition to the financial penalties, a real estate broker's or salesperson's livelihood will be in danger if his or her license is suspended or revoked. That the offense was unintentional is no defense. Licensees must scrutinize their practices and be particularly careful not to fall victim to clients or customers who expect to discriminate.

All parties deserve the same standard of service. Everyone has the right to expect equal treatment, within his or her property requirements, financial ability, and experience in the marketplace. A good test is to answer the question, "Are we doing this for everyone?" If an act is not performed consistently, or if an act affects some individuals differently from others, it could be construed as discriminatory. Standardized inventories of property listings, standardized criteria for financial qualification, and written documentation of all conversations are three effective means of self-protection for licensees.

HUD requires that its fair housing posters be displayed in any place of business where real estate is offered for sale or rent. Following HUD's advertising procedures and using the fair housing slogan and logo keep the public aware of the broker's commitment to equal opportunity.

Beyond being the law, fair housing is *good business*. It ensures the greatest number of properties available for sale and rent and the largest possible pool of potential purchasers and tenants.

■ PROFESSIONAL ETHICS

Professional conduct involves more than just complying with the law. In real estate, state licensing laws establish those activities that are illegal and therefore prohibited. However, merely complying with the letter of the law may not be enough: Licensees may perform *legally* yet not *ethically*. **Ethics** refers to a system of moral principles, rules, and standards of conduct. The ethical system of a profession establishes conduct that goes beyond merely complying with the law. These moral principles address the following two sides of a profession:

1. They establish standards for integrity and competence in dealing with consumers of an industry's services.
2. They define a code of conduct for relations within the industry, among its professionals.

Code of Ethics

One way that many organizations address ethics among their members or in their respective businesses is by adopting codes of professional conduct. A **code of ethics** is a written system of standards for ethical conduct. The code contains statements designed to advise, guide, and regulate behavior. To be effective, a code of ethics must be specific by dictating rules that either prohibit or demand certain behavior. Lofty statements of positive goals are not especially helpful. By including sanctions for violators, a code of ethics becomes more effective.

The National Association of REALTORS® (NAR), the largest trade association in the country with over one million members, adopted a Code of Ethics for its members in 1913. REALTORS® are expected to subscribe to this strict code of conduct. Not all licensees are REALTORS®—only those who are members of NAR. NAR has established procedures for professional standards committees at the local, state, and national levels of the organization to administer compliance. Practical applications of the Articles of the code are known as *Standards of Practice*. The Code of Ethics has proved helpful because it contains practical applications of business ethics. Many other professional organizations in the real estate industry have codes of ethics as well. In addition, many state real estate commissions are required by law to establish codes or canons of ethical behavior for their states' licensees.

■ KEY POINT REVIEW

Equal opportunity in housing is intended to create a marketplace in which all persons of similar financial means have a similar range of housing choices. Equal opportunity laws apply to owners, real estate licensees, apartment management companies, real estate organizations, lending agencies, builders, and developers.

The **Civil Rights Act of 1866**

■ guaranteed **equal housing opportunities** to all U.S. citizens;
■ was upheld in ***Jones v. Mayer,*** 1968; and
■ prohibits all racial discrimination with no exceptions.

Race—defined by the U.S. Supreme Court to include ancestral and ethnic characteristics, including certain physical, cultural, or linguistic characteristics that are shared by a group with a common national origin.

The **federal Fair Housing Act** is Title VIII of the **Civil Rights Act of 1968.**

■ Prohibits discrimination in housing based on **race, color, religion,** or **national origin** but **does not** prohibit discrimination based solely on a person's **citizenship status.**
■ Prohibits illegal activities that include **steering, blockbusting,** and **redlining.**

The **Housing and Community Development Act of 1974** added **sex** to the list of protected classes.

The **Fair Housing Amendments Act of 1988** added **disability** and **familial status** (presence of children) to protected classes and prohibits discrimination against an individual because of their association with persons in the protected classes.

■ Administered by HUD, which
  — establishes **rules and regulations** to further clarify the law; and
  — created the **equal housing opportunity poster.**

The **1995 Fair Housing Amendment repealed** facilities and services requirements designed for older persons and **prohibits** award of monetary damages against those who reasonably rely in good faith on property being exempt from familial status provisions of Fair Housing Act as housing for older persons.

Exemptions from the Fair Housing Act (but not the Civil Rights Act of 1866) include

■ rentals in **owner-occupied buildings** with no more than four units;
■ housing operated by **organizations and private clubs** that limit occupancy to members;
■ dwelling units; and
■ sale or rental of a **single-family home** when fewer than three homes are owned by an individual, discriminatory advertising is **not** used, and a real estate broker or salesperson is not involved in the transaction.

Housing is **exempt** from familial status protection if it is restricted to persons age 62 or older, or if 80 percent of units are occupied by persons over age **55**.

In Georgia   The **Georgia Fair Housing Law** is "substantially equivalent" to federal fair housing laws.

The **Equal Credit Opportunity Act of 1974** prohibits discrimination in **lending** on the basis of **race, color, religion, national origin, sex, age, marital status**, and **public assistance**. The **Home Mortgage Disclosure Act** requires annual reporting of institutional mortgage lenders with assets greater than $10 million.

Familial status extends fair housing protections to families with children, meaning a family in which one or more individuals under the age of 18 live with either a parent or guardian, or a woman who is pregnant. Note the following:

■ Families with children must be considered under the **same terms and conditions** as anyone else
■ The property cannot be **advertised** as *adults only*, and the ads cannot indicate limitation on the number of children accepted
■ **Limitations** on the number of persons permitted to reside in a house or apartment must be based on **objective factors** such as sanitation or safety

A **disability** is a physical or mental impairment that substantially limits one or more of an individual's major life activities. Persons with AIDS are considered disabled. Note the following:

■ The law **does not** protect individuals who are **current users** of illegal or controlled substances, or have been **convicted** of the illegal manufacture or distribution of a controlled substance. However, the law **does** protect individuals who are participating in addiction recovery programs.
■ **Reasonable modifications** to property to make it usable by an individual with a disability must be allowed, but the individual must return the property to its former condition on vacating it

The **Americans with Disabilities Act (ADA)** has the following characteristics:

■ **Title I** applies to **employers** with 15 or more employees and provides for employment of qualified job applicants regardless of disability, with **reasonable accommodations**.
■ **Title III** prohibits discrimination in **commercial properties and public accommodations**; access to facilities and services must be provided when **reasonably achievable** in existing buildings, with higher standard for new construction/remodeling.
■ Accessibility requirements for buildings are found in the **Americans with Disabilities Act Accessibility Guidelines (ADAAG)**.
■ The ADA exempts the following two types of property from its requirements: Property that is covered by the Fair Housing Act and property that is exempt from coverage by the Fair Housing Act.

Megan's Law promotes state registration systems to maintain home addresses of any person who has been incarcerated for kidnapping a child, committing a sexual crime against a child, or committing a sexually violent crime. Local law enforcement agencies may publish the location of registered offenders.

HUD enforces the Fair Housing Act in the following way:

- A **complaint** must be brought within **one year** of the alleged act of discrimination.
- Within **100 days** of filing complaint that is not referred by HUD to a local enforcement agency, HUD dismisses or goes forward with charge of illegal discrimination.
  - **Conciliation** is the resolution of a complaint in the 100-day period when respondent promises to remedy any violation.
- A complaint may be heard by an **administrative law judge (ALJ)** whose remedies include the following:
  - **Penalties** range up to
    - $11,000 for first offense
    - $27,500 for second violation within five years
    - $55,000 for further violations within seven years
  - **Injunction** may also be issued
- **Civil action** may be brought in federal court within **two years** of discriminatory act.

The **attorney general** may bring civil action in federal court and **penalties** may include a fine not to exceed

- $50,000 for first violation, and
- $100,000 for second and subsequent violations.

Complaints under the **Civil Rights Act of 1866** go directly to federal court.

Real estate professionals must act **legally** and **ethically** to ensure access to housing.

■ RELATED WEB SITES

Georgia Real Estate Commission, Request for Investigation: *www.grec.state. ga/PDFS/Other/ReqForInvestigation.pdf*

Legal Information Institute: *www.law.cornell.edu*

National Association of REALTORS®: Code of Ethics: *www.realtor.org*

National Fair Housing Advocate Online: *www.fairhousing.com*

U.S. Department of Housing and Urban Development: Accessibility Guidelines: *www.hud.gov/library/bookshelf09/fhefhag.cfm*

U.S. Department of Housing and Urban Development: Fair Housing: *www.hud.gov/groups/fairhousing.cfm*

U.S. Department of Housing and Urban Development: Fair Housing and Equal Opportunity: *www.hud.gov/offices/fhel/progdesc/title8.cfm*

U.S. Department of Housing and Urban Development: Fair Housing Laws and Executive Orders: *www.hud.gov/offices/fheo/FHLaws/index.cfm*

U.S. Department of Housing and Urban Development: Fair Housing Library: *www.hud.gov/library/bookshelf09/index.cfm*

U.S. Department of Housing and Urban Development: Fair Housing Logo (download): *www.hud.gov/library/bookshelf15/hudgraphics/fheologo.cfm*

U.S. Department of Housing and Urban Development: Frequently Asked Questions: *www.hud.gov/offices/fheo/disabilities/sect504faq.cfm*

U.S. Department of Housing and Urban Development: Housing Discrimination Complaints: *www.hud.gov/complaints/housediscrim.dfm*

U.S. Department of Housing and Urban Development: Public Service Announcement: *www.hud.gov/offices/fheo/adcampaign.cfm*

CHAPTER 21 QUIZ

1. Which of the following actions is legally permitted?
   a. Advertising property for sale only to a special group
   b. Altering the terms of a loan for a member of a minority group
   c. Refusing to make a mortgage loan to a minority individual because of a poor credit history
   d. Telling an individual that an apartment has been rented when in fact it has not

2. Which of the following statements is *TRUE* of complaints relating to the Civil Rights Act of 1866?
   a. They must be taken directly to federal courts.
   b. They are no longer reviewed in the courts.
   c. They are handled by HUD.
   d. They are handled by state enforcement agencies.

3. Why is the Civil Rights Act of 1866 unique?
   a. It has been broadened to protect the aged.
   b. It adds welfare recipients as a protected class.
   c. It contains "choose your neighbor" provisions.
   d. It provides no exceptions that would permit racial discrimination.

4. "I hear *they're* moving in. There goes the neighborhood! Better put your house on the market before values drop!" This is an example of what illegal practice?
   a. Steering
   b. Blockbusting
   c. Redlining
   d. Fraudulent advertising

5. The act of directing home seekers toward or away from particular areas either to maintain or to change the character of the neighborhood is
   a. blockbusting.
   b. redlining.
   c. steering.
   d. permitted under the Fair Housing Act of 1968.

6. A lender's refusal to lend money to potential homeowners attempting to purchase properties located in predominantly African American neighborhoods is known as
   a. redlining.
   b. blockbusting.
   c. steering.
   d. prequalifying.

7. All of the following would be permitted under the federal Fair Housing Act *EXCEPT*
   a. an expensive club in New York rents rooms only to members who are graduates of a particular university.
   b. the owner of a 20-unit residential apartment building rents to men only.
   c. a Catholic convent refuses to furnish housing for a Jewish man.
   d. an owner refuses to rent the other side of her duplex to a family with children.

8. A real estate broker wants to end racial segregation. As an office policy, the broker requires that salespersons show prospective buyers from racial or ethnic minority groups only properties that are in certain areas of town where few members of their groups currently live. The broker has prepared a map illustrating the appropriate neighborhoods for each racial or ethnic group. Through this policy, the broker hopes to achieve racial balance in residential housing. Which of the following statements is *TRUE* regarding this broker's policy?

   a. While the broker's policy may appear to constitute blockbusting, application of the effects test proves its legality.
   b. Because the effect of the broker's policy is discriminatory, it constitutes illegal steering regardless of the broker's intentions.
   c. The broker's policy clearly shows the intent to discriminate.
   d. While the broker's policy may appear to constitute steering, application of the intent test proves its legality.

9. If a mortgage lender discriminates against a loan applicant on the basis of marital status, it violates what law?

   a. ADA
   b. Civil Rights Act of 1866
   c. ECOA
   d. Fair Housing Act

10. Housing that qualifies for exemption from familial status provisions

   a. includes housing intended for persons 50 years old or older.
   b. includes a restriction that 80% of the units be occupied by persons 55 or older.
   c. is not permitted under the federal Fair Housing Act.
   d. is permitted for owner-occupied buildings with four or more units.

11. Which of the following statements describes the Supreme Court's decision in the case of *Jones v. Alfred H. Mayer Company*?

   a. Racial discrimination is prohibited by any party in the sale or rental of real estate.
   b. Sales by individual residential homeowners are exempted, provided the owners do not use brokers.
   c. Laws against discrimination apply only to federally related transactions.
   d. Persons with disabilities are a protected class.

12. After a broker takes a sale listing of a residence, the owner specifies that he will not sell his home to any Asian family. The broker should do which of the following?

   a. Advertise the property exclusively in Asian-language newspapers.
   b. Explain to the owner that the instruction violates federal law and that the broker cannot comply with it.
   c. Abide by the principal's directions despite the fact that they conflict with the fair housing laws.
   d. Require that the owner sign a separate legal document stating the additional instruction as an amendment to the listing agreement.

13. The fine for a first violation of the federal Fair Housing Act could be as much as

   a. $5,000.
   b. $27,500.
   c. $55,000.
   d. $11,000.

14. The following ad appeared in the newspaper: "For sale: 4 BR brick home; Redwood school district; excellent Elm Street location; short walk to St. John's Church, and right on the bus line. Move-in condition; priced to sell." Which statement is *TRUE*?

    a. The ad describes the property for sale and is very appropriate.

    b. The fair housing laws do not apply to newspaper advertising.

    c. The ad should state that the property is available to families with children.

    d. The ad should not mention St. John's Church.

15. Which of the following acts is *NOT* a violation of the Georgia Fair Housing Law?

    a. Stating a property is not for sale to one person when it in fact is for sale

    b. Raising the rent for one specific person but not for others

    c. Raising the conditions of a loan for one specific person but not for others

    d. Refusing to rent to a minority household because they have bad credit

CHAPTER 22

Environmental Issues and the Real Estate Transaction

■ **LEARNING OBJECTIVES** *When you have finished reading this chapter, you should be able to:*

■ **identify** the basic environmental hazards an agent should be aware of in order to protect his or her client's interests.

■ **describe** the warning signs, characteristics, causes, and solutions for the various environmental hazards most commonly found in real estate transactions.

■ **explain** the fundamental liability issues arising under environmental protection laws.

■ **distinguish** lead-based paint issues from other environmental issues.

■ **define** the following *key terms:*

asbestos	electromagnetic fields (EMFs)	polychlorinated biphenyls (PCBs)
brownfields	encapsulation	radon
Brownfields Legislation	environmental impact statement (EIS)	retroactive liability
capping		strict liability
carbon monoxide (CO)	environmental site assessments	Superfund Amendments and Reauthorization Act (SARA)
chlorofluorocarbons (CFCs)	groundwater	
Comprehensive Environmental Response, Compensation, and Liability Act (CERCLA)	joint and several liability	underground storage tanks (USTs)
	landfill	urea-formaldehyde foam insulation (UFFI)
	lead	
	mold	water table

■ ENVIRONMENTAL ISSUES

Most states have recognized the need to balance the legitimate commercial use of land with the need to preserve vital resources and protect the quality of the states' air, water, and soil. A growing number of homebuyers base their decisions in part on the desire for fresh air, clean water, and outdoor recreational opportunities. Preservation of a state's environment both enhances the quality of life and helps strengthen property values. The prevention and cleanup of pollutants and toxic wastes not only revitalizes the land but creates greater opportunities for responsible development and are steps to ensure that the interests of all parties involved in real estate transactions are protected.

Environmental issues are health issues, and health issues based on environmental hazards have become real estate issues. For this reason, it is extremely important that licensees not only make property disclosures but also see that prospective purchasers get authoritative information about hazardous substances so that they can make informed decisions.

A state-mandated disclosure is usually required by a seller only for transactions involving property with one to four dwelling units. In the past, licensees tended to accept seller-supplied disclosure forms without question, trusting that all was accurate and complete. But today, that trust is risky business. In fact, some states impose a burden on the licensee to discover problems and ask questions. Similarly, licensees should inform buyers of the need to ask and discover and not rely on disclosure forms as a warranty or guarantee. Sellers are to disclose what they are aware of, and buyers are put on notice to discover hazards they are concerned about.

Licensees should be familiar with state and federal environmental laws and the regulatory agencies that enforce them. Licensees are not expected to have the technical expertise necessary to determine whether a hazardous substance is present. However, they must *be aware* of environmental issues.

| In Georgia | In Georgia, BRRETA does not require a licensee to discover problems, but licensees must disclose what they know. |

■ HAZARDOUS SUBSTANCES

Pollution and hazardous substances in the environment are of interest to real estate licensees because they affect the attractiveness, desirability, and market value of cities, neighborhoods, and backyards. A toxic environment is not a place where anyone would want to live. (See Figure 22.1.)

Environmental Hazards: Asbestos

Asbestos is a mineral that was once used as insulation because it was resistant to fire and contained heat effectively. Before 1978, the year when the use of

Environmental Hazards

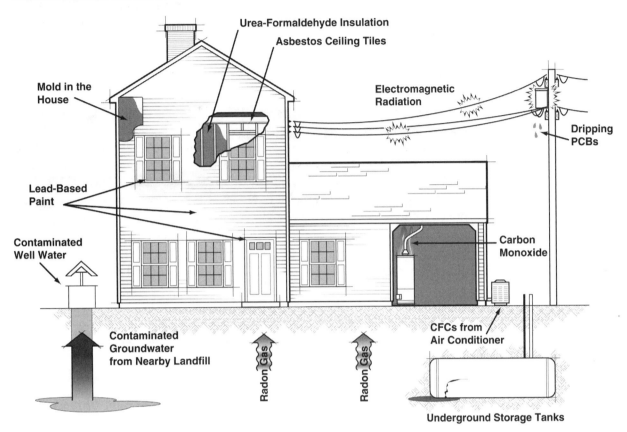

asbestos insulation was banned, asbestos was found in most residential construc-tion. It was a component of more than 3,000 types of building materials. The Environmental Protection Agency (EPA) estimates that about 20 percent of the nation's commercial and public buildings contain asbestos.

> **Asbestos** insulation can create airborne contami-nants that may result in respiratory diseases.

Today, we know that inhaling microscopic asbestos fibers can result in a variety of respiratory diseases. The presence of asbestos insulation alone is not necessar-ily a health hazard. Asbestos is harmful only if it is disturbed or exposed, as often occurs during renovation or remodeling. Asbestos is highly friable. This means that as it ages, asbestos fibers break down easily into tiny filaments and particles. When these particles become airborne, they pose a risk to humans. Airborne asbestos contamination is most prevalent in public and commercial buildings, including schools, built before 1978. If the asbestos fibers in the indoor air of a building reach a dangerous level, the building becomes difficult to lease, finance, or insure.

Federal government regulations establish guidelines for owners of public and commercial buildings to test for asbestos-containing materials.

Asbestos contamination also can be found in residential properties. It was used to cover pipes, ducts, and heating and hot water units. Its fire-resistant properties made it a popular material for use in floor tile, exterior siding, roofing products, linoleum flooring materials, joint compounds, wallboard material, backing, and mastics. Though it may be easy to identify some asbestos-containing materials (for instance, insulation around heating and water pipes), identification may be more difficult when asbestos is behind walls or under floors.

Asbestos is costly to remove because the process requires state-licensed technicians and specially sealed environments. In addition, removal itself may be dangerous: Improper removal procedures may further contaminate the air within the structure. The waste generated should be disposed of at a licensed facility, which further adds to the cost of removal. **Encapsulation,** or the sealing off of disintegrating asbestos, is an alternate method of asbestos control that may be preferable to removal in certain circumstances. However, an owner must periodically monitor the condition of the encapsulated asbestos to make sure it is not disintegrating. Of course, encapsulated asbestos will still have to be dealt with during any renovation or demolition of a building, so it will be a future cost.

A certified asbestos inspector can perform an asbestos inspection of a structure to identify which building materials may contain asbestos. The inspector can also provide recommendations and costs associated with remediation. It is vital that a buyer knows where asbestos-containing materials are located so that they are not disturbed during any repair, remodeling, demolition, or even routine use. Appraisers also should be aware of the possible presence of asbestos.

More information on asbestos-related issues is available from the EPA at 202-554-1404 or on its Web site. In addition, the EPA has numerous publications that provide guidance, information, and assistance with asbestos issues.

Lead-Based Paint and Other Lead Hazards

Lead was used as a pigment and drying agent in alkyd oil-based paint. Lead-based paint may be on any interior or exterior surface, but it is particularly common on doors, windows, and other woodwork. The federal government estimates that lead is present in about 75 percent of all private housing built before 1978; that's approximately 57 million homes, ranging from low-income apartments to million-dollar mansions.

Children younger than six are the most vulnerable to damage from excessive lead levels. Elevated levels of lead in children cause learning disabilities, developmental delays, reduced height, and poor hearing, and the effects are generally irreversible. Excessive exposure in adults can induce anemia and hypertension, trigger gallbladder problems, and cause reproductive problems in both men and women.

Lead from paint or other sources can result in damage to the brain, nervous system, kidneys, and blood. Children under the age of six are particularly vulnerable.

Lead dust can be ingested from the hands by a crawling infant, inhaled by any occupant of a structure, or ingested from the water supply because of lead pipes or lead solder. Soil and groundwater may be contaminated by everything from lead plumbing in leaking landfills to discarded skeets and bullets from an old shooting range. High levels of lead have been found in the soil near waste-to-energy incinerators.

In 1996, the EPA and the Department of Housing and Urban Development (HUD) issued final regulations, known as the Lead-Based Paint Hazard Reduction Act (LBPHRA) of 1992, requiring disclosure of the presence of any known lead-based paint hazards to potential buyers or renters. The federal law does not require that anyone test for the presence of lead-based paint.

LBPHRA requires the following from sellers and landlords of residential dwellings built before 1978:

- Landlords must disclose known information on lead-based paint and hazards before leases take effect. Leases must include a disclosure form regarding lead-based paint.
- Sellers have to disclose known information on lead-based paint and hazards prior to an execution of a contract for sale. Sales contracts must include a completed disclosure form about lead-based paint. (See Figure 22.2.) This is the form for sellers and is slightly different from the form for landlords. Licensees should use EPA-written disclosure forms rather than creating their own forms.
- Buyers have up to ten days to conduct a risk assessment or an inspection for the presence of lead-based paint hazards.
- Licensees provide buyers and lessees with *Protect Your Family from Lead in Your Home,* the pamphlet created by the EPA, HUD, and the U.S. Consumer Product Safety Commission.
- Renovators must give homeowners the *Protect Your Family from Lead in Your Home* pamphlet before starting any renovation work.
- Beginning April 2010, federal law requires anyone who is paid to perform work that disturbs paint in housing and child-occupied facilities to be trained and certified in the EPA's new lead-based work practices. This includes residential rental property owners/managers, general contractors, and special trade contractors (e.g., painters, plumbers, carpenters, electricians). The Renovation, Repair, and Painting (RR&P) program involves pre-renovation education. This education includes distribution of the pamphlet *Renovate Right* to the property owners before work commences.
- Licensees must ensure that all parties comply with the law.
- Sellers, lessors, and renovators are required to disclose any prior test results or any knowledge of lead-based paint hazards. With only a very narrow exception, all real estate licensees are required to advise sellers to make the required disclosures. Only buyer's agents who are paid entirely by the buyer are exempt.

FIGURE 22.2

Disclosure of Lead-Based Paint and Lead-Based Paint Hazards

LEAD-BASED PAINT
EXHIBIT "_____"

Georgia
Association
of REALTORS®

2010 Printing

This Exhibit is part of the Agreement with an Offer Date of _____ for the purchase and sale of that certain
Property known as: _____, _____, Georgia_____.

1. Purchase and Sale or Lease Transaction Lead Warning Statement.
Every purchaser of any interest in residential property on which a residential dwelling was built prior to 1978 is notified that such property may present exposure to lead from lead-based paint that may place young children at risk of developing lead poisoning. Lead poisoning in young children may produce permanent neurological damage, including learning disabilities, reduced intelligence quotient, behavioral problems, and impaired memory. Lead poisoning also poses a particular risk to pregnant women. The Seller of any interest in residential real property is required to provide the Buyer with any information on lead-based paint hazards from risk assessments or inspections in the Seller's possession and notify the Buyer of any known lead-based paint hazards. A risk assessment or inspection for possible lead-based paint hazards is recommended prior to purchase.

2. Seller's/Lessor's Disclosure. *[Seller/Lessor to initial section A. and B. below]*

☐ (Seller/Lessor Initials) **A.** Presence of lead-based paint and/or lead paint hazard *[check one below]*:
  ☐ Known lead-based paint and/or lead-based paint hazards are present in the housing (explain below):
  _____
  ☐ Seller/Lessor has no knowledge of lead-based paint and/or lead-based paint hazards in the housing.

☐ (Seller/Lessor Initials) **B.** Records and Reports available to the Seller/Lessor *[check one below]*:
  ☐ Seller/Lessor has provided the Buyer/Lessee with all the available records and reports pertaining to lead-based paint and/or lead-based paint hazards in the housing (list document below):
  _____
  ☐ Seller/Lessor has no reports or records pertaining to lead-based paint and/or lead-based paint hazards in the housing.

Buyer's/Lessee's Acknowledgment. *[Buyer/Lessee to initial sections below]*

☐ (Buyer/Lessee Initials) **C.** Buyer/Lessee has received copies of all information listed above.

☐ (Buyer/Lessee Initials) **D.** Buyer/Lessee has read and understands the above lead warning statement and has received the pamphlet *"Protect Your Family From Lead in Your Home"*.

☐ (Buyer/Lessee Initials) **E.** Buyer/Lessee has *[check one below]*:
  ☐ Received a ten (10) day opportunity (or mutually agreed upon period) to conduct a risk assessment or inspection for the presence of lead-based paint and/or lead-based paint hazards; or
  ☐ Waived the opportunity to conduct a risk assessment or inspection for the presence of lead-based paint and/or lead-based paint hazards.

Broker's Acknowledgment. *[Broker to initial below]*

☐ (Broker's Initials) **F.** Broker has informed the Seller/Lessor of the Seller's/Lessor's obligations under 42 U.S.C. § 4852(d) and is aware of his/her responsibility to ensure compliance.

3. Certification of Accuracy.
The following parties have reviewed the information above and certify, to the best of their knowledge, that the information provided by the signatory is true and accurate.

_____ _____   _____ _____
Seller/Lessor   Date   Buyer/Lessee   Date

_____ _____   _____ _____
Seller/Lessor   Date   Buyer/Lessee   Date

_____ _____   _____ _____
Listing Broker   Date   Selling/Leasing Broker   Date

NOTE: It is the intent of this Exhibit that it be applicable to both the sale and leasing of Property. The use of terms like "Buyer/Lessee" shall mean either a Buyer or a Lessee or both as the context may indicate.

Copyright© 2010 by Georgia Association of REALTORS®, Inc.   F54, Lead-Based Paint Exhibit, 01/01/10

IN PRACTICE   In 2006, a Georgia broker was fined $55,000 ($5,000 per transaction) for failing to have appropriate disclosure forms in transaction files. Licensees must remember to always provide buyers and lessees with the pamphlet, "Protect Your Family From Lead in Your Home."

A home can be inspected for lead hazards in the following ways:

- *Paint Inspection*—A paint inspection will provide the lead content of every different type of painted surface in a home. However, this inspection will not indicate whether the paint is a hazard or how the homeowner should deal with it.
- *Risk Assessment*—A risk assessment indicates whether there are any sources of serious lead exposure, such as peeling paint or lead dust. It also describes what actions can be taken to address the hazards.

EPA guidance pamphlets, a list of professionals qualified to inspect or assess for lead-based paint, and other information about lead-based hazards are available from the National Lead Information Center at 800-424-5323 or *www.epa.gov/lead/nlic.htm*.

In Georgia   The Georgia Lead Poisoning Prevention Act of 1994 (O.C.G.A. 31-41-1 et seq.) provides rules regarding lead paint prevention and reduction programs, training programs, and licensure and certification requirements. The Georgia Department of Natural Resources is the state agency responsible for implementation, administration, and enforcement.

Radon

Radon is a radioactive gas produced by the natural decay of other radioactive substances. Radon is found in every state, with the highest concentrations in the Great Plains states, the upper Midwest, and the Northeast of the United States. If radon dissipates into the atmosphere, it is not likely to cause harm. However, when radon enters buildings and is trapped in high concentrations (often in basements with inadequate ventilation) it can cause health problems.

Radon is a naturally occurring gas that is a suspected cause of lung cancer.

Opinions differ as to minimum safe levels. But growing evidence suggests that radon may be the most underestimated cause of lung cancer, particularly for children, individuals who smoke, and those who spend a considerable amount of time indoors.

Because radon is odorless and tasteless, it is impossible to detect without testing. Radon levels vary, depending on the amount of fresh air that circulates through a house, the fissures or soil density beneath the house, the weather conditions, and the time of year. Because the risk of radon increases as it builds up in an enclosed space, testing vacant land for radon is not an accurate indicator of the risk once a building is constructed on the site. It is relatively easy to reduce levels of radon by installing ventilation systems or exhaust fans.

Interestingly, the modern practice of creating energy-efficient homes and buildings with practically airtight walls and windows may increase the potential for radon gas accumulation. Once radon accumulates in a basement, efficient heating and ventilation systems can rapidly spread the gas throughout the building.

Home radon-detection kits are available, although more accurate testing can be conducted by radon-detection professionals. The EPA's pamphlet "A Citizen's Guide to Radon" is available at your local EPA office or on the EPA Web site. There is no federal requirement that properties be tested for radon. Local health departments, however, may maintain records of radon levels identified in particular areas.

Formaldehyde

Formaldehyde is a colorless chemical used widely in the manufacture of building materials and many household products. It has a strong odor and is often used because of its preservative characteristics. Formaldehyde is one of the few indoor air pollutants that can be measured.

In homes, the largest source of formaldehyde is likely to be pressed wood products made using adhesives that contain urea-formaldehyde (UF) resins. Pressed-wood products include particleboard, hardwood plywood paneling, and medium density fiberboard. It is also used in carpeting and ceiling tiles. Because formaldehyde is used in embalming, homes that are near funeral homes should consider whether toxic soil or other issues exist from the leakage of nearby formaldehyde storage tanks.

Another product that contains formaldehyde is insulation. In the 1970s, many homeowners had **urea-formaldehyde foam insulation (UFFI)** installed in their homes to conserve energy. However, many of the homes were found to have high concentrations of formaldehyde shortly after the UFFI installation. As a result, few homes are now insulated with this product. Studies have shown that formaldehyde emissions generally decrease over time, so homes where UFFI was installed many years ago are unlikely to have high levels of formaldehyde now.

UFFI is an insulating foam that can release harmful formaldehyde gases.

Formaldehyde causes some individuals to suffer respiratory problems (shortness of breath, wheezing, chest tightness, asthma) as well as eye and skin irritations (burning sensations in the eyes and throat). It has been shown to cause cancer in animals and may cause cancer in humans. Formaldehyde is a major contributor to sick building syndrome (SBS) (see Chapter 18) in commercial properties.

Licensees should be careful that any conditions in an agreement of sale that require tests for formaldehyde are worded properly to identify the purpose for which the tests are being conducted, such as to determine the presence of the insulation or some other source. Licensees should check their state's property disclosure form to see if UFFI must be disclosed. Georgia does not have a UFFI disclosure law. Appraisers should also be aware of the presence of formaldehyde.

Carbon Monoxide

Carbon monoxide is a by-product of fuel combustion that may result in death in poorly ventilated areas.

Carbon monoxide (CO) is a colorless, odorless gas that occurs as a by-product of burning such fuels as wood, oil, and natural gas owing to incomplete combustion. CO is a problem often encountered by property managers if tenants use kerosene heaters. Furnaces, water heaters, space heaters, fireplaces, and wood stoves all produce CO as a natural result of their combustion of fuel. However, when these appliances function properly and are properly ventilated, their CO emissions are not a problem. When improper ventilation or equipment malfunctions permit large quantities of CO to be released into a residence or commercial structure, it poses a significant health hazard. Its effects are compounded by the fact that CO is so difficult to detect. CO is quickly absorbed by the body. It inhibits the blood's ability to transport oxygen and results in dizziness and nausea. As the concentrations of CO increase, the symptoms become more severe. More than 300 deaths from carbon monoxide poisoning occur each year, with thousands of others requiring hospital emergency room care.

Carbon monoxide detectors are available, and their use is mandatory in some areas. Annual maintenance of heating systems helps avoid CO exposure.

Polychlorinated Biphenyls

Polychlorinated biphenyls (PCBs) linger in the environment for long periods of time and can cause health problems.

Polychlorinated biphenyls (PCBs) were often used as an insulating material in dielectric oil. PCBs may be present in electrical equipment, such as transformers, fluorescent light ballasts, and hydraulic oil in older equipment. PCBs are suspected of causing health problems and are known to linger in the environment for long periods of time. For example, in tests conducted on offspring of fish who were exposed to PCBs, the offspring also had elevated levels of PCBs.

In January 1978, the manufacture, processing, commercial distribution, and use of PCB materials was prohibited, except when contained in a *totally enclosed manner*. The EPA, however, made case-by-case exceptions to these limitations if it determined that an unreasonable risk of injury to public health or the environment was not present. On January 1, 1979, the manufacture of PCBs was completely banned; commercial distribution of PCBs was banned on July 1, 1979.

Chlorofluorocarbons

Chlorofluorocarbons (CFCs) are nontoxic, nonflammable chemicals containing atoms of carbon, chlorine, and fluorine. CFCs are most often used in air conditioners, refrigerators, aerosol sprays, paints, solvents, and foam blowing applications. CFCs are safe in most applications and are inert in the lower atmosphere, but once CFC vapors rise to the upper atmosphere, they are broken down by ultraviolet light into chemicals that deplete the ozone layer.

Global treaties have sought to reduce the production levels of CFCs. The manufacture of these chemicals ended for the most part in 1996, with exceptions for production in developing countries, medical products (for example, asthma inhalers), and research.

Licensees need to be aware that homes may have products, especially air conditioners and refrigerators, that contain CFCs. Licensees may want to advise consumers to consider upgrading to newer, environmentally friendly appliances. Consumers should also be aware of safe CFC disposal procedures.

Mold

Mold can be found almost anywhere and can grow on almost any organic substance, so long as moisture, oxygen, and an organic food source are present. Moisture feeds mold growth. If a moisture problem is not discovered or addressed, mold growth can gradually destroy what it is growing on.

In addition, some molds can cause serious health problems. They can trigger allergic reactions and asthma attacks. Some molds are known to produce potent toxins and/or irritants.

Some moisture problems in homes and buildings have been directly linked to recent changes in construction practices. Some of these practices have resulted in buildings that are too tightly sealed, preventing adequate ventilation. Building materials, such as drywall, may not allow moisture to escape easily. The material used in dry walls *wicks* moisture to the nutrition source of glue and paper. Vinyl wallpaper and exterior insulation finish system (EIFS), that is, synthetic stucco, do not allow moisture to escape. Other moisture problems include roof leaks, unvented combustion appliances, and landscaping or gutters that direct water to the building.

The EPA has published guidelines for the remediation and/or cleanup of mold and moisture problems in schools and commercial buildings. See the list of EPA Web sites at the end of this chapter for these guidelines.

Mold is an increasingly important issue for licensees. Initially, lawsuits were brought against construction and insurance companies. But then insurance companies started amending their homeowner's insurance policies to exclude mold from coverage. Now, plaintiffs name sellers, landlords, property management companies, and real estate licensees as defendants, in addition to construction and insurance companies.

There are no federal requirements to disclose mold contamination at this time, and only a few states require disclosure, but not Georgia. Licensees should remind buyers that sellers cannot disclose what they do not know. Also, licensees should advise buyers that they not only have the right but the burden to discover.

Electromagnetic Fields

Electromagnetic fields (EMFs) are generated by the movement of electrical currents. The use of any electrical appliance creates a small field of electromagnetic radiation; clock radios, blow-dryers, televisions, and computers all produce EMFs. A major concern regarding electromagnetic fields involves high-tension

Electromagnetic fields (EMFs) are produced by electrical currents and may be related to a variety of health complaints.

power lines. The EMFs produced by these high-voltage lines, as well as by secondary distribution lines and transformers, are suspected of causing cancer, hormonal changes, and behavioral abnormalities. There is considerable controversy (and much conflicting evidence) about whether EMFs pose a health hazard. Buyers who are aware of the controversy may, however, be unwilling to purchase property near power lines or transformers. As research into EMFs continues, real estate licensees should stay informed about current findings.

■ GROUNDWATER PROTECTION

Groundwater is the water that exists under the earth's surface within the tiny spaces or crevices in geological formations. Groundwater forms the **water table,** the natural level at which the ground is saturated. This may be near the surface (in areas where the water table is very high) or several hundred feet underground. Surface water can also be absorbed into the groundwater.

Any contamination of the underground water can threaten the supply of pure, clean water for private wells or public water systems. If groundwater is not protected from contamination, the earth's natural filtering systems may be inadequate to ensure the availability of pure water. Numerous state and federal laws have been enacted to preserve and protect the water supply.

Water can be contaminated from a number of sources. Runoff from waste disposal sites, leaking underground storage tanks, septic systems, drywells, and storm drains, as well as the illegal disposal of hazardous material and regular use of insecticides and herbicides are some of the main culprits. Because water flows from one place to another, contamination can spread far from its source. Numerous regulations are designed to protect against water contamination. Once contamination has been identified, its source can be eliminated. The water may eventually become clean. However, the process can be time consuming and extremely expensive.

In 1974, the Safe Drinking Water Act (SDWA) was created to protect public health by regulating the nation's public drinking water supply. The act authorizes the EPA to set national health-based standards for drinking water. SDWA was amended in 1996, enhancing existing law by recognizing source water protection, operator training, funding for water system improvements, and public information. The amendments were then strengthened in the year 2000. For example, the EPA requires that water suppliers report any health risk situation within 24 hours, instead of the 72 hours mandated in the past.

Many property disclosure forms require sellers to identify the property's water source, such as well water, municipal water supply, or some other source. Anything other than municipal water supply should be tested. Also, septic systems are often required to be disclosed and buyers would want to ensure that a septic system functions well.

IN PRACTICE   Real estate agents need to be aware of disclosure issues related to groundwater contamination sources both on and off a property. These include underground storage tanks, septic systems, holding ponds, drywells, buried materials, and surface spills. Remember, because groundwater flows over wide areas, the source of contamination may not be nearby.

■ UNDERGROUND STORAGE TANKS

Approximately three million to five million **underground storage tanks (USTs)** exist in the United States. According to the Environmental Protection Agency, approximately 40 percent of the tanks are leaking. Underground storage tanks are commonly found on sites where petroleum products are used or where gas stations and auto repair shops are located. They also may be found in a number of other commercial and industrial establishments—including printing and chemical plants, wood treatment plants, paper mills, paint manufacturers, dry cleaners, food processing plants, and chemical storage or process waste plants. Military bases and airports are also common sites for underground tanks. In residential areas, tanks are used to store heating oil.

Some tanks are currently in use, but many are long forgotten. It is an unfortunate fact that it was once common to dispose of toxic wastes by simple burial: out of sight, out of mind. Over time, however, neglected tanks may leak hazardous substances into the environment. This permits contaminants to pollute not only the soil around the tank but also adjacent parcels and groundwater. Licensees should be particularly alert to the presence of fill pipes, vent lines, stained soil, and fumes or odors, any of which may indicate the presence of a UST. Detection, removal, and cleanup of surrounding contaminated soil can be expensive.

State and federal laws impose strict requirements on landowners where underground storage tanks are located. The federal UST program is regulated by the EPA. The regulations apply to tanks that contain hazardous substances or liquid petroleum products and that store at least 10 percent of their volume underground. Some states have adopted laws regulating underground storage tanks that are more stringent than the federal laws. UST owners are required to register their tanks and adhere to strict technical and administrative requirements that govern

■ installation,
■ maintenance,
■ corrosion prevention,
■ overspill prevention,
■ monitoring, and
■ record keeping.

Owners are also required to demonstrate that they have sufficient financial resources to cover any damage that might result from leaks.

The following types of tanks are among those that are exempt from the federal regulations:

- Tanks that hold less than 110 gallons
- Farm and residential tanks that hold 1,100 gallons or less or motor fuel used for noncommercial purposes
- Tanks that store heating oil burned on the premises
- Tanks on or above the floor of underground areas, such as basements or tunnels
- Septic tanks and systems for collecting storm water and wastewater

Some states have adopted laws regulating underground storage tanks that are more stringent than the federal laws.

In addition to being aware of possible noncompliance with state and federal regulations, the parties to a real estate transaction should be aware that many older tanks have never been registered; exempt tanks are not required to be registered. There may be no visible sign of their presence.

■ WASTE DISPOSAL SITES

Americans produce vast quantities of garbage every day. Despite public and private recycling and composting efforts, huge piles of waste materials—from beer cans, junk mail, and diapers to food, paint, and toxic chemicals—must be disposed of. Landfill operations have become the main receptacles for garbage and refuse. Special hazardous waste disposal sites have been established to contain radioactive waste from nuclear power plants, toxic chemicals, and waste materials produced by medical, scientific, and industrial processes. Additional waste disposal sites used as on-site garbage dumps are located on rural property, such as farms, ranches, and residences. It is important for buyers to ask sellers about the potential existence of waste disposal sites on their property.

A **landfill** is an enormous hole, either excavated for the purpose of waste disposal or left over from surface mining operations. The hole is lined with clay or a synthetic liner to prevent leakage of waste material into the water supply. A system of underground drainage pipes permits monitoring of leaks and leaching. Waste is laid on the liner at the bottom of the excavation, and a layer of topsoil is then compacted onto the waste. The layering procedure is repeated until the landfill is full, the layers mounded up sometimes as high as several hundred feet. **Capping** is the process of laying two feet to four feet of soil over the top of the site and then planting grass on it to enhance the landfill's aesthetic value and prevent erosion. A ventilation pipe runs from the landfill's base through the cap to vent off accumulated natural gases created by the decomposing waste.

IN PRACTICE Environmental issues have a significant impact on the real estate industry. In 1995, a jury awarded $6.7 million to homeowners whose property values had been lowered because of the defendant tire company's negligent operation and maintenance of a hazardous waste dump site. The 1,713 plaintiffs relied on testimony from economists and a real estate appraiser to demonstrate how news stories about the site had lowered the market values of their homes. Nationwide, some landfill operators now offer price guarantees to purchasers of homes near waste disposal sites. A university study found that a home's value increases by more than $6,000 for each mile of its distance from a garbage incinerator.

Federal, state, and local regulations govern the location, construction, content, and maintenance of landfill sites. Test wells around landfill operations are installed to constantly monitor the groundwater in the surrounding area, and soil analyses can be used to test for contamination. Capped landfills have been used for such purposes as parks and golf courses. Rapid suburban growth has resulted in many housing developments and office campuses being built on landfill sites. Most newer landfill sites are well documented, but the locations of many older landfill sites are no longer known.

Hazardous and radioactive waste disposal sites are subject to strict state and federal regulation to prevent the escape of toxic substances. Some materials, such as radioactive waste, are sealed in containers and placed in *tombs* buried deep underground. The tombs are designed to last thousands of years. These disposal sites are usually limited to extremely remote locations, well away from populated areas or farmland.

IN PRACTICE Yucca Mountain, in a remote desert in Nevada, is the nation's first planned long-term geologic repository for spent nuclear fuel and high-level radioactive waste. Currently stored at 126 sites across the country, these materials are the result of nuclear power generation and national defense programs. In 2002, President Bush signed into law the resolution that allows the Department of Energy (DOE) to take the next step in establishing the site at Yucca Mountain. The DOE is in the process of preparing an application to obtain the Nuclear Regulatory Commission (NRC) license to proceed with construction of the repository. In September 2005, the NRC approved a private company's plan to store nuclear waste on Skull Valley Goshute Indian Reservation in Utah. State and local Utah officials strongly oppose the plan, and Nevada officials wonder how this will affect the plans for Yucca Mountain, many of whom also oppose the nuclear waste site in their state.

■ BROWNFIELDS

For decades, old industrial sites have plagued communities as eyesores and as potentially dangerous and hazardous property. These old industrial sites are known as **brownfields** and are defined as defunct, derelict, or abandoned commercial or industrial sites. Many of the sites have toxic wastes. According to the U.S. General Accounting Office, there may be more than 500,000 brownfields across the country.

In 2002, the **Brownfields Legislation** became law. The law gives states and localities up to $250 million a year for five years to clean up polluted industrial sites. The law is also important for property owners and developers because it shields innocent developers from liability for toxic wastes that existed at a site prior to the purchase of property. In effect, if a property owner neither caused nor contributed to the contamination, the property owner is not liable for the cleanup.

Significantly, the law encourages the development of abandoned properties, some of which are located in prime real estate areas.

■ ENVIRONMENTAL PROTECTION

The majority of legislation dealing with environmental problems has been instituted within the past three decades. Although the EPA was created at the federal level to oversee such problems, several other federal agencies' areas of concern generally overlap. The federal laws were created to encourage state and local governments to enact their own legislation.

Comprehensive Environmental Response, Compensation, and Liability Act

The **Comprehensive Environmental Response, Compensation, and Liability Act (CERCLA)** was created in 1980. It established a fund of $9 billion, called the *Superfund*, to clean up uncontrolled hazardous waste sites and to respond to spills. It created a process for identifying *potential responsible parties (PRPs)* and ordering them to take responsibility for the cleanup action. CERCLA is administered and enforced by the EPA.

Liability   A landowner is liable under CERCLA when a release or a threat of release of a hazardous substance has occurred on his or her property. Regardless of whether the contamination is the result of the landowner's actions or those of others, the owner can be held responsible for the cleanup. This liability includes the cleanup not only of the landowner's property but also of any neighboring property that has been contaminated. A landowner who is not responsible for the contamination can seek recovery reimbursement for the cleanup costs from previous landowners, any other responsible party, or the Superfund. However, if other parties are not available, even a landowner who did not cause the problem could be solely responsible for the cleanup costs.

Once the EPA determines that hazardous material has been released into the environment, it is authorized to begin remedial action. First, it attempts to identify the PRPs. If the PRPs agree to cooperate in the cleanup, they must agree about how to divide the cost. If the PRPs do not voluntarily undertake the cleanup, the EPA may hire its own contractors to do the necessary work. The EPA then bills the PRPs for the cost. If the PRPs refuse to pay, the EPA can seek damages in court for up to three times the actual cost of the cleanup.

Liability under the Superfund is considered to be strict, joint and several, and retroactive. **Strict liability** means that the owner is responsible to the injured party without excuse. **Joint and several liability** means that each of the individual owners is personally responsible for the total damages. If only one of the owners is financially able to handle the total damages, that owner must pay the total and collect the proportionate shares from the other owners whenever possible. **Retroactive liability** means that the liability is not limited to the current owner but includes people who have owned the site in the past.

Superfund Amendments and Reauthorization Act

In 1986, the U.S. Congress reauthorized the Superfund. The amended statute contains stronger cleanup standards for contaminated sites and five times the funding of the original Superfund, which expired in September 1985.

The amended act, the **Superfund Amendments and Reauthorization Act (SARA),** also sought to clarify the obligations of lenders. As mentioned, liability under the Superfund extends to both the present and all previous owners of the contaminated site. Real estate lenders found themselves either as present owners or somewhere in the chain of ownership through foreclosure proceedings.

The amendments created a concept called *innocent landowner immunity*. It was recognized that in certain cases, a landowner in the chain of ownership was completely innocent of all wrongdoing and therefore should not be held liable. The innocent landowner immunity clause established the criteria by which to judge whether a person or business could be exempted from liability. The criteria included the following:

- The pollution was caused by a third party.
- The property was acquired after the fact.
- The landowner had no actual or constructive knowledge of the damage.
- Due care was exercised when the property was purchased (the landowner made a reasonable search, called an *environmental* or *Phase I site assessment*) to determine that no damage to the property existed.
- Reasonable precautions were taken in the exercise of ownership rights.

Georgia's Department of Natural Resources (DNR)

In Georgia, the Department of Natural Resources (DNR) is the agency that oversees environmental protection. Its mission is to sustain, enhance, protect and conserve Georgia's natural, historic, and cultural resources for present and future generations, while recognizing the importance of promoting the development of commerce and industry that utilize sound environmental practices. The Georgia DNR has the following departments:

In Georgia

- Environmental Protection, which focuses on air and water quality, water management, and auto emission policies and testing
- Pollution Prevention, which provides free, nonregulatory, and confidential technical assistance in the areas of pollution prevention, resource conservation, waste reduction, by-product reuse, and recycling. It also assists firms to achieve reductions in energy and water use, major cuts in solid waste and air emissions, and significant increases in the use of recycled materials in their facilities.
- Historic preservation policies and practices

- Coastal resource management and preservation policies and practices
- State parks and recreation sites
- Wildlife resources planning, policies, and practices with regard to fishing, hunting, boating, plants, and animals

Georgia's Department of Natural Resources (DNR)

The Georgia Land Conservation Council is an umbrella organization that has the following responsibilities:

- Promote community green space preservation
- Provide for state and local government activities with respect to land conservation
- Create the Georgia Land Conservation Council and provide for its membership, powers, duties, and operations
- Create the Georgia Land Conservation Trust Fund
- Create the Georgia Land Conservation Revolving Loan Fund and provide for appropriations and other additions to said funds, as well as grants and other disbursements from said funds
- Provide eligibility criteria and award and disburse grants to counties, cities, and the Department of Natural Resources
- Provide for related matters; repeal conflicting laws; and for other purposes

■ LIABILITY OF REAL ESTATE PROFESSIONALS

Environmental law is a relatively new phenomenon. Although federal and state laws have defined many of the liabilities involved, common law is being used for further interpretation. The real estate professional and all others involved in a real estate transaction must be aware of both actual and potential liability.

Sellers, as mentioned earlier, often carry the most exposure. Innocent landowners might be held responsible, even though they did not know about the presence of environmental hazards. Purchasers may be held liable, even if they didn't cause the contamination. Lenders may end up owning worthless assets if owners default on the loans rather than undertaking expensive cleanup efforts. Real estate licensees could be held liable for improper disclosure; therefore, it is necessary to be aware of the potential environmental risks from neighboring properties, such as gas stations, manufacturing plants, or even funeral homes.

Additional exposure is created for individuals involved in other aspects of real estate transactions. For example, real estate appraisers must identify and adjust for environmental problems. Adjustments to market value typically reflect the cleanup cost plus a factor of the degree of panic and suspicion that exist in the current market. Although the sales price can be affected dramatically, it is possible that the underlying market value would remain relatively equal to others in the neighborhood. The real estate appraiser's greatest responsibility is to the lender, which depends on the appraiser to identify environmental hazards. Although the lender may be protected under certain conditions through the

1986 amendments to the Superfund Act, the lender must be aware of any potential problems and may require additional environmental reports.

Insurance carriers also might be affected in the transactions. Mortgage insurance companies protect lenders' mortgage investments and might be required to carry part of the ultimate responsibility in cases of loss. More important, hazard insurance carriers might be directly responsible for damages if such coverage was included in the initial policy.

Discovery of Environmental Hazards

Real estate licensees are not expected to have the technical expertise necessary to discover the presence of environmental hazards. However, because they are presumed by the public to have special knowledge about real estate, licensees must be aware both of possible hazards and of where to seek professional help.

Obviously, the first step for a licensee is to ask the owner. He or she may already have conducted tests for lead-based paint or radon. The owner may also be aware of a potential hazardous condition. An environmental hazard can actually be turned into a marketing plus if the owner has already done the detection and abatement work. Potential buyers can be assured that an older home is no longer a lead-paint or an asbestos risk.

> A real estate licensee can avoid liability with environmental issues by
> - becoming familiar with common environmental problems in the licensee's area;
> - looking for signs of environmental contamination;
> - advising (and including as a contingency) an environmental audit if the licensee suspects contamination; and
> - giving *no* advice on environmental issues.

The most appropriate people on whom a licensee can rely for sound environmental information are scientific or technical experts. *Environmental auditors* (or *environmental assessors*) can provide the most comprehensive studies. Their services are usually relied on by developers and purchasers of commercial and industrial properties. An environmental assessment includes the property's history of use, a current use review, and an investigation into the existence of reported or known contamination sources in the subject area that may affect the property: testing of soil, water, air, and structures can be conducted, if warranted. Trained *inspectors* conduct air-sampling tests to detect radon, asbestos, or EMFs. They can test soil and water quality and can inspect for lead-based paints. Lead inspections covered by the Residential Lead-Based Paint Hazard Reduction Act must be conducted by *certified* inspectors. While an environmental auditor assessment may occur at any stage in a transaction, they are most frequently a condition of closing. Not only can environmental experts detect environmental problems, but they can usually offer guidance about how best to resolve the conditions.

IN PRACTICE Environmental assessments and tests conducted by environmental consultants can take time. Licensees should be aware of the time involved and contact environmental consultants as soon as they know such tests are needed in order to prevent delays in closing a transaction.

Environmental Site Assessments

An **environmental site assessment** is often performed on a property to show that due care was exercised in determining if any environmental impairments exist. The assessment can help prevent parties from becoming involved in contaminated property and work as a defense to liability. It is often requested by a lending institution, developer, or a potential buyer. The assessment is commonly performed in phases, such as Phase 1 or Phase 2. A Phase 1 Environmental Report is requested first to determine if any potential environmental problems exist at or near the subject property that may cause impairment. Additional phases are performed, as warranted and requested.

There are no federal regulations that define what an environmental assessment must include. However, one of the most accepted industry standards is provided by the American Society for Testing Materials International. For standards and other information, visit *www.astm.org.*

Environmental Impact Statements

A federally funded project requires that an **environmental impact statement (EIS)** be performed. These statements detail the impact the project will have on the environment. They can include information about air quality, noise, public health and safety, energy consumption, population density, wildlife, vegetation, and need for sewer and water facilities. Increasingly, these statements are also being required for private development.

Disclosure of Environmental Hazards

State laws address the issue of disclosure of known material facts regarding a property's condition. These same rules apply to the presence of environmental hazards. A real estate licensee may be liable if he or she should have known of a condition, even if the seller neglected to disclose it. Property condition disclosures are discussed in Chapter 4.

Limited Liability for Purchasers of Contaminated Property in Georgia

In Georgia

Under Georgia law (O.C.G.A. 12-8-96.3), a purchaser of "affected property" (property listed on the hazardous site inventory maintained by the state) who meets a set of criteria can buy the property without liability to third parties from damages arising from the release of hazardous wastes. The set of criteria focuses on the purchaser's past actions with regard to hazardous properties, and relationships with those who currently operate hazardous property or had contractual relationships with people who operated or operate hazardous properties. If the purchaser passes this set of criteria, he or she is considered a "bona fide purchaser."

Before purchasing the affected property, the bona fide purchaser must present a corrective action plan. The plan must include a schedule for completion, which cannot be more than one year following the date the plan is finally approved.

■ KEY POINT REVIEW

Asbestos is a mineral composed of fibers that have fireproofing and insulating qualities. Note the following:

- Asbestos is a **health hazard** when fibers break down and are inhaled.
- Asbestos is **banned** for use in insulation as of 1978.
- **Encapsulation** can prevent asbestos fibers from becoming airborne.

Lead can be found in pipes, pipe solder, paints, air, and soil. Note the following:

- **Lead-based paint** is found in 75 percent of housing built before 1978.
- Lead **accumulates** in the body and can damage the brain, nervous system, kidneys, and blood.
- The **Lead-Based Paint Hazard Reduction Act of 1992 (LBPHRA)** requires **disclosure** of known lead-based paint hazards to potential buyers or renters.
  - **Real estate licensees** provide buyers and lessees with the pamphlet created by EPA, HUD, and U.S. Consumer Product Safety Commission, "Protect Your Family from Lead in Your Home"

In Georgia
- Georgia's Department of Natural Resources implemented the Georgia Lead Poisoning Prevention Act of 1994.

Radon is an odorless, tasteless, **radioactive gas** produced by the natural decay of radioactive substances in the ground and is found through the United States. Note that radon is suspected of causing lung cancer. Testing for radon in buildings is not a federal requirement.

Formaldehyde—described as a hazardous air pollutant in the Clean Air Act Amendments of 1990—is used for building and household products such as **urea formaldehyde foam insulation (UFFI),** may cause respiratory problems, eye and skin irritations, and possibly cancer, and has been regulated by HUD since 1985 for use in wood products.

Real estate licensees should check state formaldehyde disclosure requirements, and **appraisers** should note the presence of formaldehyde.

Carbon monoxide (CO), a colorless, odorless gas that is a byproduct of fuel burning:

- is produced by furnaces, water heaters, space heaters (including kerosene heaters), fireplaces, and wood stoves.
- may cause **carbon monoxide poisoning,** which can result in death, unless the gas is property vented.
- is detectable with available **carbon monoxide detectors** that may be required by state law.

Polychlorinated biphenyls (PCBs) may be found in electrical equipment. Note the following:

- PCBs are suspected of causing health problems.
- The **manufacture** of PCBs is completely **banned as of January 1, 1979.**
- The **commercial distribution** of PCBs is **banned as of July 1, 1979.**

Chlorofluorocarbons (CFCs), used in refrigerators, aerosol sprays, paints, solvents and foam applications, are **no longer manufactured** worldwide for the most part since **1996** and have been replaced by available environmentally friendly substitutes for home appliances.

Mold is present in the air everywhere and grows in the presence of moisture, oxygen, and a cellulosic (organic) food source. Note the following:

- Some molds can cause serious health problems.
- The **EPA** has guidelines for remediation and/or cleanup of mold and moisture problems in schools and commercial buildings.
- **Real estate licensees** should recommend a **mold inspection** if mold is evident or is suspected because of water problems.

Electromagnetic fields (EMFs) are produced by all electrical appliances:

- **High-voltage electrical lines** producing EMFs are under investigation for health risks.

Groundwater is found under the earth's surface and forms the water table.

- The **Safe Drinking Water Act (SDWA)** of 1974 regulates public drinking water supply.
- On **property transfer**, any water source other than a municipal supply should be tested, as should any septic system.

Underground storage tanks (USTs), containing petroleum products, industrial chemicals, and other substances, are of concern because the three to five million USTs in the U.S. are leaking.

- ESTs are subject to **federal law and state law,** which is sometimes stronger than federal law.
- The **EPA** regulates the federal UST program.
- When a property purchase is being considered, there should be a careful **inspection** of any property on which USTs are suspected.

Waste disposal sites can be municipally owned, part of commercial enterprises, or can be found on farms and other rural properties. Note the following:

- A **landfill** disposal site, excavated or making use of previously mined property, is
  — **lined** to prevent seepage,
  — **capped** with soil for aesthetic reasons, and
  — **vented** to release gases created by decomposing waste.

Brownfields legislation took effect in 2002. Note the following:

- An estimated 500,000 old industrial sites exist in the United States.
- The legislation **shields** innocent developers from **liability** for sites discovered after purchase.

The **Comprehensive Environmental Response, Compensation, and Liability Act (CERCLA)** was created in 1980 and is administered and enforced by the EPA. CERCLA:

- Established a **Superfund** of $9 billion to
  — **clean up** uncontrolled hazardous waste sites, and
  — **respond** to spills.
- Identifies **potential responsible parties (PRPs)**
- Administered and enforced by the EPA
- Established that **liability** is the landowner's for **cleanup** of landowner's and other affected properties as follows:
  — **Strict liability** where the landowner has no defense to the responsibility for cleanup
  — **Joint and several liability** in which each of several landowners is responsible for entire cleanup
  — **Retroactive liability** where the present owner and previous owners are responsible
- Established that **innocent landowner immunity** applies when
  — **pollution** was caused by third party;
  — property was acquired **after the fact;**
  — the landowner had **no actual or constructive knowledge** of the damage;
  — **due care (environmental site assessment)** was exercised at time of purchase; and
  — **reasonable precautions** were taken in the exercise of ownership rights.

| In Georgia |
- In Georgia, the Department of Natural Resources oversees environmental protection. The Georgia Land Conservation Council promotes preservation and conservation.

Environmental **liability** issues for real estate professionals include the following:

- Discovery of environmental hazards that includes
  — questioning the owner
  — recommending **environmental audit (environmental site assessment)**
  — **Environmental impact statement (EIS)** is required for federally funded projects and may be required by state or locality.

Disclosure of environmental hazards—state laws cover disclosure of known material facts regarding property condition.

| In Georgia |
In Georgia, a purchaser of "affected property" who meets certain criteria can buy the property without liability for damages arising from release of hazardous waste.

■ **RELATED WEB SITES**

Consumer Product Safety Commission: *www.cpsc.gov*

Legal Information Institute: *www.law.cornell.edu/co.html*

National Safety Council Environmental Health Center: Lead: *www.nsc.org/ehc/lead.htm*

U.S. Environmental Protection Agency: *www.epa.gov*

U.S. Environmental Protection Agency: Asbestos: *www.epa.gov/oppt/asbestos*

U.S. Environmental Protection Agency: CERCLA/Superfund: *www.epa.gov/superfund/action/law/cercla.htm*

U.S. Environmental Protection Agency: Compliance: *www.epa.gov/compliance/*

U.S. Environmental Protection Agency: Formaldehyde: *www.epa.gov/iaq/formalde.html*

U.S. Environmental Protection Agency: Indoor Air Quality: Mold: www.epa.gov/iaq/molds

U.S. Environmental Protection Agency: Indoor Air Quality: Radon: *www.epa.gov/iaq/radon*

U.S. Environmental Protection Agency: Lead: *www.epa.gov/lead*

U.S. Environmental Protection Agency: Lead-Based Paint Disclosure Forms: *www.epa.gov/lead/leadbase.htm*

U.S. Environmental Protection Agency: Mold Remediation: *www.epa.gov/mold/mold_remediation.html*

CHAPTER 22 QUIZ

1. Under the federal Lead-Based Paint Hazard Reduction Act, which of the following statements is *TRUE*?
   a. All residential housing built prior to 1978 must be tested for the presence of lead-based paint before being listed for sale or rent.
   b. A disclosure statement must be attached to all sales contracts and leases involving residential properties built prior to 1978.
   c. A lead hazard pamphlet must be distributed to all prospective buyers, but not tenants.
   d. Purchasers of housing built before 1978 must be given five days to test the property for the presence of lead-based paint.

2. The term *encapsulation* refers to the
   a. process of sealing a landfill with three to four feet of topsoil.
   b. way in which insulation is applied to pipes and wiring systems.
   c. method of sealing disintegrating asbestos.
   d. way in which lead-based paint particles become airborne.

3. John is a real estate salesman. He shows a pre-World War I house to Tina, a prospective buyer. Tina has two toddlers and is worried about potential health hazards. Which of the following is *TRUE*?
   a. There is a risk that urea-foam insulation was used in the original construction.
   b. Because John is a licensed real estate salesperson, he can offer to personally inspect for lead and remove any lead risks.
   c. Because of the age of the house, there is a good likelihood of the presence of lead-based paint.
   d. Removal of lead-based paint and asbestos hazards is covered by standard title insurance policies.

4. Which of the following is *TRUE* regarding asbestos?
   a. The removal of asbestos can cause further contamination of a building.
   b. Asbestos causes health problems only when it is eaten.
   c. The level of asbestos in a building is affected by weather conditions.
   d. HUD requires that all asbestos-containing materials be removed from all residential buildings.

5. All of the following may contribute to the growth of mold *EXCEPT*
   a. CFCs.
   b. EIFS.
   c. roof leaks.
   d. improperly installed gutters.

6. Federal underground storage tank (UST) regulations require that
   a. home fuel oil tanks in basements be registered with the EPA.
   b. septic tanks be pumped every five years.
   c. liquid petroleum tanks that store at least 10% of their volume underground be in compliance.
   d. states not develop regulations more stringent than the federal requirements.

7. Which of the following describes the process of creating a landfill site?
   a. Waste is liquefied, treated, and pumped through pipes to *tombs* under the water table.
   b. Waste and topsoil are layered in a pit, mounded up, and then covered with dirt and plants.
   c. Waste is compacted and sealed into a container, then placed in a *tomb* designed to last several thousand years.
   d. Waste is buried in an underground concrete vault.

8. Liability under the Superfund is
    a. limited to the owner of record.
    b. joint and several and retroactive, but not strict.
    c. voluntary.
    d. strict, joint and several, and retroactive.

9. Radon poses the greatest potential health risk to humans when it is
    a. contained in insulation material used in residential properties during the 1970s.
    b. found in high concentrations in unimproved land.
    c. trapped and concentrates in inadequately ventilated areas.
    d. emitted by malfunctioning or inadequately ventilated appliances.

10. What do UFFI, lead-based paint, and asbestos have in common?
    a. They all pose a risk to humans because they may emit harmful gases.
    b. They all were banned in 1978.
    c. All three were used in insulating materials.
    d. They were all used at one time in residential construction.

11. Which state agency is responsible for implementation of the Georgia Lead Paint Prevention Act of 1994?
    a. Georgia Real Estate Commission
    b. Georgia EPA
    c. Georgia Department of Natural Resources
    d. Georgia Department of Pollution Prevention

12. Regarding disclosure of environmental problems in Georgia, BRRETA requires a licensee to
    a. discover problems.
    b. disclose what they know.
    c. disclose issues only when asked.
    d. discover problems and disclose them immediately.

Closing the Real Estate Transaction

■ **LEARNING OBJECTIVES** *When you have finished reading this chapter, you should be able to:*

■ **identify** the issues of particular interest to the buyer and the seller as a real estate transaction closes.

■ **describe** the steps involved in preparing a closing statement.

■ **explain** the general rules for prorating.

■ **distinguish** the procedures involved in face-to-face closings from those in escrow closings.

■ **define** the following *key terms:*

accrued items	credit	survey
closing	debit	survivability
closing statement	escrow	Uniform Settlement
computerized loan origination (CLO)	prepaid item prorations	Statement
controlled business arrangement (CBA)	Real Estate Settlement Procedures Act (RESPA)	

■ PRECLOSING PROCEDURES

Closing actually involves two events: First, the promises made in the sales contract are fulfilled; second, the mortgage loan funds (if any) are distributed to the buyer. Before the property changes hands, however, important issues must be resolved, and both the buyer and the seller have specific issues to deal with.

Buyer's Issues

The buyer will want to be sure that the seller delivers title. The buyer also should ensure that the property is in the promised condition. This involves inspecting

> **Closing** is the point at which ownership of a property is transferred in exchange for the selling price.

- the title evidence;
- the seller's deed;
- any documents demonstrating the removal of undesired liens and encumbrances;
- the survey;
- the results of any required inspections, such as termite or structural inspections, or required repairs; and
- any leases if tenants reside on the premises.

IN PRACTICE   One of the first efforts to put the NAR-HUD Homebuyer Protection Initiative into action is the Consumer Notice form that explains the difference between the appraisal and a home inspection and that emphasizes the importance of an inspection to protect buyers. The one-page notice must be signed on or before closing in all transactions in which an FHA-insured mortgage is involved.

Final property inspection   Shortly before the closing takes place, the buyer usually makes a *final inspection* of the property with the broker—often called the *walk-through*. The right to have a final property inspection is normally created in the real estate sales contract. Through this inspection, the buyer makes sure that necessary repairs have been made, that the property has been well maintained, that all fixtures are in place, and that there has been no unauthorized removal or alteration of any part of the improvements. Licensees should amend the contract at closing, requiring that the seller complete any repairs or replacements that are not completed by closing. This provides **survivability** for the buyer: the right to enforce uncompleted contractual conditions after closing.

Survey   A **survey** gives information about the exact location and size of the property. The sales contract specifies who will pay for the survey. It is usual for the survey to *spot* the location of all buildings, driveways, fences, and other improvements located primarily on the premises being purchased. Any improvements located on adjoining property that may encroach on the premises being bought will be noted also. The survey should set out, in full, any existing easements and encroachments. Whether or not the sales contract or the lender call for a survey, buyers are well-advised to procure a current survey.

IN PRACTICE   A buyer should make sure that the survey is accurate so that property purchased is exactly what the buyer wanted. Relying on old surveys is not necessarily a good idea; the property should be resurveyed prior to closing by a competent surveyor, whether or not the title company or lender requires it.

Seller's Issues

Obviously, the seller's main interest is in receiving payment for the property. He or she will want to be sure that the buyer has obtained the necessary financing and has sufficient funds to complete the sale. The seller also will want to be certain that he or she has complied with all the buyer's requirements so the transaction will be completed.

Both parties will want to inspect the closing statement to make sure that all monies involved in the transaction have been accounted for properly. The parties may be accompanied by their attorneys or their real estate agents.

Title Procedures

Both the buyer and the buyer's lender will want assurance that the seller's title complies with the requirements of the real estate sales contract. Though the practice varies from state to state, the seller is usually required to produce a current *abstract of title* or *title commitment* from the title insurance company.

In Georgia

This responsibility can be handled in the real estate contract, but in Georgia the responsibility usually falls on the buyer.

> The *title* or *opinion of title* discloses all liens, encumbrances, easements, conditions, or restrictions on the property.

When an abstract of title is used, the purchaser's attorney examines it and issues an opinion of title. The attorney's opinion of title is a statement of the quality of the seller's title, and it lists all liens, encumbrances, easements, conditions, or restrictions that appear on the record and to which the seller's title is subject. The attorney's opinion is not a guarantee of title.

On the date when the sale is actually completed (the date of delivery of the deed), the buyer has a title commitment or an abstract that was issued several days or weeks before the closing. For this reason, there are sometimes two searches of the public records. The first shows the status of the seller's title on the date of the first search. Usually, the seller pays for this search. The second search, known as a *bring down*, is made after the closing and generally paid for by the purchaser. The abstract should be reviewed before closing to resolve any problems that might cause delays or threaten the transaction.

As part of this later search, the seller may be required to execute an *affidavit of title*. This is a sworn statement in which the seller assures the title insurance company (and the buyer) that there have been no judgments, bankruptcies, or divorces involving the seller since the date of the title examination. The affidavit promises that no unrecorded deeds or contracts have been made, no repairs or improvements have gone unpaid, and no defects in the title have arisen that the seller knows of. The seller also affirms that he or she is in possession of the premises. In some areas, this form is required before the title insurance company will issue an owner's policy to the buyer. The affidavit gives the title insurance company the right to sue the seller if his or her statements in the affidavit are incorrect.

When the purchaser pays cash or obtains a new loan to purchase the property, the seller's existing loan is paid in full and satisfied on record. The exact amount required to pay the existing loan is provided in a current *payoff statement* from the lender, effective on the date of closing. This payoff statement notes the unpaid amount of principal, the interest due through the date of payment, the fee for issuing the certificate of satisfaction or release deed, credits (if any) for tax and insurance reserves, and the amount of any prepayment penalties. The same procedure is followed for any other liens that must be released before the buyer takes title.

In a transaction in which the buyer assumes the seller's existing mortgage loan, the buyer will want to know the exact balance of the loan as of the closing date. In some areas, it is customary for the buyer to obtain a *mortgage reduction certificate* from the lender that certifies the amount owed on the mortgage loan, the interest rate, and the last interest payment made.

In some areas, real estate sales transactions are customarily closed through an escrow (discussed below). In these areas, the escrow instructions usually provide for an extended coverage policy to be issued to the buyer as of the date of closing. The seller has no need to execute an affidavit of title.

IN PRACTICE   Licensees often assist in preclosing arrangements as part of their service to customers. In some states, licensees are required to advise the parties of the approximate expenses involved in closing when a real estate sales contract is signed. In other states (*not* Georgia), it is the licensees' statutory duty to coordinate and supervise closing activities. Aside from state laws on this issue, even if a licensee does not have a specific role in the closing, the licensee may be the person with the most knowledge about the transaction. Because of this, many licensees feel it is part of their fiduciary duty to be present for a face-to-face closing.

■ CONDUCTING THE CLOSING

Closing is known by many names. For instance, in some areas closing is called *settlement and transfer*. In other parts of the country, the parties to the transaction sit around a single table and exchange copies of documents, a process known as *passing papers*. ("We passed papers on the new house Wednesday morning.") In still other regions, the buyer and seller may never meet at all; the paperwork is handled by an escrow agent. This process is known as *closing escrow*. ("We'll close escrow on our house next week.") Whether the closing occurs face to face or through escrow, the main concerns are that the buyer receives marketable title, the seller receives the purchase price, and certain other items are adjusted properly between the two.

In Georgia Georgia uses the "face-to-face" closing procedure except when a closing must occur by a specified date and not all conditions have been met, in which case the closing escrow is used. The closing escrow procedure is rarely used.

Face-to-Face Closing

A face-to-face closing involves the resolution of two issues. First, the promises made in the real estate sales contract are fulfilled. Second, the buyer's loan is finalized, and the mortgage lender disburses the loan funds. The difference between a face-to-face closing and an escrow closing is that in a face-to-face closing, these two issues are resolved during a single meeting of all the parties and their attorneys. As discussed earlier, the parties in an escrow closing may never meet. The phrase *passing papers* vividly describes a face-to-face closing.

In a *face-to-face closing*, the parties meet face to face.

Face-to-face closings may be held at a number of locations, including the office of the title company, the lending institution, one of the parties' attorneys, the broker, the county recorder, or the escrow company. Those attending a closing *may* include

- the buyer;
- the seller;
- the real estate salespersons or brokers (both the buyer's and the seller's agents);
- the seller's and the buyer's attorneys;
- representatives of the lending institutions involved with the buyer's new mortgage loan, the buyer's assumption of the seller's existing loan, or the seller's payoff of an existing loan; and
- a representative of the title insurance company.

Closing agent or closing officer   One person usually conducts the proceedings at a closing and calculates the division of income and expenses between the parties (called *settlement*). In some areas, real estate brokers preside. In others, the closing agent is the buyer's or seller's attorney, a representative of the lender, or a representative of the title company. Some title companies and law firms employ paralegal assistants who conduct closings for their firms.

Preparation for closing involves ordering and reviewing an array of documents, such as the title insurance policy or title certificate, surveys, property insurance policies, and other items. Arrangements must be made with the parties for the time and place of closing. Closing statements and other documents must be prepared.

The exchange   When the parties are satisfied that everything is in order, the exchange is made. All pertinent documents are then recorded in the correct order to ensure continuity of title. For instance, if the seller pays off an existing loan and the buyer obtains a new loan, the seller's satisfaction of mortgage must be recorded before the seller's deed to the buyer. The buyer's new mortgage or deed of trust must then be recorded after the deed because the buyer cannot pledge the property as security for the loan until he or she owns it.

Closing in Escrow

An **escrow** is a method of closing in which a disinterested third party is authorized to act as escrow agent and to coordinate the closing activities. The escrow agent also may be called the *escrow holder*. The escrow agent may be an attorney, a title company, a trust company, an escrow company, or the escrow department of a lending institution. Many real estate firms offer escrow services. However, a broker cannot be a disinterested party in a transaction from which he or she expects to collect a commission. Because the escrow agent is placed in a position of great trust, many states have laws regulating escrow agents and limiting who may serve in this capacity. Although a few states do not permit certain transactions to be closed in escrow, escrow closings are used to some extent in most states. As noted earlier, escrow closings are rarely used in Georgia.

Escrow procedure   When a transaction will close in escrow, the buyer and seller execute escrow instructions to the escrow agent after the sales contract is signed. One of the parties selects an escrow agent. Which party selects the agent is determined either by negotiation or by state law. Once the contract is signed, the broker turns over the earnest money to the escrow agent, who deposits it in a special trust, or escrow, account.

In an *escrow closing*, a third party coordinates the closing activities on behalf of the buyer and seller.

The buyer and the seller deposit all pertinent documents and other items with the escrow agent before the specified date of closing. The seller usually deposits

- the deed conveying the property to the buyer;
- title evidence (abstract and attorney's opinion, certificate of title, title insurance, or Torrens certificate);
- existing hazard insurance policies;
- a letter or mortgage reduction certificate from the lender stating the exact principal remaining (if the buyer assumes the seller's loan);
- affidavits of title (if required);
- a payoff statement (if the seller's loan is to be paid off); and
- other instruments or documents necessary to clear the title or to complete the transaction.

The buyer deposits

- the balance of the cash needed to complete the purchase, usually in the form of a certified check;
- loan documents (if the buyer secures a new loan);
- proof of hazard insurance, including (where required) flood insurance; and
- other necessary documents, such as inspection reports required by the lender.

The escrow agent has the authority to examine the title evidence. When marketable title is shown in the name of the buyer and all other conditions of the escrow agreement have been met, the agent is authorized to disburse the purchase price to the seller, minus all charges and expenses. The agent then records the deed and mortgage or deed of trust (if a new loan has been obtained by the purchaser).

If the escrow agent's examination of the title discloses liens, a portion of the purchase price can be withheld from the seller. The withheld portion is used to pay the liens to clear the title.

If the seller cannot clear the title, or if for any reason the sale cannot be consummated, the escrow instructions usually provide that the parties be returned to their former statuses, as if no sale occurred. The escrow agent reconveys title to the seller and returns the purchase money to the buyer.

Internal Revenue Service Reporting Requirements

Certain real estate closings must be reported to the Internal Revenue Service (IRS) on Form 1099-S. The affected properties include sales or exchanges of

- land (improved or unimproved), including air space;
- an inherently permanent structure, including any residential, commercial, or industrial building;
- a condominium unit and its appurtenant fixtures and common elements (including land); or
- stock in a cooperative housing corporation.

Information to be reported includes the sales price, the amount of property tax reimbursement credited to the seller, and the seller's Social Security number. If the closing agent does not notify the IRS, the responsibility for filing the form falls on the mortgage lender, although the brokers or the parties to the transaction ultimately could be held liable.

Broker's Role at Closing

Depending on local practice, the broker's role at closing can vary from simply collecting the commission to conducting the proceedings. Real estate brokers are not authorized to give legal advice or otherwise engage in the practice of law. This means that in some states, a broker's job is essentially finished as soon as the real estate sales contract is signed. After the contract is signed, the attorneys take over. Even so, a broker's service generally continues all the way through closing. The broker makes sure all the details are taken care of so that the closing can proceed smoothly. This means making arrangements for title evidence, surveys, appraisals, inspections or repairs for structural conditions, water supplies, sewerage facilities, or toxic substances.

Though real estate licensees do not always conduct closing proceedings, they usually attend. Often, the parties look to their agents for guidance, assistance, and information during what can be a stressful experience. Licensees need to be thoroughly familiar with the process and procedures involved in preparing a closing statement, which includes the expenses and prorations of costs to close the transaction. It is also in the brokers' best interests that the transactions they worked so hard to bring about move successfully and smoothly to a conclusion. Of course, a broker's (and a salesperson's) commission is generally paid out of the proceeds at closing.

Typically, licensees should avoid *recommending* sources for any inspection or testing services. If a buyer suffers any injury as a result of a provider's negligence, the licensee may also be liable. The better practice is to give clients the names of several professionals who offer high-quality services.

IN PRACTICE In Georgia, under the Brokerage Relationships in Real Estate Transactions Act (BRRETA), brokers may provide ministerial acts to their customers, including locating inspectors, architects, engineers, surveyors, lenders, attorneys, and insurance agents. Brokers will usually provide information on two or three service providers in any one field of expertise so the customer may choose the one best for his or her circumstances. In addition, if licensees receive any compensation or reward from a source they had recommended to a client, this must be disclosed to the client. Licensees must never receive compensation from an attorney or lender.

> **In Georgia**

Lender's Interest in Closing

Whether a buyer obtains new financing or assumes the seller's existing loan, the lender wants to protect its security interest in the property. The lender has an interest in making sure the buyer gets good, marketable title and that tax and insurance payments are maintained. Lenders want their mortgage liens to have priority over other liens. They also want to ensure that insurance is kept up to date in case property is damaged or destroyed. For this reason, a lender generally requires a title insurance policy and a fire and hazard insurance policy (along with a receipt for the premium). In addition, a lender may require other information: a survey, a termite or another inspection report, or a certificate of occupancy (for a newly constructed building). A lender also may request that a reserve account be established for tax and insurance payments. Lenders sometimes even require representation by their own attorneys at closings.

■ RESPA REQUIREMENTS

The federal **Real Estate Settlement Procedures Act (RESPA)** was enacted to protect consumers from abusive lending practices. RESPA also aids consumers during the mortgage loan settlement process. It ensures that consumers are provided with important, accurate, and timely information about the actual costs of settling or closing a transaction. It also eliminates kickbacks and other referral fees that tend to inflate the costs of settlements unnecessarily. RESPA prohibits lenders from requiring excessive escrow account deposits.

RESPA requirements apply when a purchase is financed by a federally related mortgage loan. *Federally related loans* means loans made by banks, savings and loan associations, or other lenders whose deposits are insured by federal agencies. It also includes loans insured by the FHA and guaranteed by the VA; loans administered by HUD; and loans intended to be sold by the lenders to Fannie Mae, Ginnie Mae, or Freddie Mac. RESPA is administered by HUD.

RESPA regulations apply to first-lien residential mortgage loans made to finance the purchases of one-family to four-family homes, cooperatives, and condominiums, for either investment or occupancy. RESPA also governs second or subordinate liens for home equity loans. A transaction financed solely by a purchase-money mortgage taken back by the seller, an installment contract (contract for deed), and a buyer's assumption of a seller's existing loan are not covered by RESPA. However, if the terms of the assumed loan are modified, or if the lender charges more than $50 for the assumption, the transaction is subject to RESPA regulations.

IN PRACTICE While RESPA's requirements are aimed primarily at lenders, some provisions of the act affect real estate brokers and agents as well. Real estate licensees fall under RESPA when they refer buyers to particular lenders, title companies, attorneys, or other providers of settlement services. Licensees who offer computerized loan origination (CLO) services also are subject to regulation. Remember: Buyers have the right to select their own providers of settlement services.

Controlled Business Arrangements

A service that is increasing in popularity is one-stop shopping for consumers of real estate services. A real estate firm, title insurance company, mortgage broker, home inspection company, or even a moving company may agree to offer a package of services to consumers. RESPA permits such a **controlled business arrangement (CBA)** *as long as a consumer is clearly informed of the relationship among the service providers and that other providers are available*. Fees may not be exchanged among the affiliated companies simply for referring business to one another. This referral fee prohibition may be a particularly important issue for licensees who offer **computerized loan origination (CLO)** services to their clients and customers (discussed in Chapter 16). While a borrower's ability to comparison shop for a loan may be enhanced by a CLO system, his or her range of choices must not be limited. Consumers must be informed of the availability of other lenders. Licensees who have an ownership interest in a service provider must disclose that interest as well as potential profit resulting from the referred business in the transaction.

Disclosure Requirements

Lenders and settlement agents have the following disclosure obligations at the time of loan application and loan closing or within three business days of receiving the loan application. If the lender denies the loan within three days, then RESPA does not require that the lender provide the following documents:

- *Special information booklet.* This HUD booklet, which must be given at the time of application or provided within three days of loan application, provides the borrower with general information about settlement (closing) costs. It also explains the various provisions of RESPA, including a line-by-line description of the Uniform Settlement Statement.

■ *Good-faith estimate of settlement costs.* The new three-page **good-faith estimate (GFE)** must contain the exact language specified by HUD, making it easier for borrowers to compare loan conditions from one lender to another. (See Figure 23.1) The only fee that the lender may collect before the applicant receives the GFE is for a credit report. Once the GFE is issued, lenders are committed and may only modify the GFE in certain specific instances. If certain information or circumstances change after the original GFE is issued, then a new GFE must be issued. Issuing a new GFE triggers a new three-day waiting period; in which case, closing may not occur until after three days have passed. The new GFE indicates which closing costs may or may not change prior to settlement and, if they do, by how much. The fees are divided into three categories:

— *No tolerance:* fees that may not increase before closing: lender charges for taking, underwriting, and processing the loan application, including points, origination fees, and yield spread premiums

— *10 percent tolerance:* fees that cannot increase by more than 10 percent in any given category: settlement services for which the lender selects the provider or for which the borrower selects the provider from the lender's list, title services and title insurance if the lender selects the provider, and recording fees

— *Unlimited tolerance:* fees for services that are out of the lender's control: services for which the borrower chooses the provider (such as escrow and title insurance), impounds for taxes, mortgage interest, and the cost of homeowners' insurance

■ *Mortgage servicing disclosure statement.* This statement tells the borrower whether the lender intends to service the loan or to transfer it to another lender. It will also provide information about resolving complaints.

The last page of the GFE is a worksheet consumers can use to compare different loans and terms to aid in price shopping. The lender is responsible for the accuracy of the GFE and the actual costs that the lender charges on the HUD-1.

■ *Uniform Settlement Statement (HUD-1 Form).* RESPA requires that the Uniform Settlement Statement itemize all charges that are normally paid by a borrower and a seller in connection with settlement, whether required by the lender or another party, or paid by the lender or any other person. Charges required by the lender that are paid before closing are indicated as paid outside of closing (POC). The third page of the new HUD-1 form provides for a comparison of the original GFEs to the actual charges appearing on the HUD-1. Lenders are permitted to "correct" any violation of the tolerances by reimbursing the borrower within 30 days of settlement.

RESPA prohibits lenders from requiring borrowers to deposit amounts in escrow accounts for taxes and insurance that exceed certain limits, thus preventing the lenders from taking advantage of the borrowers. While RESPA does not require that escrow accounts be set up, certain government loan programs and some lenders require escrow accounts as a condition of the loan. RESPA places limits on the amounts that a lender may require: on a monthly basis, the lender may require only one-twelfth of the total of the disbursements for the year, plus an amount necessary to cover a shortage in the account. No more than one-sixth

FIGURE 23.1

Good-Faith Estimate (GFE)

OMB Approval No. 2502-0265

Good Faith Estimate (GFE)

Name of Originator		Borrower	
Originator Address		Property Address	
Originator Phone Number			
Originator Email		Date of GFE	

Purpose

This GFE gives you an estimate of your settlement charges and loan terms if you are approved for this loan. For more information, see HUD's *Special Information Booklet* on settlement charges, your *Truth-in-Lending Disclosures*, and other consumer information at www.hud.gov/respa. If you decide you would like to proceed with this loan, contact us.

Shopping for your loan

Only you can shop for the best loan for you. Compare this GFE with other loan offers, so you can find the best loan. Use the shopping chart on page 3 to compare all the offers you receive.

Important dates

1. The interest rate for this GFE is available through [   ]. After this time, the interest rate, some of your loan Origination Charges, and the monthly payment shown below can change until you lock your interest rate.

2. This estimate for all other settlement charges is available through [   ].

3. After you lock your interest rate, you must go to settlement within [   ] days (your rate lock period) to receive the locked interest rate.

4. You must lock the interest rate at least [   ] days before settlement.

Summary of your loan

Your initial loan amount is	$
Your loan term is	years
Your initial interest rate is	%
Your initial monthly amount owed for principal, interest, and any mortgage insurance is	$ per month
Can your interest rate rise?	☐ No ☐ Yes, it can rise to a maximum of %. The first change will be in .
Even if you make payments on time, can your loan balance rise?	☐ No ☐ Yes, it can rise to a maximum of $
Even if you make payments on time, can your monthly amount owed for principal, interest, and any mortgage insurance rise?	☐ No ☐ Yes, the first increase can be in and the monthly amount owed can rise to $. The maximum it can ever rise to is $.
Does your loan have a prepayment penalty?	☐ No ☐ Yes, your maximum prepayment penalty is $.
Does your loan have a balloon payment?	☐ No ☐ Yes, you have a balloon payment of $ due in years.

Escrow account information

Some lenders require an escrow account to hold funds for paying property taxes or other property-related charges in addition to your monthly amount owed of $ [   ].

Do we require you to have an escrow account for your loan?

☐ No, you do not have an escrow account. You must pay these charges directly when due.

☐ Yes, you have an escrow account. It may or may not cover all of these charges. Ask us.

Summary of your settlement charges

A	Your Adjusted Origination Charges *(See page 2.)*	$
B	Your Charges for All Other Settlement Services *(See page 2.)*	$
A + B	Total Estimated Settlement Charges	$

FIGURE 23.1 (CONTINUED)

Good-Faith Estimate (GFE)

Understanding your estimated settlement charges

Your Adjusted Origination Charges	
1. Our origination charge This charge is for getting this loan for you.	
2. Your credit or charge (points) for the specific interest rate chosen ☐ The credit or charge for the interest rate of ☐ % is included in "Our origination charge." (See item 1 above.) ☐ You receive a credit of $ ☐ for this interest rate of ☐ %. This credit **reduces** your settlement charges. ☐ You pay a charge of $ ☐ for this interest rate of ☐ %. This charge (points) **increases** your total settlement charges. The tradeoff table on page 3 shows that you can change your total settlement charges by choosing a different interest rate for this loan.	
A Your Adjusted Origination Charges	$

Some of these charges can change at settlement. See the top of page 3 for more information.

Your Charges for All Other Settlement Services	
3. Required services that we select These charges are for services we require to complete your settlement. We will choose the providers of these services. Service Charge	
4. Title services and lender's title insurance This charge includes the services of a title or settlement agent, for example, and title insurance to protect the lender, if required.	
5. Owner's title insurance You may purchase an owner's title insurance policy to protect your interest in the property.	
6. Required services that you can shop for These charges are for other services that are required to complete your settlement. We can identify providers of these services or you can shop for them yourself. Our estimates for providing these services are below. Service Charge	
7. Government recording charges These charges are for state and local fees to record your loan and title documents.	
8. Transfer taxes These charges are for state and local fees on mortgages and home sales.	
9. Initial deposit for your escrow account This charge is held in an escrow account to pay future recurring charges on your property and includes ☐ all property taxes, ☐ all insurance, and ☐ other ☐ .	
10. Daily interest charges This charge is for the daily interest on your loan from the day of your settlement until the first day of the next month or the first day of your normal mortgage payment cycle. This amount is $ ☐ per day for ☐ days (if your settlement is ☐).	
11. Homeowner's insurance This charge is for the insurance you must buy for the property to protect from a loss, such as fire. Policy Charge	
B Your Charges for All Other Settlement Services	$
A + **B** Total Estimated Settlement Charges	$

 Good Faith Estimate (HUD-GFE) 2

F I G U R E 23.1 (CONTINUED)

Good-Faith Estimate (GFE)

Instructions

Understanding which charges can change at settlement

This GFE estimates your settlement charges. At your settlement, you will receive a HUD-1, a form that lists your actual costs. Compare the charges on the HUD-1 with the charges on this GFE. Charges can change if you select your own provider and do not use the companies we identify. (See below for details.)

These charges **cannot increase** at settlement:	The total of these charges **can increase up to 10%** at settlement:	These charges **can change** at settlement:
■ Our origination charge ■ Your credit or charge (points) for the specific interest rate chosen *(after you lock in your interest rate)* ■ Your adjusted origination charges *(after you lock in your interest rate)* ■ Transfer taxes	■ Required services that we select ■ Title services and lender's title insurance *(if we select them or you use companies we identify)* ■ Owner's title insurance *(if you use companies we identify)* ■ Required services that you can shop for *(if you use companies we identify)* ■ Government recording charges	■ Required services that you can shop for *(if you do not use companies we identify)* ■ Title services and lender's title insurance *(if you do not use companies we identify)* ■ Owner's title insurance *(if you do not use companies we identify)* ■ Initial deposit for your escrow account ■ Daily interest charges ■ Homeowner's insurance

Using the tradeoff table

In this GFE, we offered you this loan with a particular interest rate and estimated settlement charges. However:

■ If you want to choose this same loan with **lower settlement charges,** then you will have a **higher interest rate.**
■ If you want to choose this same loan with a **lower interest rate,** then you will have **higher settlement charges.**

If you would like to choose an available option, you must ask us for a new GFE.

Loan originators have the option to complete this table. Please ask for additional information if the table is not completed.

	The loan in this GFE	The same loan with lower settlement charges	The same loan with a lower interest rate
Your initial loan amount	$	$	$
Your initial interest rate[1]	%	%	%
Your initial monthly amount owed	$	$	$
Change in the monthly amount owed from this GFE	No change	You will pay $ **more** every month	You will pay $ **less** every month
Change in the amount you will pay at settlement with this interest rate	No change	Your settlement charges will be **reduced** by $	Your settlement charges will **increase** by $
How much your total estimated settlement charges will be	$	$	$

[1] *For an adjustable rate loan, the comparisons above are for the initial interest rate before adjustments are made.*

Using the shopping chart

Use this chart to compare GFEs from different loan originators. Fill in the information by using a different column for each GFE you receive. By comparing loan offers, you can shop for the best loan.

	This loan	Loan 2	Loan 3	Loan 4
Loan originator name				
Initial loan amount				
Loan term				
Initial interest rate				
Initial monthly amount owed				
Rate lock period				
Can interest rate rise?				
Can loan balance rise?				
Can monthly amount owed rise?				
Prepayment penalty?				
Balloon payment?				
Total Estimated Settlement Charges				

If your loan is sold in the future

Some lenders may sell your loan after settlement. Any fees lenders receive in the future cannot change the loan you receive or the charges you paid at settlement.

 Good Faith Estimate (HUD-GFE) 3

of the year's total disbursements may be held as a cushion (a cushion is not required). Once a year, the lender must perform an escrow account analysis and return any amount over $50 to the borrower.

By law, borrowers have the right to inspect a completed HUD-1 form, to the extent that the figures are available, one business day before the closing. (Sellers are not entitled to this privilege.) Lenders must retain these statements for two years after the closing date. In addition, state laws generally require that licensees retain all records of a transaction for a specific period.

Kickbacks and referral fees   RESPA prohibits the payment of kickbacks, or unearned fees, in any real estate settlement service. It prohibits referral fees *when no services are actually rendered.* The *payment* or *receipt* of a fee, a kickback, or anything of value for referrals for settlement services includes activities such as mortgage loans, title searches, title insurance, attorney services, surveys, credit reports, and appraisals.

■ PREPARATION OF CLOSING STATEMENTS

A typical real estate transaction involves, in addition to the purchase price, expenses for both parties. These include items prepaid by the seller for which he or she must be reimbursed (such as taxes) and items of expense the seller has incurred, but for which the buyer will be billed (such as mortgage interest paid in arrears when a loan is assumed).

The financial responsibility for these items must be prorated (or divided) between the buyer and the seller. All expenses and prorated items are accounted for on the settlement statement. This is how the exact amount of cash required from the buyer and the net proceeds to the seller are determined.

How the Closing Statement Works

The completion of a **closing statement** involves an accounting of the parties' debits and credits. A **debit** is a charge, that is, an amount that a party owes and must pay at closing. A **credit** is an amount entered in a person's favor—an amount that has already been paid, an amount being reimbursed, or an amount the buyer promises to pay in the form of a loan.

A **debit** is an amount to be paid by the buyer or seller.

A **credit** is an amount payable to the buyer or seller.

To determine the amount a buyer needs at closing, the buyer's debits are totaled. Any expenses and prorated amounts for items prepaid by the seller are added to the purchase price. Then the buyer's credits are totaled. These include the earnest money (already paid), the balance of the loan the buyer obtains or assumes, and the seller's share of any prorated items the buyer will pay in the future. (See Figure 23.2.) Finally, the total of the buyer's credits is subtracted from the total debits to arrive at the actual amount of cash the buyer must bring to closing. Usually, the buyer brings a cashier's or certified check.

FIGURE 23.2

Credits and Debits

Item	Credit to Buyer	Debit to Buyer	Credit to Seller	Debit to Seller	Prorated
Principal amount of new mortgage	X				
Payoff of existing mortgage				X	
Unpaid principal balance if assumed mortgage	X			X	
Accrued interest on existing assumed mortgage	X			X	X
Tenants' security deposit	X			X	
Purchase-money mortgage	X			X	
Unpaid water and other utility bills	X			X	X
Buyer's earnest money	X				
Selling price of property		X	X		
Fuel oil on hand (valued at current market price)		X	X		X
Prepaid insurance and tax reserve for mortgage assumed by buyer		X	X		X
Refund to seller of prepaid water charges and similar utility expenses		X	X		X
Prepaid general real estate taxes		X	X		X

*This chart is based on generally applicable practices. Please note that closing practices may be different in your state, and vary by region in states and by express agreement in the real estate sales contract.

A similar procedure is followed to determine how much money the seller will actually receive. The seller's debits and credits are each totaled. The credits include the purchase price plus the buyer's share of any prorated items that the seller has prepaid. The seller's debits include expenses, the seller's share of prorated items to be paid later by the buyer, and the balance of any mortgage loan or other lien that the seller pays off. Finally, the total of the seller's debits is subtracted from the total credits to arrive at the amount the seller will receive.

Broker's commission   The responsibility for paying the broker's commission will have been determined by previous agreement. If the broker is the agent for the seller, the seller is normally responsible for paying the commission. If an agency agreement exists between a broker and the buyer, or if two agents are involved, one for the seller and one for the buyer, the commission *may* be apportioned as an expense between both parties or according to some other arrangement.

Attorney's fees   If either of the parties' attorneys will be paid from the closing proceeds, that party will be charged with the expense in the closing statement. This expense may include fees for the preparation or review of documents or for representing the parties at settlement.

Recording expenses   The *seller* usually pays for recording charges (filing fees) necessary to clear all defects and furnish the purchaser with a marketable title. Items customarily charged to the seller include the recording of release deeds or satisfaction of mortgages, quitclaim deeds, affidavits, and satisfaction of mechanics' liens. The *purchaser* pays for recording charges that arise from the actual transfer of title. Usually, such items include recording the deed that conveys title to the purchaser and a mortgage or deed to secure debt executed by the purchaser.

| In Georgia | Local custom may determine which party pays for specific recording charges.

Transfer tax   Most states require some form of transfer tax, conveyance fee, or tax stamps on real estate conveyances. This expense is most often borne by the seller, although customs vary. In addition, many cities and local municipalities charge transfer taxes. Responsibility for these charges varies according to local practice.

| In Georgia | The transfer tax in Georgia is a state transfer tax. In Georgia, there is no city or local municipality transfer tax. The transfer tax in Georgia is discussed in Chapter 12.

Title expenses   Responsibility for title expenses varies according to local custom. In most areas, the seller is required to furnish evidence of good title and pay for the title search. If the buyer's attorney inspects the evidence or if the buyer purchases title insurance policies, the buyer is charged for the expense.

Loan fees   When the buyer secures a new loan to finance the purchase, the lender ordinarily charges a loan origination fee of 1 percent to 2 percent of the loan. The fee is usually paid by the purchaser at the time the transaction closes. The lender may also charge discount points if the buyer has secured a loan with a below-market interest rate. If the buyer assumes the seller's existing financing, the buyer may pay an assumption fee. Also, under the terms of some mortgage loans, the seller may be required to pay a prepayment charge or penalty for paying off the mortgage loan before its due date.

Tax reserves and insurance reserves (escrow or impound accounts)
Most mortgage lenders require that borrowers provide reserve funds or escrow accounts to pay future real estate taxes and insurance premiums. A borrower starts the account at closing by depositing funds to cover at least the amount of unpaid real estate taxes from the date of lien to the end of the current month. (The buyer receives a credit from the seller at closing for any unpaid taxes.) Afterward, an amount equal to one month's portion of the estimated taxes is included in the borrower's monthly mortgage payment.

The borrower is responsible for maintaining adequate fire or hazard insurance as a condition of the mortgage loan. Generally, the first year's premium is paid in full at closing. An amount equal to one month's premium is paid after that. The borrower's monthly loan payment includes the principal and interest on the loan, plus one-twelfth of the estimated taxes and insurance (PITI). The taxes and insurance are held by the lender in the escrow or impound account until the bills are due.

IN PRACTICE RESPA permits lenders to maintain a cushion equal to one-sixth of the total amount of taxes and insurance paid out of the account, that is, approximately two months of escrow payments. However, if state law or mortgage documents allow for a smaller cushion, that lesser amount prevails.

Appraisal fees Either the seller or the purchaser pays the appraisal fees, depending on who orders the appraisal. When the buyer obtains a mortgage, it is customary for the lender to require an appraisal. In this case, the buyer usually bears the cost, although this is always a negotiable item. If the fee is paid at the time of the loan application, it is reflected on the closing statement as having already been paid.

Survey fees The purchaser who obtains new mortgage financing customarily pays the survey fees. The sales contract may require that the seller furnish a survey.

Additional fees An FHA borrower owes a lump sum for payment of the *mortgage insurance premium* (MIP) if it is not financed as part of the loan. A VA mortgagor pays a funding fee directly to the VA at closing. If a conventional loan carries *private mortgage insurance (PMI)*, the buyer prepays one year's insurance premium at closing.

Accounting for Expenses

Expenses paid out of the closing proceeds are debited only to the party making the payment. Occasionally, an expense item, such as an escrow fee, a settlement fee, or a transfer tax, may be shared by the buyer and the seller. In this case, each party is debited for their share of the expense.

■ PRORATIONS

Accrued items = buyer credits

Prepaid items = seller credits

Most closings involve the division of financial responsibility between the buyer and seller for such items as loan interest, taxes, rents, fuel, and utility bills. These allowances are called **prorations.** Prorations are necessary to ensure that expenses are divided fairly between the seller and the buyer. For example, the seller may owe current taxes that have not been billed; the buyer would want this settled at the closing. Where taxes must be paid in advance, the seller is entitled to a rebate at the closing. If the buyer assumes the seller's existing mortgage or deed of trust, the seller usually owes the buyer an allowance for accrued interest through the date of closing.

Accrued items are expenses to be prorated (such as water bills and interest on an assumed mortgage) that are owed by the seller, but later will be paid by the buyer. The seller therefore pays for these items by giving the buyer credits for them at closing.

Prepaid items are expenses to be prorated, such as fuel oil in a tank, that have been prepaid by the seller but not fully used up. They are therefore credits to the seller.

The Arithmetic of Prorating

Accurate prorating involves the following four considerations:

1. Nature of the item being prorated
2. Whether it is an accrued item that requires the determination of an earned amount
3. Whether it is a prepaid item that requires the determination of an unearned amount (that is, a refund to the seller)
4. What arithmetic processes must be used

The computation of a proration involves identifying a yearly charge for the item to be prorated, then dividing by 12 to determine a monthly charge for the item. Also, it is usually necessary to identify a daily charge for the item by dividing the monthly charge by the number of days in the month. These smaller portions are then multiplied by the number of months or days in the prorated time period to determine the accrued or unearned amount that will be figured in the settlement.

Using this general principle, there are two methods of calculating prorations:

1. The yearly charge is divided by a *360-day year* (commonly called a *banking year*), or 12 months of 30 days each.
2. The yearly charge is divided by *365* (366 in a leap year) to determine the daily charge. Then the actual number of days in the proration period is determined, and this number is multiplied by the daily charge.

The final proration figure varies slightly, depending on which computation method is used. The final figure also varies according to the number of decimal places to which the division is carried. *All of the computations in this chapter are computed by carrying the division to three decimal places*. The third decimal place is rounded off to cents only after the final proration figure is determined.

Accrued Items

When the real estate tax is levied for the calendar year and is payable during that year or in the following year, the accrued portion is for the period from January 1 to the date of closing (or to the day before the closing in states where the sale date is excluded). If the current tax bill has not yet been issued, the parties must agree on an estimated amount based on the previous year's bill and any known changes in assessment or tax levy for the current year.

Sample proration calculation   Assume a sale is to be closed on September 17. Current real estate taxes of $3,600 are to be prorated. A 360-day year is used. The accrued period, then, is 8 months and 17 days. First determine the prorated cost of the real estate tax per month and day:

$3,600 ÷ 12 months = $300 per month
$300 ÷ 30 days = $10 per day

Next, multiply these figures by the accrued period, and add the totals to determine the prorated real estate tax:

$300 × 8 months = $2,400
$10 × 17 days = $170
$2,400.000 + 170 = $2,570

Thus, the accrued real estate tax for 8 months and 17 days is $2,570. This amount represents the seller's accrued earned tax. It will be a *credit to the buyer* and *a debit to the seller on the closing statement*.

To compute this proration using the actual number of days in the accrued period, the following method is used: The accrued period from January 1 to September 17 runs 260 days (January's 31 days plus February's 28 days and so on, plus the 17 days of September).

$3,600 tax bill ÷ 365 days = $9.863 per day
$9.863 × 260 days = $2,564.38

While these examples show proration as of the date of settlement, the agreement of sale may require otherwise. For instance, a buyer's possession date may not coincide with the settlement date. In this case, the parties could prorate according to the date of possession.

IN PRACTICE   On state licensing examinations, tax prorations are usually based on a 30-day month (360-day year) unless specified otherwise. This may differ with local customs regarding tax prorations. Many title insurance companies provide proration charts that detail tax factors for each day in the year. To determine a tax proration using one of these charts, multiply the factor given for the closing date by the annual real estate tax. (See Figure 23.3.)

With this formula, we can find the amount the buyer will reimburse the seller for the *unearned* portion of the real estate tax. The prepaid period, as determined

FIGURE 23.3

Calculating Real Estate Taxes

Real Estate Taxing Method	Closing Date	Proration of Accrual Calculation for Closing
Taxes for the property paid in advance (by December 31 for the coming year).	June 30	Buyer will reimburse the seller at the closing for the taxes already paid for the half of the year from July 1 to December 31 when the buyer owned the property.
Taxes for the property paid in arrears (by December 31 for the previous year).	June 30	Seller will pay the buyer at the closing for taxes not yet paid for the half of the year from January 1 to June 30 when the seller owned the property.
Blended or staggered system.	June 30	Each tax due date is compared to the closing date, and if the taxes have been paid in advance, the buyer reimburses the seller for the taxes already paid. If the taxes are not yet paid for a portion of the time on which the property is being taxed, the seller pays the buyer for those yet unpaid taxes.

Prepaid Items

A tax proration could be a prepaid item. Because real estate taxes may be paid in the early part of the year, a tax proration calculated for a closing taking place later in the year must reflect the fact that the seller has already paid the tax. For example, in the preceding problem, suppose that all taxes had been paid. The buyer, then, would have to reimburse the seller; the proration would be *credited to the seller* and *debited to the buyer*.

In figuring the tax proration, it is necessary to ascertain the number of future days, months, and years for which taxes have been paid. The formula commonly used for this purpose is as follows:

	Years	Months	Days
Taxes paid to (Dec. 31, end of tax year)	200–	12	30
Date of closing (Sept. 17, 200–)	200–	–9	–17
Period for which tax must be paid	3	13	

With this formula, we can find the amount the buyer will reimburse the seller for the *unearned* portion of the real estate tax. The prepaid period, as determined using the formula for prepaid items, is 3 months and 13 days. Three months at $300 per month equals $900, and 13 days at $10 per day equals $130. Add this to determine that the proration is $1,030 *credited to the seller* and *debited to the buyer*.

Sample prepaid item calculation   One example of a prepaid item is a water bill. Assume that the water is billed in advance by the city without using a meter. The six months' billing is $120 for the period ending October 31. The sale is to be closed on August 3. Because the water bill is paid to October 31, the prepaid time must be computed. Using a 30-day basis, the time period is the 27 days left in August plus two full months: $120 ÷ 6 = $20 per month. For one day, divide $20 by 30, which equals $0.666 per day. The prepaid period is 2 months and 27 days, so:

$$27 \times \$0.666 \text{ per day} = \$17.982$$
$$2 \text{ months} \times \$20 = \underline{\$40.000}$$
$$\$57.982 \text{ or } \$57.98$$

This is a prepaid item; it is *credited to the seller* and *debited to the buyer* on the closing statement.

To figure this based on the actual days in the month of closing, the following process would be used:

$20 per month ÷ 31 days in August = $0.645 per day
August 4 through August 31 = 28 days
28 days × $0.645 = $18.06
2 months × $20 = $40.000
$18.06 + $40 = $58.06

General Rules for Prorating

The rules or customs governing the computation of prorations for the closing of a real estate sale vary widely from state to state. The following are some general guidelines for preparing the closing statement:

In Georgia

■ In most states, the seller owns the property on the day of closing, and prorations or apportionments are usually made *to and including the day of closing*. In a few states, however, it is provided specifically that the buyer owns the property on the closing date. In that case, adjustments are made as of the day preceding the day on which title is closed. In Georgia, who owns property on the day of the sale varies.

■ Mortgage interest, general real estate taxes, water taxes, insurance premiums, and similar expenses are usually computed by using *360 days in a year and 30 days in a month*. However, the rules in some areas provide for computing prorations on the basis of the *actual number of days* in the calendar month of closing. The agreement of sale should specify which method will be used.

- Accrued or prepaid *general real estate taxes* are usually prorated at the closing. When the amount of the current real estate tax cannot be determined definitely, the proration is usually based on the last obtainable tax bill.
- *Special assessments* for municipal improvements such as sewers, water mains, or streets are usually paid in annual installments over several years, with annual interest charged on the outstanding balance of future installments. The seller normally pays the current installment, and the buyer assumes all future installments. *The special assessment installment generally is not prorated at the closing.* A buyer may insist that the seller allow the buyer a credit for the seller's share of the interest to the closing date. The agreement of sale may address the manner in which special assessments will be handled at settlement.
- *Rents* are usually adjusted on the basis of the *actual number of days* in the month of closing. It is customary for the seller to receive the rents for the day of closing and to pay all expenses for that day. If any rents for the current month are uncollected when the sale is closed, the buyer often agrees by a separate letter to collect the rents if possible and remit the pro rata share to the seller.
- *Security deposits* made by tenants to cover the last month's rent of the lease or to cover the cost of repairing damage caused by the tenant are generally transferred by the seller to the buyer.

Real estate taxes　Proration of real estate taxes varies widely depending on how the taxes are paid in the area where the real estate is located. In some states, real estate taxes are paid *in advance*; that is, if the tax year runs from January 1 to December 31, taxes for the coming year are due on January 1. In this case, the seller, who has prepaid a year's taxes, should be reimbursed for the portion of the year remaining after the buyer takes ownership of the property. In other areas, taxes are paid *in arrears*, on December 31 for the year just ended. In this case, the buyer should be credited by the seller for the time the seller occupied the property. Sometimes, taxes are due during the tax year, partly in arrears and partly in advance; sometimes they are payable in installments. It gets even more complicated: City, state, school, and other property taxes may start their tax years in different months. Whatever the case may be in a particular transaction, the licensee should understand how the taxes will be prorated.

In Georgia

In Georgia, the tax year is January 1 to December 31. Tax due dates vary from county to county, but are usually payable in September or October for the current tax year. For example, 2008 property taxes in county X would be due October 1, 2008.

Mortgage loan interest　On almost every mortgage loan the interest is paid *in arrears*, so the buyer and seller must understand that the mortgage payment due on June 1, for example, includes interest due for the month of May. Thus, the buyer who assumes a mortgage on May 31 and makes the June payment pays for the time the seller occupied the property and should be credited with a month's interest. On the other hand, the buyer who places a new mortgage loan on May 31 may be pleasantly surprised to hear that he or she will not need to make a mortgage payment until a month later.

■ SAMPLE CLOSING STATEMENT

Settlement computations take many possible formats. The remaining portion of this chapter illustrates a sample transaction using the RESPA Uniform Settlement Statement in Figure 23.4. Because customs differ in various parts of the country, the way certain expenses are charged in some locations may be different from the illustration.

Basic Information of Offer and Sale

John and Joanne Iuro list their home at 3045 North Racine Avenue in Riverdale, Georgia, with the Open Door Real Estate Company. The listing price is $237,000, and possession can be given within two weeks after all parties have signed the contract. Under the terms of the listing agreement, the sellers agree to pay the broker a commission of 6 percent of the sales price.

On May 18, the Open Door Real Estate Company submits a contract offer to the Iuros from Brook Redemann, a bachelor residing at 22 King Court, Riverdale. Redemann offers $230,000, with earnest money and down payment of $46,000 and the remaining $184,000 of the purchase price to be obtained through a new conventional loan. No private mortgage insurance is necessary because the loan-to-value ratio does not exceed 80 percent. The Iuros sign the contract on May 29. Closing is set for June 15 at the office of the Open Door Real Estate Company, 720 Main Street, Riverdale.

The unpaid balance of the Iuros' (sellers') mortgage as of June 1, 200– will be $115,400. Payments are $825 per month with interest at 7 percent per annum on the unpaid balance.

The sellers submit evidence of title in the form of a title insurance binder at a cost of $30. The title insurance policy, to be paid by the sellers at the time of closing, costs an additional $540, including $395 for lender's coverage and $145 for homeowner's coverage. Recording charges of $20 are paid for the recording of two instruments to clear defects in the sellers' title. State transfer tax stamps in the amount of $115 ($0.50 per $500 of the sales price or fraction thereof) are affixed to the deed. In addition, the sellers must pay an attorney's fee of $600 for preparing of the deed and for legal representation. This amount will be paid from the closing proceeds.

The buyer must pay an attorney's fee of $500 for examining the title evidence and for legal representation. He also must pay $20 to record the deed. These amounts also will be paid from the closing proceeds.

Real estate taxes in Riverdale are paid in arrears. Taxes for this year, estimated at last year's figure of $3,450, have not been paid. According to the contract, prorations will be made on the basis of 30 days in a month.

FIGURE 23.4

RESPA Uniform Settlement Statement

OMB Approval No. 2502-0265

A. Settlement Statement (HUD-1)

B. Type of Loan

1. ☐ FHA	2. ☐ RHS	3. ☐ Conv. Unins.	6. File Number:	7. Loan Number:	8. Mortgage Insurance Case Number:
4. ☐ VA	5. ☐ Conv. Ins.				

C. Note: This form is furnished to give you a statement of actual settlement costs. Amounts paid to and by the settlement agent are shown. Items marked "(p.o.c.)" were paid outside the closing; they are shown here for informational purposes and are not included in the totals.

D. Name & Address of Borrower:	E. Name & Address of Seller:	F. Name & Address of Lender:
G. Property Location:	H. Settlement Agent:	I. Settlement Date:
	Place of Settlement:	

J. Summary of Borrower's Transaction		**K. Summary of Seller's Transaction**	
100. Gross Amount Due from Borrower		**400. Gross Amount Due to Seller**	
101. Contract sales price		401. Contract sales price	
102. Personal property		402. Personal property	
103. Settlement charges to borrower (line 1400)		403.	
104.		404.	
105.		405.	
Adjustment for items paid by seller in advance		**Adjustments for items paid by seller in advance**	
106. City/town taxes to		406. City/town taxes to	
107. County taxes to		407. County taxes to	
108. Assessments to		408. Assessments to	
109.		409.	
110.		410.	
111.		411.	
112.		412.	
120. Gross Amount Due from Borrower		**420. Gross Amount Due to Seller**	
200. Amounts Paid by or in Behalf of Borrower		**500. Reductions In Amount Due to Seller**	
201. Deposit or earnest money		501. Excess deposit (see instructions)	
202. Principal amount of new loan(s)		502. Settlement charges to seller (line 1400)	
203. Existing loan(s) taken subject to		503. Existing loan(s) taken subject to	
204.		504. Payoff of first mortgage loan	
205.		505. Payoff of second mortgage loan	
206.		506.	
207.		507.	
208.		508.	
209.		509.	
Adjustments for items unpaid by seller		**Adjustments for items unpaid by seller**	
210. City/town taxes to		510. City/town taxes to	
211. County taxes to		511. County taxes to	
212. Assessments to		512. Assessments to	
213.		513.	
214.		514.	
215.		515.	
216.		516.	
217.		517.	
218.		518.	
219.		519.	
220. Total Paid by/for Seller		**520. Total Reduction Amount Due Seller**	
300. Cash at Settlement from/to Borrower		**600. Cash at Settlement to/from Seller**	
301. Gross amount due from borrower (line 120)		601. Gross amount due to seller (line 420)	
302. Less amounts paid by/for borrower (line 220)	( )	602. Less reductions in amount due seller (line 520)	( )
303. Cash ☐ From ☐ To Borrower		**603. Cash** ☐ To ☐ From Seller	

The Public Reporting Burden for this collection of information is estimated at 35 minutes per response for collecting, reviewing, and reporting the data. This agency may not collect this information, and you are not required to complete this form, unless it displays a currently valid OMB control number. No confidentiality is assured; this disclosure is mandatory. This is designed to provide the parties to a RESPA covered transaction with information during the settlement process.

F I G U R E 23.4 (CONTINUED)

RESPA Uniform Settlement Statement

L. Settlement Charges			Paid From Borrower's Funds at Settlement	Paid From Seller's Funds at Settlement
700. Total Real Estate Broker Fees				
Division of commission (line 700) as follows:				
701. $	to			
702. $	to			
703. Commission paid at settlement				
704.				
800. Items Payable in Connection with Loan				
801. Our origination charge	$	(from GFE #1)		
802. Your credit or charge (points) for the specific interest rate chosen $		(from GFE #2)		
803. Your adjusted origination charges		(from GFE A)		
804. Appraisal fee to		(from GFE #3)		
805. Credit report to		(from GFE #3)		
806. Tax service to		(from GFE #3)		
807. Flood certification		(from GFE #3)		
808.				
900. Items Required by Lender to Be Paid in Advance				
901. Daily interest charges from to @ $ /day		(from GFE #10)		
902. Mortgage insurance premium for months to		(from GFE #3)		
903. Homeowner's insurance for years to		(from GFE #11)		
904.				
1000. Reserves Deposited with Lender				
1001. Initial deposit for your escrow account		(from GFE #9)		
1002. Homeowner's insurance months @ $ per month $				
1003. Mortgage insurance months @ $ per month $				
1004. Property taxes months @ $ per month $				
1005. months @ $ per month $				
1006. months @ $ per month $				
1007. Aggregate Adjustment –$				
1100. Title Charges				
1101. Title services and lender's title insurance		(from GFE #4)		
1102. Settlement or closing fee $				
1103. Owner's title insurance		(from GFE #5)		
1104. Lender's title insurance $				
1105. Lender's title policy limit $				
1106. Owner's title policy limit $				
1107. Agent's portion of the total title insurance premium $				
1108. Underwriter's portion of the total title insurance premium $				
1200. Government Recording and Transfer Charges				
1201. Government recording charges		(from GFE #7)		
1202. Deed $ Mortgage $ Releases $				
1203. Transfer taxes		(from GFE #8)		
1204. City/County tax/stamps Deed $ Mortgage $				
1205. State tax/stamps Deed $ Mortgage $				
1206.				
1300. Additional Settlement Charges				
1301. Required services that you can shop for		(from GFE #6)		
1302. $				
1303. $				
1304.				
1305.				
1400. Total Settlement Charges (enter on lines 103, Section J and 502, Section K)				

F I G U R E   23.4 (CONTINUED)

RESPA Uniform Settlement Statement

Comparison of Good Faith Estimate (GFE) and HUD-1 Charges		Good Faith Estimate	HUD-1
Charges That Cannot Increase	**HUD-1 Line Number**		
Our origination charge	# 801		
Your credit or charge (points) for the specific interest rate chosen	# 802		
Your adjusted origination charges	# 803		
Transfer taxes	#1203		

Charges That in Total Cannot Increase More Than 10%		Good Faith Estimate	HUD-1
Government recording charges	# 1201		
	#		
	#		
	#		
	#		
	#		
	#		
	#		
Total			
Increase between GFE and HUD-1 Charges		$ or	%

Charges That Can Change		Good Faith Estimate	HUD-1
Initial deposit for your escrow account	#1001		
Daily interest charges	# 901 $ /day		
Homeowner's insurance	# 903		
	#		
	#		
	#		

Loan Terms

Your initial loan amount is	$
Your loan term is	_____ years
Your initial interest rate is	_____ %
Your initial monthly amount owed for principal, interest, and and any mortgage insurance is	$ _____ includes ☐ Principal ☐ Interest ☐ Mortgage Insurance
Can your interest rate rise?	☐ No. ☐ Yes, it can rise to a maximum of ___%. The first change will be on _____ and can change again every _____ after _____ . Every change date, your interest rate can increase or decrease by ___%. Over the life of the loan, your interest rate is guaranteed to never be **lower** than ___% or **higher** than ___ %.
Even if you make payments on time, can your loan balance rise?	☐ No. ☐ Yes, it can rise to a maximum of $ _____ .
Even if you make payments on time, can your monthly amount owed for principal, interest, and mortgage insurance rise?	☐ No. ☐ Yes, the first increase can be on _____ and the monthly amount owed can rise to $ _____ . The maximum it can ever rise to is $ _____ .
Does your loan have a prepayment penalty?	☐ No. ☐ Yes, your maximum prepayment penalty is $ _____ .
Does your loan have a balloon payment?	☐ No. ☐ Yes, you have a balloon payment of $ _____ due in _____ years on _____ .
Total monthly amount owed including escrow account payments	☐ You do not have a monthly escrow payment for items, such as property taxes and homeowner's insurance. You must pay these items directly yourself. ☐ You have an additional monthly escrow payment of $ _____ that results in a total initial monthly amount owed of $ _____ . This includes principal, interest, any mortgage insurance and any items checked below: ☐ Property taxes ☐ Homeowner's insurance ☐ Flood insurance ☐ _____ ☐ _____ ☐ _____

Note: If you have any questions about the Settlement Charges and Loan Terms listed on this form, please contact your lender.

Computing the prorations and charges   The following list illustrates the various steps in computing the prorations and other amounts to be included in the settlement to this point:

■ Closing date: June 15
■ Commission: 6% (0.06) × $230,000 sales price = $13,800
■ Seller's mortgage interest: 7% (0.07) × $115,400 principal due after June 1 payment = $8,078 interest per year; $8,078 ÷ 360 days = $22.44 interest per day; 15 days of accrued interest to be paid by the seller × $22.44 = $336.60 interest owed by the seller; $115,400 + $336.60 = $115,736.60 payoff of seller's mortgage
■ Real estate taxes (estimated at $3,450): $3,450 ÷ 12 months = $287.50 per month; $287.50 ÷ 30 days = $9.58 per day
■ The earned period, from January 1 to and including June 15, equals 5 months and 15 days: $287.50 × 5 months = $1,437.50; $9.58 × 15 days = $143.70; $1437.50 + $143.70 = $1,581.20 seller owes buyer
■ Transfer tax ($0.50 per $500 of consideration or fraction thereof): $230,000 ÷ $500 = $460; $460 × $0.50 = $230 transfer tax owed by seller

The sellers' loan payoff is $115,736.60. They must pay an additional $25 to record the mortgage release, as well as $100 for a pest inspection and $200 for a survey, as negotiated between the parties. The buyer's new loan is from Thrift Federal Savings, 1100 Fountain Plaza, Riverdale, in the amount of $184,000 at 7 percent interest. In connection with this loan, Redemann will be charged $500 to have the property appraised by Swift Appraisal. Acme Credit Bureau will charge $120 for a credit report. (Because appraisal and credit reports are performed before loan approval, they are paid at the time of loan application, whether or not the transaction eventually closes. These items are noted as POC—paid outside closing—on the settlement statement.) In addition, Redemann will pay for interest on his loan for the remainder of the month of closing: 15 days at $40.79 per day, or $611.85. His first full payment (including July's interest) will be due on August 1. He must deposit $2,012.50 into a tax reserve account. That's $7/12$ of the anticipated county real estate tax of $3,450. A one-year hazard insurance premium at $3 per $1,000 of appraised value ($230,000 ÷ 1,000 × 3 = $690) is paid in advance to Hite Insurance Company. An insurance reserve to cover the premium for two months is deposited with the lender. Redemann will have to pay an additional $50 to record the mortgage. He will also pay a loan origination fee of $2,300 and two discount points of $3,680.

The Uniform Settlement Statement

The Uniform Settlement Statement is divided into 12 sections. Sections J, K, and L contain particularly important information. The borrower's and seller's summaries (J and K) are very similar. In Section J, the buyer-borrower's debits are listed on lines 100 through 112. They are totaled on line 120 (gross amount due from borrower). The total of the settlement costs itemized in Section L of the statement is entered on line 103 as one of the buyer's charges. The buyer's credits are listed on lines 201 through 219 and totaled on line 220 (total paid by or for borrower). Then the buyer's credits are subtracted from the charges to arrive at the cash due from the borrower to close (line 303).

In Section K, the seller's credits are entered on lines 400 through 412 and totaled on line 420 (gross amount due to seller). The seller's debits are entered on lines 501 through 519 and totaled on line 520 (total reduction amount due seller). The total of the seller's settlement charges is on line 502. Then the debits are subtracted from the credits to arrive at the cash due to the seller to close (line 603).

Section L summarizes all the settlement charges for the transaction; the buyer's expenses are listed in one column and the seller's expenses in the other. If an attorney's fee is listed as a lump sum in line 1107, the settlement should list by line number the services that were included in that total fee.

■ KEY POINT REVIEW

Closing (settlement and transfer) is the point at which ownership of a property is transferred in exchange for the selling price.

To complete the transaction, the **buyer** requires the following:

- Title evidence—a current **abstract of title** with **opinion of title** from the buyer's attorney or **title commitment** from the **title insurance company.**
- Seller's deed
- **Affidavit of title** by seller and documents showing removal of prior encumbrances
- **Mortgage reduction certificate** from lender, if buyer assuming loan
- **Survey** and results of required **inspections**
- **Leases** if tenants reside on premises
- Successful final property inspection (**walk-through**)
- **Closing statement** showing amount and distribution of funds

To complete the transaction the **seller** requires:

- **Payoff statement** from seller's lender noting amount owed
- Evidence that buyer has necessary funds
- **Closing statement** showing distribution of funds

Depending on state law and local custom, closing may be conducted through a

- **licensed escrow company**, in which case parties may execute documents separately and never meet, or
- **face-to-face** meeting of parties at escrow company, title company, lender's office, or attorney's office.

In Georgia | Georgia uses the face-to-face closing, except on rare occasions when an escrow closing is used.

An **escrow holder (escrow agent)** is a disinterested third party authorized to coordinate the closing activities.

The **Internal Revenue Service (IRS)** may require completion and submission of the **Form 1099-S** statement of income to seller showing seller's Social Security number. **Form 1099-S** is filed by a closing agent or the mortgage lender, with brokers or parties being ultimately liable for filing.

The **Real Estate Settlement Procedures Act (RESPA)** is a federal law enacted to protect consumers in the settlement process as follows:

- Requires accurate and timely **information** about actual costs of transaction
- Eliminates **kickbacks** and other referral fees
- Prohibits lenders from requiring excessive **escrow account deposits**
- Requires that licensees disclose ownership in any referred vendor service

RESPA does not apply to a transaction financed solely by a **purchase-money mortgage** taken back by seller, installment contracts (contract for deed), or buyer's **assumption** of a seller's existing loan.

RESPA permits an offer of a transaction-related package of services through a **controlled business arrangement (CBA)** provided the consumer is clearly informed of the relationship of service providers and that other providers are available.

RESPA requires that lenders and settlement agents provide a

- **special information booklet** produced by HUD to every person from whom they receive or for whom they prepare a loan application (except for refinancing),
- **good-faith estimate of settlement costs** to the borrower no later than three business days after receiving a loan application, and
- **Uniform Settlement Statement (HUD-1 form)** to the borrower and the seller itemizing all charges to be paid in connection with closing.

A **closing (settlement) statement** involves **accounting** of amounts paid by or received by the parties, as follows:

- **Debit** is a charge that must be paid by buyer or seller at closing.
- **Credit** is amount entered in favor of buyer or seller.
- In most instances, a debit to one party is a credit to the other party.
- Certain charges are **prorated** (divided between) buyer and seller in one of two ways:
  1. Yearly charge is divided by **360-day year** (banking year), or 12 months of 30 days each, **or**
  2. Yearly charge is divided by **365-day year** (366 days in leap year) to determine daily charge, actual number of days in proration period is determined, and number of days is multiplied by daily charge.
- In most states, charges are prorated as of **date of closing**, with **seller** responsible for date of closing.

■ RELATED WEB SITES

U.S. Department of Housing and Urban Development: RESPA:
www.hud.gov/offices/hsg/sfh/res/respa_hm.cfm

U.S. Department of Housing and Urban Development: RESPA: Frequently
Asked Questions: *www.hud.gov/offices/hsg/sfh/res/respafaq.cfm*

CHAPTER 23 QUIZ

1. Which of the following statements is *TRUE* of real estate closings in most states?
   a. Closings are generally conducted by real estate salespersons.
   b. The buyer usually receives the rents for the day of closing.
   c. The buyer must reimburse the seller for any title evidence provided by the seller.
   d. The seller usually pays the expenses for the day of closing.

2. All encumbrances and liens shown on the report of title other than those waived or agreed to by the purchaser and listed in the contract must be removed so that the title can be delivered free and clear. The removal of such encumbrances is typically the duty of the
   a. buyer.
   b. seller.
   c. broker.
   d. title company.

3. Legal title *ALWAYS* passes from seller to buyer
   a. on the date of execution of the deed.
   b. when the closing statement has been signed.
   c. when the deed is placed in escrow.
   d. when the deed is delivered and accepted.

4. Which of the following would a lender generally require at the closing?
   a. Title insurance commitment
   b. Market value appraisal
   c. Application
   d. Credit report

5. The RESPA Uniform Settlement Statement must be used to illustrate all settlement charges for
   a. every real estate transaction.
   b. transactions financed by VA and FHA loans only.
   c. residential transactions financed by federally related mortgage loans.
   d. all transactions involving commercial property.

6. A mortgage reduction certificate is executed by a(n)
   a. abstract company.
   b. attorney.
   c. lending institution.
   d. grantor.

7. The principal amount of a purchaser's new mortgage loan is a
   a. credit to the seller.
   b. credit to the buyer.
   c. debit to the seller.
   d. debit to the buyer.

8. The earnest money left on deposit with the broker is a
   a. credit to the seller.
   b. credit to the buyer.
   c. balancing factor.
   d. debit to the buyer.

9. The annual real estate taxes on a property amount to $1,800. The seller has paid the taxes in advance for the calendar year. If closing is set for June 15, which of the following is *TRUE*?
   a. Credit seller $825; debit buyer $975
   b. Credit seller $1,800; debit buyer $825
   c. Credit buyer $975; debit seller $975
   d. Credit seller $975; debit buyer $975

10. If a seller collected rent of $900, payable in advance, on August 1, which of the following is *TRUE* at the closing on August 15, if the closing date is an expense to the seller?
    a. Seller owes buyer $900
    b. Buyer owes seller $900
    c. Seller owes buyer $450
    d. Buyer owes seller $450

11. Security deposits should be listed on a closing statement as a credit to the
    a. buyer.
    b. seller.
    c. lender.
    d. broker.

12. A building was purchased for $85,000, with 10 percent down and a loan for the balance. If the lender charged the buyer two discount points, how much cash did the buyer need to come up with at closing if the buyer incurred no other costs?

    a. $1,700
    b. $8,500
    c. $10,030
    d. $10,200

13. A buyer of a $100,000 home has paid $2,000 as earnest money and has a loan commitment for 70 percent of the purchase price. How much more cash does the buyer need to bring to the closing, provided the buyer has no closing costs?

    a. $18,000
    b. $28,000
    c. $58,000
    d. $61,600

14. At closing, the listing broker's commission usually is shown as a

    a. credit to the seller.
    b. credit to the buyer.
    c. debit to the seller.
    d. debit to the buyer.

15. At the closing of a real estate transaction, the person performing settlement gave the buyer a credit for certain accrued items. These items were

    a. bills relating to the property that have already been paid by the seller.
    b. bills relating to the property that will have to be paid by the buyer.
    c. all of the seller's real estate bills.
    d. all of the buyer's real estate bills.

16. A prepaid item by the seller is a(n)

    a. debit to the seller.
    b. evenly divided proration between the buyer and seller.
    c. credit to the buyer.
    d. credit to the seller.

17. The purpose of the Real Estate Settlement Procedures Act (RESPA) is to

    a. make sure buyers do not borrow more than they can repay.
    b. make real estate brokers more responsive to buyers' needs.
    c. help buyers know how much money is required.
    d. see that buyers know all settlement costs that will be charged to them.

18. The document that provides borrowers with general information about settlement costs, RESPA provisions, and the Uniform Settlement Statement is the

    a. HUD-1 form.
    b. special information booklet.
    c. good-faith estimate of settlement costs.
    d. closing statement.

19. Which of the following statements is *TRUE* of a computerized loan origination (CLO) system?

    a. The mortgage broker or lender may pay any fee charged by the real estate broker in whose office the CLO terminal is located.
    b. Consumers must be informed of the availability of other lenders—those not shown in the real estate broker's CLO.
    c. The real estate broker in whose office the CLO terminal is located may charge a fee of up to two points for the use of the system.
    d. The fee charged by the real estate broker for using the CLO terminal may not be financed as part of the loan.

In Georgia

20. Under the Georgia Brokerage Relationships in Real Estate Transactions Act, the broker can perform which ministerial acts?

    a. Locating inspectors
    b. Locating architects
    c. Locating lenders
    d. All of the above

MATH FAQs

Answers to Your Most Frequently
Asked Real Estate Math Questions

Fractions, Decimals, and Percentages

■ WHAT ARE THE PARTS OF A FRACTION?

The denominator shows the number of equal parts in the whole or total. The numerator shows the number of those parts with which you are working. In the example below, the whole or total has been divided into eight equal parts, and you have seven of those equal parts.

$$\frac{7}{8} \qquad \frac{\text{Numerator}}{\text{Denominator}} \qquad \frac{\text{(Top Number)}}{\text{(Bottom Number)}}$$

■ WHAT IS MEANT BY A "PROPER FRACTION"?

⅞ is an example of a proper fraction. In a proper fraction the numerator is less than the whole or less than 1.

■ WHAT IS AN "IMPROPER FRACTION"?

$$\frac{11}{8} \qquad \frac{\text{Numerator}}{\text{Denominator}}$$

This is an example of an **improper fraction.** In an improper fraction, the numerator is greater than the whole or greater than 1.

■ WHAT IS A MIXED NUMBER?

11½ is a **mixed number.** You have a whole number plus a fraction. A mixed number is greater than the whole or greater than 1.

■ HOW DO I MULTIPLY FRACTIONS?

When multiplying fractions, the numerator is multiplied by the numerator, and the denominator by the denominator. Let's start with an easy question. What is ½ × ¾?

First multiply the numerators (top numbers) $1 \times 3 = 3$; then the denominators (bottom numbers) $2 \times 4 = 8$. Thus, $3/2 \times 3/4 = 1/8$.

What is $4\,2/3 \times 10\,5/8$? The first step is to convert the whole number 4 into thirds. This is done by multiplying $4 \times 3 = 12$. (Multiply the whole number, 4, by the denominator of the fraction, 3.) Thus, the whole number 4 is equal to $12/3$.

$4\,2/3$ is equal to $12/3 + 2/3 = 14/3$.

The next step is to convert the whole number 10 into eighths. This is done by multiplying $10 \times 8 = 80$. (Multiply the whole number, 10, by the denominator of the fraction, 8.) Thus, the whole number 10 is equal to $80/8$. $80/8 + 5/8 = 85/8$.

So, what is $14/3 \times 85/8$? First multiply $14 \times 85 = 1{,}190$. Then, $3 \times 8 = 24$. $1{,}190/24 = 49.58$. (That is, $1{,}190 \div 24 = 49.58$.)

An easier way to work the question is to convert the fractions to decimals.

$2/3$ is equal to $2 \div 3$ or .67.

$5/8$ is equal to $5 \div 8$ or .625.

$4.67 \times 10.625 = 49.62$.

Whenever working with fractions or decimals equivalents, the answers will be close but not exact.

HOW DO I DIVIDE BY FRACTIONS?

Dividing by fractions is a two-step process. What is $3/4 \div 1/4$?

First, invert the $1/4$ to $4/1$. Then, multiply $3/4 \times 4/1 = 12/4$. Finally, $12 \div 4 = 3$.

You may also convert $3/4$ to the decimal .75 and $1/4$ to the decimal .25.

$.75 \div .25 = 3$. (There are three .25 in .75.)

What is $100\,7/8 \div 3/4$?

$100 \times 8 = 800$.

$800 + 7 = 807/8$.

$3/4$ is inverted to $4/3$.

$807/8 \times 4/3 = 807 \times 4 = 3{,}228$; $8 \times 3 = 24$. $3{,}228/24 = 3{,}228 \div 24 = 134.5$

Or $7 \div 8 = .875$ and $3 \div 4 = .75$.

$100.875 \div .75 = 134.50$.

■ HOW DO I CONVERT FRACTIONS TO DECIMALS?

Fractions will sometimes be used in real estate math problems. Since calculators may be used on most licensing examinations, it is best to convert fractions to decimals.

MATH TIP   To convert a fraction to a decimal, the top number, called the numerator, is divided by the bottom number, the denominator.

For example:

$$\tfrac{7}{8} = 7 \div 8 = \mathbf{0.875}$$
$$\tfrac{11}{8} = 11 \div 8 = \mathbf{1.375}$$
$$11\tfrac{1}{2} = 1 \div 2 = 0.5 + 11 = \mathbf{11.5}$$

Once fractions have been converted to decimals, other calculations can be easily completed using the calculator. Note that many calculators automatically add the zero before the decimal point as in the first example above.

■ HOW DO I ADD OR SUBTRACT DECIMALS?

Line up the decimals, add or subtract, and bring the decimal down in the answer. You may add zeros if necessary as place holders. For example, 0.5 is the same as 0.50, or .5.

$$\begin{array}{r} 0.50 \\ +3.25 \\ \hline =3.75 \end{array} \qquad \begin{array}{r} 8.20 \\ -0.75 \\ \hline =7.45 \end{array}$$

MATH TIP   When you use a calculator, the decimal will be in the correct place in the answer. 0.5 + 3.25 = 3.75, and 8.2 − 0.75 = 7.45

■ HOW DO I MULTIPLY DECIMALS?

Multiply the numbers, then count the number of decimal places in each number. Next, start with the last number on the right and move the decimal the total number of decimal places to the left in the answer.

Multiply as you normally would to get the 1,500, then count the four decimal places in the numbers (.20 and .75). In the 1,500, start at the last zero on the right, and count four decimal places to the left. The decimal is placed to the left of the **1**.

$$\begin{array}{r} 0.20 \\ \times\,0.75 \\ \hline 100 \\ \underline{140} \\ .1500 \text{ or } .15 \end{array}$$

Note: When you use a calculator, the decimal will be in the correct place in the answer (0.2 × 0.75 = **0.15**).

■ HOW DO I DIVIDE DECIMALS?

Divide the **dividend** (the number being divided) by the **divisor** (the number you are dividing by) and bring the decimal in the dividend straight up in the **quotient** (answer). If the divisor has a decimal, move the decimal to the right of the divisor and move the decimal the same number of places to the right in the dividend. Now divide as stated above.

$$
\begin{array}{r} = 0.75 \\ 2\overline{)1.5} \\ 1.4 \\ 10 \\ \underline{10} \\ 0 \end{array}
\qquad
0.5\overline{)15.5}
\qquad
\begin{array}{r} = 31 \\ = 5\overline{)155.} \\ 15 \\ 05 \\ \underline{5} \\ 0 \end{array}
$$

MATH TIP When you use a calculator, you can have a decimal in the divisor and the decimal will be in the correct place in the answer.

$1.5 \div 2 = 0.75$, and $15.5 \div 0.5 = 31$

■ WHAT IS A PERCENTAGE?

Percent (%) means *per hundred* or *per hundred parts*. The whole or total always represents 100 percent.

5% = 5 parts of 100 parts, or $5 \div 100 = 0.05$ or $\frac{1}{20}$
75% = 75 parts of 100 parts, or $75 \div 100 = 0.75$ or $\frac{3}{4}$
120% = 120 parts of 100 parts, or $120 \div 100 = 1.2$ or $1\frac{1}{5}$

■ HOW CAN I CONVERT A PERCENTAGE TO A DECIMAL?

Move the decimal *two places* to the *left* and drop the % sign.

20% = $2 \div 100$ = 0.20 or **0.2**
1% = $1 \div 100$ = **0.01**
$12\frac{1}{4}\%$ = 12.25%, $12.25 \div 100$ = **0.1225**

See Figure 1.1.

■ HOW CAN I CONVERT A DECIMAL TO A PERCENTAGE?

Move the decimal *two places* to the *right* and *add* the % sign.

0.25 = **25%**
0.9 = **90%**
0.0875 = **8.75%** or $8\frac{3}{4}\%$

See Figure 1.1.

Converting Percentage to Decimal

Decimal to Percentage	Percentage to Decimal
.10 ⟹ 10%	.10 ⟸ 10%
Move decimal two places right to find the percentage	Move percentage two places left to find the decimal

■ HOW DO I MULTIPLY BY PERCENTAGES?

$$500 \times 25\% = 500 \times {}^{25}\!/_{100} = {}^{12,500}\!/_{100} = \mathbf{125}$$

or

$$500 \times 25\% = \mathbf{125}, \text{ or } 500 \times .25 = \mathbf{125}$$

■ HOW DO I DIVIDE BY PERCENTAGES?

$$100 \div 5\% = 100 \div 5/100 = 100 \times {}^{100}\!/_{5} = {}^{10,000}\!/_{5} = \mathbf{2,000}$$

or

$$100 \div 5\% = \mathbf{2,000}, \text{ or } 100 \div .05 = \mathbf{2,000}$$

■ IS THERE ANY EASY WAY TO REMEMBER HOW TO SOLVE PERCENTAGE PROBLEMS?

The following three formulas are important for solving all percentage problems:

$$\text{TOTAL} \times \text{RATE} = \text{PART}$$
$$\text{PART} \div \text{RATE} = \text{TOTAL}$$
$$\text{PART} \div \text{TOTAL} = \text{RATE}$$

There is a simple way to remember how to use these formulas:

- *MULTIPLY* when PART is UNKNOWN.
- *DIVIDE* when PART is KNOWN.
- When you divide, always enter PART into the calculator first.

■ WHAT IS THE "T-BAR" METHOD?

The T-Bar is another tool to use to solve percentage problems. For some people, the "three-formula method" is more difficult to remember than the visual image of a *T*.

÷ PART ÷
TOTAL	RATE
×	

FIGURE 1.2

Using the T-Bar

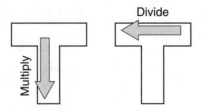

■ HOW DO I USE THE T-BAR?

The procedure for using the T-Bar is as follows:

Enter the two *known* items in the correct places.

1. If the line between the two items is *vertical*, you *multiply* to equal the missing item.
2. If the line between the two items is *horizontal*, you divide to equal the missing item. When you divide, the top **(Part)** always goes into the calculator first and is divided by the bottom **(Total or Rate).**

See Figure 1.2.

The following examples show how the T-Bar can be used to solve percentage problems. These examples deal with discounts because everyone can relate to buying an item that is on sale. Later we will see how the T-Bar can be used for many types of real estate problems.

■ **FOR EXAMPLE** John purchased a new suit that was marked $500. How much did John save if it was on sale for 20 percent off?

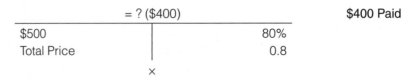

$500 × 20% (.20) = $100

How much did John pay for the suit?

$500 Total Price – $100 Discount   **$400 Paid**
or
100% Total Price – 20% Discount = 80% Paid

	= ? ($400)		$400 Paid
$500		80%	
Total Price		0.8	
	×		

$500 × 80% (.80) = $400

■ **FOR EXAMPLE**   Susie paid $112.50 for a dress that was reduced 25 percent. How much was it originally marked?

100% Original Price – 25% Discount = 75% Paid

$112.50 Paid ÷

| = ? ($150) | 75% |
| | 0.75 |

$150 Original Price

$112.50 ÷ 75% (.75) = $150

■ **FOR EXAMPLE**   Chris paid $127.50 for a coat that was marked down from the original price of $150. What percent of discount did Chris receive?

$150 Original Price – $127.50 Discount Price = $22.50 Discount

÷ 22.50 Discount

| $150 Original Price | = ? (0.15 = 15%) |

15% Discount

$22.50 ÷ $150 = .15 or 15%

or

÷ $127.50 Paid

| $150 | = ? (0.85 = 85%) |

85% of Original Price Paid

$127.50 ÷ $150 = .85 or 85%

85% was the percent paid; therefore

100% Original Price – 85% Paid = **15% Discount**

■ WORD PROBLEMS CAN BE TRICKY. HOW SHOULD I DEAL WITH THEM?

There are five important steps that must be taken to solve word problems.

1. **Read** the problem carefully and completely. Never touch the calculator until you have read the entire problem.
2. **Analyze** the problem to determine what is being asked, what facts are given that *will* be needed to solve for the answer, and what facts are given that *will not* be needed to solve for the answer. Eliminate any information and/or numbers given that are not needed to solve the problem. Take the remaining information and/or numbers and determine which will be needed first, second, etc., depending on the number of steps it will take to solve the problem.
3. **Choose** the proper formula(s) and steps it will take to solve the problem.
4. **Insert** the known elements and calculate the answer.
5. **Check** your answer to be sure you keyed in the numbers and functions properly on your calculator. Be sure you finished the problem. For example, when the problem asks for the salesperson's share of the commission, do not stop at the broker's share of the commission and mark that answer just because it is one of the choices.

Percentage Problems

■ HOW DO I WORK COMMISSION PROBLEMS?

The full **commission** is a percentage of the sales price unless stated differently in the problem. Remember that full commission rates, commission splits between brokers, and commission splits between the broker and salespersons are always negotiable. Always read a problem carefully to determine the correct rate(s).

÷ Full Commission ÷

Sales Price	Full Commission Rate

×

Sales Price × Full Commission Rate = **Full Commission**
Full Commission ÷ Full Commission Rate = **Sales Price**
Full Commission ÷ Sales Price = **Full Commission Rate**

÷ Broker's Share of the Commission ÷

Full Commission	% of Full Commission to the Broker

×

Full Commission	×	% of Full Commission to the Broker	=	**Broker's Share of the Commission**
Broker's Share of the Commission	÷	% of Full Commission to the Broker	=	**Full Commission**
Broker's Share of the Commission	÷	Full Commission	=	**% of Full Commission to the Broker**

÷ Salesperson's Share of the Commission ÷

Broker's Share of the Commission	Salesperson's % of the Broker's Share

×

| Broker's Share of the Commission | × | Salesperson's % of the Broker's Share | = | **Salesperson's Share of the Commission** |

| Salesperson's Share of the Commission | ÷ | Salesperson's % of the Broker's Share | = | **Broker's Share of the Commission** |

| Salesperson's Share of the Commission | ÷ | Broker's Share of the Commission | = | **Salesperson's % of the Broker's Share** |

■ **FOR EXAMPLE**   A seller listed a home for $200,000 and agreed to pay a full commission rate of 5 percent. The home sold four weeks later for 90 percent of the list price. The listing broker agreed to give the selling broker 50 percent of the commission. The listing broker paid the listing salesperson 50 percent of her share of the commission, and the selling broker paid the selling salesperson 60 percent of his share of the commission. How much commission did the selling salesperson receive?

= $180,000 Sales Price	
$200,000 List Price	90% or 0.9

×

$200,000 × 90% (.90) = $180,000

= $9,000 Full Commission	
$180,000 Sales Price	5% or 0.05

×

$180,000 × 5% (.05) = $9,000

= $4,500 Broker's Share of the Commission	
$9,000 Full Commission	50% or 0.5

×

$9,000 × 50% (.50) = $4,500

= $2,700 Selling Salesperson's Commission	
$4,500 Broker's Share of Comm.	60% or 0.6

×

4,500 × 60% (.60) = $2,700

$2,700 Selling Salesperson's Commission is the answer.

■ WHAT IS MEANT BY "SELLER'S DOLLARS AFTER COMMISSION"?

The first deduction from the sales price is the real estate commission. For example, if a house sold for $100,000 and a 7% commission was paid, that means $7,000 was paid in commissions. The seller still has 93% or $93,000. The seller's dollars after commission will be used to pay the seller's other expenses and hopefully will leave some money for the seller.

÷ Seller's Dollars after Commission ÷	
Sales Price	Percent after Commission
×	

Remember, the sales price is 100%. Thus 100% – Commission % = Percent after Commission.

Sales Price	×	Percent after Commission	=	**Seller's Dollars after Commission**

Seller's Dollars after Commission	÷	Percent after Commission	=	**Sales Price**

Seller's Dollars after Commission	÷	Sales Price	=	**Percent after Commission**

■ **FOR EXAMPLE** After deducting $5,850 in closing costs and a 5 percent broker's commission, the sellers received their original cost of $175,000 plus a $4,400 profit. What was the sales price of the property?

$5,850 Closing Costs + $175,000 Original Cost + $4,400 Profit = $185,250 Seller's Dollars after Commission

100% Sales Price – 5% Commission = 95% Percent after Commission

$185,250 Seller's Dollars after Commission ÷	
= **$195,000** **Sales Price**	95% or 0.95

$185,250 ÷ 95% (.95) = $195,000

$195,000 Sales Price is the answer.

■ HOW DO I DETERMINE INTEREST?

Interest is the cost of using money. The amount of interest paid is determined by the agreed-on annual interest rate, the amount of money borrowed (loan amount) or amount of money still owed (loan balance), and the period of time the money is held. When a lender grants a loan for real estate, the loan-to-value (LTV) ratio is the percentage of the sales price or appraised value, whichever is less, that the lender is willing to lend.

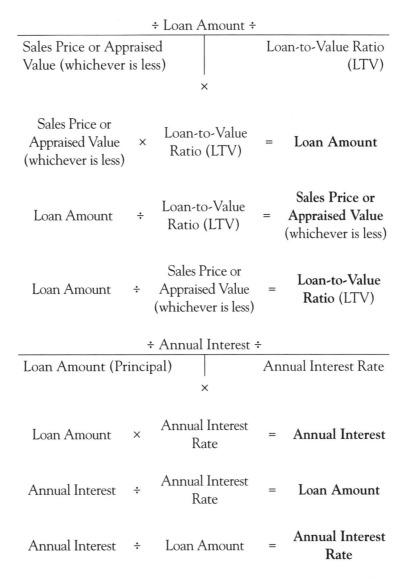

÷ Loan Amount ÷	
Sales Price or Appraised Value (whichever is less)	Loan-to-Value Ratio (LTV)

×

| Sales Price or Appraised Value (whichever is less) | × | Loan-to-Value Ratio (LTV) | = | **Loan Amount** |

| Loan Amount | ÷ | Loan-to-Value Ratio (LTV) | = | **Sales Price or Appraised Value** (whichever is less) |

| Loan Amount | ÷ | Sales Price or Appraised Value (whichever is less) | = | **Loan-to-Value Ratio** (LTV) |

÷ Annual Interest ÷	
Loan Amount (Principal)	Annual Interest Rate

×

| Loan Amount | × | Annual Interest Rate | = | **Annual Interest** |

| Annual Interest | ÷ | Annual Interest Rate | = | **Loan Amount** |

| Annual Interest | ÷ | Loan Amount | = | **Annual Interest Rate** |

■ **FOR EXAMPLE** A parcel of real estate sold for $335,200. The lender granted a 90 percent loan at 7.5 percent for 30 years. The appraised value on this parcel was $335,500. How much interest is paid to the lender in the first monthly payment?

= $301,680 Loan Amount	
$335,200 Sales Price	90% or 0.9

×

$335,200 × 90% (.90) = $301,680 Loan

= $22,626 Annual Interest	
$301,680 Loan Amount	7.5% or 0.075

×

$301,680 × 7.5% (.075) = $22,626

$22,626 Annual Interest ÷ 12 Months = $1,885.50 Monthly Interest

$1,885.50 Interest in the First Monthly Payment is the answer.

■ HOW DO I DETERMINE MONTHLY PRINCIPAL AND INTEREST PAYMENTS?

A **loan payment factor** can be used to calculate the monthly principal and interest (PI) payment on a loan. The factor represents the monthly principal and interest payment to amortize a $1,000 loan and is based on the annual interest rate and the term of the loan.

See Table 16.2 for a loan factor chart found on page 297.

Loan Amount ÷ $1,000 × Loan Payment Factor = **Monthly PI Payment**
Monthly PI Payment ÷ Loan Payment Factor = **Loan Amount**

■ **FOR EXAMPLE**   If the lender in the previous example uses a loan payment factor of $6.99 per $1,000 of loan amount, what will be the monthly PI (principal and interest) payment?

$301,680 Loan Amount ÷ $1,000 × $6.99 = $2,108.74 Monthly PI Payment

$2,108.74 Monthly PI Payment is the answer.

■ HOW DO I WORK PROBLEMS ABOUT POINTS?

One **point** equals 1 percent of the loan amount.

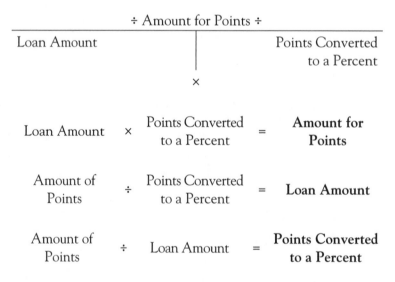

■ **FOR EXAMPLE**   The lender will charge 3½ loan discount points on an $80,000 loan. What will be the total amount due?

= $2,800 for Points	
$80,000 Loan Amount	3.5% or 0.035

×

$80,000 × 3.5% (.035) = $2,800

$2,800 for Points is the answer.

■ HOW DO I DETERMINE PROFIT?

A **profit** is made when we sell something for more than we paid for it. If we sell something for less than we paid, we have suffered a **loss.**

Sales Price – Cost = Profit

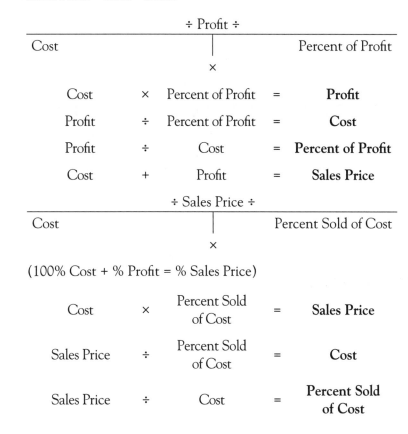

	÷ Profit ÷	
Cost		Percent of Profit
	×	

Cost	×	Percent of Profit	=	**Profit**
Profit	÷	Percent of Profit	=	**Cost**
Profit	÷	Cost	=	**Percent of Profit**
Cost	+	Profit	=	**Sales Price**

	÷ Sales Price ÷	
Cost		Percent Sold of Cost
	×	

(100% Cost + % Profit = % Sales Price)

Cost	×	Percent Sold of Cost	=	**Sales Price**
Sales Price	÷	Percent Sold of Cost	=	**Cost**
Sales Price	÷	Cost	=	**Percent Sold of Cost**

■ **FOR EXAMPLE**   Your home listed for $125,000 and sold for $123,200, which gave you a 10 percent profit over the original cost. What was the original cost?

100% Original Cost + 10% Profit = 110% Sales Price

$123,200 Sales Price	
= $112,000	110%
Original Cost	or 1.1
	×

$123,200 ÷ 110% (1.1) = $112,000

$112,000 Original Cost is the answer.

■ WHAT IS THE DIFFERENCE BETWEEN APPRECIATION AND DEPRECIATION?

Appreciation is increase in value. **Depreciation** is decrease in value. Both are based on the original cost. We only will cover the **straight-line method,** which is what should be used in math problems unless you are told differently. The straight-line method means that the value is increasing (appreciating) or decreasing (depreciating) the same amount each year. The amount of appreciation or depreciation is based on the original cost.

■ HOW DO I SOLVE APPRECIATION PROBLEMS?

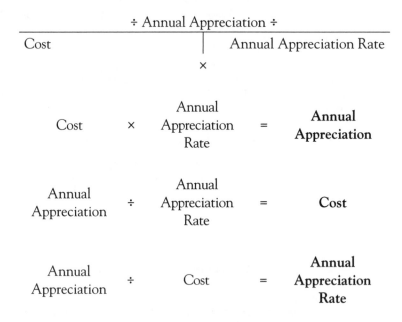

Annual Appreciation Rate × Number of Years = **Total Appreciation Rate**
100% Cost + Total Appreciation Rate = **Today's Value as a Percent**

■ HOW DO I SOLVE DEPRECIATION PROBLEMS?

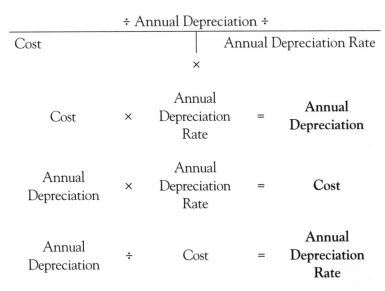

Cost	÷ Annual Depreciation ÷	Annual Depreciation Rate

Cost	×	Annual Depreciation Rate	=	**Annual Depreciation**
Annual Depreciation	×	Annual Depreciation Rate	=	**Cost**
Annual Depreciation	÷	Cost	=	**Annual Depreciation Rate**

Annual Depreciation Rate × Number of Years = **Total Depreciation Rate**
100% Cost ÷ Total Depreciation Rate = **Today's Value as a Percent**

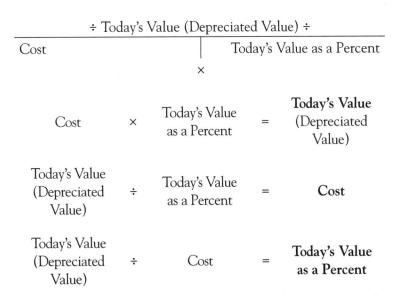

Cost	÷ Today's Value (Depreciated Value) ÷	Today's Value as a Percent

Cost	×	Today's Value as a Percent	=	**Today's Value (Depreciated Value)**
Today's Value (Depreciated Value)	÷	Today's Value as a Percent	=	**Cost**
Today's Value (Depreciated Value)	÷	Cost	=	**Today's Value as a Percent**

■ **FOR EXAMPLE**   Seven years ago you purchased a piece of real estate for $93,700, including the original cost of the land, which was $6,700. What is the total value of the land today using an appreciation rate of 8 percent per year?

8% Appreciation per Year × 7 Years = 56% Total Appreciation Rate

100% cost + 56% Appreciation = 156% Today's Value

= $10,452 Today's Value	
$6,700 Original Cost	156% or 1.56

$6,700 × 156% (1.56) = $10,452

$10,452 Today's Value is the answer.

■ **FOR EXAMPLE**   The value of a house without the lot at the end of four years is $132,300. What was the original cost of the house if the yearly rate of depreciation was 2.5 percent?

2.5% depreciation per year × 4 years = 10% total depreciation rate

100% cost − 10% depreciation = 90% today's value

$132,300 Today's Value ÷

| **$147,000** **Original Cost** | 90% or 0.9 |

×

$132,300 ÷ 90% (.90) = $147,000

$147,000 Original Cost is the answer.

■ HOW DO I DETERMINE VALUE FOR INCOME-PRODUCING PROPERTIES?

When appraising income-producing property, the value is determined by using the annual net operating income (NOI) and the current market rate of return or capitalization rate. Annual scheduled gross income is adjusted for vacancies and credit losses to arrive at the annual effective gross income. The annual operating expenses are deducted from the annual effective gross income to arrive at the annual NOI.

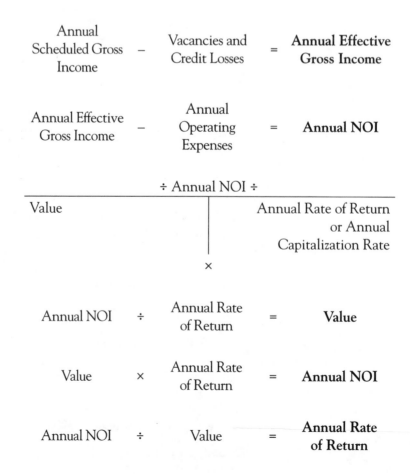

■ **FOR EXAMPLE**   An office building produces $132,600 annual gross income. If the annual expenses are $30,600 and the appraiser estimates the value using an 8.5 percent rate of return, what is the estimated value?

$132,600 Annual Gross Income − $30,600 Annual Expenses = $102,000 Annual NOI

$102,000 Annual NOI ÷	
= $1,200,000 Value	8.5% or 0.085
×	

$102,000 ÷ 8.5% = $1,200,000

$1,200,000 Value is the answer.

The above formulas also can be used for investment problems. The total becomes *original cost* or *investment* instead of value.

■ **FOR EXAMPLE**   You invest $335,000 in a property that should produce a 9 percent rate of return. What monthly NOI will you receive?

= $30,150 Annual NOI	
$335,000 Investment	9% or 0.09
×	

$335,000 × 9% (.09) = $30,150

$30,150 Annual NOI ÷ 12 Months = $2,512.50

$2,512.50 Monthly NOI is the answer.

■ HOW DO I SOLVE PROBLEMS INVOLVING PERCENTAGE LEASES?

When establishing the rent to be charged in a lease for retail space, the lease may be a **percentage lease** instead of a lease based on dollars per square foot. In the percentage lease, there is normally a base or minimum monthly rent plus a percentage of the gross sales in excess of an amount set in the lease. The percentage lease also can be set up as a percentage of the total gross sales or of the base/minimum rent, whichever is larger. We shall look at the minimum plus percentage lease only.

Gross Sales	−	Gross Sales Not Subject to the Percentage	=	**Gross Sales Subject to the Percentage**

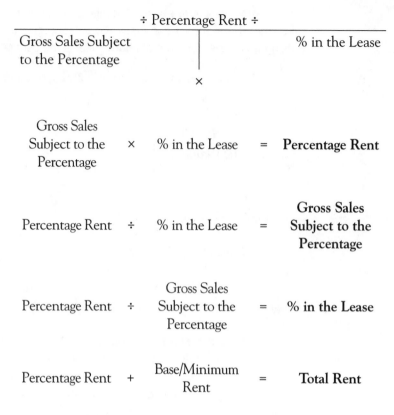

■ FOR EXAMPLE   A lease calls for monthly minimum rent of $900 plus 3 percent of annual gross sales in excess of $270,000. What was the annual rent in a year when the annual gross sales were $350,600?

$900 Monthly Minimum Rent × 12 Months = $10,800 Annual Minimum Rent

$350,600 Annual Gross Sales – $270,000 Annual Gross Sales Not Subject to the Percentage = $80,600 Annual Gross Sales Subject to the Percentage

= $2,418 Annual Percentage Rent

$80,600 Annual Gross Subject to the Percentage	3% or 0.03

×

$10,800 Annual Minimum Rent + $2,418 Annual Percentage Rent = $13,218

$13,218 Total Annual Rent is the answer.

Measurement Problems

■ WHAT ARE LINEAR MEASUREMENTS?

Linear measurement is line measurement. When the terms

■ *per foot,*
■ *per linear foot,*
■ *per running foot,* or
■ *per front foot*

are used, you are being asked to determine the *total length* of the object whether measured in a straight line, crooked line, or curved line. The abbreviation for feet is '. Thus, 12 feet could be written as 12'. The abbreviation for inches is ". Thus, 12 inches could be written as 12".

■ WHAT DOES THE PHRASE "FRONT FOOT" REFER TO?

When the term *per front foot* is used, you are dealing with the number of units on the **frontage** of a lot. The frontage is normally the street frontage, but it could be the water frontage if the lot is on a river, lake, or ocean. If two dimensions are given for a tract of land, the first dimension given is the frontage if the dimensions are not labeled.

■ HOW DO I CONVERT ONE KIND OF LINEAR MEASUREMENT TO ANOTHER?

12 inches = 1 foot

Inches ÷ 12 = Feet (144 inches ÷ 12 = 12 feet)
Feet × 12 = Inches (12 feet × 12 = 144 inches)

36 inches = 1 yard

Inches ÷ 36 = Yards (144 inches ÷ 36 = 4 yards)
Yards × 36 = Inches (4 yards × 36 = 144 Inches)

3 feet = 1 yard

Feet ÷ 3 = Yards (12 feet ÷ 3 = 4 yards)
Yards × 3 = Feet (4 yards × 3 = 12 feet)

5,280 feet = 1 mile

> Feet ÷ 5,280 = Miles (10,560 feet ÷ 5,280 = 2 miles)
> Miles × 5,280 = Feet (2 miles × 5,280 = 10,560 feet)

16½ feet = 1 rod

> Feet ÷ 16.5 = Rods (82.5 feet ÷ 16.5 = 5 rods)
> Rods × 16.5 = Feet (5 rods × 16.5 = 82.5 feet)

320 rods = 1 mile

> Rods ÷ 320 = Miles (640 rods ÷ 320 = 2 miles)
> Miles × 320 = Rods (2 miles × 320 = 640 rods)

■ **FOR EXAMPLE**   A rectangular lot is 50 feet × 150 feet. The cost to fence this lot is priced per linear/running foot. How many linear/running feet will be used to calculate the price of the fence?

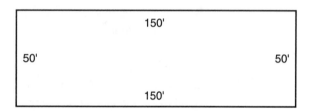

50 Feet + 150 Feet + 50 Feet + 150 Feet = 400 Linear/Running Feet

400 Linear/Running Feet is the answer.

■ **FOR EXAMPLE**   A parcel of land that fronts on Interstate 90 in Elgin, Illinois, is for sale at $5,000 per front foot. What will it cost to purchase this parcel of land if the dimensions are 150' by 100'?

150 is the frontage because it is the first dimension given.

150 Front Feet × $5,000 = $750,000 Cost

$750,000 Cost is the answer.

■ HOW DO I SOLVE FOR AREA MEASUREMENT?

Area is the two-dimensional surface of an object. Area is quoted in square units or in acres. We will look at calculating the area of squares, rectangles, and triangles. Squares and rectangles are four-sided objects. All four sides of a square are the same. Opposite sides of a rectangle are the same. A triangle is a three-sided object. The three sides of a triangle can be the same dimension or three different dimensions.

MATH TIP   When two dimensions are given, we assume it to be a rectangle unless told otherwise.

■ HOW DO I CONVERT ONE KIND OF AREA MEASUREMENT TO ANOTHER?

144 square inches = 1 square foot

Square Inches ÷ 144 = Square Feet (14,400 square inches ÷ 144 = 100 square feet)
Square Feet × 144 = Square Inches ÷ (100 square feet × 144 = 14,400 square inches)

1,296 square inches = 1 square yard

Square Inches ÷ 1,296 = Square Yards (12,960 ÷ 1,296 = 10 square yards)
Square Yards × 1,296 = Square Inches (10 square yards × 1,296 = 12,960 square yards)

9 square feet = 1 square yard

Square Feet ÷ 9 = Square Yards (90 square feet ÷ 9 = 10 square yards)
Square Yards × 9 = Square Feet (10 square yards × 9 = 90 square feet)

43,560 square feet = 1 acre

Square Feet ÷ 43,560 = Acres (87,120 ÷ 43,560 = 2 acres)
Acres × 43,560 = Square Feet (2 acres × 43,560 = 87,120 square feet)

640 acres = 1 section = 1 square mile

Acres ÷ 640 = Sections (Square Miles) (1,280 acres ÷ 640 = 2 sections)
Sections (Square Miles) × 640 = Acres (2 sections × 640 = 1,280 acres)

■ HOW DO I DETERMINE THE AREA OF A SQUARE OR RECTANGLE?

Length   ×   Width   =   **Area of a Square or Rectangle**

■ **FOR EXAMPLE**   How many square feet are in a room 15'6" × 30'9"?

Remember, we must use like dimensions, so the inches must be converted to feet.

6" ÷ 12 = 0.5' + 15' = 15.5' wide
9" ÷ 12 = 0.75' + 30' = 30.75' long
30.75' × 15.5' = 476.625 Square Feet

476.625 Square Feet is the answer.

■ **FOR EXAMPLE**   If carpet costs $63 per square yard to install, what would it cost to carpet the room in the previous example?

476.625 Square Feet ÷ 9 = 52.958333 Square Yards × $63 per Square Yard = $3,336.375 or $3,336.38 rounded

$3,336.38 Carpet Cost is the answer.

■ **F O R   E X A M P L E**   How many acres are there in a parcel of land that measures 450' × 484'?

484' × 450' = 217,800 Square Feet ÷ 43,560 = 5 Acres

5 Acres of Land is the answer.

■ HOW DO I DETERMINE THE AREA OF A TRIANGLE?

½ Base   ×   Height   =   Area of a Triangle

or

Base   ×   Height   ÷   2   =   Area of a Triangle

■ **F O R   E X A M P L E**   How many square feet are contained in a triangular parcel of land that is 400 feet on the base and 200 feet high?

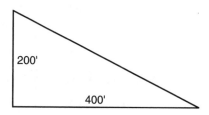

400' × 200' ÷ 2 = 40,000 Square Feet

40,000 Square Feet is the answer.

■ **F O R   E X A M P L E**   How many acres are in a three-sided tract of land that is 300' on the base and 400' high?

300' × 400' ÷ 2 = 60,000 Square Feet ÷ 43,560 = 1.377 Acres

1.377 Acres is the answer.

■ HOW DO I SOLVE FOR VOLUME?

Volume is the space inside a three-dimensional object. Volume is quoted in cubic units. We will look at calculating the volume of boxes and triangular prisms.

■ HOW DO I CONVERT FROM ONE KIND OF VOLUME MEASUREMENT TO ANOTHER?

1,728 cubic inches = 1 cubic foot

Cubic Inches ÷ 1,728 = Cubic Feet
(17,280 cubic inches ÷ 1,728 = 10 cubic feet)

Cubic Feet × 1,728 = Cubic Inches
(10 cubic feet × 1,728 = 17,280 cubic inches)

46,656 cubic inches = 1 cubic yard

Cubic Inches ÷ 46,656 = Cubic Yards
(93,312 cubic inches ÷ 46,656 = 2 cubic yards)

Cubic Yards × 46,656 = Cubic Inches
(2 cubic yards × 46,656 = 93,312 cubic inches)

27 cubic feet = 1 cubic yard

Cubic Feet ÷ 27 = Cubic Yards (270 cubic feet ÷ 27 = 10 cubic yards)
Cubic Yards × 27 = Cubic Feet (10 cubic yards × 27 = 270 cubic feet)

■ HOW DO I DETERMINE THE VOLUME OF A ROOM?

For purposes of determining volume, think of a room as if it were a box.

Length   ×   Width   ×   Height   =   **Volume of a Box**

■ **FOR EXAMPLE**   A building is 500 feet long, 400 feet wide, and 25 feet high. How many cubic feet of space are in this building?

500' × 400' × 25' = 5,000,000 Cubic Feet

5,000,000 Cubic Feet is the answer.

■ **FOR EXAMPLE**   How many cubic yards of concrete would it take to build a sidewalk measuring 120 feet long; 2 feet, 6 inches wide; and 3 inches thick?

6" ÷ 12' = .5' + 2' = 2.5' Wide
3" ÷ 12' = .25' Thick
120' × 2.5' × .25' = 75 Cubic Feet ÷ 27 = 2.778 Cubic Yards (rounded)
2.778 Cubic Yards is the answer.

■ HOW DO I DETERMINE THE VOLUME OF A TRIANGULAR PRISM?

The terms *A-frame*, *A-shaped*, or *gable roof* on an exam describe a triangular prism.

½ Base   ×   Height   ×   Width   =   **Volume of a Triangular Prism**

or

Base   ×   Height   ×   Width   ÷   2   =   **Volume of a Triangular Prism**

■ **FOR EXAMPLE**   An A-frame cabin in the mountains is 50 feet long and 30 feet wide. The cabin is 25 feet high from the base to the highest point. How many cubic feet of space does this A-frame cabin contain?

50' × 30' × 25' ÷ 2 = 18,750 Cubic Feet

18,750 Cubic Feet is the answer.

■ **FOR EXAMPLE**   A building is 40 feet by 25 feet with a 10-foot-high ceiling. The building has a gable roof that is 8 feet high at the tallest point. How many cubic feet are in this structure, including the roof?

40' × 25' × 10' = 10,000 Cubic Feet in the Building
40' × 25' × 8' ÷ 2 = 4,000 Cubic Feet in the Gable Roof
10,000 Cubic Feet + 4,000 Cubic Feet = 14,000 Total Cubic Feet

14,000 Cubic Feet is the answer.

Real Estate Math Practice Problems

1. The value of your house, not including the lot, is $91,000 today. What was the original cost if it has depreciated 5 percent per year for the past seven years?
   a. $67,407.41
   b. $95,789.47
   c. $122,850.00
   d. $140,000.00

2. What did the owners originally pay for their home if they sold it for $98,672, which gave them a 12 percent profit over their original cost?
   a. $86,830
   b. $88,100
   c. $89,700
   d. $110,510

3. What would you pay for a building producing $11,250 annual net income and showing a minimum rate of return of 9 percent?
   a. $125,000
   b. $123,626
   c. $101,250
   d. $122,625

4. An owner agrees to list his property on the condition that he will receive at least $47,300 after paying a 5 percent broker's commission and paying $1,150 in closing costs. At what price must it sell?
   a. $48,450
   b. $50,815
   c. $50,875
   d. $51,000

5. The Loving Gift Shop pays rent of $600 per month plus 2.5 percent of gross annual sales in excess of $50,000. What was the average monthly rent last year if gross annual sales were $75,000?
   a. $1,125.00
   b. $756.25
   c. $600.00
   d. $652.08

6. If your monthly rent is $525, what percent would this be of an annual income of $21,000?
   a. 25 percent
   b. 30 percent
   c. 33 percent
   d. 40 percent

7. Two brokers split the 6 percent commission on a $73,000 home. The selling salesperson, Joe, was paid 70 percent of his broker's share. The listing salesperson, Janice, was paid 30 percent of her broker's share. How much did Janice receive?
   a. $657
   b. $4,380
   c. $1,533
   d. $1,314

8. The buyer has agreed to pay $175,000 in sales price, 2.5 loan discount points, and a 1 percent origination fee. If the buyer receives a 90 percent loan-to-value ratio, how much will the buyer owe at closing for points and the origination fee?
   a. $1,575.00
   b. $3,937.50
   c. $5,512.50
   d. $6,125.00

9. Calculate eight months' interest on a $5,000 interest-only loan at 9.5 percent.
   a. $475.00
   b. $316.67
   c. $237.50
   d. $39.58

10. A 100-acre farm is divided into lots for homes. The streets require ⅛ of the whole farm, and there are 140 lots. How many square feet are in each lot?
   a. 43,560
   b. 35,004
   c. 31,114
   d. 27,225

11. What is the monthly net income on an investment of $115,000 if the rate of return is 12.5 percent?
   a. $1,150.00
   b. $1,197.92
   c. $7,666.67
   d. $14,375.00

12. A salesperson sells a property for $58,500. The contract he has with his broker is 40 percent of the full commission earned. The commission due the broker is 6 percent. What is the salesperson's share of the commission?
   a. $2,106
   b. $1,404
   c. $3,510
   d. $2,340

13. What is the interest rate on a $10,000 loan with semiannual interest of $450?
   a. 7%
   b. 9%
   c. 11%
   d. 13.5%

14. A warehouse is 80' wide and 120' long with ceilings 14' high. If 1,200 square feet of floor surface has been partitioned off, floor to ceiling, for an office, how many cubic feet of space will be left in the warehouse?
   a. 151,200
   b. 134,400
   c. 133,200
   d. 117,600

15. The lot you purchased five years ago for $15,000 has appreciated 3.5 percent per year. What is it worth today?
   a. $12,375
   b. $15,525
   c. $17,250
   d. $17,625

16. A lease calls for $1,000 per month minimum plus 2 percent of annual sales in excess of $100,000. What is the annual rent if the annual sales were $150,000?
   a. $12,000
   b. $13,000
   c. $14,000
   d. $15,000

17. There is a tract of land that is 1.25 acres. The lot is 150 feet deep. How much will the lot sell for at $65 per front foot?
   a. $9,750
   b. $8,125
   c. $23,595
   d. $8,725

18. Sue earns $20,000 per year and can qualify for a monthly PITI payment equal to 25 percent of her monthly salary. If the annual tax and insurance is $678.24, what is the loan amount she will qualify for if the monthly PI payment factor is $10.29 per $1,000 of loan amount?
   a. $66,000
   b. $43,000
   c. $40,500
   d. $35,000

19. You pay $65.53 monthly interest on a loan bearing 9.25 percent annual interest. What is the loan amount rounded to the nearest hundred dollars?
   a. $1,400
   b. $2,800
   c. $6,300
   d. $8,500

20. What percentage of profit would you make if you paid $10,500 for a lot, built a home on the lot that cost $93,000, and then sold the lot and house together for $134,550?
   a. 13 percent
   b. 23 percent
   c. 30 percent
   d. 45 percent

21. An income-producing property has $62,500 annual gross income and monthly expenses of $1,530. What is the appraised value if the appraiser uses a 10 percent capitalization rate?
   a. $441,400
   b. $625,000
   c. $183,600
   d. $609,700

22. Alfred pays $2,500 each for four parcels of land. He subdivides them into six parcels and sells each of the six parcels for $1,950. What was Alfred's percentage of profit?

    a.   14.5 percent
    b.   17 percent
    c.   52 percent
    d.   78 percent

23. A property sells for $96,000. If it has appreciated 4 percent per year straight line for the past five years, what did the owner pay for the property five years ago?

    a. $76,800
    b. $80,000
    c. $92,300
    d. $115,200

24. If you purchase a lot that is 125' ×150' for $6,468.75, what price did you pay per front foot?

    a. $23.52
    b. $43.13
    c. $51.75
    d. $64.69

25. Calculate the amount of commission earned by a broker on a property selling for $61,000 if 6 percent is paid on the first $50,000 and 3 percent on the remaining balance.

    a. $3,330
    b. $3,830
    c. $3,600
    d. $3,930

Answer Key for Real Estate Math Practice Problems

1. **d** $140,000.00 Original Cost

   5% Depreciation per Year × 7 Years = 35% Total Depreciation
   100% Original Cost − 35% Total Depreciation = 65% Today's Value

$91,000 Today's Value ÷	
= $140,000 **Original Cost**	65% or 0.65

   $91,000 ÷ 65% (.65) = $140,000 Original Cost

2. **b** $88,100 Original Cost

   100% Original Cost + 12% Profit = 112% Sales Price

$98,672 Sales Price ÷	
= $88,100 **Original Cost**	112% or 1.12

   $98,672 ÷ 112% (1.12) = $88,100 Original Cost

3. **a** $125,000 Price

$11,250 Annual Net Income ÷	
= $125,000 **Price**	9% or 0.09

   $11,250 ÷ 9% (.09) = $125,000 Price

4. **d** $51,000 Sales Price

   $47,300 Net to Seller + $1,150 Closing Costs =
   $48,450 Seller's Dollars after Commission
   100% Sales Price − 5% Commission = 95% Seller's Percent after Commission

$48,450 Seller's Dollars after Commission ÷	
= $51,000 **Sales Price**	95% or 0.95

   $48,450 ÷ 95% (0.95) = $51,000 Sales Price

5. **d** $652.08 Average Monthly Rent

   $75,000 Gross Annual Sales − $50,000 =
   $25,000 Gross Annual Sales Subject to 2.5%

	= $625 Annual Percentage Rent	
$25,000 Gross Annual Sales		2.5% or 0.025

   ×

$25,000 \times 2.5\% \ (.025) = \$625$

$625 Annual Percentage Rent ÷ 12 Months =
$52.08 Monthly Percentage Rent
$600 Monthly Minimum Rent + $52.08 Monthly Percentage Rent =
$652.08 Average Monthly Rent

6. **b** 30%

$525 Monthly Rent × 12 Months = $6,300 Annual Rent

÷ $6,300 Annual Rent	
$21,000 Annual Income	**= 0.3 or 30%**

$6,300 ÷ $21,000 = .30 or 30%

7. **a** **$657 Commission to Janice**

= $4,380 Full Commission	
$73,000 Sales Price	6% 0.06
×	

$73,000 × 6% (.06) = $4,380
$4,380 Full Commission ÷ 2 Brokers =
$2,190 Broker's Share of the Commission

= **$657 Janice's Commission**	
$2,190 Broker's Share of the Commission	30% 0.3
×	

$2,190 × 30% (.30) = $657 Commission

8. **c** **$5,512.50 for Points and the Origination Fee**

2.5 Points Loan Discount + 1 Point Origination Fee = 3.5 Points

= $157,500 Loan	
$175,000 Sales Price	90% or 0.9
×	

$175,000 × 90% or (.90) = $157,500

$5,512.50 for Points and Origination Fees	
$157,500 Loan	3.5% or 0.035
×	

$157,500 × 3.5% (.035) = $5,512.50 for Points and Origination Fees

9. **b** **$316.67 Interest**

$5,000 × 9.5% (.095) = $475
$475 Annual Interest ÷ 12 Months × 8 Months = **$316.67 Interest**

10. **d** **27,225 Square Feet per Lot**

1⅛ = 1 ÷ 8 = 0.125 for Streets
100 Acres × 0.125 = 12.5 Acres for Streets
100 Acres − 12.5 Acres for Streets = 87.5 Acres for Lots × 43,560 =
3,811,500 Square Feet ÷ 140 Lots = **27,225 Square Feet per Lot**

11. **b** **$1,197.92 Monthly Net Operating Income**

$115,000 × 12.5% (.125) = $14,375
$14,375 Annual Net Operating Income ÷ 12 Months =
$1,197.92 Monthly Net Operating Income

12. **b** **$1,404 Salesperson's Commission**

$58,500 × 6% (.06) = $3,510

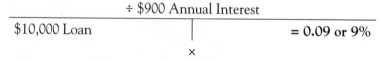

$3,510 × 40% (.40) = $1,404 Salesperson's Commission

13. **b** **9% Annual Interest Rate**

$450 × 2 = $900 Annual Interest

	÷ $900 Annual Interest	
$10,000 Loan		**= 0.09 or 9%**

$900 ÷ $10,000 = 0.09 or 9% Interest Rate

14. **d** **117,600 Cubic Feet**

120' × 80' = 9,600 Square Feet in Building – 1,200 Square Feet for Office = 8,400 Square Feet Left in Warehouse × 14' Ceiling = 117,600 Cubic Feet Left in Warehouse

15. **d** **$17,625 Today's Value**

3.5% Appreciation per Year × 5 Years = 17.5% Total Appreciation
100% Cost + 17.5% Total Appreciation = 117.5% Today's Value

= $17,625 Today's Value	
$15,000 Original Cost	117.5% or 1.175
×	

$15,000 × 117.5% (1.175) = $17,625 Today's Value

16. **b** **$13,000 Annual Rent**

$1,000 Monthly Minimum Rent × 12 Months =
$12,000 Annual Minimum Rent
$150,000 Annual Sales – $100,000 = $50,000 Annual Sales Subject to 2%

= $1,000 Annual Percentage Rent	
$50,000 Annual Sales Subject to 2%	2% or 0.02
×	

$50,000 × 2% (.02) = $1,000

$12,000 Annual Minimum Rent + $1,000 Annual Percentage Rent = $13,000 Annual Rent

17. **c** **$23,595 Sales Price**

1.25 Acres × 43,560 = 54,450 Square Feet ÷ 150' Deep = 363' Frontage × $65 per Front Foot = $23,595 Sales Price

18. **d** **$35,000 Loan**

$20,000 Annual Salary ÷ 12 Months = $1,666.67 Monthly Salary

= $416.67 Monthly PITI Payment	
$1,666.67 Monthly Salary	25% or 0.25
×	

$1,666.67 × 25% = $416.67

$678.24 Annual Tax and Insurance ÷ 12 Months =
$56.52 Monthly Tax and Insurance
$416.67 Monthly PITI Payment – $56.52 Monthly TI =
$360.15 Monthly PI Payment
$360.15 Monthly PI Payment ÷ $10.29 × $1,000 = **$35,000 Loan**

19. d **$8,500 Loan**

$65.53 Monthly Interest × 12 Months = $786.36 Annual Interest

$786.36 Annual Interest ÷	
= 8,501.19 **or $8,500 Loan**	9.25% or 0.0925

$786.36 ÷ 9.25% (.0925) = $8501.19 Loan

20. c **30%**

$10,500 Cost of Lot + $93,000 Cost of Home = $103,500 Total Cost
$134,550 Sales Price − $103,500 Total Cost = $31,050 Profit

÷ $31,050 Profit	
$103,500 Total Cost	**= 0.3 or 30%**

$31,050 ÷ $103,500 = 0.3 or 30%

21. a **$441,400 Value**

$1,530 Monthly Expenses × 12 Months = $18,360 Annual Expenses
$62,500 Annual Gross Income − $18,360 Annual Expenses =
$44,140 Annual Net Operating Income

$44,140 Annual Net Operating Income ÷	
= $441,400 Value	10% or 0.1

$44,140 ÷ 10% (.10) = $441,400 Value

22. b **17% Profit**

$2,500 Cost × 4 Parcels = $10,000 Total Cost
$1,950 Sales Price × 6 Parcels = $11,700 Sales Price
$11,700 Sales Price − $10,000 Cost = $1,700 Profit

÷ $1,700 Profit	
$10,000 Cost	**= 0.17 or 17% Profit**

$1,700 ÷ $10,000 Cost = 0.17 or 17% Profit

23. b **$80,000 Original Cost**

4% Annual Appreciation × 5 Years = 20% Total Appreciation
100% Cost + 20% Total Appreciation = 120% Today's Value

$96,000 Today's Value ÷	
= $80,000 Original Cost	120% 1.2

$96,000 ÷ 120% (1.20) = $80,000 Original Cost

24. c **$51.75 per Front Foot**

$6,468.75 Price ÷ 125 Front Feet = $51.75 per Front Foot

25. a $3,330 Total Commission

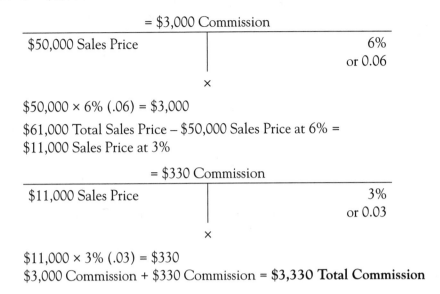

= $3,000 Commission

| $50,000 Sales Price | 6% |
| | or 0.06 |

×

$50,000 × 6% (.06) = $3,000

$61,000 Total Sales Price – $50,000 Sales Price at 6% = $11,000 Sales Price at 3%

= $330 Commission

| $11,000 Sales Price | 3% |
| | or 0.03 |

×

$11,000 × 3% (.03) = $330
$3,000 Commission + $330 Commission = **$3,330 Total Commission**

Georgia Real Estate Licensing Examination

Modern Real Estate Practice in Georgia is designed to prepare you for a career in real estate. However, before you can become a salesperson, broker, associate broker, or community association manager, you must, under Georgia law, obtain a license. Passing the licensing examination plays a large role in determining your eligibility to become licensed. The examination is designed to test your knowledge of real estate practices, principles, and laws.

The state test is prepared and administered by Applied Measurement Professionals, Inc. (AMP), an independent testing company. You can contact AMP to determine the appropriate test site and time. AMP's Web site (*www.goamp.com*) provides a candidate handbook that includes topic outlines, procedures for establishing an examination appointment, and rules for the examination.

■ WHAT TO EXPECT FROM THE EXAM

Georgia salespersons, community association managers, and brokers and associate brokers are given separate examinations.

Salesperson Exam

The salesperson exam has 100 multiple-choice questions written on three levels: recall (recalling specific information), application (applying knowledge to a situation), and analysis (analyzing information and determining solutions). In order to pass the exam, you must have a total score of at least 75 percent. Your total percentage score reflects the total number of questions answered correctly divided by the total number of questions.

The salesperson exam consists of two content areas: national, and Georgia real estate. The national content area tests knowledge of general real estate law, finance, and practices. In addition to the questions used in computing your score, the exam may contain five questions that are being pretested for future use and are not included in your score.

The Georgia supplement salesperson examination relates specifically to the law and real estate practices of Georgia. It contains 52 multiple-choice questions and tests areas of state laws and rules, real estate practice in Georgia, and finance and closing.

Community Association Manager Examination

The community association manager examination contains 48 multiple-choice questions on Georgia law. There is no national portion on this exam. The exam covers the following topics: property law, law of agency, Georgia Real Estate

License Law, forms of ownership, contracts and transaction documents, real estate instruments and conveyances, and financing and accounting.

Broker and Associate Broker Examination

The broker and associate broker examination consists of 12 simulation problems; ten of these problems are used to complete your score. The other two problems are pretested problems for future use and are not scored. Each problem has three parts: scenario, information gathering, and decision making. The scenario lays the scene and setting; for example, presenting client information and problems. Information gathering involves gathering all relevant information for answering the question. Decision making provides opportunities for making decisions and is formatted in two ways: single best option and multiple options.

Each section in the simulation has a minimum passing level. Scores are provided for each of the sections. It is the total raw score in both sections that determines passing or failing the simulation exam. If you pass the exam, you will receive a Certification of Accuracy Statement with your passing score and application information.

Veterans' Preference Points

The Commission's Rules and Regulations allow for veterans' preference points in the examination, provided certain eligibility requirements are met. If you are a disabled veteran and served on active duty of the armed forces of the United States, including the National Guard, during wartime or any conflict when military personnel were committed by the President, you may be entitled to either five or ten points of credit on your examination. See Rule 520-1-.04(3) of the Commission's Rules and Regulations.

■ EXAMINATION PROCEDURE

All examinations are given by computer at an AMP Assessment Center in a testing carrel. You do not need computer experience or typing skills to take the examination. Prior to taking the examination, you will be given an opportunity to practice taking the exam on the computer.

The computer monitors the time and terminates the exam session if you exceed the allotted time. There is a "time box" on the computer screen to check on the time remaining to complete the exam. Only one exam question is presented at a time. You may change your answer as much as you like throughout the testing period and may leave questions blank and return to them later. Be sure to answer every question; there is no penalty for guessing.

The broker or associate broker simulation exam appears in three windows on the computer screen. One window is the scenario section describing the situation, asking a question and indicating the manner for response (for example, "choose only one response"). The second window is the options window, which contains all answer options. The third window is the simulation history window, which shows all previous sections and options chosen. After selecting an option, you cannot reconsider and select a different option.

■ EXAMINATION OUTLINES

The following is the AMP Detailed Content Outline for the national portion of the exam, along with the chapters of *Modern Real Estate Practice in Georgia* in which the subjects are covered:

Topic Headings—National Portion	Chapter
1. Listing Property	
a. Listing	
1. Legal description	9
2. Lot size	9
3. Physical dimensions of structure	9
4. Appurtenances	7
5. Utilities	7
6. Type of construction	8
7. Encumbrances	7
8. Compliance with building codes	20
9. Ownership of record	13
10. Homeowners' association documents and expenses	8
11. Brokerage fee	5
12. Property taxes	10
b. Assessment of Property Value	
1. Location	2
2. Anticipated changes	2
3. Depreciation	2
4. Deterioration	2
5. Obsolescence	2
6. Improvements	2
7. Economic trends	2
8. Market data	2
c. Services to the Seller	
1. Responsibilities of the licensee and the listing firm	14
2. Property subdivision	20
3. Hidden defects known by the owner	4
4. Information about required disclosures	4, 6
5. Property included in and excluded from sale	2
6. Personal property and real property differences	2, 6
7. Net proceed estimation	4
8. Completion of listing agreement, provision to seller, explanation	6
9. Determination that parties holding title have signed listing agreement	6
10. Showing of house and safeguarding property	4
11. Methods of marketing property	5
12. Presentation of offers to the seller	11, 14
13. Property tax information	10
14. Transaction files	5
15. Deed restrictions and covenants	7, 20
16. Forms of ownership interests in real estate, issues related to conveyance of real property	8

The most recent AMP Content Outline for the Georgia Salesperson Examination covers topics that can be found in Chapter 14, Georgia Real Estate License Laws, of this book. The topics include:

State Laws and Rules
— Unfair Practices
— Substantive Regulations
— Qualifications and Fees
— Fair Housing Laws
— Real Estate Education, Research, and Recovery Fund
— Investigation and Hearing Process
— Commission Organization and Procedures
— Required Licensure

Real Estate Practice in Georgia
— Real Estate Practice
— Sales Contracts
— Listings and Agency
— Property Management
— Community Association Management

Finance and Closing
— Finance
— Closing Procedures

The most recent AMP Detailed Content Outline for the Broker Simulation Examination contains: ethics, negotiation, document preparation, fair housing, environmental issues, representation of services, valuation, advertising, finance, agency/nonagency relationships, disclosures (including stigmatized property), property representations, trust accounts, training/supervision of licensees, and risk management.

■ SAMPLE EXAMINATIONS

The following examinations have been designed for additional practice and to help you prepare for the actual licensing examination. The first examination covers general topics for the national portion of your examination. The second examination contains Georgia-specific questions for additional preparation for the Georgia-specific portion of the examination. On your actual exam, there are five "pretest" questions in each section of the exam. They do not factor into your final score. For review purposes here, however, there are no pretest-type items: every question counts.

■ MULTIPLE-CHOICE QUESTIONS: TEST-TAKING STRATEGIES

There are as many different ways to prepare for and take multiple-choice examinations as there are test takers. Before you try the following sample exam, take some time to read this overview of test-taking strategies. While no one can tell you which method will work best for you, it's always a good idea to think about what you're going to do before you do it.

One of the most important things to remember about multiple-choice test questions is this: they always give you the correct answer. You don't have to remember how things are spelled, and you don't have to try to guess what the question is about. The answer is always there, right in front of you.

Of course, if it were as easy as that, it wouldn't be much of a test. The key to success in taking multiple-choice examinations is actually twofold: first, *know the correct answer*. You do that by going to class, paying attention, taking good notes and studying the material. Then, if you don't know the correct answer, be able to analyze the questions and answers effectively so you can apply the second key: *be able to make a reasonable guess*. Even if you don't know the answer, you will probably know which answers are clearly wrong and which ones are more likely than the others to be right.

If you can eliminate one answer as wrong, you have improved your odds of "guessing correctly" by 25 percent, from 4-to-1 to 3-to-1. If you can eliminate two wrong answers, you have a 50/50 shot at a correct guess. Of course, if you can eliminate *three* wrong answers, your chance of a correct response is 100 percent. In any case, there is no secret formula: *the only sure way to improve your odds of a correct answer is to study and learn the material.*

Structure of the Question

A multiple-choice question has a basic structure. It starts with what test writers call the *stem*. That's the text of the question that sets up the need for an answer. The stem may be an incomplete statement that is finished by the correct answer; it may be a story problem or hypothetical example (called a *fact-pattern*) about which you will be asked a question. Or it may be a math problem in which you are given basic information and asked to solve a mathematical issue, such as the amount of a commission or capital gain.

The stem is always followed by *options*: four possible answers to the question presented by the stem. Depending on the structure and content of the stem, the options may be single words or numbers, phrases or complete sentences. Three of the options are *distractors*: incorrect answers intended to "distract" you from the correct choice. One of the options is the correct answer, called the *key*.

Reading a Multiple-Choice Question

Here are three suggestions for how to read a multiple-choice test question.

1. **The traditional method** Read the question through from start to finish, then read the options. When you get to the correct answer, mark it and move on. This method works best for short questions, such as those that require completion or simply define a term. For long, more complicated questions or those that are not quite so clear, however, you may miss important information.

2. **The focus method** As we've seen, multiple-choice questions have different parts. In longer math or story-type questions, the last line of the stem will contain the question's *focus*: the basic issue the item asks you to address. That is, *the question is always in the last line of the stem*. In the focus method, when you

come to a longer item, read the last line of the stem first. This will clue you in to what the question is about. Then go back and read the stem from beginning to end. The advantage is this: while you are reading the complicated facts or math elements, you know what to look for. You can watch for important items and disregard unnecessary information. It's a sad fact of multiple-choice exams that sometimes test writers include distracting elements in the stem itself. If you check for the question's focus first, you'll spot the test-writer's tricks right away.

3. **The upside-down method**   This technique takes the focus method one step further. Here, you do just what the name implies: you start reading the question from the bottom up. By reading the four options first, you can learn exactly what the test writer wants you to focus on. For instance, a fact-pattern problem might include several dollar values in the stem, leading you to believe you're going to have to do a math calculation. You'll be trying to recall all the equations you've memorized, only to find at the end of the stem that you're only expected to define a term. If you've read the options first, you would have known what to look for.

Sample Exam 1—General Real Estate Practice and Principles

1. Which of the following is a lien on real estate?
   a. Recorded easement
   b. Recorded mortgage
   c. Encroachment
   d. Deed restriction

2. A sales contract was signed by a minor. Which of the following describes this contract?
   a. Voidable
   b. Breached
   c. Discharged
   d. Void

3. A broker receives a check for earnest money from a buyer and deposits the money in the broker's personal interest-bearing checking account over the weekend. This action exposes the broker to a charge of
   a. commingling.
   b. novation.
   c. subrogation.
   d. accretion.

4. A borrower takes out a mortgage loan that requires monthly payments of $875.70 for 20 years and a final payment of $24,095. This is what type of loan?
   a. Wraparound
   b. Accelerated
   c. Balloon
   d. Variable

5. If a borrower computed the interest charged for the previous month on a $260,000 loan balance as $1,300, what is the borrower's interest rate?
   a. 7 percent
   b. 7½ percent
   c. 6 percent
   d. 6½ percent

6. A broker signs a contract with a buyer. Under the contract, the broker agrees to help the buyer find a suitable property and to represent the buyer in negotiations with the seller. Although the buyer may not sign an agreement with any other broker, the buyer may look for and purchase a property without the broker's assistance. The broker is entitled to payment only if the broker locates the property that is purchased. What kind of agreement has this broker signed?
   a. Exclusive buyer agency agreement
   b. Exclusive-agency buyer agency agreement
   c. Open buyer agency agreement
   d. Option contract

7. A grantor conveys property by delivering a deed. The deed contains five covenants. This is most likely a
   a. general warranty deed.
   b. quitclaim deed.
   c. special warranty deed.
   d. deed in trust.

8. Pat, a real estate broker, does not show non-Asian clients any properties in several traditionally Asian neighborhoods. Pat bases this practice on the need to preserve the valuable cultural integrity of Asian immigrant communities. Which of the following statements is *TRUE* regarding Pat's policy?
   a. Pat's policy is steering and violates the fair housing laws regardless of Pat's motivation.
   b. Because Pat is not attempting to restrict the rights of any single minority group, the practice does not constitute steering.
   c. Pat's policy is steering, but it does not violate the fair housing laws because Pat is motivated by cultural preservation, not by exclusion or discrimination.
   d. Pat's policy has the effect, but not the intent, of steering.

9. Helen grants a life estate to her son-in-law and stipulates that upon his death, the title to the property will pass to her grandson. This second estate is known as a(n)

    a. remainder.
    b. reversion.
    c. estate at sufferance.
    d. estate for years.

10. A primary feature of property held in joint tenancy is that

    a. a maximum of two people can own the real estate.
    b. the fractional interests of the owners can be different.
    c. additional owners may be added later.
    d. there is always right of survivorship.

11. Alan is a licensed real estate salesperson who has a written contract with his broker that specifies that he will not be treated as an employee. Alan's entire income is from sales commissions rather than an hourly wage. Based on these facts, Alan will be treated by the IRS as

    a. a real estate assistant.
    b. an employee.
    c. a subagent.
    d. self-employed.

12. A tenant's landlord plans to sell the building in which the tenant lives to the state so that a freeway can be built. The tenant's lease has expired, but the landlord permits the tenant to stay in the apartment until the building is torn down. The tenant continues to pay the rent as prescribed in the lease. What kind of tenancy does this tenant have?

    a. Holdover tenancy
    b. Month-to-month tenancy
    c. Tenancy at sufferance
    d. Tenancy at will

13. The owner of a house wants to fence the yard for the family pet. When the fence is erected, the fencing materials become real estate through

    a. severance.
    b. subrogation.
    c. annexation.
    d. attachment.

14. A suburban home that lacks sufficient indoor plumbing suffers from which of the following?

    a. Functional obsolescence
    b. Curable physical deterioration
    c. Incurable physical deterioration
    d. External obsolescence

15. A developer built a structure that has six stories. Several years later, an ordinance was passed in that area banning any building six stories or higher. This building is a

    a. nonconforming use.
    b. situation in which the structure would have to be demolished.
    c. conditional use.
    d. violation of the zoning laws.

16. Assuming that the listing broker and the selling broker in a transaction split their commission equally, what was the sales price of the property if the commission rate was 6.5 percent and the listing broker received $12,593.50?

    a. $139,900
    b. $256,200
    c. $387,492
    d. $193,746

17. Robert, a real estate broker, specializes in helping both buyers and sellers with the necessary paperwork involved in transferring property. While Robert is not an agent of either party, Robert may not disclose either party's confidential information to the other. Robert is BEST described as a(n)

    a. buyer's agent.
    b. independent contractor.
    c. dual agent.
    d. transactional broker.

18. Glen is interested in selling his house as quickly as possible and believes that the best way to do this is to have several brokers compete against each other for the commission. Glen's listing agreements with four different brokers specifically promise that if one of them finds a buyer for Glen's property, Glen will be obligated to pay a commission to that broker only. What type of agreement has Glen entered into?

    a. Executed
    b. Discharged
    c. Unilateral
    d. Bilateral

19. The listing and selling brokers agree to split a 7 percent commission 50-50 on a $295,900 sale. The listing broker gives the listing salesperson 50 percent of the listing broker's share, and the selling broker gives the selling salesperson 65 percent. How much does the selling salesperson earn from the sale after deducting expenses of $1,300?

    a. $5,431.73
    b. $10,356.50
    c. $5,178.00
    d. $6,731.73

20. Police powers include all of the following EXCEPT

    a. zoning.
    b. deed restrictions.
    c. building codes.
    d. subdivision regulations.

21. A seller wants to net $165,000 from the sale of a house after paying the broker's fee of 6 percent. The seller's gross sales price will be

    a. $182,242.
    b. $174,900.
    c. $155,000.
    d. $175,532.

22. Three acres equals how many square feet?

    a. 43,560
    b. 130,680
    c. 156,840
    d. 27,878,400

23. A buyer is purchasing a condominium unit in a subdivision and obtains financing from a local savings and loan association. In this situation, which of the following BEST describes this buyer?

    a. Vendor
    b. Mortgagor
    c. Grantor
    d. Lessor

24. The current value of a property is $140,000. The property is assessed at 40 percent of its current value for real estate tax purposes, with an equalization factor of 1.5 applied to the assessed value. If the tax rate is $4 per $100 of assessed valuation, what is the amount of tax due on the property?

    a. $840
    b. $3,360
    c. $2,240
    d. $2,100

25. A building was sold for $260,000 with the purchaser putting 10 percent down and obtaining a loan for the balance. The lending institution charged a 1 percent loan origination fee. What was the total cash used for the purchase?

    a. $2,340
    b. $23,400
    c. $28,340
    d. $26,000

26. A parcel of vacant land has an assessed valuation of $274,550. If the assessment is 85 percent of market value, what is the market value?

    a. $315,732.50
    b. $320,000.00
    c. $323,000.00
    d. $830,333.33

27. Which of the following BEST describes a capitalization rate?

    a. Amount determined by the gross rent multiplier
    b. Rate of return an income property will produce
    c. Mathematical value determined by a sales price
    d. Rate at which the amount of depreciation in a property is measured

28. In some states, by paying the debt after a fore-closure sale, the delinquent borrower has the right to regain the property under which of the following?
    a. Novation
    b. Redemption
    c. Reversion
    d. Recovery

29. If a house was sold for $180,000 and the buyer obtained an FHA-insured mortgage loan for $120,000, how much money would the buyer pay in discount points if the lender charged two points?
    a. $1,200
    b. $1,000
    c. $2,400
    d. $1,800

30. The commission rate is 7 percent on a sale of $250,000. What is the dollar amount of the commission?
    a. $35,000
    b. $17,500
    c. $1,750
    d. $3,571

31. A prospective buyer signs an offer to purchase a residential property. All of the following cir-cumstances would automatically terminate the offer EXCEPT the
    a. buyer signed a written offer to buy a house and then died.
    b. buyer revoked the offer between the presen-tation and a possible acceptance.
    c. seller made a counteroffer.
    d. seller received a better offer from another buyer.

32. Wally, owner of the Circle M Ranch, enters into a sale-and-leaseback agreement with Glenda. Which of the following statements is TRUE of this arrangement?
    a. Wally retains title to the ranch.
    b. Glenda receives possession of the property.
    c. Glenda is the lessor.
    d. Wally is the lessor.

33. A buyer and a seller sign a contract for the sale of real property. A few days later, they decide to change many of the terms of the contract, while retaining the basic intent to buy and sell. The process by which the new contract replaces the old one is called
    a. assignment.
    b. novation.
    c. assemblage.
    d. rescission.

34. Using the services of a mortgage broker, Glen borrowed $25,000 from a private lender. After deducting the loan costs, Glen received $24,255. What is the face amount of the note?
    a. $24,255
    b. $25,000
    c. $4,255
    d. $645

35. Whose signature is necessary for a signed offer to purchase real estate to become a contract?
    a. Buyer's only
    b. Buyer's and seller's
    c. Seller's only
    d. Seller's and seller's broker's

36. A borrower has just made the final payment on a mortgage loan. Regardless of this fact, the records will still show a lien on the mortgaged property until which of the following events occurs?
    a. A mortgage satisfaction document is recorded.
    b. A reconveyance of the mortgage document is delivered to the mortgage holder.
    c. A novation of the mortgage document takes place.
    d. An estoppel of the mortgage document is filed with the clerk of the county in which the mortgagee is located.

37. If the annual net income from a commercial property is $75,000 and the capitalization rate is 8 percent, what is the property worth if the income approach is used?
    a. $694,000
    b. $600,000
    c. $810,000
    d. $937,500

38. A broker enters into a listing agreement with a seller in which the seller will receive $120,000 from the sale of a vacant lot and the broker will receive any sale proceeds exceeding that amount. This is what type of listing?

a. Exclusive-agency
b. Net
c. Exclusive-right-to-sell
d. Multiple

39. Under a cooperative form of ownership, an owner

a. is a shareholder in the corporation.
b. owns his or her unit outright and a share of the common areas.
c. will have to take out a new mortgage loan on a newly acquired unit.
d. receives a fixed-term lease for the unit.

40. A known defect or a cloud on title to property may be cured by

a. obtaining quitclaim deeds from all appropriate parties.
b. recording the title after closing.
c. paying cash for the property at the settlement.
d. purchasing a title insurance policy at closing.

41. A seller signed an exclusive-right-to-sell agreement with a licensee. If the seller finds a suitable buyer with no assistance, the licensee is entitled to

a. full compensation from the buyer.
b. no compensation from the seller.
c. partial compensation.
d. full compensation from the seller.

42. Under the terms of a net lease, a commercial tenant would usually be directly responsible for paying all of the following property expenses *EXCEPT*

a. maintenance expenses.
b. mortgage debt service.
c. fire and extended-coverage insurance.
d. real estate taxes.

43. The Civil Rights Act of 1866 prohibits discrimination based on

a. sex.
b. religion.
c. race.
d. familial status.

44. What would it cost to put new carpeting in a room measuring 15 feet by 20 feet if the carpet costs $16.95 per square yard, plus a $250 installation charge?

a. $589
b. $815
c. $505
d. $5,335

45. What is the difference between a general lien and a specific lien?

a. A general lien cannot be enforced in court, while a specific lien can.
b. A specific lien is held by only one person, while a general lien must be held by two or more.
c. A general lien is a lien against personal property, while a specific lien is a lien against real estate.
d. A specific lien is a lien against a certain parcel of real estate, while a general lien covers all of a debtor's property.

46. In an option to purchase real estate, which of the following statements is *TRUE* of the optionee?

a. The optionee must purchase the property but may do so at any time within the option period.
b. The optionee is limited to a refund of the option consideration if the option is exercised.
c. The optionee cannot obtain third-party financing on the property until after the option has expired.
d. The optionee has no obligation to purchase the property during the option period.

47. The village board of Wright Park has decided that a parking lot would enhance the beauty, safety, and vitality of the community by keeping cars from parking on the streets. Unfortunately, Ann's house is located on land needed for the new parking lot. Based on these facts, which of the following statements is *TRUE*?

    a. Ann's constitutional right to own property cannot be infringed by the village under any circumstances.

    b. The village may tear down Ann's house and build the parking lot without paying her any compensation, through the village's constitutional authority under the takings clause.

    c. The village may tear down Ann's house, but must first pay her a fair amount for her home.

    d. The village may not seize Ann's house because it has insufficient reason to do so.

48. A parcel of vacant land 80 feet wide and 200 feet deep was sold for $500 per front foot. How much money would a salesperson receive as a 60 percent share in the 10 percent commission?

    a. $1,600
    b. $2,400
    c. $6,000
    d. $4,000

49. Betty's home is the smallest in a neighborhood of large, expensive houses. The effect of the other houses on the value of Betty's home is known as

    a. regression.
    b. progression.
    c. substitution.
    d. contribution.

50. A lien that arises as a result of a judgment, estate or inheritance taxes, a decedent's debts, or federal taxes is what sort of lien?

    a. Specific
    b. General
    c. Voluntary
    d. Equitable

51. All of the following will terminate an offer to purchase real estate *EXCEPT*

    a. failure to accept the offer within a prescribed period.

    b. revocation by the offeror communicated to the offeree after acceptance.

    c. a conditional acceptance of the offer by the offeree.

    d. the death of the offeror or offeree.

52. Which of the following situations does *NOT* violate the federal Fair Housing Act of 1968?

    a. The refusal of a property manager to rent an apartment to a Catholic couple who are otherwise qualified

    b. The general policy of a loan company to avoid granting home improvement loans to individuals living in transitional neighborhoods

    c. The intentional neglect of a broker to show an Asian family any property listings in all-white neighborhoods

    d. A widowed woman's insistence on renting her spare bedroom only to another widowed woman

53. Steve and Win enter into a six-month oral lease. If Win defaults, Steve may

    a. not bring a court action because leases must be in writing for a court to review them.

    b. not bring a court action because the statute of frauds governs six-month leases.

    c. bring a court action because six-month leases need not be in writing to be enforceable.

    d. bring a court action because the statute of limitations does not apply to oral leases, regardless of their term.

54. On Monday, the buyer offers to purchase a vacant lot for $25,000. On Tuesday, the owner counteroffers to sell the lot for $29,000. On Friday, the owner withdraws the counteroffer and accepts the buyer's original offer of $25,000. Under these circumstances

   a. a valid agreement exists because the seller accepted the buyer's offer exactly as it was made, regardless of the fact that it was not accepted immediately.
   b. a valid agreement exists because the seller accepted before the buyer provided notice that the offer was withdrawn.
   c. no valid agreement exists because the buyer's offer was not accepted within 72 hours of its having been made.
   d. no valid agreement exists because the seller's counteroffer was a rejection of the buyer's offer, and once rejected, it cannot be accepted later.

55. Yuri's neighbors use his driveway to reach their garage, which is on their property. Yuri's attorney explains that the neighbors have the right to use the driveway. Yuri's property is the

   a. dominant tenement.
   b. servient tenement.
   c. fee simple defeasible estate.
   d. fee simple determinable estate.

56. If the quarterly interest at 7.5 percent is $562.50, what is the principal amount of the loan?

   a. $7,500
   b. $15,000
   c. $30,000
   d. $75,000

57. A deed conveys ownership to the grantee "as long as the existing building is not torn down." What type of estate does this deed create?

   a. Fee simple determinable estate
   b. Homestead estate
   c. Fee simple absolute estate
   d. Life estate pur autre vie, with the measuring life being the building's expected structural lifetime

58. If the mortgage loan is 80 percent of the appraised value of a house and the interest rate of 6 percent amounts to $460 for the first month, what is the appraised value of the house?

   a. $92,000
   b. $73,600
   c. $115,000
   d. $55,200

59. Local zoning ordinances may regulate all of the following EXCEPT the

   a. height of buildings in an area.
   b. density of population.
   c. appropriate use of buildings in an area.
   d. market value of a property.

60. A broker took a listing and later discovered that the client had been declared incompetent by a court. What is the current status of the listing?

   a. The listing is unaffected because the broker acted in good faith as the owner's agent.
   b. The listing is of no value to the broker because the contract is void.
   c. The listing entitles the broker to collect a commission from the client's guardian or trustee if the broker produces a buyer.
   d. The listing must be renegotiated between the broker and the client, based on the new information.

61. If a storage tank that measures 12 feet by 9 feet by 8 feet is designed to store a gas that costs $1.82 per cubic foot, what does it cost to fill the tank to one-half of its capacity?

   a. $685
   b. $786
   c. $864
   d. $1,572

62. Which of the following is forbidden by the federal Fair Housing Act of 1968?

   a. Limitation by religion and nationality in the sale of a single-family home where the property is not advertised by the listing broker

   b. Limitation to members only in noncommercial lodgings of a private club

   c. Limitations against familial status and disability in the rental of a unit in an owner-occupied three-family dwelling when no discriminatory advertising is used

   d. Limitation by religion and sex in noncommercial housing in a convent or monastery

63. A buyer purchases a $137,000 property, depositing $3,000 as earnest money. If the buyer obtains a 75 percent loan-to-value loan on the property, no additional items are prorated, and there are no closing costs to the buyer, how much more cash will the buyer need at the settlement?

   a. $34,250
   b. $33,500
   c. $10,275
   d. $31,250

64. Broker Kay arrives to present a purchase offer to Dora, who is seriously ill, and finds Dora's son and daughter-in-law also present. The son and daughter-in-law angrily urge Dora to accept the offer, even though it is much less than the asking price for the property. If Dora accepts the offer, she may not be bound by it because

   a. Kay improperly presented an offer that was less than the asking price.

   b. Kay's failure to protect Dora from the son and daughter-in-law constituted a violation of Kay's fiduciary duties.

   c. Dora's rights under the ADA have been violated by the son and daughter-in-law.

   d. Dora was under undue influence from the son and daughter-in-law, so the contract is voidable.

65. A buyer bought a house for $125,000. The house, which had originally sold for $118,250, appraised for $122,500. Based on these facts, if the buyer applies for an 80 percent mortgage, what will be the amount of the loan?

   a. $94,600
   b. $98,000
   c. $100,000
   d. $106,750

66. A purchaser offers to buy a seller's property by signing a purchase contract. The seller accepts the offer. What kind of title interest does the buyer have in the property at this point?

   a. Legal
   b. Equitable
   c. Defeasible
   d. The buyer has no title interest at this point.

67. Todd agrees to purchase a house for $184,500. Todd pays $2,000 as earnest money and obtains a new mortgage loan for $167,600. The purchase contract provides for a March 15 settlement. Todd and the sellers prorate the previous year's real estate taxes of $1,880.96, which have been prepaid. Todd has additional closing costs of $1,250, and the sellers have other closing costs of $850. How much cash must Todd bring to the settlement?

   a. $16,389
   b. $17,639
   c. $17,839
   d. $19,639

68. A broker listed a house for $247,900. A member of a racial minority group saw the house and was interested in it. When the prospective buyer asked the broker the price of the house, the broker said it was listed for $253,000 and that the seller was very firm on the price. Under the federal Fair Housing Act of 1968, such a statement is

    a. legal because the law requires only that the buyer be given the opportunity to buy the house.
    b. legal because the representation was made by the broker and not directly by the owner.
    c. illegal because the difference in the offering price and the quoted price was greater than 10 percent.
    d. illegal because the terms of the potential sale were changed for the prospective buyer.

69. Which of the following federal laws requires that finance charges be stated as an annual percentage rate?

    a. Truth-in-Lending Act
    b. Real Estate Settlement Procedures Act (RESPA)
    c. Equal Credit Opportunity Act (ECOA)
    d. Federal Fair Housing Act

70. An appraiser has been hired to prepare an appraisal report of a property for loan purposes. The property is an elegant old mansion that is now used as a restaurant. To which approach to value should the appraiser probably give the greatest weight when making this appraisal?

    a. Income
    b. Sales comparison
    c. Replacement cost
    d. Reproduction cost

71. A borrower applies for a mortgage, and the loan officer suggests that the borrower consider a term mortgage loan. Which of the following statements BEST explains what the loan officer means?

    a. All of the interest is paid at the end of the term.
    b. The debt is partially amortized over the life of the loan.
    c. The length of the term is limited by state law.
    d. The entire principal amount is due at the end of the term.

72. Valley Place is a condominium community with a swimming pool, tennis courts, and biking trail. These facilities are most likely owned by the

    a. Valley Place condominium board.
    b. corporation in which the unit owners hold stock.
    c. unit owners in the form of proportional divided interests.
    d. unit owners in the form of percentage undivided interests.

In questions 73 and 74, identify how each item would be entered on a closing statement in a typical real estate transaction.

73. The buyer's earnest money deposit is a

    a. credit to buyer only.
    b. credit to seller, debit to buyer.
    c. credit to buyer and seller.
    d. debit to buyer only.

74. Prepaid insurance and tax reserves, where the buyer assumes the mortgage, is a

    a. credit to buyer, debit to seller.
    b. credit to seller only.
    c. debit to seller only.
    d. debit to buyer, credit to seller.

75. Real property can become personal property by the process known as

    a. annexation.
    b. severance.
    c. hypothecation.
    d. accretion.

76. Julie and Steve are next-door neighbors. Steve gives Julie permission to park a camper in Steve's yard for a few weeks. Steve does not charge Julie rent for the use of the yard. Steve has given Julie a(n)

    a. revocable trust.
    b. estate for years.
    c. license.
    d. permissive encroachment.

77. What is the cost of constructing a fence 6 feet, 6 inches high, around a lot measuring 90 feet by 175 feet, if the cost of erecting the fence is $1.25 per linear foot and the cost of materials is $0.825 per square foot of fence?

    a. $1,752
    b. $2,054
    c. $2,084
    d. $3,505

78. Sally signs a listing agreement with broker Eric. Broker Nancy obtains a buyer for the house, and Eric does not receive a commission. Eric does not sue Sally, even though Sally compensated Nancy. The listing agreement between Sally and Eric was probably which of the following?

    a. Exclusive-right-to-sell
    b. Open
    c. Exclusive-agency
    d. Dual-agency

79. Antitrust laws do NOT prohibit real estate

    a. companies agreeing on fees charged to sellers.
    b. brokers allocating markets based on the value of homes.
    c. companies allocating markets based on the location of commercial buildings.
    d. salespersons within the same office agreeing on a standard commission rate.

80. Tony leased an apartment from Laverne. Because Laverne failed to perform routine maintenance, the apartment building's central heating plant broke down in the fall. Laverne neglected to have the heating system repaired, and Tony had no heat for the first six weeks of winter. Tony had reported this problem repeatedly to Laverne. Although eight months remained on Tony's lease, Tony moved out of the apartment and refused to pay any rent. If Laverne sues to recover the outstanding rent, which of the following would be Tony's BEST defense?

    a. Because Tony lived in the apartment for more than 25 percent of the lease term, he was entitled to move out at any time without penalty.
    b. Tony was entitled to vacate the premises because the landlord's failure to repair the heating system constituted abandonment.
    c. Because the apartment was made uninhabitable, the landlord's actions resulted in actual eviction.
    d. The landlord's actions resulted in constructive eviction.

Sample Exam 2—Georgia Real Estate Law and Practice

1. If the sales price for a new house in a Georgia subdivision is $180,000 and the buyer is able to obtain a 7 percent per annum loan for 80 percent of the sales price while paying four discount points, a 1 percent loan origination fee and three prepayment penalty points, what is the amount of money the lender will provide?
   a. $171,000
   b. $165,600
   c. $136,800
   d. $132,480

2. Actions permitted under the Georgia fair housing laws affecting people with disabilities include all of the following *EXCEPT*
   a. a landlord discriminating by denying apartments to tenants without disabilities in a building renting units to only persons with disabilities.
   b. a landlord requiring that any modifications made by a disabled tenant that limit the general marketability of the property be returned to the original condition.
   c. a landlord refusing to rent to a person whose disability is addiction to an illegal substance.
   d. a landlord increasing the security deposit for a person with a disability because he or she will have to make modifications to the property.

3. An item of functional obsolescence is considered incurable if the
   a. repair is difficult to make or easy to replace.
   b. cost of the repair is high.
   c. cost to repair is more than the value it adds.
   d. value of the property decreases after the repair.

4. If a rental property in Georgia with eight units has a monthly rent of $1,000 per unit, a net operating income of $40,000, and a current market value of $420,000, what is the capitalization rate for this property?
   a. 9.5 percent
   b. 22.9 percent
   c. 10.5 percent
   d. 4.375 percent

5. Property taxes in Georgia are known as "ad valorem" taxes, meaning the tax is based on the
   a. property owner's ability to pay taxes.
   b. value of the property.
   c. actual age of the property.
   d. length of time the property is owned.

6. Mr. and Mrs. Taylor in Rome, Georgia, wish to exercise the clause in the lease that allows a tenant to buy the property at a future time by stating a sales price and applying the rent payments to the price of the property. This clause is known as the
   a. renewal option clause.
   b. first right of refusal clause.
   c. lease purchase clause.
   d. nondisturbance clause.

7. How far back does a normal Georgia title search go?
   a. 30 years
   b. 50 years
   c. 80 years
   d. To the date of the land grant from the state or the King of England

8. Ed and Cheryl live in Albany, Georgia. They were married on June 15, 2005. On July 10, 2002, Ed purchased Blackacre. On October 10, 2006, Cheryl inherited Whiteacre. On February 20, 2007, Ed purchased Sumter Farm. Under the marital laws of Georgia, which *BEST* describes the interests held by Ed and Cheryl (assume that all the property described is real property)?

    a. Ed and Cheryl are equal co-owners of all the properties.
    b. Ed owns Blackacre, Cheryl owns Whiteacre, and they own Sumter Farm in equal shares.
    c. Ed owns Blackacre and Sumter Farm, and Cheryl owns Whiteacre.
    d. Ed owns Blackacre, and they own Whiteacre and Sumter Farm in equal shares.

9. Phyllis buys a house in Macon. The purchase price is $264,550. What is the amount of Georgia real estate transfer tax that must be paid upon filing the deed?

    a. $264.00
    b. $265.00
    c. $264.55
    d. $264.60

10. An auctioneer who auctions real estate must have

    a. a real estate salesperson's or broker's license.
    b. an auctioneer's license.
    c. both a and b.
    d. neither a nor b.

11. What is the primary purpose of the Real Estate Education, Research, and Recovery Fund?

    a. Ensure that Georgia real estate licensees have adequate funds available to pay their licensing and continuing education fees
    b. Compensate consumers who suffer damages from a licensee and are not able to recover them through normal legal channels
    c. Protect the Georgia Real Estate Commission from claims by individuals as a result of a licensee who violated the license law or committed other illegal acts related to a real estate transaction
    d. Provide an interest-generating source of revenue to fund the activities of the Georgia Real Estate Commission

12. Several years ago, Unit 1260 of the Peachtree Towers Condominium was the site of a highly publicized murder. After the murder, the unit was purchased by an elderly lady who contracted AIDS from a blood transfusion and died in the unit. The unit is currently listed for sale with real estate broker Clarice. Clarice knows of both the murder and the AIDS-related death. She shows the unit to a potential buyer, Stan, who asks her if there has ever been a murder in the condominium.

    a. Clarice must disclose the murder but is not obligated to disclose the AIDS-related death.
    b. Clarice must disclose the AIDS-related death but is not obligated to disclose the murder.
    c. Clarice must disclose both the murder and the AIDS-related death.
    d. Clarice is not required to disclose either event.

13. Broker Kristen obtained a listing from seller Sue and placed a For Sale sign on the property. The listing expired on June 30. As of July 7, she had not removed the sign from the property. On July 8, Sue gave a new listing to broker Bill. Kristen called Sue and talked her into breaking the listing contract with Bill by offering to sell the house at a cheaper commission. Did Kristen commit any unfair practices?

    a. Yes, because she did not remove the sign on time
    b. Yes, because she induced Sue to break the listing contract
    c. Yes, because both acts are unfair practices
    d. No, because neither act is an unfair practice

14. Melanie owns a company that provides services to three condominium developments. She collects the monthly condominium fees, hires the landscaping companies, supervises the move-ins and move-outs, and conducts other business for the homeowners' associations. In Georgia, Melanie is required to have

    a. a broker's or salesperson's license.
    b. a community association manager's license.
    c. Both a and b
    d. Neither a nor b

15. Which individual would *NOT* need a sales associate's license?

    a. Attorney-in-fact acting under duly executed power of attorney to convey real estate from owner or lessor
    b. Person selling or leasing real estate for a blood relative
    c. Both a and b
    d. Neither a nor b

16. Sally, a Georgia broker, deposits earnest money checks into her general business account in order to maintain a minimum balance and earn interest. After the check clears, she writes a check into her escrow account and accounts to the buyer for all the proceeds. Is Sally engaging in an unfair practice?

    a. No, because the earnest money is eventually deposited in her escrow account and she accounts for it to the buyer
    b. No, because it is acceptable to use client money to maintain a minimum balance in a business checking account
    c. Yes, because earnest money must be deposited directly into an escrow or trust account
    d. Yes, because it is an unfair practice to have a business account that earns interest

17. If the sales price for the Georgia house is $200,000, and the buyer is able to obtain a 7 percent per annum loan for 80 percent of the sales price while paying $5,400 discount points, a $1,800 loan origination fee, and $5,000 as prepayment penalty points at the end of ten years, what is the number of points?

    a. 2.7
    b. 3.4
    c. 3.6
    d. 4.5

18. You are the property manager of an apartment complex in Atlanta that rents units to the general public. Which action are you *NOT* required to take?

    a. Make the leasing office accessible to all potential tenants
    b. Allow tenants with disabilities to make modifications that they will return to the original condition
    c. Make the administrative office (not the leasing office) accessible for your three employees
    d. Allow people with disabilities entry to all public areas of the complex such as common areas in the building(s), parking areas, restrooms, and elevators

19. If a rental property in Georgia with four units has a monthly rent of $1,000 per unit, a net operating income of $40,000, and a current market value of $420,000, the gross rent multiplier (GRM) for this property is

    a. 9.5.
    b. 22.9.
    c. 10.5.
    d. 105.

20. When a Georgia appraiser uses land value, the prices of materials and the price of labor as a basis for a value estimate, which appraisal method is being used?

    a. Cost approach
    b. GRM
    c. Income approach
    d. Sales comparison approach

21. Under Georgia mortgage law, the borrower owns the property but the lender has the right to conduct a foreclosure sale upon the borrower's default. Which theory of the mortgage is this?

    a. Equitable theory
    b. Intermediate theory
    c. Lien theory
    d. Title theory

22. Real property legal descriptions in Georgia can be based on all of the following EXCEPT

    a. townships.
    b. land lots.
    c. districts.
    d. Georgia militia districts.

23. Which is/are true about an associate broker in Georgia?

    a. An associate broker acts on behalf of a broker.
    b. An associate broker may perform any real estate brokerage act that requires a license.
    c. Both a and b
    d. Neither a nor b

24. Which is NOT true regarding a community association manager?

    a. He or she must also be licensed as a real estate sales associate or broker.
    b. He or she must be affiliated with a sole proprietorship, corporation, partnership, or limited liability company that is also licensed as a broker.
    c. He or she must furnish evidence of completion of at least 25 in-class hours in a community association manager's course or courses of study approved by the Georgia Real Estate Commission.
    d. He or she must pass a real estate exam by the Commission covering community association management services.

25. The Georgia Real Estate Commission may initiate an investigation of an applicant for licensure or a licensee

    a. by its own motion.
    b. upon written request.
    c. both a and b.
    d. neither a nor b.

26. If a licensee is found guilty of a violation, which is NOT a remedy available to the Georgia Real Estate Commission?

    a. Imposing jail time of up to 30 days
    b. Revoking a license
    c. Suspending a license
    d. Issuing a censure

27. If a licensee has been found in violation of the license law and has exhausted all administrative remedies, the licensee

    a. can appeal to the Georgia court of appeals.
    b. can submit a petition for review to the Georgia attorney general.
    c. can have a judicial review in the superior court of the county of the Commission's domicile.
    d. can have a judicial review in the superior court of the county of the licensee's domicile.

28. When a licensee believes a person who placed trust funds in his or her care has abandoned those funds, the licensee may not disburse the funds unless
    a. there exists a particular disbursal statement that contains the licensee's written authorization to disburse the funds.
    b. the licensee has complied with the requirements of the Disposition of Unretained Property Act.
    c. the licensee has complied with state law or court-ordered requirements appropriate to the circumstances.
    d. All of the above

29. Julie is a licensed Tennessee broker who resides in Chattanooga. Larry is a Georgia licensed real estate broker who has an office in Dalton, Georgia. Julie's client, who is a resident of Georgia, purchases a tract of land in Dalton that has been listed by Larry. Julie negotiates the contract and represents the purchaser at the closing. This is Julie's only Georgia transaction this year. Can Larry pay Julie a portion of the commission from the sale?
    a. No, because Julie is not a licensed broker in Georgia
    b. No, because Julie's client is a resident of Georgia
    c. Yes, because Julie is acting only as a referral agent
    d. Yes, because Julie has done less than three transactions in Georgia this year

30. Broker Gary sells a house that he owns to Phillip. Gary represented himself in the sale and disclosed the fact that he is a broker to Gary in writing. Later that month, Gary represents a buyer and a seller in the sale of real estate after obtaining their express written consent to represent both parties. Has Gary committed a violation of the license law?
    a. Yes, as to selling his own house because a licensee must be represented by another licensee to sell property
    b. Yes, as to representing both parties because dual agency violates Georgia law
    c. Yes, as to both representing himself in the sale of his house and as to the dual agency
    d. No, because there is no violation

31. What is the composition of the Georgia Real Estate Commission?
    a. Eight members appointed by the state legislature
    b. Six members appointed by the governor
    c. Six members elected by the public
    d. Eight members elected by local REALTOR® associations

32. A person aggrieved by an act, representation, or conduct of a licensee in violation of the license law or Commission rules may recover damages of up to
    a. $10,000 per transaction.
    b. $15,000 per transaction.
    c. $20,000 maximum.
    d. $25,000 maximum.

33. A broker's agency with a client can terminate upon
    a. completion of performance of the engagement.
    b. any date of expiration agreed upon by the parties in the brokerage engagement.
    c. both a and b.
    d. neither a nor b.

34. Which is NOT a requirement for a broker acting as a dual agent?
    a. Statement that the broker represents two clients whose interests are or at times could be different or adverse
    b. Statement that the client does not have to consent to the dual agency
    c. Statement that the client should seek legal advice before signing the statement
    d. Description of the transactions or types of transactions in which the broker will serve as a dual agent

35. Broker Jones represented Mrs. Bailey as a buyer's broker in the purchase of a house. Jones did not disclose the fact (known to Jones) that a murder occurred in the house ten years ago. Mrs. Bailey did not inquire about any murders occurring in the house. Is Jones liable to Mrs. Bailey for failing to disclose the murder?

a. No, in this case a broker is not liable for failing to disclose the fact or suspicion that the property was the site of a homicide.

b. No, a broker does not have any duty of disclosure under BRRETA.

c. Yes, a broker must disclose any material facts of which he or she has knowledge.

d. Yes, a broker is under an affirmative duty to disclose the fact or suspicion that the property was the site of a homicide, suicide, or was occupied by someone with a virus or disease.

36. Jane, the owner of a tract of land, asks broker Tom if he can get her a net price of $200,000 for the sale of her land. Jane and Tom sign an agreement under which Tom agrees to obtain a net price of $200,000 for Jane, and any proceeds above $200,000 from the sale will go to Tom. This arrangement is

a. legal in Georgia as an open listing.

b. legal in Georgia as an exclusive agency listing.

c. illegal in Georgia as a net listing.

d. illegal in Georgia as an open listing.

37. Gene owns a tract of land in Conyers, Georgia. For 11 years, Gene's next-door neighbor Sam has walked across Gene's land to get to the road without Gene's permission. Sam sold his house to Cynthia, who continued to walk across Gene's land without permission for 10 years. Gene then demanded that Cynthia stop walking across his land. What must Cynthia do?

a. Cynthia must stop, as she as a trespasser.

b. Cynthia must stop, as her use has not continued for a 20-year period.

c. Cynthia may continue, as she has acquired an easement by prescription.

d. Cynthia may continue, as she has an easement by necessity.

38. In Georgia, property is taxed at what percent of its fair market value?

a. 100 percent

b. 80 percent

c. 60 percent

d. 40 percent

39. A licensee who is transferring a license to a new broker may continue to act as a licensee for the former broker on transactions begun prior to the transfer, provided

a. both brokers agree in writing to the licensee's action on behalf of the former broker.

b. the former broker agrees in writing to assume full responsibility for the licensee's activities in the agreement.

c. both a and b.

d. neither a nor b.

40. If a cease and desist order is violated by a licensee in Georgia, the Real Estate Commission can impose a fine of up to

a. $5,000 for each transaction constituting a violation of the order.

b. $750 for each transaction constituting a violation of the order.

c. $1,000 for each transaction constituting a violation of the order.

d. $1,500 for each transaction constituting a violation of the order.

41. To qualify for a community association manager's license, the Real Estate Commission requires an applicant to complete

a. 25 instructional hours in an approved course of study.

b. 25 instructional hours in an approved course of study, plus a course in property management.

c. 25 instructional hours in an approved course of study plus five hours related to fair housing.

d. 35 instructional hours in an approved course of study.

42. If a licensee in Florida wishes to practice in Georgia, he or she
    a. must take a six-hour Georgia law class only.
    b. must take a six-hour Georgia agency course.
    c. must pass only the Georgia portion of the exam.
    d. There are no requirements for Georgia–Florida reciprocity.

43. What is the continuing education requirement for licensees in Georgia?
    a. 3 instructional hours for each year of the renewal period
    b. 6 instructional hours for each year of the renewal period
    c. 9 instructional hours for each year of the renewal period
    d. 12 instructional hours for each year of the renewal period

44. Which is NOT a requirement for an escrow account deposit?
    a. Names of buyer and seller, tenant and landlord, member and community association, or broker
    b. County of buyer and seller, tenant and landlord, member and community association, or broker
    c. Identification of property involved
    d. Amount, payee, and date of each check drawn on the trust account in connection with the deposit

Please answer questions 45–47, pertaining to a loan specified by a Georgia bank.

45. A Georgia bank specifies a loan with an annual mortgage interest rate of 6.5 percent and a loan term of 30 years. The monthly mortgage factor for the loan is 6.32. What is the monthly payment for interest and principal on a loan for $156,000?
    a. $140.92
    b. $845.00
    c. $985.92
    d. $1,014.00

46. A Georgia bank specifies a loan with an annual mortgage interest rate of 6.5 percent and a loan term of 30 years. The monthly mortgage factor for the loan is 6.32. What is the monthly payment for interest on a loan for $156,000?
    a. $140.92
    b. $845.00
    c. $985.92
    d. $1,014.00

47. The bank specifies a loan with an annual mortgage interest rate of 6.5 percent and a loan term of 30 years. The monthly mortgage factor for the loan is 6.32. What is the monthly payment for principal on a loan for $156,000?
    a. $140.92
    b. $845.00
    c. $985.92
    d. $1,014.00

Please answer questions 48–50, using the following information.

A household has a stabilized monthly income of $5,000. The household is trying to buy a $200,000 house in an Atlanta suburb and seeking a $180,000 loan at 6.5 percent for 30 years. The monthly payment for interest and principal is $925. The lender's total debt ratio is 36 percent. The other expenses the household has are as follows:

Property tax per month	$400
Homeowners' insurance per month	$60
PMI insurance per month	$60
Homeowners' association dues per month	$30
Installment payments per month	$300
Auto loan payment #1 per month	$500
Auto loan payment #2 per month	$400
Child care payment per month	$500

48. What is the total housing expense ratio?

   a. 28.0 percent
   b. 29.5 percent
   c. 32.5 percent
   d. 39.0 percent

49. What is the total debt expense ratio?

   a. 29.5 percent
   b. 32.5 percent
   c. 39.0 percent
   d. 63.5 percent

50. How much income would this household need to earn in order to qualify for the loan?

   a. $5,270 per month
   b. $6,075 per month
   c. $8,820 per month
   d. Not enough information to determine

Glossary

Note: Most of the entries in this Glossary reference specific chapters in *Modern Real Estate Practice in Georgia*; however, chapter references are not provided for all terms. This is because we've included some terms that are used in everyday professional practice or are of purely historical interest. *Modern Real Estate Practice in Georgia* emphasizes the vocabulary that is necessary both for passing your real estate exam as well as for a successful career in real estate.

abstract of title The condensed history of a title to a particular parcel of real estate, consisting of a summary of the original grant and all subsequent conveyances and encumbrances affecting the property and a certification by the abstractor that the history is complete and accurate. **13**

acceleration clause The clause in a mortgage or deed of trust that can be enforced to make the entire debt due immediately if the borrower defaults on an installment payment or other covenant. **15**

accession Acquiring title to additions or improvements to real property as a result of the annexation of fixtures or the accretion of alluvial deposits along the banks of streams. **2**

accretion The increase or addition of land by the deposit of sand or soil washed up naturally from a river, lake, or sea. **7**

accrued items On a closing statement, items of expense that are incurred but not yet payable, such as interest on a mortgage loan or taxes on real property. **23**

acknowledgment A formal declaration made before a duly authorized officer, usually a notary public, by a person who has signed a document. **12**

acre A measure of land equal to 43,560 square feet, 4,840 square yards, 4,047 square meters, 160 square rods, or 0.4047 hectares. **9**

actual eviction The legal process that results in the tenant's being physically removed from the leased premises. **17**

actual notice Express information or fact; that which is known; direct knowledge. **13**

adjustable-rate mortgage (ARM) A loan characterized by a fluctuating interest rate, usually one tied to a bank or savings and loan association cost-of-funds index. **16**

adjusted basis *See* basis.

ad valorem tax A tax levied according to value, generally used to refer to real estate tax. Also called the *general tax*. **10**

adverse possession The actual, open, notorious, hostile, and continuous possession of another's land under a claim of title. Possession for a statutory period may be a means of acquiring title. **12**

affidavit of title A written statement, made under oath by a seller or grantor of real property and acknowledged by a notary public, in which the grantor (1) identifies himself or herself and indicates marital status, (2) certifies that since the examination of the title, on the date of the contract no defects have occurred in the title, and (3) certifies that he or she is in possession of the property (if applicable). **23**

agency The relationship between a principal and an agent wherein the agent is authorized to represent the principal in certain transactions. **4**

agency coupled with an interest An agency relationship in which the agent is given an estate or interest in the subject of the agency (the property). **4**

agent One who acts or has the power to act for another. A fiduciary relationship is created under the *law of agency* when a property owner, as the principal, executes a listing agreement or management contract authorizing a licensed real estate broker to be his or her agent. **4**

air lot A designated airspace over a piece of land. An air lot, like surface property, may be transferred. **9**

air rights The right to use the open space above a property, usually allowing the surface to be used for another purpose. **2**

alienation The act of transferring property to another. Alienation may be voluntary, such as by gift or sale, or involuntary, as through eminent domain or adverse possession. **12**

alienation clause The clause in a mortgage or deed of trust that states that the balance of the secured debt becomes immediately due and payable at the lender's option if the property is sold by the borrower. In effect this clause prevents the borrower from assigning the debt without the lender's approval. **15**

allodial system A system of land ownership in which land is held free and clear of any rent or service due to the government; commonly contrasted to the feudal system. Land is held under the allodial system in the United States.

American Land Title Association (ALTA) policy A title insurance policy that protects the interest in a collateral property of a mortgage lender who originates a new real estate loan. **13**

Americans with Disabilities Act Act addresses rights of individuals with disabilities in employment and public accommodations. **21**

amortized loan A loan in which the principal as well as the interest is payable in monthly or other periodic installments over the term of the loan. **16**

annexation Process of converting personal property into real property. **2**

annual percentage rate (APR) The relationship of the total finance charges associated with a loan. This must be disclosed to borrowers by lenders under the Truth-in-Lending Act. **16**

anticipation The appraisal principle that holds that value can increase or decrease based on the expectation of some future benefit or detriment produced by the property. **19**

antitrust laws Laws designed to preserve the free enterprise of the open marketplace by making illegal certain private conspiracies and combinations formed to minimize competition. Most violations of antitrust laws in the real estate business involve either *price-fixing* (brokers conspiring to set fixed compensation rates) or *allocation of customers or markets* (brokers agreeing to limit their areas of trade or dealing to certain areas or properties). **5**

appraisal An estimate of the quantity, quality, or value of something. The process through which conclusions of property value are obtained; also refers to the report that sets forth the process of estimation and conclusion of value. **19**

appraisal report An opinion of market value on a property given to a lender or client with detailed and accurate information. **19**

appraiser An independent person trained to provide an unbiased estimate of value. **19**

appreciation An increase in the worth or value of a property due to economic or related causes, which may prove to be either temporary or permanent; opposite of depreciation. **23**

appurtenance A right, privilege, or improvement belonging to, and passing with, the land. **2**

appurtenant easement An easement that is annexed to the ownership of one parcel and allows the owner the use of the neighbor's land. **7**

asbestos A mineral once used in insulation and other materials that can cause respiratory diseases. **22**

assemblage The combining of two or more adjoining lots into one larger tract to increase their total value. **19**

assessment The imposition of a tax, charge, or levy, usually according to established rates. **10**

assignment The transfer in writing of interest in a bond, mortgage, lease, or other instrument. **11**

assumption of mortgage Acquiring title to property on which there is an existing mortgage and agreeing to be personally liable for the terms and conditions of the mortgage, including payments. **16**

attachment The act of taking a person's property into legal custody by writ or other judicial order to hold it available for application to that person's debt to a creditor. **10**

attorney's opinion of title An abstract of title that an attorney has examined and has certified to be, in his or her opinion, an accurate statement of the facts concerning the property ownership. **13**

automated underwriting Computer systems that permit lenders to expedite the loan approval process and reduce lending costs. **16**

automatic extension A listing agreement clause stating that the agreement will continue automatically for a certain period of time after its expiration date. In many states, use of this clause is discouraged or prohibited. **6**

avulsion The sudden tearing away of land, as by earthquake, flood, volcanic action, or the sudden change in the course of a stream. **7**

balance The appraisal principle that states that the greatest value in a property will occur when the type and size of the improvements are proportional to each other as well as the land. **19**

balloon payment A final payment of a mortgage loan that is considerably larger than the required periodic payments because the loan amount was not fully amortized. **16**

base line The main imaginary line running east and west and crossing a principal meridian at a definite point, used by surveyors for reference in locating and describing land under the rectangular (government) survey system of legal description. **9**

basis The financial interest that the Internal Revenue Service attributes to an owner of an investment property for the purpose of determining annual depreciation and gain or loss on the sale of the asset. If a property was acquired by purchase, the owner's basis is the cost of the property plus the value of any capital expenditures for improvements to the property, minus any depreciation allowable or actually taken. This new basis is called the *adjusted basis*. **23**

benchmark A permanent reference mark or point established for use by surveyors in measuring differences in elevation. **9**

beneficiary (1) The person for whom a trust operates or in whose behalf the income from a trust estate is drawn. (2) A lender in a deed of trust loan transaction. **8**

bilateral contract *See* contract.

blanket loan A mortgage covering more than one parcel of real estate, providing for each parcel's partial release from the mortgage lien upon repayment of a definite portion of the debt. **16**

blockbusting The illegal practice of inducing homeowners to sell their properties by making representations regarding the entry or prospective entry of persons of a particular race or national origin into the neighborhood. **21**

blue-sky laws Common name for those state and federal laws that regulate the registration and sale of investment securities. **23**

boot Money or property given to make up any difference in value or equity between two properties in an *exchange*. **23**

branch office A secondary place of business apart from the principal or main office from which real estate business is conducted. A branch office usually must be run by a licensed real estate broker working on behalf of the broker. **14**

breach of contract Violation of any terms or conditions in a contract without legal excuse; for example, failure to make a payment when it is due. **11**

broker One who acts as an intermediary on behalf of others for a fee or commission. **5**

brokerage The bringing together of parties interested in making a real estate transaction. **5**

brokerage engagement A written contract where the seller, buyer, landlord, or tenant becomes the broker's client and promises to pay the broker valuable consideration for producing a seller, buyer, tenant, or landlord ready, able, and willing to sell, buy, or rent, or performing other brokerage services. Also known as listing or agency agreement. **14**

broker's price opinion An opinion of real estate value commissioned by a bank or attorney and provided by a broker. **19**

brownfields Defunct, derelict, or abandoned commercial or industrial sites; many have toxic wastes. **22**

Brownfields Legislation Provides federal funding to states and localities to clean up brownfields sites. **22**

BRRETA The Georgia Brokerage Relationships in Real Estate Transactions Act, Title 10, Chapter 6A of the Georgia Code. Provides laws for agency relationships. **14**

buffer zone A strip of land, usually used as a park or designated for a similar use, separating land dedicated to one use from land dedicated to another use (e.g., residential from commercial). **20**

building code An ordinance that specifies minimum standards of construction for buildings to protect public safety and health. **20**

building permit Written governmental permission for the construction, alteration, or demolition of an improvement, showing compliance with building codes and zoning ordinances. **20**

building-related illness (BRI) An illness due to air quality problems, typically toxic substances or pathogens and is a clinically diagnosed condition. Symptoms include asthma, allergies, and hypersensitivity. **22**

bulk transfer *See* Uniform Commercial Code.

bundle of legal rights The concept of land ownership that includes ownership of all legal rights to the land—for example, possession, control within the law, and enjoyment. **2**

buydown A financing technique used to reduce the monthly payments for the first few years of a loan. Funds in the form of discount points are given to the lender by the builder or seller to buy down or lower the effective interest rate paid by the buyer, thus reducing the monthly payments for a set time. **16**

buyer-agency agreement A principal-agent relationship in which the broker is the agent for the buyer, with fiduciary responsibilities to the buyer. The broker represents the buyer under the law of agency. **6**

buyer's agent A residential real estate broker or salesperson who represents the prospective purchaser in a transaction. The buyer's agent owes the buyer-principal the common-law or statutory agency duties. **4**

buyer's broker A residential real estate broker who represents prospective buyers exclusively. As the *buyer's agent*, the broker owes the buyer-principal the common-law or statutory agency duties. **4**

capitalization A mathematical process for estimating the value of a property using a proper rate of return on the investment and the annual net operating income expected to be produced by the property. The formula is expressed as: Income ÷ Rate = Value. **19**

capitalization rate The rate of return a property will produce on the owner's investment. **19**

cash flow   The net spendable income from an investment, determined by deducting all operating and fixed expenses from the gross income. When expenses exceed income, a *negative cash flow* results. **23**

cash rent   In an agricultural lease, the amount of money given as rent to the landowner at the outset of the lease, as opposed to sharecropping. **17**

caveat emptor   A Latin phrase meaning *Let the buyer beware*. **5**

Certificate of permanent location   A certificate obtained from the county where a manufactured home is located, which, once filed, makes the home part of the real property. **2**

certificate of reasonable value (CRV)   A form indicating the appraised value of a property being financed with a VA loan. **19**

certificate of sale   The document generally given to the purchaser at a tax foreclosure sale. A certificate of sale does not convey title; normally it is an instrument certifying that the holder received title to the property after the redemption period passed and that the holder paid the property taxes for that interim period. **10**

certificate of title   A statement of opinion on the status of the title to a parcel of real property based on an examination of specified public records. **13**

chain of title   The succession of conveyances, from some accepted starting point, whereby the present holder of real property derives title. **13**

change   The appraisal principle that holds that no physical or economic condition remains constant. **19**

chattel   *See* personal property.

chlorofluorocarbons (CFCs)   Nontoxic, nonflammable chemicals containing atoms of carbon, chlorine, and fluorine, such as air conditioners and refrigerators. CFCs are safe in application but cause ozone depletion. **22**

Civil Rights Act of 1866   An act that prohibits racial discrimination in the sale and rental of housing. **21**

client   The principal. **4**

closing   An event where promises made in a sales contract are fulfilled and mortgage loan funds (if any) are distributed to the buyer. **23**

closing statement   A detailed cash accounting of a real estate transaction showing all cash received, all charges and credits made, and all cash paid out in the transaction. **23**

cloud on title   Any document, claim, unreleased lien, or encumbrance that may impair the title to real property or make the title doubtful; usually revealed by a title search and removed by either a quitclaim deed or suit to quiet title. **12**

clustering   The grouping of home sites within a subdivision on smaller lots than normal, with the remaining land used as common areas. **20**

code of ethics   A written system of standards for ethical conduct. **21**

codicil   A supplement or an addition to a will, executed with the same formalities as a will, that normally does not revoke the entire will. **12**

coinsurance clause   A clause in insurance policies covering real property that requires the policyholder to maintain fire insurance coverage generally equal to at least 80 percent of the property's actual replacement cost. **3**

commingling   The illegal act by a real estate broker of placing client or customer funds with personal funds. By law, brokers are required to maintain a separate *trust* or *escrow account* for other parties' funds held temporarily by the broker. **11**

commission   Payment to a broker for services rendered, such as in the sale or purchase of real property; usually a percentage of the selling price of the property. **5**

common elements   Parts of a property that are necessary or convenient to the existence, maintenance, and safety of a condominium or are normally in common use by all of the condominium residents. Each condominium owner has an undivided ownership interest in the common elements. **8**

common law   The body of law based on custom, usage, and court decisions. **4**

community association management   The provision of management services for the operation of the affairs of a community association, which includes overseeing the daily operations of an association. **14**

community association manager   A person who acts on behalf of a real estate broker in providing only community association management services. **1**

Community Reinvestment Act of 1977 (CRA)   Under the act, financial institutions are expected to meet the deposit and credit needs of their communities; participate and invest in local community development and rehabilitation projects; and participate in loan programs for housing, small businesses, and small farms. **16**

comparables   Properties used in an appraisal report that are substantially equivalent to the subject property. **19**

competition   The appraisal principle that states that excess profits generate competition. **19**

competitive market analysis (CMA)   A comparison of the prices of recently sold homes that are similar to a listing seller's home in terms of location, style, and amenities. **6**

Comprehensive Environmental Response, Compensation, and Liability Act (CERCLA)   A federal law administered by the Environmental Protection Agency that establishes a process for identifying parties responsible for creating hazardous waste sites, forcing liable parties to clean up toxic sites, bringing legal action against responsible parties, and funding the abatement of toxic sites. *See* Superfund. **22**

Comprehensive Loss Underwriting Exchange (CLUE) A database of consumer claim history that allows insurance companies to access prior claim information in the underwriting and rating process. **3**

comprehensive plan *See* master plan.

computerized loan origination (CLO) system An electronic network for handling loan applications through remote computer terminals linked to various lenders' computers. **16**

condemnation A judicial or administrative proceeding to exercise the power of eminent domain, through which a government agency takes private property for public use and compensates the owner. **7**

conditional-use permit Written governmental permission allowing a use inconsistent with zoning but necessary for the common good, such as locating an emergency medical facility in a predominantly residential area. **20**

condominium The absolute ownership of a unit in a multiunit building based on a legal description of the airspace the unit actually occupies, plus an undivided interest in the ownership of the common elements, which are owned jointly with the other condominium unit owners. **8**

confession of judgment clause Permits judgment to be entered against a debtor without the creditor's having to institute legal proceedings.

conformity The appraisal principle that holds that the greater the similarity among properties in an area, the better they will hold their value. **19**

consideration (1) That received by the grantor in exchange for his or her deed. (2) Something of value that induces a person to enter into a contract. **11**

construction loan *See* interim financing.

constructive eviction Actions of a landlord that so materially disturb or impair a tenant's enjoyment of the leased premises that the tenant is effectively forced to move out and terminate the lease without liability for any further rent. **17**

constructive notice Notice given to the world by recorded documents. All people are charged with knowledge of such documents and their contents, whether or not they have actually examined them. Possession of property is also considered constructive notice that the person in possession has an interest in the property. **13**

contingency A provision in a contract that requires a certain act to be done or a certain event to occur before the contract becomes binding. **11**

contract A legally enforceable promise or set of promises that must be performed and for which, if a breach of the promise occurs, the law provides a remedy. A contract may be either *unilateral*, by which only one party is bound to act, or *bilateral*, by which all parties to the instrument are legally bound to act as prescribed. **11**

contribution The appraisal principle that states that the value of any component of a property is what it gives to the value of the whole or what its absence detracts from that value. **19**

controlled business arrangement An arrangement where a package of services (such as a real estate firm, title insurance company, mortgage broker, and home inspection company) is offered to consumers. **23**

conventional loan A loan that requires no insurance or guarantee. **16**

conveyance A term used to refer to any document that transfers title to real property. The term is also used in describing the act of transferring. **12**

cooperating broker *See* listing broker.

cooperative A residential multiunit building whose title is held by a trust or corporation that is owned by and operated for the benefit of persons living within the building, who are the beneficial owners of the trust or stockholders of the corporation, each possessing a proprietary lease. **8**

co-ownership Title ownership held by two or more persons. **8**

corporation An entity or organization, created by operation of law, whose rights of doing business are essentially the same as those of an individual. The entity has continuous existence until it is dissolved according to legal procedures. **8**

correction lines Provisions in the rectangular survey (government survey) system made to compensate for the curvature of the earth's surface. Every fourth township line (at 24-mile intervals) is used as a correction line on which the intervals between the north and south range lines are remeasured and corrected to a full six miles. **9**

cost approach The process of estimating the value of a property by adding to the estimated land value the appraiser's estimate of the reproduction or replacement cost of the building, less depreciation. **19**

counteroffer A new offer made in response to an offer received. It has the effect of rejecting the original offer, which cannot be accepted thereafter unless revived by the offeror. **11**

covenant A written agreement between two or more parties in which a party or parties pledge to perform or not perform specified acts with regard to property; usually found in such real estate documents as deeds, mortgages, leases, and contracts for deed. **7**

covenant of quiet enjoyment The covenant implied by law by which a landlord guarantees that a tenant may take possession of leased premises and that the landlord will not interfere in the tenant's possession or use of the property. **12**

credit On a closing statement, an amount entered in a person's favor—either an amount the party has paid or an amount for which the party must be reimbursed. **23**

customer The third party or nonrepresented consumer for whom some level of service is provided. **4**

datum A horizontal plane from which heights and depths are measured. **9**

debit On a closing statement, an amount charged; that is, an amount that the debited party must pay. **23**

decedent A person who has died. **12**

dedication The voluntary transfer of private property by its owner to the public for some public use, such as for streets or schools. **1**

deed A written instrument that, when executed and delivered, conveys title to or an interest in real estate. **12**

deed in lieu of foreclosure A deed given by the mortgagor to the mortgagee when the mortgagor is in default under the terms of the mortgage. This is a way for the mortgagor to avoid foreclosure. **15**

deed in trust An instrument that grants a trustee under a land trust full power to sell, mortgage, and subdivide a parcel of real estate. The beneficiary controls the trustee's use of these powers under the provisions of the trust agreement. **12**

deed of trust lien *See* trust deed lien.

deed restrictions Clauses in a deed limiting the future uses of the property. Deed restrictions may impose a vast variety of limitations and conditions—for example, they may limit the density of buildings, dictate the types of structures that can be erected, or prevent buildings from being used for specific purposes or even from being used at all. **7**

default The nonperformance of a duty, whether arising under a contract or otherwise; failure to meet an obligation when due. **15**

defeasance clause A clause used in leases and mortgages that cancels a specified right upon the occurrence of a certain condition, such as cancellation of a mortgage upon repayment of the mortgage loan. **15**

defeasible fee estate An estate in which the holder has a fee simple title that may be divested upon the occurrence or nonoccurrence of a specified event. There are two categories of defeasible fee estates: fee simple on condition precedent (fee simple determinable) and fee simple on condition subsequent. **7**

deficiency judgment A personal judgment levied against the borrower when a foreclosure sale does not produce sufficient funds to pay the mortgage debt in full. **15**

demand The amount of goods people are willing and able to buy at a given price; often coupled with *supply*. **19**

density zoning Zoning ordinances that restrict the maximum average number of houses per acre that may be built within a particular area, generally a subdivision. **20**

Department of Housing and Urban Development (HUD) Governmental department that has established rules and regulations that further interpret the practices affected by the law. In addition, HUD distributes an equal housing opportunity poster. **16**

depreciation (1) In appraisal, a loss of value in property due to any cause, including *physical deterioration, functional obsolescence,* and *external obsolescence.* (2) In real estate investment, an expense deduction for tax purposes taken over the period of ownership of income property. **19**

descent Acquisition of an estate by inheritance in which an heir succeeds to the property by operation of law. **12**

designated agent Under Georgia law, means one or more licensees affiliated with a broker who are assigned by the broker to represent solely one client to the exclusion of all other clients in the same transaction and to the exclusion of all other licensees affiliated with the broker. **4**

developer One who attempts to put land to its most profitable use through the construction of improvements. **20**

devise A gift of real property by will. The donor is the devisor, and the recipient is the devisee. **12**

discount point A unit of measurement used for various loan charges; one point equals 1 percent of the amount of the loan. **15**

dispossession A landlord's eviction of a tenant under Georgia lease law. **17**

districts and land lots A legal description system used in Georgia. Grid lines divide areas into rectangles or squares and large square areas are divided into districts. Land lots further divide each district. **9**

dominant tenement A property that includes in its ownership the appurtenant right to use an easement over another person's property for a specific purpose. **7**

Do Not Call Registry A registry, managed by the Federal Trade Commission, that lists the phone numbers of consumers who have indicated their preference to limit the telemarketing calls they receive. **5**

dual agency Representing both parties to a transaction. This is unethical unless both parties agree to it, and it is illegal in many states. **4**

due-on-sale clause A provision in the mortgage that states that the entire balance of the note is immediately due and payable if the mortgagor transfers (sells) the property. **15**

duress Unlawful constraint or action exercised upon a person whereby the person is forced to perform an act against his or her will. A contract entered into under duress is voidable.

earnest money Money deposited by a buyer under the terms of a contract, to be forfeited if the buyer defaults but applied to the purchase price if the sale is closed. **11**

easement A right to use the land of another for a specific purpose, such as for a right-of-way or utilities; an incorporeal interest in land. **7**

easement by condemnation An easement created by the government or government agency that has exercised its right under eminent domain. **7**

easement by necessity An easement allowed by law as necessary for the full enjoyment of a parcel of real estate; for example, a right of ingress and egress over a grantor's land. **7**

easement by prescription An easement acquired by continuous, open, and hostile use of the property for the period of time prescribed by state law. **7**

easement in gross An easement that is not created for the benefit of any land owned by the owner of the easement but that attaches *personally to the easement owner*. For example, a right granted by Eleanor Franks to Joe Fish to use a portion of her property for the rest of his life would be an easement in gross. **7**

economic life The number of years during which an improvement will add value to the land. **19**

electronic contracting A process of integrating information in a real estate transaction between clients, lender, and title and closing agents electronically. **5**

Electronic Signatures in Global and National Commerce Act (E-Sign) An act that makes contracts (including signatures) and records legally enforceable regardless of the medium in which they are created. **5**

emblements Growing crops, such as grapes and corn, that are produced annually through labor and industry; also called *fructus industriales*. **2**

eminent domain The right of a government or municipal quasi-public body to acquire property for public use through a court action called *condemnation*, in which the court decides that the use is a public use and determines the compensation to be paid to the owner. **7**

employee Someone who works as a direct employee of an employer and has employee status. The employer is obligated to withhold income taxes and Social Security taxes from the compensation of employees. *See also* independent contractor. **5**

employment contract A document evidencing formal employment between employer and employee or between principal and agent. In the real estate business this generally takes the form of a listing agreement or management agreement. **5**

enabling acts State legislation that confers zoning powers on municipal governments. **20**

encapsulation A method of controlling environmental contamination by sealing off a dangerous substance. **22**

encroachment A building or some portion of it—a wall or fence for instance—that extends beyond the land of the owner and illegally intrudes on some land of an adjoining owner or a street or alley. **7**

encumbrance Anything—such as a mortgage, tax, or judgment lien, an easement, a restriction on the use of the land, or an outstanding dower right—that may diminish the value or use and enjoyment of a property. **7**

environmental impact statement A statement that details the impact a federally funded project will have on the environment. **22**

environmental site assessment An evaluation of property to show that due care was exercised in the determination of environmental impairments. **22**

Equal Credit Opportunity Act (ECOA) The federal law that prohibits discrimination in the extension of credit because of race, color, religion, national origin, sex, age, or marital status. **16**

equalization The raising or lowering of assessed values for tax purposes in a particular county or taxing district to make them equal to assessments in other counties or districts. **10**

equalization factor A factor (number) by which the assessed value of a property is multiplied to arrive at a value for the property that is in line with statewide tax assessments. The *ad valorem tax* would be based on this adjusted value. **10**

equitable lien *See* statutory lien.

equitable right of redemption The right of a defaulted property owner to recover the property prior to its sale by paying the appropriate fees and charges. **15**

equitable title The interest held by a vendee under a contract for deed or an installment contract; the equitable right to obtain absolute ownership to property when legal title is held in another's name. **11**

equity   The interest or value that an owner has in property over and above any indebtedness. **3**

erosion   The gradual wearing away of land by water, wind, and general weather conditions; the diminishing of property by the elements. **7**

escheat   The reversion of property to the state or county, as provided by state law, in cases where a decedent dies intestate without heirs capable of inheriting, or when the property is abandoned. **7**

escrow   The closing of a transaction through a third party called an *escrow agent*, or *escrowee*, who receives certain funds and documents to be delivered upon the performance of certain conditions outlined in the escrow instructions. **23**

escrow account   The trust account established by a broker under the provisions of the license law for the purpose of holding funds on behalf of the broker's principal or some other person until the consummation or termination of a transaction. **11**

escrow contract   An agreement between a buyer, seller, and escrow holder setting forth rights and responsibilities of each. An escrow contract is entered into when earnest money is deposited in a broker's escrow account. **11**

escrow instructions   A document that sets forth the duties of the escrow agent, as well as the requirements and obligations of the parties, when a transaction is closed through an escrow. **23**

estate (tenancy) at sufferance   The tenancy of a lessee who lawfully comes into possession of a landlord's real estate but who continues to occupy the premises improperly after his or her lease rights have expired. **17**

estate (tenancy) at will   An estate that gives the lessee the right to possession until the estate is terminated by either party; the term of this estate is indefinite. **17**

estate (tenancy) for years   An interest for a certain, exact period of time in property leased for a specified consideration. **17**

estate (tenancy) from period to period   An interest in leased property that continues from period to period— week to week, month to month, or year to year. **17**

estate in land   The degree, quantity, nature, and extent of interest a person has in real property. **7**

estate taxes   Federal taxes on a decedent's real and personal property. **10**

estoppel   Method of creating an agency relationship in which someone states incorrectly that another person is his or her agent and a third person relies on that representation.

estoppel certificate   A document in which a borrower certifies the amount owed on a mortgage loan and the rate of interest.

ethics   The system of moral principles and rules that becomes standards for professional conduct. **21**

eviction   A legal process to oust a person from possession of real estate. **17**

evidence of title   Proof of ownership of property; commonly a certificate of title, an abstract of title with lawyer's opinion, title insurance, or a Torrens registration certificate. **13**

exchange   A transaction in which all or part of the consideration is the transfer of *like-kind* property (such as real estate for real estate). **23**

exclusive-agency listing   A listing contract under which the owner appoints a real estate broker as his or her exclusive agent for a designated period of time to sell the property, on the owner's stated terms, for a commission. The owner reserves the right to sell without paying anyone a commission if he or she sells to a prospect who has not been introduced or claimed by the broker. **6**

exclusive-right-to-sell listing   A listing contract under which the owner appoints a real estate broker as his or her exclusive agent for a designated period of time, to sell the property on the owner's stated terms, and agrees to pay the broker a commission when the property is sold, whether by the broker, the owner, or another broker. **6**

executed contract   A contract in which all parties have fulfilled their promises and thus performed the contract. **11**

execution   The signing and delivery of an instrument. Also, a legal order directing an official to enforce a judgment against the property of a debtor. **2**

executory contract   A contract under which something remains to be done by one or more of the parties. **11**

exhibits   In Georgia, information or provisions attached to a real estate sales contract that either add to, change, or delete preprinted contract language. **11**

express agency   An agency relationship based on a formal agreement between the parties. **4**

express agreement   An oral or written contract in which the parties state the contract's terms and express their intentions in words. **11**

express contract   *See* express agreement.

external depreciation   Reduction in a property's value caused by outside factors (those that are off the property). **19**

external obsolescence   Incurable depreciation caused by factors not on subject property, such as environmental, social, or economic factors. **19**

facilitator   *See* nonagent.

Fair Housing Act   The federal law that prohibits discrimination in housing based on race, color, religion, sex, handicap, familial status, and national origin. **21**

Fannie Mae   A government-sponsored enterprise established to purchase any kind of mortgage loans in the secondary mortgage market from the primary lenders. **16**

Farm Credit   A federal agency of the Department of Agriculture that offers programs to help families purchase or operate family farms. **16**

Farmer Mac   A government-sponsored enterprise that operates similarly to Fannie Mae and Freddie Mac but for agricultural loans. **16**

Farm Service Agency (FSA)   An agency of the federal government that provides credit assistance to farmers and other individuals who live in rural areas. **16**

Federal Deposit Insurance Corporation (FDIC)   An independent federal agency that insures the deposits in commercial banks. **16**

Federal Home Loan Mortgage Corporation   *See* Freddie Mac.

Federal National Mortgage Association   *See* Fannie Mae.

Federal Reserve System   The country's central banking system, which exercises responsibility for the nation's monetary policy by regulating the supply of money and interest rates. **16**

fee-for-service   Arrangement where a consumer asks a licensee to perform specific real estate services for a set fee. **5**

fee simple   The highest interest in real estate recognized by the law; the holder is entitled to all rights to the property. **7**

fee simple absolute   The maximum possible estate or right of ownership of real property, continuing forever. **7**

fee simple defeasible   *See* defeasible fee estate.

fee simple determinable   A fee simple estate qualified by a special limitation. Language used to describe limitation includes the words "so long as" or "while" or "during." **7**

feudal system   A system of ownership usually associated with pre-colonial England, in which the king or other sovereign is the source of all rights. The right to possess real property was granted by the sovereign to an individual as a life estate only. Upon the death of the individual, title passed back to the sovereign, not to the decedent's heirs.

FHA loan   A loan insured by the Federal Housing Administration and made by an approved lender in accordance with the FHA's regulations. **16**

fidelity bond   A bond required of a broker who provides community association management services in Georgia. **18**

Financial Institutions Reform, Recovery, and Enforcement Act (FIRREA)   This act restructured the savings and loan association regulatory system; enacted in response to the savings and loan crisis of the 1980s. **19**

financing statement   *See* Uniform Commercial Code.

fiscal policy   The government's policy in regard to taxation and spending programs. The balance between these two areas determines the amount of money the government will withdraw from or feed into the economy, which can counter economic peaks and slumps.

fixture   An item of personal property that has been converted to real property by being permanently affixed to the realty. **2**

foreclosure   A legal procedure whereby property used as security for a debt is sold to satisfy the debt in the event of default in payment of the mortgage note or default of other terms in the mortgage document. The foreclosure procedure brings the rights of all parties to a conclusion and passes the title in the mortgaged property to either the holder of the mortgage or a third party who may purchase the realty at the foreclosure sale, free of all encumbrances affecting the property subsequent to the mortgage. **15**

formaldehyde   An air pollutant that is a colorless chemical used to manufacture building materials and many household products, such as particleboard, hardwood plywood paneling, and urea-formaldehyde foam insulation. **22**

fractional section   A parcel of land less than 160 acres, usually found at the edge of a rectangular survey. **9**

fraud   Deception intended to cause a person to give up property or a lawful right. **4**

Freddie Mac   A government-sponsored enterprise established to purchase primarily conventional mortgage loans in the secondary mortgage market. **16**

freehold estate   An estate in land in which ownership is for an indeterminate length of time, in contrast to a *leasehold estate*. **7**

front footage   The measurement of a parcel of land by the number of feet of street or road frontage.

functional obsolescence   A loss of value to an improvement to real estate arising from functional problems, often caused by age or poor design. **19**

future interest   A person's present right to an interest in real property that will not result in possession or enjoyment until some time in the future, such as a reversion or right of re-entry. **7**

gap A defect in the chain of title of a particular parcel of real estate; a missing document or conveyance that raises doubt as to the present ownership of the land. **13**

general agent One who is authorized by a principal to represent the principal in a specific range of matters. **4**

general lien The right of a creditor to have all of a debtor's property—both real and personal—sold to satisfy a debt. **10**

general partnership *See* partnership.

general real estate tax A tax that is made up of the taxes levied on the real estate by government agencies and municipalities. **10**

general warranty deed A deed in which the grantor fully warrants good clear title to the premises. Used in most real estate deed transfers, a general warranty deed offers the greatest protection of any deed. **12**

Georgia Condominium Act Provides rules and regulations for the creation and legal structure of condominiums. **8**

Georgia Department of Natural Resources A state agency that oversees environmental protection. **22**

Georgia Fair Housing Law A law that is substantially equivalent to federal fair housing laws. **21**

Georgia Joint Tenancy Act of 1976 Allows an individual or couple holding property as tenants in common to convey property to themselves as joint tenants. **8**

Georgia Land Conservation Council Act Creates an umbrella council that promotes land preservation and conservation. **22**

Georgia Land Sales Act Regulates subdivided land. **20**

Georgia Lead Poisoning Prevention Act of 1994 Provides rules regarding lead paint prevention and reduction programs, training programs, and licensure requirements. **22**

Georgia Military Districts (GMDs) Used to define a property description in some areas of Georgia. **9**

Georgia Property Owners' Association Act of 1994 Provides laws governing community associations and management. **18**

Georgia Residential Mortgage Fraud Act Allows for the prosecution of mortgage fraud and provides criminal penalties and civil forfeitures of property. **15**

Georgia Real Estate License Law Title 43, Chapter 40 of the Georgia Code. Provides standards for licensees to perform their duties and regulates the real estate industry. **14**

Georgia Time-Share Projects and Programs Statute Regulates the promotion or sale of all time-share units. **8**

Ginnie Mae A government agency that plays an important role in the secondary mortgage market. It guarantees mortgage-backed securities using FHA and VA loans as collateral. **16**

government check The 24-mile-square parcels composed of 16 townships in the rectangular (government) survey system of legal description. **9**

government lot Fractional sections in the rectangular (government) survey system that are less than one quarter-section in area. **9**

Government National Mortgage Association *See* Ginnie Mae.

government survey system *See* rectangular (government) survey system.

graduated-payment mortgage (GPM) A loan in which the monthly principal and interest payments increase by a certain percentage each year for a certain number of years and then level off for the remaining loan term.

grantee A person who receives a conveyance of real property from a grantor. **12**

granting clause Words in a deed of conveyance that state the grantor's intention to convey the property at the present time. This clause is generally worded as "convey and warrant"; "grant"; "grant, bargain, and sell"; or the like. **12**

grantor The person transferring title to or an interest in real property to a grantee. **12**

gross income multiplier A figure used as a multiplier of the gross annual income of a property to produce an estimate of the property's value. **19**

gross lease A lease of property according to which a landlord pays all property charges regularly incurred through ownership, such as repairs, taxes, insurance, and operating expenses. Most residential leases are gross leases. **17**

gross rent multiplier (GRM) The figure used as a multiplier of the gross monthly income of a property to produce an estimate of the property's value. **19**

ground lease A lease of land only, on which the tenant usually owns a building or is required to build as specified in the lease. Such leases are usually long-term net leases; the tenant's rights and obligations continue until the lease expires or is terminated through default. **17**

growing-equity mortgage (GEM) A loan in which the monthly payments increase annually, with the increased amount being used to reduce directly the principal balance outstanding and thus shorten the overall term of the loan. **16**

habendum clause That part of a deed beginning with the words "to have and to hold," following the granting clause and defining the extent of ownership the grantor is conveying. **12**

headrights The earliest property descriptions in Georgia in the eastern area used the headrights approach, which depends on natural boundaries and markers. **9**

heir One who might inherit or succeed to an interest in land under the state law of descent when the owner dies without leaving a valid will. **12**

highest and best use The possible use of a property that would produce the greatest net income and thereby develop the highest value. **19**

holdover tenancy A tenancy whereby a lessee retains possession of leased property after the lease has expired and the landlord, by continuing to accept rent, agrees to the tenant's continued occupancy as defined by state law. **17**

holographic will A will that is written, dated, and signed in the testator's handwriting. **12**

home equity loan A loan (sometimes called a *line of credit*) under which a property owner uses his or her residence as collateral and can then draw funds up to a prearranged amount against the property. **16**

homeowner's insurance policy A standardized package insurance policy that covers a residential real estate owner against financial loss from fire, theft, public liability, and other common risks. **3**

homestead Land that is owned and occupied as the family home. In many states a portion of the area or value of this land is protected or exempt from judgments for debts. **7**

hypothecate To pledge property as security for an obligation or loan without giving up possession of it. **15**

implied agency Based on the actions of the parties that imply that they have mutually consented to an agency relationship, an implied agency relationship is formed. **4**

implied agreement A contract under which the agreement of the parties is demonstrated by their acts and conduct. **11**

implied contract *See* implied agreement.

implied warranty of habitability A theory in landlord/tenant law in which the landlord renting residential property implies that the property is habitable and fit for its intended use.

improvement (1) Any structure, usually privately owned, erected on a site to enhance the value of the property—for example, building a fence or a driveway. (2) A publicly owned structure added to or benefiting land, such as a curb, sidewalk, street, or sewer. **2**

income approach The process of estimating the value of an income-producing property through capitalization of the annual net income expected to be produced by the property during its remaining useful life. **19**

incorporeal right A nonpossessory right in real estate; for example, an easement or a right-of-way.

independent contractor Someone who is retained to perform a certain act but who is subject to the control and direction of another only as to the end result and not as to the way in which the act is performed. Unlike an employee, an independent contractor pays for all expenses and Social Security and income taxes and receives no employee benefits. Most real estate salespeople are independent contractors. **5**

index method The appraisal method of estimating building costs by multiplying the original cost of the property by a percentage factor to adjust for current construction costs. **19**

inheritance taxes State-imposed taxes on a decedent's real and personal property. **10**

inquiry notice Notice the law presumes a reasonable person would obtain by inquiring into a property. **13**

interest A charge made by a lender for the use of money. **15**

interest-only mortgage A mortgage that only requires the payment of interest for a stated period of time with the principal due at the end of the term. **16**

interim financing A short-term loan usually made during the construction phase of a building project (in this case often referred to as a *construction loan*). **16**

intermediate theory Adopted by a number of states, a theory based on the principles of title theory but requires the mortgagee foreclose to obtain legal title. **15**

Internet Listing Display Policy A policy from the National Association of REALTORS® that allows all MLS members to have equal right to display MLS data, and respects the rights of property owners and their listing brokers to market a property as they wish. **5**

Interstate Land Sales Full Disclosure Act A federal law that regulates the sale of certain real estate in interstate commerce. **20**

intestate The condition of a property owner who dies without leaving a valid will. Title to the property will pass to the decedent's heirs as provided in the state law of descent. **12**

inverse condemnation An action brought by a property owner seeking just compensation for land taken for public use when the taker of the property does not intend to bring eminent domain proceedings. Property is condemned because its use and value have been diminished due to an adjacent property's public use. **20**

investment Money directed toward the purchase, improvement, and development of an asset in expectation of income or profits. **2**

involuntary alienation *See* alienation.

involuntary lien A lien placed on property without the consent of the property owner. **10**

joint and several liability Each of the individual owners is personally responsible for the total damages. **22**

joint tenancy Ownership of real estate between two or more parties who have been named in one conveyance as joint tenants. Upon the death of a joint tenant, the decedent's interest passes to the surviving joint tenant or tenants by the *right of survivorship*. **8**

joint venture The joining of two or more people to conduct a specific business enterprise. A joint venture is similar to a partnership in that it must be created by agreement between the parties to share in the losses and profits of the venture. It is unlike a partnership in that the venture is for one specific project only, rather than for a continuing business relationship. **8**

judgment The formal decision of a court upon the respective rights and claims of the parties to an action or suit. After a judgment has been entered and recorded with the county recorder, it usually becomes a general lien on the property of the defendant. **10**

judicial precedent In law, the requirements established by prior court decisions.

junior lien An obligation, such as a second mortgage, that is subordinate in right or lien priority to an existing lien on the same realty. **10**

laches An equitable doctrine used by courts to bar a legal claim or prevent the assertion of a right because of undue delay or failure to assert the claim or right. **20**

land The earth's surface, extending downward to the center of the earth and upward infinitely into space, including things permanently attached by nature, such as trees and water. **2**

latent defect A hidden structural defect that could not be discovered by ordinary inspection and that threatens the property's soundness or the safety of its inhabitants. Some states impose on sellers and licensees a duty to inspect for and disclose latent defects. **4**

law of agency *See* agency.

law of diminishing returns Law that applies when at the point where additional improvements do not increase income or value. **19**

law of increasing returns Law that applies as long as money being spent on improvements produces an increase in income or value. **19**

lease A written or oral contract between a landlord (the lessor) and a tenant (the lessee) that transfers the right to exclusive possession and use of the landlord's real property to the lessee for a specified period of time and for a stated consideration (rent). By state law, leases for longer than a certain period of time (generally one year) must be in writing to be enforceable. **17**

leasehold estate A tenant's right to occupy real estate during the term of a lease, generally considered to be a personal property interest. **17**

lease option A lease under which the tenant has the right to purchase the property either during the lease term or at its end. **17**

lease purchase The purchase of real property, the consummation of which is preceded by a lease, usually long-term, that is typically done for tax or financing purposes. **17**

legacy A disposition of money or personal property by will. **12**

legal description A description of a specific parcel of real estate complete enough for an independent surveyor to locate and identify it. **9**

legally competent parties People who are recognized by law as being able to contract with others; those of legal age and sound mind. **11**

lessee *See* lease.

lessor *See* lease.

levy To assess; to seize or collect. To levy a tax is to assess a property and set the rate of taxation. To levy an execution is to officially seize the property of a person in order to satisfy an obligation. **10**

license (1) A privilege or right granted to a person by a state to operate as a real estate broker or salesperson. (2) The revocable permission for a temporary use of land—a personal right that cannot be sold. **7**

lien A right given by law to certain creditors to have their debts paid out of the property of a defaulting debtor, usually by means of a court sale. **7**

lien theory Some states interpret a mortgage as being purely a lien on real property. The mortgagee thus has no right of possession but must foreclose the lien and sell the property if the mortgagor defaults. **15**

life cycle costing In property management, comparing one type of equipment with another based on both purchase cost and operating cost over its expected useful lifetime.

life estate An interest in real or personal property that is limited in duration to the lifetime of its owner or some other designated person or persons. **7**

life tenant A person in possession of a life estate. **7**

limited partnership *See* partnership.

liquidated damages An amount predetermined by the parties to a contract as the total compensation to an injured party should the other party breach the contract. **11**

lis pendens A recorded legal document giving constructive notice that an action affecting a particular property has been filed in either a state or a federal court. **10**

listing agreement A contract between an owner (as principal) and a real estate broker (as agent) by which the broker is employed as agent to find a buyer for the owner's real estate on the owner's terms, for which service the owner agrees to pay a commission. **4**

listing broker The broker in a multiple-listing situation from whose office a listing agreement is initiated, as opposed to the *cooperating broker,* from whose office negotiations leading up to a sale are initiated. The listing broker and the cooperating broker may be the same person. **6**

littoral rights (1) A landowner's claim to use water in large navigable lakes and oceans adjacent to his or her property. (2) The ownership rights to land bordering these bodies of water up to the high-water mark. **7**

living trust A trust that is created during one's lifetime. **8**

loan origination fee A fee charged to the borrower by the lender for making a mortgage loan. The fee is usually computed as a percentage of the loan amount. **15**

loan-to-value ratio The relationship between the amount of the mortgage loan and the value of the real estate being pledged as collateral. **16**

Local Improvement District (LID) An assessment (i.e., tax) on a local improvement district for a public improvement project the district has approved. **10**

lot-and-block (recorded plat) system A method of describing real property that identifies a parcel of land by reference to lot and block numbers within a subdivision, as specified on a recorded subdivision plat. **9**

management agreement A contract between the owner of income property and a management firm or individual property manager that outlines the scope of the manager's authority. **18**

management plan A highly detailed plan that lays out the owner's objectives with the property, as well as what the property manager wants to accomplish and how, including all budgetary information. **18**

manufactured housing Dwellings that are built off-site and trucked to a building lot where they are installed or assembled. **2**

market A place where goods can be bought and sold and a price established. **1**

marketable title Good or clear title, reasonably free from the risk of litigation over possible defects. **13**

market data approach (also known as the *sales comparison approach*) An estimate of value obtained by comparing property being appraised with recently sold comparable properties. **19**

market value The most probable price property would bring in an arm's-length transaction under normal conditions on the open market. **6**

master plan A comprehensive plan to guide the long-term physical development of a particular area. **20**

material facts Facts a party does not know, could not reasonably discover, and would reasonably want to know.

mechanic's lien A statutory lien created in favor of contractors, laborers, and materialmen who have performed work or furnished materials in the erection or repair of a building. **10**

Megan's Law Federal legislation that promotes the establishment of state registration systems to maintain residential information on every person who kidnaps children, commits sexual crimes against children, or commits sexually violent crimes. **21**

meridian One of a set of imaginary lines running north and south and crossing a base line at a definite point, used in the rectangular (government) survey system of property description. **9**

metes-and-bounds description A legal description of a parcel of land that begins at a well-marked point and follows the boundaries, using directions and distances around the tract, back to the place of beginning. **9**

mill One-tenth of one cent. Some states use a mill rate to compute real estate taxes; for example, a rate of 52 mills would be $0.052 tax for each dollar of assessed valuation of a property. **10**

minimum level of service Some states are requiring licensees perform some minimum level of service to clients. **5**

ministerial acts Those acts outlined in BRRETA and other acts that do not require a broker's or broker's affiliated licensee's professional judgment or skill. **14**

minor Someone who has not reached the age of majority and therefore does not have legal capacity to transfer title to real property. **11**

Model Real Estate Time-Share Act An act that governs the management, use, and termination of time-share units. **5**

monetary policy Governmental regulation of the amount of money in circulation through such institutions as the Federal Reserve Board. **16**

month-to-month tenancy   A periodic tenancy under which the tenant rents for one month at a time. In the absence of a rental agreement (oral or written) a tenancy is generally considered to be month to month. **17**

monument   A fixed natural or artificial object used to establish real estate boundaries for a metes-and-bounds description. **9**

mortgage   A conditional transfer or pledge of real estate as security for the payment of a debt. Also, the document creating a mortgage lien. **15**

mortgage banker   Mortgage loan companies that originate, service, and sell loans to investors. **16**

mortgage broker   An agent of a lender who brings the lender and borrower together. The broker receives a fee for this service. **16**

mortgagee   A lender in a mortgage loan transaction. **15**

mortgage lien   A lien or charge on the property of a mortgagor that secures the underlying debt obligations. **10**

mortgagor   A borrower in a mortgage loan transaction. **15**

multiperil policies   Insurance policies that offer protection from a range of potential perils, such as those of a fire, hazard, public liability, and casualty. **18**

multiple-listing clause   A provision in an exclusive listing for the authority and obligation on the part of the listing broker to distribute the listing to other brokers in the multiple-listing organization. **6**

multiple listing service (MLS)   A marketing organization composed of member brokers who agree to share their listing agreements with one another in the hope of procuring ready, willing, and able buyers for their properties more quickly than they could on their own. Most multiple listing services accept exclusive-right-to-sell or exclusive-agency listings from their member brokers. **6**

National Do Not Call Registry   *See* Do Not Call Registry. **5**

negotiable instrument   A written promise or order to pay a specific sum of money that may be transferred by endorsement or delivery. The transferee then has the original payee's right to payment. **15**

net lease   A lease requiring the tenant to pay not only rent but also costs incurred in maintaining the property, including taxes, insurance, utilities, and repairs. **17**

net listing   A listing based on the net price the seller will receive if the property is sold. Under a net listing the broker can offer the property for sale at the highest price obtainable to increase the commission. This type of listing is illegal in many states. **6**

net operating income (NOI)   The income projected for an income-producing property after deducting losses for vacancy and collection and operating expenses. **19**

nonagent   An intermediary between a buyer and seller, or landlord and tenant, who assists one or both parties with a transaction without representing either. Also known as a *facilitator, transaction broker, transaction coordinator,* and *contract broker.* **4**

nonconforming use   A use of property that is permitted to continue after a zoning ordinance prohibiting it has been established for the area. **20**

nondisturbance clause   A mortgage clause that states the mortgagee agrees not to terminate the tenancies of the lessees in the event the mortgagee forecloses on the mortgagor-lessor's building. **17**

nonhomogeneity   A lack of uniformity; dissimilarity. Because no two parcels of land are exactly alike, real estate is said to be nonhomogeneous. **2**

note   *See* promissory note.

novation   Substituting a new obligation for an old one or substituting new parties to an existing obligation. **11**

nuncupative will   An oral will declared by the testator in his or her final illness, made before witnesses and afterward reduced to writing. **12**

obsolescence   The loss of value due to factors that are outmoded or less useful. Obsolescence may be functional or economic. **19**

occupancy permit   A permit issued by the appropriate local governing body to establish that the property is suitable for habitation by meeting certain safety and health standards. **19**

offer and acceptance   Two essential components of a valid contract; a "meeting of the minds." **11**

offeror/offeree   The person who makes the offer is the offeror. The person to whom the offer is made is the offeree. **11**

Office of Thrift Supervision (OTS)   A government agency that governs the practices of fiduciary lenders. OTS was created by the Financial Institutions Reform, Recovery, and Enforcement Act (FIRREA). **16**

open-end loan   A mortgage loan that is expandable by increments up to a maximum dollar amount, the full loan being secured by the same original mortgage. **16**

open listing   A listing contract under which the broker's commission is contingent on the broker's producing a ready, willing, and able buyer before the property is sold by the seller or another broker. **6**

option   An agreement to keep open for a set period an offer to sell or purchase property. **11**

option listing   Listing with a provision that gives the listing broker the right, but not the obligation, to purchase the listed property within a certain time. **6**

ostensible agency   A form of implied agency relationship created by the actions of the parties involved rather than by written agreement or document.

package loan   A real estate loan used to finance the purchase of both real property and personal property, such as in the purchase of a new home that includes carpeting, window coverings, and major appliances. **16**

parol evidence   Oral or verbal evidence.

parol evidence rule   A rule of evidence providing that a written agreement is the final expression of the agreement of the parties, not to be varied or contradicted by prior or contemporaneous oral or written negotiations.

participation mortgage   A mortgage loan wherein the lender has a partial equity interest in the property or receives a portion of the income from the property. **16**

partition   The division of cotenants' interests in real property when the parties do not all voluntarily agree to terminate the co-ownership; takes place through court procedures. **8**

partnership   An association of two or more individuals who carry on a continuing business for profit as co-owners. Under the law, a partnership is regarded as a group of individuals rather than as a single entity. A *general partnership* is a typical form of joint venture in which each general partner shares in the administration, profits, and losses of the operation. A *limited partnership* is a business arrangement whereby the operation is administered by one or more general partners and funded, by and large, by limited or silent partners, who are by law responsible for losses only to the extent of their investments. **8**

party wall   A wall that is located on or at a boundary line between two adjoining parcels of land and is used or is intended to be used by the owners of both properties. **7**

patent   A grant or franchise of land from the U.S. government.

payment cap   The limit on the amount the monthly payment can be increased on an adjustable-rate mortgage when the interest rate is adjusted. **16**

payoff statement   *See* reduction certificate.

percentage lease   A lease, commonly used for commercial property, whose rental is based on the tenant's gross sales at the premises; it usually stipulates a base monthly rental plus a percentage of any gross sales above a certain amount. **17**

percolation test   A test of the soil to determine if it will absorb and drain water adequately to use a septic system for sewage disposal.

periodic estate (tenancy)   *See* estate from period to period. **17**

personal property   Items, called *chattels*, that do not fit into the definition of real property; movable objects. **2**

physical deterioration   A reduction in a property's value resulting from a decline in physical condition; can be caused by action of the elements or by ordinary wear and tear. **19**

planned unit development (PUD)   A planned combination of diverse land uses, such as housing, recreation, and shopping, in one contained development or subdivision. **20**

plat   A detailed map that illustrates the geographic boundaries of individual lots. **20**

plat map   A map of a town, section, or subdivision indicating the location and boundaries of individual properties. **9**

plottage   The increase in value or utility resulting from the consolidation (*assemblage*) of two or more adjacent lots into one larger lot. **19**

point of beginning (POB)   In a metes-and-bounds legal description, the starting point of the survey, situated in one corner of the parcel; all metes-and-bounds descriptions must follow the boundaries of the parcel back to the point of beginning. **9**

police power   The government's right to impose laws, statutes, and ordinances, including zoning ordinances and building codes, to protect the public health, safety, and welfare. **7**

power of attorney   A written instrument authorizing a person, the *attorney-in-fact*, to act as agent for another person to the extent indicated in the instrument. **4**

prepaid items   On a closing statement, items that have been paid in advance by the seller, such as insurance premiums and some real estate taxes, for which he or she must be reimbursed by the buyer. **23**

prepayment penalty   A charge imposed on a borrower who pays off the loan principal early. This penalty compensates the lender for interest and other charges that would otherwise be lost. **15**

price-fixing   *See* antitrust laws.

primary mortgage market   The mortgage market in which loans are originated, consisting of lenders such as commercial banks, savings associations, and mutual savings banks. **16**

principal   (1) A sum loaned or employed as a fund or an investment, as distinguished from its income or profits. (2) The original amount (as in a loan) of the total due and payable at a certain date. (3) A main party to a transaction—the person for whom the agent works. **4**

principal meridian   The main imaginary line running north and south and crossing a base line at a definite point, used by surveyors for reference in locating and describing land under the rectangular (government) survey system of legal description. **9**

prior appropriation A concept of water ownership in which the landowner's right to use available water is based on a government-administered permit system. **7**

priority The order of position or time. The priority of liens is generally determined by the chronological order in which the lien documents are recorded; tax liens, however, have priority even over previously recorded liens. **13**

private mortgage insurance (PMI) Insurance provided by private carrier that protects a lender against a loss in the event of a foreclosure and deficiency. **16**

probate A legal process by which a court determines who will inherit a decedent's property and what the estate's assets are. **12**

procuring cause The effort that brings about the desired result. Under an open listing the broker who is the procuring cause of the sale receives the commission. **5**

progression An appraisal principle that states that, between dissimilar properties, the value of the lesser-quality property is favorably affected by the presence of the better-quality property. **19**

promissory note A financing instrument that states the terms of the underlying obligation, is signed by its maker, and is negotiable (transferable to a third party). **15**

property manager Someone who manages real estate for another person for compensation. Duties include collecting rents, maintaining the property, and keeping up all accounting. **18**

property reports The mandatory federal and state documents compiled by subdividers and developers to provide potential purchasers with facts about a property, prior to their purchase.

proprietary lease A lease given by the corporation that owns a cooperative apartment building to the shareholder for the shareholder's right as a tenant to an individual apartment. **3**

prorations Expenses, either prepaid or paid in arrears, that are divided or distributed between buyer and seller at the closing. **23**

protected class Any group of people designated as such by the Department of Housing and Urban Development (HUD) in consideration of federal and state civil rights legislation. Currently includes ethnic minorities, women, religious groups, the handicapped, and others. **21**

puffing Exaggerated or superlative comments or opinions. **4**

pur autre vie "For the life of another." A life estate pur autre vie is a life estate that is measured by the life of a person other than the grantee. **7**

purchase-money mortgage (PMM) A note secured by a mortgage or deed of trust given by a buyer, as borrower, to a seller, as lender, as part of the purchase price of the real estate. **16**

quantity-survey method The appraisal method of estimating building costs by calculating the cost of all of the physical components in the improvements, adding the cost to assemble them, and then including the indirect costs associated with such construction. **19**

quiet title A court action to remove a cloud on the title. **13**

quitclaim deed A conveyance by which the grantor transfers whatever interest he or she has in the real estate, without warranties or obligations. **12**

radon A naturally occurring gas that is suspected of causing lung cancer. **22**

range A strip of land six miles wide, extending north and south and numbered east and west according to its distance from the principal meridian in the rectangular (government) survey system of legal description. **9**

rate cap The limit on the amount the interest rate can be increased at each adjustment period in an adjustable-rate loan. The cap may also set the maximum interest rate that can be charged during the life of the loan. **16**

ratification Method of creating an agency relationship in which the principal accepts the conduct of someone who acted without prior authorization as the principal's agent.

ready, willing, and able buyer One who is prepared to buy property on the seller's terms and is ready to take positive steps to consummate the transaction. **5**

real estate Land; a portion of the earth's surface extending downward to the center of the earth and upward infinitely into space, including all things permanently attached to it, whether naturally or artificially. **2**

Real Estate Education, Research, and Recovery Fund A fund the Georgia Real Estate Commission maintains to compensate consumers who suffer damages from a licensee and who have exhausted legal remedies. The fund also provides for professional education of licensees. **14**

real estate investment syndicate *See* syndicate.

real estate license law State law enacted to protect the public from fraud, dishonesty, and incompetence in the purchase and sale of real estate. **2**

real estate mortgage investment conduit (REMIC) A tax entity that issues multiple classes of investor interests (securities) backed by a pool of mortgages. **4**

Real Estate Settlement Procedures Act (RESPA) The federal law that requires certain disclosures to consumers about mortgage loan settlements. The law also prohibits the payment or receipt of kickbacks and certain kinds of referral fees. **23**

real property The interests, benefits, and rights inherent in real estate ownership. **2**

REALTOR® A registered trademark term reserved for the sole use of active members of local REALTOR® boards affiliated with the National Association of REALTORS®. **1**

reconciliation The final step in the appraisal process, in which the appraiser combines the estimates of value received from the sales comparison, cost, and income approaches to arrive at a final estimate of market value for the subject property. **19**

recording The act of entering or recording documents affecting or conveying interests in real estate in the recorder's office established in each county. Until it is recorded, a deed or mortgage ordinarily is not effective against subsequent purchasers or mortgagees. **13**

rectangular (government) survey system A system established in 1785 by the federal government, providing for surveying and describing land by reference to principal meridians and base lines. **9**

redemption The right of a defaulted property owner to recover his or her property by curing the default. **10**

redemption period A period of time established by state law during which a property owner has the right to redeem his or her real estate from a foreclosure or tax sale by paying the sales price, interest, and costs. Many states do not have mortgage redemption laws. **10**

redlining The illegal practice of a lending institution denying loans or restricting their number for certain areas of a community. **21**

reduction certificate (payoff statement) The document signed by a lender indicating the amount required to pay a loan balance in full and satisfy the debt; used in the settlement process to protect both the seller's and the buyer's interests. **23**

regression An appraisal principle that states that, between dissimilar properties, the value of the better-quality property is affected adversely by the presence of the lesser-quality property. **19**

Regulation Z Implements the Truth-in-Lending Act requiring credit institutions to inform borrowers of the true cost of obtaining credit. **16**

release deed A document, also known as a *deed of reconveyance*, that transfers all rights given a trustee under a deed of trust loan back to the grantor after the loan has been fully repaid. **15**

remainder interest The remnant of an estate that has been conveyed to take effect and be enjoyed after the termination of a prior estate, such as when an owner conveys a life estate to one party and the remainder to another. **7**

renewal option A clause in a lease that grants the lessee the privilege of renewing the lease. **17**

rent A fixed, periodic payment made by a tenant of a property to the owner for possession and use, usually by prior agreement of the parties. **17**

rent schedule A statement of proposed rental rates, determined by the owner or the property manager or both, based on a building's estimated expenses, market supply and demand, and the owner's long-range goals for the property. **17**

replacement cost The construction cost at current prices of a property that is not necessarily an exact duplicate of the subject property but serves the same purpose or function as the original. **3**

reproduction cost The construction cost at current prices of an exact duplicate of the subject property. **19**

rescission The practice of one party canceling or terminating a contract, which has the effect of returning the parties to their original positions before the contract was made. **11**

Resolution Trust Corporation The organization created by the Financial Institutions Reform, Recovery, and Enforcement Act (FIRREA) to liquidate the assets of failed savings and loan associations.

restrictive covenants A clause in a deed that limits the way the real estate ownership may be used. **7**

retroactive liability Liability is not limited to the current owner, but includes people who have owned the site in the past. **22**

reverse-annuity mortgage (RAM) A loan under which the homeowner receives monthly payments based on his or her accumulated equity rather than a lump sum. The loan must be repaid at a prearranged date, or upon the death of the owner, or upon the sale of the property. **16**

reversionary interest The remnant of an estate that the grantor holds after granting a life estate to another person. **7**

reversionary right The return of the rights of possession and quiet enjoyment to the lessor at the expiration of a lease. **17**

right of possession A right given by a landlord to a tenant at the beginning of a lease under Georgia lease law. **17**

right of survivorship *See* joint tenancy.

right-of-way   The right given by one landowner to another to pass over the land, construct a roadway, or use as a pathway, without actually transferring ownership.

riparian rights   An owner's rights in land that borders on or includes a stream, river, or lake. These rights include access to and use of the water. **7**

risk management   Evaluation and selection of appropriate property and other insurance. **18**

rules and regulations   Real estate licensing authority orders that govern licensees' activities; they usually have the same force and effect as statutory law.

Safe Drinking Water Act   An act to protect public health by authorizing the EPA to set national health-based standards for drinking water. **22**

sale-and-leaseback   A transaction in which an owner sells his or her improved property and, as part of the same transaction, signs a long-term lease to remain in possession of the premises. **16**

sales comparison approach   The process of estimating the value of a property by examining and comparing actual sales of comparable properties. **19**

salesperson   A person who performs real estate activities while employed by or associated with a licensed real estate broker. **1**

satisfaction of mortgage   A document acknowledging the payment of a mortgage debt. **15**

secondary mortgage market   A market for the purchase and sale of existing mortgages, designed to provide greater liquidity for mortgages; also called the *secondary money market*. Mortgages are first originated in the *primary mortgage market*. **16**

section   A portion of township under the rectangular (government) survey system. A township is divided into 36 sections, numbered 1 through 36. A section is a square with mile-long sides and an area of one square mile, or 640 acres. **9**

security agreement   *See* Uniform Commercial Code.

security deed or deed to secure debt   The Georgia form of a mortgage instrument in which a borrower conveys legal title to the property to the lender for the purpose of securing a mortgage loan. **15**

security deposit   A payment by a tenant, held by the landlord during the lease term, and kept (wholly or partially) on default, or on destruction of the premises by the tenant. **17**

separate property   Under community property law, property owned solely by either spouse before the marriage, acquired by gift or inheritance after the marriage, or purchased with separate funds after the marriage. **8**

servient tenement   Land on which an easement exists in favor of an adjacent property (called a *dominant estate*); also called a *servient estate*. **7**

setback   The amount of space local zoning regulations require between a lot line and a building line.

severalty   Ownership of real property by one person only, also called *sole ownership*. **8**

severance   Changing an item of real estate to personal property by detaching it from the land; for example, cutting down a tree. **2**

sharecropping   In an agricultural lease, the agreement between the landowner and the tenant farmer to split the crop or the profit from its sale, actually sharing the crop. **17**

shared-appreciation mortgage (SAM)   A mortgage loan in which the lender, in exchange for a loan with a favorable interest rate, participates in the profits (if any) the borrower receives when the property is eventually sold.

sick building syndrome (SBS)   An illness caused by poor air quality, typically in office building settings. Symptoms include fatigue, nausea, headache, and sensitivity to odors. **18**

situs   The personal preference of people for one area over another, not necessarily based on objective facts and knowledge. **2**

special agent   One who is authorized by a principal to perform a single act or transaction; a real estate broker is usually a special agent authorized to find a ready, willing, and able buyer for a particular property. **4**

special assessment   A tax or levy customarily imposed against only those specific parcels of real estate that will benefit from a proposed public improvement like a street or sewer. **10**

special warranty deed   A deed in which the grantor warrants, or guarantees, the title only against defects arising during the period of his or her tenure and ownership of the property and not against defects existing before that time, generally using the language, "by, through, or under the grantor but not otherwise." **12**

specific lien   A lien affecting or attaching only to a certain, specific parcel of land or piece of property. **10**

specific performance   A legal action to compel a party to carry out the terms of a contract. **11**

square-foot method   The appraisal method of estimating building costs by multiplying the number of square feet in the improvements being appraised by the cost per square foot for recently constructed similar improvements. **19**

state-certified general real property appraiser (SCGRPA)   A certified general appraiser who performs appraisals on any type of property for any purpose. **19**

state-certified residential real property appraiser (SCR-RPA) A certified residential appraiser who performs any appraisal, including those with limited federally related financial transactions. **19**

state-licensed real property appraiser (SLRPA) A licensed appraiser who performs appraisals on any property, including those with limited federally related financial transactions. **19**

state-registered real property appraiser A registered appraiser who performs appraisals on any type of property except on property involving federally related financial transactions. **19**

statute of frauds That part of a state law that requires certain instruments, such as deeds, real estate sales contracts, and certain leases, to be in writing to be legally enforceable. **11**

statute of limitations That law pertaining to the period of time within which certain actions must be brought to court. **11**

statutory lien A lien imposed on property by statute—a tax lien, for example—in contrast to an *equitable lien*, which arises out of common law. **10**

statutory right of redemption The right of a defaulted property owner to recover the property after its sale by paying the appropriate fees and charges. **10**

steering The illegal practice of channeling home seekers to particular areas, either to maintain the homogeneity of an area or to change the character of an area, which limits their choices of where they can live. **21**

stigmatized property A property that has acquired an undesirable reputation due to an event that occurred on or near it, such as violent crime, gang-related activity, illness, or personal tragedy. Some states restrict the disclosure of information about stigmatized properties. **4**

straight-line method A method of calculating depreciation for tax purposes, computed by dividing the adjusted basis of a property by the estimated number of years of remaining useful life. **19**

straight (term) loan A loan in which only interest is paid during the term of the loan, with the entire principal amount due with the final interest payment. **16**

strict liability The owner is responsible to the injured party without excuse. **22**

subagent One who is employed by a person already acting as an agent. Typically a reference to a salesperson licensed under a broker (agent) who is employed under the terms of a listing agreement. **4**

subdivider One who buys undeveloped land, divides it into smaller, usable lots, and sells the lots to potential users. **20**

subdivision A tract of land divided by the owner, known as the *subdivider*, into blocks, building lots, and streets according to a recorded subdivision plat, which must comply with local ordinances and regulations. **20**

subdivision and development ordinances Municipal ordinances that establish requirements for subdivisions and development. **20**

subdivision plat *See* plat map.

sublease *See* subletting.

subletting The leasing of premises by a lessee to a third party for part of the lessee's remaining term. *See also* assignment. **17**

subordination Relegation to a lesser position, usually in respect to a right or security. **10**

subordination agreement A written agreement between holders of liens on a property that changes the priority of mortgage, judgment, and other liens under certain circumstances. **10**

subrogation The substitution of one creditor for another, with the substituted person succeeding to the legal rights and claims of the original claimant. Subrogation is used by title insurers to acquire from the injured party rights to sue in order to recover any claims they have paid. **13**

substitution An appraisal principle that states that the maximum value of a property tends to be set by the cost of purchasing an equally desirable and valuable substitute property, assuming that no costly delay is encountered in making the substitution. **19**

subsurface rights Ownership rights in a parcel of real estate to the water, minerals, gas, oil, and so forth that lie beneath the surface of the property. **2**

suit for possession A court suit initiated by a landlord to evict a tenant from leased premises after the tenant has breached one of the terms of the lease or has held possession of the property after the lease's expiration. **17**

suit to quiet title A court action intended to establish or settle the title to a particular property, especially when there is a cloud on the title. **13**

Superfund Popular name of the hazardous-waste cleanup fund established by the Comprehensive Environmental Response, Compensation, and Liability Act (CERCLA). **22**

Superfund Amendments and Reauthorization Act (SARA) An amendatory statute that contains stronger cleanup standards for contaminated sites, increased funding for Superfund, and clarifications of lender liability and innocent landowner immunity. *See* Comprehensive Environmental Response, Compensation, and Liability Act (CERCLA). **22**

supply The amount of goods available in the market to be sold at a given price. The term is often coupled with *demand*. **1**

supply and demand The appraisal principle that follows the interrelationship of the supply of and demand for real estate. As appraising is based on economic concepts, this principle recognizes that real property is subject to the influences of the marketplace just as is any other commodity. **1**

surety bond An agreement by an insurance or bonding company to be responsible for certain possible defaults, debts, or obligations contracted for by an insured party; in essence, a policy insuring one's personal and/or financial integrity. In the real estate business a surety bond is generally used to ensure that a particular project will be completed at a certain date or that a contract will be performed as stated. **18**

surface rights Ownership rights in a parcel of real estate that are limited to the surface of the property and do not include the air above it (*air rights*) or the minerals below the surface (*subsurface rights*). **2**

survey The process by which boundaries are measured and land areas are determined; the on-site measurement of lot lines, dimensions, and position of a house on a lot, including the determination of any existing encroachments or easements. **23**

syndicate A combination of people or firms formed to accomplish a business venture of mutual interest by pooling resources. In a *real estate investment syndicate*, the parties own and/or develop property, with the main profit generally arising from the sale of the property. **8**

tacking Adding or combining successive periods of continuous occupation of real property by adverse possessors. This concept enables someone who has not been in possession for the entire statutory period to establish a claim of adverse possession. **7**

taking A concept that comes from the takings clause of the Fifth Amendment to the U.S. Constitution and means that when land is taken for public use through the government's power of eminent domain or condemnation, the owner must be compensated. **20**

taxation The process by which a government or municipal quasi-public body raises monies to fund its operation. **7**

tax deed An instrument, similar to a certificate of sale, given to a purchaser at a tax sale. *See also* certificate of sale. **10**

tax lien A charge against property, created by operation of law. Tax liens and assessments take priority over all other liens. **10**

tax sale A court-ordered sale of real property to raise money to cover delinquent taxes. **10**

tenancy in common A form of co-ownership by which each owner holds an undivided interest in real property as if he or she were sole owner. Each individual owner has the right to partition. Unlike joint tenants, tenants in common have right of inheritance. **8**

tenant One who holds or possesses lands or tenements by any kind of right or title. **18**

tenant improvements Alterations to the interior of a building to meet the functional demands of the tenant. Also known as *build-outs*. **18**

tenant's insurance Insurance coverage that protects the personal belongings of tenants. **18**

testate Having made and left a valid will. **12**

testator A person who has made a valid will. A woman often is referred to as a *testatrix*, although testator can be used for either gender. **12**

tier (township strip) A strip of land six miles wide, extending east and west and numbered north and south according to its distance from the base line in the rectangular (government) survey system of legal description. **9**

time is of the essence A phrase in a contract that requires the performance of a certain act within a stated period of time. **11**

time-share A form of ownership interest that may include an estate interest in property and that allows use of the property for a fixed or variable time period. **8**

title (1) The right to ownership or the ownership of land. (2) The evidence of ownership of land. **12**

title insurance A policy insuring the owner or mortgagee against loss by reason of defects in the title to a parcel of real estate, other than encumbrances, defects, and matters specifically excluded by the policy. **13**

title search The examination of public records relating to real estate to determine the current state of the ownership. **13**

title theory Some states interpret a mortgage to mean that the lender is the owner of mortgaged land. Upon full payment of the mortgage debt, the borrower becomes the landowner. **15**

Title VIII of Civil Rights Act of 1968 (called the federal Fair Housing Act) Prohibits discrimination in housing based on race, color, religion, or national origin. **21**

Torrens system A method of evidencing title by registration with the proper public authority, generally called the *registrar*, named for its founder, Sir Robert Torrens. **13**

town house A type of residential dwelling with two floors that is connected to one or more dwellings by a common wall(s). Title to the unit and lot vest in the owner who shares a fractional interest with other owners for the common areas. **8**

township The principal unit of the rectangular (government) survey system. A township is a square with six-mile sides and an area of 36 square miles. **9**

township lines All the lines in a rectangular survey system that run east and west, parallel to the base line six miles apart. **9**

township strips *See* tier.

township tiers Township lines that form strips of land and are designated by consecutive numbers north or south of the base line. **9**

trade fixture An article installed by a tenant under the terms of a lease and removable by the tenant before the lease expires. **2**

transfer tax A tax on real estate payable when a deed is recorded. **12**

trigger terms Specific credit terms, such as down payment, monthly payment, and amount of finance charge or term of loan. **16**

trust A fiduciary arrangement whereby property is conveyed to a person or institution, called a *trustee*, to be held and administered on behalf of another person, called a *beneficiary*. The one who conveys the trust is called the *trustor*. **8**

trust deed lien A lien on the property of a trustor that secures a deed of trust loan. **10**

trustee One to whom something is entrusted, and holds legal title to property and administers the property for the benefit of a beneficiary. Or a member of a board entrusted with the administration of an institution or organization, such as a cooperative. **8**

trustee's deed A deed executed by a trustee conveying land held in a trust. **12**

trustor A borrower in a deed of trust loan transaction; one who places property in a trust. Also called a grantor or settler. **8**

Truth-in-Lending Act Federal government regulates the lending practices of mortgage lenders through this act. **16**

unbundling services Offering real estate services in a piecemeal fashion. **5**

undivided interest *See* tenancy in common.

unenforceable contract A contract that has all the elements of a valid contract, yet neither party can sue the other to force performance of it. For example, an unsigned contract is generally unenforceable. **11**

Uniform Commercial Code (UCC) A codification of commercial law, adopted in most states, that attempts to make uniform all laws relating to commercial transactions, including chattel mortgages and bulk transfers.

Security interests in chattels are created by an instrument known as a *security agreement*. To give notice of the security interest, a *financing statement* must be recorded. Article 6 of the code regulates *bulk transfers*—the sale of a business as a whole, including all fixtures, chattels, and merchandise. **13**

Uniform Electronic Transactions Act (UETA) Sets forth rules for entering into an enforceable contract using electronic means. **5**

uniform settlement statement A special HUD form that itemizes all charges to be paid by a borrower and seller in connection with the settlement. **23**

unilateral contract A one-sided contract wherein one party makes a promise so as to induce a second party to do something. The second party is not legally bound to perform; however, if the second party does comply, the first party is obligated to keep the promise. **11**

unit-in-place method The appraisal method of estimating building costs by calculating the costs of all of the physical components in the structure, with the cost of each item including its proper installation, connection, etc.; also called the *segregated cost method*. **19**

unity of ownership The four unities that are traditionally needed to create a joint tenancy—unity of title, time, interest, and possession.

universal agent A person empowered to do anything the principal could do personally. **4**

usury Charging interest at a higher rate than the maximum rate established by state law. **15**

valid contract A contract that complies with all the essentials of a contract and is binding and enforceable on all parties to it. **11**

VA loan A mortgage loan on approved property made to a qualified veteran by an authorized lender and guaranteed by the Department of Veterans Affairs in order to limit the lender's possible loss. **16**

value The power of a good or service to command other goods in exchange for the present worth of future rights to its income or amenities. **19**

variance Permission obtained from zoning authorities to build a structure or conduct a use that is expressly prohibited by the current zoning laws; an exception from the zoning ordinances. **20**

vendee A buyer, usually under the terms of a land contract. **11**

vendor A seller, usually under the terms of a land contract. **11**

vendor's lien A lien that belongs to a vendor for the unpaid purchase price of land, where the vendor has not taken any other lien or security beyond the personal obligation of the purchaser. **10**

vested interest A present right, interest, or title to property that gives the holder the right to convey it to another, even though the right might not be enjoyed until a future time. **12**

voidable contract A contract that seems to be valid on the surface but may be rejected or disaffirmed by one or both of the parties. **11**

void contract A contract that has no legal force or effect because it does not meet the essential elements of a contract. **11**

voluntary alienation *See* alienation.

voluntary lien A lien placed on property with the knowledge and consent of the property owner. **10**

waste An improper use or an abuse of a property by a possessor who holds less than fee ownership, such as a tenant, life tenant, mortgagor, or vendee. Such waste ordinarily impairs the value of the land or the interest of the person holding the title or the reversionary rights. **7**

water rights Common law rights held by owners of land adjacent to rivers, lakes, or oceans, and includes restrictions on those rights and land ownership. **2**

will A written document, properly witnessed, providing for the transfer of title to property owned by the deceased, called the *testator*. **12**

workers' compensation acts Laws that require an employer to obtain insurance coverage to protect his or her employees who are injured in the course of their employment. **18**

wraparound loan A method of refinancing in which the new mortgage is placed in a secondary, or subordinate, position; the new mortgage includes both the unpaid principal balance of the first mortgage and whatever additional sums are advanced by the lender. In essence it is an additional mortgage in which another lender refinances a borrower by lending an amount over the existing first mortgage amount without disturbing the existence of the first mortgage. **16**

year's support Has replaced dower and curtesy in Georgia. A surviving spouse and/or minor can petition the probate court to have real and/or personal property set aside from the estate to provide for 12 months' support from the date of the decedent's death. **7**

zoning ordinance An exercise of police power by a municipality to regulate and control the character and use of property. **20**

Answer Key

Following are the correct answers to the review questions included in each chapter of the text. In parentheses following the correct answers are references to the pages where the question topics are discussed or explained. The references for the Sample Exam 1 refer to chapter numbers. If you have answered a question incorrectly, be sure to go back to the page or pages noted and restudy the material until you understand the correct answer.

CHAPTER 1
Introduction to the Real
Estate Business

1. b (2)
2. b (6)
3. d (7)
4. c (8)
5. b (2)
6. d (4)
7. b (6)
8. a (3)
9. d (4)
10. a (5)
11. d (3)
12. a (3)

CHAPTER 2
Real Property and the Law

1. c (18)
2. b (20)
3. c (22)
4. c (17)
5. d (15)
6. b (14)
7. a (19)
8. a (21)
9. a (18)
10. a (19)
11. c (16)
12. b (18)
13. c (19)
14. d (16)
15. a (14)

CHAPTER 3
Concepts of Home Ownership

1. d (31)
2. b (32)
3. a (30)
4. b (29)
5. b (30)
6. c (32)
7. d (35)
8. b (32)
9. a (32)
10. b (32)
11. c (32)
12. c (33)
13. a (33)
14. b (29)
15. c (34)

CHAPTER 4
Agency

1. a (47)
2. a (44)
3. b (48)
4. c (50)
5. b (46)
6. d (52)
7. c (50)
8. c (53)
9. d (58)
10. b (51)
11. c (44)
12. b (52)
13. d (45)

CHAPTER 5
Real Estate Brokerage

1. b (79)
2. c (70)
3. b (70)
4. b (70)
5. a (79)
6. d (70)
7. d (82)
8. a (81)
9. c (69)
10. b (80)
11. d (81)
12. a (80)
13. c (80)
14. b (80)
15. a (69)
16. b (83)

CHAPTER 6
Listing Agreements and
Buyer Representation

1. a (92)
2. c (93, 94)
3. c (96)
4. a (94)
5. d (95)
6. a (94)
7. c (97)
8. c (93)
9. b (106)
10. a (108)
11. b (107)
12. b (97)
13. b (99)
14. b (99)
15. c (93)
16. b (96)

17. c (107)
18. d (93)
19. d (99)
20. b (99)

CHAPTER 7
Interests in Real Estate

1. b (116)
2. a (118)
3. c (119)
4. d (123)
5. c (126)
6. a (120)
7. d (123)
8. d (125)
9. c (129)
10. a (115)
11. b (118)
12. b (123)
13. b (120)
14. b (127)
15. d (126)
16. a (122)
17. d (117)
18. b (123)
19. a (123)
20. b (127)
21. d (128)
22. a (125)
23. d (126)
24. a (121)
25. c (122)

CHAPTER 8
Forms of Real Estate Ownership

1. d (139)
2. b (136)
3. a (138)
4. b (145)
5. b (141)
6. b (136)
7. a (141)
8. b (145)
9. c (149)
10. c (144)
11. d (136)
12. b (147)
13. b (136)
14. c (147)
15. b (147)

16. d (145)
17. a (138)
18. d (136)
19. c (149)
20. d (146)

CHAPTER 9
Legal Descriptions

1. b (160)
2. b (166)
3. b (167)
4. b (160)
5. b (Math FAQs)
6. c (160)
7. c (163)
8. a (163)
9. d (160)

CHAPTER 10
Real Estate Taxes and Other Liens

1. d (172)
2. b (174)
3. b (180)
4. c (172)
5. b (174)
6. d (179)
7. c (175)
8. c (172)
9. d (179)
10. c (173)
11. d (182)
12. d (183)
13. c (180)
14. b (172)
15. b (172)
16. d (178)
17. a (172)
18. b (175)
19. c (181)
20. b (179)

CHAPTER 11
Real Estate Contracts

1. c (190)
2. b (194)
3. d (190)
4. b (191)
5. c (193)

6. d (195)
7. d (208)
8. a (206)
9. a (208)
10. d (206)
11. b (209)
12. d (209)
13. c (190)
14. b (197)
15. b (205)
16. a (193)
17. b (197)
18. d (194)
19. c (205)
20. c (195)

CHAPTER 12
Transfer of Title

1. a (216)
2. a (218)
3. d (216)
4. a (218)
5. d (220)
6. d (221)
7. c (219)
8. b (217)
9. b (219)
10. b (219)
11. c (223)
12. b (223)
13. d (223)
14. a (222)
15. b (224)
16. d (224)
17. b (225)
18. c (225)
19. c (226)
20. b (216)
21. d (220)
22. b (221)
23. a (222)
24. c (224)
25. a (224)

CHAPTER 13
Title Records

1. a (234)
2. a (234)
3. c (235)
4. a (235)

5. a (235)
6. d (237)
7. d (237)
8. d (235)
9. c (237)
10. a (236)
11. c (234)
12. c (239)
13. b (238)
14. d (238)
15. c (238)
16. a (238)
17. b (240)
18. a (235)
19. b (234)
20. c (236)

CHAPTER 14
Georgia Real Estate License Law

1. b (248)
2. c (248)
3. d (249)
4. d (250)
5. c (262)
6. b (249)
7. a (262)
8. d (249)
9. b (255)
10. c (248)
11. b (257)
12. c (259)
13. d (259)
14. d (260)
15. b (258)
16. d (263)
17. d (265)
18. a (255)
19. b (248)
20. c (258)

CHAPTER 15
Real Estate Financing: Principles

1. b (277)
2. a (274)
3. c (274)
4. c (283)
5. b (276)
6. d (284)
7. a (283)
8. c (278)

9. d (282)
10. b (284)
11. a (275)
12. b (277)
13. c (282)
14. b (283)
15. b (281)
16. d (275)
17. b (274)
18. c (282)

CHAPTER 16
Real Estate Financing: Practice

1. d (307)
2. d (309)
3. c (294)
4. c (299)
5. b (293)
6. a (296)
7. b (292)
8. c (296)
9. b (307)
10. c (303)
11. b (310)
12. b (296)
13. b (294)
14. a (296)
15. b (295)
16. d (312)
17. b (300)
18. b (297)
19. b (297)
20. b (300)
21. c (304)
22. a (292)
23. b (296)
24. c (298)
25. d (310)

CHAPTER 17
Leases

1. c (330)
2. c (330)
3. d (332)
4. c (332)
5. a (328)
6. d (323)
7. c (322)
8. b (333)
9. b (323)

10. b (328)
11. a (331)
12. b (330)
13. d (324)
14. c (330)
15. a (329)
16. c (330)
17. c (324)
18. c (332)
19. a (333)
20. d (327)

CHAPTER 18
Property Management

1. b (355)
2. c (354)
3. d (347)
4. c (355)
5. d (356)
6. b (351)
7. c (346)
8. a (346)
9. c (355)
10. c (355)
11. c (347)
12. b (350)
13. b (344)
14. b (346)
15. b (355)
16. c (352)
17. c (352)
18. d (353)
19. c (341)
20. c (349)

CHAPTER 19
Real Estate Appraisal

1. c (381)
2. b (374)
3. b (376)
4. b (374)
5. d (376)
6. a (376)
7. d (380)
8. c (384)
9. b (379)
10. a (381)
11. c (381)
12. c (381)
13. c (374)

14. b (381)
15. c (378)
16. d (377)
17. d (379)
18. b (375)
19. c (375)
20. b (380)
21. c (380)
22. d (384)
23. d (382)
24. c (366)
25. b (382)

CHAPTER 20
Land-Use Controls and Property Development

1. a (400)
2. a (396)
3. b (400)
4. c (393)
5. c (397)
6. a (393)
7. a (396)
8. d (394)
9. b (401)
10. a (401)
11. a (397)
12. c (398)
13. b (399)
14. b (399)
15. b (392)
16. d (398)
17. a (399)
18. a (399)
19. a (402)
20. c (396)

CHAPTER 21
Fair Housing and Ethical Practices

1. c (416)
2. a (421)
3. d (413)
4. b (417)
5. c (418)
6. a (419)
7. b (414)
8. b (420)
9. c (416)
10. b (414)

11. a (413)
12. b (422)
13. d (421)
14. d (415)
15. d (415)

CHAPTER 22
Environmental Issues and the Real Estate Transaction

1. b (434)
2. c (433)
3. c (433)
4. a (433)
5. a (438)
6. c (441)
7. b (442)
8. d (444)
9. c (436)
10. d (431, 433, 437)
11. c (436)
12. b (431)

CHAPTER 23
Closing the Real Estate Transaction

1. d (469)
2. b (456)
3. d (456)
4. a (456)
5. c (461)
6. c (457)
7. b (464)
8. b (464)
9. d (469, Math FAQs)
10. c (470, Math FAQs)
11. a (464)
12. c (465, Math FAQs)
13. b (Math FAQs)
14. c (464)
15. b (466)
16. d (466)
17. d (461)
18. b (462)
19. b (462)
20. d (460)

SAMPLE EXAM 1
1. b (Chapter 10)
2. a (11)
3. a (11)

4. c (16)
5. c (16, Math FAQs)
6. b (6)
7. a (12)
8. a (21)
9. a (7)
10. d (8)
11. d (5)
12. d (15)
13. c (17)
14. a (19)
15. a (20)
16. c (5, Math FAQs)
17. d (4)
18. c (8)
19. a (5, Math FAQs)
20. b (7)
21. d (6, Math FAQs)
22. b (9, Math FAQs)
23. b (15)
24. b (10)
25. c (Math FAQs)
26. c (10)
27. b (19)
28. b (9, Math FAQs)
29. c (15, Math FAQs)
30. b (6, Math FAQs)
31. d (11)
32. c (11)
33. b (11)
34. b (15, 16)
35. b (11)
36. a (15)
37. d (19, Math FAQs)
38. b (6)
39. a (8)
40. a (12)
41. d (6)
42. b (17)
43. c (21)
44. b (Math FAQs)
45. d (10)
46. d (11)
47. c (7)
48. b (5, Math FAQs)
49. b (19)
50. b (10)
51. b (11)
52. d (21)
53. c (17)

54. d (11)
55. b (7)
56. c (16, Math FAQs)
57. a (7)
58. c (Math FAQs)
59. d (20)
60. b (11)
61. b (15)
62. a (21)
63. d (23, Math FAQs)
64. d (11)
65. b (12)
66. b (8)
67. b (23, Math FAQs)
68. d (21)
69. a (12)
70. a (19)
71. d (16)
72. d (8)
73. a (23)
74. d (23)
75. b (2)
76. c (7)
77. d (Math FAQs)
78. b (6)
79. d (5)
80. d (17)

S A M P L E   E X A M   2

1. c $180,000 × 80% equals a loan amount of $144,000. The front-end charges are the loan origination fee and the discount points (1% + 4%). $144,000 × 0.05 = $7,200. $144,000 − $7,200 = $136,800.

2. d The law prohibits any increase to a person with disabilities in the customary security deposit charged to people without disabilities. However, the landlord can require that the tenant with a disability pay into an escrow account a periodic amount that would cover the cost to return the property to its original condition.

3. c The repair is considered incurable if the cost to repair is more than the value added to the property.

4. a The capitalization rate is $40,000 ÷ $420,000 = 0.095 = 9.51%.

5. b "Ad valorem" means "on the value," so the property tax is based on the value of the property.

6. c The lease purchase clause allows the tenant to buy the property at a future time by stating a sales price and applying the rent payments to the price of the property.

7. b Fifty years is the normal Georgia search period.

8. c Georgia law allows married persons to own real property individually; marriage does not change the form of ownership.

9. d The Georgia real estate transfer tax rate is $1 for every $1,000 and $0.10 for each additional $100 or fraction thereof. There are 264 whole $1,000s for a tax of $264, plus five whole $100s and one partial $100 for a tax of $0.60. $264 + $0.60 = $264.60.

10. c The auctioneer must have an auctioneer's license to conduct auctions, plus a real estate license if real estate is auctioned.

11. b The primary purpose of the fund is to compensate consumers who suffer damages from a licensee.

12. a Clarice is not required to disclose the murder or AIDS as stigmatized properties, but she must truthfully answer questions if asked. Stan asked about murders, so Clarice must disclose the murder.

13. b Kristen had ten days to remove the sign after the expiration of the listing, so a violation had not yet occurred. Inducing a party to break a listing agreement for the purpose of substituting another agreement is an unfair practice.

14. b Melanie is only required to have a community association manager's license.

15. a An attorney-in-fact would not need a sales associate's license, but a person cannot sell or lease property on behalf of a relative without a license.

16. c Earnest money checks must be deposited directly into an escrow or trust account.

17. d $200,000 × 80% = a loan amount of $160,000. The front-end charges are $5,400 in discount points and a $1,800 loan origination fee for a total charge of $7,200. Then, $7,200 divided by $160,000 yields 4.5% as the total number of front-end points.

18. c The ADA Act requires that the administrative office be made fully accessible to people with disabilities if you employ 15 or more people in that space.

19. d The GRM is $420,000 ÷ $4,000 = 105.

20. a The cost approach uses land value, the price of materials, and the price of labor as a basis for a value estimate.

21. d The title theory of the mortgage gives the lender the right to conduct a foreclosure sale upon the borrower's default.

22. a Townships are not used in Georgia legal descriptions.

23. c An associate broker acts on behalf of a broker and can perform any real estate brokerage act that requires a license.

24. a A community association manager does not have to be licensed also as a sales associate or broker.

25. c The Commission may initiate an investigation either by its own motion or upon written request.

26. a The Commission cannot impose jail time.

27. c The licensee is entitled to a review in the superior court of the county of the Commission's domicile.

28. d All of the choices are appropriate.

29. a Julie is not acting as merely a referral agent because she is negotiating and representing a client. There is no minimum number of transactions, and the client's state of residence is irrelevant.

30. d There is no requirement that a licensee be represented by another licensee, only that the licensee *disclose* that he or she is licensed. Dual agency is permitted if all parties consent in writing. See BRRETA for a full list of the requirements for dual agency.

31. b The Commission is appointed by the governor and confirmed by the Georgia senate. It is composed of six members with five-year terms.

32. b A person aggrieved by an act, representation, or conduct of a licensee in violation of the licensing law or rules may recover up to $15,000 per transaction.

33. c BRRETA provides that an agency may be terminated several ways, two of which are by completion of performance of the engagement and upon any expiration date agreed upon by the parties in the brokerage engagement.

34. c BRRETA contains no requirement that the broker advise the client to seek legal advice.

35. a O.C.G.A. 44-1-16 states that no broker or affiliated licensee is liable for failing to disclose the fact or suspicion of property being occupied by someone with a virus or disease or that was the site of a homicide or death by accidental or natural causes. The situation would be different if Mrs. Bailey had inquired.

36. c Net listings are illegal in Georgia because they create a conflict of interest between the client's best interests and the broker's best interests.

37. c The statute of limitations for acquiring a prescriptive easement in Georgia is 20 years. Tacking of use is allowed, so the total use time of Sam and Cynthia exceeds the 20 years.

38. d The assessed value for tax purposes is 40 percent of fair market value.

39. c Both brokers must agree in writing to the licensee's actions, and the former broker must assume full responsibility for the licensee's activities in the agreement.

40. c If a cease and desist order for the unlicensed practice of real estate is violated, the fine can be up to $1,000 for each violation.

41. a The community manager's license requires at least 25 instructional hours in a community association manager's course or approved course of study.

42. c If a licensee is a Florida resident, he or she must submit the proper documents and pass the Georgia portion of the exam.

43. b Six hours of continuing education for each year of the renewal period is required.

44. b Names, addresses, identification of property, and amount of each check are all required. The county of the individuals involved is not a requirement.

45. c $156 \times 6.32 = \$985.92$.

46. b $\$156,000 \times 6.5\%$ (0.065) $= \$10,140$. $\$10,140 \div$ by 12 months $= \$845$.

47. a $\$156 \times 6.32 = \$985.92$. $\$985.92$ (interest and principal) $- \$845$ (interest) $= \$140.92$ (principal).

48. b Total housing expenses per month are $925 for interest and principal plus the following housing expenses:

Property tax per month	$400
Homeowners' insurance per month	$60
PMI insurance per month	$60
Homeowners' association dues per month	$30
	$550

    Total housing expenses per month are $925 + $550 = $1,475. The housing expenses ratio is $1,475 ÷ $5,000 = 29.5%.

49. d The housing expenses per month are $1,475 and the other debts are as follows:

Installment payments per month	$300
Auto loan payment #1 per month	$500
Auto loan payment #2 per month	$400
Child care payment per month	$500
	$1,700

Total debt is $1,475 + $1,700 = $3,175. $3,175 ÷ $5,000 = 63.5% (total debt ratio).

50. c Total debt = $3,175. This debt must be less than 36 percent of stabilized monthly income. $3,175 ÷ by 0.36 = $8,819.44 per month.

Index

Notes